STRANGE VICTORY

STRANGE VICTORY

HITLER'S CONQUEST OF FRANCE

ERNEST R. MAY

I.B.Tauris Publishers
LONDON • NEW YORK

Published in 2000 by I.B.Tauris & Co Ltd
Victoria House, Bloomsbury Square, London WC1B 4DZ
175 Fifth Avenue, New York NY 10010
Website: http://www.ibtauris.com

Copyright © Ernest R. May 2000
Designed by Jonathan D. Lippincott
Maps by the author

ISBN 1-85043-329-1

A full CIP record for this book is available from the British Library
Manufactured in the USA

To Richard E. Neustadt,

colleague, collaborator, friend

CONTENTS

STRANGE VICTORY

INTRODUCTION

O n the afternoon of May 9, 1940, at the resort town of Clervaux, in the forested north of Luxembourg, Camille Schneider entered the telephone booth outside the post office. An undercover representative of the French Secret Service, Schneider had tried in vain to reach his chief in Luxembourg's capital and was risking a direct call to the next echelon, the regional intelligence center at Longwy, just over the border in France. Schneider's message was urgent. With his own eyes he had seen soldiers on the German side of the Sûre River preparing pontoon bridges on which heavy vehicles could cross into Luxembourg.

Two days earlier, Schneider's chief, Fernand Archen, a pretended wine merchant in Luxembourg, the duchy's capital, had reported to Longwy the arrival of German commandos disguised as tourists. On signal, he had been told, these commandos were to seize bridges on the Sûre and the two other rivers that separated Luxembourg from Germany, the Our and the Moselle. On May 9, he missed Schneider's calls because he and his radio operator had taken the evening off to see Errol Flynn in a dubbed version of *Dawn Patrol*. As soon as he returned to his quarters, he heard not only from Schneider but from others, including informants in the Luxembourg gendarmerie, who reported exchanging shots with armed Germans discovered at a lonely farm not far from the Moselle. Using a clandestine transmitter, Archen radioed Longwy at 11:45 P.M.: "Reports of important German troop movements on the German-Luxembourg frontier." Through the night, his messages became more detailed and frantic.

At Vormeldange, on the Luxembourg side of the Moselle, meanwhile, two Luxembourg customs officers had been trying to make out what was happening on the German side of the river. They heard horses neighing and men calling to one another, but the fog was heavy and their field glasses showed them nothing. Then, just before dawn, as the fog was turning into mist, a German lieutenant ran across the international bridge with twenty soldiers behind him. Since the bridge is a good seventy yards long, the guards had plenty of time to use their rifles, but they did no more than yell "Halt!" Then the German lieutenant had them at gunpoint, and his sergeant sent up a flare. At this signal, foot soldiers and horse-drawn guns and wagons of the German Twelfth Army began to file across.

North of Vormeldange, German soldiers simultaneously seized other crossing points or laid pontoon bridges of the type spotted by Schneider at Clervaux. Infantry marched over, followed by horses pulling guns or supply wagons. At Echternach, Bollendorf, Wallendorf, and Wanden on the Sûre, it was not shoes and horse hooves that rattled the bridges but mile-long files of tanks accompanied by trucks, cars, and motorcycles carrying motorized infantry. Nazi Germany had commenced its war to conquer France.

The messages from Schneider, Archen, and other spies in Luxembourg and elsewhere made little impression in France. Responsibility for guarding the France-Luxembourg frontier lay with General Robert Petiet, commander of the Third Light Cavalry Division. He was taken completely by surprise when awakened around daybreak by the sound of German bombers passing overhead to raid air bases in France. In Paris, similarly, the first news was of attacks on French air bases, then of German parachutists dropping on Rotterdam in the Netherlands.[1]

Orders went out to respond to the German attack by executing a long-prepared plan, the result of which would be to send the best-trained troops and newest tanks of France and Britain to the southern Netherlands and eastern Belgium just as Germany's best-trained troops and newest tanks entered Luxembourg, headed for the Ardennes Forest and the Meuse River of eastern France.

Within a few days, French and British leaders would recognize that they had made a tragic mistake. German tanks by then were chugging several abreast across fields in the French heartland. Allied forces in Belgium were cut off from those in central France, partly by civilian refugees clogging the roads. The situation proved beyond rescue. Britain eventually evacuated as many troops as possible from the port of Dunkerque. French armies retreated farther and farther to the west and south. A new French government, formed under the aged Marshal Philippe Pétain, agreed to armistice terms. On June 22, not quite seven weeks after the first German soldiers had crossed into Luxembourg, German cavalry clattered down the Champs-Élysées in Paris in a victory parade, with their Führer, Adolf Hitler, looking on.

More than anything else, this happened because France and its allies misjudged what Germany planned to do. If leaders in the Allied governments had anticipated the German offensive through the Ardennes, even as a worrisome contingency, it is almost inconceivable that France would have been defeated when and as it was. It is more than conceivable that the outcome would have been not France's defeat but Germany's and, possibly, a French victory parade on the Unter den Linden in Berlin.

This book tries to explain how and why leaders in Paris and other Western capitals made such fateful misjudgments, even though France had an intelligence network that included not only Schneider and Archen but men and women high in the German government and at the very top of Germany's own intelligence apparatus.

In June 1940, and for a long time thereafter, the fact of France's rapid defeat seemed to speak for itself. Three conclusions were thought obvious. First, Germany must have had crushing superiority, not only in modern weaponry but in an understanding of how to use it. Second, France and its allies must have been very badly led. Third, the French people must have had no stomach for fighting. Marshal Philippe Pétain, who headed the satellite French government of 1940–44, ascribed France's defeat to "moral laxness."[2] Though not everyone would have used Pétain's particular term ("*relâchement*"), most people around the world agreed that France's defeat owed something to lack of moral fiber.

Now, sixty years later, in light of what is known about the circumstances of France's defeat, none of these conclusions holds up well. Overall, France and its allies turn out to have been better equipped for war than was Germany, with more trained men, more guns, more and better tanks, more bombers and fighters. On the whole, they did not lag even in thinking about the use of tanks and airplanes. A few German military men may have been ahead in this respect, but not many. The Allied commander in chief, General Maurice Gamelin, had worked hard to increase and improve France's tank forces. The German army commander in chief, General Walther von Brauchitsch, by contrast had tolerated the formation of all-tank divisions but said to his staff that this was wasteful—wars would continue to be decided by foot soldiers and horses. In computer simulations of the war of 1940, if the computer takes control, the Allies win.[3]

While evidence that France was not inferior militarily might seem to strengthen the conclusion that leadership was bad, this proposition also has come to seem doubtful. It should probably have seemed so long ago, for the implicit corollary is that Germany was comparatively well led. At a tactical level, this might be defensible, for the best field commanders in the German army—Heinz Guderian and Erwin Rommel, for example—were very good indeed. But it is hard to make a case that, all in all, Germany's timid, wrangling generals had an edge on men similarly placed in France or Britain, let alone that Hitler and his henchmen were more astute or adroit than political leaders in Paris and London. Recent studies of General Gamelin, of France's prime minister, Édouard Daladier, and of Britain's long-maligned prime minister, Neville Chamberlain, not only explain why they were thought to be heroes before the débâcle of 1940 but why they *deserved* to be held in high regard. None, to be sure, was Churchill, but Churchill was not then what he would be later. In fact, as a member of Chamberlain's wartime cabinet, he was often harebrained, urging, for example, that the Allies go to war with the Soviet Union as well as with Germany. And the more we have learned about the Nazi regime, the more its appearance of strength and efficiency seems an illusion created by its own propagandists.

The third proposition—that France fell in 1940 because of moral rot—is not so easy to dismiss, in part because France earlier in the 1930s had unquestionably suffered deep malaise and in part because the moral condition of any country or people is hard to gauge. France had had four and a half million men killed or wounded in the Great War of 1914–18. The Great Depression had bruised French workers and farmers. Clashes between dogmatic leftists and rightists sometimes became so intense as to seem omens of a new French Revolution. When Hitler began to threaten war, the French government and people were alarmed and appalled, and many reacted like the students at the Oxford Union who in February 1933 had voted 275 to 153 never again to fight for king or country.

But the more we have studied the period 1938–40, as opposed to the earlier 1930s, the more we have seen indications of a profound change in mood and spirit among people in both France and Britain. By the summer of 1939, when a new Great War clearly impended, Daladier complained that he could not appear in an open place or in a bistro without seeing people stand up and cry, "Lead! We will follow you!" When war came in September, reporters said the prevailing mood in both countries was one of resigned determination. When fighting actually commenced in May 1940, after more than eight months of military inactivity, reporters told of celebrations. A Danish journalist described Paris as "bubbling with enthusiasm."[4]

In the field, soldiers of France and Britain fought well. They won battles. At Hannut in Belgium on May 12–13, 1940, for example, two divisions of French tanks clashed with two divisions of German tanks and carried the day, losing 105 tanks to the Germans' 160. Even when losing, most French military units showed gallantry. At Monthermé, a plaque commemorates a French African regiment's Thermopylae-like defense of a crossing over the Meuse River. At Stonne, a few miles south of Sedan, stands a small monument which says accurately that the town changed hands seventeen times between mid-May and mid-June 1940 and became "a cemetery of tanks." During the six weeks of fighting, France lost approximately 124,000 men, with another 200,000 wounded. The total number of French battle deaths was two and a half times that of the United States in either the Korean War of 1950–53 or the Vietnam War of 1965–75. Do these bits of evidence suggest "moral laxness"?

And again arises the matter of comparison. Foreigners in Germany in 1939–40, including Italians and Hungarians, whose governments sided with Hitler, described a public with little or no appetite for the war, carried along by sureness that their adored Führer would find a way out of it. In the winter of 1939–40, after the Allies had rejected Hitler's proposal for a negotiated peace, an Italian diplomat in Berlin wrote of "frightening demoralization" among the German people.[5] As for Germany's generals, they believed to a man that Hitler had gotten the country into a war for which it was not prepared and which it might well lose. Among themselves, they talked of a possible coup. When Germany opened its offensive against the Low Countries and France in May 1940, not a single general expected victory to result. The chief of staff of the German army wrote to his wife that his fellow generals thought what they were doing was "crazy and reckless."[6] Can one say that morale was stronger in Germany than in France?

But if the Allies in May 1940 were in most respects militarily superior, were not badly led, and did not suffer from demoralization (not yet, at least), what then accounts for Germany's six-week triumph? I entitle this book *Strange Victory* in conscious if presumptuous imitation of the great French medievalist Marc Bloch, who, before his execution by the Germans in 1944, wrote a wonderfully perceptive essay on the fall of France with the title *Strange Defeat*. My book is intended as a complement to Bloch's, not a challenge to it, for the only serious defects in Bloch's analysis were due to his understandable lack of awareness of weaknesses on the German side. He did not appreciate that it was in many ways easier to tick off French vulnerabilities than to explain how a disorganized, divided German government, poorly equipped for war, managed to identify those vulnerabilities, take advantage of them, and achieve the equivalent of a successful Pearl Harbor attack—that is, a victory of the weak over the strong.

Even so, much of what Bloch wrote continues to seem clear-eyed—more so than most of what was written later about the same event. His very title captures an important fact largely lost to sight in the postwar years, namely, that France's defeat astonished both the French and their allies. The postwar consensus was that France was doomed from the start and that the French and their leaders were defeatist because they recognized their relative weakness. Bloch, by contrast, remembered that he and most people he knew had expected France to win. They had assumed that France was stronger than Germany. The key question for him was not why France had succumbed to fate but why the common expectation had proven wrong.

The point is crucial, for the whole history of the period 1938–40 is misunderstood if one fails to keep in mind the high level of confidence that prevailed in France and Britain prior to May 1940. Whatever doubts may have obtained earlier, French leaders in 1939–40 were sure of French power, indeed arrogantly so. And this arrogance seems to me one of the three keys to explaining both France's strange defeat and Germany's strange victory.

By the time serious fighting commenced in May 1940, most French and British leaders had become convinced that Hitler would never dare an offensive against France and that Germany's seeming preparations for such an offensive were deceptive maneuvers intended to pin down Allied forces and prevent their deployment in other, potentially decisive theaters such as Scandinavia or the Balkans. This accounts for the fact that, while Allied air forces were numerically superior to those of Germany, the French air force's official history is technically accurate in crediting Germany with a five-to-two edge in combat aircraft on the Western front, for the air force's high command had transferred most bombers and fighters to other sectors and had, in fact, designated the Western front as a mere training area.[7] The British Royal Air Force, meanwhile, hoarded bombers and fighters at home on the presumption that a German air offensive against the British Isles was more likely than a reckless land offensive against France.

Confidence that France had superiority and that Germany recognized this superiority made it difficult for French and British leaders to put themselves in the place of German planners, whom Hitler had commanded to prepare an offensive no matter what their opinions about its wisdom or feasibility might have been. Imagination was not paralyzed; far from it. Witness the enthusiasm for opening fronts in Scandinavia or the Balkans. But the possibility that the Germans might use ingenuity to shape a surprise version of a frontal offensive seemed too fanciful for consideration.

A second factor, also stressed by Bloch, was the French and British emphasis on minimizing loss of life. This was inevitable, given the losses in the Great War and the extent to which leaders in Paris and London were responsible to voters whose fathers, brothers, lovers, and friends had been among the lost. But writers after Bloch failed to understand the force and effect of this eagerness to minimize battle deaths, for they assumed that it was part and parcel of a defeatism that also showed in an alleged "Maginot Line mentality." In fact, the Maginot Line, the chain of fortifications on France's border with Germany, was indicative neither of despair about defeating Germany nor of thought mired in the past. It was instead evidence of faith that technology could substitute for manpower. It was a forerunner of the strategic bomber, the guided missile, and the "smart bomb." The same faith led to France's building tanks with thicker armor and bigger guns than German tanks had, deploying immensely larger quantities of mobile big guns, and above all committing to maintain a continuous line—that is, advancing or retreating in such coordination as to prevent an enemy from establishing a salient from which it could cut off a French unit from supplies and reinforcements. (Today, military strategists call this "force protection.") But having machines do the work of men and putting emphasis on minimal loss of life carried a price in slowed-down reaction times and lessened initiative for battlefield commanders.

Though Bloch is often cited as documenting French "moral laxness," he actually insisted that, insofar as he could tell, the French people and their soldiers were committed to winning the war. He disputed the proposition that their sense of commitment was less than at the beginning of the Great War, in 1914. Indeed, he hazarded the observation that commitment was stronger in 1939 because the war's " 'ideological' complexion . . . [gave] a touch of beauty to the sacrifices entailed."[8]

A third factor, emphasized by Bloch and reemphasized recently in Jean-Louis Crémieux-Brilhac's monumental work *Les Français de l'an 40*, was the cumbersomeness of French (and British and Belgian) procedures for making decisions and carrying them out. Like most democracies, France had institutions better suited for protecting citizens against the government than for mobilizing them to defend against foreigners. Its elected leaders necessarily spent most of their energies constructing cabinet or parliamentary coalitions. Their assertions about and their prescriptions for dealing with foreign nations tended to be functions of their domestic political needs. (The German air force was seen and described as a fearsome threat when domestic politics dictated finding reasons for avoiding conflict. It ceased to be seen or described in this way when public opinion appeared to prefer resoluteness.)

But French procedures were particularly sclerotic when it came to making and effecting military decisions, for the military establishment was a foreign body inside the Third Republic. Its officer corps tended to be conservative, Roman Catholic, even royalist, and to be so perceived by politicians and the public. Hence the military high command was watched and constrained. To guard against republican intrusion, the military establishment in response sheathed itself in bureaucratic armor. One result was to protect the promotion prospects for a number of senior officers who probably deserved involuntary retirement. Another, which was to have serious effects in 1940, was copperbound compartmentalization within the armed services, so that line commanders and their operations officers formed an elite from which staff officers such as those dealing with intelligence or supply were shut out, left to the company of surgeons and veterinarians. Bloch, who served for a time in army intelligence, described how officers in that branch responded by developing their own arcana and their own walls of separateness. As readers of this book will see, this compartmentalization, combined with arrogant assumptions of superiority, virtually blinded the French high command and gave German leaders opportunities to achieve what Hitler and others characterized as a "miracle."

Germany's strange victory occurred because the French and British failed to take advantage of their superiority. The Germans, meanwhile, spied out and exploited the psychological and procedural weaknesses that Bloch would catalogue. The story is particularly well worth recalling now, for in the post–Cold War era, the United States and the other seemingly victorious Western democracies exhibit many of the same characteristics that France and Britain did in 1938–40—arrogance, a strong disinclination to risk life in battle, heavy reliance on technology as a substitute, and governmental procedures poorly designed for anticipating or coping with ingenious challenges from the comparatively weak.

But I am getting ahead of the story. I first began to muse about the episode a decade and a half ago, when putting together a book about intelligence analysis before the two world wars.[9] Since then, I have discussed the puzzle of Germany's strange victory not only with college students and graduates specializing in modern history but with thousands of men and women in mid-career or executive programs at Harvard's John F. Kennedy School of Government. Several hundred of these came to Harvard from U.S. intelligence agencies, chiefly the CIA, in a special program—utterly unclassified—aimed at improving delivery of intelligence analysis to decision-makers. They were especially interested in the puzzle of 1940— and their comments were particularly interesting to me—because the story speaks to their professional concerns.

This book was shaped by all these people. It is written for them and others like them and for my wife and children, none of whom habitually goes to bed with a book about warfare. That means that I assume readers who are not experts or even necessarily history buffs. Hence I retell some tales that experts or buffs already know.

Even for the experts and buffs, however, the book should hold some novelty. It is the only account that deals in equal depth with both Germany and France. The best works in German use little source material or literature in French, and the reverse is true of the best works in French.[10] This book is also the only one with a focus on intelligence analysis as an element in explaining what happened in 1940. Though there are good histories of the German and French intelligence services, no previous work connects the intelligence story in either country to the story of high-level decision-making, let alone compares performance on the two sides.[11] Though the whole book is based on research in original sources, the segments that will be new even to experts are those based on archives of the German and French intelligence services. (Incidentally, these archives do not confirm the claims of prescience that have been made by former French intelligence officers.)

Most important, this book tries to explain Germany's strange victory in terms applicable beyond its characters or epoch. This claim of real-world usefulness is brash and needs qualification. For that, I borrow from the lore of *The Times* of London, where, it is said, a new leader-writer turned in some bold copy and waited heart in mouth for the reaction of her distant and forbidding editor, William Rees Mogg. She then saw her copy printed with no word changed but three words added: "Or perhaps not."

Judgment by the reader of whether this story serves as a parable for our own and other times will come more easily after it has been told.

PART ONE

HITLER'S GERMANY

CHAPTER ONE

ORDERS

"The Führer already said in my hearing on September 29 [1939], this offensive [against France] could well cost him a million men, but also the enemy, who cannot bear it."   —*Diary of Ernst von Weizsäcker, October 17, 1939*

"Prolonged conference with the commander in chief [Brauchitsch] on the overall situation: commander in chief: Three possibilities: attack; wait and see; fundamental changes."
                    —*Diary of General Franz Halder, chief of staff of the German army, October 14, 1939*

Anyone with a taste for old movies can visualize the scene. It is late afternoon, Wednesday, September 27, 1939. What is already being called the Second World War is entering its fourth week. Berlin is a city no longer at peace but not yet at war. Heavy five-liter Horch and Mercedes limousines with wide running boards roll along the Wilhelmstrasse. On their gull-wing fenders flutter miniature flags with white-circled black swastikas on bright-red backgrounds, the symbol of the Nazi state. At the old Chancellory, they turn into the narrow, dead-end roadway fronting the courtyard of the New Chancellory. The giant white building, just nine months old, looms over the old limestone-block Chancellory next door as, in his imagination, Chancellor and Führer Adolf Hitler looms over predecessors such as Frederick the Great, the eighteenth-century monarch who made Prussia a great power, and Otto von Bismarck, the nineteenth-century chancellor who transformed Prussia into the German Empire, the most powerful state in Europe from 1871 until the end of the Great War in 1918.

The passengers leave their limousines. Army generals are in field gray with glistening black boots; air-force officers wear pale blue, naval officers blue-black. Every chest is spangled with medals. Up marble stairs, through massive Corinthian columns, past huge gilded statues of Aryan athletes, the visitors walk through seventeen-foot-high bronze doors flanked by guards wearing the black uniforms and black boots of the Nazi Schutz-staffel—the SS. The five-hundred-foot-long entry hall has a polished marble floor which Hitler has left uncarpeted because he relishes seeing dignitaries slip and fall. At the far end, doors open on an oversize reception area, beyond which is Hitler's four-thousand-square-foot study, character-ized by *Life* magazine as the "biggest private office in the world."[1]

Beside the study doorway stand other SS troopers. Each has Hitler's name braided on his left sleeve, on his helmet a white death's head, and on both lapels the emblem of the Hitler bodyguard. Inside, above the doors, a mural depicts the Virtues—Wisdom, Prudence, Fortitude, and Justice. Over a fireplace, not quite so out of place, hangs an oil portrait of Bismarck. Hitler's huge desk is ornamented, even more appropriately, with an inlay of a sword emerging from its scabbard.

One can imagine Hitler standing in front of this desk this early-autumn afternoon. Northern light streaming through the high windows silhouettes him. He is of medium height and slender, though with the beginning of a paunch. Previously, his standard costume had been the brown uniform of the Nazi Party's now largely ceremonial Sturmabteilung—SA, or storm troopers. Now he has on a simple field-gray uniform, which he has vowed to continue wearing until the war is over. Except for a swastika armband and the Iron Cross he won as a front-line soldier in the last war, he is without decorations. His brown hair slants down over the left side of his forehead, matching in color the brush mustache which, for foreign cartoonists, has become his emblem. (Hitler grew and kept the mustache to distract from his too-large nose.) One can imagine him nodding to the arrivals, gesturing them to seats, tossing his head, then beginning to speak. It was his custom to speak softly at first, then to let his voice and emotions rise in tandem.[2]

Those in attendance include the commanders in chief of the armed ser-vices: General Walther von Brauchitsch for the army; Field Marshal Her-mann Göring for the air force; and Admiral Erich Raeder for the navy. Brauchitsch is slight, rigidly erect, with a handsome face that is beginning to sag. Göring, almost comically fat, is stuffed into a white, gold-trimmed uniform of his own design and has a Crusader's sword at his waist. He has natural dimples and a set smile but, above it, small, malicious, pale-blue eyes. Raeder is squarely built but wide-bottomed, like one of his cruisers. The most detailed notes are taken by the army chief of staff, General Franz Halder, who has cropped hair, wears rimless spectacles, and, out of uni-form, might be taken for a schoolteacher rather than a soldier.[3]

Less than four weeks earlier, on September 1, German armed forces had invaded Poland, and France and Great Britain, after demanding a cease-fire and German withdrawal, had declared war. All the men gathered in Hitler's study had feared that French armies would march against Germany. At the time, German defense forces on the Western front had been feeble. Their commander, General Wilhelm Ritter von Leeb, had warned Brauchitsch that he could do little to stop French troops from walking in and taking over the Ruhr River Valley. A 1,280-square-mile area less than forty miles from Germany's western border, this valley included cities such as Essen, Dortmund, Duisburg, and Bochum, where a large percentage of German heavy industry was concentrated.[4] Hitler, who had gone to the Polish front on the *Amerika*, a special twelve-car double-locomotive armored train, had opened every morning's meeting in the train's command coach by asking, "What's new in the West?" Brauchitsch had said to his staff, "Every day of calm in the West is for me a gift from God."[5]

Apart from a noisy show of force on the border with Germany and some leaflet dropping, France and Britain had done nothing. Meanwhile, the Germans had thrown more than a million and a half soldiers and almost two thousand aircraft into a campaign aimed at the quick and complete defeat of Poland. In the first few days, German bombers had decimated the small Polish air force and disrupted life in the Polish capital, Warsaw. From then on, German planes made it difficult for Polish forces to move either by road or by rail.

A German Army Group commanded by General Fedor von Bock attacked from the north. After breaking through Polish lines, its two armies turned south to envelop Warsaw. A corps under General Heinz Guderian, composed primarily of armored divisions and supported by air-force dive-bombers, stormed northern Poland, not stopping until it reached Brest, more than a hundred miles west of Warsaw. A second Army Group, commanded by General Gerd von Rundstedt, meanwhile struck from the west and southwest, closing in on central Poland like the lower jaw of a wire-cutter.

Just a week before the start of the war, Nazi Germany had astonished the world by signing a nonaggression pact with the communist Soviet Union, supposedly its mortal ideological enemy. This pact had ensured the Soviet Union's not joining France and Britain in declaring war. The commitment made by Germany to obtain this result became apparent when, on September 17, four Soviet armies marched into Poland from the east. Germany and the Soviet Union soon afterward agreed on a partition line, and, for the time being, Poland disappeared from the map.

Though the Polish army mounted a briefly successful counteroffensive, it was soon overwhelmed. During the second week of the war, Brauchitsch and Halder had felt able to begin transferring some forces to Leeb in the West. As early as September 12, Brauchitsch said to one of his aides that he could now "nip in the bud any attempt by the enemy to invade German territory."[6] He and Halder began to plan for recruiting, training, and equipping forces with an eye to a possible offensive against France in 1941, if the war was still going on. They drew up orders for partial demobilization so that skilled workers could go back to their factories. On an assumption that any fighting in the West in the next year or two would be defensive, they also planned to "demotorize" some infantry divisions that had fought in Poland, thus conserving both vehicles and fuel.[7]

Göring's air staff had returned to planning a bomber force that would be large enough by 1942 for a strategic air campaign against Britain.[8] Raeder, who had advised Hitler that a serious effort to blockade the British Isles would require three hundred submarines and that Germany currently had only fifty-seven, wanted raw materials diverted from both the army and the air force so that, in a year or two, the navy could play a decisive role in a war.[9] The military chiefs lined up in front of Hitler were all looking forward to a very long period of, at most, defensive warfare.

Halder's notes show their gradual discovery of the different message that Hitler had in mind, for Hitler described the victory over Poland as giving Germany only a temporary advantage. "All historical successes come to nothing when they are not continued," he said. "Great victories have little enduring luster." He attributed the French and British inaction to weakness, which would not last: "The enemy adjusts. After the first engagement with an enemy, even bad troops get better."

For the present, said Hitler, France held back because England would not yet "bear enough of the cost in blood." That would change when British troops arrived. Learning from the Polish war, the two enemy powers would strengthen their anti-aircraft and antitank defenses, and that would make another quick German victory increasingly difficult. Therefore, Hitler concluded, Germany should take the offensive against France now. "The sooner, the better," Halder recorded his saying. "Do not wait for the enemy to come to us, but rather immediately take the offensive ourselves. . . . Ruthless methods. Once time is lost, it cannot be recovered."

After being dismissed by Hitler, the generals and admirals made their way back to the courtyard of the New Chancellory. The staff cars of Brauchitsch and Halder went down the Wilhelmstrasse and around Belle Alliance Platz, with its sixty-foot-high Peace Column, put up just one century earlier to celebrate the twenty-five-year peace following what was remembered by Germans as their war of liberation and by other Europeans as the last of the Napoleonic Wars. The route went out of the city along the Berlinerstrasse, passing first industrial suburbs and then farmland still green with late cabbage rows and beanstalks, where, between stands of linden, maple, and oak, Holstein and Jersey cows grazed in high grass.

The destination of Brauchitsch and Halder, about twenty miles from Berlin, was a huge fenced-in army-training facility neighboring the village of Zossen. The grounds had barracks, stables, vehicle-weighing stations, a large recreation center, and fields for sports, parades, and maneuvers. They also had sugarloaf-shaped structures mounting anti-aircraft guns, near which stood two large A-shaped buildings mistakable, at a distance, for ski chalets.

Built on marshland, these A-shaped buildings had to be approached across wooden planks. They contained offices and living quarters. But their north doors gave admission to elevators that descended sixty feet downward and opened onto long, steel-walled corridors lined with insulated cables and broken at intervals by airtight steel doors. These corridors led to a warren of offices, communication centers, and service and storage areas. Under the code name "Zeppelin," this was the army high command's supposedly bomb-proof, gas-proof quarters for wartime. (It was sufficiently well built so that, throughout the Cold War, the Soviet Union would use it as a command post for its armies in East Germany.) Brauchitsch and Halder had moved there six days before the attack on Poland.[10]

Early in the afternoon on the day following Hitler's order for an early Western offensive, Halder gathered some key officers of the general staff in his office, a Spartan pine-paneled room with barracks furniture. He directed these officers to analyze possibilities for an offensive against France. If his own diary account is trustworthy, he himself made a strong case for such an offensive. He said that Hitler hoped France and Britain would agree to some negotiated settlement, but if not, Germany would face the reality that time worked in favor of the enemy. Even with the Western front being reinforced by troops transferring from Poland, France and Britain could still seize the Ruhr Valley if they made a determined strike. Since the two powers had only recently begun to modernize their military forces, they would grow progressively stronger, and their prospects for success would improve. Hence, said Halder, the general staff needed to develop a contingency plan for a possible German offensive to be launched as early as late

October, seeking to take as much territory as possible in the Netherlands and Belgium and conceivably in northern France, with a view to providing defense in depth for the Ruhr and gaining coastal bases for air and naval operations against the British home islands.

Halder asked General Kurt von Tippelskirch, head of the general staff's intelligence directorate, and Lieutenant Colonel Ulrich Liss, chief of Tippelskirch's Foreign Armies West branch, for a quick, rough estimate of enemy numbers and materiel and of fortifications in the Netherlands and Belgium. He asked General Karl Heinrich von Stülpnagel, head of the general staff's plans-and-operations directorate (and effectively his own number two), to outline a plan based on Tippelskirch's estimates of likely enemy forces and of German forces that could be shifted quickly from the Polish front to the West. He allowed less than two days for this work. Suspecting a negative reaction to the very idea of an offensive, he closed the meeting by emphasizing: "Extreme urgency to obtain basic data for a thorough discussion with the Führer about what is possible. No reservations or hesitations."[11]

When the group assembled again on the morning of Saturday, September 30, the reports all discouraged even thinking of an offensive in the West any time soon. General Eduard Wagner, the army's chief supply officer, confirmed the conclusions of General Georg Thomas, who headed the economic section in Hitler's own armed-forces staff, that the Polish campaign had sapped Germany's reserves of fuel and ammunition and that Germany lacked the industrial base, particularly in chemicals and steel, to produce adequate quantities of gunpowder or artillery shells before 1941. Noting that about half of Germany's tanks had broken down or been disabled in Poland, General Adolf von Schell, who was in charge of motor transport, predicted that most of these tanks would still be out of action at the end of October. In any case, only the newer-model tanks—Panzer IIIs and Panzer IVs—had a hope of standing up against French and British tanks and anti-tank guns, and they could not come on line in any numbers until much later in the year, if then.

Tippelskirch, the intelligence chief, and Liss, his expert on Western armies, ticked off obstacles to a successful offensive against the Low Countries and France. For one, Belgium had a respectable army and some of the strongest fortifications in Europe. For another, France and Britain had sixty divisions on the French-Belgian border, eighteen of which were mechanized or motorized and could quickly come to Belgium's rescue. Stülpnagel and his operations staff, having already analyzed on their own the possibilities for a German offensive in the West, reported that there was no way in which it could be conducted with any prospect of success before 1942 at the earliest.[12]

Anticipating negative reports from the general staff, Halder and Brauchitsch had already put their heads together to outline arguments that might persuade Hitler to change his mind. They agreed to point out to him the extreme vulnerability of the Ruhr Basin. They would explain that, though fast-moving German tank formations with air support had had success in Poland, they could not be equally effective in the West, where the terrain was different and the opposing forces would be much better equipped, trained, and led. Tanks moving into Belgium or France would encounter concrete fortifications, deep trenches, and steel barricades, none of which had existed in Poland. German tanks would become sitting targets for French and British bombers and for the thousands of artillery pieces arrayed along the French and Belgian frontiers. Moreover, the days were getting shorter. The weather was becoming more unpredictable. These factors would hamper ground operations and make air operations more and more chancy. Still, if the offensive were postponed even to 1940, Brauchitsch and Halder proposed to point out, the German army would not only have time to build up supplies and to train recruits but would also have significant numbers of Panzer IIIs and IVs and, among other things, new mortars capable of firing poison-gas shells. With their brief thus assembled, Brauchitsch and Halder arranged to see Hitler.

When Hitler's armed-forces high-command staff gave him advance notice of what the generals planned to say, he reacted with rage. He was already angry, because some generals had raised questions about his orders systematically to murder or enslave Jews in occupied Poland.[13] His personal aides saw him pacing his private quarters in the Chancellory, fulminating against army officers who lacked faith in their own soldiers and were afraid of the French and British. Though he had agreed to see Brauchitsch and Halder, he gave them only the briefest of audiences. Dismissing their arguments almost out of hand, Hitler said that he intended to offer France and Britain a chance to retract their declarations of war but that, if they declined to do so, his position would be "absolute resoluteness" for an early offensive.[14]

Returning to Zossen, Brauchitsch and Halder began to make some token preparations for an offensive in the West. For practical purposes, their planning focused on making ready to counter an Allied offensive. When the chief of the naval staff asked Halder if he was thinking of reaching the Belgian coast, where the navy wanted bases, Halder told him that such notions were "utopian."[15]

Brauchitsch and Halder continued to hope that Hitler could be persuaded to change his orders. To gather additional arguments, they consulted General Leeb, whose Army Group was still the only one holding down the Western front. Leeb told them that most of his troops were not ready for anything but position warfare. They might fight if attacked, but not otherwise. Though Leeb's chief of staff, Lieutenant General Georg von Sodenstern, had a slightly higher opinion of the troops, he warned that the German army as a whole was crippled because of France's overwhelming superiority in artillery, which had been the decisive weapon in earlier wars. General Wagner, the chief supply officer, came in with a calculation that the army had only enough ammunition for one-third of its divisions to conduct operations for two weeks. From other sources, Brauchitsch and Halder learned that Göring and his senior staff officers doubted the air force's capacity to wage offensive operations before the spring of 1940. Of planes committed in Poland, 564 (almost 30 percent) had been lost or seriously disabled—and this against an enemy with a small air force and minimal anti-aircraft artillery.[16]

On October 6, Hitler made his promised speech proposing that the Allies retract their declarations of war. He said that there were no direct issues between Germany and the Western powers. Germany had no designs on France or Britain. But the price of peace would be French and British acquiescence in Germany's control over all Central and Eastern Europe. Brauchitsch had said hopefully to Leeb and Sodenstern that Hitler's preparations for an offensive might just be part of a big bluff intended to bring the Allies to the bargaining table. According to Adolf Heusinger, then in the operations section of the general staff, all the junior officers at Zossen expected Hitler somehow to patch up a peace with the Western powers.[17] Now it was evident that this expectation was wrong. Quick, uncompromising responses from Paris and London guaranteed that the war would go on.[18]

On October 10, Hitler ordered Brauchitsch and Halder to appear in his office at 11 A.M. For most of the two previous nights, he had kept his two secretaries awake taking dictation. When the generals appeared, he had in hand a fifty-eight-page manuscript, which he proceeded to read aloud. His principal points were as follows:

1) If France and Britain were forced to give battle, they would be defeated. Germany was stronger, no matter what Halder's intelligence officers told him, for France was weaker than it appeared to

be. France's population was smaller than Germany's, and France could not or would not lose millions of men in battle again as in 1914–18. Faced with a Germany prepared for war to the death, French leaders and the French populace would lose heart and give up. (A week later, Hitler would say casually to a senior official in the Foreign Ministry that this offensive could well cost him a million men, "but also the enemy, who cannot bear it.")

2) Belgium could be disregarded. Belgian defenses would collapse almost at a touch.

3) If the British Expeditionary Force tried to rescue Belgium, it could be cut off before it reached Antwerp and would have to retreat.

4) Even if France and Britain could rally and defend the French frontier, Germany would be in occupation of the Low Countries and would have a base for bombing Britain.

5) When Germany mounted an offensive, Italy would join, forcing France to fight on a second front, for Italy's Fascist dictator, Benito Mussolini, Hitler asserted, was only "waiting for the suitable moment to take the plunge."

6) It was important to act soon, because there was no Eastern front. In return for the eastern half of Poland, the Soviet Union had agreed to stay out of the war. The Soviets could be counted on to remain quiet for a time, but not forever.

7) The army could manage this offensive even given some critical shortages if it used primarily small-caliber ammunition, deployed tanks only in open country, bypassed urban areas, and swept forward on a broad front but with concentrations at particular points of vulnerability.

Hitler made only one concession to the generals. The timing of the offensive would depend, he said, on readiness for combined armor-air operations such as those that had been successful in Poland.[19]

On the day after the Chancellory meeting at which Hitler first called for an early offensive, Halder's diary recorded that he and Brauchitsch had spent the evening in "talk regarding [our] stand on the subject set forth at the Führer conference." After their first failed effort to change Hitler's mind, the two generals again devoted the evening to "prolonged conversation . . . about our stand on the Führer's plans in the West." A few days after sitting through the reading of Hitler's long memorandum, Brauchitsch and Halder had another very long talk. Halder recorded in his diary:

Prolonged conference with the commander in chief [Brauchitsch] on the overall situation: commander in chief: Three possibilities: attack; wait and see; fundamental changes. None of these three possibilities offers prospects of decisive success, least of all the last, since it is essentially negative and tends to render us vulnerable. Quite apart from all this it is our duty to set forth military prospects soberly and to promote every possibility for peace.[20]

The language in Halder's diary entries has to be understood against the long history of the army in Germany, and against the shorter but eventful history of the army's relations with Hitler since the advent of the Third Reich.

When Brauchitsch and Halder talked to each other of what "stand" they should take toward Hitler, they did so with assumptions they shared as generals in the German army. For them, the army was the nucleus of the nation. Duty therefore demanded not only preservation of the army but preservation of its pre-eminence among German institutions. As possible models for their action in 1939, they could look back at predecessors— Friedrich Wilhelm von Seydlitz in the eighteenth century; Yorck von Wartenburg in the early 1800s; and Wilhelm Groener in 1918, at the Great War's end.

Seydlitz symbolized obedience by the soldier to the head of state. The roots of Germany had been in the kingdom of Prussia, which, as recently as the mid-1600s, had been only a collection of properties scattered across Northern Europe from the Baltic Sea to the Rhine River. During the seventeenth and eighteenth centuries, the Hohenzollern dynasty had created a Prussian state, primarily by forming and using an outsize army. The fact that more than 80 percent of all royal revenues went to the army accounted for the often quoted observation by the Marquis de Mirabeau that Prussia was not a state with an army but an army with a state.[21]

Then, as later, the Prussian army was noted for its discipline. King Frederick the Great likened its workings to the machinery inside a watch. He laid down as a principle that his soldiers should be more afraid of their own leaders than of the enemy. "If a soldier . . . so much as sets foot outside the line," he ordered, "the non-commissioned officer standing behind him will run him through with his bayonet and kill him on the spot." The king's commands were as if from God.

Seydlitz, the first of possible models for Brauchitsch and Halder, had been Frederick's foremost cavalry commander. At the battle of Kunersdorf in 1759, during the Seven Years' War which Prussia waged against Russia and Austria in 1756–63, Seydlitz was ordered by Frederick to charge Russian and Austrian forces half again stronger than Prussia's, and entrenched to boot. Seydlitz warned the king that the charge would be disastrous. When Frederick repeated the order, Seydlitz obeyed, even though the result was as he had predicted and he himself was killed.[22]

Yorck symbolized service rendered by soldiers guiding their head of state. During the wars of the French Revolution and Napoleon between 1793 and 1815, the Prussian army had gained some independence. In 1806, in the battles of Jena and Auerstädt, Napoleon had routed the Prussians, and, as an English campaign historian writes, a "perfect epidemic of surrender set in amongst the higher commanders," while the Prussian people "welcomed the conquerors as deliverers, and turned their own soldiers, even the wounded, away from their doors."[23] With Napoleon occupying Berlin, Prussia seemed destined to survive, if at all, as a dependency of France.

Prussia's rescue from this threat was remembered, especially by German soldiers, as primarily an accomplishment of its officer corps. With little help from the ruling Hohenzollern monarch, a small group of reformers began to build a new Prussian state and Prussian army. The new army embodied and symbolized Prussian nationhood. The reformers redesigned recruitment to make service a duty associated with citizenship—not, as previously, a fate akin to being enslaved. Imitating France, they opened the officer corps to nonaristocrats. Moreover, the army put a premium on brainwork and began the practice of attaching to every commander a staff officer experienced in planning and preparing campaigns. When Napoleon began to founder after his failed invasion of Russia in 1812, this new Prussian army proved able to defeat a French army in battle and to participate in victories culminating in Napoleon's surrender at Waterloo in 1815.

Yorck's role in these events had been to sign, at the very end of 1812, the Convention of Tauroggen, which effectively allied Prussia with Russia against France. Yorck had not done this on orders from the then Prussian king, who would almost certainly have chosen for Prussia to remain Napoleon's puppet. Yorck had not been a reformer—he had even protested the notion that Prussian officers should be required to be able to read and write—but he nevertheless presented his king with a fait accompli.

Afterward, into the late nineteenth century, when Brauchitsch and Halder were cadets, German school textbooks insisted that Yorck could not have acted on his own in 1812. Nationalist historians hypothesized that oral instructions had been given authorizing Yorck to act against his monarch's written orders. Yorck, wrote historian Heinrich von Treitschke, "would never have thought of setting himself against the king's will." Yet during the Great War, when the generals-to-be of 1939 were lieutenants, captains, or majors, the army high command, headed by Field Marshal Paul von Hindenburg and General Erich Ludendorff, assumed dictatorial powers more in place of Kaiser Wilhelm II than on his behalf, largely because it had become evident that the Kaiser could not manage a war. In light of current events, Yorck came to be recognized as having acted on his own and done what the king should have done.[24] He, along with Hindenburg and Ludendorff, became a model of the soldier doing for the statesman what the statesman should have done for himself.

General Groener exemplified the soldier who went one step further and took control of the state. In 1918, when both the Western front and the German home front began to collapse, Groener succeeded Ludendorff. At Spa, in November 1918, he told Kaiser Wilhelm II that the officer corps no longer felt bound by its oath to him. "The personal oath of loyalty," he said, "is now just a notion"—"*nur eine Idee.*" Thus deserted, the Kaiser surrendered his legal powers to Marshal Hindenburg, abdicated, and went into exile. Groener negotiated with the civilian chancellor of Germany's new republic what both men characterized as "an alliance." The army would protect the republic from radical revolutionaries. Apart from exacting an oath to the new Constitution, the republic would leave the army to rule itself.[25] When Brauchitsch and Halder used the phrase "fundamental changes" to describe one option they had vis-à-vis Hitler, they probably had in mind the example of Groener at Spa.

In the German officer corps of the 1920s and 1930s, it was accepted truth that the army had always been the soul of the nation. General Hans von Seeckt, who headed the army staff during the first of these decades, wrote an essay, published in 1928 as "The Army in the State," which asserted that the army had evolved beyond its earlier bonding with monarchy: "Drawing men from all sources and stations, the army embodies the manifest national unity of the state and serves as one of the strongest clamps holding together the national edifice. . . . The army serves the state, only the state; for it is the state." An eminent Frankfurt jurist, writing on the army and the state in 1938—five years after Hitler came to power—echoed Seeckt, writing, "The basic political order springs from the structure of the military establishment."[26]

A majority of the German army's senior officers in 1939 were Prussians.

Those who were not, like Halder, a Bavarian, had the traditions of the Prussian army equally fixed in their minds. They had studied the career of Seydlitz. Whenever they visited Hitler, they passed a bronze statue of him in the Wilhelm-Platz, just opposite the old Chancellory. They also had before them the models of Yorck at Tauroggen and of Hindenburg and Ludendorff later, taking decisions into their own hands. And they had the model of Groener at Spa, saying that the higher interests of the state required "fundamental changes."

CHAPTER TWO

HONEYMOON

"I have wished for years for the political revolution, and now my wishes have come true. It is the first ray of hope since 1918."
—*General Ludwig Beck, on Hitler's accession to power in 1933*

"The Führer is cleverer than we are; he will plan and do everything correctly."
—*Field Marshal Werner von Blomberg, 1935*

In January 1933, when Hitler became chancellor, few army officers had imagined that, within a few years, they might face choices such as those Brauchitsch and Halder debated at Zossen in October 1939. Most officers had been pleased by Hitler's success. They agreed with him that Germany should try to regain great-power status abroad, restore order at home, and renew national pride. They endorsed enthusiastically his call for repudiating the articles of the Versailles Peace Treaty that limited Germany to an army of a hundred thousand men and forbade the building of an air force. Many had been contemptuous of Weimar Republic cabinets content merely to seek modifications in these restraints.

Hitler bent himself right away to cementing support within the armed services. During his first month as chancellor, he was invited by the then commander in chief of the army, General Kurt Baron von Hammerstein-Equord, to dine with about twenty senior officers. After the meal, Hitler spoke for more than two hours. According to notes kept by General Curt Liebmann, he promised "complete reversal of the present domestic political situation . . . extermination of Marxism root and branch . . . removal of the cancer of democracy." Hitler declared rearmament his most important aim and gave assurance that he had no thought either of having the Nazi Party's uniformed storm troopers assume functions of the army or of asking the army to act against the communists or other opposition parties. The army, he said, should "stay unpolitical and above party," with "the internal struggle not its affair."[1]

Hitler's actions accorded with his words. He told heads of domestic agencies that his guiding principle would be "everything for the armed forces." After a pretense of negotiating for revision of the Versailles Treaty, Hitler in March 1935 proclaimed it a dead letter. He announced a plan to expand the army to three hundred thousand men. He reintroduced conscription. He proclaimed that Germany would build an air force. When government economists protested the rocketing demands of rearmament, Hitler told them that the army had to be made ready for war, no matter what the cost at home.

At the time, the Nazi party's brown-shirted SA outnumbered the regular army. Their chief, Ernst Röhm, an ex–army captain and a carousing homosexual, made no secret of wanting the SA to become the "people's army." Nor did he make a secret of his belief that the SA's rough-and-tumble leaders ought to supplant the aristocratic officers whose snubs he had suffered when in uniform. When Röhm ignored orders to scale back SA activity, Hitler called in Heinrich Himmler, head of, among other things, the Blackshirts—the SS—the party's other fighting force. In a two-day "Blood Purge" in June 1934, Himmler's SS murdered at least fifty Brownshirts, including Röhm. Hitler personally supervised doing away with Röhm's entourage. Göring oversaw the butchery in Berlin. Other scores were settled. SS men murdered General Kurt von Schleicher, who had been Hitler's predecessor as chancellor and who had intrigued to keep the post. With Schleicher went his wife and Schleicher's former assistant, General Kurt von Bredow. Some persons were shot by mistake, as, for example, a music critic whose name resembled that of a renegade Nazi.

To the public, Hitler explained that Röhm had planned a coup. He alleged that Röhm, Schleicher, and Bredow had been in treasonous communication with a foreign government, presumed to be France.[2] Though the murders of Schleicher and his wife and Bredow made some army officers queasy, the majority seemed glad to take Hitler's word. Their chief feeling was relief at being freed of the threat from Röhm and the SA. This relief was compounded when Hitler allowed army leaders to choose Röhm's successor. They did so, using as criteria, as one general said, "stupidity and lack of dangerous leadership qualities."[3]

After the Blood Purge, Hitler nearly always sided with the army when issues arose between it and the Nazi Party. When Himmler's SS showed signs of emerging as another rival to the army, Hitler arranged a joint assembly of army and party leaders. It took place early in 1935 at the Opera House on Berlin's boulevard, Unter den Linden. Hitler said there that he viewed the army and the party as "the two pillars of the state"—equally indispensable. The figure of speech was significant because Röhm had once said that the SA and the SS were "the foundation pillars of the coming National Socialist state." Hitler also declared that he would not even listen to criticism of the army by the party or vice versa. He asked the audience to imagine his being visited by someone from the party. "He says to me: All fine and well, my Führer, but General So-and-so is speaking and working against you! Then I say: I do not believe it! If then the other says, I can bring you written proof, my Führer!, then I would tear it up, because my faith in the armed forces is unshakable." Hitler took occasion to say also that he now believed Schleicher and Bredow to have been falsely accused.[4] He followed up by ordering that the secret police, the Gestapo, also under Himmler's control, keep away from the army. He directed party members to respect army regulations that forbade political activity by anyone conscripted or called up as a reservist.[5]

To the extent that the army lost independence during Hitler's early years in power, the fault lay with the army more than with Hitler or the party. The principal agents were the war minister, General Werner von Blomberg, and his deputy, General Walther von Reichenau. Blomberg and Reichenau had come into office at about the same time as Hitler but independently. Hindenburg, the aged field marshal, still president of the republic, had selected Blomberg for his position on the basis of seniority and military record. Previously, Blomberg had been the equivalent of chief of staff of the army and commander of the military district girdling Berlin. No other officer of his age had comparable qualifications or anything like Blomberg's imposing presence—"Siegfried with a monocle," as one British historian writes.[6]

Reichenau was Blomberg's designee, not Hitler's. A bright and aggressive modernizer, Reichenau would probably not have held such a high post except for Blomberg's patronage, for he ruffled his military colleagues. He addressed them as "you" instead of, in the third person, as "*der Herr Gen-*

eral." He sometimes fraternized with juniors; he ran in marathons; and he drove his own compressor-equipped Mercedes at high speeds. A fellow officer said scornfully that Reichenau could "be taken as . . . an American general."[7]

Blomberg adored Hitler. At one time, as a result of a trip to the Soviet Union, he had become a champion of a Sovietized Germany; then, partly through listening to Ludwig Müller, an army chaplain who had become a Nazi zealot, Blomberg concluded that Hitler had a better formula.[8] To questioners of Hitler's policies, Blomberg would respond, "The Führer is cleverer than we are; he will plan and do everything correctly." To fellow officers anxious lest Hitler antagonize the other European powers, he would say dismissively, "The more enemies, the more honor."[9] Reichenau had a better head than Blomberg but lived under at least as great an illusion— namely, that the army would be able to manipulate Hitler. Before Hitler became chancellor, Reichenau boasted to an acquaintance that Hitler's Brownshirts "will eat out of our hand one day." After January 1933, he believed that the army's optimal strategy was to ingratiate itself with the dictator.[10]

In combination, Blomberg's sentimentality and Reichenau's Machiavellianism produced a series of gratuitous acts that made the army seem more an instrument of Hitler than most senior officers imagined it actually to be. At the time of the Blood Purge, Blomberg issued formal congratulations: "The Führer has personally attacked and wiped out the mutineers and traitors with soldierly decision and exemplary courage." He added this Seecktlike caveat: "The armed forces as the sole bearer of arms within the Reich, remain aloof from internal political conflict but pledge anew their devotion and their fidelity." Reichenau said of Hitler: "We love him because he has shown himself a true soldier."[11]

It was Blomberg who decreed that officers of the Wehrmacht (the armed forces) wear the Nazi Party badge on the left breast of their uniform jackets: a stylized eagle with talons atop a globe-encircled swastika. Soldiers less reverent than Blomberg called the badge "the bird."[12] According to Colonel Friedrich Hossbach, who served on Hitler's staff as liaison with the army high command, Blomberg came up on his own with the idea of having Hitler addressed as "Mein Führer" rather than simply "Herr Hitler." Hossbach wrote after the war, "I can still hear Blomberg asking: 'Will you then agree?,' whereupon Hitler with a nod of the head and a brief 'Yes' gave his assent to the usage." Blomberg made "Heil Hitler!" a standard military greeting. Hossbach describes this, too, as impulsive. Blomberg accompanied Hitler on a visit to the fleet, heard sailors calling out "Heil" instead of "Good morning," and, on the spot, ordered that the practice be adopted throughout the armed forces.[13]

When President Hindenburg died, soon after the Blood Purge, Hitler announced that no new president would be chosen. As chancellor and Führer, he would take over all presidential functions and powers. Blomberg not only accepted Hitler's decision but applauded it. Apparently on his own, he decided that army officers should take an oath of allegiance to Hitler. Reichenau approved and helped him compose it. It began, "I swear by God this holy oath, that I will render to Adolf Hitler, Führer of the German nation and people, supreme commander of the armed forces, unconditional obedience."

Though no officers refused to take this oath, some voiced misgivings. Many said later that this oath had prevented their becoming parties to plots against Hitler. For a few, this may have been true. For most, it was an excuse. Hardly any officers had taken seriously their oaths to support the Weimar Constitution. For most of them, the new oath must have seemed an improvement. It said nothing about constitutions, and it resembled the old personal oaths taken by officers of the Prussian kingdom and the German Empire.[14]

Differences between Hitler and the army leadership did not begin to develop until the fourth or fifth year of the dictatorship. During this time, the Nazi Party had achieved dominance over nearly all other segments of Germany's state and society—government at all levels, including the courts; labor unions; much of the business and banking worlds; most newspapers; nearly all schools and universities; and most churches and voluntary organizations, including professional associations. This had brought with it a social revolution scarcely matched anywhere—ever. Except in the army, the diplomatic service, and a few other spheres, old elites had been displaced and their places taken by men and women who, given their lack of breeding or education or culture, would not even have thought of being officials or judges or business leaders or members of professions.[15]

The army's first effort to assert itself against Hitler rose from an issue not unlike that which would preoccupy Brauchitsch and Halder at Zossen. The officer leading it was General Ludwig Beck, Halder's predecessor as head of the army general staff. A tall Rhinelander with facial skin so tight as to seem ghoulish, especially on the rare occasions when he smiled, Beck was, ironically, one of the senior officers most admiring of Hitler and most in Hitler's debt. In 1930, when three young officers of his regiment had been put on trial for illegal activities on behalf of the Nazis, Beck had testified for them. Hitler also spoke at the trial, and Beck liked what Hitler said. When Hitler came to power, Beck wrote, "I have wished for years for the political revolution, and now my wishes have come true. It is the first ray of hope since 1918." When the post of army chief of staff came open in 1933, Hitler urged Blomberg to appoint Beck, and Blomberg did so.[16]

Beck's loyalty to the army, however, was incomparably stronger than his loyalty to Hitler. Originally, Beck's appointment was merely as chief of the Defense Ministry's Troop Office (Truppenamt), for the Versailles Treaty had required dissolution of the prewar general staff. Officers who had once worn the red trouser stripe denoting membership in the general staff suffered during the Weimar era, passing through the old Königs-Platz and seeing its new name, Platz der Republik, with the great "red house" at Number 6 which had been the staff's home from the Napoleonic wars onward, now headquarters for the Ministry of the Interior. The general staff did not regain its name, or Beck the title of chief, until June 1935, after Hitler's repudiation of the military clauses of the Versailles Treaty. Even then, the general staff did not regain the "red house," for Hitler's minister of the interior would not move. Beck worked from drab concrete buildings wedged between the Tirpitz Ufer, along the Spree River, and on the Bendlerstrasse, in a complex about half a mile from the Wilhelmstrasse that also housed the War Ministry.

In Beck's conception, however, the general staff was that which, under Bismarck and Kaiser Wilhelm II, had been managed from the "red house" by the great chiefs of staff, Field Marshals Helmuth von Moltke and Alfred von Schlieffen. Then the war minister had overseen army finances, but the Kaiser himself had been commander in chief and, with regard to operations, had taken guidance entirely from his army chief of staff, who had had the right of access to him no matter what any chancellor might prefer— even Bismarck. Under the chief's direction, the general staff prepared plans for war, and general-staff officers, assigned to headquarters up and down the line, saw to it that orders from field commanders were consistent with those plans. Moltke had faced down Bismarck during the Franco-Prussian War of 1870–71, insisting successfully on military actions that the chancellor thought imprudent. And Schlieffen had prepared the plans that, once activated, took matters out of the hands of the Kaiser and his ministers in the crisis of July–August 1914 that eventuated in the Great War.

At times, Beck seemed to take as his model the even more powerful

general staff of the Great War, headed by Ludendorff. Through the Kaiser
and his surrogate commander in chief, Hindenburg, Ludendorff had directed not only military campaigns but the whole mobilization of Germany's
war economy. Beck was eventually to argue that war had become too complicated to be run as it had been in 1916–18, but he did so only in face of
a threat that Blomberg or some other armed-forces commander in chief
would control. As long as he imagined that an *army* commander in chief
would be in power, Beck saw much to be said for a general staff à la Ludendorff.

Though Beck never in fact succeeded in making the general staff what
it had been before the Great War, he ran it in the tradition of Moltke and
Schlieffen. His personal example resembled Schlieffen's. Refusing to take
an official residence, he slept in a modest private villa in Lichterfelde, a
southwestern suburb of Berlin. Rising early each morning, he would ride a
horse for two hours, then be driven to the Tirpitz Ufer around 9 A.M. and remain until 7 P.M., usually without a break. A briefcase went home with him,
and an officer who had delivered a memorandum late on one day could get
it back the following morning with as many as ten pages of handwritten
commentary. The staff marveled but grumbled at Beck's passion for detail,
which led him sometimes to have a document redrafted a dozen times.

The man who would have played the part of Hindenburg had Beck become Ludendorff was the army commander in chief, Brauchitsch's predecessor, Colonel General Werner Baron von Fritsch. Also a Rhinelander,
shorter than Beck, strikingly ruddy, and with a thick monocle always
gripped in his weak left eye, Fritsch was two months younger than Beck but
slightly senior by date of rank. He, too, had welcomed Hitler's coming to
power, but he had none of Blomberg's reverence for Hitler. When directed
by Blomberg to reprove some officers who had been overheard referring to
the Führer as a "housepainter," Fritsch reportedly told the officers to speak
less loudly. But Fritsch simply evidenced the prejudices of an aristocrat.[17]
He liked Hitler's programs, and shared his detestation of Jews. What was
important to him, as to Beck, was Hitler's apparent commitment to building
up the army and to keeping it independent.

After Hitler's Opera House speech about the "two pillars of the state,"
General Fritsch expressed hope of "good, even trusting" relations with the
party. And Beck applauded Hitler's assumption of broader powers after
the death of Hindenburg, saying that this created "favorable conditions" for
the army.[18] Repeatedly, he took occasion to praise Hitler in public, though.
In private he expressed fear only that Hitler might prove "too high-minded"
to cope effectively with intriguers around him.[19]

From the beginning, General Beck did from time to time voice concern lest Germany get into a war prematurely. In 1934, soon after the Blood Purge, he had taken alarm because of a crisis over Austria. Members of an Austrian Nazi Party tried unsuccessfully to seize power, believing that the Austrian army would back them, and on July 25, they murdered the Austrian chancellor, Engelbert Dollfuss. But the Austrian army, instead of helping them, arrested them. To their surprise and Hitler's, Mussolini denounced this coup attempt, advertised precautionary troop moves, and joined French and British leaders in affirming a commitment to preserving Austria's independence.[20]

Hitler had to repudiate his fellow Nazis on the other side of the Inn River. Signing a formal agreement that promised no interference in Austria's internal affairs, he dissolved the Austrian Legion, a group that had been training in Bavaria. He even issued an order forbidding Nazis in Germany to have any contact with Nazis in Austria. In foreign newspapers and magazines supplied to him regularly by his press aide, Otto Dietrich, Hitler saw himself ridiculed. *Punch* pictured Germany as a dachshund cowering before a mastiff labeled "Italy." Alluding to one of Jean de La Fontaine's seventeenth-century fables, the *Review of Reviews* showed "the frog who wished to be as big as the ox," with Hitler recognizable as the frog and Mussolini the ox.[21]

Beck commented to an official in the Foreign Ministry that the attempted Nazi coup in Vienna had created the danger of military action against Germany. He said that Germans in "leading positions" needed to understand that their country was as yet in no position to carry on a successful war. A clash forcing Germany into a "humiliating retreat" might, he warned, finish off the Third Reich.[22] But there is no indication that Beck or Fritsch blamed Hitler for creating this danger, or that they believed Germany's status or honor to have been impaired by Hitler's climb-down. Within less than a year, both of them began to discount the danger of foreign military action against Germany. When Hitler repudiated the Treaty of Versailles in March 1935, reinstituted conscription, and started openly to build an air force, Blomberg seemed jittery, but Beck and Fritsch did not.

The same held true in 1936, when Germany suddenly remilitarized the Rhineland. Though cautiously, both Beck and Fritsch approved this surprise move. The Treaty of Versailles had prescribed that, in the area from the Rhine and the French and Belgian borders on the west, to, on the east, fifty kilometers into Germany from the Rhine, Germany should build no fortifications and introduce no uniformed military forces. Despite Germany's repudiation of most of the Treaty of Versailles, the Rhineland had remained demilitarized for two reasons. One was legal: Germany, France, Britain, and Italy had guaranteed its permanent demilitarization under the separate Locarno Pact of 1925. The second was practical: the status of the Rhineland was a sensitive political issue in France. The détente symbolized by the Locarno Pact had involved France's withdrawing occupation troops from the Rhineland sooner than the Versailles Treaty required. Right-wing members of the French Parliament had fought this concession. Since the centrists and leftists who prevailed had argued that permanent demilitarization adequately protected France's security, members of their parties had a stake in its continuance.

The legal case against remilitarization was increasingly weak, however. In 1935, France had reached an understanding with the Soviet Union, envisioning a future military alliance. As commentators not only in Germany but in France and Britain had been quick to point out, this understanding was inconsistent with the Locarno Pact, for it implied that, in the event of a German-Russian war, France would not live up to the Locarno promise to respect Germany's western frontier. In the press and Parliament, French opponents of a Soviet alliance said that Germany might be entitled to treat as a dead letter its Locarno obligations regarding the Rhineland.

While watching to see how France and Britain responded to Germany's open rearmament, General Fritsch advised against immediate remilitarization. But after the Western powers raised no serious objections to German rearmament, he and Beck became less timid. Constantin Baron von Neurath, Hitler's foreign minister, having seen intelligence reports that the French army was of two minds about whether to resist remilitarization, was urging that Germany take advantage of the opportunity presented by the debate over the Franco-Soviet pact.[23] Fritsch said that other nations now had enough respect for Germany's growing military strength so that any forceful response to its remilitarization was unlikely. Indicating confidence that it would soon occur, Beck initiated planning to incorporate into the army the Rhineland's large militia. His own personal feelings were engaged, for it infuriated him to be forbidden to wear his uniform when he visited his birthplace.

In mid-February 1936, Hitler and Fritsch had a conversation about the Rhineland. Fritsch said that its remilitarization was an indispensable accompaniment to Germany's ongoing rearmament. When Hitler suggested that the army prepare to move into the area, Fritsch voiced the standard comment that Germany was not yet ready for war. Nevertheless, when he returned to the Bendlerstrasse, he reported the conversation, and Beck agreed that the general staff should develop an operational plan for remilitarization.[24]

In view of later mythology about the remilitarization of the Rhineland, the comparative complacency of the army's leaders calls for explanation. After-the-fact criticism of the Western powers' appeasement of Hitler would portray the Rhineland affair as a crucial turning point. If France had insisted on enforcing the Locarno Pact and had marched troops into the Rhineland, it was said, Germany would have faced exactly what Beck had feared in 1934—a humiliating retreat. In Winston Churchill's lastingly influential formulation: "There is no doubt that Hitler would have been compelled by his own General Staff to withdraw, and a check would have been given to his pretensions which might well have proved fatal to his rule."[25]

After the war, German military men endorsed and embraced Churchill's version of the story, for Fritsch and Beck and the other generals figured in it as "good Germans." Since Beck and some other officers had later opposed Hitler, even to the point of trying to assassinate him, they were represented as having always been ready to act against Hitler but prevented from doing so in 1936 by weak-spined appeasers in Paris and London.

Not a scrap of evidence dating from 1936 supports such a story. Neither Fritsch nor Beck evidenced serious misgivings. They were pleased that Hitler had turned to them and not to Blomberg to plan the operation. Germany at the time was host for the Olympic Games, and Blomberg had gone to Garmisch-Partenkirchen to observe ski trials. For some time, he had been trying to act as an armed-forces commander in chief and to appropriate for himself and his staff some of the powers traditionally monopolized by the army commander in chief and chief of staff. By talking to Fritsch before himself departing for Garmisch, Hitler seemed deliberately to be demonstrating trust in and reliance on the army rather than on Blomberg. His action also implied that, if danger developed, the army would have responsibility for controlling it.

On February 27, the French Chamber of Deputies ratified the Franco-Soviet mutual security agreement. In the debate, opponents had insisted that ratification would invalidate the Locarno Pact. The final vote was narrow, with many traditionally anti-German deputies on the right voting no or abstaining. This vote did not complete ratification, for the Senate had yet to act, but the world press, including that in France, represented it as an accomplished fact.

Without waiting to see what the French Senate would do, Fritsch and Beck convened their field commanders. On March 2, Blomberg, back from

Garmisch, issued operational orders based on Beck's plans. Hitler set March 7 as the date for action: it had the advantage of being a Saturday and also the day before a long-scheduled major speech he was to give in Berlin. There would be some delay in foreign reactions, and Hitler would meanwhile have had more than one chance to reach both German and foreign audiences with explanations and assurances of Germany's peaceful intentions.

Hitler reportedly asked his adjutants if the operation could be canceled at the last moment. This may have indicated nervousness on his part. Blomberg, who may have expressed disquiet, almost certainly became anxious after the operation had commenced. News reports told of France's putting eleven divisions on alert, and Germany's military attaché in London sent an urgent telegram predicting that Great Britain would insist on upholding Locarno. Blomberg showed the telegram to Hitler. Hossbach thought he remembered Blomberg's urging Hitler to recall the army units already deploying into the Rhineland. Whatever the specifics, Hitler two years later described Blomberg as having behaved like "a hysterical maiden."[26]

That Hitler never said anything of the sort about Fritsch or Beck seems in itself evidence that they did not express doubts about the action. An officer on Blomberg's staff did testify after the war that General Beck had suggested that Hitler volunteer a promise not to fortify the left bank of the Rhine, and had his suggestion rejected. Another officer thought, however, that he remembered Beck's saying that the person who showed hesitancy was Hitler. According to this officer's recollection, Beck quoted Hitler: "If the French mean business, then I shall pull back." Commanders marching into the Rhineland were instructed to hold their ground if attacked. Withdrawal in the face of forcible French resistance would have come on orders from Fritsch and Beck. It is not even logical to suppose that their issuing such orders would have been followed by an effort to unseat Hitler. Nor is there any logical reason to suppose that a setback in the Rhineland in 1936 would have had any worse effect on Hitler's standing with the German public than the setback in Austria in 1934.[27]

Until late 1937, most German army officers thought Hitler was collaborating with the army rather than the army with him. In spite of the Nazi emblem on their uniforms, the oath to Hitler, and the ritual of calling out "Heil

Hitler!," the army seemed more independent, more supreme within its sphere, than it had ever been in the past. Not only did Hitler give its leaders the resources they asked for, he actually gave them more. Though he showed interest in new weaponry and exercises and war games, he merely asked questions: he did not issue orders, and rarely even gave advice. Army officers had little reason to complain of civilian meddling, as they had during the Weimar years.

In some respects, the army seemed even more autonomous than under the monarchy or the empire. Prior to 1918, soldiers had had to pretend that monarchs were their superiors, whether they believed it or not. The Weimar Constitution made soldiers legally answerable to elected members of the Reichstag. But since 1933, they had owed deference to no one, except possibly Hitler. And few officers treated Hitler as they would have treated a Hohenzollern. Hossbach, though only a colonel and assigned to Hitler's own staff, refused to get up in the night when Hitler summoned him. When a messenger came to his room at 2:15 A.M., Hossbach told him to tell the Führer it was too late; he would drop in next morning! On another occasion, when invited to dine with Hitler, Hossbach declined, explaining that he had promised his wife he would go home for dinner. When Hitler sent a staff officer to invite General Beck to a meeting, Beck laughed and said to the emissary, "Give the Führer my best, but whether I will come or not, I do not know, for I have much to do."[28] And this was in mid-1938, less than eighteen months before the outbreak of war. It is evidence of belief, even at that late date, that the army thought itself at least still a state within the state.

CHAPTER THREE

RIFTS

"Military premises are not subjects for statesmen."
— *General Ludwig Beck, November 12, 1937*

The first evident differences of opinion were not between the German armed forces and Hitler but among the military officers themselves. They concerned the issue that had figured in the Rhineland affair—the respective roles of the War Ministry and its staff on the one hand and of the army and its general staff on the other. The War Ministry had nominal jurisdiction over all three armed services. Titled a Ministry of Defense during the Weimar era, it had been designed as an organ of civilian control, but in the crisis atmosphere preceding Hitler's takeover, General Groener had become defense minister. Though he had bossed the army more than had his predecessors, he had worn civilian clothes and in most respects acted as a civilian overseer. General Blomberg, by contrast, treated the post as a military assignment. He remained in uniform, and accepted promotions—to colonel general in August 1933 and to field marshal in 1936. He outranked both Fritsch and Beck.

When changing the name Ministry of Defense to War Ministry, Hitler designated the war minister as nominally also commander in chief of the armed forces. Wanting to give the title substance, Blomberg began to build an interservice staff and to arrange war games involving combined land, air, and sea operations. In May 1937, he ordered preparation of a plan for military intervention in Austria—Plan Otto. The code name derived from one of the contingencies envisioned, which was a coup in Vienna making Otto von Hapsburg monarch.

General Beck refused to draw up any such plan. For Germany to intervene in Austria, he wrote, would provoke a general European war, probably involving Russia, Poland, and Lithuania as well as Czechoslovakia and Western nations. He would not allow the army general staff even to toy with such a contingency.

Yet Blomberg did not back off. Within weeks, he sent Fritsch and Beck a broader directive ordering planning against possible attack from either France or Czechoslovakia (Plan Red and Plan Green), saying that, though there was no immediate prospect of attack, it was desirable to get ready. He recommended preparation of a plan for an attack on Czechoslovakia, referring vaguely to "being able militarily to exploit favorable political opportunities." And he repeated the injunction to prepare Plan Otto.[1]

Fritsch and Beck saw a bureaucratic problem and nothing more. They had no reason to suppose that Hitler had inspired Blomberg's directives. And there is no evidence that he did. Blomberg had said there was no prospect of attack, and Fritsch and Beck had no reason to doubt him. In their eyes, the chief issue was not what should be planned but who should do it. They continued to resist what they interpreted as Blomberg's encroachments on army prerogatives, and they heard not a word from Hitler suggesting that they should desist.

In the summer of 1937, Blomberg tried again. He ordered the army and the other services to prepare joint plans. His directive said operational orders would come from him.[2] But General Fritsch would have none of this. The services, he insisted, were not equal: the army alone would win or lose a war. Operations by the other services would either support the army or be of secondary importance. It followed, said Fritsch, that the army's commander in chief should control combined operations. Its general staff could consult, as needed, with the air force and the navy.[3]

Fritsch threatened to take the issue to Hitler if Blomberg did not give in. Though he might have feared Hitler's siding with Blomberg as the more pro-Nazi, he evidently assumed the contrary. He expected Hitler yet again to confirm the army's special status. Blomberg must have agreed, for he temporized, thus keeping the issue away from Hitler, at least for the time being. What is significant is that Fritsch and Beck were willing to make Hitler arbiter in a matter internal to the military establishment.

The army also differed with the other services. At issue were scarce resources. Though rearmament had had priority, there was still the question:
whose rearmament? The army planned to have a hundred divisions by the
early 1940s. The air force wanted by then to have more than tripled its battle force. The navy projected a fivefold increase in the submarine fleet and,
in addition, a score of major capital ships. But Germany had nothing like
the raw materials and industrial plant for all three programs.[4]

All army generals, including Blomberg, believed that the army deserved
priority. In the early years of the Third Reich, army officers had presided
over the cabinet committee that allocated resources, and the army chief of
staff originally held the chair; more recently, that place had been taken by
a designee of Blomberg's. Neither the air force nor the navy, however, was
prepared to let this arrangement stand. The obvious person to whom to appeal was Hitler. Even if army officers might hope that Hitler would continue to show preference to the army, they could not be blind to the
possibility of his doing otherwise. The air force had the advantage of being
represented by Göring, who, in addition to all else, was commissar for Germany's economic four-year plan and hence overseer of all economic priorities. And the navy could have hopes based on Hitler's sometimes speaking
of England as Germany's most dangerous foe.[5]

By the autumn of 1937, decisions had to be made. Raeder wrote
Blomberg that there was not enough steel for the naval building program al-
ready authorized. Blomberg arranged a meeting with Hitler: he, Göring,
Raeder, and Fritsch would attend; Hossbach would take notes.

As he was to do two years later at the new Chancellory, Hitler turned
the meeting in an unexpected direction. He invited Foreign Minister Neurath to join the group, and instead of talking about how to allocate steel and
rubber and such, he talked about Germany's need to expand in order to
gain new resources and new living space (*Lebensraum*). According to Hossbach's memorandum of record—which became a key text in later war-
crimes trials, presented as proof that Germany's military and diplomatic
leaders joined Hitler in a conspiracy to commit aggression—Hitler said,
"Germany's problem could only be solved by means of force." This force
had to be applied no later than 1943–45—"Our relative strength would decrease in relation to the rearmament ... carried out by the rest of the
world. ... It was while the rest of the world was fencing itself off that we
were obliged to take the offensive."

The immediate places for expansion were to the east—Austria and
Czechoslovakia. Circumstances might permit seizing these territories soon.

Eventually, if not at that time, Germany might have to fight Britain and France. But these "two hate-inspired antagonists," Hitler said, were not so powerful as they seemed. The British Empire was menaced by Italy in the Mediterranean, by Japan in Asia, and by the United States all over the world. France, though more secure, confronted "internal political difficulties." But because France and Britain were beginning to rearm to match Germany's rearmament and would eventually become stronger, Germany would have to initiate a war at least by 1943–45, he declared. In the shorter run, its armed forces should prepare to seize Czechoslovakia and Austria whenever opportunity offered—if, for example, France should experience an internal crisis or become involved in a war with Italy.[6]

Hitler's words should not have struck his hearers as particularly new. When he first addressed senior officers after the dinner arranged by General Hammerstein in February 1933, he had said that he envisioned "conquest of new living space in the East and its ruthless Germanization." After declaring in his speech in 1935 at the Opera House that the army and the party were the twin "pillars of the state," he had gone on to speak of the hostility of Britain and France and the probable need for "short, decisive blows to the West and then to the East," blows that would probably have to come in the early 1940s. Hossbach, who had heard Hitler's monologues dozens of times, was not surprised at all. He waited three days before bothering to write out his memorandum of the meeting and did so only when Fritsch prodded him.[7]

Blomberg, Fritsch, and Neurath, however, were all taken aback. If they had listened to Hitler earlier, they had not taken in the possibility that he might mean what he said. According to Hossbach's memorandum, Blomberg and Fritsch both "repeatedly emphasized the necessity that Britain and France must not appear in the role of our enemies," and Neurath said something similar. The two generals asserted that France would have superiority no matter what. A French war with Italy would engage only a small part of France's armed forces. Since Germany had as yet no useful fortifications and no motorized forces, whereas France was prepared for rapid mobilization and had several motorized and mechanized divisions, Fritsch warned, nothing could keep France from seizing Germany's industrial centers.

After the war, Hossbach was to say that his memorandum minimized the extent and strength of the generals' protests. He recalled sharp exchanges between the generals and Göring, none of which he mentioned in his memorandum.[8] Testifying at his war-crimes trial, Göring said that Hitler had told him ahead of time that he intended to push the generals toward much faster preparations for war. He implied that, for this reason, he took Hitler's words to be mostly theatrics. Admiral Raeder, in his own testimony, recalled being reassured by Blomberg's quoting to him the proverb *"Kommt Zeit, kommt Rat"*—in effect, "Time brings second thoughts."[9]

Fritsch came to a similar view. Before the meeting, he had been planning a vacation in Egypt. Hearing Hitler talk of attacking Czechoslovakia, he said he would obviously have to change his plans, though Hitler told him that he need not do so: "The possibility of a conflict need not yet be regarded as so imminent." Fritsch saw Hitler again on November 9, then left Berlin and stayed away for two full months, giving little indication in letters home of serious worries about the future.[10]

Beck, however, became alarmed. Though he had not been at the meeting, Fritsch had told him about it, and he had seen Hossbach's memorandum.[11] He immediately composed a long memorandum of his own. Whether intended for Hitler's eyes or Blomberg's or just for his own use, one cannot tell. Beck labeled it simply as "Marginal Notes" on the Hossbach memorandum.[12]

These "Marginal Notes" disputed almost every one of Hitler's assertions. According to Hossbach, Hitler had said that Germany's future was "wholly conditional upon the solving of the need for space"; trade would not meet Germany's economic needs, for dependence on trade made a country militarily vulnerable. Italy and Japan were expanding and Germany needed to do likewise, but in Europe, not in distant colonial areas. Beck agreed that Germany "undoubtedly" needed more land, but he questioned whether truly large changes in the map of Europe would be in Germany's best interest. To "Germanize" the East, Beck observed, could imperil "the German racial core." As for trade, he wrote: "To the extent that I understand these matters, we have need for all time of the greatest possible participation in the world economy. Otherwise, the German people must slowly atrophy."

According to Hossbach's notes, Hitler had outlined three possible scenarios. In the first, Germany would come to the period 1943–45 with its boundaries not materially changed and would then have to launch a war of conquest. In the second and third scenarios, Germany would go to war earlier, either because of an internal crisis in France that created an opportunity, or because France and Italy went to war and Germany intervened on the side of Italy. Beck's comments on these scenarios bordered on contempt. With regard to Hitler's statement that war had to come by 1943–45 because after that time France and Britain would have military forces more modern than Germany's, Beck huffed: "*Military* premises are not subjects for statesmen but must be assessed and determined by professionals. . . . The conclusion that by 1943–45 at the latest the German space problem must be solved is . . . unconvincing." (In pencil, Beck wrote in the last word as a replacement for a stronger one—"*niederschmetternd,*" equivalent to "baseless.") Beck characterized the scenario of French internal collapse as "completely improbable . . . a fantasy," and, regarding a French war with Italy, repeated what Fritsch had said at the Chancellory: "France will always have available adequate forces to counter Germany."

Beck took issue equally forcefully with Hitler's analogies. It was wrong to compare German expansion in Europe to that of Italy in Africa or of Japan in Asia, he wrote. The long-settled, populous, economically developed European continent had little in common with primitive areas elsewhere. It was also wrong for Hitler to liken his thinking to that of Frederick the Great or Bismarck, saying, according to Hossbach's memorandum, that Frederick's seizure of Silesia in 1754 and Bismarck's wars against Austria and France in 1866 and 1870–71 had "involved unheard-of risk." No such thing: "It is not historically accurate to say that Bismarck's wars against Austria and France were irresponsibly risky," Beck wrote. "They were perhaps the best-prepared wars that a statesman has ever waged and were for that reason successful."

Before long, Beck would compose even stronger memoranda criticizing Hitler's thoughts and projects. Meanwhile, during the winter of 1937–38, changes in the German government increased Hitler's power relative to all his generals and any others who might question his proposed war for "living space."

January 1938 saw the "Blomberg-Fritsch affair."[13] Blomberg, approaching sixty and long a widower, had fallen into a habit of putting on civilian clothes and wandering into taverns for company. At one of these, the White Deer, he met Margarette Gruhn, the twenty-four-year-old daughter of a one-time Royal Palace housemaid now proprietress of a massage parlor in the southeastern Berlin suburb of Neuköln. Blomberg became infatuated.

Fräulein Gruhn became pregnant. Though knowing it would cause talk, Blomberg proposed marriage. It was, after all, "the New Germany," and when Blomberg told Hitler and Göring that he wished to wed "a child of the people," they congratulated him and agreed to be witnesses. The ceremony took place quietly at the War Ministry. Blomberg kept it so private that his former deputy, Reichenau, now commanding an army corps at Munich, learned about it only after the couple had left for their honeymoon.

Unfortunately for Blomberg, Fräulein Gruhn was not only "of the people" but, at least figuratively, of the streets. When registering her change of address, the Berlin police found arrest records. Under various names, she had modeled for pornographic photographs. Count Wolf-Heinrich von Helldorf, the police president of Berlin, took these records to General Wilhelm Keitel, Blomberg's principal aide, who had also recently become Blomberg's son-in-law, urging him to show the file to Göring. (He probably hoped that it would thus escape falling into the hands of Himmler, who was energetically conniving to acquire power at anyone's expense, including police agencies such as Helldorf's.)

Though Göring knew from other sources that the new Frau Blomberg had a questionable past, he had had to keep quiet: Hitler still held to his rule of hearing no party official speak evil of an army man. But now, since Helldorf's evidence came to him via General Keitel, a military man, the rule did not apply. Göring presented the file to Hitler, and this time Hitler did not play deaf. He blew up—or pretended to. He said he could not tolerate such dishonoring of the uniform.

Even before Hitler confronted Blomberg, the affair became the Fritsch affair also. Himmler had long been ready to lay an accusation against General Fritsch. His Gestapo had an affidavit from a police informer who had spied on a male prostitute working the men's room of the Potsdamer Platz railway station. The informer said he had followed one of the prostitute's clients and blackmailed him, the victim being an army officer who lived not far from the Potsdamer Platz. With help from his interrogators, the informer identified this victim as General Fritsch. (Actually, the prostitute's patron had been a cavalry captain named Achim von Frisch.) Himmler had informed Hitler at the time, but Hitler had refused to listen. Now, given the Blomberg scandal, he paid attention. He himself may have asked Himmler for the file. As of Blomberg, so of Fritsch, Hitler declared that he could not tolerate the stain on the honor of the army.

In part of his mind, Hitler may have welcomed the opportunity to shake up his military leadership. Blomberg and Fritsch had both questioned the program of conquest he had outlined the previous November. Aware that Stalin had begun to purge the Soviet officer corps and that Britain had recently shaken up its whole army command, Hitler may have been looking for a chance to show publicly that he, too, was master of his armed forces.[14] But the timing of this affair had not been Hitler's choice. Blomberg had been useful to him and would not be easy to replace. Nor was there an obvious successor to Fritsch. The diaries of Joseph Goebbels, Hitler's minister of propaganda, describe Hitler as being for several days ashen, distraught, and occasionally tearful.[15]

Blomberg tendered his resignation. Hitler accepted it. On the same day, Hitler summoned Fritsch to the Chancellory (still the old shabby one where Bismarck had worked, flush with the sidewalk on the Wilhelmstrasse). Göring and Himmler were present. The Gestapo informer came forward. Pointing at Fritsch, Hitler asked, "Was this the man?" The informer said "Yes." Fritsch's naturally red face must have turned the color of a poinsettia. Although he tried to maintain his customary icy calm, he burbled a guess that there might have been some misunderstanding owing to the fact that, like other bachelor officers, he had played host to fatherless boys from the Hitler Youth. Hitler took Fritsch's words as confession (or pretended to) and offered him the face-saving resort of resigning on pretense of ill health. At this Fritsch stiffened and said, "I refuse to account for myself in this way. . . . I demand a court of honor."

Not long after this awful scene, Fritsch did resign. He expected the military court of honor to hear his case and establish his innocence, and in time, this happened. The only result, however, was to gratify those who had never believed Fritsch guilty. The general himself shrank into plaintive retirement.

Hitler used the Blomberg-Fritsch affair as opportunity to effect a major reorganization. Instead of naming a successor to Blomberg, he abolished the War Ministry and took for himself the title of commander in chief of the armed forces. Like "Heil Hitler!" and the officers' oath, this may have been at Blomberg's suggestion when Hitler asked him to propose a successor. And it was made independently by Goebbels, who called it "the logical solution" (not least because another logical solution would have been the promotion of Goebbels's rival, Göring).[16] The formula was acceptable to the army's generals. They, too, feared Göring's moving into Blomberg's post, for they could envision Göring as both continuing Blomberg's effort to create a real armed-forces high command and, as budget coordinator, favoring the air force over the army. (In fact, the fear was groundless. Hitler said to an aide that he had no thought of giving Göring the job: "No question of it. He understands almost nothing about the air force. He can't even conduct a proper inspection. I know more about that than he does."[17])

To the generals, Hitler's solution seemed to spell an end to Blomberg's armed-forces high-command scheme. Few of them supposed that Hitler, who had never risen above the rank of private first class, would try to dictate operational strategy. The chances of his even being tempted to do so seemed to disappear when Hitler announced his personnel plans, for there was to be no armed-forces chief of staff. As commander in chief, he would be served only by a small secretariat, the head of which would be Keitel. Previously the equivalent of a chief clerk for Blomberg, Keitel had had a career mostly in administration. An officer who had served with him in the 1920s characterized him as "industrious" and "skilled at writing and speaking, but not a strong personality."[18] Behind his back, some fellow officers called him "Lakeitel," in a play on *Lakai*, the German word for "lackey." Hitler added yet more reassurance by saying that he expected to be commander in chief only temporarily. At some point, he said, he would probably copy French practice and designate an army general to serve as generalissimo over all the armed forces.

To replace Fritsch, Hitler chose Brauchitsch. Some officers wanted no permanent replacement, preferring that the office be held open until Fritsch was vindicated; others thought differently, given that Fritsch had actually resigned. Hitler discussed the possibilities with several advisers. Goebbels's diary records Hitler's talking of Beck, Brauchitsch, and Reichenau, saying that Reichenau was too political and not sturdy enough in character and Brauchitsch perhaps not political enough but "an absolute professional." Goebbels spoke strongly in favor of Beck, saying, "He comes straight from the Schlieffen school."[19]

When Hitler asked senior generals for advice, they, too, discouraged his choosing Reichenau and endorsed Brauchitsch, for Brauchitsch had an outstanding record and, as compared with Beck, had the advantage of coming not from one of Prussia's Rhineland colonies but from the old Prussian heartland east of the Elbe River. As a youth, Brauchitsch had been a page at the court of Kaiser Wilhelm II. As a staff officer in the Great War, he had earned high combat decorations. Since then, in addition to staff service, he had commanded a division, a corps, and an army group. He had experience of both artillery and tanks and was credited with planning the training that had enabled the hundred-thousand-man army to expand almost tenfold so smoothly. Brauchitsch would have been a leading candidate had Fritsch left his post in a routine way. If he himself had misgivings about not leaving the post open for Fritsch, he swallowed them by rationalizing that the alternative was Reichenau, and that he was protecting the army against politicization.

Though the appointment of Brauchitsch seemed on the surface merely to put one disciple of Seeckt in the place of another, Hitler probably expected Brauchitsch to be more responsive than his predecessor, for the new man would soon be in debt to him not only for being nominated but also for a personal favor. Like Blomberg, Brauchitsch had fallen in love. His inamorata, Charlotte Rüffer Schmidt, did not have Fräulein Gruhn's social disabilities. She was a Silesian of good family and the widow of a bank director. To marry her, Brauchitsch needed a divorce from his current wife. He and she had been on cool terms for years. Even in the 1920s, fellow officers had pitied his unhappy home life.[20] Frau Brauchitsch, however, demanded a comfortable financial settlement. Brauchitsch had almost decided to retire from the army to take a higher-paying civilian job, but Hitler resolved his dilemma with an outright gift of enough money to underwrite the divorce. (Hitler had a large private fund created by, among other things, royalties paid him by the post office for permission to use his picture on stamps.) Though Brauchitsch was undoubtedly pleased, he may not have felt particularly obligated to Hitler, for it was a venerable custom for the state to make gifts to eminent soldiers. He is said to have thought of Hitler's eighty thousand Reichsmarks as akin to the grants of land and estates by which earlier Prussian generals had been rescued from their creditors. But, whatever he may have thought, Hitler, as a politician, surely assumed that he would have an extra claim on Brauchitsch's loyalty.[21]

Reorganization in the high command and the replacement of Fritsch were only two of many changes. Keitel's younger brother, Major General Bodewin Keitel, "little Keitel," came in with Brauchitsch as army chief of personnel. Several general-staff officers known to have spoken critically of the Nazi Party were transferred to troop duty. Major General Erich von Manstein, Beck's chief operational planner, went off to command a division. He was replaced by Halder. Göring, in compensation for not becoming war minister, was promoted to field marshal.

Hitler, meanwhile, also changed personnel in the Foreign Ministry. He had previously dealt with that ministry much as he had with the military estab-

lishment, keeping it independent of the party. Neurath had been in place
when he became chancellor, and he kept him on. There had been no reason
not to do so, for Neurath served Hitler willingly. At the time of the Blood
Purge, he defended Hitler's actions as zealously as Blomberg and Reichenau. At the ceremonies marking Hitler's assumption of the powers that
had been vested in Hindenburg, a foreign journalist remarked that Neurath
was "so self-conscious, so servile, as he always is when Hitler is around,
that you could almost see him wag his tail."[22] Also, Neurath's presence
helped to give the outside world an impression of foreign-policy continuity.
And party members who aspired to take Neurath's place managed mostly to
disqualify themselves. Alfred Rosenberg, for example, Hitler's principal
adviser on foreign policy prior to the takeover, had gone to London in May
1933 to promote Anglo-German understanding. He placed a swastika-
bedecked wreath at the Cenotaph, the memorial to Britain's Great War
dead, which stands in front of the Foreign Office, just where Parliament
Street becomes Whitehall. A British war veteran promptly picked up the
wreath, carried it the long block to the bank of the Thames, and threw it
into the river, as onlookers cheered. This was the only moment of Rosenberg's mission reported by the world press, which, by contrast, customarily
treated Neurath with respect. Hitler thus had little cause for complaining
about Neurath, and he was rarely bothered by him, for Hitler's erratic
schedule kept him often away from the capital, and when in Berlin, he was
likely to work, if at all, during the night, whereas Neurath, a man of rigid
habits, always went to bed at 10 P.M. As a result, weeks could pass without
Hitler's even seeing his foreign minister.

The decision suddenly to replace Neurath seems best explained by the
Blomberg-Fritsch affair. As a career diplomat, Neurath was scheduled to
retire because of age. Though he had spoken against Hitler's expansionist
program and taken occasion later to caution that it might "lead to world
war," Hitler had said publicly that he intended to waive the retirement rule
and keep Neurath on. Now, when announcing that he himself would take
the place of Blomberg and that Brauchitsch would replace Fritsch, he
added that Neurath would leave the Foreign Ministry to assume undefined
duties as a "counselor." Neurath's successor would be Joachim von Ribbentrop, currently German ambassador in London.[23]

The appointment of Ribbentrop made it likely that Hitler would hear
much more often the voice of the Foreign Ministry—or at least that of the
foreign minister. For, day and night, Ribbentrop was at hand if Hitler would
see him. As ambassador in London since 1936, he had flown to Germany so

often to try to be with Hitler that *Punch* labeled him "the wandering Aryan."

Forty-four, and thus four years younger than Hitler, Ribbentrop had ash-blond hair and the puffy handsomeness of an overage gigolo. He was one of the handful of prominent Nazis with experience of the world outside Germany. The son of a workaday army officer, he had spent some of his youth in Lorraine and had then emigrated to Canada. After returning to Germany to serve as a junior officer in the Great War, he had been wounded and awarded the same decoration that Hitler prized—the Iron Cross, First Class.

After the war, Ribbentrop became a wine merchant in Berlin, prospered, and married his boss's daughter. Later, he was sometimes called "a champagne salesman." And he was. But his firm also had exclusive rights to prized foreign labels such as Chartreuse liqueur and Johnny Walker whisky. He made or married enough money to cut a figure in Berlin's haut monde. His villa in Berlin-Dahlem had its own swimming pool and tennis court, and he drove the latest Mercedes sports cars. By paying a distant relative to adopt him, he meanwhile became not just plain Ribbentrop but *von* Ribbentrop.

An important member of Ribbentrop's social circle was the political dilettante Franz von Papen, whom he had met during the war. The bankruptcy of the late Weimar Republic had no clearer symptom than the fact that Papen briefly became chancellor, for he was a poseur who had been promoted from post to post in the diplomatic service by superiors trying to get rid of him because of his incompetence. Like many others in the German elite, Papen had had the illusion that he could use Hitler instead of the other way around and, knowing that Ribbentrop was acquainted with Hitler, had enlisted him as a go-between in the negotiations that led eventually to Hitler's becoming chancellor. In the process, Ribbentrop fell completely under Hitler's spell. Later—and when he was foreign minister—much of what Ribbentrop said was an echo, almost word for word, of what he had heard from Hitler. And when he spoke to Hitler or sent him memoranda, Ribbentrop's aim was less to modify or shape Hitler's opinion than to put in words and clarify what he understood Hitler to believe.

His eagerness to please Hitler and his willingness to return after a rebuke, like a puppy after a slap on the nose, earned him Hitler's praise and protection. On more than one occasion, Hitler was to extol Ribbentrop as "a genius" and as "the greatest foreign minister since Bismarck." This would enable Ribbentrop to remain foreign minister even though he was a latecomer to the party and a butt of jokes from, among others, Göring and Goebbels. (Rumor had it, for example, that Göring had questioned Ribbentrop's appointment to the embassy in London; Hitler had said, "But he knows all the top people in England," to which Göring rejoined, "The trouble is that they know him.")

Ribbentrop could have suffered the same fate as Rosenberg. For using the stiff-armed salute and otherwise parading his Nazism, he had been an object of ridicule in London. The *Manchester Guardian* cartoonist David Low nicknamed him "Brickendrop." Other cartoonists enjoyed picturing him as a schoolboy giving a Nazi salute and being allowed by a teacher to go to the loo. Though Ribbentrop's English was excellent, he may not have been so fluent in French as he pretended. One Englishman remembered visiting the French Embassy in London and saying that he had never met Ribbentrop, to which the French ambassador responded, in Ribbentrop's hearing, "*Comment, vous ne connaissez pas ce sinistre fantoche?*" (What? You don't know this sinister puppet?)[24]

But Ribbentrop, unlike Rosenberg, provided Hitler what Hitler wanted. In 1935, he had gone to London as a special emissary commissioned to seek an agreement allowing Germany a larger navy than permitted by the Treaty of Versailles. Neurath's professionals had said it couldn't be done. Göring et al. had said that, even if it could be done, Ribbentrop couldn't do it. But, as it happened, the British government was looking for a symbolic way of saying that it favored scrapping the Versailles settlement, and Ribbentrop obtained a naval treaty that Hitler applauded. Promoted to be ambassador, Ribbentrop not only supplied Hitler with the details he craved about English politicians but also arranged visits to Hitler by sympathetic members of the British aristocracy and governing class.

Ribbentrop, though in most respects weak and stupid, had the wisdom to choose very good subordinates. His top aides at the London embassy, Erich Kordt and Ernst Woermann, were two of Germany's best-thought-of career diplomats. When he became foreign minister, Ribbentrop brought Kordt and Woermann back with him to Berlin. Within weeks of taking office, he also promoted Ernst Baron von Weizsäcker to the key post of state secretary, the number-two position in the ministry.

Almost a dozen years older than Ribbentrop, and from a Württemberg family that had long boasted both famous scholars and intimates of kings, Weizsäcker had originally been a career naval officer. He had entered the navy in 1900, at the height of popular enthusiasm for Grand Admiral Alfred von Tirpitz's new fleet and Germany's quest for a "place in the sun" as a colonial power, and he had worn the uniform for almost twenty years. Only after the defeat and upheaval of 1918 had Weizsäcker shifted to the diplomatic service.

Like Beck, Weizsäcker remained a monarchist. He never felt loyalty to the Weimar Republic. But, unlike Beck, Weizsäcker did not cheer the advent of Hitler. His vantage point in 1933 was the German mission in Oslo, Norway, and his early reaction was discomfort at representing a government that foreigners did not yet take seriously.[25] Subsequently, he watched with approval the new regime's programs for treaty revision and rearmament. At the same time, he found it an irksome duty to defend before foreign audiences—chiefly in Switzerland, where he was minister from 1933 to 1936—the excesses of the party and such events as the Blood Purge and the murder of Dollfuss.

Weizsäcker had returned to Berlin in August 1936 to become, in effect, the Foreign Ministry's number three. Neurath's state secretary, Bernhard von Bülow, had died suddenly, and Neurath replaced him with his own son-in-law, Hans Georg Viktor von Mackensen, who happened to be one of the career service's few zealous Nazis. Though Mackensen shared with Bülow the circumstance of having a famous general as a father, he shared little else—not Bülow's brains or energy, and least of all Bülow's high standing among other career officials. Weizsäcker's appointment as number three had been compensation, for Weizsäcker had been the careerists' leading candidate for the succession to Bülow. Ribbentrop had the intelligence to rid himself of Mackensen by sending him off to Italy and giving Weizsäcker the post he probably should have had in 1936.

Ribbentrop had access to Hitler such as Neurath had never had. In person or through his trusted agent in Hitler's Chancellory, Walter Hewel, he constantly measured Hitler's moods and thoughts. Weizsäcker would then equip him to present to Hitler evidence and arguments designed—often to a degree that Ribbentrop did not comprehend—to shape Hitler's views. During much of 1938, therefore, Hitler would be given at least two sets of opinions at variance with his own—those of Beck and those of Weizsäcker.

CHAPTER FOUR

CONFLICT

"All drivers should be sure to wear goggles, otherwise they might be blinded by the flowers thrown at them."
—Colonel Alfred Jodl of the armed-forces high command, on precautions to be taken by the German army when marching into Austria in February 1938

"It is my unalterable decison to smash Czechoslovakia by military action in the near future." *—Hitler's directive to the armed forces, May 30, 1938*

When Hitler talked with Blomberg and Fritsch in November 1937 during the meeting recorded by Colonel Hossbach, he had known that crises were likely over Austria or Czechoslovakia or both. He may well have questioned whether his generals or even his foreign minister recognized their imminence or urgency. Beck's refusal to work on Plan Otto would have given him evidence, had he known of it, since it showed Beck's total unawareness that Austrian politicians were in fact flirting with a possible Hapsburg restoration. Göring did understand the critical state of German-Austrian and German-Czech relations, for, unlike Blomberg or Fritsch and more than Neurath, he understood Nazi Party relationships with political groups in both countries.

Hitler had recently seen the prospects improve for accomplishing in Austria what he had failed to accomplish in 1934. Mussolini had prosecuted a war of conquest in Ethiopia in defiance of a League of Nations resolution and had, as a result, become estranged from France and Britain. When Hitler's emissaries queried him, he had indicated that he might be more tolerant now of an increase in German influence in Austria. Face-to-face conversations between Mussolini and Hitler in September 1937 confirmed this—or seemed to. Since Mussolini insisted on practicing imperfect and sometimes incomprehensible German, his meaning was not always clear. Also, he put Hitler off balance with a gesture open to the interpretation that he thought himself the dominating figure in the pair—he the ox and Hitler the frog, as in the *Review of Reviews* cartoon of 1934. With great ceremony, he made Hitler an honorary corporal in his Fascist militia. Nevertheless, Hitler obtained from this encounter, together with news reports and what he heard from individuals, increasing confidence that, if he managed Austrian affairs dexterously, he would not face opposition from Italy.[1]

About other foreign governments, Hitler could feel less sure. Visiting Berlin in November 1937, Viscount Halifax, an influential member of the British Cabinet, soon to be foreign secretary, had said to Hitler "of his own accord that certain changes in the European system could probably not be avoided in the long run." Halifax had referred specifically to Austria and Czechoslovakia, but had emphasized the need for changes to be brought about peacefully.

Members of the French Cabinet used similar language with regard to Austria, though not Czechoslovakia. Some of them said to the German ambassador in Paris that France would have "no essential objection to further assimilation of certain of Austria's domestic institutions with Germany's." But *peaceful* change was emphasized in Paris, and officials in the German Foreign Ministry cautioned that Italy, too, might object if Germany did not preserve at least "the façade of Austrian independence."[2]

Hitler appeared inclined to act with the recommended prudence. In late December, in a meeting with his ambassador to Austria, none other than former Chancellor Franz von Papen, Hitler said, "It is to remain our aim to pursue a policy that will preclude a solution by force so long as such a solution is undesirable for European reasons."[3] His language was awkward but precise. Though he personally might have nothing against a "solution by force," he would not insist on it, if it risked complications.

The rub for Hitler was that he lacked control over what might happen inside Austria. Internal politics there were volatile and unpredictable, and no element in the compound was more unstable than the faction-ridden Austrian Nazi Party.

To summarize a story with a plot line as complicated as that in any nineteenth-century Gothic novel: Most Austrians thought of themselves as both German and Austrian. Large numbers yearned for closer ties with Germany. Few, however, wanted Austria simply to become a province of Germany. The governing Fatherland Front Party imitated the Nazis, even to using a reverse swastika as a symbol. But its head, Dollfuss's successor, Chancellor Kurt von Schuschnigg, had nothing like Hitler's powers. One of many Viennese coffeehouse jokes told of Schuschnigg comparing notes with Hitler and boasting that the opposition in Austria was as small as that in Germany—about six million.[4]

Though no one could judge the exact strength of the Austrian Nazi Party, given that it had been outlawed in 1934, its ranks clearly included many teachers, lawyers, civil servants, and members of the police and security services, and its popularity increased. Nazi Germany was becoming stronger, and the hearts of non-Nazi Austrians were becoming fainter. Asked why he had done nothing to interfere with an unauthorized Nazi demonstration, a Vienna policeman confided to a Fatherland Front leader: "Before we know where we are, the Nazis will be in the government. How can we know if a Nazi will not be made minister for security? Then, anyone who has been too active against them . . . will pay for it."[5]

But the Austrian Nazis had no Hitler of their own. They had many competing leaders, each with his own program and strategy. Several had alliances in Germany. One, Franz Hüber, was a brother-in-law of Göring. Another commanded an Austrian SS and looked to Himmler for guidance. Yet another commanded an Austrian SA and communicated with what remained of the German SA. Others were in touch with Rudolf Hess, deputy head of the German Nazi Party; Goebbels; or Martin Bormann, Hitler's secretary. One had had Blomberg as his patron.[6]

After the failed coup of 1934, Hitler had temporarily imposed order. One Austrian Nazi reminisced in 1942 about how Hitler had received him and some of his colleagues. "He spoke to us clearly and icily . . . : My foreign policy cannot carry the burden of Austria. I . . . must build a friendly relationship with Italy and need time to build up the armed forces. . . . I need at least two years for political work. For that long, the party in Austria must maintain discipline."[7]

The discipline did not last. Partly on their own, partly with uncoordinated encouragement from Göring, Himmler, and others, factions in the Austrian party gathered weapons and laid plans for a new coup. Hitler tried to reimpose order by sending to Vienna a high-level personal representative, Wilhelm Keppler, a Bavarian industrialist who had helped raise money from big business before 1933 and had since been one of his economic advisers. But Keppler had little success. One of the more radical Austrian Nazis, Captain Josef Leopold, told Keppler brusquely that he took orders from no one.[8]

Hitler could easily imagine Captain Leopold or someone like him acting without German say-so and creating a crisis like that of 1934. In late January 1938, Schuschnigg ordered a surprise raid on Nazi headquarters in Vienna. The Vienna police got up the courage to obey his order. In the party's rabbit-hutch offices in the Teinfaltstrasse, the police found not only caches of guns and explosives but detailed plans for a new attempt to seize power. Some of these plans provided for murdering one or more German official representatives and making it appear as if the Austrian government were responsible, thus, it was hoped, triggering German military intervention. An early draft targeted the German ambassador, Papen. In the final draft, the substitute was the German military attaché, General Wolfgang Muff.[9]

On course toward the "gradual economic and military rapprochement" he had decided upon in 1937, Hitler invited Schuschnigg to come to Germany to revise yet again the formal accord on German-Austrian relations. Schuschnigg reluctantly agreed. Originally scheduled for mid-January 1938, the visit was put off until mid-February because of the Blomberg-Fritsch affair. The Vienna police raid occurred in the interval, adding some extra chill to Schuschnigg's customarily cool demeanor. The meeting, which took place at Berchtesgaden, Hitler's retreat in the Bavarian Alps, nevertheless went off calmly. A formal agreement provided, among other things, for Nazi sympathizers to have a larger role in the Austrian government. The terms, however, were ones that Schuschnigg had already decided he could live with.

Yet the terms did not satisfy the Austrian Nazis. In the province of Styria, south of the capital, Nazi demonstrations occurred in rising crescendo. Nazi students took over the University of Graz, where most students soon sported swastikas. Local Nazi leaders did their best to provoke government forces into killing some of their rank and file so as to provoke a nationwide Nazi uprising and perhaps bring about Hitler's intervention.

Foreseeing collapse of his government's authority and possible civil war, Schuschnigg gambled. The Nazis had all along been calling for a plebiscite on *Anschluss*—union with Germany. Schuschnigg announced that a plebiscite would be held. It would be on the question of whether Austrians favored "a free and German, independent and social, Christian and united Austria; . . . freedom and work, and . . . equality of all who declare for race and Fatherland"—not an easy question on which to vote no.

Between them, the Austrian Nazis and the Schuschnigg government created the crisis that Hitler and German officials had hoped to postpone. Otto von Meissner, the Chancellory chief of staff, describes Hitler as enraged, pouring out invective against Schuschnigg, declaring that he had been betrayed. Alfred-Ingemar Berndt, a Nazi journalist, heard that Hitler became literally hopping mad—so incensed he could not stand still. Directly or by phone, Hitler spoke with Göring, Neurath, Hess, and Himmler. At his direction, Keitel summoned Generals Brauchitsch and Beck.[10]

Within a day, Hitler had worked out a plan of action. His immediate aims were to stop Schuschnigg's plebiscite, to install a thoroughly pro-Nazi government in Vienna, and to bring the Austrian Nazis to heel. He intended to act along three lines. First, he would talk toughly to all parties, from Schuschnigg down to the lowest-level Nazi leaders. Second, he would mobilize German forces along the frontier, making ready to move into Austria if necessary to safeguard a pro-Nazi government. Third, he would neutralize Italy by diplomacy.

Hitler used Goebbels and Göring for the tough talk.[11] Goebbels' propaganda organs loosed fury on Schuschnigg. By telephone, Göring gave precise instructions to Arthur Seyss-Inquardt, an eminent Viennese lawyer, and Edmund Glaise-Horstenau, an equally eminent Austrian historian, who had already agreed to lead a pro-Nazi Austrian government. (Transcripts of these telephone conversations survived to be used in evidence at Nuremberg.) Göring had Seyss-Inquardt and Glaise-Horstenau reinforce Goebbels's message that the proposed plebiscite was totally unacceptable.[12]

Hitler's second line of action had to be implemented by the armed forces. In addition to having Keitel call in Brauchitsch and Beck, Hitler spoke with Göring in his capacity as head of the air force and with the army generals who commanded troops in Bavaria, one of whom was Reichenau. Göring arranged for concentrations of warplanes at Bavarian bases. Hitler himself ordered a call-up of army reserves and mobilization of uniformed party formations. For the moment, these actions simply supplemented Goebbels's propaganda. Austrians were expected to hear radio broadcasts and read front-page stories telling of German bombers descending onto runways, Bavarian civilians putting on uniforms and mustering in town squares, of army trucks, horses, and wagons rattling along Bavarian roads, and of SS and SA troopers buckling on Sam Browne belts and Mausers. Only after having created this display did Hitler direct Keitel to plan for actual use of military force in case Schuschnigg proved unyielding.

Keitel turned to his principal staff officers, Colonels Walter Warlimont and Alfred Jodl. One or both or all three remembered Blomberg's Plan Otto. They pulled it out of the files, then asked Beck to come to the Chancellory. Beck arrived, accompanied by Manstein, who had not yet left Berlin for his new command. When shown the rudimentary "Otto" file, Beck and Manstein responded as they had before: the army, they said, was totally unprepared even to move against Austria, let alone to do so while guarding against possible action on other fronts.

Hitler exerted his persuasive powers. He, too, was taken by surprise, he said to Beck, but Schuschnigg's deceit and defiance left him no choice, and he was certain that no other great power would involve itself. If German forces had to move into Austria, he predicted—accurately, as it turned out—that they would be cheered, not resisted. (Jodl contributed to the planning a suggestion that each column be preceded by a military band and a warning that "all drivers should be sure to wear goggles, otherwise they might be blinded by the flowers thrown at them."[13]) Hitler indicated that the move might in fact be simply a police action, perhaps to be carried out by Himmler's SS and other party elements.

Given Hitler's assurances and his implicit threat that credit might go to the party instead of the army, Beck changed stance. Returning to the Tirpitz Ufer, he and Manstein and officers under them whipped together in five hours a plan for the coordinated movement to the Austrian frontier of two divisions, the Second Panzer, under Guderian, and Hitler's SS Life guard, with Bock, an army general, at its head. The operation cannot be described as having gone like clockwork. Jodl estimated that 70 percent of the two divisions' vehicles broke down and were left by the roadside.[14] But it seemed an imposing force when it arrived at the Austrian border, and it certainly sufficed to achieve Hitler's purpose.

As for Mussolini, the Führer dealt with him directly. Despite all the assurances he had received from so many sources, including Mussolini himself, Hitler remained uneasy. Since he knew, probably from communications intercepts, that some dominions in the British Commonwealth had said they would not back Britain in a crisis over Austria, and he was sure that France would not move without Britain, Hitler did not feel much immediate concern about his western flank. But he had not forgotten how Mussolini had treated him in 1934, and he recognized that a sudden turn by Italy could change the whole international framework.[15] He therefore sent Mussolini a special personal appeal for support. The bearer of his message was Prince Philip of Hesse. Mussolini replied, through the prince, that Germany had Italy's complete understanding and support. Hitler responded by gushing to Mussolini that he would "never, ever, ever forget" what he had done.

The outcome was a success past all Hitler's immediate hopes. Despite his words to Beck, he had obviously seen some possibility of actual shooting. While he told military and party commanders to avoid bloodshed if possible, he ordered that resistance "be broken most ruthlessly by force of arms."[16] Yet, after less than forty-eight hours of psychological pressure, Schuschnigg began to cave, telling Seyss-Inquardt that he would postpone the plebiscite. After hearing from Seyss by phone, Göring consulted Hitler, then called Seyss back to say that nothing short of Schuschnigg's resignation could prevent a Nazi uprising, which would have immediate reinforcement from party units in Germany. Göring directed Keppler to send the Austrian Nazis into the streets. He meanwhile had General Muff, Germany's military attaché in Vienna, demand of the president of the Austrian republic that Seyss be made chancellor in Schuschnigg's place, threatening that two hundred thousand German troops would otherwise cross the border.[17]

Though Muff followed Göring's instructions, he feared that the actual arrival of German troops might electrify Austrian patriotism, and so warned German army headquarters. According to Weizsäcker's later recollection, Brauchitsch passed this warning on to Hitler and seconded the recommendation for patience. According to Göring, these cautions gave Hitler "misgivings." Göring himself meanwhile maintained phone communication with Vienna, talking with both Muff and Seyss. He concluded that the Austrian president's commission to Seyss effectively made the latter the government of Austria, so he drafted a message for Seyss that invited Germany to send troops into Austria. Without waiting for Seyss to agree, he released the communication, and Hitler ordered German army and party forces to move.[18]

When Wehrmacht and SS units trooped into Austria on March 12, 1938, they met only cheering crowds and makeshift swastika banners. Hitler flew to Guderian's headquarters. A specially equipped six-wheel black command car took him from there to his native village of Braunau, then across the Inn River slowly via Linz to Vienna. Joyful shouts of "Heil Hitler!" exceeded even what he was used to hearing at home. Theodor Cardinal Innitzer ordered churches in Austria to be draped with swastika banners, and bells pealed to celebrate Hitler's arrival. Originally, Hitler had had in mind leaving Austria independent but under a Nazi-controlled government that would recognize him, personally, as Führer. During his procession to Vienna, he concluded that he could and should annex Austria outright. From Vienna he proclaimed *Anschluss*—merger of Austria into Germany.

Not long after the *Anschluss*, Hitler decided to make an early military move against Czechoslovakia. Like Austria, Czechoslovakia posed for him both opportunity and threat. He wanted to conquer the country, absorb its German population, and, in effect, enslave the rest. As in Austria, however, Hitler had to reckon with forces not entirely in his own control.

Sudeten Germans formed a large, concentrated minority within Czechoslovakia. Approximately 30 percent of the country's total population, they were bunched together in a horseshoe-shaped hill region wedged next to Germany and Austria. Although they had an effective lobby in Prague and although the Czech central government bent over backward to accommodate them, the Sudeten Germans resented their status as an ethnic minority in an area where, under the Hapsburg monarchy, they had been part of a privileged majority. They bridled at every indication that Czechoslovaks might be getting preference in the civil service or in awards for government contracts, or that their children were being fed Czechoslovak nationalist versions of history. Many of them became idolators of Hitler. The Sudeten German party, which represented them in the Parliament in Prague, was for all practical purposes a Nazi party, and it had links not only with the party in Germany but with the outlawed party in Austria.[19]

Hitler had better control of the Sudeten Nazis than of the Austrian Nazis. One Sudeten party leader paraphrased him as saying in 1933 that "the Reich could not help them for a long time."[20] He concentrated relations with the Sudeten party leaders—and the flow of money—under Hess, the dark-browed onetime prisonmate to whom he had dictated *Mein Kampf* (and whom one aristocratic general described as a character suitable only for a murder mystery[21]). And the Sudeten party, in contrast to the Nazi Party in Austria, had a single controlling leader, Konrad Henlein, who was comparatively level-headed, patient, and tractable.

Nevertheless, Hitler faced the constant and increasing risk that events would get out of his control. Despite Henlein's seeming subservience, rumors continually circulated that he might make a deal by which he would accept concessions on Sudeten German grievances in return for becoming part of a ruling coalition in Prague. In the fractious Czechoslovak Parliament, his party formed the largest single bloc. This fact, together with concern about foreign opinion and worry about what Hitler might do, was indeed encouraging Czechoslovak politicians to become more openhanded in their approaches to him. The more Henlein and his followers resisted these approaches, the more likely it became that the Czechoslovaks would shift to treating his party as a threat to the state and begin a crackdown. Either way, Hitler could face a situation he did not want. If Henlein did make a deal, Hitler would find it harder to attack Czechoslovakia. If the Czechoslovak government began to jail Sudeten agitators and break up

Sudeten meetings, he might have to choose between a premature crisis with Czechoslovakia and the appearance once again, as in Austria in 1934, of weakly deserting his comrades abroad.

After the *Anschluss*, Hitler could expect the Czechoslovakian government to deal more urgently and perhaps more resolutely with the Sudeten Germans, for everyone could see that Czechoslovakia had become much more vulnerable militarily. It now neighbored Germany not only across rough and comparatively defensible mountains on its west but also across the plains of the middle Danube on its south. Given that Germany's arms buildup was still in its early stages, Czechoslovakia might well prefer confrontation sooner rather than later. Also, Prague felt increasing pressure from Paris and London to settle with the Sudeten Germans in order to achieve "appeasement"—the permanent easing of resentments left behind by the 1919 peace treaties.

At the same time, the outcome of the *Anschluss* crisis gave Hitler greater confidence in his ability to manage successfully an early contest with Czechoslovakia. His triumph in Austria had been more complete than he had ever hoped. Mussolini had supported Germany steadfastly. The French and British governments had hardly voiced objection, even in whispers.

Within a month of the *Anschluss*, Hitler was thinking seriously of initiating military action against Czechoslovakia during 1938. Perhaps because of the sudden insistent rumors that Henlein was making a deal with the Czechoslovak government, Hitler in late March summoned him to Berlin. In company with Hess and Ribbentrop, he talked with Henlein and other Sudeten leaders for almost three hours. Hitler said that "he intended to settle the Sudeten German problem in the not-too-distant future." Henlein, he promised, would become his "Viceroy." As Henlein summarized "the instructions, which the Führer has given," the Sudetens were to make "demands . . . which are unacceptable to the Czech Government."

Though Henlein and the others accepted these instructions, they detailed for Hitler the bases for their concern that the government might be preparing to break off negotiations. According to their informants, truckloads of rifles, machine guns, and ammunition were being delivered to Czechoslovak military and paramilitary units in the Sudetenland. Henlein said that the armed forces were in control in Prague and were preparing to act, regardless of civilian wishes. He claimed that the Italian press attaché in Prague had seen a secret Comintern plan for having agents disguised as Sudeten Germans provoke a conflict with Czechoslovak soldiers. D-day was supposed to be May 4.[22]

Immediately after this meeting, Hitler left Berlin for two weeks of electioneering. He had scheduled a nationwide referendum for April 10. The people were to vote on whether they approved of the *Anschluss* and of the candidates chosen by "our Führer Adolf Hitler." Hitler conducted himself as if the outcome were in doubt, going from city to city, making increasingly impassioned speeches. Nationwide, almost every eligible person voted, in what appeared to foreign observers to be an honestly managed secret ballot, and 99.08 percent voted yes. In the new Austrian provinces of Greater Germany, the percentage was even higher.[23]

When back in Berlin, Hitler occupied himself with preparations for a great parade, to be held on April 20, celebrating his forty-ninth birthday. During that very day, he talked with Keitel about Czechoslovakia. Just before Schuschnigg's surprise plebiscite proposal, Hitler had told Keitel that he did not want to discuss planning with regard to Czechoslovakia until later.[24] According to Keitel's later recollection, Hitler now directed that the armed-forces high-command staff begin preliminary planning for an offensive. He said that he was not thinking of acting on his own accord but "political constellations might emerge where one would have to strike like lightning."[25] Possibly, Hitler was influenced by reports from Czechoslovakia that more and more Sudeten Germans expected German military intervention and that Henlein, partly because of his efforts to dampen such expectations, was losing control. Possibly, too, Hitler saw indications that Czechoslovak politicians were ever more desperate for a deal with Henlein. Very likely, the fact of the birthday also made Hitler think of hurrying up his general timetable for conquest, for he always worried about dying young.

Whatever his train of reasoning, Hitler began to think more actively of a military attack on Czechoslovakia. On the day after his birthday, he met again with Keitel. A memorandum of record was prepared by Colonel Rudolf Schmundt, who had recently replaced Hossbach. According to this memorandum, Hitler reiterated that he did not have in mind an "attack out of the blue," if only because "hostile world opinion . . . might lead to [a] serious situation." It was also undesirable to have a long period of diplomatic discussion, for the Czechoslovaks would then have too much time to prepare for war. Therefore, he said, military planners should focus on a third contingency: "lightning action based on an incident."

That Hitler had in mind an incident of his own contriving is suggested by Schmundt's parenthetical note: "(for example the murder of the German minister in the course of an anti-German demonstration)." Ernst Eisenlohr, the German minister in Prague, seemed cast for the role barely escaped in Vienna first by Papen, then by General Muff. And Hitler made quite clear the campaign he visualized. It would involve concentrating troops as rapidly as possible without sacrifice of surprise. Columns of troops directly supported by the air force would break through Czechoslovak defenses at several points. Motorized forces might make a bold strike for Pilsen, by-passing Prague. The objective had to be an effective victory within four days. Otherwise, Hitler explained, "a European crisis is certain to arise. Faits accomplis must convince foreign powers of the hopelessness of military intervention."[26]

Within about six weeks, between his birthday and the end of May, Hitler went from this request for contingency planning to a definite order for an early military offensive. After the conversation recorded by Schmundt, Hitler departed again for Vienna to deal with details and ceremonies concerning Austria's incorporation into the Reich. He returned to Berlin for May Day, making an early-morning speech in Olympia Stadium to a crowd of young people and a noontime speech to a throng in the Lustgarten. One theme in the second speech was "no more war." Hitler declaimed, "I know this saying. . . . It is mine also! That is exactly why I have made Germany strong and safe and stood it on its own feet!"[27] These words fitted in well with his words in private about quieting the Western powers and getting ready for war without giving Czechoslovakia too much time to prepare. In these speeches as well as in his earlier electioneering, he returned constantly to his achievement in having brought six and a half million more Germans into "our holy Reich." Such words always brought stormy applause, most loudly in Austria. But knowing that he could not continue forever to play thus upon the *Anschluss* may have stimulated Hitler's interest in having a new achievement to boast of.

On May 2, Hitler departed by special train for Italy, naming Göring acting Führer. He took with him Ribbentrop, Goebbels, and Himmler, and since he also included in his entourage not only Keitel but also the chief operations officers of the army, navy, and air force, he may have had in mind discussion of possible military cooperation. But no such discussion took place. The diplomats accompanying Ribbentrop had feared that Mussolini might try to get backing for further adventures in Africa or the Mediterranean, but they soon concluded that what preoccupied the Italian dictator was assuring Hitler of his good will without having to promise actually to do anything. Weizsäcker commented later that Mussolini had presented a draft agreement that "resembled a peace treaty with an enemy rather than a pact of loyalty with a friend."[28]

As in all encounters between Hitler and Mussolini, life outdid art. The 1940 American film *The Great Dictator*, with Charlie Chaplin and Jack Oakie clowning as Adenoid Hynkel and Napaloni, had fewer comic touches than the real-life events. Again, Mussolini spoke incomprehensible German, leaving everyone in some fog as to what had actually taken place. Hitler took offense at Mussolini's deference to King Victor Emmanuel III, who was frequently present at various rituals of the visit. Trying to assert his precedence, Hitler turned one formal reception into a scene that could have featured the Marx Brothers.[29] Noting that Mussolini's soldiers used the Fascist salute while his merely touched their caps, Hitler, after returning to Germany, ordered that thenceforth all German soldiers should salute him stiff-armed.

Hitler was accompanied throughout by his mistress, Eva Braun. At Naples, where he, Mussolini, and the king were to tour the Italian cruiser *Cavour*, a lunatic tried to attack Fräulein Braun but by mistake stabbed Frau Fritz Dreesen, one of her companions. The wound was minor, and the whole affair was hushed up, but Hitler was visibly upset. He had been reminded yet again of mortality.[30] The trip lasted nine days. Its chief fruit was reassurance for Hitler that Mussolini did not plan to oppose him. When he said to Mussolini that the Czech question would be settled in a matter of months, Mussolini apparently grunted "*Gut,*" thus confirming what his foreign minister had been telling the Germans for months.[31]

Following the Italian trip, Hitler rested for a while at Berchtesgaden. There Keitel brought him a draft order for Plan Green—the offensive against Czechoslovakia. Tailored strictly to the guidelines recorded by Colonel Schmundt, the draft order commenced: "It is not my intention to smash Czechoslovakia by military action in the immediate future without provocation, unless an unavoidable development of the political conditions within Czechoslovakia forces the issue, or political events in Europe create a particularly favorable opportunity which may perhaps never recur." It provided in general terms for exactly the kind of four-day war for which Hitler had called,[32] but it did not have the detail and weight of a general-staff plan. Having worked mainly in administration, Keitel did not know how to prepare such a plan, and most members of his meager staff were less experienced than he.

While this document sat on a desk in Hitler's Alpine retreat, there occurred what was later called the "May Crisis." Czechoslovak soldiers shot two German cyclists. Riots broke out in Sudeten towns. Over the weekend of May 20–21, Czechoslovak officials expressed alarm over supposed German troop movements on the Sudetenland border. Czechoslovak military forces commenced mobilization. Assuming that Hitler was preparing a coup comparable to the *Anschluss*, the French and British ambassadors in Berlin sent urgent telegrams to their home governments and obtained the authority to warn Ribbentrop that, in the event of a clash, France and Britain might support Czechoslovakia. News of these warnings immediately reached newspapers and made headlines everywhere, even in Germany, at least in newspapers like the *Frankfurter Allgemeine* which were not yet altogether under Goebbels's control.[33] In fact, when the French and British military attachés toured eastern Germany, they could find no signs of unusual German troop movements. Probably, the Czechoslovaks had received a false alarm from an agent in the intelligence section of the new armed-forces high command.[34]

Ribbentrop reacted angrily, dressing down the British ambassador, Sir Nevile Henderson. Britain's message, he said, was "directed altogether to the wrong address." London should communicate with Prague, not Berlin. With customary restraint, Ribbentrop added: "The Czechs were playing with fire if they relied upon foreign aid, for before such aid arrived there would certainly not be a living soul in that state."[35]

Hitler may have reacted likewise. It was later commonly surmised that the May Crisis had infuriated him because he actually had been planning an attack and warnings from the Western powers forced him to back down. This was not true. He was as much taken by surprise as anyone else. But it must have angered him to have anyone think that gestures by other governments had caused him once again to back down, as vis-à-vis Austria in 1934.

Ten days later, Hitler sent the armed services a revised version of the directive Keitel had drafted. The most important change was in the first paragraph, which now commenced: "It is my unalterable decison to smash Czechoslovakia by military action in the near future." Otherwise, it conformed to the earlier draft except in stating more candidly that a "convenient apparent excuse" would be found.[36]

The question when Hitler made up his mind has been debated. Two of the most learned and meticulous students of Hitler's diplomacy hold entirely opposite views. The great British historian Donald Cameron Watt sees the available evidence as showing a gradual process. He believes that Hitler was at first uncertain, that he thought reassurance from Mussolini a necessary precondition, and that the May Crisis then provoked him to a resolute decision. The great American historian Gerhard Weinberg, author of a two-volume analysis of Hitler's prewar foreign policy (and a masterful survey of the war itself), believes that Hitler had settled his intention to attack Czechoslovakia as early as late April; he interprets the differences between the Schmundt memorandum, the first draft directive, and the final directive simply as results of Schmundt's and Keitel's inexperience. The final directive, he believes, said what Hitler had meant it to say when he first set Keitel to work.[37] Whichever interpretation is more nearly right, there is no doubt that, by the end of May 1938, Hitler had moved further in the direction he had sketched during the November 1937 meeting recorded by Hossbach.

Hitler's hardening intention to have a war with Czechoslovakia became known quickly to both Beck and Weizsäcker, and they began immediately to try to change his mind.

CLASHES

"There is an 80 to 90 percent chance of a very big mess."
—*Hermann Göring, July 8, 1938*

L earning that Hitler continued to think of a possible attack on Czecho-slovakia, Beck once again put pen to paper. On May 5, he had com-pleted a memorandum obviously intended partly to orient Brauchitsch, the newcomer, but also probably to be seen by Hitler. Drawn up while Hitler was visiting Mussolini, it breathed concern lest Hitler overestimate the strength and fidelity of Italy and believe that Italian support would even the balance against the Western powers.[1]

Mainly, Beck sought to correct what he thought to be the mistaken esti-mate of France apparent in Hossbach's memorandum. France "wishes for peace or, perhaps more accurately, abhors a new war," but, he cautioned, "in case of a real threat or what is perceived by the people to be foreign-policy pressure, the French nation comes together as if one." The *Anschluss* had irritated the French but not affected them directly. They were likely to see a challenge to Czechoslovakia, however, as "a question of honor . . . for which a strong government will have no difficulty pulling itself together." Scoffing at Hitler's surmise that France might suffer an internal collapse, Beck warned: "The French army is and remains intact and is at the moment the strongest in Europe." He predicted that Britain would join France in fighting for Czechoslovakia, and even if Germany succeeded in conquering Czechoslovakia, the larger war would be lost. "The military-economic situation of Germany is bad, worse than in 1917–1918," he wrote. "In its current military, military-political, and military-economic condition, Germany cannot expose itself to the risk of a long war."

This memorandum may not have reached Hitler. Brauchitsch and Keitel both testified later that they had discussed it, recognized that it would anger Hitler, and decided to give him only its final part, on the ground that it dealt more with strictly military matters.[2] Though we have evidence of Hitler's being irritated by a Beck memorandum, it may not have been this one.

Hitler invited Beck and some others to come to the Chancellory on May 28, the Saturday following the May Crisis. It was this invitation that Beck said he might or might not accept, given how busy he was.[3] But he did show up, as did the three service commanders—Brauchitsch, Göring, and Raeder. Keitel and Ribbentrop were also present, as was Neurath in his new capacity as counselor. The visitors were ushered into the Wintergarten, Hitler's favorite room in the old Chancellory. A thirty-by-eighty-foot glassed enclosure, it looked out across a walled-in park, which Hitler had opened up by clearing beeches and elms planted by Bismarck and putting in a marble fountain. He liked to seat visitors against a wall and address them, pacing a long red plush runner.[4]

Beck himself kept the best record of the meeting.[5] According to his notes, Hitler said less than he had the previous November about long-term goals and addressed himself mostly to the urgency of dealing with Czechoslovakia. He said that, as Germany's political leader, he had responsibility for grasping opportunities. Though some risk was inevitable, his risk-taking had thus far been successful, and Germany was becoming strong enough to assume still greater risks. Beck's shorthand notes say: "Germany stronger today than in 1914. Unified state. Psychological effects of the World War begin [to lessen]. Trust in ourselves. We have the respect of others." France, Hitler said, was not so strong as it had been in 1914, "but manifestly weaker." England was also not so strong as in 1914, partly because of strains within the empire and commonwealth.

Hitler reviewed the arguments against and for acting now against Czechoslovakia. On the con side, he mentioned that plans for an offensive operation had not yet been drawn up, that fortifications in the West were still unfinished, and that a war could cost lives. In his recital, however, the positive side of the ledger had many more entries: Czechoslovak fortifications were still improvised, and in two to three years would be stronger; "France and England do not want war," and their rearmament was still years from completion. "Lightning-fast action" would therefore succeed.

Hitler's conclusion was categorical: "The propitious moment must be seized. (A political leader has such only briefly in his hand.)" From there, he proceeded to a series of specific orders, almost as if he truly were commander in chief of the armed forces. For example, he called for production of three thousand machine guns per month, for preparing sabotage operations, and for equipping motorized forces with anti-aircraft guns.

Though Beck simply made notes, with no marginal commentary, it is likely that he returned to the Tirpitz Ufer in high indignation about the extent to which Keitel or Ribbentrop or other amateurs had been misleading his Führer. Overnight and during the next day, he set forth in great detail his reasons for directly opposite conclusions.[6]

Beck began by identifying the points on which he thought Hitler was right. He agreed that Germany needed *Lebensraum*, and in Europe, he conceded, *Lebensraum* could be obtained only by force, not won by negotiation alone. The modern republic of Czechoslovakia as the peace treaties of 1919 had created it was "intolerable," and "a way must be found to eliminate it as a threat to Germany, even, if necessary, by war." But, said Beck, the war would have to be successful, and he questioned whether Keitel and his clerks had accurately assayed for Hitler the chances of success. Though there were indeed good arguments for acting soon against Czechoslovakia, they were more than offset by arguments against getting into a war with France and Britain at the present time. Restating what he had written earlier, Beck predicted that the two Western powers would back Czechoslovakia and in the resultant war Germany would lose.

Beck attacked with particular vigor Hitler's stated presumptions about Germany's relative power. "It is not accurate to judge Germany today as stronger than in 1914," he wrote. He acknowledged that much had been accomplished, especially in restoring national self-confidence, but the state of the armed forces was something on which he could speak as an expert, and the armed forces were not so large, well equipped, or well trained as those of 1914. Nor, Beck asserted, could a soldier "accept these estimates of the military power of France and England. . . . Germany, whether alone or in alliance with Italy, is not in a position militarily to match England or France."

A subtheme in the memorandum concerned the armed-forces high command. Beck continued to regard it as an outrage that Keitel and his aides would presume to draw up directives and plans for military operations. He closed by writing:

> Once again, the comments of the Führer demonstrate the complete inadequacy of the current top military advisory hierarchy.
>
> What is needed is continual, competent advising of the comman- der in chief of the Wehrmacht on questions of war leadership and above all on weapons of war, with clear delineation of responsibili- ties. If steps are not taken soon to produce a change in conditions, which have grown intolerable; if the current anarchy becomes a per- manent condition; then the future destiny of the Wehrmacht in peace and war, indeed the destiny of Germany in a future war, must be painted in the blackest of colors.[7]

A few days later, Beck composed a longer memorandum addressed to Brauchitsch but intended also for Hitler.[8] In it, Beck amplified his reasons for a professional judgment that an early war with Czechoslovakia would be disastrous. The Czechoslovaks, he said, had long been making preparations to cope with a German attack. Their fortifications were formidable. The re- serve forces behind their lines were motorized and mechanized to an extent that enabled them to rush to any breach in their fixed defenses.

Against Czechoslovakia, wrote Beck, Germany could field thirty divi- sions, three of them armored and one of reservists, to which could be added seven understrength Austrian divisions. Though more forces could be built up during the year, they would be poorly equipped, without ammunition, and hence wholly unsuitable for offensive operations. In Czechoslovakia alone, Beck said, these thirty-plus German divisions would have to contend with thirty-eight enemy divisions, seventeen of reservists, twenty-one of regulars, with four of the latter motorized. In the very best circumstances, a German offensive would not make much headway in less than three weeks. If France came to Czechoslovakia's aid, its army could mount a massive of- fensive against Germany's Western front in two weeks, where Germany had only rudimentary fixed fortifications. Because rolling stock would be needed in the East, trains could not be used to move troops to sites under attack. The French army would have an overwhelming advantage.

It was his duty, Beck said, to assert that the military premises of the di- rective for an attack on Czechoslovakia would not withstand scrutiny and that he regarded "as fateful the military action against Czechoslovakia planned on the basis of these military premises and must explicitly disavow any responsibility of the general staff of the army for such action."

Hitler had already made up his mind to fire Beck. Even before the May 28 meeting in the Wintergarten, Hitler had said to his military aide Captain Engel that Beck was "one of the officers still imprisoned in the idea of the hundred-thousand-man army." He had nothing against him, he said (which seems evidence that he had not yet seen any of Beck's memoranda). He simply wanted someone more in tune with his own views and with the times.[9] Yet Hitler had no wish for an open break with Beck: the Blomberg-Fritsch affair was too recent. So he began to take precautions to ensure that, when a break did occur, Beck would have as few supporters as possible.

On June 13, a little more than two weeks after the Wintergarten meeting, Hitler went to Barth, on the Pomeranian coast, to address a large gathering of generals and admirals. Many of these officers were still vexed about the Fritsch affair, and newly vexed because, though the Court of Honor had vindicated Fritsch, nothing had been done either to make reparations to him or to punish Himmler and the Gestapo officers who had falsely accused him. Some talked of resigning in protest, others of organizing a collective démarche to demand action by Hitler. Before Hitler entered the meeting room at Barth, Brauchitsch referred to the Fritsch affair, saying that he himself had considered resigning but was deterred from doing so by the imminence of a war with Czechoslovakia that might become a larger war.

Hitler then appeared and addressed the Fritsch affair at length. He praised Fritsch and apologized for having put him through such an ordeal. He said that, if he had it to do over, he would act differently. He explained, however, that he could not say this in public, for the masses could never hear the Führer admit to error. Fritsch, he said, would be made honorary colonel in chief of an artillery unit. Schmidt, his accuser, would be executed.

Though these were considered feeble gestures, most in the audience seemed to accept them as satisfactory. They then heard Hitler confirm what Brauchitsch had said earlier: Czechoslovakia had to be dealt with promptly; doing so could bring on a larger war; he would do his utmost to prevent that larger war, but his duty to the Sudeten Germans and to Germany's own destiny demanded that he not shrink from the risk. Hitler took occasion also to sound the theme that always went down well with the officer corps, stressing the independence of the armed forces and his own dependence on them as a pillar of the state. As usual, he captivated his hearers and brought them to their feet, giving the straight-arm salute and crying "Heil Hitler!"[10]

A few days later, Keitel circulated a draft directive for an operation against Czechoslovakia to commence on or near October 1. Meeting a major concern voiced by Beck and shared by many of the officers who had been at Barth, this draft had Hitler declaring: "I shall . . . only decide to take action against Czechoslovakia if, as in the case of the occupation of the demilitarized zone and the entry into Austria, I am firmly convinced that France will not march and therefore Britain will not intervene either."[11]

Hitler soon had second thoughts about this commitment. During this period, he may well have been paying more attention than at other times to the boxes full of telegrams and cables regularly brought over from the Foreign Ministry. His eyes may have been caught by reports from diplomats and military attachés in Paris, London, and other capitals predicting that France and Britain would fight for Czechoslovakia. Though Hitler himself put little faith in career diplomats or military attachés, he recognized that others might attach weight to warnings in these telegrams and dispatches and, by citing them, try to prevent or delay action against Czechoslovakia.

When the armed-forces high command circulated yet another draft directive on July 7, this version no longer promised that the war would be only with Czechoslovakia. "It cannot be foreseen how the political situation will develop," the new document began. Hence, it called for "at least theoretical planning . . . if—contrary to our expectations—other states, after all, intervene against us." It continued insouciantly to declare that, if France were to intervene, the operational problem would be primarily to hold the Western fortifications until Czechoslovakia was defeated and forces could be shifted west. Gallingly for the army, the directive specified that the other services should plan for the possibility of British intervention but that planning against the contingency of French intervention should be concentrated in the armed-forces high command.[12]

This draft directive set off alarms all over Berlin. The air-force staff had been working on a plan that envisioned fighting Britain no earlier than 1942. Elements there concerned with aircraft production had already warned that goals for 1939 and 1940 were unlikely to be met. Now they were told to think about challenging the RAF in 1938![13] Göring put nothing in writing to indicate that the new directive worried him. Nor, probably, did he say anything cautionary to Hitler. Elsewhere, however, he let slip evidence of concern. To a group of aircraft manufacturers, he said that war with Czechoslovakia was imminent, that there was a 10–15 percent chance of its being an isolated small war, but "there is an 80 to 90 percent chance of a very big mess [*einen grösseren Kladderadatsch*]."[14]

Beck, who may have been partially appeased by the earlier draft directive, sent Brauchitsch a series of memoranda that crossed an important line. He had previously been offering professional advice to the head of his government, perhaps rudely. But now he was taking the position that the head of government should be *made* to accept this advice. He proposed that Brauchitsch join him in rallying other senior officers, including some in other services. Hitler should learn, he argued, that nearly all of his professional military advisers opposed the projected Czechoslovak campaign. He further recommended that, if these representations produced no result, the military leaders should resign en masse.[15]

> Now at stake are final decisions regarding the fate of the nation. History will burden these leaders with blood guilt if they do not act according to their professional and statesmanly principles and knowledge.
>
> Their soldierly loyalty must end at the boundary where their knowledge, conscience, and sense of responsibility forbid the execution of an order.
>
> In case their advice and warnings fall on deaf ears in such circumstances, then they have the right and the duty, before the people and history, to resign their offices.
>
> If they all act together, then it will be impossible to carry out military action. They will have thereby saved the Fatherland from the worst, from total ruin.
>
> If a soldier in a position of highest authority in such times sees his duties and tasks only within the limits of his military responsibilities, without consciousness of his higher responsibility to the whole people, then he shows a lack of greatness, a lack of comprehension of responsibility.
>
> Extraordinary times demand extraordinary actions!

In a matter of days, Beck went even further, proposing to Brauchitsch that the military leaders effectively carry out a coup. They should do so in the name of freeing the Führer from false advisers, he insisted, but in practice they should take control of the organs of state.[16]

It puzzled and angered Hitler that generals should raise objections to his plans for national expansion. He had poured money into the armed forces while denying it to the party and the mass public. He expected the generals to be grateful and to be willing to use their new formations and weapons. Instead, he encountered what seemed to him excessive caution, if not timidity.

To intimates, including his young military aides, and even to foreign visitors, Hitler expressed disappointment and vexation. He said that he wished his generals had the spirit of Nazi Party Gauleiters. Goebbels noted, "He doesn't listen to his generals, because they always say they are not ready and they are always worrying." When describing to Goebbels how the generals had reacted to his directives for war with Czechoslovakia, he used earthy language, saying, "Naturally, our generals in Berlin shit in their pants."[17]

Though few senior army officers became as agitated as Beck or reached the same radical conclusion, many shared his worry that Germany would be defeated if France and Britain intervened. In early August, Brauchitsch gathered in Berlin the army's most senior commanders and general-staff officers. A meeting with Hitler of these and other officers was scheduled for a few days later, at the artillery proving ground at Jüterborg, south of Berlin. Beck had drafted for Brauchitsch a speech in which Brauchitsch was to propose saying to Hitler, on behalf of the entire army leadership, that Germany was not at present militarily capable of fighting the Western powers. Instead of using this text, Brauchitsch read aloud parts of Beck's most recent memorandum to Hitler, though without identifying it as Beck's work. When he then asked for comments, several generals endorsed Beck's points, some emphatically. No one expressed disagreement.

There were differences, however, as to whether or how these opinions were to be conveyed to Hitler. General Ernst Busch, who commanded an army corps based at Breslau, said he thought the army should have confidence in the Führer. Beck rose and insisted that it was a general-staff officer's duty to ensure that the supreme warlord received and was guided by advice from professional military officers. Reichenau, now commander of an army based at Leipzig, did not come to Busch's defense but did recommend that officers not give Hitler such advice one on one. In view of Reichenau's experience, his advice on dealing with Hitler carried weight. The meeting ended with Brauchitsch saying there was agreement that a major war now would mean "Finis Germaniae." The implication was that this would be said to Hitler at Jüterborg.[18]

Hitler, however, learned of this almost immediately. Reichenau told him about it, perhaps hoping for a new shake-up that might end with him in Beck's place or Brauchitsch's or perhaps being the generalissimo of which Hitler had spoken earlier. Thus, Hitler was forearmed when Brauchitsch called to hand him Beck's most recent memoranda. Scarcely looking at them, Hitler said that he had had enough of "memoranda from Herr Beck." In fact, he had already seen Beck's estimate of Germany's weakness relative to Czechoslovakia on one side and France on the other. He had thought Beck's statistics "mendacious" and had exclaimed to his aides: "Childish calculations of strength! Whereas the French Garde Mobile, police, and gendarmerie are counted, there is nothing in the German reckoning for the SA, SS, etc. The police are not mentioned once. Beck must take him to be stupid."[19] To Brauchitsch, Hitler said that he was ready to remove Beck. He quickly settled, however, for Brauchitsch's agreement that Beck should write no more memoranda.

Hitler invited the commanding generals' chiefs of staff to dine with him at his mountain retreat at Berchtesgaden on August 6. Hitler assumed that these officers, being somewhat younger than their bosses, were less captive to the "hundred-thousand-man-army" mentality. He treated them to a three-hour exposition of the reasons why action against Czechoslovakia had to be taken now and why, in his judgment, the attendant risks were tolerable. He predicted that France and Britain would not act, but he asserted, as earlier, that even in the worst case German fortifications in the West would be adequate to hold back France while German armies completed defeat of the Czechs.

In Beck's memorandum that Brauchitsch had read aloud in Berlin and later handed to Hitler occurred a warning that Germany had only begun to build fortifications in the West and that this so-called Westwall would not hold off France for as much as three weeks. During Brauchitsch's Berlin meeting, General Wilhelm Adam, who had charge of defenses in the West, had seconded Beck's assertion. Here, at Berchtesgaden, Adam's chief of staff, General Wendt von Wietersheim, voiced the same three-week estimate. Hitler had already worried that the document by Beck might have had wide circulation. This seemed proof. Unused to contradiction in any case, Hitler lost his temper and shouted that the Westwall would hold for three years and that anyone who could not make it do so was a criminal.[20]

The Jüterborg meeting occurred a little more than a week later, on August 15. Now Hitler was in the presence of the generals who had heard Brauchitsch read Beck's memorandum. Hitler prepared them for his own rebuttal by having them watch carefully prepared trials in which German artillery smashed replicas of the fortifications on the Czechoslovak frontier. Then, in the officers' mess, he spoke at length about why it was Germany's duty to act now against Czechoslovakia. Acknowledging that the Western powers seemed to have a quantitative edge over Germany, he asserted that France was not psychologically ready for war and that, given the current leadership in Paris and London, there was little risk of war. Some of the generals were persuaded. Others were not. Hitler returned to the Chancellory to give his aides what one of them recalled as "a long, reproachful litany on the timidity and slackness of the army's generals."[21]

To try to bring the army into line, Hitler made two moves. First, on August 18, he personally toured the Westwall. This enabled him to claim firsthand knowledge when he next asserted that it would hold much longer than three weeks. He also involved himself in planning the project. Indulging his amateur enthusiasm for architecture, he drew up a design for a bunker. When told that the design was impractical because it would require many types of nonstandard fittings, he said: "Industry has to produce what is commanded. I order the production of the new bunker."[22] Second, during the same period, he contrived to get rid of Beck without any of the to-do that had surrounded the removal of Fritsch. Just before leaving to tour the Westwall, he had told Brauchitsch that Beck had to be replaced, but asked that the change not be made public during the current period of crisis. Beck accepted this condition. He probably thought that news of his stepping down could increase the chance that France and Britain would decide to go to war. Also, Hitler had encouraged him to believe that, if he stayed quiet, he would be rewarded with a major field command, perhaps an Army Group. Maybe Beck cherished a small hope that Hitler would yet come to his senses, recognize that his other advisers were misleading him, back off from war, ask Beck to remain chief of staff, and then rely on him as Kaiser Wilhelm I had relied on Moltke.[23]

Beck would come to regret his decision not to make an open break with Hitler. He did not get a new assignment; he simply found himself on the retired list. Staying in touch with officers at the Tirpitz Ufer and with

Weizsäcker and others, he became increasingly critical not only of the regime but of Hitler himself. Much later, in July 1944, he was one of the heroes of the botched attempt to end Hitler's life. Effectively, however, Beck steps out of our line of view when he leaves office, for he ceases to have any major role in German decision-making.

CHAPTER SIX

WAR!

"This fool wants a war!"
*—General Gerd von Rundstedt, August 22, 1939,
after hearing Hitler's rationale for invading Poland*

"Don't bother me with this ridiculous rubbish. Thoughts on the world-political situation from the Reich chancellor interest me, but not his organizational thoughts or his military enthusiasms."
*—General Franz Halder, army chief of staff, in late August 1938,
after being brought a memorandum from Hitler concerning
the conduct of the prospective war in Czechoslovakia*

With Beck's effective removal, the burden of trying to deflect Hitler fell to Weizsäcker. Like Beck earlier, Weizsäcker remained loyal to Hitler even as he questioned the courses of action that Hitler seemed to be choosing. The *Anschluss* had elated him. The day of the annexation of Austria, he wrote in his diary, was the greatest day since that in 1871 when defeated France had signed Alsace and Lorraine over to Germany. In July 1938, when already voicing warnings not unlike Beck's, Weizsäcker wrote to his wife, "I am, of course, happy to be able in my present position to be able to be nearer the Führer than before, to the extent that I can be near him."[1]

Weizsäcker had heard Beck and others from the general staff state their dark views concerning the military balance. When Ribbentrop said to him petulantly that the generals were timid and lacked faith in the Führer, Weizsäcker responded stiffly, "Whoever loves the German Reich and its Führer cannot counsel war." In June, perhaps knowing the gist of or even having seen Beck's recent, strident memorandum (saying military action against Czechoslovakia would be "fateful"), Weizsäcker cautioned Ribbentrop: "We have no military recipe for defeating France and Britain. . . . The war would therefore end with our exhaustion and defeat. . . . The first care, therefore, of German policy must be to ensure that the Third Reich is not attacked."[2]

When Weizsäcker saw the revised directive from the armed-forces high command that said it might not be possible to prevent a war against Czechoslovakia from becoming a wider war, he immediately wrote to Ribbentrop, using still sharper language. Obviously presuming that Keitel and his aides were responsible for the directive, he warned of dangerous "military schemes being hatched in our country" and said, "In my opinion the situation must be made plain to the Führer."[3] Not long afterward, when Ribbentrop proposed to instruct German representatives abroad to boast of Germany's military superiority over France, Weizsäcker said to him that it might be all right to have such statements made but that it was their "duty not to dupe one another." He continued, "I did not believe that we should win this war."[4]

By mid-August, Weizsäcker had come to the same conclusion as Beck: that Hitler had been taken in by Ribbentrop and others and was being insulated against corrective information and advice. When Ribbentrop told him that Hitler was determined to go to war, Weizsäcker should have known that it was Ribbentrop parroting Hitler rather than the other way around, but he presumed that Ribbentrop had succeeded in talking Hitler into such a decision. To Weizsäcker's warning that this was to have Germany assume "unjustifiable risks," Ribbentrop replied that he should trust the Führer: "It was necessary to believe in his genius." Though one of Hitler's military aides not only confirmed for Weizsäcker what Ribbentrop had said but asserted that there was no way now of changing Hitler's mind, Weizsäcker did not give up his supposition that the fault lay with Hitler's advisers rather than with Hitler himself.[5]

Like Beck, Weizsäcker sympathized with Hitler's aim of getting rid of Czechoslovakia. His only concern was that in accomplishing this aim Germany not get into a losing war. Regarding Czechoslovakia as an artificial state doomed by ethnic and cultural divisions and knowing this view was widely shared in France and Britain, Weizsäcker had argued all along that Germany should seek to dispose of Czechoslovakia by "chemical" processes—by intensifying internal turbulence rather than by pressing from outside. The Sudetenlanders would serve as a key catalyst. They would be abetted by separatist agitation among the country's many Poles and Hungarians and the large, generally neglected Slovak minority. Weizsäcker's line in conversations with French and British representatives and in communications with German missions abroad was that Czecho-slovakia, as currently composed, was an unstable element in the heart of Europe. Its effective dissolution was necessary for regional and continent-wide stability. The Bohemian-dominated government in Prague would resist change as long as it counted on France and perhaps Britain to guarantee the territorial arrangements jury-rigged in 1919. If Paris and London would make it clear that their primary interest was peace and stability in the region, new territorial arrangements could be worked out, genuinely reflect-ing the principles of "self-determination" and "nationality."

At every opportunity, Weizsäcker tried to get Hitler to consider this "chemical" formula as an alternative to the "mechanical" approach of us-ing military power to detach the Sudetenland or to demolish Czechoslova-kia. When the Regent of Hungary, Admiral Miklós Horthy, visited Germany in late August to discuss with Hitler cooperation against Czechoslovakia, Weizsäcker spoke to him and to every other available Hungarian about the desirability of the "chemical" solution and the high risks involved in mili-tary action. He succeeded in persuading Horthy and other Hungarians to caution Hitler against provoking a Europe-wide war. Accompanying them when they went aboard Hitler's official yacht, *Grille*, at Kiel, Weizsäcker himself had a chance to be alone with Hitler briefly and to say that, if war came, he would regard his own career as a failure.[6] Visiting Stuttgart, Weizsäcker found himself in company with Rudolf Hess, and he applied all his skills to show the deputy Führer the merits of the "chemical" solution.[7]

Frustrating though he found it to do so, Weizsäcker continued to try to reason with Ribbentrop. He wrote to him at the end of August, "The coali-tion of the western powers can, if it will, decide the war against Germany without any great bloodshed by the mere employment of siege tactics. The consequences of such a defeat for Adolf Hitler's reconstruction work are obvious." Perhaps, he suggested, Germany could use military force after the Czechoslovak government had taken some action against an ethnic mi-nority that would cause it to forfeit Western support. Weizsäcker also as-serted to Ribbentrop that all the experienced career diplomats endorsed his views as to what should be done and what were the grave risks of doing oth-erwise.[8]

Losing hope of winning his case in Berlin, Weizsäcker devoted more and more effort to trying to manage the British government, hoping that, through London, he might have an effect on Hitler. Weizsäcker knew that the French and British missions in Berlin had given up trying to com-municate with or through Ribbentrop.[9] He presumed accurately that other diplomats respected, if not trusted, him. And he knew that the British ambassador, Sir Nevile Henderson, wanted desperately to help his prime minister avoid a war. But some Germans hoping to organize a coup against Hitler were telling the British Embassy in Berlin, probably without Weizsäcker's knowledge, that Britain should stand absolutely firm behind France and Czechoslovakia, that this would force Hitler to back down, and that backing down would cause his downfall. Weizsäcker did not share any part of this reasoning, and his counsel to Henderson was exactly the contrary: "I have said to Henderson once again that this is not a game of chess but a rising sea. One cannot make the same kinds of assumptions as in normal times with normal reasons and normal people." His recommendation was a "friendly message" for Hitler describing Britain's "difficulties and apprehensions."[10]

Like Hitler himself and almost everyone else in the world, Weizsäcker was surprised when British Prime Minister Chamberlain offered to fly to Germany on September 14 to discuss directly with Hitler possibilities for preventing a war. He had earlier heard a suggestion that Chamberlain might propose such a meeting, but he had questioned whether Chamberlain was the right person, thinking it would be better if Britain were represented by a field marshal, wrapped in decorations, ready to pound the table with a riding crop. Referring to Hitler's inclination to let everything ride on one gamble or, as Germans say, to "play Vabanquespiel," Weizsäcker said, "Only sensible trading combined with firmness can stop him from playing the same 'Vabanquespiel' that he has played at home with so much success."[11]

Though sixty-nine and facing his first airplane flight, Chamberlain accepted Hitler's invitation to come to Berchtesgaden. There Hitler laid out a demand for an early plebiscite in the Sudetenland and a transfer to Germany of all territory where the population so voted. These terms were entirely consistent with Weizsäcker's "chemical" formula, and Weizsäcker was at Berchtesgaden and helped draft the papers from which Hitler spoke. Chamberlain thanked Hitler and said he would talk with the Czechoslovaks and the French and see what he could do.[12]

On September 22, Chamberlain returned to Germany to meet Hitler at the Hotel Dreesen in Bad Godesberg, in the Rhineland. With the satisfaction of a mother announcing the betrothal of a spinster daughter, Chamberlain told Hitler that Czechoslovakia and France had agreed in principle to a plebiscite. He was prepared to describe how it would be conducted and supervised so as to ensure fairness. But Hitler said this solution was "no longer practicable." He could not allow the Germans in the Sudetenland to suffer the long preparations that were necessary for a plebiscite, nor could he ignore the pitiable condition of Polish and Hungarian minorities elsewhere in Czechoslovakia. German troops would move into the Sudetenland nine days hence, he said, at the beginning of October.

Weizsäcker had already been warned by Erich Kordt, his closest associate in the Foreign Ministry, that Hitler had had second thoughts about the Berchtesgaden formula. Kordt reported that Hitler chided the Hungarian government for not giving him vocal and unreserved support and said he "was determined to settle the Czech question even at the risk of a world war" but "was convinced that neither England nor France would intervene." Concerned lest Czechoslovakia agree to the conditions set at Berchtesgaden, Hitler had decided to tell Chamberlain "with brutal frankness" that "it was quite impossible to tolerate the existence of this aircraft carrier in the heart of Europe."[13] Being in Hitler's entourage at Godesberg, Weizsäcker was able to slip a little modifying language into the aide-mémoire supplied afterward to the British—but not much. For practical purposes, Hitler had said he intended to make war on Czechoslovakia no matter what the Western powers did. Chamberlain returned to London and on September 27 announced mobilization of the British fleet to complement the partial mobilization of ground forces that was commencing in France, lamenting, as he did so, how "horrible, fantastic, incredible" it was to be preparing for another Great War.

If Weizsäcker during this period discussed with anyone the possibility of a coup against Hitler, he guarded the fact from even close Foreign Ministry associates. When Kordt cautiously touched on such a possibility, Weizsäcker said to him: "And what if the state should collapse? We must have done everything possible at our level to prevent war and must not play 'va banque.' "[14]

At the last moment came glimmerings of a possible settlement. Chamberlain sent a special personal representative for last-minute talks. Weizsäcker did his utmost to keep the exchanges from totally breaking down. Then a proposal arrived from Mussolini in Rome for possible four-power discussions. This carried weight with Hitler. At the same time, Hitler observed the evident lack of enthusiasm for war on the part of the public in Berlin. He could have discounted this, for he detested Berlin and Berliners, but Goebbels made no secret of believing that the mood was not confined to Berlin. Weizsäcker heard him speak of this loudly when dining with Hitler and a number of others.[15]

For whatever reasons, Hitler decided not to hold his ground. In a four-power conference hastily convened at Munich on September 29–30, he agreed to accept not much more than the terms Chamberlain had offered at Godesberg. And for whatever other reason, he confirmed what he had said gratuitously at Godesberg—that he had no more territorial demands or claims to assert in Europe. The British and French premiers went home to be cheered by hundreds of thousands, welcoming the apparent escape from war.

Weizsäcker's reaction was intense relief. In retrospect, he continued to believe that Hitler had been egged on by Ribbentrop, Himmler, and others in "the group that wanted war." Regarding his own attitudes and role, Weizsäcker wrote in December:

> It is true that people here say I was an opponent of war against the Czechs because of possible intervention by the Western powers. Everyone who thinks this has lost his nerve. Toward me, as the head of officials in the Foreign Ministry, that is especially bad. I do not deny that I was for the 'small solution': that is, the peaceful takeover of Czechoslovakia. I reproach myself less because the Führer himself chose this route.[16]

Hitler had not liked backing away from his Godesberg positions. It soon came to be orthodoxy around the Chancellory that Germany's concessions at Munich had been unnecessary, and that France and Britain would have found excuses for not acting if German troops *had* marched into the Sudetenland when and as Hitler had once said they would. Colonel Schmundt, his chief adjutant, said to one of his war college classmates:

> It is a shame that war didn't come. . . . There was so much talk about reports and rumors of lack of zest for war—especially within the army. Because of the unsteadiness—particularly of the generals— much trust is shaken. The Führer has spoken of it very often in quite bitter words and called to mind the Prussian generals of 1806– 13. . . . In opposition to his own theories of military leadership he had to confront during the Sudeten crisis the numbers produced from the single general-staff way of thinking. A Czech division had been put on a par with a German, and, from the offensive readiness of forty French divisions, our power was [deemed] inadequate.[17]

Back in mid-September, when temporarily happy about his arrangement with Chamberlain at Berchtesgaden, Hitler had explained to Weizsäcker that he would have license to send in troops if the Czechoslovak government refused to hold a plebiscite; and if it agreed to hold one, Germany would get the Sudetenland in the autumn of 1938 and could then take the remainder of Czechoslovakia in the spring of 1939.[18] Now, three weeks after Munich, with resentment growing in him, Hitler sent all the service chiefs a list of near-term tasks, one of which was to liquidate the remainder of Czechoslovakia. Shortly before Christmas 1938, he directed the army to prepare for such action. He predicted that there would be little resistance in Czechoslovakia or elsewhere, and that it could be made to appear "merely an action of pacification and not a warlike undertaking."[19]

In the new year, Hitler and the armed-forces high-command staff commenced a campaign to teach the army leadership not to repeat the mistakes General Beck had made. Between early January and mid-February 1939, Hitler delivered three addresses to gatherings of military officers, the first to the heads of the services and a number of newly commissioned officers. The official record says: "In the Mosaic Hall at the new Chancellory, the Führer extensively detailed to his lieutenants their duties and obligations as German officers in the Great German Wehrmacht."[20] The second address was given to senior officers of all the services. Again, we have only the notice published in the official gazette, which says that Hitler "held a lengthy lecture on the political and military situation."[21] The third address was delivered at the Kroll Oper to a very large number of officers from the rank of lieutenant colonel on up. It had a formal title: "Responsibilities and Duties of the Officer in the National Socialist State." Implicitly directed at Beck and all his sympathizers, Hitler's speech damned "lack of spirit" and "overbreeding" in the officer corps. What was needed, he declared, was "officers who believe" with "blindly confident trust"—"I want no more warning memoranda." In other words, officers should fulfill their technical duties zealously but, even at the very highest ranks, should leave judgment to their political superiors.[22]

Whether influenced by these injunctions or simply chastened by experience, no one at the senior levels of the armed services raised any questions about Germany's taking over the remainder of Czechoslovakia. The army high command developed a plan consistent with the armed-forces high command's guidelines, presuming there would be little or no resistance to a German invasion. On March 14, after arranging for Slovak leaders to make a bid for independence, Hitler brought to Berlin Emil Hácha, president of the rump Czechoslovakian republic. With Göring and others harassing him to such an extent that he collapsed and had to be revived by

injections, Hácha agreed to invite Germany to make his country a protec-
torate. On March 15, army and SS troops paraded into Prague, with not a
shot fired. Hitler asked Otto Dietrich, his press chief, "Have you word of
military movements in France or the Soviet Union or about mobilization of
the British fleet?" When Dietrich said no, Hitler exclaimed, "I knew it! In
two weeks no one will say another word about it."[23]

Ten days later, on March 25, 1939, Hitler ordered preparations for a war
with Poland. His directive said reassuringly that issues with Poland were
not to be settled right away. Privately, however, Hitler called in Brauchitsch
and told him that operations might begin in less than six months.[24] That he
spoke to Brauchitsch and said nothing to Keitel indicates that, even if he
believed that he would see no more memoranda like Beck's, he still worried
lest the army rebel against losing its prerogatives. Approaching Brauchitsch and bypassing Keitel was of a piece with the maneuver in 1938 in
which he gave Beck the lead in planning the *Anschluss.*

With Brauchitsch and the army already at work, Hitler gradually disclosed that he had actually decided on early action against Poland. He issued through the armed-forces high command a directive to plan for
possible war with Poland as early as the approaching August. The directive
said reassuringly: "The political leaders consider it their task to isolate
Poland if possible, that is to say, to limit the war to Poland only." Consistent
with what Hitler had said earlier about the Western powers, it went on:
"The development of increasing internal crises in France and resulting
British restraint might produce such a situation in the not too distant future."[25]

Hitler rehearsed and updated his general appreciation of the European
situation when he brought together in late May, at his study in the new
Chancellory, the most senior officers of the armed-forces high command
and the services. Now he was again in the mode of the late summer of 1938.
He wanted his soldiers to see action as necessary and urgent. He wanted
them to have no mental reservations. "The idea that we can get off cheaply
is dangerous; there is no such possibility. We must burn our boats, and it is
no longer a question of justice or injustice, but of life or death for eighty
million human beings." The relative capacities of Germany and its enemies
and the vulnerabilities of the latter needed to be studied by "men with
great imaginative power and the best technical knowledge." But such work

"must not be left to the general staffs," for they were unable to keep secrets. Hence, he directed that the armed-forces high command form a small staff to prepare for an attack on Poland at the earliest opportunity, consistent with the principle that there should be "no simultaneous conflict with the western powers (France and England)."[26]

By now, few officers doubted Hitler's acumen in assessing other powers. Generals whom Brauchitsch enlisted as prospective commanders in operations against Poland took it for granted that Hitler could prevent intervention by France or Britain.[27] General Geyr von Schweppenburg, who had supported Beck in 1938 and was now to command armored formations scheduled to lead the attack, reported that his men were eager to have at the despised Poles.[28] Though the new young chief of staff of the air force, Colonel Hans Jeschonnek, had the air staff make plans on the assumption that the Western powers would intervene, Göring assured them that this would not be so.[29]

Halder was now the army chief of staff. He had become Beck's chief of operations, succeeding Manstein, during the changes that attended the Blomberg-Fritsch affair. Years before, he had served under Brauchitsch in the training branch of the Weimar-era army and had succeeded him as head of it. Though Brauchitsch did not particularly like Halder, he actively disliked the clever and arrogant Manstein. Halder was available, had run the army's maneuvers in 1937, and had much impressed Hitler. So Brauchitsch and Beck agreed to replace Manstein with Halder. When Hitler arranged to get rid of Beck, Halder became first acting chief of staff, then, *faute de mieux*, Beck's formal successor.

Halder would turn fifty-five on June 30, 1939. He came from a Bavarian family that had produced generals for generations. Many assumed that, because he was a Bavarian, he was a Catholic. Himmler commented to Hitler that Halder was a "Mother-of-God General" with no front-line battle experience. But Hitler was reassured to learn that Halder had been reared a Protestant and seldom attended church.[30] The second part of what Himmler said was, however, true. All Halder's service, in war and peace, had been either in staff assignments or in organizing and supervising training.

Serving on the staff of the military district that embraced the industrial Rhineland, then commanding a division based in Bavaria, Halder had seen the evolution of the Nazi state from vantage points outside Berlin. He did not care for most of the Nazis with whom he had to deal. He had rejoiced at the Blood Purge of 1934, writing Beck elliptically that the SA was "not the only and perhaps not the most dangerous suppurating boil that Germany's sick body carries." But, like Beck and Weizsäcker and millions of ordinary Germans, Halder distinguished between Hitler and the party. He and Beck agreed that the "pure, idealistically motivated solemn will of the chancellor" was often frustrated by party underlings.[31]

Brought from Bavaria in 1937 by Beck to head the organization and training of the general staff, Halder had arranged the maneuvers of that year, which Hitler had approvingly observed. General Guderian had just published his book *Achtung Panzer!*, arguing that independent tank formations—divisions, corps, even armies—should lead offensive operations, with artillery and infantry trailing. Halder delighted Guderian and other armor enthusiasts by making the maneuvers partly a test of Guderian's doctrine. They were even more delighted when the maneuvers seemed to show that the doctrine worked. And Hitler was equally pleased, for tank-led offensives could be speedy, seemed modern, and sidelined horses, of which he had always been afraid.[32]

These Wehrmacht maneuvers also gratified Beck, because they were controlled and dominated by the army, not the War Ministry. Then and later, Halder was even more firm and dogmatic than Beck or Fritsch in insisting that only the army and its general staff was competent to manage war planning. Hitler's army aide Captain Engel wrote that he was shocked by the strength of Halder's feeling. In late August 1938, when there was conflict about the respective functions of the two headquarters in planning operations against Czechoslovakia, Engel tried to make Halder see Hitler's point of view, and Halder responded: "Don't bother me with this ridiculous rubbish. Thoughts on the world-political situation from the Reich chancellor interest me, but not his organizational thoughts or his military enthusiasms."[33]

During the crisis of 1938, Halder shared many of Beck's anxieties. Somewhat undiplomatically, he said to Beck that he was not going to get his way with Hitler just by writing memoranda. Even before beginning to act as de facto chief of staff, he had talked with officers in the Abwehr, the intelligence branch of the armed-forces high command, who were actively plotting Hitler's overthrow. Through them, he had some contact—though how much is unclear—with civilians also engaged in such plotting, and he discussed with General Erwin von Witzleben, commander of the Berlin military district, how to move troops stationed at Potsdam so as to disarm the SS and take control of the Chancellory. Halder also gave Weizsäcker some of the information he used to try to sway Ribbentrop and others around Hitler.[34]

Halder was as dedicated to his work as Beck had been. Indeed, his habits almost made Beck seem a slouch. "He was a tireless worker," wrote one of his aides, "who risked his health, in that for months he would keep going into the wee hours. I have repeatedly seen him leave his desk at 7 A.M., when I went to the barracks for morning report. Around 9 A.M. he would appear, ready again for duty." Manstein belittled this characteristic of Halder's. "Moltke's motto, 'Genius is diligence,' was his byword," he wrote. "The holy fire that inspires the true warrior hardly flared inside him." Perhaps because he exhausted himself, or perhaps because he himself suspected that he lacked the "holy fire," Halder sometimes lost the cold, pedantic self-possession so often noted by those who knew him only casually. His adjutant, Peter Sauerbruch, recalled seeing him give way to emotion and even cry.[35]

As the time approached for starting the Polish campaign, Halder became more and more worried. After Germany's takeover of the remainder of Czechoslovakia, the French and British governments had declared they would go to war in behalf of Poland if Germany made an unprovoked attack. Halder's detailed plans presumed the Western powers would honor this promise. He spent anxious hours going over these plans with General Leeb, who was already designated to command the few forces available to defend the Western front. His mood varied. On one day he would say that France and Britain were sure to stay out; on another, that they would surely go to war. But he never challenged Hitler, as Beck had challenged him in 1938, nor did he show an inclination at this time to join the band of plotters who continued to look for opportunities to mount a coup. When they approached him, he sent them away, saying in effect that conditions were no longer what they had been in September 1938 and that a coup was not workable.[36]

Though Hitler had heard no rumblings like those of 1938, he nevertheless once again assembled senior officers of the services just a week before the planned attack on Poland was scheduled to commence. At Berchtesgaden on August 22, Hitler informed them of the surprise nonaggression pact Ribbentrop had just concluded with the Soviet Union, which completely undercut ongoing French and British negotiations in Moscow aimed at enlisting the Soviet Union as another guarantor of Poland.

Though Hitler acknowledged that France and Britain might come to

Poland's aid in spite of the new German-Soviet pact, he said that Germany was secure; the Westwall was impregnable; Belgium would remain neutral; and France and Britain would not violate Belgian neutrality in order to by-pass the Westwall. In any case, he rated as very small the chance of their actually acting in behalf of Poland. He exhorted the generals to wage a war of annihilation against the Polish army, to be remorseless, and to shrink at nothing in order to achieve early success.[37]

Though the meeting ended with the customary standing straight-armed salute and cries of "Heil Hitler!," Hitler was not sure he had been effective. He complained to Engel that he could usually read his audiences but that the rigid, masklike faces of senior military officers baffled him. In the more relaxed atmosphere of his private quarters, he said more categorically that he expected the war to be limited entirely to Poland. He was certain that Britain would not come in and almost certain that France would not. What worried him most, he said, was the danger of some meddlesome peacemongers' forcing a new Munich: "a 'stupid emotional acrobat' with diaperlike proposals that could destroy the concept in the last moment and force it once again to be given up."[38]

Hitler was right to doubt that he had made converts of these generals. Though none was prepared to challenge him on particulars, as Beck had earlier, many felt that no civilian politician should make decisions affecting the army. They would have found nothing odd in Beck's having said that he was too busy to see the Führer or Halder's saying that he had no interest in the "organizational thoughts or . . . military enthusiasms" of an Austrian-born private first class. Some of them doubted Hitler's prediction that the Western powers would not intervene. Others were simply irritated by the harangue. Rundstedt, who had just come out of retirement to take command of the Army Group that was to attack Poland from the west and south, was heard to mutter, after Hitler finished his speech, "This fool wants a war!" Halder recalled a "frosty atmosphere" and Dietrich, Hitler's press chief, that the generals were "fretful" and "perturbed" at the meal afterward.[39]

Weizsäcker had once favored early action against Poland and been confident that France and Britain would not interfere. That, however, had been prior to the takeover of the remainder of Czechoslovakia. He had reasoned that Germany had a basis for making demands that the Western powers would deem legitimate: the city of Memel in Lithuania, the independent city of Danzig, and the Polish Corridor, the strip of land that connected Poland to the sea and cut East Prussia off from the rest of Germany, were all peopled primarily by Germans; many were active Nazis, waging campaigns like those of the Austrian and Czechoslovakian Nazis for integration into Hitler's Reich. Germany could invoke the principles of self-determination and nationality. The Polish government was certain to resist any compromises regarding either Danzig or the Corridor, and possibly object regarding Memel. By one means or another, Polish troops could be made to fire the first shots. Germany would then appear to be acting defensively, on behalf of order, and could subdue the Poles with France and Britain simply looking on, possibly approvingly. In Weizsäcker's mind, this scenario seemed all the more plausible because, ever since Hitler's emergence, the Polish government had distanced itself from its alliance with France and had done so conspicuously in 1938, when, instead of supporting Czechoslovakia, it demanded a share in the country's carving up.

Hitler's seizing the remainder of Czechoslovakia seemed to Weizsäcker to have been a serious tactical mistake. Though he approved it in principle, he thought it made early action against Poland more difficult. When he learned that Hitler was nevertheless planning a late-summer attack on Poland, he did not react as he had the year before. He thought Ribbentrop was once again deluded—indeed, chronically so—and trying to delude Hitler. He wrote in his diary that Ribbentrop was saying Germany could defeat Poland in forty-eight hours, and Britain would lose its empire if it stood by its guarantee of Poland. Weizsäcker regarded these views as naïve, but he, too, thought that, in the end, Britain would not fight for Poland. In late July, he wrote: "If we can get past the summer hysteria of the English House of Commons and of the English people; if we can quiet the ghosts of the émigrés and the Czechs, until fall, then, despite everything, a situation will arise in which Berlin and London will try to find a new equilibrium. In general, it is possible to be optimistic."[40]

In August, Weizsäcker became increasingly concerned lest Hitler not wait out the current session of the British House of Commons. On August 13, he wrote worriedly in his diary that the Ribbentrop-Himmler war party seemed stronger and that Ribbentrop showed far too much confidence that the Western powers would welsh on their guarantee to Poland. He hoped Hitler appreciated that Germany could act against Poland with impunity if, and only if, in the eyes of the Western powers, Poland seemed the provoker of the war.[41]

At the beginning of the last week in August, Weizsäcker had an experience that shook his long-standing presumption that Ribbentrop, Himmler, and a war party had warped Hitler's thinking. With Ribbentrop away in Moscow signing the Nazi-Soviet pact, Weizsäcker sat between Hitler and British Ambassador Henderson in a meeting at Berchtesgaden on August 23. He recorded in his diary: "The Führer's thinking focused on the following: He wants to force the English government to back down from its guarantees for Poland. The Führer expects that, in view of our coup in Moscow, Chamberlain will stumble and the guarantee idea will fail." After the ambassador departed, Weizsäcker warned Hitler that he thought this an illusion:

> My own divergent opinion I conveyed to the Führer by saying, in effect, that the English are prisoners of their policy. They are not to be taken or understood either as logical or systematic but, rather, as emotional. They are psychotic, as if under whisky. What they are doing should not be appraised as tactical or anything of the sort. Chamberlain will tomorrow with his war speech have the whole Parliament behind him.[42]

From his vantage point in the Foreign Ministry, Weizsäcker could see Ribbentrop handling final negotiations about Poland in such a way as to frustrate all Western efforts to find again some last-minute escape from war. He now had a sense that this was not solely Ribbentrop's doing but Hitler's. On August 25, the day when the attack on Poland was supposed to occur, Weizsäcker wrote in his diary: "This afternoon may have been the most depressing of my life. To have my name connected with this event is a frightful idea."[43]

Though Hitler several times postponed the actual launch of the offensive, nothing Weizsäcker could see suggested any genuine second thoughts. On August 28, he wrote balefully in his diary that Germany seemed to have a natural tendency toward the kind of melodramatic self-destruction symbolized by the last in Wagner's series of operas on the Siegfried legend.[44] The next day, he recorded hearing Göring say to Hitler that Germany was playing Vabanquespiel. Hitler said, "In my life I have always played Vabanquespiel."[45]

The Munich settlement had effectively killed questioning within the German government of Hitler's premises and policies. During the eleven months from early October 1938 to September 1939, there were only minor, or at least not immediate, differences between the spectrum of judgments voiced by Hitler and those accepted by his military officers and diplomats. As in 1938, however, the fears of the generals and diplomats proved excessive. The Western powers did demand that Germany halt the war against

Poland. When Hitler rejected their ultimatum, they declared that a state of war existed. They had waited three days, however, to take this action, and then they did little more than mobilize. A few British planes flew over Germany, but only to drop leaflets. On September 7, a week after Germany invaded Poland, French troops made a cautious probe into the Saarland. Though bulletins out of Paris spoke of a great offensive that would relieve pressure on the Poles, it was in fact only a gesture. General Wagner, the German army's chief supply officer, wrote in his diary that the French bulletins were "not worthy of a great nation."[46]

Meanwhile, the German army and air force carried out their successful conquest of western Poland, creating the circumstances existing when Hitler convened his military chiefs at the New Chancellory on September 27 and shocked them with his order that they prepare an immediate offensive against France.

CHAPTER SEVEN

HITLER

"Except in cases where he had pledged his word, Hitler always meant what he said."   —*Sir John Wheeler-Bennett*, Nemesis of Power

itler assessed France and Britain differently from Beck, Halder, Weizsäcker, and other professionals. Had he been consistently wrong, the differences would be easy to account for and could be dismissed as delusions of an ignorant madman. But since Hitler often came nearer the mark than did his advisers, that will not do. One has to ask about his presumptions and about the information on which he based his assessments.

Most of Hitler's basic beliefs were on public display in *Mein Kampf* ("My Battle"), the long confessional autobiography-cum-manifesto published in the mid-1920s. He had dictated the book during a ten-month stay in prison. Not long before, he had banded with General Ludendorff—by then a lunatic—in a plot to overthrow the five-year-old Weimar Republic. With their intended first step a takeover of the state of Bavaria, they marched off from a Munich beer hall. The police barred them. After exchanges of shots, the putsch attempt collapsed. Even though fourteen of Hitler's followers and four policemen had been killed and the putschists had managed to steal several million marks, a sympathetic judge and jury exonerated Ludendorff and gave Hitler a light sentence in Landsberg Prison, a minimum-security institution. His time there, Hitler said later, served him as a "university paid for by the state."[1] *Mein Kampf* was the tangible product.

Three elements from Hitler's background emerge strikingly in *Mein Kampf*. The first is that, though he identified himself as German, he had grown up in the Austro-Hungarian Empire. His father had been a customs collector on the Austrian-German border and every year had donned a fancy uniform to honor the birthday of the Hapsburg emperor. Though Hitler could probably have won in court had he claimed that he became German when he joined the German army in 1914, he did not formally renounce his Austrian citizenship until 1925 or take out papers as a German citizen until 1932.

To Prussians like Beck and Weizsäcker and even to a Bavarian like Halder, modern history was anchored in the period when, with Bismarck guiding, Prussia had defeated Austria and, after the Franco-Prussian War of 1870–71, proclaimed the German Empire. To Hitler, this was just one phase in the eclipse of the Austrian Empire. In *Mein Kampf*, he criticizes the Hapsburgs for treating Hungarians as equals in their monarchy and then, as he saw it, making one concession after another to other inferior races, such as Czechs. Though he could speak admiringly of Bismarck's tactics, he did not share the fond memories of Germans for the decades of stability after 1871.

A second noteworthy point is that Hitler had his origins not only in Austria but in that part of the upper Danube Valley called the Waldviertel, or Forest Quarter, so known to distinguish it from the Weinviertel, or Wine Quarter, farther down the Inn River, toward Vienna. From Passau on the German border, where Hitler's father served, through Linz, where Hitler went to school after his father's death, the Danube courses between cliffs some of which are barren rock, others covered by thin growths of pine. In the Weinviertel, loess-covered hills nourish vineyards and pastures. In the Waldviertel, however, as in parts of Scotland and the Appalachians, nature excites the eye but is not generous to the stomach, and local lore stresses blood feuds.[2]

The early part of *Mein Kampf*, and later passages that hark back to Hitler's early years, are recollections by someone who, as a youngster, lived where farm families loved the land but had a hard time making a living from it. Though Hitler used the term *Lebensraum* only after being instructed by his prisonmate and sometime stenographer, Rudolf Hess, who was acquainted with the geopolitics of Karl Haushofer, his background in the Waldviertel helps to explain why the concept so easily became central to his thinking.

And concern about the balance between population and food supply must have intensified for Hitler as a result of leaving home in his early teens and moving, on his own, to Vienna. Passages in *Mein Kampf* recalling his Vienna years are almost poignant.[3] "The uncertainty of earning one's daily bread seemed to me to be the darkest side of my new life," he wrote. In one long section, Hitler coupled autobiographical fragments with an evocation of a type—the "farmer's boy . . . accustomed to a certain security of income" who "brings a little money with him to the big city," uses it up, and finds himself on the streets and penniless. Hitler, who had come to Vienna both with a small legacy and with a pension as the orphaned son of a civil servant, was describing his own experience when he wrote of this boy's lot: "It is especially hard in winter. . . . Now he loiters about hungrily, he pawns or sells the last of his belongings, his clothes get shabbier day by day. . . . If then he becomes homeless, and if this happens (as is often the case) in winter, then his misery becomes acute." Hitler himself spent at least part of one winter in a shelter for the homeless.[4]

In standard up-by-the-bootstraps format, Hitler included in his recollections of poverty an assertion that the school of hard knocks had its rewards. "How grateful I am today that Providence . . . bade me go to this school," he wrote. "It educated me quickly and thoroughly." It also fed contempt for well-born generals and diplomats who had never known want or mixed with the poor.

A third noteworthy point relates to Hitler's experience in the Great War and its importance in his life. In 1913, as a twenty-four-year-old, he had moved from Vienna to Munich, possibly to evade the Austrian draft. But the 1914 declarations of war—Austria's against Serbia, then Germany's against Russia and France, soon to be followed by Britain's against Germany— electrified him. He is recognizable in a photograph snapped in Munich on August 1, the first day of hostilities for Germany, which, as Lord Bullock writes in his biography of Hitler, shows "his eyes excited and exultant; it is the face of a man come home at last."[5]

Volunteering immediately, Hitler was enrolled in a Bavarian regiment despite his Austrian citizenship. He then spent most of four years in the fieriest sections of the Western front. Doing duty mostly as a courier, running messages from the front-line trenches to rear-area regimental-command posts, he witnessed, among other notable moments of carnage, the artillery and machine-gun duels and bayonet charges remembered as First Ypres, the Somme, and Third Ypres. He suffered a leg wound. In the last weeks of the war, he was gassed and had to be hospitalized with temporary blindness. Though never promoted beyond the rank of private first class, he received not only the commonly awarded Iron Cross, Second Class, but the much more distinctive Iron Cross, First Class, usually reserved for heroes of higher rank. He was commended for "reckless courage."

After the war, with his sight restored, Hitler stayed in uniform as long as he could. As he wrote in *Mein Kampf* and would say over and over in later years, being a soldier had been "the most unforgettable and the greatest period of my mortal life."[6] He had discovered how dread of an anonymous enemy, combined with desire to harm or kill that enemy, could bond humans together and cause them to do what few would do alone. His constant resort later to battle metaphors and his positive relish for war trace in part to his feelings of epiphany amid artillery craters and barbed wire on the blood-caked mud of the Western front.

Partly because the war had been such a glorious experience for Hitler, he reacted to the sudden capitulation of 1918 as if to a high-voltage shock. He was by no means alone. German government propaganda had so disguised reality as to make not only ordinary Germans but high-ranking officials optimistic about approaching victory. The announcement that Germany was suing for an armistice turned the world upside down. But Hitler's reaction was extreme by any standard. "While everything went black before my eyes, stumbling, I . . . threw myself on my cot and buried my burning head in the covers and pillows," he wrote.[7]

The shock helped to shape opinions that Hitler would carry in his mind from then on. Adopting the most radical version of the "stab-in-the-back" legend, he would contend that Jews, Marxists, and their dupes had snatched victory from Germany's front-line fighters. Answering a later charge that Nazi activities constituted treason against the Weimar Republic, Hitler declared on the witness stand: "There is no such thing as high treason against the traitors of 1918."[8]

Anti-Semitism already permeated his thinking. It had been stronger in the Vienna of Hitler's youth than almost anywhere else in the world, and one of his early heroes had been Karl Lüder, the popular, long-serving, and hysterically anti-Semitic mayor of Vienna. As early as 1919, Hitler articulated the reasoning (if it can be called that) that led him in 1942 to order the Holocaust. In a report submitted to the army command in Munich,

Hitler condemned the emotional anti-Semitism that led to pogroms. He argued for anti-Semitism "based on reason" which would gradually outlaw Jews, but he went on to assert that the "final goal must always remain the removal of the Jews as a whole."[9] In *Mein Kampf*, Hitler resorted repeatedly to the image of the Jew as a pest or an insect needing to be eradicated.

Before he finally shed his uniform, Hitler's basic values had hardened. Someone who compares the language in *Mein Kampf* with that in later speeches might detect vacillation on some points, but not on many. Hitler defined the objectives he would pursue when and if he had power, and they included forceful conquest of endless territory and systematic murder of Jews. That his professional advisers were surprised by the program he began to lay out at the 1937 conference recorded by Hossbach and were dismayed by the measures he authorized in occupied Poland seems strong evidence that they had not paid much attention to what he had written and said. In this, they were not unique, for officials in most countries tend to ignore the public utterances of their politicians, but in Nazi Germany this was a serious mistake. As Sir John Wheeler-Bennett remarks, "Except in cases where he had pledged his word, Hitler always meant what he said."[10]

In *Mein Kampf* and in speeches, Hitler also disclosed some of the beliefs that influenced his assessments of foreign governments and his judgments about tactics for dealing with them. Crucially important were his views on the nature of political power. Time and again, Hitler advanced the proposition that the basis of power in a modern state was emotional support from the masses:

> Every movement with great aims has anxiously to watch that it may not lose connection with the great masses . . .
>
> It has to examine every question primarily from this point of view. . . .
>
> Further, it has to avoid everything that could diminish or even weaken its ability to influence the masses . . . because of the simple reason that without the enormous power of the masses of a people no great idea, no matter how sublime and lofty it may appear, is realizable.[11]

Hitler held the masses to be as stupid as they were powerful: "The political understanding of the great masses . . . is not sufficiently developed for them to arrive at . . . general political opinions by themselves," he wrote; "the majority of humankind . . . is inert and cowardly."[12] The strength of a national leader depended, according to him, on his ability to seize and manipulate emotions. Significantly, he discounted as merely auxiliary the institutions of the state. Laws derived their force from the willingness of the people to obey them and from the comforting sense of order they attached to the idea of appealing to a statute instead of to the favoritism of a ruler. Both publicly and privately, Hitler warred in the late 1920s and early 1930s with Nazis who wanted the storm troopers to defy the laws of the Weimar Republic, insisting that the SA and SS stay within the letter of those laws. Playing on the sobriquet of the Orléans prince who joined the revolutionaries in France in the 1790s, "Philippe-Égalité," some referred to Hitler as "Adolphe Légalité."[13] He insisted that democracy had to be defeated by democracy.[14]

For Hitler, even police forces and armies counted less than the masses. Of course, he respected the power of the gun. He remembered that his Munich beer-hall putsch had been put down by policemen, and this experience contributed to his determination not to risk action that could be treated as criminal. At the same time, the example illustrated for him how hard it was for political authorities to make full use of their police or military forces when public support for them was insecure. Though his coup attempt had misfired, he had come closer to success than could have been forecast by merely counting guns. The clear lesson for Hitler was that the strength of a government should be measured primarily by the level and intensity of mass support, not by its armies or its treasury.

Strongly affecting Hitler's judgments both about the significance of events and about his own alternatives for action was the constantly rising level of his own self-confidence. Though he bragged in *Mein Kampf* about being a precocious public speaker, he acknowledged that those who heard him orating in Vienna "must have thought me a queer fellow."[15] Only after the war, when his commanders in Munich gave him the assignment of counteracting communist and socialist propaganda, did he begin to feel that he was affecting his hearers, an experience that decided him to make a profession of politics.[16]

What confirmed this decision for Hitler was his early success.[17] He recalled rising before a gathering of a little more than one hundred in a Munich beer cellar:

I had been granted twenty minutes speaking time. . . . I spoke for thirty minutes, and what formerly I had felt in my mind, without knowing it somehow, was now proved by reality. I could speak. After thirty minutes the small room filled with people was electrified, and the enthusiasm found its expression first in the fact that my appeal to the willingness to sacrifice led the audience to donate three hundred Marks.[18]

The crowds grew. Within months, Hitler had tested himself in a hotel ballroom. As he recalled it, there was a throng of two thousand, many of them initially hostile. Then "applause gradually began to drown out the shouting and calling." In the end, what he said seemed to have everyone's support. "I was confronted by a hall filled with people united by a new conviction, a new faith, a new will."[19]

By the time *Mein Kampf* was published, Hitler had become a masterful demagogue. He was candid in describing and appraising his skills. Two of his watchwords were "simplicity" and "consistency."

The great masses' receptive ability is only very limited, their understanding is small, but their forgetfulness is great. As a consequence . . . , all effective propaganda has to limit itself only to a very few points and to use them like slogans. . . . The purpose of propaganda is not continually to produce interesting changes . . . , but to convince; that means, to convince the masses. . . . A change must never alter the content. . . . In the end it always has to stay the same.[20]

Once having successfully launched the National Socialist Party, Hitler declared its twenty-five-point platform immutable. In fact, he never supported all twenty-five points, and he changed his mind about many of them. But he argued in party councils that any appearance of uncertainty or changeability would arouse doubts among the people. (Also, of course, change or even debate about change could call into question his dictatorial command of the party.) An example of how he could mask change was his invocation of his party's socialist label. In practice, he ceased to make much of the genuinely socialist planks in the platform, which put off businessmen whose monetary contributions he wanted. Instead of dropping the label, he simply broadened its meaning, declaring in one speech that anyone who understood the country's national anthem, "Deutschland über Alles," was thereby a socialist.[21]

A third principle of Hitler's, seemingly inconsistent with the first two, was to tailor every speech to its specific audience. Hitler could do this, while maintaining simplicity and consistency, by adopting the assumption so effectively used later in mass and segmented product marketing—namely, that only parts of a message get through to any listener or onlooker, and that the crucial parts may not lie in the words or logic. Hitler boasted that he was the one-in-a-thousand example of someone who could speak "to an auditorium composed of street sweepers, locksmiths, sewer cleaners, etc., and . . . on the following day . . . to university professors and students . . . in a form which is equally satisfactory to both sides."[22]

Whether or not Hitler deserved his own compliments when he dictated these words in Landsberg Prison, he certainly came to earn them. In the late 1920s and early 1930s, Hitler campaigned in practically every town and village in Germany, visiting many of them repeatedly. His experience in face-to-face, flesh-pressing politics was probably unmatched by any other politician, not only in Germany but in the world.

With intimate groups as well as throngs, it was Hitler's practice to begin speaking in a low key, often talking about his own experiences or experiences that he and his hearers might have shared. Though his Austrian origin was always evident, he also used specific intonations to establish rapport. His own regional accent was neither so marked nor so consistent as, say, that of Al Smith or John Kennedy or Lyndon Johnson or Jimmy Carter. Max Domarus, the premier collector and analyst of Hitler's speeches, comments that, in Hamburg or Hannover, Hitler would pronounce the "s" and "t" separately in words with "st," whereas in Bavaria he would mush them together.[23] After a while, Hitler would become more declamatory, phrasing his points in tune with what he sensed in the room or among the crowd. He would then wind up with vehement words, involving many gestures, calling to an American's mind a tent-meeting evangelist.[24] Well into his chancellorship, Hitler continued to learn from experience and to improve his capacity for stirring audiences. He rehearsed before his staff and in front of mirrors, and he had his clothes specially cut to allow for flailing gestures.[25]

Hitler could be guided by ethical norms of a sort—as, for example, concerning the importance of protecting the German race or the German peasantry—but he had absolutely no tactical scruples. This is evident in a passage of *Mein Kampf* that was often cited outside Germany as extolling "the big lie." To be sure, he claimed to be describing what Jews did, but in doing so he affirmed the validity of the theory:

In the size of the lie there is always contained a certain factor of credibility, since the great masses of a people may be more corrupt in the bottom of their hearts than they will be consciously and intentionally bad, therefore with the primitive simplicity of their minds they will more easily fall victims to a great lie than to a small one, since they themselves perhaps also lie sometimes in little things, but would certainly still be too much ashamed of too great lies . . . ; therefore, just for this reason some part of the impudent lie will remain and stick.[26]

In *Mein Kampf* but even more in subsequent speeches, Hitler made it evident that he believed many of his ideas to have universal applicability. He spoke of "the masses," not "the German masses." Hence his judgments about Austria or Czechoslovakia or France or Britain or the Soviet Union or the United States were likely to be influenced not only by his theories about the nature of power but also by his mounting self-confidence as a politician—his ability to *feel* mass opinion.

Though basic beliefs contributed to differences between Hitler's assessments of foreign governments and those of his professional advisers, the differences were reinforced by the fact that he and they relied on somewhat different sources of information. Hitler, of course, had access to practically all the information available to Beck or Halder or Weizsäcker. The Chancellory routinely received copies of reports from military attachés and telegrams from German diplomats and memoranda generated within the Foreign Ministry. It also received reports not ordinarily seen at the Bendlerstrasse or the Wilhelmstrasse, as, for example, from party agents abroad and from the Gestapo and other internal-security services answering to Himmler.

How much of this reportage Hitler read is uncertain. He described his Foreign Ministry as an "intellectual garbage dump" and spoke scornfully of almost all the military attachés. The only one he trusted, he once said, was General Friedrich von Bötticher, who reported from Washington that, though the American government might be riddled with Jews and President Franklin Roosevelt sympathetic to France and Britain, the American general staff appreciated the new Germany and would never permit the United States to side with Germany's enemies.[27] Although Hitler had had to pay close attention to Nazi Party leaders in Austria and Czechoslovakia, it is not apparent that he attached any weight to communications from party representatives relating to France or Britain. From Himmler he received primarily information regarding persons in Germany. Some were foreigners, including diplomats and reporters, but little of the information could have had much bearing on Hitler's judgments regarding foreign governments.

Hitler did assiduously read German translations of foreign newspapers and magazines. His press chief, Meissner, whom a journalist described as a caricature German, with "a fat body, a fat face, a square red neck," given to "bobbing up and down like a weighted cork on a heavy sea," had the duty of placing fat folders of press excerpts in front of Hitler's bedroom door every morning.[28] Hitler insisted on extracts, not summaries. He particularly demanded material on foreign leaders. Given that he did not read much or work much, tended to rise late in the day, have long lunches and dinners with party cronies, and watch one or two movies every night, it is evident that he attached much importance to these clippings. But he sometimes also referred to the movies as keys to attitudes and moods in foreign countries. His assertions about French lack of will may have owed something to his seeing pacifist films popular in France in the 1930s, such as Jean Renoir's *Grand Illusion*. What he said to Brauchitsch and Halder about the superior fighting qualities of the British may have been affected by images of spirited British soldiers in his favorite film, Louis Lighton's *Lives of a Bengal Lancer*.[29] Probably, too, he drew upon conversations with foreign admirers such as the French journalist Fernand de Brinon, and the literary sisters Nancy and Unity Mitford, who talked to him of the weaknesses of their own countries in comparison with the Third Reich.[30]

In his post-1938 capacity as commander in chief of the armed forces, Hitler had directly under his control the Abwehr, properly the armed-forces high command's Amtsgruppe Ausland/Abwehr (Foreign and Defense Office Groups), which was Germany's secret-intelligence service. Usually referred to simply as the Abwehr, the organization had been created in the 1920s in hope of consolidating all collection and analysis of secret intelligence. As everywhere else in the world, the hope had been disappointed. The armed services' intelligence branches remained intact. The Abwehr, headed after 1934 by Admiral Wilhelm Canaris, simply complemented the services by running human spies abroad and by planning and conducting secret operations.

Most reports from spies concerned specific military weapons or deployments and were of greater use to the services than to Hitler, but some had to do with politics, and parts possibly interesting for Hitler were selected for him by navy captain Leopold Bürkner, head of the Abwehr's Ausland group. Once described by Canaris as a "true-blue seaman and a rose-red optimist," Bürkner was especially prone to passing on statements by foreign sympathizers and other evidence suggesting awe of Germany and Hitler among people in France and Britain.[31] The operational capabilities of the Abwehr may also have contributed to Hitler's comparative optimism about dealing with foreign governments, for they made it possible to stage incidents that could possibly confuse debate abroad. Thus, for example, the trigger for the invasion of Poland was supposed to be some shooting by Abwehr men wearing Polish army uniforms, making it appear that the Poles had provoked the German attack, but the incident was staged too clumsily to deceive anyone.

Hitler had access also to communications intelligence. A large agency, the Forschungsamt, tapped telephone and telegraph lines and deciphered coded messages. Göring had created the Forschungsamt in 1933 after having become head of the Prussian government. When he became air minister as well, in 1935, he moved it to the Air Ministry. Its title meant "research office." Its offices, occupying a whole apartment complex on the Schillerstrasse in the Charlottenburg district, west of central Berlin, had wrought-iron doors covered with gold leaf and guards in gray uniforms, just as at the main Air Ministry building on the Wilhelmstrasse, and its employees were instructed to say that they did classified research for the Luftwaffe. In reality, it was a wholly independent agency, with Göring himself its only link to any other part of the government.[32]

The Forschungsamt's staff received transcripts of wire recordings from taps at central telephone exchanges all over Germany, copies of messages obtained from telegraph offices, and radio interceptions. Any message in code went to a well-manned cryptanalytic section. Another section reviewed everything, including decrypted messages. Its chiefs decided what was worth passing on to Göring. He decided what should be sent to Hitler and what should be parceled out to others.

Though the Forschungsamt tried to employ only zealous Nazis, its internal code of conduct called for complete objectivity in reportage, and this code seems to have been obeyed. (Late in the war, with Hitler still talking of victory, Forschungsamt reports told of defeats, with worse to come.) Most of these reports were in mimeograph on brown paper and were sometimes referred to as "brown friends."[33] Despite Hitler's order that the Forschungsamt not target any high military officers or high party members, its A Section, which ran telephone taps, used a "Woman Bible" (Damenbibel), which listed women who had husbands or friends in high circles, and some of the resulting intercepts undoubtedly violated Hitler's order.[34] They may have been given special handling. Also, Hitler himself authorized exceptions, as, for example, the tracking of Goebbels's extramarital affairs. (Magda Goebbels was a long-term member of Hitler's retinue, and when Goebbels talked of divorcing her, Hitler ordered him to forget it.[35])

Special couriers carried "brown friends" to their addressees, and the recipients had to sign for them. One month later, another courier would come to retrieve them and write out receipts. The only exception was Hitler himself, who held on to "friends" for as much as nine months.[36]

In peacetime, the Forschungsamt supplied Hitler with information giving him tactical advantage in negotiations with foreign governments. Since Forschungsamt cryptanalysts broke most of the codes used by most embassies, including those of France and Britain, Hitler frequently knew what French and British ambassadors and attachés were reporting and what instructions they were receiving from home.[37] The Forschungsamt worked quickly enough so that, for example, at Godesberg, Hitler was able to read the British delegation's report on his first meeting with Chamberlain before he met with Chamberlain on the morning of the next day.[38]

Forschungsamt interceptions may not always have benefited Hitler. They may have misled him in August 1939 as to how France and Britain would actually respond when he attacked Poland, because the French foreign minister and the British ambassador in Berlin were ardent to avoid war.[39] Cumulatively, however, intercepted messages undoubtedly gave Hitler in peacetime additional insight into the thinking of other governments' foreign offices. Reading "brown friends" also told him what foreign correspondents were phoning and wiring home. When he went through his morning piles of clippings, he could then note what their editors were selecting for publication, and this probably had some effect on his estimates of public opinion in their countries.

What Hitler absorbed from reading or listening to foreign visitors mostly supported what he already believed. This was not uniquely true of him. In some degree, it is true of everyone.[40] But Hitler's growing self-idolization gave him more than normal insulation against information and evidence at odds with his preconceptions. Hence his indignant outbursts at Beck's figures about the French armed forces and at assertions that the Westwall would not hold France back.

This is not to say that Hitler paid no attention to evidence or argumentation at variance with his presumptions. His craziest beliefs, of course, were beyond modification. Nothing could have shaken his certainty about *Lebensraum* or about Jews. But he was very sensitive—at least before

1940—to specific information affecting tactical choices. However angry it made him to hear questions about the impregnability of the Westwall, he took them seriously. His practical response was to pour more money into the project and to make it a centerpiece in Goebbels's propaganda. Also, like the news or not, he paid close attention to any evidence of weakening public support at home. His inclination in late 1937 to act against Austria and Czechoslovakia sooner rather than later was probably influenced by reports of public grumbling about shortages. He retreated from his Godesberg demands and accepted the Munich accord in September 1938 in part because of Goebbels's warnings that Germans were unenthusiastic about war. In all likelihood, his eagerness for an offensive against France was partially driven by the strong and mounting evidence of mass antipathy to the war that had begun with the conquest of Poland. Hans Frank, head of the National Socialist Lawyers Association and a Chancellory hanger-on, later characterized the war as the most unpopular in German history. There were signs of this not only among civilians but among front-line soldiers. Army censors reported enlisted men writing home that only the generals wanted to continue the war and that the Führer would stop it if he could.[41]

Hitler's assessments of France and Britain and other nations were based less on formal military and diplomatic reportage than on gleanings from the press, scraps from Ausland/Abwehr bulletins, "brown friends" from the Forschungsamt, and testimony by friendly foreign visitors. What was most important to him was almost certainly evidence on mass opinion in other countries, and on the extent to which leaders abroad seemed to have popular support comparable to his. The relative absence of open dissent in Italy surely contributed to his high opinion of Mussolini. The fact that most U.S. newspapers were editorially critical of Roosevelt must have reinforced his low evaluation of the United States (and contributed to his misplaced regard for General Bötticher).

Hitler also received information and advice from some of the Nazis at his court, particularly Goebbels and Göring. A slight, dapper Rhinelander, eight years younger than Hitler, Goebbels in the 1920s had attached himself to Gregor Strasser, a Nazi leader who took more seriously than Hitler the "Socialist" part of the party's name. Gradually, he had shifted to supporting Hitler. His political ambitions were destined to be fulfilled, if at all, in someone's shadow, for he was too intense and too sharp-tongued to gather a large following of his own, and he had other disabilities. Because of childhood polio, he walked with a limp. His head was too large for his thin body, and his mouth was too large for his head. Frederick Birchall, a *New York Times* correspondent, commented of him: "The most remarkable thing about him was his mouth, which he opened so wide that at times the rest of his face seemed a mere thin frame around it."[42] But his support of Hitler was not just opportunistic. He became a worshipper. The gossipy diary that he kept from 1924 to 1945, undoubtedly written not only for eventual publication but with an eye to its doing him no damage if it somehow fell into wrong hands (and hence, for example, saying nothing about his notoriously frequent affairs with actresses), is full of adoring comments about Hitler that seem genuine. When the Third Reich came to its end in 1945, he chose to die with Hitler rather than survive him.

In the Nazis' climb to power, Goebbels had proved himself a talented attack-dog journalist. He had also had a large role in managing Hitler's national campaigns. When Hitler became chancellor, he had created for Goebbels a new post as minister of public enlightenment and propaganda. In that capacity, Goebbels managed and eventually controlled almost all German newspapers and magazines, all radio broadcasting, and the film industry. Given Hitler's views on the nature of political power, this was as important as any set of functions performed by anyone in his government. Goebbels was in and out of the Chancellory almost every day when Hitler was in Berlin and often traveled with him. He was the only member of the government to be a regular member of Hitler's circle at lunch and dinner, and his was the only party leader's home that Hitler regularly visited.

Goebbels brought Hitler information about mass opinion not only in Germany but abroad, for his ministry monitored foreign press-and-radio commentary about Germany and kept track of foreign films. (Goebbels selected the films that Hitler watched of an evening.) It was Goebbels's duty also to provide official releases to foreign news media and broadcasts to foreign audiences, to court friendly foreign journalists, and both openly and covertly to subsidize articles, books, broadcasts, and films produced abroad.

What Goebbels told Hitler tended to reinforce his low evaluation of the French and British governments. In part, this effect was an inevitable result of Goebbels's own self-advertising, for he constantly boasted to Hitler of his success in influencing foreign opinion. Because his ministry kept track of newspapers and radio broadcasts around the whole world, not just in Europe, he often called Hitler's attention to problems in French or British colonial possessions of which the Foreign Ministry took less note. In the meeting recorded by Hossbach, some of what Hitler said about problems in the British Empire echoed what he had been told by Goebbels.[43] And Goebbels's comments on events abroad often had the same slant as Hitler's. Thus, for example, he would describe a speech by a British politician calling for firmness against Germany as "childish," another by a champion of conciliation as "masterful." Both out of conviction and as a way of bolstering his own status with Hitler, Goebbels would also denigrate diplomats and military officers, deriding the former as "comical" and saying that the latter "think too much of themselves."[44]

Hermann Göring was also frequently in contact with Hitler. One of the more bizarre characters in the Third Reich, he was preposterously self-indulgent and theatrical. Weighing nearly three hundred pounds, he was so fat that it was said he had to wear corsets on his thighs.[45] He collected every office and medal that came within grasp. The official *Prussian Yearbook for 1939* lists his titles as "Field Marshal General, Commissar for the Four-Year Plan, Minister for Air and Commander in Chief of the Air Force, Master of the Forests for the Reich and for Prussia, Master of the Hunt for the Reich, President of the Reichstag, President of the State Council, and Minister President of Prussia." In the latter capacity, the *Yearbook* continued, he controlled the Archives, the State Theater, and the Prussian Secret Police. He was also patron and chief of the Hermann Göring Master School for Painting and patron of the Prussian Academy of Arts. His friend Prince Philip of Hesse joked that, in spite of his girth, he would soon have so many medals that he would have to pin some on his backside. It was also whispered that he had rubber replicas of each so that he could wear them in his swimming pool.[46]

Göring's extravagant uniforms were also subjects of humor. He kept a great estate not far from Berlin, named Karin Hall after his deceased first wife. When there, he liked to dress, it was reported, "in a sleeveless leather doublet, snow-white shirt sleeves of homespun linen bulging around his arms, and medieval high boots to the middle of his thighs." At a hunting lodge farther away, he once appeared after dinner dressed in a bearskin, carrying a spear, dragging behind him two bison, whom he encouraged to mate for the entertainment of his guests.[47]

But this often ridiculous tub of a man had been a genuine flying ace in the Great War. During the 1920s, he had contributed to developing Lufthansa, the dominant German commercial airline. The success of the Nazi Party owed a good deal to his organizing and disciplining its cadres in

Prussia. Hitler said that he had given Göring the Prussian SA as "a disheveled rabble. In a very short time he had organized a division of eleven thousand men."[48] And after Hitler came to power, Göring collected all those offices in part because he was one of the less incompetent administrators in Hitler's entourage.

Göring probably shared Hitler's beliefs about *Lebensraum* and Jews. In any case, if he differed with Hitler on any fundamental matter, he gave no sign of doing so. As was evident during the Blood Purge, he had no more scruples than Hitler about lying and committing murder. He probably felt some institutional loyalty toward the air force, which he had helped to create and with which he was identified, but it is unlikely that this loyalty was ever stronger than his loyalty to Hitler.

The multiplicity of Göring's functions and the knowledge that came with his varied duties put him more than once in a difficult position. In the mid-1930s, Göring knew how much the rearmament effort was straining Germany's civilian economy. It was partly for this reason that he took such an energetic lead with regard to Austria. He wanted Austria's resources. He may never have described to Hitler the full extent of the problems he was hoping thereby to solve.

As head of the air force, Göring had access to detailed information on how Germany compared with France and Britain in air power. Whether he sought such information or not is an open question. Johannes Steinhoff, a young air-force ace who, after the war, would come to head the West German air force, spent some time with Göring in 1939 and concluded that he understood almost nothing about modern aircraft. Paul Deichmann, an officer on the air staff, was convinced, however, that Göring knew that many of the Luftwaffe's planes had serious shortcomings but deliberately pretended otherwise, and also exaggerated both rates of production and numbers of planes operational—building for Hitler the equivalent of the stage-scenery villages that Prince Potemkin erected in the eighteenth century to line the routes of travel of the Empress Catherine the Great so that she would have the illusion that Russia was becoming a modern European nation.[49]

It is even more uncertain whether Göring was or was not aware of facts concerning the French and British air forces. The chief of intelligence for the German air force, Colonel Josef ("Beppo") Schmid, was an alcoholic roughneck with no evident qualification for his job other than unshakable certainty that German planes and pilots were superior to all others. Most officers in the air staff scorned Schmid and paid no attention to the intelligence estimates he circulated.[50] Whether Göring believed them or just wanted documents that would please Hitler, no one knows. Given his intellect and shrewdness, however, it seems unlikely that he himself believed everything he said to Hitler about how the air-power balance favored Germany. Although Göring goaded Hitler in 1938 to disregard the cautions of Beck and other generals, he had worried aloud even then about the possibility of a "big mess."

However prejudiced Hitler's mind, however limited his background, however scattered his sources of information, however his prejudices were reinforced by courtiers such as Goebbels and Göring, Hitler had both a broader conceptual framework than his professional advisers and a broader base of knowledge. When he made predictions about France or Britain, he thought of the politicians who headed their governments and about currents of mass opinion eddying around them that would influence, possibly control, their decisions. For practical purposes, Beck and Halder knew only what attachés and military intelligence reported on the military establishments of France and Britain. Though Weizsäcker read newspapers, he depended largely on reportage from German diplomatic missions abroad and gleanings from foreigners in Berlin. These sources told him much about high politics in Paris and London, especially as it touched their foreign offices, but less about the larger environment surrounding French and British decision-making.

Hitler's own experience as a politician, creating his interest in information about political leaders and mass politics in other countries, probably explains why, despite his disabilities, he was sometimes better able than his official advisers to foresee what the French and British governments would do. But the realities behind decisions made by those governments were far more complex and contingent than he or any of his advisers appreciated.

PART TWO

THE WESTERN ALLIES

CHAPTER EIGHT

DALADIER

"Daladier breathed courage, reflectiveness, and also a certain detachment as if he saw problems from a distance."

—*Jean Daridan, Daladier's principal assistant*

When Hitler or others in Germany made judgments about "France," they were, for practical purposes, assessing decisions that would percolate through the mind of Édouard Daladier, for, on April 10, 1938, not quite a month after the *Anschluss*, Daladier became prime minister of France, and he held that office until the spring of 1940.

Daladier's origins were almost as humble as Hitler's. Five years older than the German dictator, he had grown up in a village in Provence, in Mediterranean France, where his parents ran a bakery. As Hitler's mother indulged his desire to go to Vienna to study art, so Daladier's parents scrimped in order to send him to the University of Lyon. But there any similarity ended, for Daladier proved a hardworking student and successfully completed the training needed to become a professor, specializing in modern French and Italian history.

Daladier's experience of the Great War had some similarities to Hitler's. Called up in 1914, he went immediately to the front and remained there throughout. But, having been a reservist before the war, he started off as a sergeant and was eventually commissioned from the ranks. Like Hitler, he was frequently exposed to danger. As a company intelligence officer, he scouted areas in front of the French trenches, was wounded several times, commended often, and given two of France's highest decorations, the Croix de Guerre and the Légion d'Honneur.

The effects of the Great War on Daladier were very different from those on Hitler. Whereas Hitler's associations with the war were joyous, Daladier's were grim. Élisabeth du Réau, author of the best biography of Daladier, cites lines from the field records of a unit with which Daladier served during the second battle of Verdun in 1916:

> In darkness, the men had to cover a distance of eleven kilometers, part of which consisted of very muddy roads . . . obstructed by numerous bodies, German, but mostly French. . . . The ground was strewn with tree trunks and branches, weapons, clothing, ammunition, grenades, and cartridges. In the paths one had to step over human bodies half buried in the mud. Two men, one a German and the other a French staff officer, were hanging on the branches of a tree.[1]

Memories such as these would haunt Daladier when he faced the question whether France should go to war again and then, when war was a fact, whether it was to be fought as bloodily as the war of 1914–18.

Daladier, like Hitler, decided after the war to go into politics, but he did so through conventional routes. Before the war, he had been a socialist. Now he affiliated himself with the Radical Socialist Party. Usually simply called Radicals, most members of the party were not socialist at all but centrist, representing rural and middle-class voters united primarily by support for public schools as opposed to Catholic schools, reluctance to pay taxes, and unwillingness to identify clearly with either left or right. Daladier won a seat in the Chamber of Deputies (the French equivalent of the House of Commons or the U.S. House of Representatives). His eventual base was the Provençal town of Orange, where he also served continuously as mayor. Even when wartime prime minister, he would ride by train for ten hours from Paris's Gare de Lyon down to the south, and spend days dealing with local affairs there and comforting constituents. One French journalist characterized Daladier as "the machine politician *par excellence*."[2]

Within his party and in the Chamber of Deputies, Daladier rapidly rose to leadership. Other young war veterans lined up behind him, and he became the party's chief spokesman on defense matters. In 1927, he was elected party chairman, temporarily displacing Édouard Herriot, a whale-shaped bon vivant who had been his teacher at Lyon and his first political mentor.

In February 1934, at the age of forty-nine, Daladier briefly became prime minister. He did so at a time of internal crisis in France. He managed badly and almost finished off his political career. The experience affected him perhaps even more profoundly than had that of the Great War.

For France and the rest of the economically developed world, the Wall Street crash of October 1929 had opened what would be remembered as the Great Depression, which at first had little affected France. Large gold reserves and an economy only partially dependent on export earnings had initially provided cushioning. But the reserves eventually ran low, and the beggaring of neighbors had delayed effects. Just as most other developed nations were beginning to recover, France plunged into a slump. From having been the most prosperous country in Europe in the 1920s, France became, along with the United States, the Marxists' favorite example of the apparent failure of capitalism. National product declined. Prices sagged. The proud French countryside displayed neglected vineyards and fields, with cows and horses so lean that their ribs showed. Rivers running through French cities were lined with jobless workers trolling for fish. The pavements teemed with beggars. France seemed, in the phrase of one economist, to have "a vegetative economy."[3]

Largely but not entirely because of the economy, many French people seemed to be losing confidence in their political institutions. The malaise was not so deep as that which had dissolved the Weimar Republic. It resembled more that of the United States in the despairing months before Franklin Roosevelt became president, promising a "New Deal." But by 1934, many in France were asking whether their Third Republic, created hopefully in the aftermath of the defeat by Prussia in the war of 1870–71, which had celebrated its sixtieth birthday in 1931, would live to celebrate a seventieth.

Most ominous was the possibility of the country's splitting along ideological lines, maybe even experiencing a civil war. The Communist Party, though still a small minority in Parliament, was noisy and obviously growing stronger. Its umbrella trade-union organization, the CGTU (Confédération Générale du Travail Unitaire), enrolled more than 40 percent of France's organized workers. Its two national dailies, the morning *L'Humanité* and evening *Ce Soir*, were the fourth and fifth most widely sold newspapers in France.[4] As in Germany earlier, the radical right was also gaining in numbers and visibility. The streets of Paris saw demonstrations by paramilitary groups menacingly similar to the Blackshirts and Brownshirts of Italy and Germany. The Jeunesses Patriotes affected blue raincoats, the Solidarité Française SA-style jackboots. The largest group, the Croix de Feu, consisted of disciplined, militant war veterans who paraded wearing uniforms and decorations.

The immediate background for Daladier's short-lived premiership was an incident on which extremists of both left and right seized as a gross symptom of the Third Republic's corruptness: the arrest in Marseilles of a confidence man named Alexandre Stavisky uncorked a stream of evidence incriminating bribe-takers at all levels of government. Communists and socialists charged a cover-up by the right-wing head of the Paris police, Jean Chiappe. The Jeunesses Patriotes, Solidarité Française, Croix de Feu, and other such bodies immediately came to Chiappe's defense. Factional leaders in Parliament picked Daladier to be prime minister in the hope that he could mediate.

Daladier failed. When he proposed that Chiappe leave Paris to become governor general of Morocco, Chiappe refused. Moreover, as Daladier heard him, he threatened armed revolt: Daladier said Chiappe had said to him that he would go *"à la rue"*—take to the streets. Chiappe claimed to have used the phrase *"dans la rue,"* meaning he would be jobless and out on the street. Whatever the case, contingents of right-wing toughs did go *à la rue*. They surged through central Paris, apparently intent on attacking the Parliament. Left-wing toughs streamed out to block them. In and around the Place de la Concorde, where the Alexandre III Bridge crosses the Seine to the Parliament and government buildings, demonstrators hurled bricks and bottles and scattered marbles, which caused the horses of mounted policemen to tumble. As night fell, someone fired a gun. No one was ever sure who. Probably, it was some frightened young policeman. Other guns came out. By morning, eighteen were dead and more than fourteen hundred wounded.

Daladier passed the night never quite sure how bad things were or would become. Some of the ministers and deputies milling around him in the Parliament building proposed that he call out the army. Aware of the strength of right-wing sympathy in the regular army, he feared that this would be—or seem—intervention against the left. In the confused, tired wee hours of the morning, some of the young Radicals whom he had included in his cabinet began to urge that they all resign lest their party carry blame for a civil war. Eventually, Daladier accepted their advice. It was a mistake. The police lines held. The commander of the Croix de Feu ordered his veterans not to mix in the fighting. Demonstrators began to disperse. The cabinet that took over from Daladier's got the credit for the subsequent peace, and he found himself in subsequent days denounced from the right as "murderer" and from the left as "coward."[5]

This experience scarred Daladier. After 1940, many would cite the episode as evidence that he had always been weak, indecisive, and inclined to evade responsibility. If he himself had put into words the lessons it seemed to teach, he might have said that it showed the wisdom of being deliberate rather than precipitate, and casting widely for advice instead of listening to just one person or faction. But this may be a way of saying that it encouraged future indecisiveness. Certainly, recollection of February 1934 left Daladier permanently fearful of emotionally charged public demonstrations. Long after the French economy had recovered and public pessimism about the future of France had lessened, Daladier remained hypersensitive about arousing the ire of right-wing extremists.

February 1934 might have marked the end of Daladier's political career, but it did not. Supporters in Provence remained loyal. As party and parliamentary colleagues looked left and right, they saw few others with Daladier's capacity for brokering coalitions among the many factions in the Chamber of Deputies and the Senate. Herriot, who had returned as chairman of the Radical party (the Radical Socialist Party), had proved unable to bargain effectively with other party leaders. By 1936, the Radical rank and file had once again chosen Daladier as chairman.

French politics had meanwhile changed in ways that created new opportunities for Radicals. Not long after the 1934 riots, the French Communist Party received new orders from Moscow. Previously, party members had condemned socialists as worse than fascists. Now they were told to speak well of them and to seek an alliance with all parties of the left and even of the center. In parliamentary elections in April–May 1936, the communists increased their strength sixfold. Their seventy-two representatives thereafter made up almost one-eighth of the Chamber of Deputies. The socialists also gained seats. The Socialist Party leader Léon Blum formed a Popular Front government.[6] Though communists took no seats in the cabinet, they supported it. So did most Radicals. As one token of Radical support, Daladier entered Blum's cabinet as minister of war.

From May 1936 until April 1938, when he became prime minister as well as minister of war, Daladier conceived his chief task to be rebuilding and strengthening the French army so that it would not be surpassed by the army that Germany had been in the process of creating even before March 1935, when Hitler declared the Versailles Treaty null and void.

The challenge facing Daladier was partly due to ups and downs in earlier French military policy. During most of the 1920s, France had maintained a much larger army than most people elsewhere in the world thought either necessary or desirable. British and American commentators routinely described France as "militaristic" and "obsessed with security." In the French Parliament, parties on the left consistently called for cutting military spending. After the Franco-German détente of the mid-1920s, symbolized by the Locarno Pact and its guarantee of the French-German border, some members of center parties began to take a similar position. In 1930, Pierre Cot, a left-wing Radical (who may have been a Soviet secret agent), proposed that the party take as its slogan, "Not another man, not another sou for defense." Though Daladier did not go quite so far, he came close.[7]

Meanwhile, the right-center cabinets in power had kept military spending at high levels but had made a dramatic programmatic change. Previously, the army's chief purpose had been readiness to enforce the peace terms of 1919 in case Germany tried to evade them. After the Locarno Pact, French governments began to invest instead in permanent fortifications designed to protect the frontier in the event that Germany, now apparently tame but clearly growing in power, should again threaten invasion.

These fortifications were the famous Maginot Line, so called after the then minister of war, André Maginot. Because "Maginot Line" later came to be a synonym for muddle-headed military thinking, a brief digression is needed to defend it both as a concept and as a reality.[8] Two of its key premises were beyond dispute: that France could not match Germany in numbers, and that geography made France vulnerable in several wide areas. Even within the smaller boundaries fixed by the Versailles Treaty, Germany's population was larger by a third. For military purposes, the disparity was particularly great in the "hollow years" between 1934 and 1938, when the numbers of men eligible for army call-up in France would be few because so few potential fathers had been at home between 1914 and 1918. Though the Pyrenees Mountains and the Alps provided natural protection to the southwest and southeast, the Rhine (complemented by the Vosges and Jura ranges) formed a natural barrier in the east, and the Ardennes massif obstructed passage into France from the northeast via Luxembourg and southern Belgium, the whole of Lorraine, from the neighborhood of Strasbourg up to the Ardennes, lay invitingly open.

The logic of the Maginot Line grew directly from these facts. It was designed to compensate both for a comparative shortage of manpower and for geography. Embodying the highest technology of the era, it consisted of

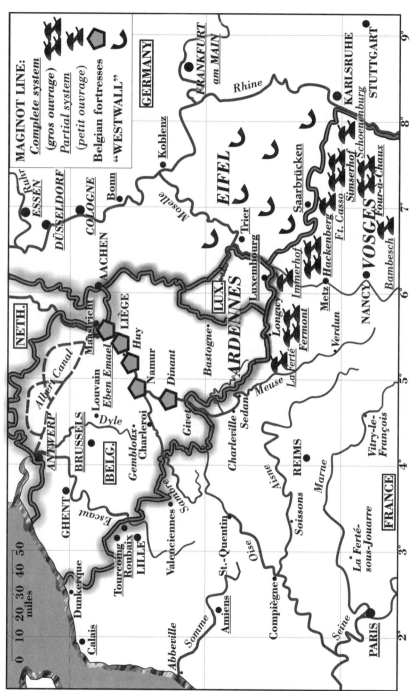

The Maginot Line and the "Westwall"

carefully sited, heavily armored gun turrets connected by underground rail lines. Elaborate quarters for troops, including kitchens, medical facilities, and vast chambers for storage of ammunition and supplies, were also underground. Well-protected telephone lines permitted men to be summoned in strength to any sector that came under attack. Sheltered aboveground roads permitted rapid transfer of manpower from one chain of turrets to another in case the attack was particularly heavy. One writer likened the Maginot Line to a land-based battle fleet. Leopold Amery (always referred to as Leo), a British Tory member of Parliament who toured the Line in 1939, described it as "the prodigious child of a marriage betweem a cruiser and a mine."[9] Anyone who tours a surviving fragment such as the small chain (*petit ouvrage*) at Rohrbach, not far from Strasbourg, will see that the Line was a technical marvel of the interwar era, on a par with American or Soviet intercontinental ballistic missile complexes of the Cold War. Because of its design and the strength of each complex, only a small proportion of the troops that France could mobilize needed to be committed to defense of the borders directly opposite Germany.

The Maginot Line thus did not in itself commit France to a defensive strategy. On the contrary, the existence of the Line made it possible for France, despite its overall inferiority in numbers, to contemplate matching the Germans in a war of maneuver, for only so many troops on either side could mass within the area not covered by fixed defenses—that between the Ardennes massif and the Channel coast. Though some French politicians and even some military men advocated complete commitment to a defensive strategy with construction of fixed fortifications all along the Belgian frontier, what in fact happened was erection there of a very thin defensive line combined with preparation for a war of movement, perhaps in northeastern France but preferably on the Belgian plain.

The building of the Line may have encouraged a tendency among the French people to believe that France could be safe no matter what happened on the other side of the Rhine—a "Maginot Line mentality." But the illusion was never universal, nor did it last long. The remilitarization of the Rhineland occurred in March 1936. By that spring, when Daladier became war minister, few knowledgeable people in France believed that the Maginot Line did more than ensure that, if the Germans attacked, it would not be through Lorraine. And this was an accurate perception, for the Line always seemed to German military men to be almost impenetrable.

As France began to feel the full effect of the Great Depression, however, overall spending for military forces leveled off and then declined. Because of heavy commitments already made for constructing and outfitting the Maginot Line, even the leveling off meant an absolute decrease in regular spending for the army and navy.

The decrease was all the sharper because in 1928 the French air force had become an independent service and therefore a rival claimant for money. And all three services argued uncompromisingly for priority. Admiral François Darlan, head of the navy, insisted that a 630,000-ton fleet had to take first place. Without it, he said, France could not ensure communications with North Africa and elsewhere or be protected if relations worsened with Great Britain, France's chief enemy in ages past. Senior air-force officers such as General Jules Armengaud, the service's inspector general, risked court-martial by publishing pseudonymous articles denouncing the failure of governments and the Parliament to appreciate the need for long-range bombers, the weapons that, in their view, would determine the outcome of any future war. Within the army, Colonel Charles de Gaulle made himself famous by writing a book with a theme anticipating that of Guderian's *Achtung Panzer!* It called for relying less on draftees and instead building up elite professional armored forces equipped for rapid offensive operations. (He served his cause badly by coupling the two propositions, for he thus made armored forces a target of attack not only by generals still partial to the horse but by anyone who believed in citizen armies.)[10]

In these circumstances, governments of the early 1930s resorted to expedients. The period of mandatory service for males reaching age twenty, already cut from eighteen months to one year, was reduced in 1932 to just eleven months. This was followed in 1933 by a 15-percent cut in the officer corps of the regular army. To satisfy both army requirements for air support and air-force enthusiasm for an independent strategic-bombing capability, contracts were let to design aircraft that could serve either as fighters or as bombers. When drawings arrived, the proposed planes seemed likely to do well in neither role. The result was to postpone France's effort to match the aggressive air-force buildup being advertised by Hitler and Göring.

All these economies affected the efficiency of French fighting forces in the short run, and they would have some effects lingering into 1939–40. Because some of the eleven months of training went simply to getting troops enrolled, tested for aptitudes, and assigned and quartered, and because each recruit was entitled to about a month of furlough, the net effect was to reduce severely the time recruits actually gave to soldiering. And the problem was compounded by economies down the line when scheduled three-week refresher courses and seven-day exercises, supposed to occur periodically over a twenty-eight-year period of eligibility for call-up, either failed to occur or became perfunctory. In 1939, some infantrymen reported for active duty never having fixed a bayonet or handled a grenade. The author-philosopher Jean-Paul Sartre commented on the "respectful terror" he observed in fellow reservists handling weapons they had never seen before.[11]

Reductions in the officer corps and some accompanying reorganizations meant that practically all regular-army captains, lieutenants, and noncommissioned officers drew duty drilling recruits and hence had little opportunity to exercise regular-army formations, or even to study or practice field maneuvers. This, too, affected performance when the French armed forces were mobilized later.

The short-run effects were probably more important than those in the long run, however, for, after September 1939, the army was to have nine months in which to remedy deficiencies discovered at mobilization, and most commanders—though not all—would put those months to good use. What was most harshly affected was immediate confidence. Career officers in the French army, more than career officers in most other armies, traditionally looked down on draftees and reservists. It was a result of the army's having remained monarchist after the country became republican and of the officer corps's being prevented by republican politicians from disciplining civilian soldiers as they wished, and it was a reason why French career officers had such a strong preference for serving in colonies rather than at home. In the 1930s, even the officers and noncommissioned officers least prejudiced against civilians were skeptical of men with only eleven months of training to cope with an emergency, and this in a period when there was much speculation about an emergency at home, and when photographs and films coming out of Germany seemed to show disciplined mass armies in formation and new tanks and other equipment rolling off assembly lines.

Daladier was to claim to have started France's rearming against the Nazi threat. That was an exaggeration, for his predecessors had already commenced a turnaround. What Daladier did was to intensify the effort and, perhaps most important, to begin to remedy inefficiency and fragmentation. Though most of the socialist bloc within the Popular Front remained dogmatically antimilitary, the communists were now under orders to support, not resist, military spending. Since Daladier could count on backing from most fellow Radicals and from others in the center and right who were traditionally promilitary, he had the parliamentary votes for an ambitious rearmament program.

The highest obstacles were in the cabinet, for Blum and eleven of his twenty ministers were socialists, and several of the Radicals came from the party's left. (Cot, once the opponent of spending any sou for the military, was air minister.) Yet Daladier succeeded in winning a cabinet vote in August 1936 in favor not only of increased military spending but of a shift to longer-term commitments. Theretofore, defense budgets had run year to year, with service proposals framed in late winter and spring, cabinet action in summer, parliamentary debate in fall, and final authorizations at the beginning of the new year; the Treasury was still able to withhold funds in event of shortfalls in tax revenues or increases in costs of borrowing. Daladier somehow persuaded his colleagues that this was no way for France to try to keep up with Germany, and the cabinet authorized him to put before Parliament a four-year spending program not subject to adjustment by the Treasury.

Within the War Ministry, when Daladier first asked for a four-year program, the army proposed one totaling nine billion francs. He rejected it as too unambitious. The army's second budget—for twenty billion francs—he pared back. What he won from Blum and the others was approval for spending fourteen billion francs over the four-year-period, approximately one-quarter for tanks and motorized troop transport and 30 percent for new artillery, especially antitank and anti-aircraft guns.[12]

The nationalization of some armaments factories appeased socialists, who had been willing to arm against Germany but objected to rewarding "merchants of death." Since manufacturers had never made more than meager profits from chancy, often canceled government contracts, opposition was less than might have been expected. Actual nationalization proved very limited—chiefly small aircraft plants and a few tank factories.[13] Combined with multiyear funding, however, even limited consolidation in the defense industry smoothed the stream from service orders to actual deliveries.

Blum meanwhile succeeded in pushing through Parliament some of the domestic legislation that he and his partners had promised. His accomplishments included passage in 1936 of laws limiting the factory workweek to forty hours and guaranteeing industrial workers two weeks a year of paid vacation. After a while the momentum for such reform diminished. To stay in office, Blum had to make increasing concessions to factions and parties of the center-right. In June 1937, he lost a vote in the Senate. Although he did not have to do so, he chose to resign. Camille Chautemps, a Radical, formed a new government with Blum as vice-premier. This held together until January 1938, when Blum and the other socialists all resigned.

Daladier remained in place throughout as war minister. When legislation early in 1938 created a minister of national defense, he took that title as well. This supposedly meant that he would have power to coordinate the three services, but he never tested whether that was so. It was almost if not quite true that, as had been said of an earlier experiment in unifying the French defense establishment, nothing changed except "the headings printed on letters and envelopes."[14] The navy, like navies everywhere, guarded its independence. The air force came under Daladier's effective budgetary control only because Cot joined the socialists in resigning, and the new air minister, Guy La Chambre, a tall, dark, elegant young Radical senator, characterized by one War Ministry staff officer as "a sort of Hollywood parliamentarian," regarded himself as Daladier's disciple.[15]

Daladier immediately set out to do for the air force what he had done for the army. Though Cot had had authority for multiyear funding, he had not made much use of it, in part because of design problems and in part because of his preoccupation with efforts to nationalize the aircraft industry. Appearing before a combined session of the army, navy, and air-force committees of the Chamber of Deputies in March 1938, Daladier described bluntly the inherited problem. The air staff as well as the minister and his civilian aides, he said, had been far too perfectionist. The Breguet 691, a three-seat fighter-bomber, had been modified more than a hundred times before going into production. Though prototypes of the Amiot 350 and 351 twin-engine bombers had broken world records, that had been a year ago, and planes were not yet coming off the line. The same was true for the Morane-Saulnier 405, a highly maneuverable single-seat fighter, which had been ready for production for two years.[16] This confession before the responsible committees of the Parliament proved a prelude to head-cracking in the air force, which would result in a broadening stream of deliveries to operational squadrons.

In March 1938, the air force adopted a plan for a sixfold increase in strength, with its target almost five thousand new planes with speeds above three hundred miles per hour, retractable landing gear, motor-regulated cannon, and other advanced features. After the *Anschluss*, at the insistence of Daladier and La Chambre, the program was speeded up, calling for all these new planes to be delivered within two years—by the spring of 1940.[17]

When Daladier became prime minister in April 1938, he kept his posts as war minister and defense minister, and he kept also a preoccupation with building up France's ground and air forces. His own experience in the Great War made him loath even to think of sending these forces into battle. The trauma of February 1934 had left him deeply cautious about adopting any policy that might arouse violent public dissent. At the same time, he was proud of the military instruments that he had helped to create, and sure that the armament program he had sponsored would have a deterrent effect on Hitler.

Burly and dark-complected, with his shoulders usually hunched, and his balding head pulled toward his chest, Daladier was thought by many to be a tough and somewhat willful leader. He had been nicknamed "the Bull of the Camargue" by journalists in his home region. The reference was to the marshland west of Provence famous as a breeding ground for fighting bulls. Parisian journalists substituted "Bull of the Vaucluse." Jean Montigny, a deputy from the right wing of the Radical party, commented on Daladier's "Roman head" and wrote: "He gives an impression of energy, will, and controlled power."[18]

Some men who had opportunities to observe Daladier closely thought his apparent forcefulness and resoluteness were masks. Jules Jeanneney, the president of the Senate, concluded that Daladier retreated into taciturnity and gruffness because he was embarrassed by his natural indecisiveness. Cot, reminiscing about dealing with Daladier, said: "One thought he was going to say no; in fact, he began gamely by saying no, after which he said perhaps, and then he ended up by compromising if not by giving in."[19]

Jean Daridan, who was Daladier's principal assistant and probably observed him more closely than anyone else, believed that he was best understood as a man of analytic mind, given pause less by inability to decide than by consciousness of complexities. Daridan wrote:

Of medium height but massive presence, with very blue and penetrating eyes, little hair, a sensual nose, and a wry mouth, Daladier breathed courage, reflectiveness, and also a certain detachment as if he saw problems from a distance. He could make fun of himself, but his irony, when applied to others, could be corrosive. With a pleasant manner and no bombast, he excelled, when interrogating people, at making his interlocutors talk and giving them the impression that he had complete confidence in them. His knowledge, especially of history, was vast, his intelligence lively, and I have never seen anyone approach him in ability to make quick study of a question or to make sense out of a file.[20]

An American journalist adds to the picture of Daladier as interrogator:

He was tactful in public. In private, however, he was blunt, his endless suspicion of others determining his attitude. Eying that drooping cigarette of his, he often risked losing it when he spat out some comment that put his visitor on the defensive. Rich tales were whispered of how he slouched in his chair, then surprised the unwary with some unexpected thrust. Hunched forward, he searched out the truth. . . . His voice seemed to struggle for expression, as if strangled by emotions at war within him.[21]

This was the man whose mind Hitler was trying to read when he assessed France through his press clippings and other sources, and whose choices Weizsäcker presumed to forecast on the basis of reports from German diplomats and attachés and German generals on the basis of their own calculations of French military capabilities.

CHAPTER NINE

GAMELIN

"This man, in whom intelligence, subtlety, and self-control reached a very high level, had absolutely no doubt that, in the approaching battle, he was bound eventually to win. . . . This great chief . . ."
—*Charles de Gaulle,* Mémoires de guerre, *describing General Gamelin in April 1940*

A s war minister, defense minister, and prime minister, Daladier had as his chief military adviser General Maurice Gamelin. Since Gamelin had been the senior serving officer of the army since 1935, he and Daladier had been constant collaborators in the War Ministry. When Daladier also became minister of national defense, Gamelin added to his own titles that of chief of staff of national defense, thus additionally becoming Daladier's collaborator in nominal management of the defense establishment as a whole.

More than a decade older than Daladier, Gamelin had been born the year after France's defeat in the Franco-Prussian War of 1870–71. His father had been a general. His grandfather had been a general. There had been generals named Gamelin since the reign of Louis XIV.[1] An oil painting hanging in the family home in Paris showed a nine-year-old Gamelin outfitted as a drummer boy, and he was said to have had as a child the largest collection of lead soldiers in the city. Gamelin père had nevertheless discouraged an army career, perhaps because he thought his son too small, too bookish, or too unskilled at garrison sports such as riding, shooting, and fencing. But Gamelin insisted on keeping the family tradition.

He graduated from the French military academy, St.-Cyr, in 1893, first in a class of 449. After duty in North Africa, he attended the War College and again starred. There he studied under Ferdinand Foch, one of the military intellectuals who served as role models for young officers of his generation. Afterward, he made a bid to enter this circle by publishing *A Philosophical Study on the Art of War*. Like Foch's famous *Principles of War*, Gamelin's small treatise emphasized the unpredictability of warfare and the crucial role of the commander. In the spirit also of earlier French military theorists such as Ardant du Picq and of his own favorite modern philosopher, Henri Bergson, coiner of *"élan vital,"* Gamelin argued that purpose, will, and intelligence could overcome almost any odds. By thinking hard enough and acting decisively enough, a determined commander could overcome superior numbers even in disadvantageous terrain. He cited specifically battles won by commanders taking the offensive in thickly wooded hill country such as that in France's Ardennes Forest. In the book, one can see attitudes that would remain with Gamelin all through his life, particularly faith in his own capacity to master or adapt any averse circumstances.

In 1906, the year when he published his book, Gamelin got the first of the series of assignments that led him eventually to the top of the military establishment. As a thirty-four-year-old captain, he became aide to General Joseph Joffre, then commander of an infantry division. After five years, he returned to the field, taking over a troubled battalion of Alpine troops and turning it, in six months, into a model fighting organization. In 1913, he went to the "holy of holies," the general staff, and to its inner temple, the Troisième (Operations) Bureau, then soon afterward to the personal staff of Joffre, now army chief of staff.

When the Great War opened in 1914, the forty-two-year-old Gamelin was thus on a central stage. The general staff expected Germany to attack through Alsace-Lorraine as they had in 1870, headed for Sedan. Instead, seven German armies struck Belgium, attempting a sweep across that country into northeastern France to Paris, which would box in the French forces that had moved eastward toward Sedan and Strasbourg. From a small command post at Vitry-le-François, eighty miles east of Paris, Joffre maneuvered his armies so as to reposition them in the line of the actual German advance. He used every available form of transport, including Paris taxicabs. In the first battle of the Marne, in September 1914, Joffre's armies held their line. The Germans went no farther. The Western front became what it would remain for another four years.

Gamelin was one of the heroes of this defensive success. Joffre, though decisive and self-confident, was better at barking orders than at explaining what they meant. Gamelin, at this stage in life, was a superb staff officer, able quickly to translate Joffre's Delphic orders into step-by-step instructions that moved soldiers, cannon, horses, shells, hay, and rations from one precise point to another. Without Joffre's vision and insight, the first battle of the Marne might not have been fought. Without Gamelin's meticulous staffwork, it might not have been won.

Gamelin later commanded a division that distinguished itself in bloody engagements in the Aisne sector of the Western front. He was repeatedly commended and decorated. But the time with Joffre in 1914 had been a molding period. Ever afterward, in moments of crisis, Gamelin's mind would go back to the days of 1914 at Vitry-le-François. This one experience ratified for him the theory he had advanced in his book—that will power and cool intelligence counted ahead of everything else in determining the outcome of battle. He consciously modeled himself on Joffre, trying always to be calm, aloof, and reassuring, especially in the presence of nervous politicians.

After the war, Gamelin headed a military mission in Brazil, commanded troops in the Levant, and then returned to France, where in 1929 he moved into the number-three post in the army, just under General Maxime Weygand, who was in turn just under Marshal Philippe-Henri Pétain. When Weygand succeeded Pétain in 1931, Gamelin moved into Weygand's chair. When Weygand retired in 1935, Gamelin took over from him.

Gamelin owed his status and long tenure in part simply to his credentials as a soldier. De Gaulle refers to Gamelin in the memoirs he wrote after the war as "the great chief," commenting particularly on his "intelligence, subtlety, and self-control."[2] Commentary on Gamelin before the war, both in France and abroad, approached the reverential. His admirers in Germany included Generals Rundstedt and Beck, the latter of whom kept a portrait of Gamelin in his study at home.[3]

In part, however, Gamelin's success and standing were due to his being different from other generals. In France, as in Germany, the strongest loyalty of many army officers was to the army. Many had never reconciled themselves to the parliamentary republic that had come into being after the war of 1870–71. They would have preferred a monarchy, with an established Roman Catholic Church dominating the spiritual realm. They remained anti-Dreyfusards. Even if acknowledging that the army had made a mistake in the 1890s when convicting Captain Alfred Dreyfus of espionage and condemning him to Devil's Island, they believed that the journalists and politicians who exposed the mistake and obtained the release of Dreyfus had acted against the interests of France. In their view, it would have been much better to let the Jewish captain suffer than to bring the army into public disrepute. Their chief hero from the Great War was Marshal Foch, Gamelin's War College teacher, for Foch had openly despised and battled politicians—even Georges Clemenceau, "the Tiger," the uncompromising nationalist who had led France to victory in 1918. Foch had also made bold display of his Catholicism.

By virtue of his closeness to Joffre, Gamelin was identified with a different camp, for Joffre had been an avowed republican and atheist and had publicly expressed regret about the injustice to Dreyfus. In the army of the 1920s and 1930s, Weygand was seen as the heir of Foch, Gamelin as the heir of Joffre.

For Weygand, this was deserved. He imitated Foch in every respect, including his tactless belligerence toward politicians.

For Gamelin, it was true only to the extent that he tried to behave like Joffre. Privately, he was as much a monarchist as Weygand, and as devout a Catholic. He writes in his memoirs of a meeting in 1939 with Daladier, at which Daladier remarked that he felt like King Louis XV in 1772, looking on while other powers partitioned Poland. Gamelin recalls starting to sneer inwardly at a party politician's likening himself to a Bourbon monarch but then realizing on second thought that "Prime Minister Daladier was thinking in the name of immortal France."[4] When war actually came, one of Gamelin's first acts was to say prayers at Notre-Dame. But Gamelin kept his beliefs to himself. He never openly criticized the republic, and when he prayed at Notre-Dame he took the precaution of leaving his uniform hat in the car and draping himself in a raincoat in order not to be remarked.[5] Because he so successfully concealed his real attitude toward the godless republic, and because he imitated the manners of Joffre, he, unlike Weygand, was able to develop amiable personal relations with a wide variety of political leaders. As a German military attaché commented in 1937, Gamelin "was the exceptional French soldier who was accepted by politicians because he did not arouse their suspicions or give rise to the belief that he was making himself too powerful." Also, as historian Nicole Jordan writes: "His inveterate habit was to tell interlocutors whatever he sensed that they wanted to hear."[6]

The more Gamelin was trusted by politicians, the less he was trusted by his fellow generals. Although he and Weygand cooperated at first, a breach occurred when Weygand wanted to take an uncompromising position against cuts in personnel while Gamelin argued for seeming accommodating but employing sleight of hand, as, for example, by beefing up forces in North Africa. War Ministry staff officers partial to Weygand said sneeringly of Gamelin that he was "like a silk shirt; the more you crumple him, the more supple he becomes."[7] Though Weygand could not block Gamelin's succession, he left Gamelin surrounded by a coterie of his own supporters. The new number two under Gamelin, General Alphonse-Joseph Georges, was thought to be such, perhaps because he appropriated for his own staff Colonel Jean de Lattre de Tassigny, widely thought to have been Weygand's chief liaison with groups such as the Jeunesses Patriotes.[8] The number three, General Louis Colson, army chief of staff, certainly was. Although until the war Gamelin had no sharp conflict with either, he had continual difficulty with Weygand men who were professionally and politically conservative and hence resistant to his desire to mechanize and motorize the army. General Marie-Robert Altmayer, the inspector general of cavalry, for example, insisted that tanks could not adequately take the place of horses; General Julien Dufieux, the inspector general of infantry, opposed having infantrymen travel by truck instead of on foot. Colson supported Dufieux, at least to the extent of contending that the army did not need to train truck drivers; it could just call them up.[9]

To retain office, to keep some degree of control within the army, and to influence the extent and character of military spending, Gamelin needed support from politicians, particularly, of course, the politician who happened to be war minister. From mid-1936 onward, that was Daladier.

The relationship between the two men became increasingly one of mutual dependence. Gamelin could not do without Daladier; Daladier found that he could not do without Gamelin. He never trusted him—or any general. "I had the impression," Gamelin writes, "that he had confidence in me and at the same time mistrust . . . mistrust because that was his nature." At first, Daladier hoped that his chief military adviser could be General Victor Bourret, who served on his personal staff. The son of a gendarme and the only senior general to have entered the officer corps through the technical school at St.-Maxent rather than the academy at St.-Cyr, Bourret paraded his republicanism, made a point of having plebeian manners, and was continually on the lookout for evidence of right-wing conspiracies. But Bourret proved of no help to Daladier in his main task of furthering rearmament. Gamelin did.[10] Moreover, it was quickly clear to Daladier that he and Gamelin agreed not only on the urgency of a military buildup but on the importance of high-quality new weaponry, especially tanks and troop-carrying vehicles and antitank and anti-aircraft guns. The postwar researches of Élisabeth du Réau, Martin Alexander, and Pierre Dutailly leave little doubt that Daladier and Gamelin were both in the forefront of efforts to prepare France's ground forces for what would soon be called *Blitzkrieg*. When opportunity offered, Daladier and Gamelin were equally eager to take control of and rationalize a program to provide France with a modern air force.

And, however much Daladier distrusted Gamelin, he distrusted other generals more. He recognized that most of them admired Weygand, and, partly because of information and gossip relayed to him by Bourret, he suspected them of plotting against the republic. Whenever he found himself at odds with Gamelin, he realized that, if Gamelin stepped down, he would probably have to replace him with Georges or Colson. The result was that Daladier always yielded or compromised.

It is not clear that either man ever liked the other. Daladier's highest tribute to Gamelin came in a statement before the military-affairs committee of the Chamber, in which he characterized him as "completely in the line of the great military leaders that France had in the last war," adding, "He is an exceptionally cultivated man with a remarkably open mind."[11] Gamelin's view of Daladier was ambivalent at best. Though he might applaud Daladier's identifying himself with France, he could speak harshly of the prime minister when he thought his words were safe. "He changes his mind depending on which way the wind is blowing . . . a total lightweight," he said of Daladier to Lieutenant Colonel Paul de Villelume, an officer who served as liaison between Gamelin and the Foreign Ministry and who made no secret of his own dislike for Daladier.[12] Élie Bois, Daladier's newspaper-editor friend, probably had it right when he commented, "The relations between General Gamelin and M. Daladier were subject to variations, rain, if not storm, alternating with fine weather."[13]

Colonel Pierre Le Goyet, a French military historian who was acquainted with Gamelin, provides the following description of him in roughly 1938–39:

Of medium height, quite stocky, he gave an impression of solidity. A round face, slightly ruddy, with a narrow brush mustache. Very clear eyes, very blue, but indefinable, neither inquiring, nor questioning, nor encouraging. The painter Brisgand, who did his portrait in 1936, said: "These are eyes that wait." Nothing describes better than this remark the dominant personality trait of the General: he has time.

He expresses himself with measured but simple words, in a calm and resonant voice. Affable and courteous, he is the picture of self-control. Always well turned out, elegantly dressed, he seems not to suffer any inferiority complex. Sure of his memory, of his experience, and of his powers of concentration, he exudes balance. . . . He could pass for a philosopher. He is an admirer of Bergson and likes to talk about Bergson's theories. An expert in Italian painting and Greek philosophy, he constantly amazes his listeners.[14]

In France, the head of the army had responsibility for all secret intelligence, for unchallenged primacy in secret intelligence belonged to the Deuxième (or Second) Bureau of the army general staff.[15] This Deuxième Bureau differed from the intelligence directorate of the German general staff in two respects that combine to make a paradox. The Deuxième Bureau had much wider reach and authority. The German army intelligence directorate, headed by General Tippelskirch, competed with the other services' intelligence branches and with Canaris's Abwehr, Göring's Forschungsamt, and other organizations. The Deuxième Bureau, by contrast, was more nearly a genuine central intelligence agency than any other, anywhere, before or since. It effectively controlled all spies and all interception and decryption of communications. Its chief received reports on all photographic intelligence collected by the air force. He also had the lead role in counterespionage.[16]

Organizationally, however, the Deuxième Bureau was not well situated to make use of its resources. The chain of command went from Gamelin to Colson to General Henri-Ferdinand Dentz, one of Colson's deputies. But Dentz was not a counterpart to General Tippelskirch, for Dentz had a number of other responsibilities and Tippelskirch had none. Moreover, Dentz was presumed to be in his last post before retirement, whereas Tippelskirch was recognized as a rising star.[17] The actual chief of the Deuxième Bureau, and thus France's principal intelligence officer, was Lieutenant Colonel Maurice-Henri Gauché. Originally an infantry officer, Gauché was, writes a British general who knew him well, "a pleasant though ponderous officer, . . . who had an extraordinary affection for a tame parrot. He was of medium height, but thick-set, with greying hair cut short . . . [and an] intelligent twinkle in his eyes, which peered through pince-nez so precariously balanced that it seemed as if a sneeze might dislodge them."[18]

The Deuxième Bureau's Service des Renseignements (the SR) controlled all human agents collecting intelligence abroad. The chief of the SR, Louis Rivet, subordinate to Gauché, was senior to him in rank, having been a lieutenant colonel for three years longer. But Rivet's career had been spent mostly in the shadows, even though he was almost unforgettable in person. He was tall, practically hairless, and had a booming voice. "A rough bruiser," wrote one SR veteran, "miserly with words, an incorrigible smoker of little cigars, impressive with his piercing eyes, etched features, and forceful jaw." Captured in an early battle, he had spent most of the Great War in a German prison camp. Afterward, he worked under cover in Poland and Germany and then headed the SR stations at Belfort and Lille, on the French side of the Franco-German border.[19]

There was a more-than-implicit understanding that Rivet would manage the SR with little interference from Gauché or others in the War Ministry. The SR remained physically separate, with its main offices in concrete battlements that had been added during the nineteenth century to the Invalides, the great memorial–cum–museum–cum–office complex that frowns across a long esplanade leading to the Alexander III Bridge and the Place de la Concorde. The entrance to the SR, guarded but unmarked, was at 2 bis avenue de Tourville, a brisk ten blocks distant from Gauché's offices in the War Ministry. Rivet himself had a separate channel to Daladier through General Bourret, who was always in search of food for his conspiracy theories, and through Raymond Clapier, who managed Daladier's office.[20] But Rivet's fragmentary diaries and other sources seem to show that he would communicate with or through Gauché whenever an SR source turned up an item of information potentially significant for appraising the capabilities or plans of another government.

The SR had a remarkable agent network. Its stations in French border cities obtained regular streams of reports about movements of troops, supplies, and vehicles, conditions on military bases and airfields, and economic and social conditions in Germany. Routine Deuxième Bureau data on German weaponry and military forces were more up-to-date and precise than comparable German data about France.

In addition, the SR had access to some information about German decision-making. Later, its sources would include members of the anti-Hitler conspiracy within the German government, even though most of them preferred initial contact with other Western intelligence services, particularly the Dutch or the British. Up to and through 1938, before the conspiracy in Germany developed, the most productive SR informant was Hans-Thilo Schmidt, who was kept on SR files as "H.E."[21]

Schmidt had been recruited at the beginning of the 1930s, before Hitler came to power. A letter arrived at 75 rue de l'Université, a seedy office building on the Left Bank where the SR had its headquarters before moving to the avenue de Tourville. The writer of the letter claimed to have obtained the address by asking at the French Embassy in Berlin how to reach the French secret service. He offered to sell "documents of the greatest importance." Though skeptical, the chiefs of the Deuxième Bureau and SR did not throw the letter away. They arranged for a follow-up by "Rex," a Berlin-born confidence man used from time to time as an SR vetter. "Rex" pronounced the writer of the letter genuine.

Schmidt was a well-educated, well-connected Prussian ex-officer. Gassed in the Great War, he had had to leave the army. Then the Depression cost him his civilian job. His brother, Rudolf Schmidt, who had stayed in the army, wangled him a place as civilian assistant to the head of the German War Ministry cipher service. Since the salary did not sustain his preferred manner of living, he bethought himself of testing whether the papers that crossed his desk had cash value.

A compact with the SR then enabled Schmidt both to live in greater luxury and to indulge a taste for risk-taking. Once, later, he would have a rendezvous with a French intelligence officer at the bar of the Hotel Adlon in Berlin. While the two were together, a big blond man came in accompanied by a woman. They sat down at a nearby table. Identifying the man as Reinhard Heydrich, head of Himmler's special security service, Schmidt continued pouring out sensitive information without lowering his voice.[22]

By mail, or more often at some rendezvous in southern Germany or Switzerland, "H.E." delivered quantities of classified military documents to the French. Sensing the wind, he had joined the Nazi Party while it was still out of office. As his brother moved up, first to the general staff and then, in October 1937, to command of a Panzer division, he picked up more and more valuable military gossip. Joining Göring's Forschungsamt, he came into position to inform the French about German cryptography and sometimes to supply keys that helped break German codes.

Another SR find was a young man whose father kept the records for a German army corps. The SR used evidence that he had embezzled money to blackmail him, and though he initially refused to yield to SR pressure, he found that his conscience did not forbid his inducing his mother to act on behalf of France. Another useful agent, also recruited by blackmail, was the homosexual brother of Erhard Milch, overseer of German aircraft production.[23] An agent who signed on as a volunteer was a German woman who taught French in Berlin. Her pupils included officers who worked in the Intelligence Directorate of the German army general staff. In the classroom or sometimes the bedroom, she induced them to talk of their work. She also passed on to her SR case officer documents she picked up from her husband, who worked in the German Foreign Ministry.[24]

Among SR agents planted in Abwehr stations, the most enterprising was one Joseph Doudot.[25] While attached to the SR station at Metz, Doudot managed to get himself recruited by an Abwehr handler based in Munster. With help from French army staffs, he gave his German employers information that seemed valuable. They came to depend on him not only as a source but also as a recruiter. He, of course, nominated others from the SR. One of these became a case officer at the Abwehr station in Stuttgart. When that man unexpectedly died, Doudot went to Stuttgart, pretended to be the man's nephew and a collaborator in his work for Germany, and succeeded in being taken on as the man's successor. Thereafter, he traveled to both Munster and Stuttgart, changing disguises, planting information at both places, and reporting to the Deuxième Bureau exactly what the Abwehr was up to. He used the money the Germans paid him to finance other SR activities.

As a counterpart to its penetration of the Abwehr, the SR had a nearly complete picture of German espionage in France, and as soon as France declared war on Germany in September 1939, the French police rounded up all known German agents in France. These included French journalists some of whom could be proved to have taken German money in return for slanting stories. One was Loys Aubin, news director of Le Temps, one of the most prestigious Paris dailies.[26] Paul Paillole, then a young army captain, headed the SR's counterespionage division. When I had lunch with him a few years ago at his villa at La Queue les Yvelines, I asked about a rumor that the mistress of a member of the French government had acted as a wartime German spy. "No!" he said, lifting his chin. "There were no German spies. We knew them all!"

The SR also managed collection of signal intelligence. Its cryptographic division, headed by Major Gustave Bertrand, a fine technician but a thoroughly disagreeable human being, intercepted and deciphered quantities of German army and air-force radio traffic. It also intercepted and decoded some diplomatic messages. Just what the harvest was, is hard to judge, for only a few copies of intercepts survive, and those are Italian or Belgian messages which might have come via human agents.

Photographic intelligence came to Gauché from the Deuxième Bureau of the air force, which was nominally independent but for practical purposes under his control. Its head, Colonel Georges Ronin, operated on his own only in developing capabilities for aerial reconnaissance. Under Cot, he got money during the Popular Front government of 1936–38, to purchase secretly from the United States two high-flying Lockheed 12As. While these planes were still on order, he learned that Richard Labrély, a manufacturer of photographic equipment, and Roger Henrard, a noted civilian flier, had adapted a Farman 402 for high-altitude photography. In the autumn of 1937, when he saw two hundred pictures that Henrard had taken of German airfields and military bases, he signed him up. By 1938, when the Lockheeds arrived, Henrard and other French pilots were carrying out about one mission a month, taking as many as three hundred pictures per mission and penetrating as much as a hundred miles into Germany. Also during that year, Britain's Royal Air Force began to share with Ronin its high-altitude photography, some of which covered targets even farther inside Germany.[27]

By 1939, the French air-force reconnaissance service had new three-seater Bloch 174s and Potez 63-11s, which could fly at speeds of more than four hundred miles an hour and take pictures from above twenty-five thousand feet. When active fighting commenced on the Western front in May 1940, this fleet took as many as four hundred pictures a day. The results of aerial photography—or at least written summaries based on the photographs—went to Gauché as well as to the air-force Deuxième Bureau, and figured in their regular and special memoranda on Germany's capabilities and intentions. The assessments themselves were written by air-force and army officers working together in the SR, either in a special air section or in the German section, headed by Rivet's chief deputy, Major Guy Schlesser, a sometime racing jockey and godson of French President Albert Lebrun.[28]

Daily or almost daily meetings with liaison officers from the Foreign Ministry gave Gauché or his subordinates virtually complete knowledge of what French diplomats were reporting, but the relationship was cool. Like their counterparts in other countries, French ambassadors disliked giving diplomatic cover to SR officers, and they resented having occasionally to apologize when some SR activity was exposed. But the Foreign Ministry's senior officials had to cooperate with Gauché. Otherwise, they would not have known what the spies were reporting and might even have been in the dark about information from military attachés, for attachés did not have to show all their dispatches to ambassadors.[29]

By means of regular meetings with representatives of the Sûreté and other police agencies, the SR, and therefore the Deuxième Bureau, had access to the results of mail searches, telephone taps, and other surveillance of people in France. In Paris, the Sûreté, which came under the Ministry of the Interior, tapped some phone lines of the metropolitan Prefecture of Police, and the Prefecture in revenge tapped the Sûreté. The ostensible purpose of much of this tapping was counterintelligence, but the telephones covered included those of communists and of politicians and journalists thought overly friendly toward any foreign country. Rivet undoubtedly obtained by these means information useful for assessing Germany. Very likely, he also picked up, and passed on through Bourret or Clapier, other information useful to Daladier for political or parliamentary management.[30]

Almost any information about a foreign government gleaned by any element of the French government was thus available to Gauché for use in his oral and written reports. Probably no chief of intelligence anywhere has ever had comparably inclusive access within his own government. To assist in preparing reports, he had in the Deuxième Bureau itself a staff considerably larger than that doing comparable work in Germany. It was divided into four sections, one specifically for Germany, one for Britain, and two for the rest of the world.[31] And all Gauché's reports went to General Gamelin.

For Gamelin—and for Daladier before he became prime minister—the principal use for intelligence was to support the case for rearmament, and the Deuxième Bureau provided plenty of material useful for such a purpose.

Long before Hitler came to power in 1933, the Deuxième Bureau had been doing its best to locate every single German soldier, gun, or military vehicle. French officers had assumed (quite rightly) that the German army would do everything possible to evade the clauses of the Versailles Treaty limiting its size and composition. The Deuxième Bureau successfully tracked arrangements under which the German army trained men not technically under the colors, entered into sub-rosa agreements with industrialists whose factories might someday again produce war materiel, and struck secret deals for, among other things, clandestine training on Soviet soil.[32]

In the first few months of 1933, when it remained unclear how long Hitler would remain chancellor, the Deuxième Bureau estimated that the German army was already far over the hundred-thousand-man limit set by the Versailles Treaty. And it regarded the Nazi Party paramilitary organizations as the equivalent of an additional army several times that size.

As Hitler consolidated his power and made a rapid military buildup his first priority, the Deuxième Bureau passed upward report after alarming report. In a spring-1935 summary, it credited the German army with three hundred thousand regulars, one hundred thousand Landespolizei (equivalent to British Territorials or active-duty French reservists), and two million well-trained men in paramilitary formations.[33] By the beginning of 1936, the Deuxième Bureau reckoned German regulars to have reached 480,000, with the Landespolizei and paramilitary organizations at least as numerous as before.[34] Officers who had done attaché duty in Berlin seconded the presumption that men in paramilitary organizations were hard to distinguish from regular soldiers in their equipment and training.[35]

At the same time, the Deuxième Bureau reported unfavorably on the military forces of France's possible allies. Poland, having signed a nonaggression pact with Germany in 1934, was deemed unlikely to join France in a war and in any case militarily backward. Though the Soviet Union was recognized to have a large army and the world's largest air force, a memorandum of April 1935 warned against the dangers of "linking ourselves to a government that betrayed us in the middle of a war, that ruined our investors, whose doctrine undermines our institutions, particularly our military, and whose Francophilism, as is well known, is completely opportunistic."[36] This view coincided with that of senior officers. When a French general who made a fact-finding trip to the U.S.S.R. came back saying that it might not be so weak and unreliable as was widely thought, Chief of Staff Colson took pains to see that his report did not go on to Gamelin or to a minister.[37]

The intelligence that Gamelin saw and passed on to Daladier emphasized the growing power of Germany, and by implication the vulnerability of France. This was what both men wanted and needed in order to press their case for higher levels of military spending. Gamelin almost certainly discounted some of what he was told by the Deuxième Bureau. He understood, as General Joseph Vuillemin, chief of staff of the French air force, and many other officers did not, that the figures used in military assessments were to some degree what would now be called "social constructions." Talking in 1937 to officers at the Center for Advanced Military Studies, Gamelin made some deeply revealing remarks. As summarized by Colonel Le Goyet in his biography of Gamelin:

He juxtaposes two original formulas, used by two great military men: Marshals Foch and Lyautey. The former said: "You can undertake anything and succeed in anything, provided you never forget that two and two make four." The latter: "You can dare to do anything and succeed in anything, provided you never forget that two and two do not make four; in clumsy hands, they often make three or even less; but they can make five or six." He continues: the first, a *polytechnicien*, never felt able to free himself from mathematics; the second was a statesman and had the habit of juggling figures, especially budgets.[38]

Later, he was to give Daladier his own estimates of German armed forces, many of which were at variance with those of the Deuxième Bureau.

Daladier must at least have suspected that the Deuxième Bureau erred on the high side when counting potential enemy forces, and that the operating branches of the army erred on the low side when pleading their needs. Nevertheless, it is likely that both men were in some degree persuaded that what they said to committees of the cabinet and the Parliament was true. Thus when Daladier went from being war and defense minister to being also prime minister, he was committed to saying that France was poorly prepared for war with Germany, and he continued to have as his principal military adviser someone committed to the same position, and with access to all relevant secret intelligence that could be gathered.

CHAPTER TEN

CROSS-CURRENTS

"You can dare to do anything and succeed in anything, provided you never forget that two and two do not make four; in clumsy hands, they often make three or even less; but they can make five or six."
—*Marshal Louis-Herbert Lyautey, quoted approvingly in 1937 by General Gamelin*

Daladier as prime minister needed advice on foreign policy as well as on military policy. And General Gamelin had had practice in giving foreign-policy advice disguised as military advice. In 1936, he had helped to shape the French government's response to the remilitarization of the Rhineland. The then prime minister, Albert Sarraut, had reacted to the news by declaring over the radio: "We are not prepared to allow Strasbourg to come under the fire of German cannon"—words that seemed to signal an intention to force the German troops that had unexpectedly marched in to withdraw. By their own accounts, written much later, Foreign Minister Pierre-Étienne Flandin and some other cabinet members favored such action.

For Gamelin, remilitarization had been no surprise. He had seen SR and attaché reports telling of German preparations for remilitarization, and he had noted the public debates predicting that it would occur if the French Parliament ratified the pending mutual security accord with the Soviet Union. For more than a year, army general-staff planning had assumed eventual remilitarization, and Gamelin himself had criticized the accord with the Soviet Union on the ground that it would hasten the event. He had even commissioned some planning for forcing German withdrawal.[1]

The presumption in these plans was that the Germans would hold their ground and that French troops would have to shoot. When German forces actually did march in, the Deuxième Bureau estimated German strength in the Rhineland at about three hundred thousand men. This seems a huge overestimate: the actual German army forces that crossed into the Rhineland consisted of only three battalions, or fewer than a thousand men, with sixteen other battalions—another five thousand men—following once it seemed sure there would be no resistance. But it has to be remembered that local German security forces already functioning in the Rhineland totaled around one hundred thousand and were well armed and well trained; also, the Deuxième Bureau was in the habit of counting uniformed Nazi Party formations as equivalents of regular army units. Gamelin himself thought it possible that, if French troops crossed the boundary, the German regular forces would pull back, and that the militia and party formations would not put up a fight. But he did not press this opinion, nor did he express it outside the general staff.

The then war minister was Gamelin's onetime War College classmate, General Joseph Maurin. (Daladier would not become war minister for another three months.) Gamelin reported to Maurin the estimate of the Deuxième Bureau, and summarized the reasoning of the general staff: the army could not act in the Rhineland and maintain necessary readiness elsewhere unless the government ordered a mobilization of reserves. Sarraut, Flandin, and others writing postwar memoirs claim to have been shocked when Maurin relayed this advice to them. In the "missed-opportunity" mythology that has grown up around the Rhineland affair, Gamelin figures as a chief villain.

In the circumstances of the time and in light of his own responsibilities, however, Gamelin's advice to the government is more than understandable. In the first place, the views expressed around Sarraut's cabinet table were more nuanced than most memoirs suggest. Members of the government probably did not envision French soldiers shooting at German soldiers, neither when considering the possibility ahead of time nor when faced with Hitler's surprise action in the Rhineland. They talked chiefly about acting in concert with Britain and about opening a debate in the League of Nations. Some of them may well have wanted some accompanying movements of French troops up to but probably not beyond the French border.

Even about such a gesture, the cabinet members quickly had second thoughts. Nowhere in France was there the slightest indication that the public wanted or would even tolerate military action on account of German remilitarization of the Rhineland. The satirical weekly *Le Canard enchaîné* expressed a common view when it said: "The Germans have invaded—Germany!" Communist leaders, supposedly in the forefront of opposition to Nazism, called stridently for preventing "the scourge of war from falling anew on us." They urged that the whole nation unite "against those who want to lead us to massacre." Socialist spokesmen termed "inadmissible any response that risked war," saying that even reinforcing the Maginot Line would be "provocative." The right-wing dailies *Le Matin* and *Le Jour* declared that conflict with Germany would benefit only communist Russia. As the eminent French historian Jean-Baptiste Duroselle writes, France was swept by "a pacifist tornado."[2]

Members of the government were much more sensitive to these winds than most of them remembered or confessed when later giving testimony or writing memoirs. Marcel Déat, Sarraut's air minister, writing before it became conventional to regard the Rhineland affair as a great lost opportunity, recalled saying to his colleagues: "If we declared a general mobilization two months before the elections, we would be swept out of Parliament by the voters, if it didn't happen beforehand through a revolution in the streets." Georges Mandel, minister in charge of the post office—who had been an aide to Clemenceau, always modeled himself on "the Tiger," and was reputed to be the most bellicose member of the government—said to a fellow politician less than a week after Hitler's march into the Rhineland, "Do you think that, in this country, one can mobilize just a few months before the elections?"[3]

Gamelin's telling Maurin and the cabinet that mobilization was a necessary first step toward military action in the Rhineland did thus paralyze the government. But all Gamelin did was to prevent the government from starting a gesture that it would never have been able to carry through. One can argue, of course, that even a gesture might have frightened Hitler and caused him to order his troops out. Had this occurred, however, it is hard to imagine anything like the sequel supposed in "missed-opportunity" mythology. On the contrary, the most probable result would have been an outcry against the Sarraut government across France and the world, and gushes of sympathy for Germany, making it much more difficult for French cabinets to obtain money for rearmament.

Moreover, what Gamelin said to Maurin has to be understood in light of the army's past experience in the region and of recent budget-cutting. Back in 1923, when France had taken over the Rhineland in hope of forcing a recalcitrant Weimar Republic government to make reparations payments prescribed by the Versailles Treaty, the French occupation troops had found themselves surrounded by a hostile and uncooperative population. Criticized around the world and eventually in France as well, they had pulled out after only partially accomplishing their mission. In 1936, Gamelin could imagine that, even if French soldiers went into the Rhineland unopposed, they could find themselves in the situation of 1923. With such a prospect, he would have had no choice but to send to the Rhineland the army's best disciplined regulars, who were currently either training elevenmonth recruits or serving in the colonies. In these circumstances, it was hardly irresponsible to insist that the cabinet order the army to move only if it were prepared to commit itself to more than a gesture.

Not more than six weeks later, Gamelin would profess to be outraged by a charge that the army had dictated to the government. At the time, however, he had said to officers on the general staff that the cabinet was "very bellicose and full of illusions" and that "the soldiers had been forced to restrain the politicians."[4] Though Gamelin might pretend to be merely someone calling attention to military realities, he knew perfectly well that his opinions carried weight on political and diplomatic issues and could even be decisive, particularly given the army's monopoly on secret intelligence.

After the Rhineland affair, when the spring elections brought the Popular Front into office and Gamelin and Daladier commenced their long collaboration within the War Ministry, Gamelin used his authoritative position almost exclusively to promote the arms buildup. Estimates of German strength compiled by the Deuxième Bureau had helped him with Daladier's predecessors, and he continued to pass these estimates along without hinting that they might overstate reality. In March 1937, for example, he gave Daladier a Deuxième Bureau memorandum reckoning the twenty-four German divisions of 1936 to have now become thirty-six, of which three were armored. Those figures themselves were accurate, but the memorandum did not mention that some of the new divisions were still shells, and it asserted, erroneously, that paramilitary forces such as the National Socialist Automobile Corps were being equipped and trained not only as regular forces but as elite units.[5]

To the extent that Gamelin steered government policy, it was mostly by trying to keep its focus on longer-term rearmament rather than on possible short-run crises. Like most professional military men at most times in modern history, he was much more interested in force structure than in readiness—in having well-equipped armies at some later date rather than having troops on the line prepared to fight with what they had in hand.

This inclination would account for his not calling the government's attention to evidence that Hitler might be planning early action against Austria or Czechoslovakia if, as is alleged, he received such evidence. In a fascinating but not entirely trustworthy book on the exploits of "H.E.," Paillole, the former SR counterintelligence chief, claims that Gamelin was told of the November 1937 Chancellory meeting recorded by Colonel Hossbach. According to Paillole, General Schmidt heard about the meeting from Hossbach and told his brother, "H.E.," who promptly passed on the news to Maurice Dejean of the French Embassy in Berlin.[6] Unlikely as the story seems, especially since Hossbach did not think the meeting important enough to deserve an immediate memorandum of record, Paillole has in his possession an Abwehr document of about this period that shows that Göring's Forschungsamt had picked up telephone traffic from the French Embassy about a secret meeting between Hitler and the heads of the Foreign Ministry and military services, and that the Abwehr conducted a quiet but intensive search for the source of the leak. Also, after a visit to Daladier, Rivet wrote in his diary: "The minister makes hardly any allusion to the intelligence from H.E."[7] Possibly, Gamelin had chosen not to trouble Daladier lest Daladier's mind turn to worrying about an early crisis rather than about the army's needs for equipment not deliverable for another year or more. Perhaps he did not himself believe it or think the report significant. In mid-December, at a meeting of the Permanent Committee on National Defense (CPDN), a body consisting of service ministers, service chiefs, and "the Marshal" (Pétain), Gamelin said reassuringly that it would be some time before Germany could contemplate going to war with Czechoslovakia and thus risking war with Poland and France.[8]

In early 1938, Gamelin had ample warning of Germany's approaching move against Austria. He had seen a report of Göring's saying, "The solution of the Austrian question cannot be postponed beyond the coming spring." Austrians inundated the SR with warnings of maneuvers planned by Austrian Nazis. A verbatim transcript of Hitler's threatening interview with Chancellor Schuschnigg at Berchtesgaden in February 1938 reached Paris almost overnight. On March 9, on the basis of information from Göring's entourage, the French air attaché in Berlin predicted that Germany would move within three days.[9] The *Anschluss* occurred exactly as he forecast. The fact that Daladier's staff complained to Rivet that Germany's action had come with "inconceivable suddenness" suggests that Gamelin continued to avoid raising short-term alarms.

When Daladier became prime minister, his sources of information and advice broadened. Though he himself had spent time in Italy when a graduate student and had made a brief trip to the Soviet Union in the 1920s in company with Herriot, he was not widely traveled, nor did he customarily read foreign newspapers or seek out foreigners. The one exception was William C. Bullitt, the American ambassador in Paris, who was fluent in French, a generous host, an apparent admirer, and representative of a country from which Daladier hoped for help in his rearmament program.[10] From French newspapers and from conversations with acquaintances more traveled than he, Daladier undoubtedly picked up impressions of the outside world. He often talked, for example, with Fernand de Brinon, a journalist who headed a Franco-German friendship committee and was one of the foreigners whom Hitler liked to see. But most of Daladier's information about occurrences and developments outside of France came through official channels.

Daladier's chief link with the Foreign Ministry was Alexis Léger, who had a post analogous to that of Weizsäcker in Germany. Brought up in the French Antilles, Léger had come to France at age fifteen, when an eruption of Mont Pelée scared his parents away from Martinique. Amazingly, given the French educational system, where children start up a ladder almost at birth and are usually left at whatever point they miss a step, Léger sprinted through demanding schools. He then studied medicine but, changing career plans, stood for and easily passed the daunting entry examinations for the diplomatic corps.

After a posting in China, Léger was sent to the Washington Conference of 1921–22, where the agenda included Asian affairs as well as the limitation of naval armaments. He there caught the eye of Aristide Briand, head of the French delegation. By the end of the ocean voyage back to France, he had become one of Briand's favorites. Since Briand was either foreign minister or prime minister during most of the 1920s, Léger received promotion after promotion. Recognizedly the brightest among the young men who shared Briand's vision of a United States of Europe under French leadership (and therefore, of course, better regulated and more civilized than the United States of America), Léger reached the top of his profession when named secretary general of the Foreign Ministry in 1933. His intellectual gifts were extraordinary, for he combined with his spectacular diplomatic career a second career as a poet, writing under the name St. John Perse. In 1960, he would be awarded a Nobel Prize in literature.

Léger's predecessor, Philippe Berthelot, had been famous for his mastery of detail. He had complemented Briand, who often had a clearer vision of the future than of the present. Léger was more like Briand. Gossip said that he came to work at 11 A.M., then left for a long lunch, returned around 4 P.M., but stayed late chiefly to talk with friends from the press or the literary world. Étienne Crouy-Chanel, who was his chief assistant, asserts that this gossip was malicious, that Léger arrived at 9 A.M. and often worked into the night, and that he always knew his dossiers. It is a fact, nevertheless, that the archives of the Foreign Ministry contain very few official memoranda or letters by Léger. Colleagues remembered more his presence than his thoughts or deeds. For Jean Chauvel, a fellow diplomat and writer, Léger was a man "dressed in black, wearing a thin black necktie, with a waxen face, a muffled voice, elegant in expression, refined in language." Crouy-Chanel recalled that his "two dark eyes, wide open, seemed to be contemplating, beyond yourself, distant perspectives," and a journalist who covered the Quai d'Orsay in the 1930s retained only a memory of a "slim, dark young man from the tropics, who was always tracing circles on pieces of paper."[11]

What we know of Léger's attitudes and influence comes almost entirely from records made by others and from a presumption that gossip, if possibly wrong about his work habits, was not wrong in saying that many of the more businesslike senior officials of the Foreign Ministry were his devoted acolytes. He and they appear to have been open-minded regarding revision of the post–Great War peace treaties but to have thought of France's concessions as rewards it got for good behavior, not as Germany's due. They were offended less by what Hitler did in his early years as chancellor than by his theatrics. Until at least 1937, perhaps 1938, they were annoyed less at Germany than at Italy, which had defied a League of Nations call to halt its war against Ethiopia. Sir Eric Phipps, the British ambassador in Paris, commented that whenever Italy was mentioned Léger would look like "a cross between a mule and a viper."[12]

In March 1936, Léger and his number two, René Massigli, wanted France to demand that Germany withdraw its troops from the Rhineland. Massigli drafted the sentence in Sarraut's radio address about not allowing German cannon to menace Strasbourg. Neither Léger nor Massigli, however, recommended that the government order the mobilization proposed by Gamelin or that it question his advice that mobilization was a necessary precondition for a show of force. The chief reason was probably not so much sensitivity to French public opinion as a quick recognition that there was no chance of obtaining backing from Britain.

Adopting a "plague-on-both-your-houses" attitude, British Prime Minister Stanley Baldwin reproached Germany for its surprise action but reproached France as well, saying, "Our best hopes have been blighted time after time, sometimes by the French, in our view, missing an opportunity of accepting some offer or, on the other side, by Germany doing some act to liberate herself as in the breaking of a treaty which has shocked our conscience."[13] Since Léger and others at the Quai d'Orsay regarded French-British cooperation as the cornerstone of international order, they had no inclination for a dispute with London about the Rhineland, and hence shifted grumblingly to supporting their own government's acquiescent stance.

Through the long-serving French representatives in London, Ambassador Charles Corbin and his deputy, Roger Cambon, Léger and Massigli did their best to make British ministers believe that the French government felt aggrieved, even betrayed. They emphasized that the remilitarization of the Rhineland made France much more vulnerable to attack. This vulnerability became greater when, almost at once, the Belgian government renounced its de facto alliance with France, saying in effect that Belgium intended to become a new Switzerland, and greater still when civil war broke out in Spain in July, with Italy and Germany backing the rebel Spanish Nationalists, led by Francisco Franco. It seemed possible that France would soon face potential enemies across the Rhine, the Alps, and the Pyrenees, with no allies nearby. Léger and Massigli sought to convince the British government that, unless Hitler was convinced that Britain would stand by France, he could be reckless enough to start a new war.

The French diplomats had some success. The British government reaffirmed its Locarno Pact commitment to come to France's aid in the event of an unprovoked attack. British ministers began, moreover, to make a point of communicating with Paris prior to taking any initiative regarding Germany or responding to any initiative by Germany. Previously, they had made a point of not doing so, as, for example, when they signed the naval treaty with Ribbentrop and let the French government learn about it from newspapers.

Thereafter, Léger, Massigli, and their colleagues at the Quai d'Orsay maneuvered to keep the French and British governments in step. Doing so was not easy, for Blum and others in the Popular Front sympathized strongly with the Spanish Republic, which was steadily losing ground to Franco's Nationalists, and the British government did not share Blum's sentiments. Fearing lest the Spanish civil war turn into an international war, Britain preferred to pretend it was ignorant of Italian and German aid to the Nationalists and Soviet aid to the Republicans. Hence it brokered creation of a Nonintervention Committee composed of all interested powers, including those that in practice were intervening. The diplomats at the Quai d'Orsay enlisted help from politicians, journalists, and others who were pro-British or anti-Soviet or both, and by doing so managed to damp down pro-Republican interventionism. Paris thus joined London in turning blind eyes to the presence in Spain of Italian military advisers, German bomber pilots, and Soviet commissars.

Events on the other side of the globe helped to further Franco-British cooperation, for both nations had interests affected by a war between Japan and China that broke out in the summer of 1937. Both were concerned about citizens resident in China and about nearby colonial territories such as Hong Kong, French Indochina, Malaya, and Burma. Both were worried about having to send troops or warships to the Far East and thus weaken themselves in Europe, particularly since Japan seemed to be coming increasingly close to Germany and Italy. In the fall of 1936, the three had displayed symbolic solidarity by signing an Anti-Comintern Pact, promising collaborative opposition to the Communist International.

Another bond tying France to Britain was France's financial vulnerability. France's lag in recovering from the Great Depression had resulted in a massive flight of capital. In the autumn of 1936, this had been checked by a French-British-American accord involving, among other things, devaluation of the franc. Rightly or wrongly, many ministers, officials, and others in France believed the subsequent recovering health of the French economy to be dependent on continued British willingness both to prevent the pound sterling from being more attractive than the franc and to use influence in Washington and New York to prevent the dollar's being so.[14]

As of early 1938, however, Britain was far from being committed to acting in tandem with France vis-à-vis Germany. When Léger was shown the Deuxième Bureau's nearly conclusive evidence that Hitler was on the verge of acting against Austria, he arranged for Corbin to receive instructions to propose to the brand-new British foreign secretary, Lord Halifax, that France and Britain join in declaring to Ribbentrop: "Neither the French nor the British Governments can tolerate a *coup de main* or an act of war which would challenge the status quo in Central Europe."[15] But Halifax refused categorically. Words would not restrain Hitler, he said, and Britain had no intention of going beyond words to protest an arrangement made by German-speaking Germans with German-speaking Austrians.

Léger and his colleagues did not therefore press their own government to prepare anything more than an expression of regret that Germany was again acting unilaterally. Gamelin, for his part, carried to Daladier intelligence reports of March 11, forecasting a German move against Austria on March 12. He dutifully declared that the French army would be ready to go on alert. Daladier alerted the caretaker prime minister, Camille Chautemps, who called a special meeting of the inner cabinet. The result of the meeting was a decision that the army should be put on alert "on condition that the British join in."[16] Since the British government had already said that it would not join in, Gamelin and Daladier created a record that France had sounded firm without actually incurring any risks.

By early 1938, when Daladier became prime minister, though the diplomats at the Quai d'Orsay had come to recognize Nazi Germany as the number-one threat both to France and to international peace and order, they divided into three camps as to how best to deal with that threat.

Léger, the ministry's high priest, led only one faction. Dubbed "the Optimists" by the historian René Girault, members of this faction held Nazi Germany to be basically unstable and Hitler to be a blusterer who would become reasonable if the French and British governments firmly insisted on normal processes of negotiation.

Massigli, though personally close to Léger, led a rival faction which Girault termed "the Realists," whose members doubted that Hitler would climb down unless confronted with a threat of war from an alliance strong enough to intimidate him. Massigli believed that it would require combined opposition from France, Britain, Poland, Czechoslovakia, and the Soviet Union to achieve the outcome that he and Léger both desired.

A third faction, called by Girault "the Pessimists," agreed with Massigli that Léger and his friends probably underestimated Hitler's willingness to gamble but doubted both the practicality and the desirability of enlisting allies in Eastern Europe. They favored giving Germany virtually a free hand against Poland, Czechoslovakia, and perhaps the Soviet Union and meanwhile consolidating a new Western alliance, with Italy included, and Spain as well, once Franco won. Germany could use up its energies on the peasantry of the East. The Western powers could have stability and order on their side of the Rhine.

To the extent that the Quai d'Orsay could give Daladier facts, rather than simply alternative interpretative schemes, all three factions depended on the French Embassy in Berlin. The ambassador was André François-Poncet, a stellar graduate of the elite École Normale Supérieure who had married well, become a pet of France's steel magnates, and moved laterally into the diplomatic corps in hope of eventually becoming foreign minister. Universally thought to be Hitler's favorite among the foreign diplomats in Berlin, he sent Paris long, elegantly phrased dispatches portraying Hitler as determined to redress Germany's grievances, inclined to be impetuous, but realistic enough to be restrained by awareness both of Germany's comparative weakness and of the costs of war. François-Poncet also emphasized Hitler's high regard for Mussolini. Though his dispatches lent somewhat more support to Realists and Pessimists than to Léger and the Optimists, they were sufficiently diffuse and nuanced to be drawn upon by all three factions.[17]

When Daladier became prime minister, Léger's seemed likely to be the most influential voice at the Quai d'Orsay, not only because of his pre-eminent position but because he and Daladier were old friends. One of the few letters by Léger that survive was written in 1933, congratulating Daladier on becoming foreign minister (for what would prove to be a very brief tenure). In it, Léger said that he had been "hoping for this moment for a long time" and that "slow and calm germination" had prepared Daladier for the post "like a force of nature."[18] Through two of Daladier's aides, Daridan and Emmanuel Arago, Léger had all along been passing to Daladier any information possibly helpful in making the case for more military spending. He had—and used—authority to order wiretaps by the Sûreté, and he may also have supplied information helpful to Daladier in party and parliamentary management. Now, through Arago, a Buddha-like figure complete with shaved head, Léger had documents delivered to Daladier every morning and noontime.[19]

Whether from Léger or Massigli or the Quai d'Orsay Pessimists or from Gamelin and the intelligence services, Daladier received a monochromatic appreciation of Hitler's Germany. Though their policy prescriptions differed, all these advisers shared the premise that Hitler would ultimately cooperate in some system that maintained international order and ensured

that there would not be another Great War. Since Beck and Weizsäcker and
many others in the German government also believed something of the sort,
this is hardly surprising.

Nor is it surprising that the conception of Hitler's government prevalent
in Paris (and in London) resembled that of Beck and Weizsäcker. Like
these Germans, French officials assumed that some of Hitler's advisers believed Germany could push its claims very aggressively without bringing on
a war and that others were more cautious. Ribbentrop was often identified
as one of the former, Göring as one of the latter. Hitler was taken to be an
arbiter whose decisions would be determined by the arguments of his advisers and by his preferences among them. French officials arrived at their
differing policy prescriptions in part from differing analyses of the considerations that might affect the relative influence of Ribbentrop or Göring.
Léger's advice was based partly on his acquaintance with and contempt for
Ribbentrop. That of both Massigli and the Pessimists was influenced by evidence that Göring, the supposed moderate, had been heavily engaged in
effecting the *Anschluss*.

Differences between Realists on the one hand and Pessimists on the
other turned less on judgments about the German government than on assessments of states in Eastern Europe. Massigli and the Realists were committed to the belief that Czechoslovakia was a strong, coherent state. It had,
after all, been partly a creation of Briand's, and its president, Edvard
Beneš, had been one of Briand's close friends. The Pessimists tended to be
men who had opposed Briand and his system. They thought the creation of
Czechoslovakia had been a mistake and, like Weizsäcker, they anticipated
its chemical dissolution.

What is striking is that no one in Paris seems to have taken it as even
an outlying possibility that Hitler might make decisions without paying
much attention to any of his advisers, and that he did not simply seek an
international order in which Germany had a larger role but, in fact, wanted
a war. Nor did anyone around Daladier suggest that Hitler's assessments of
France and other nations might be based less on their diplomatic maneuvers and their apparent military capabilities than on his impressions of
their leaders and of public opinion. Some of them must have sampled *Mein
Kampf*. But, like officials in Germany, they did not take the book to be a basis even for speculation about the premises that might govern Hitler's decisions. That was an understandable mistake, but nevertheless a mistake.

CHAPTER ELEVEN

TO MUNICH

"The ambitions of Napoleon were far inferior to the present aims of the German Reich."
—*Daladier, at a meeting with British ministers, April 28, 1938*

"What kind of a negotiation is this, with a knife at the throat!"
—*Daladier, September 15, 1938, à propos of Prime Minister Chamberlain's exchanges with Hitler regarding Czechoslovakia's Sudetenland*

A t the time of the *Anschluss*, observers in Germany had noticed primarily the absence of any strong reaction from France and Britain. This was true for Beck and Weizsäcker no less than for Hitler, and it influenced their expectations. Though their specific forecasts varied, they all supposed some degree of continuity, inferring that French and British acquiescence in the *Anschluss* foreshadowed acquiescence in other territorial changes in Central and Eastern Europe, provided only that Germany managed these changes artfully. In fact, however, the *Anschluss* set in train changes in France and Britain that made it progressively less likely that their governments would stand aside while Germany continued to redraw the map of Europe.

The *Anschluss* shocked the French people. Not long before Hitler came to power, their government had refused to permit a German-Austrian customs union and had stood its ground despite worldwide criticism. In 1934, Hitler himself had had to refrain from supporting Nazis in Austria because of foreign opposition—Mussolini's, to be sure, but also that of France. Now, suddenly, Hitler entered Vienna at the head of German troops, receiving a delirious welcome from the Austrian people, and proclaiming Austria part of Germany. Newsreels seen by millions of French moviegoers showed these scenes along with ones of Hitler stridently proclaiming Germans and Austrians members of a "master race."

From far left to far right, politicians and journalists in France predicted that Hitler would spring more and worse surprises. The possibility of his turning next against Czechoslovakia was apparent to everyone, though some thought he might take up the grievances of Germans in the Polish Corridor before those of the Germans in the Sudetenland. In either case, he would threaten a nation with which France had a treaty of alliance dating back to the 1920s. The next crisis could thus be one in which France would face a choice between going to war or reneging on a sworn commitment.

Opinions ranged widely. The communists demanded that France make ready to fight, particularly, of course, in company with the U.S.S.R. (They had already been urging intervention in Spain on the side of the Soviet-backed Spanish Republic.) Socialists and most others in the noncommunist left continued to say that war should be out of the question and there had to be peacefully negotiable solutions.

Leaders on the right also spoke in favor of negotiation. Flandin, who had been prime minister in 1934–35 as well as foreign minister during the Rhineland crisis, and Pierre Laval, three times prime minister in 1931–32, both argued publicly that France had no real interest in Central Europe. The region's mongrel Slav population, they said, should concern only Germany and Soviet Russia. Flandin wrote in *Le Figaro* almost immediately after the *Anschluss*:

> Germany has to find in the world an outlet for its overindustrialization and its overpopulation. The question is whether you allow it to find this or, wherever it goes, it finds the opposition of France.
>
> I do not agree that France can play in Central Europe, any more in regard to Czechoslovakia than in regard to any other country, the role of sole policeman, which it is not in condition to sustain.[1]

Many leaders on the right argued simply that a war between France and Germany would benefit only the communist Soviet Union. "Better Hitler than Stalin" was their slogan.

Radicals and others in the center divided three ways. Some sided with the pacifist socialists. Some sided with the right. Some, however, said that France had to uphold the alliance treaties and, if necessary, go to war. Hitler would eventually have to be stopped, they contended, and it might as

well be when he next moved, for France would then at least have allies able
to force Germany to fight a two-front war. Those who took this position in
public tended to be journalists—such as André Géraud, who wrote in *L'Ordre* under the pen name "Pertinax," and Geneviève Tabouis of *L'Oeuvre*—
not politicians who had to answer to constituents, but they represented a
strong undercurrent of thought that had been almost wholly absent as recently as 1936.

Since the cabinet in office at the time of the *Anschluss* had been temporary, resulting from the socialists' walkout in January 1938, a new and
stronger government was plainly needed. Blum, still heading the largest
bloc in the Chamber of Deputies, put himself forward, this time to lead a
National Front rather than a Popular Front. He appeared before a large
gathering of leaders of right-wing parties to appeal for their participation in
a cabinet representing all major factions, from the communists around to
the far right. They voted 152–5 not to do so, some on the ground that a government trying to unite the French people against Nazi Germany should not
be headed by Blum, a Jew, others because they thought a government that
included leftists of any stripe would be weak or wrongheaded, and some
who had the view "Better Hitler than Blum."

It was Blum's failure that brought Daladier into the premiership. A new
Popular Front Cabinet put together by Blum lasted only a few weeks. Some
of those on the right who had voted against Blum's proposal came around to
saying that they would not oppose a government consisting primarily of
centrists. Their preferred candidate among Radicals was Georges Bonnet,
but Bonnet's only following was among the right wing of his own party. Daladier was almost the only Radical acceptable to leaders of right-wing parties, to all segments of the Radical party, and to Blum. Through cautious
negotiations, Daladier determined that the communists and socialists
would agree to refrain from voting against him if he promised to uphold the
forty-hour-workweek law, whereas Flandin and his allies would agree to do
likewise if he promised not to finance rearmament primarily by heavy taxes
on the rich. He then offered around to the various party leaders a cabinet
slate composed primarily of Radicals but representing the full diversity of
that quiltlike party, and it won nods left and right.

Both as insurance against being quickly turned out of office and as a
sign that his government would not just conduct business as usual, Daladier sought and obtained from the Chamber of Deputies and the Senate
not only the customary vote of confidence but a grant of four months of
power to govern by decree—in other words, to make decisions that would

have the force of law until Parliament reconvened and either ratified what had been done or reversed it and compelled formation of a new cabinet. This power, which would be given to him later more than once, did not free Daladier from constant calculation concerning sentiment among members of the two houses of Parliament. When he did so, he was often forced to think about public opinion not only of the moment but of the past, for most members of Parliament had won their seats in campaigns waged at least two years earlier.

The Chamber was a product of the 1936 elections that had produced the Popular Front. In its amphitheater in the Palais Bourbon, the communists, socialists, and others on the left continued to have almost half the seats, with Radicals and others from the center accounting for a third and the right for only about 20 percent.

The Senate had a different composition. Its members were not popularly elected but chosen in three hundred–odd communes by electoral colleges composed of local officials. Since senators had nine-year terms, with only one-third coming up for election at any one time, two-thirds of the senators were men who had been elected in 1930 or 1933, when the country had been much more conservative than in 1936 (and "men" is literal, for France did not even allow women to vote, let alone to sit in Parliament). In the Palais Luxembourg, where the Senate met, ten blocks distant from the Palais Bourbon, not even 6 percent belonged to parties of the left; almost 40 percent represented the right; the center, particularly the Radicals, had a majority.

Though governments continued in office or fell depending on their majorities in the Chamber of Deputies and could constitutionally survive a lost vote in the Senate, effective governance depended on majorities in both houses. This required Daladier to conciliate both the left and the right: the left could force him out of office by an adverse vote in the Chamber, and the right could paralyze him by not passing bills he sent to the Senate. Since only the communists and socialists maintained any degree of party discipline, Daladier had to gauge potential parliamentary support by constantly canvassing factional leaders in both houses. Friends and fellow Radicals did some of this for him, both in formal committee meetings and in lobbies and side rooms of the two palaces or in cafés or salons, but Daladier also had to keep a close eye on newspapers and magazines.

To an extent paralleled nowhere else, the press constituted in France a third chamber of Parliament. Paris had more than thirty dailies. Outside Paris, a hundred dailies had circulations in the tens of thousands. In addition, there were dozens of weeklies and monthlies. Only a handful of all these periodicals functioned primarily as providers of information. Ninety percent or more were organs of opinion, nearly all directly linked to political parties or individual political leaders.

Daladier and individual members of his government used dailies or weeklies to float trial balloons. Since Élie Bois, editor of *Le Petit-Parisien*, was known as a confidant of Daladier, his editorials were sometimes seen as indicators of Daladier's thinking. Other members of his cabinet used other journals, sometimes to send signals to their cabinet colleagues. Ministers and officials fed journalists money as well as information, and so did business firms. So did foreign governments. Witness the senior editors of the prestigious dailies *Le Temps* and *Le Figaro*, arrested in 1939 for being on Germany's payroll.[2] Chiefly, newspapers and magazines signaled to ministers and officials the inclinations of the politicians who were not members of the government but to whom the government had to be sensitive.

The clippings from French newspapers that Hitler sampled every morning thus did give him a sense of Daladier's environment and of crosscurrents influencing French governmental decisions. They did not, however, provide even Daladier a firm basis for anticipating how future decisions might be affected by Germany's own actions or by the actions of other governments.

The *Anschluss* stimulated not only a change in government in France but also a change in French-British relations. Shortly before Daladier became prime minister in France, Neville Chamberlain had succeeded Stanley Baldwin as prime minister in Britain. The French press had been speculating on Britain's position if Hitler's next move were against one of France's Eastern allies. Most commentators predicted that the British government would distance itself from France. Chamberlain, however, declared in the House of Commons on March 24, 1938: "Where peace and war are concerned, legal obligations are not alone involved, and, if war broke out, it would be unlikely to be confined to those who have assumed such obligations."

Daladier, soon after forming his cabinet, traveled to London to explore the implications of these suggestive but noncommittal words. Gamelin had given him added incentive by laying on his desk a memorandum that predicted that Germany would soon have a large enough army to attack

Czechoslovakia while holding France at bay. Within a year, said Gamelin, Germany would have more than a hundred divisions. France, under current budgeting, would have no more than eighty and would have to hold some of those in reserve to protect against the sixty-six divisions of Italy.[3] By implication, Gamelin argued, a guaranteed British alliance was indispensable, not just for diplomatic purposes but for preserving France's security.

In London, Daladier found Chamberlain interested less in discussing how Britain could support France, than in discouraging the French government from assuming that it could count on Britain to join a war in defense of Czechoslovakia or Poland. Chamberlain emphasized to Daladier that Britain's only fixed obligation was to defend France if France were directly attacked; it was not a corollary that Britain would join France in waging war in behalf of a third nation.

After returning to Paris and reporting to his cabinet on what Chamberlain had said, Daladier decided to make a second visit to London. His first trip had been on April 18–19, scarcely a week after he had become prime minister. The second was on April 28–29. Chamberlain's message was the same. To make sure that he was understood, Chamberlain sat beside Daladier at a ceremonial dinner and repeated his point in slow, stilted schoolboy French.

Three weeks later, the "May Crisis" put Chamberlain's assertions to a test. When the Deuxième Bureau and the French and British ambassadors in Berlin joined in warning that Germany might be about to take surprise military action against Czechoslovakia, Daladier summoned Gamelin back from a field inspection, making him get up from his midday meal to be driven at full speed to Paris. Following Léger's recommendation, Daladier then advised the British government via both the British mission in Paris and the French mission in London that, were Germany to act, France would feel obliged to back Czechoslovakia. These communications from Paris, along with worried messages from the British mission in Berlin, reached Chamberlain in the middle of a trout stream in Scotland, and he then and there authorized his Berlin ambassador to join his French colleague in delivering a warning to Ribbentrop and, as a sign of earnestness, to commence preparations for withdrawing diplomatic personnel.

Ribbentrop, it will be remembered, protested that Germany had no military move in preparation. The crisis, he fumed, was imaginary. And so it seemed when the French and British military attachés in Germany returned from border areas, reporting sight only of soldiers and airmen on normal furloughs. Daladier was puzzled. He continued to think that Hitler had had

something in view. He said to Gamelin that they had been within two fingers of a war and that it had been avoided only because France and Britain
had spoken with one voice. According to informants in London, Chamberlain shared this opinion. In any event, the May Crisis left behind a presumption that, whatever Chamberlain had said in his April meetings with
Daladier, Britain was committed to siding with France to defend Czechoslovakia.

Within France, the May Crisis touched off furious debate, for it put directly on the public agenda the question of whether France should be prepared to go to war in behalf of Czechoslovakia. Communists exulted.
Socialists for the most part took the position that France should at all costs
avoid risk of another bloodletting like that of 1914–18. The French and
British governments, some of them said, should insist that Czechoslovakia
negotiate with Germany and be prepared to make large concessions to the
Sudetenlanders. The socialist leader René Bélin said: "A bad arrangement
is still worth more than a victorious war."[4]

The far right exhibited outrage. In the literarily elegant but viciously
anti-Semitic weekly *Je suis partout*, the eminent historian Pierre Gaxotte
wrote that supporters of Czechoslovakia were asking France "to commit
suicide at the dictate of the Russians, those without a country, the Jews, the
corrupt, and the rotten." A similar attitude was evident even on the moderate right. In *La République*, a Radical organ once linked with Daladier,
Pierre Dominique declared that the only person who would be disappointed
by a negotiated settlement was Stalin.[5]

On the moderate right and in the center, however, many people were
saying that France should stand behind Czechoslovakia not just as a matter
of honor but because Hitler had to be stopped before he became stronger.
In addition to Pertinax and Tabouis and others who had taken this line in
the past, these individuals now included the erratic right-winger Henri de
Kérillis, editor of the daily *L'Époque*, and a number of reformist Roman
Catholics. In the Catholic daily *L'Aube*, for example, Louis Masson wrote
arrestingly that a tragedy was being enacted: Austria had been the victim in
the first act; "Czechoslovakia will be the victim in the second act, France
and Britain, the victims in the third. Before 1940, the play will be over!"[6]
There was enough such sentiment among Radicals so that Herriot told Daladier that he had had difficulty preventing the party's executive committee
from passing a resolution that promises to Czechoslovakia be kept.[7]

Since Daladier had had to assemble a cabinet acceptable across the
spectrum of factions in both the left-dominated Chamber and the center-

right–dominated Senate, it included representatives of almost all the opinions manifest in the press. According to rumor, his first choice for foreign minister had been Joseph Paul-Boncour, one of the most ardent disciples of Briand and one of the few elected politicians to have aligned himself with Pertinax and Tabouis. Sir Eric Phipps, the British ambassador in Paris, had let Daladier know that his government would not welcome the appointment. (Daladier may himself have floated the rumor in order to win Paul-Boncour's support, sure that the choice would somehow be vetoed.) Daladier's eventual selection was Bonnet, the favorite of the right.

Small and dapper, with a long pointed nose and a prominent Adam's apple, Georges Bonnet was mocked behind his back for overdoing the bidding of his young, sensual, and well-to-do wife, Odette Pelletan. In a play on the French word for "brassiere" (soutien-gorge), she was called "Madame Soutien-Georges."[8] But Bonnet was no lightweight. Élie Bois, who did not like him, writes of his "features . . . instinct with . . . the intelligence of a fox on the alert."[9] As a minister, he worked long hours, always knew his briefs, and had formidable skill in parliamentary intrigue. He had support on the right not only because he had been a leader among comparatively conservative Radicals but because he was known to doubt that French interests justified risking war for either Czechoslovakia or Poland. During the previous few years, he had been absent from France, serving as ambassador to the United States, and, apart from having never been friendly with Briand, he was influenced by the strength of criticism of the whole post–Great War peace settlement that characterized the American isolationism of that period. At the Quai d'Orsay, he immediately became leader of the Pessimists.

At the same time, Daladier's cabinet had in it Georges Mandel and Paul Reynaud, both of whom advocated uncompromising support for Czechoslovakia. Mandel, the former aide to Clemenceau who modeled himself on "the Tiger" and who had come close to calling for forceful action during the Rhineland affair, was minister of colonies. With sad eyes and a mouth with downturned corners, he was described by the American journalist Clare Boothe (later Clare Boothe Luce) as looking "like a male impersonator of Queen Victoria." To him, Czechoslovakia was part of the legacy of Clemenceau, and the French-Czechoslovak alliance therefore almost holy. He said to Bonnet's face during a ceremonial dinner, "War is inevitable. And it is desirable that it break out as soon as possible: better in a week than in a month; in a day rather than a week."[10] Reynaud, a short peacock of a man, though a favorite of financiers and industrialists who tended to be of the "better Hitler than Stalin" inclination, allied himself openly with Mandel.

Since Daladier kept his own counsel, it is not clear which way he leaned. His friend Léger encouraged him to listen to Mandel and Reynaud. Léger had a collaborative, even conspiratorial, relationship with his counterpart in London, Sir Robert Vansittart, permanent undersecretary in the Foreign Office. Léger was fluent in English, which he spoke with the accent of his native West Indies. He and Vansittart shared a passion for sailing and spent parts of each summer on the water together. Both men deplored Hitler's tactic of surprising other powers with faits accomplis. Both thought Nazi Germany basically unstable and Hitler a blusterer who would become reasonable only if the French and British governments made it clear that they insisted on normal processes of negotiation. Vansittart's estimate was influenced by informants in Germany, some of whom were in touch with the handful of men plotting against Hitler. He encouraged Léger's natural inclination to be contemptuous of a government run by rabble. Léger then assured Daladier that, if France and Britain simply formed a firm common front, Hitler would back down, and also that, if France stood firm all by itself, Britain would back France, no matter how reluctant Chamberlain seemed regarding any formal commitment.[11]

From Bonnet, however, Daladier received strong and seemingly well-grounded advice not to count on Germany's folding before French and British firmness but, rather, to assume that support of Czechoslovakia would lead to war and that France therefore should seek a way of abandoning Czechoslovakia without seeming to do so. Bonnet favored pressing the Czechoslovak government to make large concessions to the Sudetenlanders and to Hitler. If this occurred, he reasoned, Hitler would be deprived of a pretext for forcing a crisis. If not, the French government would be able to charge Prague with unreasonable stubbornness and on that ground to say that its alliance obligations no longer held.

Though Léger's position and Bonnet's seemed to be polar opposites, they were not. They agreed that the Czechoslovak government should make concessions to the Sudetenlanders, and Léger said so not only to Czechoslovak but to German diplomats. His friend Vansittart, who had a clandestine link with Henlein, the Sudeten German leader, was trying to work out an arrangement that could be made entirely within Czechoslovakia, presenting *Hitler* with a fait accompli. (Henlein, with Berlin's full knowledge, was stringing Vansittart along.) Bonnet, for his part, accepted that there had to be some limitations to France's pressure on Czechoslovakia and hence that, if Hitler proved totally uncompromising, France might have to threaten war.

For Daladier, however, the choices between Léger's view and Bonnet's *were* polar opposites. One would commit him to war unless Germany yielded ground. The other would commit him to keeping the peace unless Germany were unrelentingly exigent. Sometimes he leaned Léger's way, sometimes Bonnet's. In July 1938, he put heavy pressure on the Czechoslovak government by formally saying to President Beneš that France could not act under the treaty of alliance unless it were convinced that Czechoslovakia had gone the last mile in negotiating both with the Sudetenlanders and with Germany. At the same time, he seemed eager not to act dishonorably, and part of his mind surely told him that France would be weaker and Germany stronger if Czechoslovakia had to make too many concessions. Complicating his thinking was dread lest a war-or-peace choice split the French people and perhaps even bring into the streets mobs like those of February 1934.

As the summer of 1938 wore on, it came to seem less and less likely that such a choice could be avoided. In July, the Deuxième Bureau reported intensive German preparations for military action against Czechoslovakia, perhaps within a matter of weeks. One of the SR's female agents told of German negotiations with the Hungarian government, looking to joint action against Czechoslovakia sometime in the near future. The Deuxième Bureau received—probably via Hans-Thilo Schmidt ("H.E."), from either what he saw at the Forschungsamt or what he heard from his brother the general—and passed on to Gamelin and Daladier precise details about meetings where Hitler sought to overcome his generals' fears, and about the German general staff's reluctant plans for an attack against Czechoslovakia on or about September 25. Confirmation came from other intelligence sources in Germany cultivated by Robert Vansittart.[12]

The British government had taken the lead in trying to persuade the Czechoslovak government to defuse the crisis through concessions to the Sudetenlanders. A mission headed by Lord Walter Runciman toured Czechoslovakia and developed specific proposals to make to Prague. Bonnet supported this effort zealously. Talking directly with the Czechoslovak ambassador in Paris, or over the telephone with the French ambassador in Prague, and keeping Léger and other Quai d'Orsay officials in the dark, Bonnet said as emphatically as he could that Czechoslovakia should not count on military support from France or Britain. Sometimes Bonnet also left Daladier uninformed about what he was doing. On one occasion when he slipped, Daladier forcefully reminded him that the actual French position would have to be decided by the cabinet, "not by one minister."[13]

Daladier must certainly have hoped that diplomacy would somehow succeed in averting a direct conflict with Germany. But as evidence mounted of German preparations for military action, he had to face the possibility that all diplomatic maneuvers would fail, that Hitler would give Czechoslovakia some kind of ultimatum, that the Czechoslovak government would reject it, and that France would then have only the choice of going to war or finding some frail excuse for not doing so. Some of his calculations would thus have to be about the relative military capabilities of France, or France and Britain, on the one hand, and Germany on the other, and his judgment in these matters had to be influenced if not shaped by what Gamelin said to him, in part on the basis of information from the Deuxième Bureau.

Since Gamelin's primary objective in peacetime was always to obtain more money for the armed services, he consistently emphasized to Daladier and the rest of the cabinet the strengths of Germany and the weaknesses of France. The Deuxième Bureau, with help from French attachés in Berlin, continued with its stream of reports on the growth of Germany's armed forces. The army general staff and the air staff meanwhile served up litanies of shortcomings on the French side. These became longer and louder as a result of Gamelin's success in bringing into the general staff advocates of mechanized and motorized forces and of antitank and anti-aircraft defense, for acquisition of weaponry in these categories had been particularly slow under their predecessors. Thus, as a result of organizational routines, Daladier was shown an increasingly bleak picture of French short-term military readiness.

In public debate, Pertinax and Tabouis and their like argued that Czechoslovakia had a strong army and was an ally not to be taken lightly. Massigli and other Quai d'Orsay Realists made a similar argument. But the army general staff said the contrary to Daladier. One Deuxième Bureau report asked how one could have confidence in an army of which 23 percent consisted of members of a separatist minority.[14]

Documents going to Daladier as minister of defense stressed France's weakness in air power. Upon assuming responsibility for the air force as well as the army, he had been told by the air-force comptroller that, of the two thousand six hundred modern planes that Cot, the Popular Front's air minister, had projected for procurement, only twenty-seven had actually entered service. The air staff had recently revised sharply upward its estimate of German air strength, and it now declared the Luftwaffe able to send two thousand planes against Czechoslovakia while reserving another thousand to fifteen hundred for use in the West, perhaps in bombing raids against France's military bases, industrial centers, and cities. The famous American flier Charles Lindbergh had toured Germany's air bases and factories as Göring's guest, and on his return said that Germany was far ahead of all other nations in air power. General Vuillemin, chief of staff of the French air force, accepted an invitation from Göring for a similar tour. A short, chunky Bordelais who had been an ace bomber pilot in the Great War, Vuillemin was a hero to the public and to air-force fliers but not a man of great discernment. Like Lindbergh, he was taken in by Göring's Potemkin villages, and back in Paris told the air staff that it was still underestimating German capabilities.[15]

After Hitler's speech at Nuremberg on September 12, which clearly threatened an early attack on Czechoslovakia, Gamelin came to Daladier's office. Though entitled to use the prime-ministerial complex in the Hôtel Matignon, Daladier preferred to work from the War Ministry. The conversation therefore took place in a setting long familiar to both men. Daladier's private office, furnished in Empire style, had a marble fireplace, cherry-colored satin hangings on two walls, and, on the third, a huge tapestry showing King Louis XIV in 1670 signing the Treaty of Dover, which briefly allied France with England. Glass doors opened onto a small garden.[16]

Gamelin told Daladier that the Deuxième Bureau thought the German army was in fact poised to attack Czechoslovakia. In part because French and British diplomats had been cautioning Czechoslovakia not to make any provocative moves, Czechoslovak armed forces were only in the first stages of mobilization. Gamelin asked Daladier whether he wished to order mobilization by France. If France were to be ready to support Czechoslovakia, he said, the order would have to be given soon. Since any such order was certain to cause public furor, Gamelin wanted to put the question before Daladier before even beginning to discuss it with the other service chiefs.[17]

Daladier had not yet answered Gamelin when, on September 13, news broke that Chamberlain was flying to Munich to meet Hitler privately at Berchtesgaden. Chamberlain had not consulted Daladier or even given him private notification of this trip. Radio and newspaper reporters publicized the story well before any word arrived from the French Embassy in London or the British Embassy in Paris.

After Chamberlain returned from Berchtesgaden, Daladier made another pilgrimage to London, accompanied by Bonnet. He already knew the conditions that Chamberlain had agreed to press on the Czechoslovak government. He exclaimed to Chamberlain, "What kind of a negotiation is this, with a knife at the throat!" But he confessed that, in view of the division in French public opinion, he could do little other than accept Chamberlain's lead. "What can I do," he asked, "if I have no one behind me?"[18]

On returning to Paris, he gathered his cabinet to tell them what was afoot. Describing what Chamberlain intended to exact from the Czechoslovak government, he said he saw no alternative but to let Chamberlain proceed. As one cabinet member recorded, Daladier explained:

If we refuse, a German resort to force will occur. We would be alone in war for a month at least. It would be impossible for us to aid the Czechs other than by drawing the maximum number of Germans on ourselves and going on the offensive. Now, we have one thousand two hundred operational aircraft. The Germans can throw against us four thousand war planes that have much higher speeds. We could not break through the Siegfried Line before many weeks or many months and at the price of huge losses.[19]

Chamberlain, it will be remembered, had a second meeting with Hitler at Bad Godesberg on September 22–23. After two long sessions, he flew back to London to inform his Cabinet that Hitler would no longer settle for the terms agreed upon at Berchtesgaden but intended to march into Czechoslovakia and dictate terms there. On the next day, Chamberlain announced publicly that Britain would commence mobilization for war. Over BBC radio, he said to the people of Britain and the world, in never-to-be-forgotten words: "How horrible, fantastic, incredible, it is that we should be digging trenches and trying on gas masks here because of a quarrel in a faraway country between people of whom we know nothing."

Gamelin and Daladier had another long private talk in Daladier's War Ministry office. Gamelin set forth his own view of Czechoslovakia, which was somewhat different from that of the Deuxième Bureau or the general staff. On the positive side, he observed that the Czechoslovak air force was small but modern and that Czechoslovakia had an equivalent of the Maginot Line which was well-enough built to cause problems to German invaders. On the negative side, he pointed out that, as a result of the *Anschluss*, the Czechoslovak border with Austria lay open. Gamelin predicted that the German army would enter Czechoslovakia through this corridor and outflank the Czechoslovak fortifications, thus probably making it impossible for Czechoslovakia to hold out for more than a month.

Though Gamelin did not contest the air force's estimates of France's inferiority in the air, he assured Daladier that France could be defended, provided all reserves were called up at once. Daladier asked if Germany's armored divisions could not break through France's fixed defenses as Guderian, de Gaulle, and their like had argued. Gamelin replied, "Though the German tanks were fast, they were lightly armored. . . . We had two light mechanized divisions; at least as many tanks—better armored and better gunned; and efficient artillery."[20]

In the cabinet, Daladier found Bonnet protesting that war would be disastrously costly for France. On the other side of the table, Mandel and Reynaud insisted that Hitler had thrown down a gauntlet and there was no honorable or desirable alternative to picking it up. Both opinions had support among other cabinet members. Daladier was obviously torn. He ordered some preparations for war: reservists currently on active duty had already been directed to remain in uniform and report to regional centers for assignment to divisions in formation, and now he called up additional classes of reservists and directed that existing field units put themselves on a war footing. Convening his cabinet and ostentatiously omitting to invite Bonnet, Daladier asked for a vote regarding Hitler's Godesberg demands. Overwhelmingly, the cabinet pronounced them unacceptable.

Yet Daladier had clearly not abandoned hope that peace could be preserved. He crossed the Channel once again and, in London, assured Chamberlain that France would not stand in the way of further British efforts to avoid war, even if this required Czechoslovakia to make further concessions. He and Gamelin, who accompanied him, spent most of their energies trying to persuade the British that France would be a strong ally if war came, but that both nations would be better positioned for the conflict if Britain gave France maximum air support.

Back home from London, Daladier walked a fine line, giving a long public speech in which he announced the further steps toward mobilization, declared that the government could not accept "peace at any price," but emphasized that "the supreme goal is peace." His naval aide recalled his "tormented face." An intimate would say later:

> He took it as inevitable that there would be a conflict—a conflict that public opinion did not want. . . . Obliged to act as a patriot and also as a responsible leader, he felt himself on a razor's edge. At that

time and afterwards, Daladier struck me not as hesitant but tormented by the difficulty of making the right choice among uncertain opinions.[21]

Then came the new surprise—Mussolini's proposal of a four-power conference, Chamberlain's jubilant acceptance, Hitler's reluctant acceptance. Chamberlain gave Daladier no opportunity even to comment, let alone to propose conditions for the meeting. Daladier departed for Munich, leaving Bonnet behind but taking Léger along—perhaps in token that he did not relish doing what Bonnet had all along wanted him to do. But if he ever thought of arguing for less onerous terms for Czechoslovakia or of separating himself in any way from Chamberlain, any such thought was stifled by his military advisers.

Gauché had been saying all September that France was not ready for war. He may have been influenced by his associates in the Deuxième Bureau of the air force, or he may simply have credited the estimates of German power that he had been forwarding to Gamelin and have known of French power only what was being said by monarchist officers dubious about republican draftees and reservists. In any case, he had said offhandedly to the British military attaché at about the time of Chamberlain's return from Berchtesgaden: "Of course there will be no European war, since we are not going to fight," and, when asked, explained "that the French could not face the risk of the German air threat."[22] After Godesberg, when it seemed that France might have to go to war after all, Gauché gave Gamelin an elaborate and pessimistic estimate of the military situation, which Gamelin passed on to Daladier. As Gauché summarizes it in his postwar memoir, it made the following points:

• Germany is ready for general war. It has 120 divisions, with ninety ready for action.
• The Czechoslovak position is hopeless. The Czechoslovaks have only forty divisions. The Germans are planning to throw armored forces against the Czechoslovak frontier fortresses. The Czechoslovaks cannot hold these fortresses. Within days they will be conducting a fighting retreat into the mountains. That is now the essence of their war plan.
• On the Western side, the Germans have made their frontier impregnable. They have built two lines of fortifications. The Deuxième Bureau has good photographs of both. It would take all France's artillery to force a breach anywhere. And the breach could not be exploited. The German forces not

engaged against Czechoslovakia would be adequate to defend against any attack. Overall, Germany's land forces are superior to France's. German air forces outclass—by far—the French and British air forces combined.[23]

Just before Daladier's plane took off from Le Bourget, General Vuillemin underlined Gauché's final point, saying, "If there is war, there will be no French air force by the end of fifteen days."[24]

During the Munich meeting, Daladier sat glumly silent. He may have been drunk part of the time. Pertinax, who covered the conference for *L'Ordre*, said afterward that the Germans had planned to ply Daladier with alcohol and that they had succeeded.[25] He signed the accords without comment, then flew home. His sometime naval aide Raphaël-Leygues writes that, on his return from Munich, Daladier "had his hat down over his eyes; he looked shy and sad. . . . His nice blue eyes had, as they did sometimes, a hunted look. He was lost in thought, sad, moved. He had a horror of being photographed, of displaying himself. He was bashful." Daladier claimed to have expected a cold, jeering reception, but instead, the ten-mile roadway to and through the Porte de Bercy was lined with an estimated half-million cheerers. Daladier did not share their joy. He said to his aides, "Don't have any illusions. This is only a respite, and if we don't make use of it, we will all be shot."[26]

CHAPTER TWELVE

CHAMBERLAIN

"What a pity Hitler did not know when he met this sober English politician with his umbrella at Berchtesgaden, Godesberg and Munich, that he was actually talking to a hard-bitten pioneer from the outer marches of the British Empire!"   —*Winston Churchill, October 25, 1939*

France and Britain had surprised Hitler by threatening war over Czechoslovakia. They had surprised General Beck by being so conciliatory, given that he perceived them as having overwhelming military superiority. While Weizsäcker had been less surprised than either Hitler or Beck, he had interpreted the French and British shows of resoluteness as more a reaction to German high-handedness than an indication of real concern about central or eastern Europe. After the Munich conference, Hitler concluded that the western powers had been bluffing and he could safely have had the war he wanted with Czechoslovakia. In retrospect, he thought French and British policies in the Sudeten crisis of a piece with their policies at the time of the *Anschluss*. Hence he believed that Germany's taking the remainder of Czechoslovakia would hardly cause Paris or London to move a finger. Weizsäcker did not disagree, cautioning only that Germany had to manage the matter carefully, with due regard for diplomatic proprieties.

None of these Germans perceived that France and Britain had shown more mettle than at the time of Germany's remilitarization of the Rhineland or the *Anschluss* in part because both countries had begun to recover from the Great Depression both economically and psychologically and also because public opinion in both countries reacted adversely to Hitler's aggressiveness. Hence, in March 1939, when Hitler took the remainder of Czechoslovakia, France and Britain responded by effectively committing themselves to go to war if Hitler lifted his hand against any other nation in Europe. Hitler, with his newspaper clippings and conversations with foreign visitors and Forschungsamt intercepts, and Weizsäcker, with his diplomatic reportage, both failed to see how actions by Germany altered the attitudes taken among citizens and politicians in both France and Britain, and that the past patterns of behavior by their governments were thus a less and less reliable basis for forecasting what they would do in the future.

As Germans' judgments of France boiled down to judgments about Daladier, so their judgments of Britain were essentially judgments about Chamberlain. The image of Chamberlain surviving after 1940 came primarily from photographs and newsreels recording his return from Munich in 1938. They show him, umbrella and homburg hat in hand, a gaunt face and bristling mustache over a starched wing collar, waving a piece of paper. He says in a reedy voice that he brings home "peace with honor" and goes on to declare, "I believe it is peace for our time." Given what happened so soon afterward, the image is that of a weak, foolish old man putting a celebratory face on an act of cowardice.

Foolish perhaps, but weak—no. Except possibly for Margaret Thatcher, no peacetime British prime minister has been so strong-willed, almost tyrannical.[1] The film record of his return from Munich is in fact evidence of this. By feeding or withholding information, getting publishers to punish unfriendly reporters, steering the government-owned BBC, and rationing photographic opportunities, Chamberlain had established influence over the news media that, if not quite on a par with that of Goebbels in Germany, exceeded that of any contemporary head of government in any other democratic nation.[2] In the summer of 1938, he had sought low-key coverage of the Sudeten crisis. Though others had tried to build interest in the subject, including a cabal within his own party and senior officials such as Vansittart and Rex Leeper, the Foreign Office press chief, Chamberlain had been sufficiently successful so that his broadcast after Godesberg warning of possible war had surprised most hearers. After signing the agreements at Munich, he expected a triumphant public reception and arranged to have maximum coverage, not only by press photographers and the BBC but by British Gaumont and other film companies.[3]

David Dilks, Chamberlain's premier biographer, who has often tried to correct the conventional image, likes to cite Churchill's account of the first occasion when he and Chamberlain dined together informally. It was in October 1939, after Churchill had come into Chamberlain's cabinet as First Lord of the Admiralty. Though both men came from famous political families, were leaders in the same political party, and had frequently served in government together, they had never before had a relaxed conversation. Churchill recorded afterward his fascination at hearing Chamberlain describe how, during the first forty years of his life, he had been the family's businessman. Before settling back into Birmingham, becoming lord mayor, and entering Parliament, he had, among other things, spent five years and lost fifty thousand pounds in a futile effort to grow sisal on an islet in the Caribbean. "I thought to myself," Churchill wrote, " 'What a pity Hitler did not know when he met this sober English politician with his umbrella at Berchtesgaden, Godesberg and Munich, that he was actually talking to a hard-bitten pioneer from the outer marches of the British Empire!' "[4]

Chamberlain seldom allowed himself such moments of letup. Even less did he show such emotion as at Heston Airport and Downing Street after Munich. As a rule, his widest smile seemed strained, his normal smile not easy to distinguish from a sneer. The National Portrait Gallery's full-length oil, finished in 1939 by Henry Lamb, shows him in a starched posture, staring out with fixed cold, bright, brown eyes. Perhaps from impatience at endless sittings, he seems ready to snarl. But other than graying hair and wattles on a thin neck, he shows few signs of age. From crown to toe, he is a no-nonsense, bottom-line company director.

Chamberlain was one of the rare politicians to command respect among British senior civil servants. One wrote of him: "He was an exceptionally good Chairman of committees. He had all the qualities that Whitehall most desires for its normal tasks: industry, order, precision, correctitude. He was a lucid expositor, and a competent defender, of Departmental policy."[5] Though he had many admirers, he had few friends. His chief confidantes were his two maiden sisters, Hilda and Ida. In letters to them, at least once a week, Chamberlain detailed his ambitions and apprehensions, his high opinion of himself, and his low opinion of most other mortals.

He was not at all popular among fellow politicians. David Margesson, chief whip in the House of Commons, commented: "He engendered personal dislike among his opponents to an extent almost unbelievable." Margesson's own explanation was that "his cold intellect was too much for them." John Colville, a young assistant private secretary to the prime minister, noted in his diary the strength of Chamberlain's reaction to even mild criticism: "I was surprised at the violence of his fury which I could never have expected in such a cold man." Though in many respects a supporter, Colville wrote of Chamberlain: "He likes to be set on a pedestal and adored, with suitable humility, by unquestioning admirers." Leo Amery, one of Chamberlain's opponents within the Tory party, said of him, "He knew his own mind and saw to it that he had his own way. An autocrat with all the courage of his convictions right or wrong."[6]

From 1933 onward, first as chancellor of the exchequer and then as prime minister, Chamberlain championed concurrent pursuit of two policies—an arms buildup and "appeasement." When Hitler's intention to rearm Germany first became apparent, Chamberlain wrote in his diary in 1933, "Common prudence would seem to indicate some strengthening of our defences."[7] Early in the following year, he supported recommendations from a committee of civil-service mandarins that Germany be considered Britain's "ultimate potential enemy" and that a five-year program equip Britain for possible war. Though leaving in doubt both the ultimate scale of the program and the difficult question of service shares, the Cabinet gave its approval.[8]

Chamberlain saw it as his duty to find the necessary money. This drew criticism, for the chancellor of the exchequer was supposed to be the government's penny-pincher. The weekly *Economist* described it as "a regrettable departure from British tradition that the chancellor of the exchequer should himself be the foremost advocate of increased expenditure on armaments." Privately, Chamberlain not only agreed with *The Economist* but deplored defense spending as a matter of principle. He would later say publicly: "The very idea that the hard-won savings of our people . . . should have to be dissipated on the construction of weapons of war is hateful and damnable." But he had concluded that arms spending served not only "common prudence" but also the interests of the Conservative Party. Given the rise of Nazi Germany, he told his Cabinet colleagues, the public was made uneasy by the opposition Labour Party's doctrinaire antimilitarism. At his urging, the government called an election.[9] The result, in November 1935, was a Conservative sweep. In the new House of Commons, the Conservatives had a majority of 247.

Afterward, Chamberlain could have his policy without compromising his role as chancellor, for the Cabinet agreed to create a new post, minister for coordination of defense. This new minister could be the advocate of an all-service arms buildup. Chamberlain had only to bless his proposals as fiscally acceptable. Friends of Churchill urged that he be appointed to the post. A Cabinet member during most of the period from 1911 to the beginning of the 1930s, Churchill had been left out of recent governments. Stanley Baldwin thought him irresponsible. He claimed to want to say of Churchill in the House of Commons:

> When Winston was born lots of fairies swooped down on his cradle with gifts—imagination, eloquence, industry, ability—and then a fairy came who said "No one person has a right to so many gifts," picked him up and gave him such a shake and twist that with all these gifts he was denied judgment and wisdom. And that is why while we delight to listen to him in this House we do not take his advice.[10]

Chamberlain had a similar view and, moreover, feared that Churchill would demand excessive spending for defense and would make jingoistic speeches offending foreign governments. He successfully backed someone else for the new Cabinet post: Sir Thomas Inskip, previously the attorney general, who was sure both to watch every shilling and to speak publicly in a low key. His one memorable statement characterized a strong balance of payments as Britain's "fourth arm of defence."[11]

Like Daladier, Chamberlain was nevertheless continually engaged in cultivating parliamentary and public support for military spending. The treaty negotiated with Ribbentrop in June 1935 had sanctioned Germany's exceeding the naval limitations prescribed by the Treaty of Versailles but had bound Germany to have a fleet only one-third the size of Britain's. Although the Royal Navy had ambitious plans for modernization, this treaty constrained its demands for new funds. The army also had difficulty establishing claims, for most people in Britain thought now that it had been a mistake to send large numbers of ground forces to the continent during the Great War. Many believed, further, that any new war would be decided by airplanes rather than by either warships or ground troops. Chamberlain fended off army requests for money on the premise that it would take weeks for a British Expeditionary Force to be assembled and that by that time a war might well be over.[12]

Chamberlain's program aimed primarily at keeping up with or staying ahead of Germany in air power. As he had explained to the Cabinet in 1934, the objective was an air force "of a size and efficiency calculated to inspire respect in the mind of a possible enemy."[13] The dimensions of the program therefore depended on estimates of Germany's air buildup, and so did its specifics.

The Royal Air Force (or RAF), unlike the air forces of most other nations, was entirely independent. Not only was it not a servant of the army but it claimed the mission of controlling the air as the Royal Navy had historically controlled the sea. Its guiding doctrine came from Air Chief Marshal Sir Hugh Trenchard, who held that the RAF could do almost anything that had been done in the past by either the army or the navy and do it more efficiently, swiftly, and cheaply. Trenchard's doctrine supposed, among other things, that there would be no new Great War, because bombers would deliver a "knockout blow," making ground or sea combat unnecessary or incidental. But the RAF's senior officers, though mostly worshipful toward Trenchard, were divided between bomber pilots committed to delivering this knock-out blow and fighter pilots committed to preventing its being inflicted on Britain.

Chamberlain's formula implied that the overall allocation for the RAF would be based on estimates of Germany's spending for its Luftwaffe and also that funds for bombers and fighters would depend on estimates of how the Luftwaffe was evolving: if Germany was emphasizing long-range bombers, then the heaviest British investment should go to fighters; if Germany was emphasizing fighters, then Britain would build bombers. The deterrent effect of the British air buildup required that it discourage Germany from optimism about a knockout blow against Britain or its own invulnerability to a knockout blow from Britain.

Information about the German air force was scarce and untrustworthy.[14] In the spring of 1935, Hitler claimed publicly that the new German air force was already equal to Britain's. The British air staff had been saying (accurately) that the German air force lagged behind the RAF both in overall numbers and in quality of both bombers and fighters.[15] Vansittart, then permanent undersecretary in the Foreign Office, pronounced the air staff hopelessly complacent. The Secret Intelligence Service (SIS), which was under the Foreign Office, obtained German documents that more or less supported Hitler's claim. Persuaded by Vansittart and the SIS documents, Baldwin, while still prime minister, said in the House of Commons that he had been "completely misled" when earlier minimizing German air strength. His rhetoric and Chamberlain's promised a catch-up effort, but left it unclear whether the catch-up needed to be in bombers or in fighters.

From 1935 to 1938, the British government tended to credit the most alarming of possible predictions regarding the German air force. In 1936 and 1937, through a retired British officer with good connections in the Luftwaffe staff, Vansittart obtained and circulated tolerably accurate figures on the building plans developed for Göring by Erhard Milch. But since details were missing, papers that circulated within the British government hypothesized huge forces of both bombers and fighters when, in fact, Milch proposed chiefly to build trainers, transports, and ground-support aircraft. (The nearest German counterpart to Trenchard, General Walther Wever, had been killed in a flying accident in June 1936, and Luftwaffe building and training programs had been taken over by officers more inclined to prepare for air-ground operations than for air operations alone.[16])

By May 1937, when Chamberlain became prime minister, the Air Ministry was saying that, unless Britain were to risk bankruptcy, the RAF could not match the Luftwaffe for at least four years. In early 1938, the chiefs of staff unanimously advised the Cabinet that Germany could sustain a two-month bombing campaign against the British Isles, which might in fact serve as a knockout blow.[17] In August, when the Sudeten crisis worsened, the air staff's Intelligence Directorate circulated detailed figures on German bomber strength and warned that a full-force Luftwaffe strike against Britain could produce fifty thousand casualties in the first twenty-four hours.

Chamberlain's diplomacy has to be understood against this background. This is not to say or suggest that he was motivated primarily by a desire to buy time for catching up with Germany in air power. He could not conceive of anyone's wanting war. Indeed, he would die believing that war had resulted from Hitler's miscalculation. Wanton murder and destruction of property seemed to Chamberlain totally irrational, and demonstrated as such by the Great War. Moreover, he had almost unlimited faith in his own powers of reasoning and persuasion.

Though Chamberlain had endorsed and furthered the rearmament program premised on the possibility of a future war with Germany, he had done so in the spirit of a householder taking out earthquake insurance. Given the naval treaty and Hitler's comparatively moderate statements about possibly reclaiming lost colonies, Chamberlain could see few issues threatening to generate a German-British conflict. He thought Hitler crude and melodramatic, but he believed he understood what animated him. And he was sympathetic.

Abhorring Lloyd George, the British prime minister who was partly accountable for the Versailles Treaty, Chamberlain adopted every chapter of the "revisionist" critique. He believed that emotion had ruled in the 1919 peacemaking, that Germany had been wronged in ways harmful to the world economy and dangerous both politically and socially. He deemed Germany's grievances real and Hitler's demands not unreasonable. "Of course they want to dominate eastern Europe," he said in September 1937; "they want as close a union with Austria as they can get without incorporating her in the Reich and they want much the same things for the Sudetendeutsche as we did for the Uitlanders in the Transvaal."[18] The Boer analogy had particular resonance for Chamberlain since his father, Joseph Chamberlain, had been the colonial secretary whose championship of the English-speaking Uitlanders had contributed to bringing on the war of 1899–1902 between Britain and South Africa's Boer Republic.

The *Anschluss* unsettled Chamberlain, but more because of its suddenness than its outcome. During the spring and summer of 1938, he set himself to achieving a peaceful settlement between Germany and Czechoslovakia. It was not a matter of great import to him how or whether Czechoslovakia survived such a settlement. His ambassador in Prague, Basil Cochrane Newton, took a view of Czechoslovakia not altogether unlike Weizsäcker's. "Should war come . . . ," wrote Newton, "all we could hope to achieve would be to restore after a lengthy struggle a *status quo* which had already proved unacceptable and which, even if restored, would probably again prove unworkable." He pronounced Czechoslovakia, from "her history and the racial divisions of her population . . . not permanently tenable," and added: "It will not be a kindness in the long run to try to maintain her in it."[19]

Chamberlain thought he was acting for France as well as Britain. And though Daladier, in London as the new French prime minister, never departed from saying that France would stand firmly behind Czechoslovakia, Chamberlain supposed this to be pretense. He had said to the Cabinet in March 1938, before Daladier became prime minister, that he found it "difficult to believe . . . that . . . the French would not be glad to find some method to relieve them of their engagement," and he did not change his mind. Moreover, what Daladier said in London was contradicted behind his back by Bonnet, and Phipps, the British ambassador in Paris, supported Bonnet wholeheartedly. At one point, Phipps cautioned London of "the extreme danger of even appearing to encourage small, but noisy and corrupt, war groups here," continuing: "All that is best in France is against war, *almost* at any price."[20] Chamberlain thought it his task to work a deal that would protect France against having to admit publicly that its promise to defend Czechoslovakia was "a scrap of paper."

Chamberlain never became wholly disheartened. When Hitler, at Godesberg, rejected terms that he himself had proposed barely a week earlier, Chamberlain did not conclude that the effort for a negotiated settlement would have to be abandoned. Back in London, he described for the

Cabinet his return flight over the Thames and his inability to think of anything except the scene below had his plane been a German bomber on a wartime mission. He said that he wanted Daladier to state publicly that France was unable to defend Czechoslovakia. The Czechoslovak government would then have no choice but to bow to Hitler's Godesberg demands.[21]

But Chamberlain discovered that he could no longer count on the Cabinet's following his dictates. The *Anschluss* had bothered many Conservative backbenchers. Churchill, who had criticized the slow pace of rearmament and questioned aspects of appeasement, had gained followers. Another knot of dissent had gathered around Anthony Eden, who had been Halifax's predecessor as foreign secretary and was reputed to have stepped down because of doubts about the government's foreign policy. (The actual reason had been more irritation with Chamberlain's autocratic style.) Whereas most of the British press had acclaimed Chamberlain for flying to Berchtesgaden, its reaction to the news from Godesberg was outrage. With Chamberlain not on hand to provide guidance, even editors close to the prime minister printed editorials declaring Hitler's conduct intolerable. The staunchly Tory *Daily Telegraph*, for example, characterized Germany's policy as extortion. Chamberlain's Cabinet colleagues recognized that, if Britain yielded to the Godesberg demands, the government might face an uprising both in the House of Commons and in the country.[22]

It was Halifax who took it upon himself to disillusion Chamberlain. Tall, gangling, and horse-faced, Lord Halifax seemed a living caricature of a north-country peer. He spoke in an aristocratic mumble, was conspicuously a high-church Anglican, and went fox-hunting on every possible occasion. Only those who saw more than his exterior were aware that he also had a keen-edged intellect, had taken a first in modern history at Oxford, and had received the rare tribute of election as a Fellow of All Souls, often considered a certificate of brilliance. Previously, he had been an unhesitating supporter of both Chamberlain and appeasement. When he visited Germany shortly before becoming foreign secretary, he had mistaken Hitler for a servant and, if not held back by Neurath, would have handed him his hat and coat, but he had ended up being impressed, reporting afterward that Hitler was "very sincere, . . . believing everything he said." Halifax had also taken a liking to Göring, even though he knew of his role in the Blood Purge, and also to Goebbels. His sympathy for Germany owed something to the fact that he apparently despised all Frenchmen.[23]

Hitler's bluster about the Sudetenland had nevertheless gone down badly with Halifax, who had misgivings about Chamberlain's flight to Berchtesgaden and believed that the terms arranged there represented the absolute limit of a bargain to which Britain could lend support. When he saw the first ciphered telegrams from the British delegation at Godesberg, Halifax responded with a message saying that Hitler's refusal to accept the settlement arranged by Chamberlain "would be an unpardonable crime against humanity."[24] On the evening of Chamberlain's return from Godesberg, he had a long conversation with Alexander Cadogan, Vansittart's successor as permanent undersecretary in the Foreign Office. Cadogan had previously been an advocate of appeasement, scorning as "awful rubbish" Vansittart's thesis that Hitler would back down on the Sudetenland only if faced with a threat of war, but he had changed his mind completely, concluding that what Hitler had said at Godesberg was consistent only with an interpretation such as Vansittart's. He so argued to Halifax, and during a sleepless night Halifax concluded not only that Cadogan was right but that he could not keep silent out of loyalty to Chamberlain.[25]

At the Cabinet meeting on September 25, Halifax said that Hitler's new demands should be rejected and that Britain should prepare to join France in a war. Chamberlain, astonished, passed Halifax a note saying that his "complete change of view" was "a horrible blow."[26] But when most of the Cabinet appeared to support Halifax, Chamberlain concluded that it was necessary to prepare the country. He delivered the public speech that is best remembered for its "faraway country" line but which, in less remembered passages, summarized his sense of dilemma: "If I were convinced that any nation had made up its mind to dominate the world by fear of its force, I should feel that it must be resisted . . . ; but war is a fearful thing, and we must be very clear, before we embark on it, that it is really the great issues that are at stake."

Mussolini's last-moment proposal for a four-power conference rescued Chamberlain. He was actually in the House of Commons giving a mournful recital of his failed negotiations when one of his colleagues tugged at his sleeve and handed him a message. His face transformed, he announced Hitler's invitation to the Munich conference. As a result of it, Chamberlain got what he wanted—an escape from war. He hoped, indeed believed, that the basis now existed for long-term peaceful understanding with Germany. But it had been a near thing. British public opinion had pushed Chamberlain to the edge of war. In 1939, it would push him over that edge.

CHAPTER THIRTEEN

ENOUGH!

"When peace was threatened, we saw the shame of war. When war seemed to menace us, we felt the shame of peace."
—*Antoine de Saint-Exupéry, October 2, 1938*

In France, after Munich, Daladier's government pursued two lines of policy. Bonnet tested a hypothesis that Hitler was ready now for some form of détente. At the same time, urged on by Gamelin, Daladier redoubled the effort to arm France for a war that might come at any time, perhaps even within months.

At the suggestion of François-Poncet, who was about to leave Berlin for Rome, Bonnet began to seek a Franco-German treaty that would revive the guarantee of the border between the two countries that had been a key element in the now lapsed Locarno Pact. He indicated that this might be followed by agreements strengthening economic and cultural relationships. Bonnet meanwhile reinforced his hand within the Quai d'Orsay by ridding himself of Massigli, who learned first from a morning newspaper that he was to become ambassador to Turkey. Bonnet would also have dispensed with Léger had it not been for Léger's closeness to Daladier (and perhaps, as rumor had it, information in Léger's safe about Bonnet's stock-market speculation during the Sudeten crisis). As a replacement for François-Poncet in Berlin, Bonnet and Léger agreed on Robert Coulondre, until then ambassador in Moscow. Instructing Coulondre "to work out an accord with Hitler," Bonnet invited Ribbentrop to come to Paris.[1]

In early November, when plans for this visit were almost final, a young Polish Jew, Herschel Grynszpan, recently arrived in France from Germany, shot a third secretary of the German Embassy. Bonnet immediately expressed regret for this crime on French soil. The German ambassador in Paris gave no sign that he meant to blame the French government. At home, however, Hitler decided impetuously to use the incident as trigger for a massive display of anti-Semitism. The night of November 9–10 became *Kristallnacht*, the night of broken glass. All over Germany, groups of Nazis smashed windows in shops and houses belonging to Jews. They beat up Jews, killed at least a dozen, and dragged large numbers off to concentration camps.

Anti-Semitism was strong in France, and not only among the radical right. During the Sudeten crisis, the mayor of Strasbourg had had to call out police to protect German Jewish refugees, whom Strasbourgers seemed prepared to blame for bringing on the threat of war. The city of Nancy also saw anti-Jewish demonstrations, and rumors were rife that Jewish reservists were manning the mobilization centers but not themselves going to the front lines.[2] Except for vitriolic anti-Semites such as contributors to *Je suis partout*, however, French people found *Kristallnacht* hard to stomach. Most French dailies and weeklies condemned the occurrences in Germany as barbaric. The condemnation became stronger when, a few days later, it was learned that Nazis had roughed up Michael Cardinal von Faulhaber, desecrated his cathedral in Munich, and vandalized his home because he had denounced their actions on *Kristallnacht*. Non-Jewish members of the Parisian elite raised money for Grynszpan's defense, and leading French barristers offered him their services.

Bonnet and Ribbentrop agreed that Ribbentrop's visit to Paris should be postponed. Ribbentrop's stated excuse was a threat by French unions to call a general strike if the Daladier government departed from the programs of the Popular Front. The visit did not take place until early December, by which time the Grynszpan case had become caught in the law's delays and the unions had become quiet. As evidence that the initiative was not just Bonnet's, Daladier entertained Ribbentrop at lunch at the Hôtel Matignon, his prime-ministerial quarters, and, as Ribbentrop had requested, omitted invitations to the Jewish members of the cabinet, Mandel and Education Minister Jean Zay. (One odd feature of the luncheon was that the Marquise Jeanne de Crussol acted as hostess. Daladier's wife had died in 1932, and the marquise, a sardine-canning heiress from Brittany, had subsequently become his companion, but she rarely appeared with him at official functions.)

The formal talks between Bonnet and Ribbentrop produced an anodyne agreement guaranteeing the existing French-German boundary. There was talk of other agreements to be worked out later, but only talk. Ribbentrop would subsequently claim to have been assured by Bonnet that France no longer had any interest in Eastern Europe. This was untrue. Léger, who had no incentive to defend Bonnet and who had been present almost all the time, testified eventually that no such words had come from Bonnet's mouth. Perhaps Ribbentrop misunderstood, for some of the conversation was in French, or perhaps Ribbentrop simply heard what he wanted to hear, or perhaps he just lied.[3]

In the meantime, Hitler made new speeches about Germany's continuing need to redress the iniquities of the 1919 peace settlement. Ambassador Coulondre in Berlin, far from reporting hopefully on German interest in détente, told of indications that some new adventure was in preparation. In company with his predecessor, François-Poncet, and the French ambassadors in Warsaw and Bucharest, he hypothesized for a time that Hitler had in mind a deal with Poland under which the two nations would detach Ukraine from the Soviet Union and turn it into an agricultural colony. (Poland and Hungary had both sided with Germany against Czechoslovakia and taken territorial spoils as a result of the Munich accords.) Through most of the autumn and winter of 1938–39, Coulondre continued to warn of evidence that some such venture might be in preparation. If not that, he said, Hitler might just attack Poland.[4]

The Deuxième Bureau repeatedly raised warning flags. Though cautioning that it was "difficult and dangerous to prejudge the future and all hypotheses have to be kept in view," Gauché in late November 1938 noted that Germany was building up offensive forces in Saxony and Silesia while concentrating on defensive fortifications in the West. In late December, he mentioned the possibility of an accord between Germany and the Soviet Union as "a hypothesis that has never been considered absurd." He kept calling attention to German military preparations compatible with a hypothesis of an imminent move against Poland or Romania but also commented that apparent German preparations for a drive to the East could be camouflage while "the real aim was to conquer a colonial domain to the detriment of France, Belgium, and the Netherlands."[5]

Gamelin meanwhile prodded Daladier to accelerate France's arms buildup. After the Munich conference, the War Ministry comptroller had proposed cutting the army budget by 5 percent on the ground that the danger of war had diminished. In addition to protesting and preventing such a cut, Gamelin had circulated a memorandum to the other chiefs of staff saying that, in his view, war had become more, not less, likely. His conclusion from the 1938 crisis was: "We can never deal with Germany except with force."[6] He asked Vuillemin and Darlan to summarize the most urgent needs of the air force and navy, and the general staff to do the same for the army.

Melding the replies, Gamelin put before Daladier a gloomy description of France's current military condition and a long list of expensive programs needing immediate funding. Vuillemin had said that Germany had five thousand first-line aircraft whereas France had only five hundred, that France and Britain together were not currently a match for Germany, and that, absent a new, large acquisition effort, France would not have even minimum security against a German air attack until 1940.[7] Admiral Darlan recommended abandoning central and eastern Europe to Germany and concentrating on a fleet build-up to safeguard the French empire. Though Gamelin did not endorse Darlan's position or proposals, he put himself strongly behind Vuillemin, telling Daladier that deficiencies in air power needed to be remedied as soon as possible. As for the army, he recommended to Daladier much heavier investment in equipment and manpower. Owing to the crippling of Czechoslovakia, Gamelin wrote, France's situation had become perilous, and "the military means of yesterday are no longer enough for today." The army needed new tanks, vehicles for motorized infantry, heavy antitank and anti-aircraft weapons, and many more men. Almost saying outright that Daladier had not gone far enough toward abandoning the costly domestic programs of the Popular Front, Gamelin declared, "The moment has arrived to ask whether the security of the country should not take priority over all other considerations."[8]

Daladier was slow to respond. He may have hoped that Bonnet's diplomatic effort would succeed. He was certainly conscious of domestic political problems rising out of the arms buildup already in progress. A few days after returning from Munich, he had asked the Chamber of Deputies and the Senate for a renewed grant of power to rule by decree. Since he made it clear that he intended to move away from the programs of the Popular Front and concentrate exclusively on rearmament, the center and right parties gave him a lopsided majority, but the communists opposed him and the socialists abstained. He then made the conservative Paul Reynaud his finance minister, raised taxes, and cut back sharply on spending for all purposes other than defense. The aim, he said, was to increase industrial production and pull capital back from abroad. For the same ends, he announced extension of the work week from forty to forty-eight hours.

Since the law ordaining a five-day, forty-hour week had been the prize accomplishment of the Popular Front and was a totem for labor unions, the umbrella labor organization, the Conféderation Générale du Travail (CGT), called a twenty-four-hour general strike. The day for it was Tuesday, November 30. Daladier told public-service workers to stay on the job. They did. The Paris subways ran without interruption, for only two hundred out of twenty thousand workers went on strike. Though metalworkers and dockworkers walked out in large numbers, most members of industrial unions followed the example of the public-service workers. Daladier was perceived as having broken the strike. By all indications, the result for him was a gain in stature among working-class as well as middle-class voters. Militant labor leaders found it difficult thereafter not just to call strikes but even to get majorities in union congresses for motions critical of government policies.

Still, Daladier balked at signing on to the large-scale spending program Gamelin proposed. He set a ceiling of twenty-five billion francs. Gamelin ordained some economies. Despite Vuillemin's protests, he pared air-force bomber programs, proposing almost complete concentration on fighter aircraft to support ground troops. He also deferred formation of full armored divisions, accepting the argument of the army's conservative inspectorates that more time was needed for planning. But with every possible economy, Gamelin told Daladier, the bill for 1939 would still come to thirty-one billion francs. France "does not have the capability of initiating an attack against Germany with any serious chance of success," he asserted. "If it is contented with maintaining the current posture of its army it will soon be unable, without strong British reinforcements, to retake Belgium, which in the event of a German attack would be quickly engulfed."[9]

On December 5, 1938, less than a week after Daladier frustrated the general strike and the day before he and the Marquise de Crussol greeted Ribbentrop, he presided over a meeting of the Permanent Committee on National Defense. It took place at the War Ministry on the rue St.-Dominique, in a large room adjacent to Daladier's office that had been the billiard room when, in the eighteenth century, the whole building had been the townhouse of the Richelieu family. At Daladier's invitation, Reynaud attended, accompanied by staff from the Ministry of Finance.

The minutes, though not verbatim, indicate spirited exchanges. Gamelin argued that the emergency was such as to demand scrapping all normal rules for budgeting. Reynaud, having argued in favor of risking war in behalf of Czechoslovakia, was now in the uncomfortable position of having to resist Gamelin's plea. Daladier, who disliked Reynaud (and would soon loathe him), enjoyed seeing his finance minister in this predicament and at one point asked if he was prepared to see the French air force remain in "tragic inferiority" to that of Germany. At the same time, Daladier continued to deny Gamelin full support. By saying that bombers were surely the aircraft most likely to have an intimidating effect on an enemy, he seemed to side with Vuillemin. Although he had in the past joined Gamelin in trying to increase the number of French tanks, he seemed now to question Gamelin's thesis that France should push toward having Panzer divisions like Germany's. Not long afterward, Daladier would say to a Senate committee: "Too much has been sacrificed for mechanization. The horse is indispensable." He may have been influenced by his onetime adviser General Bourret, who had been deriding Gamelin's plans, saying, "Tanks: we already have too many."[10]

During the meeting, Gamelin advocated an immediate effort to bolster the French air force by ordering a thousand planes from the United States. Reynaud objected that the cost would be ruinous. Nevertheless, the group endorsed Gamelin's proposal. Afterward, Gamelin kept up pressure on Daladier. On December 19, he sent him a letter saying that a very reliable source in Germany predicted Hitler's moving soon against some target in the East. An SR report described a meeting at which Hitler spoke of acting against rump Czechoslovakia, Poland, and Ukraine. The information came from within the armed-forces high command, perhaps from Canaris, the head of the Abwehr. Daladier had to decide, wrote Gamelin, whether France was "to renounce the role of a great power and yield to Germany not only hegemony in Central Europe but in Eastern Europe."[11] In the end, Daladier agreed to commit more than forty million francs to the arms buildup.

After the beginning of 1939, Daladier seemed to abandon interest in discussing détente with Germany, though Bonnet continued his diplomatic efforts. A mini-crisis with Italy caused him to become more assertive about French interests and his own willingness to use force. François-Poncet, as the new ambassador to Italy, was invited to be Mussolini's guest at the Italian Chamber of Deputies, where he found himself the target of well-organized demonstrators calling for France to cede Tunisia, Corsica, even Nice and Savoy to Italy. The episode was reminiscent of demonstrations in

Berlin in behalf of the Sudeten Czechs. French journalists speculated about a Munich conference where France's territory would be carved up. This was even a theme in the generally pacifist *Canard enchaîné*.

Daladier responded by declaring to the Chamber of Deputies, and repeating word for word before the Senate, "France will not cede an inch of its territories to Italy, no matter whether armed conflict results." He then made a tour to Corsica, Algeria, and Tunisia, speaking at each stop of France's determination not to bargain away any of its domains. In Paris, journalists said that the prime minister had never been so popular. Commented *The New Yorker*'s Janet Flanner, "The military flourish which surrounded his trip . . . delighted the French nation, skeptical of an umbrella's ever again looking as powerful as a cannon."[12] Though Hitler and various German officials assured the French government that they had not prompted the Italian initiative and did not support it, Italian diplomatic messages intercepted and decrypted by the Deuxième Bureau gave Daladier reason to believe that Mussolini had been planning to foment a crisis and expected backing from Berlin.[13]

French diplomatic and intelligence services continued to warn that Hitler planned some new adventure and that Germany was arming at a sprinter's pace. Speculation about Hitler's possible targets continued to wander across the map. In January 1939, the Netherlands led the Deuxième Bureau's candidate list. This was helpful to Gamelin, who was at the time conspiring with British army generals to get a commitment from the British government to send ground troops to the continent in the event of war; fear of Germany's getting bomber bases in the Netherlands was expected to spur a decision in his favor. But the Deuxième Bureau did not invent the threat for Gamelin's benefit. Diplomats reported that the Dutch government was genuinely frightened, possibly as a result of a warning passed to the Dutch military attaché in Berlin by his good friend Colonel Hans Oster of the Abwehr.[14] Romania was another favorite candidate, the logic being that Germany needed Romanian oil, and the evidence being loud and crude German protests against the Romanian government's execution of some members of the proto-Nazi Iron Guard and editorials in a Berlin daily identified with Göring denouncing the king's mistress, Magda Lupescu, as a Jewess.[15] Oddly, though Deuxième Bureau and SR memoirs say otherwise, there is no documentary evidence of warnings that Hitler would seize the remainder of Czechoslovakia until a few days before he hailed President Hácha to Berlin and harassed him into inviting a German takeover.[16]

Deuxième Bureau data on the German armed forces meanwhile continued to buttress Gamelin's pleas for more money. At the beginning of 1939, the Deuxième Bureau estimated that Germany had an army of 1.2 million, with five Panzer divisions and four divisions of motorized infantry. It credited the Luftwaffe with having three thousand modern planes operational and having achieved capacity to produce planes at a rate of a thousand a month. It also described a rapidly growing network of more than five hundred well-protected airfields. In February, consistently with its practice in past years, the Deuxième Bureau warned that Germany had another 1.5 million men under arms in party organizations, which "consecrate the totality of their energies on the one hand to providing the army with recruits who have had thorough physical training and very advanced technical instruction and, on the other hand, to maintain this training and instruction among reservists, not to mention their propaganda activity, oriented toward the regime's objectives of conquest."[17]

Daladier continued to bend to Gamelin's urgings. By the beginning of March, he became comfortable with a plan for committing 64.8 billion francs for the next phase of rearmament. It frustrated him that the legislative chambers failed to vote the full appropriations he requested. Moreover, he concluded that the goals for domestic production of planes and other armaments would be met only by further lengthening the workweek. During the first or second week of March, he decided to seek a new and much longer extension of power to govern by decree.[18]

Then came Hitler's takeover of what remained of Czechoslovakia. Daladier now said publicly that any hope of diplomatic accord with Germany was dead, and that the word of the German government could not be trusted. In a radio address to the nation, as his biographer, Élisabeth du Réau, points out, Daladier abandoned his earlier refrain about France's desire for peace. Instead of "peace," she notes, the dominating nouns in his address were "power" and "force."[19]

Three days after German troops marched into Prague, Daladier obtained renewed power to govern by decree, this time for a period of eight months. Communists and socialists again opposed him, with Blum charging that he wanted a "personal dictatorship," and eighteen left-wing Radicals voted with the opposition. But Daladier's majority was nevertheless comfortable—321–264 in the Chamber and 268–17 in the Senate. As soon as he had the power, he ordered spending for defense at the levels that he had proposed but the chambers had dawdled over. He also issued orders extending service for reservists and otherwise increasing the number of men under arms.

To his cabinet, Daladier said, "There is nothing more to do than prepare for war." A Finance Ministry economist, Alfred Sauvy, who happened to attend a meeting of a cabinet subcommittee, recalled Daladier's response to a proposal for an agricultural subsidy: "We should not devote a single dollar of our reserves to nonmilitary purposes. It is indeed necessary to go further: the dollars and gold of which we dispose should be devoted entirely to the purchase of airplanes in the United States." Indicating that he remained more sympathetic with Vuillemin than with Gamelin, he continued: "With that sum, we will be able to create a powerful air fleet, thanks to which we will be able to crush the Ruhr under a deluge of fire, which will lead Germany to capitulate." Sauvy writes that, after a moment of silence, Daladier added, "It is the only means of finishing the war. I do not see another."[20]

The French government's shift to a much harder posture toward Germany was not due simply to reactions to events by Daladier and Gamelin and other ministers and officials. It mirrored, was made possible by, may even have been necessitated by a shift in French public opinion comparable to one of those shifts in the earth's tectonic plates that produce tremors registering on the Richter scale.

The cheering crowds that had greeted Daladier on his return from Munich had been euphoric. The numbers claimed for the crowds were a little artificial, since the Paris Prefecture of Police had stopped cross-traffic and taken other measures that had the effect of forcing people to throng the roadsides,[21] but the sentiment was genuine. It manifested itself also in the Chamber of Deputies, where only de Kérillis and one socialist deputy joined the communists in registering opposition. But it was short-lived.

After Godesberg, the French people seemed to resign themselves to war. They showed none of the exhilaration of 1914. How could they, given memories of what had happened between 1914 and 1918? But all observers agreed that the common inclination was to accept Germany's challenge, fight, and win the war. Ambassador Phipps, sure on September 24 that all the best elements of French society favored appeasement, only a "small, but noisy and corrupt" group opposing, had to report on September 26, after news arrived of Hitler's Godesberg demands, that French public opinion had "undergone a complete change" and that, in Parliament and across the country, there was "a firm and melancholy determination to resist." The French people, he said, were "resigned but resolute," and there was "a fatalistic feeling that war is inevitable now or later."[22] Elation over Munich had been due to a sense of miraculous delivery, but it had not taken long for the revelers to realize that peace had been purchased at the expense of a French ally and with the result of making Hitler's Germany stronger and possibly even more of a menace. The famous flier Antoine de Saint-Exupéry wrote in *Paris-Soir* as early as October 2: "When peace was threatened, we saw the shame of war. When war seemed to menace us, we felt the shame of peace." The British journalist Alexander Werth heard a similar point put more earthily in a conversation between two patrons at the bar of the Café des Capucines in Paris. "All the same, what a relief!" said one. "Hm, yes, but . . ." said the other. "It's the relief that one feels the moment he has wet his pants." By the end of October, well before *Kristallnacht*, the German ambassador in Paris reported hearing mounting criticism of the Munich accords.[23]

At all levels there was evidence of the shame about which Saint-Exupéry had written. Gabriel Péri, a communist deputy and an editor of *L'Humanité*, pricked consciences outside his party with the remark that it had become dangerous to be a friend of France. An idol of the intellectual right, Henry de Montherlant, a writer who, Hemingway-like, preached virility, published a tract accusing his countrymen of having become numb to notions such as honor, courage, pride, and dignity. Catholic writers such as Georges Bernanos, Emmanuel Mounier, Georges Bidault, and Hubert Beuve-Méry attacked the policy of appeasement as fundamentally immoral, ignoring right and wrong. Mounier, editor of *Esprit*, who had originally been sympathetic with German efforts to revise the 1919 peace treaties, even praising the *Anschluss*, denounced the Munich accord as worthy only of "little-minded people besotted with alcohol who think only about their savings." Realists such as Pertinax, Geneviève Tabouis, and Joseph Paul-Boncour kept hammering the argument that, by making concessions to Hitler, France and Britain merely invited ever higher demands.[24]

On the other hand, anyone not a communist who was active in a labor union or a left-wing political party had to face the troubling fact that to criticize Munich or to call for a policy other than appeasement was to side with the communists. For a conservative such as de Kérillis, this was not difficult. He could say that, on this one issue, the communists were not wrong. For those in the center, it was harder, for any lining up with communists risked alienation of the party's right wing. For those on the left, it was harder still, for to them the communists were competitors as well as adversaries. In working-class constituencies and especially within labor unions, leaders on the noncommunist left constantly vied with communists for popularity and leadership. In *Temps présent*, a journal devoted to building up a Catholic working-class movement, Georges Hourdin described the dilemma—"either to fight the communist danger and have the appearance of resigning oneself to the Germanization of France or to fight against the German danger and have the appearance of giving in to Bolshevik penetration."[25] Within all groups previously part of the Popular Front, the six months after Munich witnessed tortured efforts to escape this dilemma.

Many on the right and right center rested their hopes on Bonnet's diplomacy. Former premier Flandin had been a leading advocate of giving Hitler what he asked at Godesberg. He had gone so far as to post placards appealing to the public not to be deceived into a war contrived through "clever machinery . . . mounted . . . by secret forces." After the Munich conference, he had sent a telegram of congratulation to Hitler. Now he wrote and spoke in favor of allowing Hitler a free hand throughout Eastern Europe. The theme was picked up not only by *Notre Temps*, subsidized by Bonnet, but by *Le Matin* and *Le Journal*, each of which had circulation in the hundreds of thousands, and by *Paris-Soir*, the most popular daily in France, with circulation approaching two million. Along with the more pretentious small-circulation periodicals of the extreme right, these journals said that France had no reason to oppose Germany's satisfying its economic needs by gaining control of and developing backward areas such as the Ukraine.[26]

But calls for conceding German control over Central and Eastern Europe seemed to lack wide appeal. Several deputies and senators who belonged to Flandin's Alliance Démocratique resigned from the party. (As Élie Bois observes, it was an odd party, less one "with deep roots in the country than a kind of mutual assistance society for politicians who considered themselves eligible for ministerial rank."[27]) Radicals, meeting at Marseilles at the end of October, preserved an appearance of harmony. Daladier so organized the proceedings that most votes were direct tests of willingness to cooperate with the communists. Few Radicals were willing to vote yes, no matter how they felt about the policy symbolized by Munich. As a result, the party congress seemed to give the government solid backing.[28] Radical newspapers indicated, however, that, on resolutions differently framed, many party leaders would now have expressed misgivings about a policy of making concessions to Hitler in order to preserve peace.

Among socialists, the torment was obvious. French political parties held congresses at least once a year, when their parliamentary delegations received guidance from delegates representing local party organizations. In the case of the Socialist Party, the congress usually followed a congress of the CGT, itself preceded by congresses of its major constituent unions. Since the Communist CGTU had merged with the CGT in March 1936, these congresses often served as tests of the socialist versus communist strength within organized labor.

At a CGT meeting at Nantes in mid-November, the communists demanded condemnation of what had been done at Munich. Leaders in some of the noncommunist unions, particularly those of teachers and others in the public sector, saw this as a ploy to strengthen the communist position within the confederation. They stuck, therefore, to the line they had taken during the crisis—that the unions should not allow "military fanfare" to divert them from their struggle on behalf of the working class. With pacifist labor leaders as allies, they managed a strong minority vote—6,419 against 16,784, with 1,046 abstaining. The number of noncommunists in the majority was, however, the most significant fact. The CGT congress bore witness to labor's disillusionment with Munich and appeasement and served as a warning to socialist leaders that they would have a hard time retaining support of union members if they persisted in being *munichois*.

The extent of this disillusionment became still more apparent at the end of December, when the Socialist Party held its congress at Montrouge, just south of Paris. Blum, the party leader, had been labeled a warmonger by advocates of appeasement—less because of what he had said or done than because, as the Popular Front premier, he symbolized cooperation with communists, and because he was a Jew. He had done his best to maintain party solidarity, expressing disagreement with the pacifists only through qualifying phrases—as, for example, in a pre-Munich *Populaire* editorial saying, "Peace *can* and *ought* to be preserved, at least if Chancellor Hitler is not inflexibly resolved to impose his will by force."[29] At the Montrouge congress, Blum introduced a resolution characterizing as unacceptable any "transaction or concession extorted under the threat of war." Despite vehement opposition from Paul Faure and other pacifists, the motion carried 4,322–2,837, with 1,014 abstentions.[30]

Analysts of French politics came to speak less often of right versus left than of *munichois* versus *antimunichois*. Month by month, even week by week, the *munichois* bloc seemed to lose strength. The mini-crisis with Italy early in 1939 was costly to the *munichois*, because many on the right had been insisting that France should oppose Germany, if at all, only in partnership with Italy and, ideally, with Franco's Spain. Some of their arguments had had to do with exposed flanks, others with avoiding dependence on Britain or alignment with Soviet Russia. Applause for Daladier's defiance of Mussolini served as a means by which politicians and editors, especially those with Catholic associations, could distance themselves from the "peace at any price" position.

In March 1939, Hitler's seizure of Czechoslovakia led to mass desertions from *munichois* ranks. By an overwhelming margin, the CGT voted a no-strike pledge on the ground of the urgency of preparing national defense. The teachers' union, which had mobilized 150,000 signatures in 1938 on a petition against fighting for Czechoslovakia, declared now that the time for appeasement had passed. Robert Lazurick, a socialist deputy and editor of the weekly *Justice*, previously in the camp of Paul Faure, turned completely around. He made no apologies for having applauded Munich, he wrote, but now saw no alternative to telling Hitler that any next move would mean war.[31]

Though important French political figures such as Flandin and Laval continued to argue for accommodating Germany, and though essentially pacifist constituencies still populated the Socialist Party and a number of labor unions, the French body politic had profoundly changed. In September 1938, prior to Godesberg, Daladier had reckoned that strong right-wing and left-wing groups might be prepared to take to the streets if the government called for war in behalf of Czechoslovakia. In March 1939, he had to reckon with the possibility that crowds would take to the streets if the government did not show itself willing to risk war to prevent Hitler from making some other state his victim.

In Britain, a similar mood change was evident. As in France, indignation over Godesberg had been followed by elation over the Munich conference. Churchill spoke for only a minority when he likened Chamberlain's transactions with Hitler to those between a traveler and a highwayman. Comparing the Berchtesgaden, Godesberg, and Munich meetings, he said: "One pound was demanded at the pistol's point. When it was given, two pounds were demanded at the pistol's point. Finally, the Dictator consented to take £1 17s. 6d. and the rest in promises of good will for the future."[32] Churchill characterized the Munich agreement as "a defeat without a war." But the applause for his words was not that of a scattered minority. Labour and Liberal spokesmen also attacked Chamberlain, and more than thirty Conservatives abstained from voting confidence in the government.

Chamberlain himself was quite satisfied with what had happened at Munich. He believed that he had exercised statesmanship of a high order. "I sincerely believe that we have at last opened the way to that general appeasement which alone can save the world from chaos," he wrote to the archbishop of Canterbury.[33] He said to his Cabinet that he believed Hitler would now be willing to enter into disarmament agreements, and Britain would be relieved of an economic burden which, if not lifted, "might break our backs."[34] He congratulated himself on having prevailed over "weak-kneed colleagues" who would have abandoned appeasement.[35] On March 12, 1939, he wrote to his sister Ida, "Like Chatham, 'I know that I can save this country and I do not believe that anyone else can.' "[36]

Only three days after this boastful letter, Hitler seized the non-German remainder of Czechoslovakia. Chamberlain reacted with puzzlement more than alarm. Answering a question in the House of Commons, he declined to describe Hitler's action as violating understandings reached at Munich. He said only that it had not been "contemplated by any of the signatories." He went on, "Though one may have to suffer checks and disappointments from time to time, the object which we have in mind is of too great significance to the happiness of mankind for us lightly to give it up or set it on one side."[37]

Chamberlain quickly learned that his language had been too cool and legalistic. During the previous winter, Conservative candidates had lost by-elections in two supposedly safe constituencies, with disapproval of appeasement reportedly a factor in both cases. Halifax and others told Chamberlain that he had somehow to quiet members of his own party who interpreted Hitler's march into Prague as not only repudiation of his promises to Chamberlain but evidence that the entire policy of appeasement had been mistaken.[38]

Chamberlain responded by giving a speech at Birmingham in which he declared that, though he was "not prepared to engage this country in new unspecified commitments," it would be a great mistake for anyone to suppose that Britain would not go to war if convinced that another power was attempting "to dominate the world by force." Although first returns registered public approval of these words, Halifax wanted more. Using what he probably knew to be dubious evidence that Hitler might be planning an immediate surprise attack on either Romania or Poland, he pressed Chamberlain to consider "a public pronouncement that we should resist any further act of aggression on the part of Germany."[39]

On the last day of March, Chamberlain rose in the House of Commons and issued an apparently unqualified guarantee that Britain would defend

Poland if Poland were attacked by Germany. A government that a half-year earlier had resisted going to war for a faraway country with democratic institutions, well-armed military forces, and strong fortifications now promised with no apparent reservations to go to war for a dictatorship with less-than-modern armed forces and wide-open frontiers.

Chamberlain's statement gratified those who had criticized his earlier language. It also wakened among officials concern lest the guarantee to Poland be tested. General Sir Henry Pownall, the army's chief operations planner, who had been conniving to get a commitment of ground forces to the continent, commented in his diary, "A continental commitment with a vengeance!," adding, "But I'm sure it's the right policy. The only way to stop Hitler is to show a firm front."[40] Sir Maurice Hankey, recently retired after many years as secretary of the Committee of Imperial Defence, wrote worriedly to Ambassador Phipps in Paris, "The whole point is that we cannot save these eastern nations. . . . We shall look terribly silly if [Polish leader Józef] Beck refuses to play with us and sillier still if Hitler goes in and knocks Poland out and we fail to help."[41] This objection was all the more telling because Admiral Lord Chatfield, Inskip's successor as minister for the coordination of defense, had just told the Cabinet that Poland on its own could not hold out against Germany for more than two or three months, and all the chiefs of staff had concurred.[42]

The French government, though surprised by Chamberlain's speech, immediately seconded the guarantee to Poland. Then, on April 7, Paris and London alike received the dumbfounding news that Italy had attacked Albania. Chamberlain complained to his sister Hilda that Mussolini had behaved toward him "like a sneak and a cad. He has not made the least effort to preserve my friendly feelings."[43] Informed from Bucharest that Italy's action made the Romanian government anxious about possible attacks by both Italy and Germany, Daladier decided to show Chamberlain that he, too, could show initiative. For a long time, he had been hearing the argument that it was crucially important to prevent Germany's gaining control of Romania, for Germany's chief long-run weakness was shortage of natural resources, and possession of Romanian oilfields would significantly reduce that weakness. When the Deuxième Bureau sent him a report that a "very reliable" source described Germany as getting ready for action against Romania, he had Gauché forward the report to London, and he informed Chamberlain that he intended to announce a guarantee of Romania and of Greece.[44]

Though some officials in Whitehall questioned the wisdom of these additional guarantees, Chamberlain and his Cabinet decided to go along with

Daladier. Chamberlain explained that he did not think it important to distinguish among states being guaranteed or to make calculations about whether a particular state could or could not be protected by Britain and France. "The real issue," he said, "was that, if Germany showed signs that she intended to proceed with her march for world domination, we must take steps to stop her. . . . We should attack Germany not in order to save a particular victim but in order to pull down the bully."[45]

Thus, by mid-April 1939, the French and British governments had gone about as far as possible in warning that they would not stand by peacefully if Germany made a surprise military move. Previously, newspaper clippings and other sources had led Hitler to presume that the Western powers would not resort to war. Weizsäcker had feared in 1938 that Hitler was wrong and he had been surprised, though delighted, that war did not occur. Hitler, however, seemed unable to perceive the changes that should have been evident in those clippings. He said to his press chief, it will be recalled, à propos of the takeover of Czechoslovakia in March 1939: "In two weeks no one will say another word about it."[46] He was probably too much disposed to presume that the past predicted the future, and too much inclined to notice the clippings that jibed with this expectation while ignoring those that did not. Captain Bürkner of the Abwehr probably contributed by sending him agent reports that exaggerated the strength in France of far-right anti-Semitism, and in Britain of Sir Oswald Mosley's British Union of Fascists.

Weizsäcker, though fearful that the manner of Germany's move into Prague might stiffen backs in France and Britain, continued to believe that, with deft management, Germany could take Memel or Danzig or the Polish Corridor, perhaps even precipitate "chemical dissolution" in Poland, without war in the West. Germans assessing France and Britain failed to perceive how their own actions had affected the mix of value judgments that shaped decisions in those two nations.

CHAPTER FOURTEEN

ACCEPTING WAR

"Make it impossible for the other side to win except at such cost as to make it not worthwhile. That is what we are doing and . . . they [the Germans] will presently come to recognize that it never *will* be worthwhile. Then we can talk."   —*Chamberlain to his sister Hilda Chamberlain, July 23, 1939*

With the guarantees of Poland and Romania, Britain and France had shifted from appeasement to deterrence. Before Germany had taken Prague, Chamberlain had supposed that Hitler was primarily a nationalist intent on tearing up the Versailles *Diktat*. He sometimes entertained alternative hypotheses, but not often. Though Halifax had abandoned this supposition after having seen Hitler's Godesberg demands, Chamberlain had clung to it. But after March 1939, both men adopted the supposition that Hitler had larger ambitions. Along with most of their officials and of ministers and officials in France, they also supposed that, however large Hitler's ambitions, he would attempt to realize them only if reasonably sure that the gains would be greater than the costs. If Hitler saw that his actions would lead to war with France and Britain, they presumed, he would hold back. The less the chance of his having an illusion that Germany might win such a war, the more certain this would be. "Make it impossible for the other side to win except at such cost as to make it not worthwhile," Chamberlain explained to his sister Hilda. "That is what we are doing and . . . they [the Germans] will presently come to recognize that it never *will* be worthwhile. Then we can talk."[1]

Daladier had never accepted the premise that Hitler was just another German nationalist. In one of his first meetings with Chamberlain, he had said, "The ambitions of Napoleon were far inferior to the present aims of the German Reich."[2] He had gone along with Chamberlain partly from unwillingness to act independently of Britain, partly from hope that, whether Chamberlain's premise was right or wrong, diplomacy might somehow avert a new Great War. Since French diplomats and attachés and secret agents reported growing malaise among the German public and disaffection on the part of military officers, bureaucrats, and businessmen, Daladier may have hoped that Nazi Germany would somehow come apart, even if Hitler were meanwhile achieving diplomatic successes. As his preoccupation with French rearmament indicated, he also held steadily to an assumption that, if Hitler remained in power, the best hope of preventing war lay in making him see an unfavorable military balance. After Prague, therefore, Daladier and Chamberlain were thinking alike.

After the guarantees of Poland and Romania, the British government bolstered its effort at deterrence by instituting conscription. Since in the Great War Britain had waited two years to take this step, it seemed dramatic evidence of determination to fight.

The reasons were tangled. Partly as a by-product of staff talks with the French, British army officers had won from their own government bit-by-bit increases in the number of British troops promised to France in the event of war. The level had risen high enough so that the army staff had begun to argue for calling up reserves *and* introducing conscription.

Halifax came independently to favor conscription because he thought it would impress Hitler. This was a contention he had heard from both Daladier and Gamelin, and officials in the Foreign Office believed that the French government wanted it enough to trade for it concessions on almost any other matters.[3]

Chamberlain's own reasoning moved differently. Concerned still about a possible German attempt at a knockout blow, he wanted searchlights and anti-aircraft batteries manned. A surprise attack, he wrote Ida, "didn't seem to me in the least probable, but with this fanatic you can't exclude entirely the conception."[4] His legal advisers told him that, to call up reserves for this purpose, he would need a declaration of national emergency. This, he feared, would send too strong a signal to Berlin. He wanted Hitler to believe that Britain would go to war if necessary, but he did not want to give an impression that Britain had abandoned hope of achieving general appeasement through diplomacy. Conscription seemed to him a way of accommodating the army, Halifax, and Daladier while getting crews for those lights and guns without unduly alarming Berlin.[5]

During the spring of 1939, Britain and France also opened negotiations with the Soviet Union. In both countries, this step involved mixed motives and mixed feelings. Despite the recent difficulties with Italy, Bonnet and his supporters continued to hope that Mussolini could be somehow separated from Hitler, and they feared that any flirtation with Moscow would kill this possibility. Independently, many on the right wing in French politics still regarded the communist Soviet Union as no better than Nazi Germany and possibly worse, a view shared by many senior military officers. Moreover, it was a common opinion within the French officer corps that, if any military strength had survived in Russia, it had been vitiated by Stalin's recent purges.

Daladier, however, believed that an apparent alliance with the Soviet Union might help deter Hitler. Also, he knew that many people in France agreed and would criticize the government if it did not seek such an alliance. As for Gamelin, he doubted that either Poland or Romania could hold out long against Germany and was disinclined to plan a prompt French offensive as a means of rescuing them. Hence, Gamelin favored approaching the Soviet Union in the hope of ensuring that, if war came, Germany would have to fight continuously on two fronts. Together, Daladier and Gamelin made enough headway against skeptics in the cabinet and the bureaucracy so that, on April 24, the French government broached to London joint negotiations with the U.S.S.R. about possible military cooperation.[6]

Even before the public guarantees to Poland and Romania, the British government had suggested asking both Warsaw and Moscow to join in warning Hitler against any further aggression. Bonnet had consented, but the project died when the Polish government said that it would not agree to any association with the U.S.S.R.

Now the French government put before Chamberlain and Halifax a proposal that might result in Britain's being obliged to pressure the Polish government to change its position. The prospect made both men squeamish. They may have been inclined to think that the British and French guarantees, standing alone, had more deterrent effect on Hitler than would joint

British-French-Soviet guarantees. The astute historian R.A.C. Parker believes that Chamberlain and Halifax thought Hitler saw Britain and France
as opposing him on principle whereas, if the Soviet Union joined in, he
would see them as trying to encircle Germany.[7]

Both men abhorred communism. Halifax felt such distaste for the Soviet
Union that he always found excuses for not meeting the Soviet ambassador.
Chamberlain wrote to his sister Ida: "I must profess to the most profound
distrust of Russia."[8] But, like Daladier in Paris, Chamberlain and Halifax
had to reckon with a wider public. An approach to Moscow had all along
had support among the Labour opposition, and after the guarantee to
Poland, it gained the added support of Lloyd George, who, though without
much of a party of his own, continued to be considered a possible strongman in case the country someday needed one. Lloyd George said in the
House of Commons, "If we are going in without help from Russia we are
walking into a trap."[9] Hence, despite their personal distaste, Chamberlain
and Halifax eventually agreed that a French-British mission should go to
Moscow.

Gamelin genuinely wanted a military understanding. He chose for the
French delegation General Joseph-Aimé Doumenc, an outstanding logistical planner, one of his strong supporters in the campaign to mechanize and
motorize the army, and the man whom he would later pick to be his chief of
staff in the event that he assumed command of Allied forces in the field. He
informed the British government of Doumenc's appointment several days
before he informed Doumenc himself.[10]

Interested more in appearing to want an understanding than in actually
getting one, the British government sent a delegation of two admirals and
one relatively junior army officer. The senior admiral, though an accomplished staff officer, hardly had his heart in the task: he had recently
helped to draft a memorandum arguing that any closer relationship with the
Soviet Union would antagonize Spain, which was militarily more important.[11] As the British delegation proceeded to Moscow slowly by sea, Daladier and Gamelin displayed mild impatience. Chamberlain told his sister
Ida that the eagerness of the French to come to terms with the Soviet Union
"thoroughly disgusted" him.[12]

The Nazi-Soviet pact nevertheless shocked London as well as Paris. On
August 22, Tass, the official Soviet news service, disclosed that Ribbentrop

was flying to Moscow. Daladier and Gamelin surmised almost at once that Germany and the Soviet Union were about to make a deal. Though Coulondre had consistently pooh-poohed the possibility, and he was supposedly an expert on both the Soviet Union and Germany, others, including his own air attaché, had periodically noted signs to the contrary. In April, the Deuxième Bureau had noted that Hitler, in a speech railing against Germany's many enemies, had omitted a diatribe against the Soviet Union, and in May, it had circulated unconfirmed SR reports that German representatives in Moscow had secretly broached a possible German-Soviet partition of Poland. Probably from similar reportage, Halifax remarked to the British Cabinet on May 24 that the possibility "of some rapprochement between Germany and Russia was not one which could be disregarded." Speculation to this effect was picked up in May by an Associated Press correspondent in Berlin, and in June by a Hearst International News Syndicate correspondent in Geneva. Chamberlain commented to Hilda that members of his Cabinet were urging a more serious effort for a pact with the Soviets on the ground that Stalin might otherwise come to terms with Hitler, which, he said, was "a pretty sinister commentary on Russian reliability."[13] Nevertheless, neither Daladier nor Chamberlain seemed prepared for the amazing news that Stalin and Hitler had actually come to terms.

The Nazi-Soviet pact raised two difficult questions. First, did it make a German move against Poland or another country to the east more likely? In view of the much-publicized negotiations between the Western powers and the Soviet Union and the fact that Germany's Eastern neighbors were now isolated, Hitler might conclude that he had succeeded in undercutting the British and French guarantees to them. Second, should Britain and France in fact maintain the guarantees, given that it was now unlikely that Germany would have to fight a sustained two-front war? Both the French and the British had agreed that, if there were a war, an Eastern front would be "essential."[14]

The evidence that Hitler was preparing military action in the East, probably against Poland, had continued to accumulate while the French-British negotiations with the Soviets were going on. In the spring of 1939, Gauché had told Gamelin that "an excellent source" confirmed earlier predictions that Poland would be Hitler's next target.[15] In May, he had described a buildup of German troops on the Polish frontier, cited an "excellent source" as reporting that the German general staff expected an order to attack Poland, and mentioned an "uncontrolled source" as describing a general-staff plan for a seventy-division pincer movement,[16] despite Coulondre's saying that he could find no sign of any of this. In early June, Rivet had written in his diary, "Letter from H.E.: watch out for the end of August!"[17] Gauché covered himself by saying that other hypotheses could still not be ruled out, that Hitler had not finally committed himself, and that Germany could yet retreat or turn elsewhere, as, for example, against Hungary.[18] But by mid-August, the Deuxième Bureau had ceased to express any doubt that Hitler was preparing to act against Poland in a matter of weeks. By his own account, Gauché went to see Colson and said, "General, we find ourselves today, as last year with regard to the Sudetenland, looking at the most nearly perfect form of work that the Deuxième Bureau could hope to achieve. It is not humanly possible to come closer to the truth."[19]

As soon as he had news of the Nazi-Soviet pact, Daladier convened his cabinet. Mandel and Reynaud urged immediate mobilization: this would signal that France still intended to honor the guarantees and at the same time ready the country for war if Hitler refused to be deterred. Bonnet argued the exact contrary. A journalist who saw him at the Quai d'Orsay answering questions about the Nazi-Soviet pact wrote later that "a sort of irresistible gaiety played across his face."[20] He and his constant ally, Anatole de Monzie, minister of public works, maintained that France and Britain should find a tactful way of saying that conditions had changed and the guarantees to Poland and Romania were no longer valid. Bonnet and de Monzie were now supported by Deputy Prime Minister Camille Chautemps, a cautious Radical centrist, who said that France should not risk war in behalf of a nation in Central or Eastern Europe unless "the Russian shield were in place."[21] That night, dining with his friend Ambassador Bullitt, Daladier asked if there were any chance of President Roosevelt's calling for a conference to find a way of preserving peace. He clearly clung to hope that war might yet be avoided.[22]

The next day, kiosks in Paris were papered with banner headlines: "NAZIS AND COMMUNISTS ALLIES! POLAND SURROUNDED!" Daladier summoned Bonnet, the ministers of the air force and navy, Gamelin, and other key military and naval officers to his vast second-floor conference room at the War Ministry. He gave them little notice—Gamelin only about thirty minutes. There, surrounded by giant tapestries illustrating French victories in the wars of Louis XIV, he had Bonnet reiterate his argument for declaring the guarantee to Poland null and void. Daladier had not invited either Mandel or Reynaud, possibly because he did not want to hear again their objections to Bonnet's thesis.

Turning to the service ministers and men in uniform, Daladier asked whether France was militarily capable of maintaining the guarantee to Poland. The official notes record Gamelin's joining Darlan in "indicating that the army and navy are ready." Later, Gamelin professed to have meant only that the army was ready to mobilize with more dispatch than in 1938, not that it was ready for operations. But no contemporaneous record indicates that his statement was qualified other than by his cautioning, as did Darlan, that French armed forces "could do little against Germany" at the outset of a conflict but that "French mobilization in itself would provide a certain relief to Poland." Though Air Minister La Chambre described the French air force as still inferior to Germany's, he said that, taking account of what Britain could contribute, "the situation of our air force need no longer weigh on the decisions of the Government, as it had in 1938."[23]

The meeting decided nothing. Three days later, when Coulondre telephoned from Berlin, Daladier spoke of his continuing hope that something could be worked out. He had just sent off a letter to Hitler, appealing to him as one front-line soldier to another, both recognizing the horrors of the Great War.[24] Coulondre, wrong earlier about the possibility of a German-Russian deal, misjudged once again. He understood Hitler to be getting a variety of advice. He believed that Göring sided with the armed forces in urging caution, that Ribbentrop and Himmler were advocates of action, and that Hitler was still undecided. He believed Hitler to be impressed, as in 1938, with the antiwar sentiment evident among the Berlin public. He convinced himself that Hitler would back down if he thought that France and Britain would actually go to war in support of Poland. By every channel, he communicated this opinion to Paris and to London. Since he and Daladier were old friends who reportedly conversed over the telephone in Provençal, he certainly had the ear of his own government.[25]

At meeting after meeting in Daladier's War Ministry offices, Bonnet pleaded for time to test possibilities for negotiation. He reported that Mussolini was willing to intervene, as in 1938, if given a go-ahead by the French and British. On August 31, while Daladier listened to debate about whether or not to encourage Mussolini, a messenger brought in a personal letter from Coulondre. "We must continue to hold on, hold on, hold on. You are a fisherman, I know. Well, the fish is hooked. Now we must maneuver with finesse, so we can catch him without his breaking the line." Léger used a different analogy. He was heard saying over the phone, "We are playing a game of poker; our adversary is bluffing."[26]

Daladier told Bonnet to prepare a communication accepting Mussolini's offer but not to send it until he knew the British reaction. The next day, Halifax said that, though the British government could not agree to another Munich conference, it could not be in the position of having rejected a peaceful solution.[27] A note went off to Rome. By then, however, German troops had crossed the Polish frontier.

Though Daladier had already authorized most of the measures that put France on a war footing, he accepted Bonnet's plea for another twenty-four to forty-eight hours to see if there were not some peaceful way out. He told the rest of the Cabinet that it would not hurt to have that much time for continuing mobilization. And he decided not to convene the Chamber of Deputies and Senate for a formal declaration of war but simply to give notice, at the appropriate moment, that Germany, by attacking Poland, had created a state of war.

Chamberlain had been less shaken than Daladier by the Nazi-Soviet pact. He had presumed since spring that fear of war with France and Britain, particularly Britain, would deter Hitler, and he remained hopeful that this would be the case. Hitler might provoke a crisis with Poland on a narrow issue where the German case was strong, he thought, as, for example, the status of the essentially German city of Danzig or the rights of Germans transiting the Polish Corridor from Germany proper to isolated East Prussia. As his friends at *The Times* had hastened to emphasize back in March, the British government had guaranteed only Poland's independence, not its integrity. Regarding Danzig or the Corridor, he expected the House of Commons and the public to applaud Britain's acting as broker, and he believed that Hitler would agree to compromise. "I can't help thinking," he commented of Hitler in a July 1939 letter to Hilda, "that he is not such a fool as some hysterical people make out and that he would not be sorry to compromise if he could do so without what he would feel to be humiliation."[28]

Chamberlain was all the more hopeful because the British rearmament effort had continued, and he assumed that Hitler was mindful of this fact. "Hitler has concluded that we mean business and that time is not ripe for a major war," he wrote during the summer.[29] He saw no reason to change this opinion because of the reversal in relations with the Soviet Union.

Having been told that August 26 was Hitler's deadline for moving against Poland, Chamberlain became optimistic when the deadline passed. He and his closest aides then pursued every will-of-the-wisp suggestion that Berlin might be prepared to discuss compromise. On September 2, after German troops and planes had been on the attack in Poland for more than twenty-four hours, Chamberlain continued to flirt with the idea of proposing to Hitler an immediate armistice to be followed by a Munich-style conference. He had a grace period because of France's delay in declaring war and Halifax's accepting the view that Britain ought not to declare war ahead of France.

But time ran out. Chamberlain was told that Tory backbenchers would rise in revolt if the government did not immediately carry out its threat to declare war. Twelve Cabinet members met in caucus in the chambers of Chancellor of the Exchequer Sir John Simon. They agreed to warn Chamberlain that his government could not survive another day of delay, regardless of what France did. Shortly before midnight, Chamberlain gathered his Cabinet and accepted a vote for war. On the following morning, looking "crumpled, despondent, and old," he made a radio broadcast to the country, saying, "Everything that I have worked for, everything that I have believed in during my public life has crashed into ruins." To his sisters, he complained that "the House of Commons was out of hand" and that some of his colleagues had gotten up "a sort of mutiny." When Halifax notified the French government of Britain's action, Daladier made his planned announcement. Both Britain and France were formally at war with Germany.[30]

The actions of Britain and France puzzled Hitler and dismayed Weizsäcker. Both men thought that they were illogical, and, of course, they were. Many in the British and French governments recognized that, absent an agreement with the Soviet Union, there was not much either country could or would do to provide direct aid to Poland. General Gamelin had told both his own government and the British government that he did not plan a major offensive. Both governments, having concluded solemnly that in any war Germany should have to fight on two fronts, now entered on what seemed almost certain to become soon a one-front war. Since both nations were in the midst of building up their military forces, it should not have been hard to reason that it would be wiser to accelerate preparations for war and to defer commencing it. The decisions of September 1939 cannot easily be characterized as outcomes of cool calculation.

Of the factors explaining the British and French decisions, the most obvious was the sense that enough was enough. Hitler had not been stopped from remilitarizing the Rhineland or taking over Austria or taking portions, then all, of Czechoslovakia. He could not be allowed to get away with yet one more conquest. Britain and France, having pledged to fight for Poland, were honor bound to keep their word. These were sentiments best not rationalized, though Leslie Hore-Belisha, the British war minister, tried to do so, writing to Halifax that if Britain did not stand by Poland it would lose Romania and Turkey: "In this way, the balance of power in Europe would be finally tilted against us, and we should be left in any dispute with Germany to rely solely upon the French"[31]—hardly unanswerable reasoning.

Behind exasperation was another crucial factor in the declarations of war and much else that happened in 1939–40. This was the belief in Allied military superiority pervasive in both Britain and France. In light of the quick defeat of France in the spring of 1940, the scuttle of British troops via Dunkerque, and the subsequent close-run Battle of Britain, expressions of this belief tend to be interpreted after the fact as having been whistles in the dark from men who must have recognized Allied inferiority. Not so. These were expressions of genuine confidence that in fact remained little shaken until May 1940 and was shaken then because the German armed forces achieved a surprise that compensated—indeed, compensated many times over—for the *German* military inferiority, which the Allies had recognized. A young civil servant remembered later having heard Gamelin say that, if war actually came, French forces would re-enter Germany like a knife in butter. Michel Debré, one of Reynaud's entourage at the Ministry of Finance (and a later prime minister), recalled hearing General Georges, commander of Allied armies on the Western front, express similar confidence. Though Reynaud and his friends held that the army had been mistaken not to follow the prescription of de Gaulle (and Guderian) for full-fledged armored divisions, they never doubted, Debré says, France's superiority in ground forces.[32]

Of course, many individuals in France and Britain wanted desperately to avoid war. Some in France believed that the costs of a new Great War would ruin their country, but they mostly believed the ruin would result from the cost of victory, not from defeat. Some reckoned these potential costs primarily in terms of lost lives or money, whereas others feared social dislocation, especially if France ended up an impoverished victor in a Europe with a thriving communist U.S.S.R. As the French historian Robert Frankenstein writes, "Since the Russian example of 1917, the propertied classes saw in war risks of revolution."[33] Such concerns occupied Bonnet and others who kept pressing for negotiations that would at least postpone a war. But in records from earlier than May 1940, it is hard to find anyone in France predicting or foreseeing anything but an eventual Allied victory. Of the self-doubt so evident in the mid-1930s, there remained hardly a trace. The civil-war scare of February 1934 was now half a decade in the past. The disintegration of the Popular Front and especially the fizzling of the general strike at the end of 1938 reassured France's elites. An economic boom starting in 1938 erased most of the earlier worrisome signs of decay. The surge of new defense spending, accompanied by a return to two-year terms of service for conscripts, dissipated the earlier fretfulness of the military. France in 1939 was as different from France in 1936 as the United States in the 1980s, midway through the presidency of Ronald Reagan, was different from the United States of the late 1970s, when President Jimmy Carter bemoaned national "malaise."[34]

Order-of-battle estimates prepared by the Deuxième Bureau, it is true, tended to emphasize German strength, and one can read them as warning of a probable French defeat; Gauché, in his postwar memoir, claims to have called on Colson early in September 1939 to issue such a warning. *"Never at any period in its history,"* he recalled saying, *"has France entered a war in such unfavorable conditions."*[35] But no surviving document of the period shows Gauché actually saying anything of the sort.

Also, it has to be remembered that Deuxième Bureau estimates of German military forces served primarily to support spending briefs. Until 1939, they always emphasized the worst-case implications of any hard evidence. Every indication of a shell of a German division became a division; uniformed party formations became equivalents of reserve units; and boasts by Göring and others about the German air force and German aviation-production capabilities were recorded as descriptions of reality. In 1938, it is clear, Vuillemin and others did genuinely believe that Germany had a lead in air power. Vuillemin credited the Luftwaffe with three, perhaps four, thousand modern warplanes. In private, Gamelin told Daladier that, taking into account the Czechoslovak air force and the RAF, he did not share Vuillemin's alarm.[36] On other occasions when it mattered, Gamelin acknowledged that he also did not take Deuxième Bureau figures on German ground-force strength as bases for serious military or diplomatic planning.

In 1939, with Daladier's government ruling by decree, with Daladier committed to spending every possible franc for defense, and with war coming to seem a much more realistic possibility, the Deuxième Bureau reports ceased to stress Germany's strengths. Early in the year, the Deuxième Bureau was calling attention to serious shortages of both officers and noncommissioned officers in the German army—not surprising, given that it had had hardly any new recruits between 1919 and 1934. Both the Deuxième Bureau and the French mission in Berlin cited evidence of low morale among the German public and in the German armed forces. In June, the SR had reports of high desertion rates from the labor battalions working on the Westwall and in the army itself. Its sources, highly placed within the German government, meanwhile relayed detailed information about the opposition to war among German generals. "Military circles well informed about British and French military power," said one report, "exhibit considerable disquiet about the turn that events could take for Germany."[37]

The French air staff changed position at least ninety degrees. The airmen at last acknowledged the obvious point that, even if German aircraft production were what Göring claimed it to be, Germany did not have enough trained pilots to put even a fraction of those machines in the air. Second, as they compared notes with the RAF and reviewed evidence from SR sources and aerial reconnaissance, they saw reason to conclude that Göring had exaggerated. RAF analysts now said the Luftwaffe had at most three thousand modern planes, not five thousand. Third, they were reassured about their own forces. Air Minister La Chambre had a solid basis for saying in August that the state of the French air force no longer needed to constrain French diplomacy. By the end of 1938, aircraft production had achieved such a rapid pace that manufacturers were talking of laying off workers. Though Vuillemin voiced concern as to whether the air force would have enough trained pilots, La Chambre forced an increase in production targets. Because of the failure of the general strike, employers had become able to exact longer hours from workers. In March 1939, La Chambre had induced the air force to aim at production of eight thousand instead of five thousand new planes, and this on top of orders from the United States. The air staff, previously so glum, now told the minister that France had more than fourteen hundred new planes in service, the British more than eighteen hundred; production in French aircraft plants exceeded two hundred a month; the new French aircraft were mostly fighters, and the British had invested heavily in bombers; France had both fighters and bombers scheduled for delivery from U.S. manufacturers.[38]

However much senior French officers wanted to avoid a war, internal documents of the French general staff showed considerable sangfroid about French prospects should war occur. A highly classified study for 1939, entitled "The French Military Problem," declared that France's fixed fortifications guaranteed safety against any attack. It asserted accurately that

France had better tanks than either Germany or Italy and also that, on evidence from the Spanish Civil War, its doctrine for the use of tanks was "the only one susceptible to producing results in close combat." The study also said, however, that France would be ill-advised to rely on a defensive strategy:

> In the event that France should be exposed *alone* at the outbreak of a sudden conflict to attack by forces of the Rome-Berlin Axis . . . , it would not be good for the conduct of operations if [France] were to dedicate itself to the wearing effects of a defensive war in which it could see the best of its resources melt away before the intervention of the mass of forces of its eventual allies.
>
> Given its particular situation, serious assistance rendered more rapidly and at an opportune point could, on the other hand, provide the possibility of obtaining, with relatively short delay, a victorious outcome of the conflict. This last point is worth pausing over.[39]

This logic underpinned the effort to get a large British force deployed to France. It also underpinned the planning for an offensive against Italy to be conducted by French troops alone if Italy joined Germany in going to war.[40]

After Germany's takeover of the remainder of Czechoslovakia, another highly classified study was prepared within the French War College. Using Deuxième Bureau figures, it ascribed to Germany and Italy the possibility of ultimately mobilizing more than three hundred divisions. France and Britain together would have only 120; the Eastern allies might provide another 150, but they would be uncoordinated and possibly demoralized by air attack. Nevertheless, the study said, at worst France and Britain would prevail as a result of presenting "a solid front with possibilities for strategic defensive maneuver."[41]

On July 2, General Weygand gave a speech at Lille. He had been openly critical of the defense policies of Popular Front governments. Yet in this speech he praised what had been accomplished in the recent rearmament push. France, he declared, had the best-equipped army in the world, and if war came, there was no doubt of French victory. Of course, Weygand hoped that his words would contribute to deterring Germany. He was one of those who feared that war would disrupt France internally. After the war, he would claim to have been trying to bolster public morale and to have known that he was not speaking the truth. But there is not a trace of evidence to support this claim. At the time, he probably believed what he said. Colonel de Lattre de Tassigny, probably the officer in the army closest to Weygand, had said to his wife that Hitler had to be bluffing, for he had to know that if war came he would lose it.[42]

On Bastille Day, July 14, the French government put on public display the results of its rearmament program. Even years later, when he could claim that events had proved the wisdom of his efforts to prevent war, Bonnet recalled the procession of "Algerians, Moroccans, Senegalese, and Indo-Chinese, all those native regiments . . . which are testimony to the extent and power of the French empire . . . cannon of all calibers . . . tanks of all sizes . . . hammering the surface of the Champs-Élysées . . . squadrons, at high and low altitude, flying over Paris, from the Arc de Triomphe to the Obelisk." The army, he wrote, gave "an impression of order, discipline, and irresistible force."[43] This impression was shared by every foreign observer—every single one, including officers from Germany and Italy and from Britain and other nations that would before long be France's allies.

In the introductory part of his moving history of France under German occupation, the writer Henri Amouroux portrays the Bastille Day parade as a pageant masking the reality of France's lack of preparedness for modern war:

> An impressive parade. Well organized to strike the imagination.
>
> A pathetic parade.
>
> Impresssive for the assembled masses—the equipment, the propaganda facilely orchestrated around an event that was reassuring, and deceptive.[44]

In the BBC's evocative *World at War* series, one can see film clips of the parade, with Sir Laurence Olivier reading, in the background voiceover, a script saying that the French army relied for mobility on railways and horses, continuing, after a pregnant pause, "especially the horses."

But Amouroux and others who write or speak as if the French defeat of 1940 were inevitable and even foreknown presume that Hitler's Wehrmacht must have been better prepared, better armed, and less dependent on carts, horses, hay, and shoe leather, and that French and British leaders knew this to be so. In fact, to say again what has to be said more than once, Germany by most quantitative measurements was not nearly so well prepared for a major war as were France and Britain. The Wehrmacht had many fewer vehicles and was much more reliant on horses. Halder estimated that each German infantry division needed forty-five hundred horses and two thousand horse-drawn vehicles. The German army was to commence war in September 1939 with almost six hundred thousand horses and, early in its Western offensive of May–June 1940, was to be suffering a severe shortage of them.[45] German equipment was generally inferior. France's tanks were better gunned, better armored, and more reliable. (As many as half of Germany's basic tanks, the Panzer Is and Panzer IIs, broke down simply propelling themselves across the level plains of Poland. The Panzer IIIs and Panzer IVs, of which they had very few, were the only tanks the Germans themselves thought a match for those of France or Britain.[46]) In dogfights in the fall of 1939, German fighter planes did so badly against French fighters that the Luftwaffe was ordered to avoid one-on-one engagements.[47] If Allied leaders had not believed France and Britain to be militarily at least a match for Germany, exasperation would not have sufficed to produce declarations of war in behalf of Poland.

Even with exasperation and confidence in eventual victory, the French and British governments might still have refrained from going to war in September 1939 had it not been for a third factor: the strength of public opposition in both countries to any further appeasement of Hitler. Daladier and Chamberlain acted as they did because, though both men would have preferred to continue postponing war, both perceived that, if they tried to do so, they would probably be replaced. They would then have to watch other prime ministers do what they had declined to do.

That French and British public opinion demanded war in September 1939 seems hard to credit in light of what was to happen in only nine short months, when Marshal Pétain, Daladier's successor, signed a humiliating peace treaty and Churchill, Chamberlain's successor, acknowledged that there was real risk of the British Isles' being conquered and occupied. (When Churchill spoke in June 1940 of fighting "on the beaches, . . . on the landing grounds, . . . in the fields and in the streets," he was not overdramatizing. He *expected* such fighting, and his chiefs of staff advised him that it would fail and that German invaders would win.[48]) But evidence from 1939—not recollections formed after the fact—indicates that most attentive citizens in both France and Britain had reconciled themselves regretfully to waging and winning a second Great War.

The evidence for France is less clear than that for Britain. Daladier deliberately made it difficult for French public opinion to manifest itself. In April, not long after the German move into Prague, there had been a possibility of some kind of test of sentiment. The seven-year term of President Albert Lebrun came to its end. By tradition, presidents served only one term, and though some presidents had made themselves important, the office itself did not confer power. (Clemenceau once compared its usefulness to that of the prostate gland.) Lebrun had come increasingly to treat it as a place of retirement from which he emerged chiefly for ceremonial orations. There was expected to be a contest for succession among candidates prepared to be more energetic and to stake out stands on major current issues. Among the likely prospects were Daladier himself and his onetime patron but now hostile intraparty rival, former prime minister Herriot, identified now as a critic of appeasement.

Daladier prevented such a contest by proposing that Lebrun be given a second term. The choice of a president lay with the Chamber of Deputies and Senate, meeting together at Versailles as a National Assembly. Daladier asked that everyone vote for Lebrun. Herriot and some others declined to stand aside. Nevertheless, Lebrun received an absolute majority. As one consequence, the Daladier cabinet continued in office unchanged, and no opportunity arose to gauge how strongly the *antimunichois* current had risen after the German march into Prague.

In July, Daladier by decree postponed the parliamentary elections scheduled for the spring of 1940. Though elections had traditionally been held every four years, France's constitutional laws did not stipulate such a term. During the Great War, the two chambers had voted to postpone elections. Using this precedent, Daladier cited the existing emergency as cause for not having elections until 1942. The result was temporarily to free deputies from the need to tell their constituents exactly where they stood on issues such as those dividing *munichois* from *antimunichois*.

The Paris press, despite its links with politicians of all persuasions, seemed unquestionably to register rising opposition to appeasement. Marcel Déat, an independent socialist (USR) allied with Flandin, published in *L'Oeuvre* an editorial concluding, "Die for Danzig, no!"[49] The editors of *L'Oeuvre* published a disclaimer, saying that they did not endorse this reprise of a theme that they themselves had sounded regarding the Sudetenland. Other journals previously *munichois* denounced Déat almost as harshly as did *antimunichois* such as Pertinax and Tabouis. Among these was the *Petit Journal*, associated with Colonel de la Rocque of the Croix de Feu.[50]

Another indicator of a strong shift away from the peace-at-any-price mood of 1938 was the movie box office.[51] The success of a movie was usually due, of course, to its director, cast, or plot more than to its political message. Often, too, the message was obscure or ambiguous.[52] Nevertheless, certain themes strong in movies of the mid-1930s did seem suddenly to lose appeal in the last year or so before the war.

Between 1934 and 1938, many films popular in France had ridiculed parliamentary democracy. A great many had seemed pacifist, or at least antimilitary. As late as the winter of 1937–38, the great commercial and critical successes in Paris had been Jean Renoir's *Grand Illusion*, Abel Gance's remake of *J'accuse*, and Marcel Carné's *Quai des brumes* (*Port of Shadows*). *Grand Illusion* focused on the folly, *J'accuse* on the horror, of war. Set in the Great War, *Grand Illusion* shows the essential brotherhood of French prisoners and their German captors. In one scene, a French professional officer of aristocratic lineage says to a German of similar background, "Perhaps there is no longer a need for us." *J'accuse* ends with skeletons thronging up from battlefield cemeteries to embrace the bones of their enemies. The hero of *Quai des brumes* (played by Jean Gabin), an army deserter hiding out in Le Havre, is portrayed as a person of gleaming morality.

After the *Anschluss*, Parisian moviegoers seemed suddenly to change taste. Léon Mathot, a director who had previously shown a good feel for the Paris market, tried to capitalize on the apparent public exultation over Munich. His *Rappel immédiat* was a drama about a peace conference that saves the world from disaster. It starred Erich von Stroheim, still lionized for his performance as the German camp commander in *Grand Illusion*. It was a total flop.

Renoir, too, lost audiences. *La Marseillaise*, his DeMille-like celebration of the 150th anniversary of the French Revolution, which had been in production since the mid-1930s, had aimed originally at celebrating social revolution. By mid-1938, he added scenes showing French armies rallying in 1793 at the famous Valmy windmill to repel foreign invaders. The emphasis now fell almost as much on "*aux armes*" as on "*citoyens*." Moviegoers and reviewers alike found its message confused, and it was not a success.[53] Then, in July 1939, Renoir released *La Règle du jeu* (*The Rules of the Game*). Though a drama about a murder at a country house, its scenes and dialogue clearly showed the director's purpose, which, as he phrased it later, was to show that "we are dancing on a volcano." The audience at the première had seen a preliminary documentary glorifying the French army in the colonies, which called forth frequent applause. After Renoir's feature came on, the mood changed. Before long, spectators were whistling and booing. Some even set fire to newspapers. The movie soon closed.[54]

More to the apparent taste of Parisian moviegoers in 1939 were films expressing pride in France and especially in the armed forces. Léonide Moguy's *Je t'attendrai*, originally to be entitled *Le Deserteur*, seemed almost a retort to or apology for Carné's *Quai des brumes*. It told of a young soldier who flees for home but, after an hour and a half, remorsefully returns to his troop train. The biggest hit of the summer was Jean-Paul Paulin's *Trois de Saint-Cyr* (*Three from Saint-Cyr*). Every parade-ground episode brought loud cheers. In the same period, the "in" night spot in Paris became L'Amiral, a small club near the Place de l'Étoile where crowds stood to hear bugle sounds accompanying "Mon Légionnaire" and "La Fanion de la Légion" sung by the young Édith Piaf.[55]

Daladier complained to his cabinet that he could not go into a bar or out into a park "without seeing people stand up and cry, 'Lead! We will follow you!'" Louis Aragon, a communist intellectual, commented regretfully, "There is these days a confidence in the prime minister which approaches being a religion."[56] It was later to be argued that, in September, had Daladier asked for a declaration of war, the chambers would have refused it, but the contemporaneous evidence indicates that there would in fact have been large majorities favoring war.

Daladier's decision not to have a parliamentary test, like his allowing Bonnet to continue exploring possibilities for negotiation, were evidence of his own deep disinclination for war. His reading Coulondre's letter aloud to the cabinet and following the advice to "hold on, hold on, hold on" surely indicates his hope that Coulondre and Léger were right, that Hitler was bluffing, and that French and British firmness would persuade him to back down. Daladier's behavior also reflected indecisiveness, perhaps traceable in part to the trauma of 1934, perhaps a necessary quality in someone who spent most of his life cobbling together unstable party and parliamentary combinations. Lucien Lamoureux, a Radical leader who was deputy presiding officer of the Chamber of Deputies, characterized him at this time as "irresolute and frequently changing." More cruelly, the journalist Pierre Lazareff wrote that Daladier had shown himself to be not the Bull of the Vaucluse but "the cow named Vacillation."[57]

PART THREE

PLAN YELLOW

CHAPTER FIFTEEN

NOW FRANCE?

"None of the higher headquarters think that the offensive . . . has any prospect of success." —*General Franz Halder, Diary, November 3, 1939*

In October and November 1939, Hitler's generals debated—and had to decide—whether to model themselves on Seydlitz, Yorck, or Groener—to obey Hitler and march the army to defeat; to find some way of seeming to obey but not doing so; or, as Brauchitsch had put it to Halder at Zossen, to move for "fundamental changes," perhaps deposing Hitler as Groener had deposed the Kaiser in 1918, perhaps even trying to make Hitler a prisoner or to kill him.

In 1938, General Beck had ended up advocating that the army seize power. Halder had backed him. Preparations were being made for army units from the Berlin military district to seize the Chancellory when news arrived of Chamberlain's surprise flight to Berchtesgaden. The plans for a coup were put on hold and then, after Munich, practically ceased, though a few officers, mostly in the Abwehr, continued to talk with dissident civil servants and ex–civil servants about a possible attempt to overthrow Hitler.

Now Hitler's demand for a Western offensive caused Halder to begin thinking along these lines again, as well as other generals, who had kept a greater distance from Beck in 1938. Brauchitsch, for instance, not only broached "fundamental changes" to Halder but was heard musing aloud at

Zossen that Hindenburg and Ludendorff had made the right choice when, in the Great War, they had taken power from the Kaiser and substituted a military dictatorship.[1]

General Stülpnagel, Halder's number two, had been close to Beck, had continued to visit him, and had remained in touch with the Abwehr officers who had never given up thinking of a coup. Among these was Colonel Hans Oster, Canaris's chief deputy, and Lieutenant Colonel Helmuth Groscurth, who was the Abwehr's liaison officer with the army general staff.

In all likelihood, Canaris himself actively aided his subordinates' conspiracies. Canaris was a strange character. There were many such, of course, at the center of the Third Reich, but Canaris stands out among them. A naval officer with a background in derring-do intelligence collection but also a solid record in sea command, he had become head of the Abwehr in 1934 because the billet belonged to the navy and he was the only naval officer whom Blomberg would accept. Five feet four, with prematurely white hair, he detested tall men and, above all, tall men with small ears. The loves of his life were Seppel and Sabine, two dachshunds from whom he was almost inseparable. When traveling, he would require from his staff frequent reports on their apparent emotions and their bowel movements.

In the early 1930s, Canaris seemed to be a committed supporter of Hitler. As late as March 1938, he was exhorting Abwehr officers "to stand foursquare by the National Socialist state."[2] Yet, at the time of the Munich conference only a few months later, he was making statements that caused others to think him a committed opponent of Hitler. When leaving office, Beck said Canaris was the only man who had not disappointed him.[3]

Why he changed—indeed, whether he did—remains unclear. He spent time with Beck. He may have shared Beck's qualms about Hitler's new adventurousness. He may have been outraged by the Blomberg-Fritsch affair or by having to report to Keitel. One possibility is that he and his subordinates kept watch on Himmler and the Gestapo as a potential threat to Hitler, then became gradually convinced that Himmler was acting for Hitler, not against him.[4] There are some indications that he found the regime's anti-Semitism increasingly offensive. Yet another possibility is anger over encroachments in his domain by Reinhard Heydrich, the head of Himmler's security service. Outwardly, his relationship with Heydrich was cordial; the Canarises and the Heydrichs were neighbors and dined together. But Heydrich was thought repulsive by men who had no such reaction to Himmler or Bormann. Also, he was very tall and had small ears.

By 1939, Canaris was allowing the Abwehr to be a center for plotting Hitler's overthrow. He chose Oster to be his deputy even though he knew that Oster was both personally reckless and unguardedly anti-Hitler. As intelligence officer for Halder when Halder was a division commander in the late 1920s, Oster had had an affair with another officer's wife and behaved so badly that Halder had difficulty getting him out of the army without a court-martial. He had managed to get back into uniform by joining the Abwehr and becoming Canaris's favorite tennis partner. The treatment of Fritsch, under whom he had also served, had turned him against the regime, and he made no secret of his change. At Canaris's morning staff meetings, he would make statements that, if reported to the Gestapo, would at least have caused him to be investigated for treason. From October 1939 on, he would alert his friend the Dutch military attaché whenever he heard that Hitler had ordered a Western offensive.

Canaris had chosen Groscurth as his liaison with the armed forces and army high commands. More discreet than Oster but holding identical views, Groscurth was to leave a large set of diaries recording his subversive activities as well as his regular work. He had no doubt that Canaris was spiritually in the same camp with himself and Oster. Yet one combs the entries without finding hard evidence that this was so. To Oster and Groscurth, as to Keitel or even Hitler, Canaris spoke elliptically and ironically, so that whatever he said could be interpreted as either his actual opinion or a mockery of it.[5]

Weizsäcker, who saw a great deal of Canaris, wrote of him after the war that he combined "the cleverness of a snake and the purity of a dove. . . . Canaris had the gift of getting people to talk without revealing himself. His pale blue eyes did not reveal the depth of his being. Very seldom, and then as it were only through a narrow crack, did one get a glimpse of his character."[6]

Even before Brauchitsch and Halder began to discuss "fundamental changes," Stülpnagel had signaled to Oster and Groscurth that they might soon have powerful allies. Oster, Groscurth, and their civilian confederates roughed out a plan, probably with encouragement from Canaris. Army detachments would seize Hitler. General Beck, former Leipzig Lord Mayor Carl Goerdeler, and former Economics Minister Hjalmar Schacht would announce that the Führer was "ill" and that they were temporarily acting on his behalf. Göring and most other Nazi leaders would be arrested. The new triumvirate would then negotiate with the Allies a settlement guaranteeing future peace but leaving Germany in possession of Czechoslovakia and western Poland. As a sympathetic biographer of Beck writes sadly, this plan was marked by "impracticality and utopianism."[7] Goerdeler had for some time been sounding out the British government about these peace terms and had not noticed that every one of his London contacts thought them out of the question.[8] Nevertheless, this was as far as an operational plan had gone when Brauchitsch and Halder began urgently to discuss with other senior officers how the army should respond to Hitler's uncompromising demand for an early Western offensive.

Brauchitsch and Halder found all their field commanders in agreement that the projected offensive had little or no chance of success. Leeb, who had been in sole command in the West throughout the Polish campaign, pronounced defeat of France utterly out of the question. Bock, who was forming a new Army Group in the West, reported that he, his chief of staff, and both of the generals who were to command armies under him, Reichenau and Hans von Kluge, believed that an offensive launched any time soon would be at best costly and inconclusive and at worst a disaster.[9]

On October 17, after Brauchitsch and Halder had begun their soundings of field commanders, Hitler again summoned them to the Chancellory. Halder's notes record Hitler's saying that negotiations had proved hopeless. "The British will be ready to talk only after a beating. We must get at them as quickly as possible. No use holding back." Hitler, wrote Halder, "does not believe that the French can get there fast enough. French infantry [are] not as tough as ours." The offensive should start in mid-November, Hitler said, the exact date to be fixed later, with seven days to be allowed for preparation. On October 22, he specified November 12, which meant that Brauchitsch and Halder were to have everything ready to go by November 5—in less than two weeks.[10]

Brauchitsch and Halder tried one more appeal, this time bringing with them several other officers, including Bock, Reichenau, and Schell, the latter being chiefly responsible for motorized forces. Though the sources recording this October 25 meeting are skimpy, its length makes it likely that Hitler was given details about the balance of forces in the West as estimated by Tippelskirch and the intelligence directorate of the army general staff. By the target date, Bock and Leeb would have seventy-two divisions available for the whole front from the Netherlands to southern Belgium. Those committed to an offensive would face Dutch and Belgian divisions, the former sheltered by a flooded plain, the latter well equipped and well entrenched. Approximately ninety French and British divisions were poised along the Belgian and German borders or were readily movable either by rail or road. At least ten of the forward-deployed French and British divisions were classified as mechanized or motorized. Schell, who had earlier predicted that most German tanks and troop-transport vehicles disabled in Poland would be back in service by early November, now warned that this would probably not be the case. Though the Luftwaffe could commit sixty groups of fighters and Stukas to support an offensive, its intelligence staff estimated that an equivalent number of French and British aircraft were either at the front or in the Paris-Orléans area, and twice as many fighters and bombers on fields in Britain.[11]

Brauchitsch and Halder let Bock and Reichenau take the lead. General Bock had once been close to General Schleicher, a victim of Hitler's 1934 Blood Purge, and was privately disdainful of the Nazis. After *Kristallnacht*, he was heard to ask, "Can't this swine Goebbels be hanged?"[12] But he had a reputation as a cold, highly competent technician uninterested in politics, and he had been one of the successful Army Group commanders in Poland. General Reichenau, of course, had long courted Hitler and was thought in the army to be comparatively pro-Nazi.

Both Bock and Reichenau told Hitler unequivocally that a mid-November offensive would be a mistake. Even with an additional Panzer division, said Bock, his armies could probably not get to Antwerp ahead of French and British forces. His units were likely to be pinned down in circumstances less advantageous than those on the existing front. Only massive coordinated air strikes could prevent defeat, he said, and these would require a long spell of almost perfect weather. Reichenau agreed, and argued further that mud due to the current cold rains would hamper ground operations even if the weather improved. Noting that many of the soldiers in the West were virtually untrained, he urged Hitler to consider how much could be gained if the entire winter were devoted to preparing for a spring offensive.

But Hitler had no patience with these arguments, any more than with those of Brauchitsch and Halder. He suggested that planners narrow the front, possibly concentrating everything into an attack in southern Belgium, where a German breakthrough might prevent France and Britain from joining forces with the Belgians and Dutch. At 7 P.M., he dismissed the generals, telling them perhaps to come up with a revised operation plan, but in any event the offensive would begin on November 12.[13]

Two days later, when Brauchitsch and Halder made another try at talking Hitler out of his deadline, they got nowhere. Hitler said the offensive was to proceed on November 12 and that the final operation order would be issued within a day. Brauchitsch, Halder wrote in his diary, returned to Zossen "tired and dejected."[14]

At the beginning of November, Brauchitsch and Halder set out on a two-day tour of the Western front, accompanied by Tippelskirch and by Wagner, the army's principal supply officer. Stülpnagel, whom they left behind, arranged to see Colonel Groscurth of the Abwehr and, according to Groscurth's diary, asked him to "begin preparations" for a coup.[15] Again, we do not know whether Stülpnagel did this on his own or on instructions from Halder. Long afterward, Halder would say of Stülpnagel that he was "a high-minded intellectual" and "not a rash hothead." Nearer the time, he characterized him as "a crazy fellow who always behaved like a bull in a china shop."[16] Probably, what we see is further evidence of the mental variability, if not instability, that Halder usually kept disguised.

Brauchitsch and Halder already knew that General Leeb favored seeking "fundamental change." A pious Roman Catholic, Leeb had recoiled from the Nazis at an early point, had become more and more disenchanted with Hitler as the Nazis stepped up attacks on all religions, and was now horrified by reports of systematic murder and enslavement of Jews in occupied Poland.[17] Though Stülpnagel cautioned him that it might be futile and even imprudent, Leeb sent Brauchitsch a letter urging him to take matters into his own hands. "The fate of the entire German nation may depend on you in the next few days," he wrote, adding that the German people "are filled with a deep longing for peace."[18]

Though Bock, Reichenau, and Kluge did not give advice like Leeb's, they repeated with great emphasis what they had said to Hitler: their forces could not possibly be ready for an offensive by mid-November. Brauchitsch and Halder stopped next at the headquarters of General von Rundstedt, who was forming yet another Army Group for the Western front. He and his chief of staff, Manstein, said that an offensive conducted on Hitler's timetable simply could not succeed. Their army commanders agreed emphatically. They did not yet have all the troops that were supposed to come from the Eastern front, they lacked vehicles and spare parts, and many of their artillery pieces had never been tried out. Manstein, who had been close to Beck and had been Halder's predecessor as Beck's chief of operations, may have known of Beck's categorical assessment that an offensive in the West at this stage would cost Germany four hundred thousand men and the Ruhr.[19]

After returning to Zossen, Halder listed in his diary the key points made by the field commanders. First: "At the moment we cannot launch an offensive with a distant objective." The armies lacked manpower; training was inadequate; and there were serious deficiencies in materiel. Second: "*None* of the higher headquarters think that the offensive . . . has any prospect of success." Third: "On the whole, assessment of the enemy is the same as that of the army high command. Naturally, every Army Group expects that it will have to bear on its front the brunt of enemy countermeasures." Tippelskirch made a similar entry in his diary. The senior commanders, he wrote, were "torn between duty and conscience. Purely military considerations [argue] against using up the forces in our tool kit." He also noted hearing junior officers and soldiers say that, though they had understood going to war against Poland, "a violation of Belgian and Dutch neutrality would be dishonorable."[20]

Brauchitsch and Halder returned from the front ready to contemplate drastic action. Now Halder himself, not Stülpnagel, told Oster and Groscurth that Beck, Goerdeler, and Schacht should get ready to carry out their plan for taking over from Hitler.[21] The decisive moment was supposed to come on November 5, when Hitler was to give the definitive order for an offensive. Halder drafted a memorandum restating all the many reasons why only cancellation or postponement made military sense. Brauchitsch arranged to go by himself to the Chancellory and confront Hitler with this memorandum. If Hitler still insisted on an offensive, Brauchitsch would rejoin Halder in an anteroom at the Chancellory, and they would then set in motion "fundamental changes."

Exactly what Halder had in mind is not clear. In 1938, General Witzleben, commander of the Berlin military district, had apparently intended using the 23rd Infantry Division, based at Potsdam, to disarm the SS and occupy the Chancellory and other key government buildings. But Witzleben, whom Hitler suspected of being in league with Beck, had since been transferred and now commanded one of the armies in Leeb's Army Group. The Potsdam division had a new commander. SS units had meanwhile been given their pick of recruits and prime equipment, including tanks, and Hitler had proclaimed them "standing armed forces," subject only to his own orders.[22] Many of the troops in and around Berlin belonged to Luftwaffe anti-aircraft units and hence were controlled by Göring. Even if all the army commanders on the Western front supported a coup, it is not apparent how it could have gone forward without heavy and prolonged fighting.

Possibly, Halder never brought himself really to believe that Hitler would hold out against advice from all his generals, especially since it was rumored that Göring also doubted that an offensive would succeed. Halder may never have applied his skills as a staff officer to the operational question of forcing "fundamental changes." The military side of the plot, like the political side, may have remained utopian.

In any event, the project unraveled. Brauchitsch went to the Chancellory. He gave Hitler his memorandum. Hitler gave him a memorandum in return. If Hitler ran his eyes over the document from Brauchitsch, he did so hastily, for the entire session lasted only twenty minutes. Brauchitsch delivered his main message orally. He said that the offensive had to be postponed. The troops were not ready, and the weather was bad. Hitler rejoined that the troops would not be much better trained a few weeks hence and that bad weather would also hamper the enemy. Heusinger, who heard subsequent Zossen gossip, imagines Hitler dismissing Brauchitsch's cautions about French strength by saying to him: "Every army is a mirror of its people. The French people are preoccupied with their comfort and well-being and are for that reason torn apart by parliamentary battles."[23] Brauchitsch said the weaknesses on the German side were not just a matter of training. Troop morale was low. Visiting the front, he had seen the same lack of discipline and disinclination to fight that had been in evidence in 1917–18. At this, Hitler flew into a rage. Demanding to know in which particular units this was supposed to be true, he said that he would fly to the front and confront the soldiers in person.

Whatever resolve Brauchitsch had brought into the room melted before Hitler's fury like an icicle in a furnace. Like Beck in 1938 when counting gendarmes as French soldiers and ignoring German storm troopers, he overplayed his professional expertise. In fact, he had seen no potentially mutinous troops. When he afterward tried to gather evidence supporting his allegation, he could find none.[24] Also, he always had difficulty speaking in front of Hitler. Groscurth heard, probably from Keitel, that, in the face of Hitler's rage, Brauchitsch suffered a "complete collapse" and could not utter a word. Only in the corridor on the way out was he able to say to Engel, "It's all up. He still doesn't believe me."[25]

Collecting Halder, Brauchitsch reported his total failure. Discussion with Hitler was impossible, he said, and added that at one point Hitler had asked suspiciously, "What are you planning?"[26]

This news seems to have affected Halder much as Hitler's anger had affected Brauchitsch. He rushed back to Zossen and told Stülpnagel to call off all preparations for a coup, and to destroy all incriminating evidence. He gave the same message to Groscurth and would not listen to Groscurth's appeals.[27] Though Tippelskirch's diary for the following day records that Halder was still saying that an offensive against France would be "a political and military crime," no trace lingered of any inclination on his part to prevent the crime by forcing "fundamental change" in Germany's leadership.[28]

Soon Hitler sent word that the army could have two additional days to get troops on the line for the offensive. Jodl told Halder that Hitler was going out of town for a couple of days and would not make his order final until the evening of November 9. A transport officer who had visited the armed-forces high command reported to Halder hearing talk there that the offensive would actually be postponed until November 15, perhaps even November 19.[29]

On November 8 came news of a surprise mediation offer issued jointly by King Leopold of Belgium and Queen Wilhelmina of the Netherlands. If this made the generals momentarily hopeful, the effect was short-lived, for Goebbels's organs immediately ridiculed the offer. His propaganda line, worked out with Hitler, was to describe it as a desperate effort to fend off a French invasion.[30] Meanwhile, the cover story for the planned offensive was to be an allegation that French troops had crossed the Belgian frontier and Germany was retaliating.

General Leeb did not give up hope. Accompanied by Witzleben, he went to Koblenz, where Rundstedt had his headquarters. He proposed that Bock and Rundstedt second him in urging a coup attempt. They refused. Rundstedt said that the generals had done all they could to resist the offensive. He spoke of "a military tradition that forbade rebellion or active opposition to the head of the state."[31] Though Leeb advised Halder that he and Witzleben remained ready to act, his was almost a lone voice. General Geyr von Schweppenburg, now in command of a corps in Leeb's Army Group, reported regretfully to Stülpnagel that his men would probably mutiny if asked to oppose Hitler. Stülpnagel himself had to tell Halder that reactions among junior officers and enlisted men were uncertain. Halder said to him, "You see now: it won't work! The commanders and the troops won't answer your call!" Halder also said to Weizsäcker that he was now "resigned to fate" ("*gottergeben*").[32]

"Fundamental changes" had always seemed to Brauchitsch and Halder a desperate resort. Except for Stülpnagel, no senior officer in the general staff had given such a course more than momentary approval, nor had any of the key field commanders other than Leeb and Witzleben. By mid-November, the possibility of a coup was dead. Oster, Groscurth, Goerdeler, Beck, and their few associates would continue plotting but, at least for a long time to come, only in shadow play. An almost comic footnote came in

a memorandum circulated by Tippelskirch on November 10, which enjoined officers in the army high command to be cautious about voicing
"critical statements" over the telephone.[33]

The question now for Hitler's generals was simply whether they would have
to play the Seydlitz role or could somehow engineer a series of delays.
When November 9 came, Hitler put off the offensive for another four days,
citing both the need to deal with the Dutch-Belgian mediation proposal and
apparent problems in working out armor-air coordination. When those four
days were up, Hitler extended the deadline another three days. The army
high command notified the Army Group commanders, saying that they had
been given no explanation for the new postponement. Later, it developed
that Göring and some Luftwaffe meteorologists had briefed Hitler on probable wind and weather for the weeks ahead and had persuaded him that
conditions for Luftwaffe operations would not be satisfactory until about
November 22.[34]

On November 16 came another four-day postponement, with bad
weather cited as the reason. This occurred again four days later. By now,
the actual takeoff time had become December 3. It then became December 9, December 11, December 17, December 27. (The staff officer keeping
the war diary for Bock's Army Group noted, "This is the ninth postponement!"[35]) When the new deadline arrived, Hitler announced an indefinite
postponement but with the stipulation that, if there were to be a spell of
clear, cold weather, he would order that the offensive proceed on a stepped-
up timetable.[36]

Lest the generals take satisfaction from having won the delay for which
they had begged, Hitler summoned two hundred senior officers to appear at
the New Chancellory on January 2, 1940, for a lecture designed partly to
inspire enthusiasm for an eventual offensive in the West, partly to take the
army leadership to task for past timidity, and partly to reinforce the message embodied in his post-Munich strictures about taking account of moral
factors, not just numbers, when calculating the balance between Germany
and its enemies. The lecture updated in modest respects the views he had
repeatedly put before his military leaders. "The question of violating Dutch
and Belgian neutrality plays absolutely no role here," he said. "No one will
ask about it afterward if Germany has won." The Soviet Union remained
neutral, but that condition might not last. He would not guarantee its being
true six months hence. Italy, in his judgment, was both powerful and ready

to join in the war as soon as Germany had a success in the West. The French and British remained vulnerable but would become less and less so. The spirit of the German soldier gave Germany superiority, whatever the numbers seemed to say.[37]

Before the group as a whole, Hitler lamented only that the true strength of the armed forces was not always adequately appreciated. After the rest had been dismissed, Hitler kept Brauchitsch and Halder behind. In harsh language, he condemned "the spirit of Zossen." Brauchitsch offered again to resign. Hitler told him that he must continue to fulfill his duties, and Brauchitsch went away determined to seek some way of actually achieving the decisive victory that Hitler wanted, or so Bock thought afterward.[38] In any case, the army leaders had been put on notice that their practical success in obtaining delay did not in any way imply that Hitler had become less intent on an offensive or any more respectful of their professional military judgment.

Early January 1940 brought exactly the weather that Hitler wanted. Across all of Northern Europe, temperatures remained at near-record lows. Goebbels wrote in his diary of its being "barbarically cold" and of Berlin's running out of coal.[39] But the fog and snow of the Christmas season lifted. Fliers had unlimited visibility. And on January 10, Hitler began to give orders that sounded serious and final. Summoning senior officers to the Chancellory, he told them that the meteorologists predicted a period of high barometric pressure of rare intensity and duration, with temperatures ten to fifteen degrees below freezing for about two weeks. Hitler regarded these as near-perfect conditions for fast operations by tanks with air support, and he fixed the moment for attack as a quarter-hour before sunrise on Wednesday, January 17. The war diary for Bock's Army Group for January 12 says: "After the eleventh postponement (the first on Nov. 11, 1939), it appears now as if the operation is finally going to proceed!"[40]

The meteorologists proved to have been overoptimistic. Fog and snow returned. Meanwhile, by mishap, a plane carrying an air-staff officer and a copy of the current Luftwaffe war plan crash-landed at Mechelen-sur-Meuse, in Belgium. Although the officer destroyed part of the plan, he could not destroy all of it. It had to be assumed, therefore, that the Belgians now knew at least something about the German offensive concept and were probably sharing their knowledge with Paris and London. Having already begun a new round of postponements, Hitler told his generals that the offensive would probably have to wait until spring, but he enjoined them to keep this schedule secret and to continue to act as if an offensive were imminent. The purpose was to keep the enemy on edge.[41]

The generals congratulated themselves on having at least partially succeeded in the York role. They had diligently collected predictions of bad
weather. According to their later testimony, they made a practice of having
all visitors to the front from Hitler's entourage travel the muddiest or foggi-
est routes. Göring, who privately wanted the offensive postponed until
spring, probably helped.[42] The resistance group in the Abwehr made its
own contribution by alerting the enemy to every order for an offensive that
circulated in the armed-forces high command. The moment he learned of
any such order, Colonel Oster would immediately call on his friend Major
Gijsbertus Sas, the Dutch military attaché. Sas would share his information
with his colleague Colonel Georges Goethals, the Belgian military attaché,
or with the Belgian ambassador, Viscount Jacques Davignon, or both. Word
would then go by ciphered telegram to The Hague and Brussels, and the
Belgian army chief of staff would relay it to General Gamelin in Paris and,
through Gamelin, to London. On October 10, by these routes, all four Western capitals had been advised of Hitler's directive of October 9 for an early
attack on the Low Countries. They were told about most later directives almost equally promptly, with the result that, more often than not, soon after
Hitler ordered an offensive, Abwehr agents would report that the Allies
were making ready to counter an attack.[43]

Hitler himself may have decided much earlier, perhaps even in November, that an early offensive was not in the cards. The most careful analyst of
German military planning, the historian Hans-Adolf Jacobsen, believes
that the Forschungsamt intercepted at least some of the messages sent by
Sas or Goethals or Davignon or others, that Hitler saw them, and that, from
some comparatively early point, he was conducting a double war of nerves,
with his generals one target and the Allied high command another. Ever
since October 1939, Abwehr agents had been reporting Allied foreknowl-
edge of German plans, and in January 1940, Hitler commented to Keitel
that the Allies had had information about his order for an offensive.[44]

Whatever the case, Brauchitsch, Halder, and their colleagues had had
to plan for an offensive as if it might occur within weeks, if not days. On the
one hand, this made it difficult for them to give much thought to the longer
future. On the other hand, it also meant that they had to adapt constantly to
changes in deployments of forces and materiel and to improvements in
equipment or training. Neither they nor commanders at the front could lock
themselves into complicated, hard-to-change operational plans. As we shall
see, the Allied high command was in the process of doing exactly that.

CHAPTER SIXTEEN

NOT DEFEAT?

"Here is the weak point. Here we have to go through!"
—*General Halder, pointing to the Ardennes forest on a map at German general-staff headquarters, mid-December 1939*

I n early October 1939, after it had become clear that Hitler did not in-tend to seek negotiations with the Allies and that he might insist on a November offensive, General Halder had asked General Bock, as com-mander of the Army Group in the West with the largest number of battle-ready forces, to prepare a plan of attack.

Bock, whose best-positioned units were opposite the Netherlands and the very northernmost part of Belgium, started by discussing with his staff and commanders possible action only against the Netherlands. But Halder could not wait until Bock got around to a methodical look at a wider field of operations, and he began to outline at Zossen a plan for attack on Belgium. In German usage, a war plan was labeled Case (or Contingency) something-or-other, usually a color. The code names for plans of attack on Czechoslo-vakia and Poland had been respectively Fall Grün (Case Green) and Fall Weiss (Case White), and the code name for defensive operations in the West had been Fall Rot (Case Red). The label chosen for a plan of attack on or through the Low Countries was Fall Gelb (Case Yellow). For simplicity, I render it here as Plan Yellow.

Bock's sketchwork and Halder's were soon cobbled together in an initial

Plan Yellow. It envisioned a special Force N, under Bock, moving toward Utrecht and the Dutch coast. Three armies, also under Bock, would strike toward Brussels, with one spearhead north and a second south of Liège, each with three armored divisions in the lead. Rundstedt would by then have the better part of two armies in his Group. They were to line up southeast of Bock's armies but northwest of Leeb's. (Confusingly, Rundstedt's was Army Group A, Bock's Army Group B, and Leeb's Army Group C, which meant that the alignment from the Dutch border to Germany opposite the Maginot Line was B, then A, then C.) The mission assigned Rundstedt was to prevent the Allies from counterattacking on the line of the Meuse River or east of it.

Essentially, it was this first version of Plan Yellow that Brauchitsch, Halder, Bock, and Reichenau described to Hitler during the long afternoon of October 25, explaining that they expected overwhelming opposition from Belgian, French, and British forces and hence failure. Groscurth heard officers from Zossen saying that the preparation of this plan had been a proforma exercise. No one thought it could actually be put into effect.

During this period, serious planning, both at Zossen and at Luftwaffe headquarters, went to the Sofort Fall (Immediate Plan)—the contingency of an *Allied* offensive, such as had been feared during the Polish campaign.

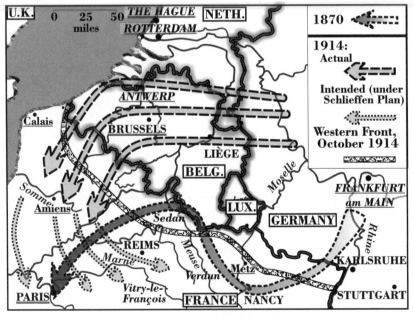

German Invasion Routes, 1870 and 1914

Since Rundstedt's newly forming Army Group was to have responsibility for the area opposite Luxembourg and the French and Belgian Ardennes, he, Manstein, and their army and corps commanders expressed high concern about a possible Allied attack and asked for more forces to be assigned to their area. The war could be lost if the Allies made a breakthrough into the Ruhr, they pointed out, and also, if French and British armies were to move in force into Belgium, they might leave weak units behind to guard their rear, in which case Army Group A might be able to attack across the Ardennes in the direction of Sedan, the site of Prussia's decisive victory in 1870.

At first, Halder and the general staff resisted the arguments from Rundstedt's headquarters. Trying to work out a plan of operations that might actually be carried out, they developed a second version of Plan Yellow. Ready at the very end of October, it envisioned bypassing the Netherlands, as in 1914. Bock would now attack only Belgium, sending five armored divisions north and four south of Liège. Rundstedt's Army Group would have the same assignment as before: to protect Bock's armies against counterattack; it had an injunction to go on the offensive if opportunity offered, but not much encouragement to do so, and was given only foot soldiers and a horse-drawn supply train. Alongside the portion of the governing directive

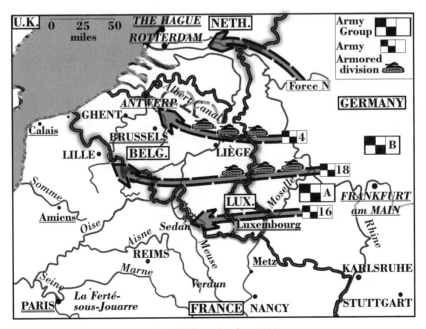

Plan Yellow, October 1939

that said Rundstedt was to move toward Sedan if opportunity offered, some-one in his headquarters penciled a large skeptical question mark.[1]

The new plan drew immediate protest from the Luftwaffe staff. Bypass-ing the Netherlands, the airmen complained, would deny them their prime objective—air bases from which to bomb the British homeland. Hitler sided with the Luftwaffe. Halder and his planners therefore had to begin further revision of Plan Yellow. Meanwhile, Rundstedt and Manstein, with some support from others, offered a fundamental objection to all versions of the existing plan: even if it succeeded perfectly, they said, the only result would be acquisition of bases for future operations and fighting along a more advanced, less well-prepared line, with stretched-out and vulnerable supply corridors. But if the German army were to run the mortal risks in-volved in any Western offensive, they contended, it should be on the basis of a plan that offered some hope of genuine victory. This was an argument with appeal for Hitler, who had long ago concluded that most of the army's generals were timid and who had already asked Brauchitsch and Halder if they were not simply contemplating a replay of the Schlieffen Plan.

In practice, Brauchitsch and Halder began to accommodate the forceful pleas of Rundstedt and Manstein, which they could not ignore. This may have gone against Brauchitsch's grain, for he and Rundstedt were not on

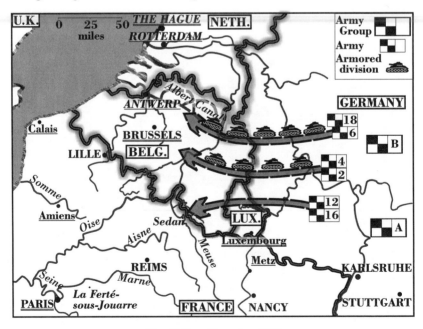

Plan Yellow, November 1939

the best of terms. Brauchitsch knew that, back in January 1938, Rundstedt, though having endorsed him as General Fritsch's successor, had subsequently been very critical of him for failing to insist on Fritsch's rehabilitation. It certainly went against Halder's grain, for he and Manstein had been rivals for more than a decade. They were near contemporaries, but Halder had become a general two years before Manstein and enjoyed the advantage of being a genuine general-staff officer (even though a graduate of the Bavarian Staff College rather than the Prussian Kriegsakademie). Yet Manstein (who had missed getting the requisite educational certificate because of front-line service in the Great War) had had general-staff assignments and gained a reputation as a strategist, whereas Halder had merely gained a reputation as a manager. He had preceded Halder as head of Beck's operations staff, and when he left for a divisional command around the time of the Blomberg-Fritsch affair, people said that Beck had forced Halder on Brauchitsch. Partly because of this background, partly because Manstein was both arrogant and persistent, Halder disliked having Manstein push proposals at him, especially with backing from a general of Rundstedt's stature.

As new units arrived on the Western front, Rundstedt's Army Group received reinforcement. In early November, it gained two Panzer divisions.

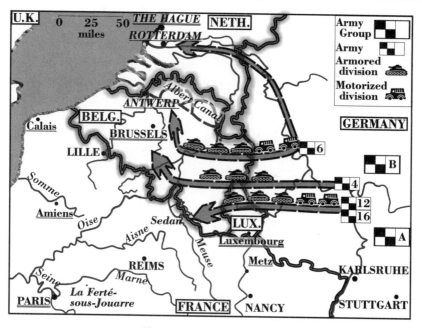

Plan Yellow, December 1939

Hitler himself, apparently captivated by the idea of a possible victory at Sedan, insisted that the complement of mobile forces in the southern sector of the front be strengthened. Halder therefore assigned Rundstedt two additional armored divisions and two motorized divisions, one army and one SS. Bock complained that he would soon have neither the front-line armor nor the reserves needed to attempt even the limited offensive mission assigned to Army Group B.

In a directive issued on November 20, looking toward a December 3 offensive, Hitler tried to blend all the alternatives then alive—a Dutch operation, Plan Yellow, *and* flexibility for Rundstedt's Group. He set as one objective the seizure of the southern Netherlands all the way to the coast. He expressed hope that the Dutch could be persuaded or coerced to consent to this. If not, the territory would have to be conquered. Bock was to have this mission, and also the mission of conducting the two-pronged attack against Belgium. But Hitler commanded that preparations be made so that, if Allied dispositions created a suitable opportunity, additional armored and motorized forces could be quickly transferred to Rundstedt and sent in the direction of Sedan. This play-by-ear version of Plan Yellow is the one that would have gone into effect had weather and the Mechelen incident not combined to cause Hitler to cancel the offensive scheduled for mid-January 1940.

No one high in the German army expected any of these plans to produce even a semblance of victory. The successive versions of Plan Yellow, however, did provide for operations sufficiently concentrated and coordinated so that, at worst, they would create a new stationary front in the vicinity of the Belgian Meuse. At best, they might give Germany control of significant portions of Belgium and the Netherlands, including coastal zones suitable for air operations against Britain.

General Manstein continued to press the thesis that the objective ought to be genuine victory, and he gradually went from arguing simply for strengthening the southern Army Group as a means of guarding against an Allied offensive to suggesting that, if the principal spearhead of an offensive were shifted to the south, victory might be attainable.

The final version of Plan Yellow, executed in May 1940, was to concentrate most armored and motorized forces in Rundstedt's sector; it would involve an all-out gamble on victory or defeat—a military Vabanquespiel. Using paratroops and glider-borne forces and the remainder of the armored and motorized units, General Bock was to make surprise strikes into the Low Countries designed to be interpreted as the main offensive. The plan presumed that France and Britain would rush to support the Dutch and Belgians and only later perceive that Bock's attacks were diversionary and that the primary German offensive was cutting across behind them and, moreover, was not sweeping toward Paris, in the Schlieffen Plan model, but racing toward Sedan, St.-Quentin, Abbéville, and Calais, severing the arteries connecting forward-deployed Allied forces with reserves and supplies in France. Rundstedt's attack was initially to go west by south, then bend west by north. On a map the pattern would resemble the blade of a scythe. Since the object was to cut communication lines as a scythe cuts stalks of grain, the final version of Plan Yellow was sometimes called the "sickle-cut" plan.

Victory has a hundred fathers but defeat is an orphan, said President John F. Kennedy when shouldering blame for the debacle at the Bay of Pigs in 1961. The aftermath of Germany's victory over France in 1940 certainly validated the first part of this saying. Hitler claimed the victory as his. General Keitel would later agree, though he assigned a few of the laurels to himself and others in the armed-forces high command. One of General Halder's aides claimed that, early in November 1939, Halder had drawn red arrows on a map sketching exactly the later lines of attack. (Other aides thought he drew these lines about three months later.) General Rundstedt asserted that the basic concept had germinated in his headquarters. General Manstein, while acknowledging support from Rundstedt and from Hitler, insisted that he and he alone had conceived the winning strategy, and General Günther Blumentritt, his chief of operations, endorsed this claim. Since Blumentritt contributed to one of the first official studies of the operation after the war, and since Manstein himself made his case insistently and artfully in postwar testimony and writings, the final version of Plan Yellow has come conventionally to be called "the Manstein Plan."[2] General Guderian, though agreeing with Manstein and Blumentritt, amends the story by noting that, without his own intervention, there would not have been a large enough concentration of tanks to make the plan succeed.

Unfortunately for anyone who likes history to be simple, there is some truth in each of these claims—and in others not immediately registered. Guderian's is far too modest. For the operational concept he had developed during the 1920s and 1930s, publicized in his 1937 book *Achtung Panzer!*, and advertised at every opportunity before and after, was crucial to the German success. Guderian made the case that large formations of tanks could

operate independently of infantry, move fast, break up enemy concentrations, disrupt enemy communications, and create conditions enabling infantry to move in with none of the grueling position warfare of 1914–18. He
envisioned armored divisions and groups of armored divisions performing
not only the functions sometimes performed by horse cavalry in earlier
epochs or in primitive theaters, but also the functions that artillery had monopolized in recent years—breaking up and scattering enemy defenses so
that they could be bypassed or taken over.

Though Guderian was primarily a warrior and did not have a complicated mind, he recognized early on that fighter-bombers and other ground-
support aircraft could also assume some of the functions of horse cavalry
and artillery. Unlike some armor advocates elsewhere, he modified his doctrine to presume coordinated armor and air strikes well ahead of slower-
moving infantry. (It helped that, more than his counterparts in France,
Britain, the United States, and elsewhere, he could look on the air force as
an auxiliary rather than as a rival service.) Without the doctrines that Guderian and officers associated with him developed and successfully mar-
keted, and without the armored and air forces built upon these doctrines, the
German plan of campaign of 1940 would have been almost inconceivable.

Hitler, regrettably, is also entitled to some of the credit he claimed—
and more. When he initially gave first priority to rearmament, he left specific allocations to an interagency Working Committee of the Defense
Council, chaired by the army chief of staff. In 1935, a reorganization gave
the chair to Blomberg's deputy, Reichenau. This was partly because Blomberg and Reichenau wanted to have resource allocation take account of the
armed services as a whole and, as a corollary, to enhance the status and importance of the war ministry. But at least in small part, it was also because
of Hitler's growing interest in rearmament, emphasizing modernization as
much as expansion. In 1934, Hitler had joined Guderian at Kummersdorf
to watch a demonstration conducted with mock tanks and had become excited. "That's what I need! That's what I want to have!" he had said.[3]

In 1938, when Hitler began visibly to assert authority over and within
the military establishment, he showed a clear preference for operations of
the type championed by Guderian. This probably had something to do with
why he spoke of replacing Beck even before he had read any of Beck's offensive memoranda, for Beck's operational concepts were more conservative than Guderian's. Though not a horse-cavalry-to-the-end conservative,
Beck did have doubts about creating only all-armor units and not brigading
some tanks with infantry, and junior officers questioned whether he under-

stood the full potential of air power.[4] Brauchitsch was even more conservative, insisting to intimates that, in a showdown, only horsemen and foot soldiers would matter.[5] Hitler had already expressed a preference that Halder
succeed Beck after seeing him oversee maneuvers in 1937. He approved
what he called Halder's "modern outlook."[6] Yet, in August and September,
when Hitler removed Beck and was preparing and hoping for a war with
Czechoslovakia, he discovered that neither Halder nor Brauchitsch had internalized Guderian's conception of the daring offensive led by armor and
air. While operational orders for an attack on Czechoslovakia were being
drawn up, he had more than one face-to-face set-to with the two generals,
demanding that armored divisions operate independently of infantry and be
concentrated in a single spearhead.[7]

A similar contest developed when the Polish campaign was being
planned in 1939. During the campaign itself, Hitler left Brauchitsch and
Halder in complete control. In Halder's view, that meant that *he* was in control, for Brauchitsch seemed to him to be acting primarily as a roving observer, and Hitler, Halder said afterward, never even communicated with
him by phone. Just before the war started, however, Hitler gave Brauchitsch and Halder another severe lecture on the importance of putting
Guderian's doctrines into effect. (In fact, armor and air in Poland moved
pretty much at the pace of infantry, but success came swiftly enough so that
Hitler did not complain.)[8]

The success of *Blitzkrieg* in Poland made converts of generals who had
previously doubted Guderian's doctrine. At the head of Halder's own list of
lessons from the Polish campaign were: "(1) Battle testing and success of
modern weaponry (armored units, motorized units, antitank and anti-
aircraft defenses), (2) Cooperation between armored forces and infantry."[9]
Even the first, nonserious version of Plan Yellow reflected these supposed
lessons. The spearheads were to be led by armored divisions with Luftwaffe
support. This remained true in all subsequent versions of the plan, at least
as much because of backing from Hitler as because of advocacy by Guderian and like-minded army officers, or the fact that Guderian's precepts
seemed to have been at least partially valiadated by experience.

Hitler then came forward with the strategic assessment that was to be
pivotal for the final version of Plan Yellow. When the generals came to him
on October 25 and said with one voice that the first version of Plan Yellow
had little or no chance of being carried out successfully, he started a discussion about concentrating forces in a single spearhead and moving that
spearhead southward. Most important, he gave as the reason for doing so

the desirability of forcing the enemy "to operate and to act quickly, something that does not come easily either to the systematic French or to the
ponderous English."[10]

At this point, Rundstedt and Manstein were just setting up Army Group
A. Manstein had had a glimpse of Plan Yellow when stopping over at
Zossen on the way from the Polish front to his new base at Koblenz, and
shared the common view that it was neither imaginative nor workable, but
he certainly had no alternative as yet in mind. Nor for months did he or
anyone else at Army Group A articulate the crucial premise that Hitler had
already voiced—namely, that the key to success for Germany could lie in
taking advantage of *procedural* weaknesses on the Allied side.

Hitler's contribution to the subsequent development of a final version of
Plan Yellow was erratic. Only a few days after suggesting concentration toward the south to exploit the enemy's sluggish procedures, Hitler went back
to pressing for a two-pronged offensive north and south of Liège, saying that
he did not want to "put everything on one card." Then, as we have seen, he
picked up the notion that opportunity might open up for a strike to Sedan,
to which he kept returning.[11] But he also talked periodically of offensive
operations on both sides of Liège, with a move in the direction of Sedan to
occur only if opportunity suddenly opened; and as Rundstedt and Manstein
requested more and more armored forces for their Army Group, he seemed
to become suspicious that talk of going to Sedan was just another ruse for
delaying the offensive. He complained to aides of "sabotage" by the army
and said he saw no reason for sending tanks through mountains.[12]

Not until February 1940 did Hitler become a decided supporter of a
concentrated offensive across the Ardennes. This was after friends in the
armed-forces high command helped Manstein go behind Halder's back to
arrange a meeting with Hitler, when Manstein put forward a case for an offensive centered in the Army Group A sector and intimated that Halder had
been resisting the idea out of timidity and hiding it from Hitler. This, and
advocacy by Guderian, led Hitler to decide that it was a genuine alternative
plan that he should force on his generals. In addition, as Hitler brooded
about the crash landing at Mechelen-sur-Meuse, where the existing German war plan had probably fallen into Allied hands, he came to think that
the incident could be turned to Germany's advantage. He said to Jodl that
everything possible should be concentrated on a drive to Sedan: "There the
enemy doesn't expect our great thrust. The documents from the landed flier
have strengthened the enemy in their conception that [the offensive] depends only on the occupation of Holland and the Belgian canal coast."[13]

Given the extent to which Hitler went back and forth among operational concepts, one can hardly call the final version of Plan Yellow the "Hitler Plan." But one can say that the plan could not have taken shape as it did without Hitler's enthusiasm for Guderian's operational concepts, and without his constant insistence that the goal should be the one ranked first by Clausewitz—to render the enemy militarily helpless. The plan might not have come together as it did without his insights into the exploitable weaknesses of the Allies. But these, as we shall shortly see, required a good deal of expert shoring up before they became accepted bases for a Vabanque-spiel that would be the army's as well as Hitler's.

Without the efforts of Rundstedt, Manstein, and other officers at Army Group A as operational planners and insistent advocates, the final Plan Yellow might not have turned out as it did. General Bock fought constantly to keep some forces in Army Group B. General Leeb chafed at his assignment to act primarily as a decoy, pretending to threaten the Maginot Line but lacking capability to actually attack it. (The general staff, having arranged for Army Group C to get equipment retired from service elsewhere, referred to it as "Museum Leeb."[14]) Army Group A battled continually to prevent Brauchitsch, Halder, and the army high command from compromising the principle of concentration of forces in order to placate Bock or Leeb or cater to whims of the Luftwaffe or the navy; but its own leadership was of at least two minds both about hinging everything on the achievement of surprise and about applying Guderian's operational concepts.

When Army Group A first began to seek increased forces and a larger operational role, General Manstein composed a memorandum that centered on the powerful argument that all versions of Plan Yellow, even if successful, would only give Germany a new Western front, whereas traditional military doctrine argued that a war plan should aim at total victory. Though Manstein later represented this memorandum as a proposal for Plan Yellow in its final version, it did not in fact go beyond asserting that existing plans were deficient. Even as late as mid-November 1939, memoranda drafted by Manstein called only for strengthening Army Group A's sector, not for giving it primary responsibility for an offensive, and when Rundstedt had the opportunity for a meeting with Hitler, his notes say no more than that he "emphasized the necessity of making the southern wing of the whole operation strong."[15]

Only in late November did General Manstein even argue that, in a revised Plan Yellow, Army Group A should have a role equal to that of Army Group B. German staff planning often focused on the choice of an operation's *Schwerpunkt*, literally "center of gravity."[16] Manstein sent the army high command a memorandum proposing that the plan call for two points of attack (*Schwerpunkten*), one in Belgium, one in the Ardennes region. (The then current version of Plan Yellow already had two *Schwerpunkten*, but both were in Belgium [see map on page 229].) On into December, Manstein was still basing the case for reinforcing Army Group A primarily on warnings that the Allies might intend an offensive there. And only on December 18 did he recommend in writing that the primary German strike should be a sickle cut through the Ardennes and across northeastern France to the Channel. Not until then was there something that might be called a "Manstein Plan."[17]

Halder was irritated at Manstein's constant pleading in behalf of Army Group A, and he had already decided to promote him out of his post as Rundstedt's chief of staff. He was to take command of an army corps and to be replaced by General Georg von Sodenstern, an officer of proven ability with none of his intellectual pretensions. Halder made the decision in mid-December, and Manstein learned of it a few days before Christmas, when he was told it would take effect in early February. During the interval, Manstein concluded that Halder and the army high command opposed even his recommendation for reinforcing Army Group A (though Stülpnagel told him that Halder and the general staff sympathized with his proposal but could not get it past Hitler, armed-forces high-command officers told him it had never gone to Hitler), and he interpreted his promotion as Halder's effort to sabotage the new plan. Manstein therefore used every available opportunity to reach Hitler directly. In February, as we have already seen, he succeeded in doing so. Others told him later that he had made an impression on Hitler even though Hitler disliked him. Thereafter, and in his postwar memoirs, Manstein took the position that it was entirely his own plan but became Hitler's because of his salesmanship, seconded by that of Guderian.[18]

Halder's initial reaction to the full-blown Manstein Plan makes it doubly unlikely that he was accurate after the war in recalling that he himself had sketched out the idea even earlier, for his diary for December 19, 1939, records his receiving Manstein's memorandum via Colonel Walter Buhle, one of Stülpnagel's deputies. The entry reads: "Buhle brings the idiotic proposal of [Army Group] A."

But eventually Halder changed his mind. He had already come to see merit in the idea of a southern *Schwerpunkt*. In the cramped underground quarters at Zossen, one large space was set aside for the *Kuhhaut* (literally "cowhide" but the German term connotes both elaborateness and expensiveness, closer to English "leopardskin"), a large terrain map of the Western front. There, Captain Alexis Baron von Roenne, of the Intelligence Directorate, Foreign Armies West section, maintained up-to-date markers for all German forces and for every identified enemy unit or potential enemy unit. Halder and others visited the space frequently. One day in early December, Halder lingered over the portion of the map showing thinly spread French deployments between Longwy, the northernmost outwork of the Maginot Line, and Bouillon on the Belgian frontier—in other words, along the French verge of the Ardennes Forest. Placing his finger on the map, Halder exclaimed, "Here is the weak point. Here we have to go through!"[19]

This was not the moment of Halder's complete conversion. At the time, he probably meant only that the Ardennes Forest was where one prong of an offensive might go, not that it was the place for the primary offensive. In early January 1940, visiting Fourth Army headquarters at Cologne, he spoke of Brussels as the central objective and an attack in the Ardennes area as materializing only if French armies invited it by putting the Ourthe River at their backs.[20] It was only after many weeks of study that Halder seemed sure Manstein's concept was not "idiotic." Many more weeks of meticulous staffwork and much rearrangement of deployments would be required before Halder would sign off on a plan of campaign based on this concept. Even then, he remained doubtful that it would work.[21]

Guderian and Hitler were so important in shaping the German plan of campaign as to make it questionable whether it should be remembered as even the Army Group A Plan, let alone the Manstein Plan. But the slowness of Halder and the army high command to adopt the basic concept surely precludes its being remembered as theirs. It was a collective product, but among those who contributed importantly to it were some who never laid much claim for credit, particularly General Tippelskirch, Colonel Liss, and the Foreign Armies West analysts who affirmed for army and armed-forces planners the crucial insight that Hitler had articulated as early as October 1939—that, despite some apparent advantages, the Allies had potentially fatal vulnerabilities—if they could be forced "to operate and act quickly."

CHAPTER SEVENTEEN

INTELLIGENCE

"It was not a pleasant task to have to go to the chief of the general staff twice a day with a situation report that resembled a map of central Africa from the eighteenth century." —*Colonel Liss, of German army intelligence, commenting on his situation in 1939*

S ince German military leaders saw no choice except to obey Hitler's command for a Western offensive and knew their own forces to be in most respects inferior to those of the Allies, they depended for hope of success on finding enemy weaknesses. Many organizations within the German government collected information that could contribute to identifying these weaknesses.[1]

Göring's Forschungsamt remained the principal collector of communications intelligence. When the war started, it expanded. Though it had tried to enforce a rule that all personnel, once employed, should spend their lives within the agency and thus never be able to talk of its work to outsiders, the rule was bent now to permit some cryptologists and linguists to take up duty with the armed services. The new recruits were set to work primarily monitoring domestic communications to detect signs of foreign espionage, breaches of security, or disloyalty.

The regular distribution list for Forschungsamt products had never included the service high commands, not even that of the Luftwaffe. The principal reason, probably, was that most Forschungsamt intercepts of foreign traffic related to business transactions in or with neutral countries.

One Forschungsamt veteran estimated that 99 percent of the agency's wartime intercepts were of this character.[2] The Forschungsamt liaison officer in the armed-forces high command was a Major Braunschweig, who worked for General Georg Thomas, head of the war economic staff in the armed-forces high command.[3]

Since the Forschungsamt was reasonably successful in persuading recipients not to keep copies of its products, and since most of its own files appear to have been destroyed, it is hard to know what contribution it made to assessments of France and Britain in 1939–40. It was probably through the Forschungsamt that Hitler learned that the Allies were being warned of his on-again, off-again orders for an offensive. Probably, too, Forschungsamt telephone taps helped him keep track of—and remain furious about—army objections to these orders and efforts to frustrate them. Otherwise, "brown friends" likely had most value in helping to maintain confidence that the Netherlands and Belgium would remain neutral, calibrating pressures to apply to Norway and Sweden to ensure continued shipment to Germany of Swedish iron ore (which had to travel in winter via Norway), and in dealing with the Balkan States. Even though Soviet codes were unreadable, Hitler saw plenty of "brown friends" telling about other countries' relations with the Soviet Union, and these may have helped him make his prediction in December 1939 that Stalin would remain on the sideline at least until mid-1940. If the Forschungsamt made any direct contributions to the assessments of France and Britain that entered into German war plans, it did so through intercepts passed along to military-communications intelligence organizations.

The military communications of enemy and neutral states were mostly intercepted and dealt with by Germany's individual military services. The navy's B-Dienst kept track of movements of all types of vessels and intercepted most coded or ciphered messages exchanged within the British navy.[4] The Luftwaffe chief of communications controlled several fixed intercept stations around Germany's borders. Antennae rising high above a stone building at Trier that pretended to be a weather station picked up messages of the air forces of France and the Low Countries and of RAF planes in France. The take from these and other stations, and from supplementary mobile intercept companies, went to analysts at the headquarters of each air fleet and at Luftwaffe headquarters in Berlin. Intercepts in code or cipher went to the Cipher Center, located in the stables of the old New Palace in Potsdam.

The army did its own communication interception, much in the fashion of the air force but on a larger scale.[5] In the West, at the outset of the war, the chief of army communications had fixed intercept stations at Munster, on a parallel with the central Netherlands; Euskirchen, almost on a parallel with Liège in east-central Belgium; and Stuttgart, on a parallel with the rear of the Maginot Line. The total take was evaluated by a small staff in Frankfurt and a larger staff in the army high command's underground complex at Zossen. Reviews of the Polish campaign criticized army-communications intelligence for being slow both to collect messages and to inform commanders of their contents. In the West, therefore, fixed stations were supplemented by mobile intercept groups, and each Army Group headquarters had a small evaluation staff that kept in touch both with the mobile stations and with the central evaluation staff at Zossen.

As forces in the West expanded, the number of mobile intercept groups multiplied. Owing to General Manstein's continually raising the alarm about a possible Allied offensive through the Ardennes, the number of groups collecting signals from Allied forces there became disproportionate even before late versions of Plan Yellow began to shift the *Schwerpunkt* in that direction.

General Erich Fellgiebel headed both army communications and a communications division in the armed-forces high command. (A table in the Appendix, "The German High Command, 1938–40," shows German command linkages.) Having been the army's outstanding signals officer ever since the Great War, he held this dual responsibility, reporting to Keitel as well as to Halder, even though Keitel knew him to be intensely anti-Nazi. (He would take part in the 1944 attempt to kill Hitler and lose his own life for doing so.) In the armed-forces high-command organization, he received decrypts from the Forschungsamt, the navy, the air force, and even the Foreign Ministry. Hence, he was in a position both to sift army intercepts for Tippelskirch and to pass on to him whatever came through other channels that seemed potentially useful for army-high-command planning.[6]

In December 1939, Fellgiebel began to supply Tippelskirch with decrypts of messages from the French War Ministry to military districts and armies in the field.[7] By February 1940, his fixed and mobile intercept stations were reading almost 90 percent of French military radio traffic and, except for brief periods when the French army changed keys, were breaking all encoded messages.[8] But because the French high command made a fetish of communications security and strictly limited the use of radio and telephone, these intercepts gave only a fragmentary picture even of Allied order of battle, let alone of Allied intentions. Although the command post for French armies at the front had been set up at La Ferté-sous-Jouarre on the first day of the war, Fellgiebel did not pinpoint it there until April 1940. Not until May 12, two days into the Battle of France, did intercepts bring the welcome news that the French force guarding the Ardennes was not the powerful First Army but the weaker Ninth Army.[9] Thus, even though Germany had an elaborate communications-intelligence system and it was organized so that it could be exploited with high efficiency, it yielded only limited information of any real value for planning.

Human intelligence made a larger contribution to the final version of Plan Yellow and to the German war in the Low Countries and France. This fell under Section I of the Abwehr, which handled both espionage and counterespionage. Its head was Colonel Hans Piekenbrock, known as "Piki," a bon vivant and Rhinelander, lazy but clever enough so that Canaris enjoyed his company. (They would make jokes to each other so subtle that others could not see their points.) The large majority of Piekenbrock's agents were scouts sent to report on terrain, deployments, or construction within twenty to thirty kilometers of a border. The actual supervision of these agents was the responsibility of Abwehr stations, the most important of which, for the Western front, were at Hamburg and Trier. At both of these stations, the real priority was counterespionage. The men in charge spent much of their time organizing and planning for the capture of enemy espionage centers and listening posts when and if an offensive occurred.[10]

Prior to the war, Abwehr stations in the West, including one at Stuttgart, had collected a good deal of information from private contractors about construction work on fortifications in both France and Belgium. In March 1939, according to testimony given by Piekenbrock after the war, an agent in place in France provided "photographs of the whole defense system of the Maginot Line, with all fortifications, equipment, rail lines, and transport and communication links." Through German contractors who had helped build the huge new Belgian fort at Eben Emael, the Abwehr obtained data essential for planning its surprise seizure by paratroops.[11]

The coming of the war interrupted information collection, and the Abwehr stations lost touch with many of their agents. It was late in 1939 before they recovered. Piekenbrock admitted after the war, "Our general staff was for a considerable time not clear about the distribution of French forces. Only at the end of 1939 and the beginning of 1940 did information really begin to arrive."[12] After the final version of Plan Yellow began to jell, the army high command and field commands indicated where Abwehr collectors should focus. The Trier station was told to find out as much as it could about the apparently weak Ardennes sector. Oscar Reile, an Abwehr officer in Trier, writes that he sought "in Luxembourg and, beyond that, in the Sedan-Charleville-Hirson region to clarify the most minute details concerning the layout of auto routes, railroads, and the mails," but he adds, "The details desired could only rarely be successfully obtained. The agent reports that came to me contained in most cases only fragments."[13]

Most valuable of all for German planners were the results of aerial reconnaissance. Liss and Roenne were able to site Allied units on their *Kuhhaut* in large part because of photographs from the Luftwaffe.

A capability for aerial reconnaissance had developed originally in the private sector. Theodor Rowehl, a Great War flier, had lost his lands when the Treaty of Versailles gave part of Prussia to the new state of Poland. Hoping that Germany would someday go to war against Poland and get him back his property, he rented a plane and, with a camera, ranged along the Polish border taking pictures of military installations. Shortly before Hitler became chancellor, Rowehl had enough such pictures to make an appointment with Captain Patzig, then head of the Abwehr, and Patzig promptly gave him a contract to continue and expand his work.

When Hitler came to power and new resources were available for all parts of the military establishment, Rowehl soon had five planes covering all frontiers. In 1936, Göring saw samples of his work, which included extensive photography of the Maginot Line and stereoscopic shots of new fortifications going up in Czechoslovakia. Göring appropriated the whole operation, made Rowehl a Luftwaffe colonel, and put him in charge of a reconnaissance group that he directly controlled.

Aerial reconnaissance was a major activity of the Luftwaffe. More than one plane out of seven was designed for and assigned to this mission. Pilots of short-range reconnaissance planes usually used only their eyes and tried to summarize what they had seen, but pilots of long-range reconnaissance planes (mostly Dornier 17F's) controlled specially built Zeiss cameras. Since they flew at fifteen thousand feet and tried not to linger over targets, even if there were clouds, the imagery was often indistinct, but in good weather Rowehl's Strategic Reconnaissance Group managed five to six missions a day.

Each air fleet had its own reconnaissance force, together with trucks and special trailers where photos could be quickly developed and interpreted. Photographs from Rowehl's Strategic Reconnaissance Group went to a laboratory-and-interpretation center in rooms once used by the now defunct Prussian Diet. The center accepted assignments from the army as well as the air force, and an army liaison officer there would bring to Zossen glossies potentially interesting to army-high-command analysts and planners.

Despite the importance of reconnaissance within the air force, officers of the air staff and commanders of air fleets were disappointed with the results of both short-range and long-range missions. The reason was that they wanted information primarily about their service's counterparts—Allied air forces. The success of Allied Curtiss-Hawk 75A's against German aircraft in dogfights during the autumn of 1939 made Rowehl cautious about risking his comparatively slow Dornier 17s. Most of his photographs were thus of sites very near the German border. As a result, very few showed airfields in the interior of France, Britain, or the Low Countries, which were the targets of greatest interest to the Luftwaffe's operational planners, and few provided useful data on Allied air-force deployments.

In part because of this concentration on border areas, air-force photography did give army analysts a great deal of detail about Allied ground forces stationed on or near borders in northeastern France or poised to move into the Low Countries to counter a German attack. It was this photography, complemented by radio-intercept data and Abwehr agent reports, that enabled Liss and Roenne to show on the *Kuhhaut* the thinness of French forces along the edge of the Ardennes. Because so little of this photography covered rear areas, Germany had little information about the size or disposition of Allied reserves. But German intelligence analysts benefited from the fact that the Allies got advance word of Hitler's attack orders, for the resultant French and British preparations for these emergencies contained clues as to what Allied commanders intended to do when and if a German attack actually occurred.

For practical purposes, intelligence analysis in Germany concentrated in Tippelskirch's section of the army general staff.[14] The navy's equivalent, the Third Section of the naval staff, devoted itself to obtaining target data and transmitting these to the operations section. That of the air force, section five of the air staff, functioned in much the same way (though it had a foreign-air-forces group that looked like the foreign-armies groups at Zossen). Its analytical products were circulars from Beppo Schmid denigrating foreign aircraft. An official historian of the postwar German air force summarizes what Schmid was saying in early 1940:

In January 1940 Schmid held British and French air forces to be "clearly inferior in strength and armament in comparison with the Luftwaffe." Even if the U.S.A., without entering the war, were to make available to the Western powers the mass of its aircraft production and sea transport were to be secured, this would "not by itself" produce a decided improvement in the relative status of the Western powers in the air arm during the course of 1940. Schmid further expressed doubt that English fighters, "in view of the better configuration and defensive armament of the Me 110," would have much of a chance against it.[15]

(As the historian adds, the latter was "an observation . . . that only a half-year later would be proved absurd.") The Luftwaffe's intelligence staff devoted itself mainly to assembling material for pilot target folders.

Army intelligence was different, however. Tippelskirch, the son of a Prussian general and before the Great War an officer in the elite corps that guarded the person of Kaiser Wilhelm II, had transferred to a front-line unit and been captured during the first battle of the Marne in 1914 (the defensive triumph of General Joffre, to which Gamelin made such a large contribution). Tippelskirch spent all the rest of the war as a French prisoner. Owing to this experience and his command of the French language, he was assigned after the war to the foreign-armies unit of the Truppenamt (the part of the army that would have been the general staff if the Versailles Treaty had not forbidden Germany to have one). In the 1920s and 1930s, he rotated into this unit whenever not on troop duty. General Beck made him head of it in 1936, and when Halder, succeeding Beck, reorganized the general staff and divided it into five major sections (operations, training, organizations, intelligence, and history[16]), Tippelskirch, who had meanwhile been promoted to major general, became head of the intelligence section, with Liss taking over his old job.

Kenneth Strong, a British military attaché in Berlin in the 1930s, writes of Tippelskirch: "In appearance he was a short bull-necked man with close-cropped hair. . . . I recall him gazing at me through a pair of thin-rimmed spectacles with little charm or friendliness." Puzzled by his "aloofness and apparent detachment," Strong concluded that it was due to his being preoccupied with France, not with Britain.[17] Contrasting him with Stülpnagel, in whom he saw "perceptiveness and sensitivity," Halder spoke of Tippelskirch as "forceful"—a "*Kraftnatur.*"[18]

Tippelskirch's function was partly to serve as an intelligence officer but also partly to validate judgments made by experts working under him. Having been made a general officer because of high marks earned not only in staff assignments but as a regimental and brigade commander (he would go on to command a division and, before the war ended, a corps and an army), he had the credentials for saying to other generals that this or that assertion by a given analyst seemed plausible and realistic in light of his own experience. And Tippelskirch's endorsement had double weight if seconded by Stülpnagel, for Stülpnagel, in addition to having once overseen Foreign Armies West, had already commanded a division and now had experience also as chief of operations.

The expert judgments were chiefly those of Liss and Roenne. Liss had served in Foreign Armies West under both Stülpnagel and Tippelskirch, and Tippelskirch had chosen him to head the organization even though he was at the time only a major and the branch included three full colonels and three other officers senior to him, one of whom was named Tippelskirch and was presumably a relative of the general.[19] A heavyset Mecklenburger, Liss did not come from a military family. He had, however, been a front-line artillery officer in the Great War and was an outstanding horseman with no fewer than forty-six major tournament prizes. The latter accomplishment gave him cachet not only in the German officer corps but in France and England. In armies all over the world, it was still the case that nothing counted so heavily in an officer's favor as his appearance on horseback. When visiting foreign countries, Liss was given unusual opportunities both to observe military maneuvers and to meet military officers and members of other elites. Fluency in French, English, Spanish, and Italian helped him make the most of these opportunities.[20]

Alexis Baron von Roenne, an army captain, came from the Baltic region, spoke fluent Russian, and in 1942 would shift to Foreign Armies East. "Sharp, clear-headed and purposeful" were words applied to him by a Russian who later worked under him. David Kahn, who interviewed many of his associates, writes that Roenne "was meticulous and somewhat rigid; he could be superior and sarcastic to his juniors; but behind his rimless spectacles and compressed lips there worked a brain as clear as glass." Like Beck and Fellgiebel, he was to take part in the plot to kill Hitler in July 1944 and die for it, telling his interrogators that he was motivated by devout Catholicism and disgust with the way Nazis dealt with aristocrats "who, because of their origins, have title to be a higher class among the people."[21]

Despite their junior ranks, Liss and Roenne had easy relationships with the colonels and generals above them. From corps or division head-quarters downward, intelligence officers in the German army were, as in military establishments elsewhere, the servants of operations officers, not their equals—unless, of course, they wore the red trouser stripe of the general staff and were therefore marked for rotation to operations or command.[22] In the First Panzer Division, the staff intelligence officer was to know nothing of the revised version of Plan Yellow until the offensive actually commenced. Only the division commander, his chief of staff, and his operations officer had been informed.[23]

At higher levels, especially in the general staff itself, intelligence officers were more nearly on a par with colleagues in operations. The manual, *Duties of the General Staff*, composed in the 1870s by General Bronsart von Schellendorf, specified:

> Faulty plans are generally the result in war of insufficient knowledge of the state of affairs on the enemy's side. . . . The incalculable advantage of a good system of obtaining intelligence, is thus at once apparent. The foundation for such a system rests, in the first instance, on an intimate knowledge and acquaintance with the organization, customs, and habits of the enemy's army.

The acquisition of such knowledge, wrote Schellendorf, was a prime function of the general staff, and he added with emphasis, "The first condition, however, of accurately appreciating such information is *the most thorough and accurate knowledge* of one's own army, for without this it is impossible to draw comparisons or estimate matters with sound professional judgment."[24] From this doctrine, it followed that intelligence officers at the general-staff level had to know about German capabilities and plans. Assignments to intelligence analysis were in the career tracks of a number of men who passed through the general staff on the way to being general officers with major command responsibilities. Intelligence analysis was integrated with operational planning. Liss provided written and oral reports not only on enemy forces but on German forces, and he played the role of enemy commander in chief when plans were tested on the giant maps or sand tables at army headquarters.

Since Tippelskirch, Liss, and Roenne received a rather thin diet of standard intelligence sources such as intercepted messages, reports from spies, and pictures taken from the air, they had to base their assessments and forecasts in large part on accumulated general knowledge. The long period of the hundred-thousand-man army, before Hitler came to power, had accustomed them to making do with little secret information. From the end of the Great War until the mid-1930s, officers in Foreign Armies West had depended primarily on reading foreign publications, contriving invitations to visit foreign military facilities, and talking with foreigners living in or traveling through Germany. From these sources, they had developed suppositions about patterns of thought and action in foreign governments and armies. As rearmament brought with it expansion in intelligence collection capabilities of all kinds, they began to get more current information, but they tended to fit the new bits and pieces of secret intelligence to schemas developed from the types of open-source information that are staples for journalists. As it turned out, this stood them in good stead.

Foreign Armies West had traditionally produced reference works on foreign countries—*Grosse Orientierungshefte* (roughly, Big Guidebooks). Fat folders or even printed volumes, these Big Guidebooks, most updated at least annually, covered military geography, governmental and military organization, armaments, training, and education. In his postwar memoir, Liss complains, "Naïve people often took us for a kind of travel bureau."[25]

Officers in Foreign Armies West supplemented the Guidebooks with long studies, sometimes in typescript, sometimes in print, that paid particular attention to officer education and debates about military doctrine. Examining textbooks used at St.-Cyr, St.-Maxent, the War College, and other military schools in France and comparable texts from other countries, analyzing field manuals, reading articles in foreign military journals, studying public statements by French and other war ministers, and discreetly questioning alumni of foreign military academies and staff schools, they tried to identify precepts that might influence military plans and routines that might figure in operations. In March 1935, Foreign Armies West published a 135-page book on training in the French army.

Building on such earlier studies, Foreign Armies West issued in May 1938 a supplement to the Big Guidebook for France. It made the following observations: "In many respects the structure and management of the French army lacks clarity and simplicity in organization. The complicated regulations governing functions as between the central government offices and army field commands, which get further entangled with the air force and navy, lead frequently to duplication and conflict."[26]

The German analysts offered two explanations for this, both of which led them to predict that the problems would not be soon remedied. First, they said, France was a democracy. Hence, its Parliament would not allow much power to collect in any individual's hands. Second, they argued, the white population of France feared the army because so many professional soldiers were Africans. (This passage could have been contributed by an officer in Foreign Armies West who was also an ardent Nazi, such as Major Rudolf Ritter von Xylander, but not necessarily. At the time, racism was potent everywhere, France included. Young officers in the U.S. Army such as Dwight Eisenhower and Omar Bradley would probably have been given less pause by the line about racial fears in the French army than by a companion comment that, as soldiers, the nonwhites were at least as good as the whites.)

A Foreign Armies West study of the French general staff released in June 1938 noted that it put more constraints on field commanders than did the German general staff.[27] "Even the commander of an army," wrote the German analysts, "must act within a framework set by the high command. This goes so far that enjoyment of responsibility and boldness in independent decisions is constrained and, in particular, training in rapid exploitation of favorable opportunities is neglected." In French planning, they wrote, "*Security takes precedence over boldness.*" (The emphasis is theirs.) "An attack can only be commenced if, as a result of superiority or possibly surprise, success is assured beforehand." In part because of the stress on avoiding risk, they added, French planning was characterized by thoroughness well in excess of that usually attributed to Germans: "Great importance is attached to the formulation of very long orders." As an example, the analysts cited instructions for a high-level French war game, which they had probably obtained via an Abwehr agent. The document was 280 pages long, not counting its twenty-two appendixes.

The German analysts did not depict the French general staff as a covey of men like Colonel Blimp, the buffoonish old fogey in a popular British comic strip. They knew its officers had looked closely at the implications of making infantry more mobile by motorization and of substituting tanks for horses. They had studied the evolution of aircraft and possible uses of airplanes in ground warfare. In these respects, the French were at least on a level with their German counterparts. Whatever their own branch (infantry, cavalry, signals, etc.), they were experts on the characteristics and uses of artillery, and they benefited from a system of rotation that exposed them to a variety of arms and levels of command.

Close observation of French mobilization in September 1938, during the Sudeten crisis, gave Foreign Armies West analysts data against which they could test the hypotheses they had drawn from studying textbooks, manuals, and like sources.[28] They circulated a report analyzing this mobilization almost minute by minute. The value of this analysis, they warned, was not to show what French mobilization would be like in the next crisis, for the French general staff was reported to be very critical of what had been done and to be studying closely how to do better in the future. But they did point to features that showed the attributes they had singled out earlier.

The analysts commented that the French army had been preoccupied with preparing for a German attack rather than for an offensive of its own. They reported evidence that the French government had overestimated the strength and degree of completion of Germany's Western fortifications (this was supportive more of Hitler's judgment than of Beck's). They noted, too, that, though French forces had concentrated along the Belgian frontier, they had positioned themselves to move in only with Belgium's cooperation. There was no evident preparedness for an invasion of Belgium, and Belgian mobilization had, indeed, seemed to signal an intention to resist by force any such move, whether German or French.

Still, the analysts observed that the French army had also mobilized to go on the offensive. Consistently with their earlier surmise that French senior officers were given to emphasizing protection of their own forces, hence to thinking defensively, and were not partial to bold initiatives, they concluded that the officers would not have initiated an offensive unless the government ordered it. They reported having been told by some source, probably someone in the Abwehr, that General Gamelin had written to Prime Minister Daladier that "if the political leadership demanded an offensive, it would be carried out despite the expected very heavy loss of life and, with this condition, a breakthrough of the [German] line could be achieved." (Although Gamelin had written no such letter, he had held such an opinion.)

During the Sudeten crisis, Tippelskirch and his analysts had again been more of Hitler's mind than of Beck's in their assessments of France and Britain. They had been partly responsible, it is true, for one of Hitler's outbursts against Beck, for the Big Guidebook included the gendarmerie, the Sûreté, and the railway police in the tally of French military forces, on the ground that they were all subject to control by the Ministry of National Defense. But a Foreign Armies West report of March 1938 had said that Germany's Western fortifications, though rudimentary, made it much less likely that France would attempt a quick offensive in support of Czechoslovakia. Tippelskirch himself doubted that the British would go to war for Czechoslovakia—at almost exactly the moment when Beck was sending Hitler a memorandum saying that they were certain to do so.[29]

In 1939, in the buildup to the Polish war, Tippelskirch and his crew abetted Halder's cautionary efforts. They supplied him with estimates of ready French forces, yielding a scary picture of what might happen if Germany attacked Poland, and the French and British entered the war. Halder relayed this picture to Göring precisely as it had come to him from Tippelskirch and Liss:

WEST:

Maximum immediate buildup against Germany: 44 divisions. Additional strength available against Germany: 40 divisions. Together with British troops a total of 90 divisions may be reached, which means 50 divisions on the northern wing.

French timetable (capability): Luxembourg on third day. Belgian border, first wave (motorized) on sixth day. All-out offensive at the end of two or three weeks.

Artillery: France can put up 1,600 guns over and above divisional artillery on northern wing, against 300 German guns; moreover, French divisional artillery is superior in firepower to German.

Tanks: France has 50 to 60 battalions (c. 2,500 tanks), Germany none (on this front).[30]

In actuality, the army's intelligence analysts were less worried than Halder about immediate intervention by France and Britain. Liss thought the Soviet pact would dissuade them. Tippelskirch repeatedly assured Halder that, in any case, the Western powers were likely to act circumspectly; he gave him a guarantee that Belgium would remain neutral, and his daily updates for Halder, even as France and Britain moved toward declaring war, then actually did so, emphasized the absence of any concentrations portending an early major offensive.[31]

At the Abwehr, however, Canaris, Oster, and Groscurth were sure that the Western powers would attack soon and in great force. That was Beck's expectation, and would continue to be. Well into October 1939, he was saying that he knew General Gamelin and was sure he must be preparing a great offensive.[32] It outraged the Abwehr officers to have Tippelskirch and Liss saying the contrary. On September 10, when French forces moved into the Saarland, commencing what turned out to be their insignificant mini-offensive, Groscurth wrote in his diary, "Tippelskirch's optimistic house of cards starts to totter."[33] In early October, when Foreign Armies West made light of Abwehr/Ausland predictions that France was now about to launch a grand offensive, Groscurth's diary entry denounced "Liss's *crazy* report on the Abwehr's misjudgment."[34]

The almost total inaction of the Western Allies exceeded even Liss's expectations. As he writes in his postwar memoir, he interpreted the mini-offensive in the Saarland as pure theater:

> The tone of French military press releases was amazing. They spoke of major battles with heavy use of artillery, predicted the fall of Saarbrücken, and talked of very significant numbers of engagements . . . in gross contradiction of the facts. . . . Obviously, it was pure propaganda for the Poles. As their resistance came to an end, they changed tone as if a different reporter had taken up the pen.[35]

A touch of scorn for the Allies began to appear in briefing notes by both Tippelskirch and Liss.

Halder had felt obliged early on to caution Tippelskirch and Liss against seeming completely at odds with the Abwehr. After Hitler's order for an early Western offensive, he became concerned lest his own intelligence staff encourage such rashness. Taking notes at the Chancellory and hearing Hitler cite figures on German superiority in anti-aircraft guns, he scribbled in the margin, "No more detailed figures!" Annotating the document after the war, he explained that he was reminding himself to tell Foreign Armies West "in future in presentations to Hitler to avoid if possible estimates of numbers. Because of Hitler's extraordinary memory for numbers, this is dangerous, for he will always take occasion to make spiteful remarks whenever later estimates fail to jibe."[36]

CHAPTER EIGHTEEN

GAMBLE

"We have to resort to extraordinary methods and accept the accompanying risks." —*General Halder to General Rundstedt, March 12, 1940*

In the weeks after Hitler issued his order, Tippelskirch shared in some degree the pain of Halder and Brauchitsch. Accompanying them in their early-November visit to the headquarters of Army Groups in the west, he heard every single commander and chief of staff say that an early German offensive against France would probably end in disaster. As he reported to Halder, he also overheard middle-level officers questioning the moral justification for an attack on the unoffending Low Countries. He participated in some discussion of the army's possibly attempting to effect "basic changes," and, as will be recalled, he cautioned his colleagues against being too candid in what they said to one another over the telephone.[1]

Officers under Tippelskirch knew only, however, that they now had the assignment of analyzing the enemy forces that German armies would encounter if they were to go on the offensive. This entailed a lot of new and hard work, which was complicated because information was scarcer than ever, what with France and Britain taking measures to guard communications security and imposing border controls and other measures that cut Abwehr stations off from their agents, and Hitler and Göring temporarily forbidding aerial reconnaissance across the western borders. Even after partially lifting the ban, Göring limited reconnaissance because of concern about losing planes to faster, higher-climbing Allied fighters. Liss wrote after the war: "It was not a pleasant task to have to go to the chief of the general staff twice a day with a situation report that resembled a map of central Africa from the eighteenth century."[2]

By November and December, conditions had improved. The Abwehr stations at Hamburg, Trier, and Stuttgart re-established communication with agents and recruited new agents. Fellgiebel's technicians began to supply decrypted intercepts of French military-radio traffic and then of communications from the French War Ministry.[3] Interrogation of prisoners taken during the skirmishing in the Saarland yielded little, but postmarked letters among their effects enabled Foreign Armies West to identify the base locations of a number of French army units.[4] Nevertheless, Liss's recollection was of working throughout the autumn of 1939 in "a sea of fog."[5]

Evaluations of the armed forces of the Allies and the Low Countries prepared by Foreign Armies West for the general staff rested largely, therefore, on knowledge accumulated before the war, chiefly from open sources. Sprinkling shrewd observations onto stereotypes, and obviously bearing in mind mutinies that had occurred in the French army late in the Great War, Foreign Armies West in October 1939 offered the following assessment of French troops:

> The behavior of the French soldier is heavily dependent on emotional influences. If there is lacking a war aim that is clear and understandable to the soldier, he may do his job all right but without enthusiasm or eagerness to attack. Heavy and unnecessary losses can in these circumstances badly shake the inner state of the troops. . . . On the other hand, the Frenchman is easily stirred to enthusiasm and to great effort by persuasive words. In the defense of his own land he will always fight with great passion and bitter intensity. . . . On the whole, the officer corps is thoroughly up to carrying on a war.[6]

It still gave a high rating to the French general staff, which "works excellently from a technical point of view. It is a closed body with shared education, upbringing, and command language."

Then, however, picking up themes from prewar analyses, Foreign Armies West pointed to a central weakness—a cautiousness that could easily become excessive. In the French army, "in every strategic or tactical action, the *leadership* will always allow concern for *security* to take precedence over the possibility of achieving success by rash or bold measures ... This cautious attitude will have been strengthened by the impression of the successful German campaign in Poland." As specific manifestations of this caution, two elements of French doctrine were cited: (1) that large force elements should move only by night, thus to gain some protection against air attack, and (2) that commanders should preserve a continuous front. The analysts forecast "a hesitant procedure in all circumstances in which there is no guarantee of an unbroken front."

The French army had a naturally slow action or response rate, said Foreign Armies West—"a comparatively long period required for the preparation or conduct of an attack, the principle of identifying short-range objectives and, after the achievement of each objective, giving thought primarily to ensuring defense; a noteworthy sensitivity regarding flanks; great caution about committing any units to battle, especially new formations." A presumption that this cautiousness would affect French responses to any German attack was to be crucial in German general-staff thinking about alternative versions of Plan Yellow.

Assessing the British army at about the same time, Foreign Armies West relied even more heavily on stereotypes.[7] "Because of the national character of the English, *losses* and *setbacks* are accepted with equanimity," said its report. Though pronouncing the higher ranks in the British army pretty good, the report said in praise of lieutenants, captains, and majors only that they could exhibit "self-sacrifice, bravery, and strong nerves in face of setbacks." Army leadership, said the authors of this report, "is in general schematic and slow. Operational deftness and spirited handling of tactical maneuvers are not to be expected. ... In the lower ranks limited independence in decision is particularly apparent. On the other hand, it is a great advantage of the English to have a gift for improvisation and for simplifying their work by practical measures."

Originally, Liss and his colleagues had rated the Belgian army not on a par, man for man, with either the French or British army, but they did not dismiss it lightly. In a report also issued in October 1939, Foreign Armies West said: "The Belgian soldier has to be rated differently, depending on whether he belongs to the Walloons or to the Flemish." The Walloons, the French-speaking population mostly in southern Belgium, wrote the analysts, were similar to the French of northeastern France but less tough and brave. The Flemings, whose language resembled Dutch and who lived mostly in northern Belgium, were like the Dutch but even "more ponderous" and were braver than the Walloons. "The Belgian general staff works carefully and intelligently," wrote Foreign Armies West. "It is well organized. In tactics it follows the French model. An inclination toward schematization and also a certain narrowness in tactical outlook are characteristics of the higher leadership. It is doubtful that they can deal with a rapidly changing situation."[8]

Even though the situation maps developed by Foreign Armies West identified with increasing accuracy forces just on the other side of the German border, the shallowness of penetration by communications-interception stations, Abwehr agents, and reconnaissance planes meant that they continued to have only an unclear picture of conditions beyond the borders. In late November, Liss and his fellow analysts advised operations officers working to revise Plan Yellow that there was probably a large concentration of French reserves behind the Maginot Line. They believed most of them were about twenty miles behind the Line, but near railheads. "From that, it follows that it is possible for the French to transfer divisions to another place rapidly without a requirement of time-consuming movements."[9]

During December and the early part of 1940, the analysts in Foreign Armies West began to be more sure that the main concentration of Allied forces was along the Belgian frontier, between the Channel coast and Maubeuge. Although they continued to caution that French reserves could move rapidly by rail, they noted that flatcars and boxcars suitable for transporting troops were bunched around Lille, through which passed the main tracks to central Belgium. They had already pinpointed seventy-five Allied divisions located where their most logical axes of movement were into Belgium, included among them almost all of France's motorized and mechanized units. New pieces of information had told mostly of additions to forces so located. Supporting an obvious inference that the Allies were preparing for a large-scale move into Belgium was intelligence the Germans acquired in December 1939 that units of the British Expeditionary Force were being given maps of the Dyle River Valley, east of Brussels more than a hundred miles from the British sector of the front.[10]

On December 15, after he had begun to hope that Hitler might continue to postpone the offensive, General Halder ordered a day-long war game to test three possible versions of Plan Yellow. Though most armies used war games, the German army took them more seriously than did most others. Sometimes the games were simulations, with teams in the field operating against each other out of doors. At headquarters, a tactical game might be played on a sand table, with the sand shaped to resemble the supposed terrain. For a wider battlefield, games had to be played on maps, with markers representing units on both sides. What Halder wanted on this occasion was a strategic game, which had to be played on a large map representing the whole of northeastern France and the Low Countries.[11]

General Stülpnagel, chief of the operations staff, was to lead the German team. Liss was to play the part of the Allied commander in chief, Gamelin. According to Adolf Heusinger, who was Stülpnagel's chief assistant in the exercise, the three alternatives to be tested were:

1) The *Schwerpunkt* for the Panzer divisions lies with Bock's Army Group B.
2) The *Schwerpunkt* for the Panzer divisions lies with Rundstedt's Army Group A.
3) The *Schwerpunkt* for the Panzer divisions is not predetermined. It will only be designated when it is known whether the enemy does us the favor of going into Belgium and whether we have in the meantime succeeded in making a crossing of the Meuse near or above Sedan.[12]

In effect, the game would test the original concept for Plan Yellow against the concept being urged by Manstein and against the play-by-ear concept preferred at that moment by Hitler.

Halder told Liss, playing the Gamelin part, to presume that French and British forces would be prepared both to hold the Maginot Line and to meet a German offensive into Belgium and Holland with a counterattack. He was further to assume that

the German attack will as quickly as possible bring the Belgians to the line Meuse-Namur-Antwerp. In the vicinity, the first-line French and British units will act with their *Schwerpunkt* between the Meuse and the Escaut. The left wing seeks early support of the defensive fortifications at Antwerp and offensive use of the fortified lines by fast, heavy forces; the right wing will attempt rapid buildup of defenses on the sector of the Meuse around Namur. . . .

Halder allowed no weaknesses on the Allied side other than those already exposed on Roenne's *Kuhhaut*. Allied reserves were to be situated north of the line Dijon-Paris-Rouen, "so located that they can rapidly be moved to counter an initial attack north of the Meuse and Sambre but also south of the line. They have to be so grouped that in case of a rapid turning back of the enemy attack they can go on the offensive on the line Metz-Charleville in the direction of Cologne without much loss of time."

Liss was told to suppose that France and Britain had no prior understandings with Belgium except possibly regarding rail transport. He was expected to know the initial locations and strengths of German forces. As long as he respected these conditions, he was free to exercise command as he chose.[13]

As was explained in a postwar monograph by General Rudolf Hofmann, a German expert on war gaming, Liss "did not have to act according to German principles, but was supposed to adopt decisions and measures which . . . the Allied command would presumably have followed." Since the purpose of the exercise was primarily to define issues and focus debate, this particular game, writes Hofmann, "did not proceed in the form of a continuous game, but rather in 'bounds,' in which connection the situations which were probably to be expected were represented anew on each occasion." A major aim was to test operational timing. Hence, the officers on each team had to work with supplementary small-scale maps showing roads and even parking places. Between "bounds," with hypothetical six-hour intervals, they had to move their forces "with due regard for their security distances and the intervals between march units" and ascertain "when, where and what kind of interruptions might be expected as the result of enemy action, traffic congestion, refueling and the condition of the roads."

Liss thought he had three broad options. The first was to keep most of the Allied forces near the frontier with Germany. The second was to move most of them up to a line from Antwerp through the Dyle Valley to Namur, on the Meuse. The third was to try to support the Belgian forces on their defense line along the Albert Canal. Putting himself in the position of Gamelin, he discarded the first option, for "this would leave the Belgians in the lurch," he writes, "and turn over all of Belgium to us as a base for air operations against England." The second had the drawback of surrendering much of Belgium to Germany. The third had all the advantages:

With this approach, very little of Belgium was given up, a connection could be established with the Dutch from Antwerp, and the possibility would be preserved for a bridgehead at Namur for a later flank attack against a German offensive wedge in the Ardennes, as well as for a comparable bridgehead around Montmedy to provide for a two-sided flank attack.

At the end of the game, according to Liss, it seemed clear that from the German point of view, whatever the Allied strategy, "a German attack through the Ardennes would offer the best prospects to achieve a break-through in open territory and to catch the whole enemy force at its hinge."[14]

Heusinger's recollection is that the game established immediately that the play-by-ear concept was unworkable. It would lose too much time and leave the initiative to the enemy. The remaining alternatives, he says, "were searchingly discussed." He was sure that the game discouraged for good the thought of a German offensive along the lines of the Schlieffen Plan—an attempt to sweep through Belgium and head toward Paris. Otherwise, he remembered its producing only agreement that "in no event would [there be] commitment of the mass of Panzer units north of the area of the Meuse between Namur and Liège, for we would here have every prospect of meeting the enemy head-on." It implied shifting the *Schwerpunkt* to Rundstedt's sector, but it left open the question of whether the Ardennes Forest was the proper area for it.[15] Tippelskirch's account stresses that it remained very

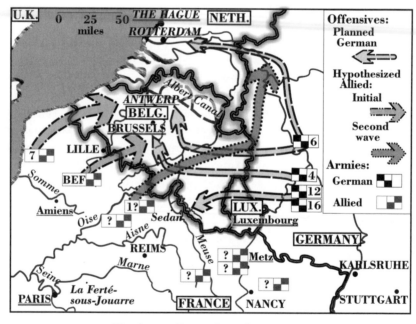

War Game at Zossen, December 27, 1939

uncertain whether large numbers of tanks could make it through that forest. Hence, he writes, "the outcome of the game brought no clarification for a new draft of the operation plan."[16]

The December war game had no immediate effects outside Zossen. Though Halder had Stülpnagel tell Jodl about the game and its results, Hitler reaffirmed his decision to let the *Schwerpunkt* be determined by events. He issued a new directive to that effect on December 28, intending it to govern the offensive supposed to commence during the clear spell in January predicted by Göring's meteorologists.[17]

The Mechelen incident, together with bad weather, caused the planned January offensive to be called off. In addition, it led Hitler to say that a new war plan was needed. This enabled General Halder to put forward the notion of shifting the *Schwerpunkt* southward. Hitler, of course, was getting similar urging from Manstein, abetted by Guderian. Also, as Hitler commented to Jodl, he believed that the documents the Allies had captured at Mechelen might have convinced French and British generals that Germany intended to attack the Netherlands and strike for the Belgian coast in order to bomb Britain. If so, Germany should turn this to advantage—and attack elsewhere. Jodl dutifully passed on briefs for an Ardennes offensive, which would do just that. Jodl himself cautioned Hitler, however, against going down "a dark path, on which one can be caught by the war god."[18]

Partly as a result of additional war games, partly just through analysis of details of transport, supply, and the like, Halder leaned increasing toward a Plan Yellow with an Ardennes *Schwerpunkt*. A game at the headquarters of the Eighteenth Army at Düsseldorf, held not long after the big game at Zossen, helped to push him in this direction, for it showed that, as Foreign Armies West had cautioned, if the *Schwerpunkt* was in central Belgium and the Allies countered by rushing their motorized and mechanized divisions northward, Bock's Army Group could find it hard to get to the Belgian coast.[19]

A subsequent game at Zossen tested further the possibility of an Ardennes-centered offensive. By this time, Foreign Armies West had obtained two new pieces of information. First, shortly before the turn of the year, it had learned that France's Seventh Army, positioned near the English Channel and outfitted for fast movement, had been designated the "Army of Intervention in Belgium." Second, it learned from radio interceptions that the French Second Cavalry Division had the assignment of covering the Ardennes when and if the Allies moved into Belgium. The first item added to Liss's confidence in the war games as, playing Gamelin, he raced the bulk of Allied mobile forces up the Belgian coast. The second caused him to show even less resistance than in December to a German drive through the Ardennes, for, as he wrote after the war (and as would in fact prove the case), the French Second Cavalry, still mostly horse-borne, seemed "sure to become a sacrifice to German tanks."[20]

Toward the end of January, Halder met with the operations-staff chiefs for the Army Groups and armies in the west. He explained that many changes were required because of the Mechelen incident. Among other things, front-line ground and air forces were going to have to go into action with much less notice than previously planned; there was too much danger otherwise of losing surprise. He then outlined a plan calling for Army Group B to make a concentrated attack on the Netherlands. For this purpose, he assigned Bock the Eighth Panzer Division. Obviously, the hoped-for effect of this concentration would be to pull the Allies as far north into the Low Countries as possible. "The greatest chance of surprise in future," said Halder, "lies in the sector of Army Group A." He therefore transferred to Rundstedt the II Corps, previously forming the left wing of Bock's Group, and he pledged to arrange not only air support for Army Group A but also paratroop landings at sites such as Arlon and Bastogne, to help Rundstedt's forces move quickly through Luxembourg, across the Belgian Ardennes, into France. "The first objective for Army Group A should be the line Bastogne-Arlon," he said. "The attainment of the line of the Meuse and Chiers would definitely mean for Army Group A the end of the first act."[21]

In early February, Halder observed the results of a game conducted at the headquarters of Army Group A at Koblenz. Manstein had gone off to his new command. Sodenstern was now Rundstedt's chief of staff. But Guderian was present, and, having been quartered next to Manstein and having heard Manstein's persistent complaints about Halder's stodginess, he expected the worst. In fact, all that developed was an argument about force mix and timing. Halder agreed to add another armored division to the assault force, but it remained an open question when the force was to reach the vicinity of Sedan and how many divisions would have to arrive before an attempt was made to cross the Meuse. When one staff officer reported to his army commander that the tight timetable troubled him, his chief said, "Don't worry. None of it will happen."[22]

A review of Luftwaffe plans gave Halder reason to expect strong air support for an attempt to cross the Meuse four days after the start of an attack. Prior to that time, the Luftwaffe would be operating primarily in support of Bock's drive into the Netherlands. Another game, run on February 14 at Twelfth Army headquarters, not far from the Luxembourg border, produced discouraging results, however. It suggested that a crossing of the Meuse might not be possible before day nine of an offensive, by which time the Allies would surely have recovered from their surprise and grouped themselves for a powerful counterattack. Halder noted in his diary that now neither Guderian nor General Gustav von Wietersheim, who was to command a motorized corps, showed any confidence in success.[23] After returning to Zossen, he himself again suffered "inner doubt about any prospects for success."[24]

A visit to Bock's headquarters at Bad Godesberg deepened Halder's skepticism, for Bock predicted that the French army would react much more quickly than Tippelskirch and Liss thought. "It is hardly to be supposed," he said, "that the French will remain on the Meuse south of Namur if a strong German attack force makes a breakthrough north of Namur . . . and if, furthermore, in the south, Army Group A breaks through the Maginot Line."[25] Rundstedt, too, seemed prey to second thoughts. His new chief of staff, Sodenstern, was much more a traditionalist than Manstein, and, on Sodenstern's advice, he began to question the feasibility of an armor-led attack. Perhaps it would be safer, the two men suggested to Halder, if the infantry led and tanks came up behind, even though this would add days to the timetable and sacrifice most of the benefits of surprise.[26]

In early March, Sodenstern sent Halder a long memorandum arguing that it would not be possible to drive through the Ardennes "entirely without an enemy reaction." Horsemen had gotten lost in the Ardennes in 1914, he pointed out. Tanks would be certain to do so if they left the roads, and they might have to do so, because the roads were bound to be mined or otherwise blocked. In any case, tanks filing through the forest would be easy targets for Allied bombers. And any tanks that reached the Meuse would find themselves in front of Allied fortifications, which they could not try to breach without support from infantry and artillery slowly coming up behind them. In effect, Sodenstern, a highly respected staff officer—and, indeed, one of the senior army officers most full of faith in Hitler—writing on behalf of the commander who would have the assignment of executing an Ardennes offensive, was giving the whole project a bath of cold water.[27] Though Rundstedt did not formally state agreement with Sodenstern, he said privately that optimism was madness (*"Unsinn"*) and that "the campaign could never be won."[28]

A new game conducted at Zossen in mid-March convinced Halder that an Ardennes offensive would have absolutely no chance of success if carried out as Sodenstern and Rundstedt were recommending. Liss, playing Gamelin again, sent the French Seventh Army far into Belgium and again needed a few days to recognize that the German *Schwerpunkt* was actually in the Ardennes. Now, however, Roenne's *Kuhhaut* showed that the most powerful French units, the two mechanized divisions of the Corps of Cavalry, were attached to the First Army, not the Seventh. So Liss deployed both the First Army and the British Expeditionary Force, the latter with four motorized divisions, southeast and south of Brussels; according to his expectations, they needed much less time to be redeployed once the Ardennes *Schwerpunkt* had been detected. Moreover, Liss, as Gamelin, had in formation in northeastern France three, perhaps four, new armored divisions equipped with Chars B, the most heavily armored tanks in the world. Once he recognized the axis of the German offensive, he organized massive drives against both flanks of Army Group A, threatening it with annihilation. It appeared that Army Group A could forestall this if—and only if—it had substantial forces west of the Meuse in less than five days. If that were the case, the Allied counteroffensive would arrive too late.[29]

General Halder concluded that he would either have to adopt a different plan altogether or accept the arguments previously advanced by Guderian and Wietersheim: in other words, to gamble that a large armored force, accompanied by some motorized infantry and lent strong air support, could not only reach the Meuse rapidly but effect a crossing before the Allies grouped for a counteroffensive. He resolved on the latter course, but not without strong misgivings. He wrote to Rundstedt, "We have to resort to extraordinary methods and accept the accompanying risks," and said to Bock, "Even if the operation were to have only a 10-percent chance of success, I would stick with it. For only this can lead to defeat of the enemy."[30]

Debate continued. Games at Fourth Army and Sixth Army headquarters uncovered new transport problems. Another big game at Zossen at the very end of March caused Bock and his commanders to revive the question of whether it was really wise to shift the *Schwerpunkt* from Belgium to the Ardennes. In the game, Rundstedt's two armored corps, now organized as Guderian recommended, managed to break through at Sedan and Charleville just before Liss (as Gamelin) could deliver a counterthrust. Bock's Army Group B, however, became stalled around the Albert Canal in northern Belgium, allowing Belgian and French forces to set up strong defenses, so that most of the French Seventh Army could be detached for the counteroffensive in the south. Halder's response was to press Göring harder to provide air support for both Army Group B and Army Group A. He pleaded for the air staff to figure out some means of spreading their limited forces so as, almost simultaneously, to fight off French and British air forces, impede the advance of French and British troops into northern and eastern Belgium, provide air cover for Rundstedt's fast-moving tank columns, then, when those columns reached the Meuse, supply them with bombers to take the place of the artillery that would not have had time to reach the scene.[31]

Sodenstern continued meanwhile to argue that Halder was making a mistake in planning for tanks to move ahead of infantry. Though he may not have known it, Guderian's staff officers themselves recognized that the pace would leave their men little time for sleep. Kielmansegg, as operations officer for the First Panzer Division, laid in twenty thousand capsules of Pervitin, a sleep-prevention pill, to distribute among them.[32]

Halder stood fast. He had decided in February to create the equivalent of an armored army. He would not call it that. It would be simply a Group, but it would include the two armored corps. To command it, he considered Manstein and Maximilian von Weichs, commander of II Corps, but he ended up choosing Ewald von Kleist, a veteran cavalryman who had shown

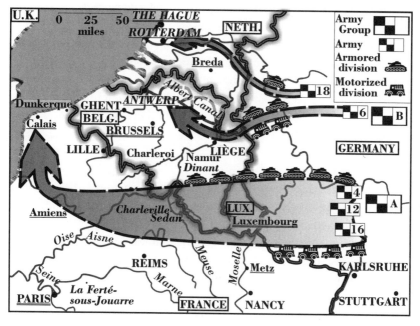

Plan Yellow, Final Version

steadiness and skill commanding motorized forces but had no experience commanding armor.[33] Hence, the organization was to be called Group Kleist.

Halder dealt with detail after detail. Elaborate plans were laid with the objective of making Bock's offensive against the Netherlands and Belgium seem, for the longest time possible, to be Germany's primary effort. Working out a suggestion that originated with Hitler, the Luftwaffe developed a plan for a dramatic glider-borne attack on Eben Emael, the strongest of Belgium's forts. Luftwaffe bombers would meanwhile concentrate on other targets in the Netherlands and Belgium—airfields and depots seemingly selected to stall an Allied movement into Belgium. They were to stage some raids in France, but He-111 bombers and Stukas were to turn in force against France only after Group Kleist reached the Meuse.

Other deceptive planning involved planting apparent indiscretions in neutral countries, giving many different dates and targets for a possible German spring offensive but mostly intended to reinforce a presumption that any offensive in the West would be some variant on the Schlieffen Plan.

Despite being a center of opposition to the regime, Canaris's Abwehr contributed by organizing this deception campaign and by collecting data requested by Foreign Armies West or field commands. In addition, Abwehr II, under Colonel Erwin Lahousen, organized covert operations to support the new version of Plan Yellow. Just beforehand, agents pretending to be tourists were to go into Luxembourg and southern Belgium and, on signal, to do what they could to prevent the destruction of bridges or mining of roadways. In the Netherlands, men costumed as Dutch policemen were to try to take possession of bridges that might otherwise be blown up.[34]

In the final stages, it remained uncertain when or whether Hitler would actually order an offensive against France. During the winter, acting at the prompting of Raeder, he had had the armed-forces high command prepare a plan for an independent offensive into Scandinavia. Keitel formed a staff for the purpose, and elements from all three services were eventually assembled to carry it out. The army high command and its air-force counterpart had only occasional advisory roles. The officers in Foreign Armies West were unaware of the operation until it was about to occur.[35]

Receiving information from Fellgiebel's communications-intelligence organizations that the Allies were planning action in Norway intended to

cut off iron-ore shipments to Germany out of the port of Narvik, Hitler decided to give a "go" signal. On March 27, he told Halder that a combined
force under General Nikolaus von Falkenhorst would move into Denmark
and make landings in Norway, with April 9 or 10 as the likely date. He said
that the offensive in the West would start a few days later, probably on Sunday, April 14.[36]

Though Germany's invasions of Denmark and Norway took place on
schedule, the offensive in the West did not. The British and French did, in
fact, move into Norway. For the better part of two weeks, German and Allied armies skirmished in central Norway. The German navy, which had
ferried in troops on destroyers and other warships, suffered catastrophic
losses. On the ground, however, the Germans prevailed, and British and
French forces withdrew. Not so in northern Norway, where the Germans had
to give up Narvik. Nevertheless, Hitler exulted. Goebbels, in his diary, described him as speaking of "a fist blow in Britain's mug [Fratze]" and "fab-
ulous success."[37]

For practical purposes, Hitler had ceded to Brauchitsch and Halder all
control over the Western offensive except the actual starting date. After
hearing out Manstein and Guderian on Plan Yellow, then learning that
Halder had virtually the same operational concept, Hitler stopped asserting
himself. In mid-March, after entertaining Brauchitsch, Halder, Bock, and
some other generals as guests at lunch, Halder noted: "No new viewpoints.
The Führer now approves the preparations made and is manifestly confident of success."[38] Subsequently, Hitler visited the headquarters of all
three Army Groups in the west and simply blessed the plans that Halder
was maturing. He did not even sit in on debates about the results of the various war games.

On April 14, however, instead of receiving an order to commence an offensive, Halder was told only that Plan Yellow would be put into effect if
things got ugly in Norway.[39] When he made inquiries at the armed-forces
high command, he was told that Hitler was uncertain about the timing: as
before, Hitler would set a date, then order a postponement, usually because
of bad weather. On May 8, though, he told his aides at the armed-forces
high command that the offensive against France could be postponed no
longer, whatever the weather. He set the early morning of May 10 as D-day.
This time, the order was not countermanded.

No German military leader was sure of success. Halder had suggested
that the odds might be ten to one against. The key field commanders,
Rundstedt and Sodenstern, repeatedly expressed doubt that the operation
would succeed, and Bock came close to predicting outright that it would

end in German defeat. Staff officers in the Fourth Army, now under Rundstedt, thought Brauchitsch's exhortations to them dismayingly similar to the parting words of a soldier entering a hopeless battle.[40] Even Guderian thought it would succeed only if everyone in Group Kleist exerted near superhuman effort—first to conceal what they were doing and then to reach and cross the Meuse. Though Manstein was naturally enthusiastic about the operational concept, he questioned whether Halder could carry it out. Only Hitler voiced complete confidence in German victory, and he had done so all along, regardless of the particular war plan.

That the revised version of Plan Yellow was being put into effect owed much to the way in which Liss had played the part of Gamelin during the exercises and war games. On the game tables and in memoranda, he and his colleagues assured the generals that French and British forces would rush into Belgium, that the Allied high command would leave weak forces behind to cover the Ardennes, and that, once they grasped what was going on, they would still be slow to redirect their efforts toward the true German *Schwerpunkt*. As Foreign Armies West had pointed out, French commanders at every level would require minute instructions that could be generated only slowly. Also, French units would have trouble turning about, because French doctrine placed such emphasis on communications security that even their mechanized and motorized units were short of radios and other means of receiving urgent orders.

Had Liss based his playing of Gamelin on a more idealized model either of Gamelin himself or of the system he worked in, he would have given an earlier Allied response to the Ardennes offensive, with the result that the game would have ended in a devastating defeat for Army Group A. The actual way he played cut across the preferences of many senior officers, for, in effect, he was saying that the French could be fooled and as a result the Allied forces could be cut in two, with French forces around the Meuse overwhelmed, leaving originally stronger Allied forces trapped in Belgium. Possibly, General Halder and the others would have continued with the revised version of Plan Yellow simply because they would have seen no other formula offering even a chance of victory within the timetable that Hitler had fixed. But Liss's confident portrayal of an Allied commander in chief who could be fooled for a fairly long time probably contributed to the acceptance and eventual implementation of the final version of Plan Yellow. As far as I know, no intelligence analyst has ever, in all of human history, had comparable influence on a great event.

PART FOUR

THE DEMOCRACIES' PREPARATIONS FOR VICTORY

CHAPTER NINETEEN

WAR BUT NOT WAR

"The French are divided into two camps, those who do not want to make peace and those who do not want to make war."
—*Alfred Sauvy, of the French Ministry of Finance, September 1939*

"A French attack against the weak German defensive front on the Siegfried Line [in September 1939] . . . would, as far as it is humanly possible to judge, have led to a very quick military defeat of Germany and therefore to an end of the war." —*Andreas Hillgruber,* Hitlers Strategie *(1965)*

In August 1939, General Gamelin had said that the French army was ready, but he had not said for what. That spring, he had promised Poland's war minister that were Germany to invade Poland, France would commence immediate air operations and, toward the third day after mobilization, "offensive actions with limited objectives." If Germany concentrated its forces against Poland, he had said, "France would unleash an offensive action against Germany with the bulk of its forces, fifteen days after mobilization."[1]

Characteristically, General Gamelin had left "offensive action" undefined. Though the French army was given to detailed plans and instructions, Gamelin himself adhered to the principle laid out in the little book he had written before the Great War—that the commander should adapt to circumstances. This gave him a rationale for postponing decisions that required either confrontation with military colleagues or specificity in understandings with allies.

Aware that General Vuillemin, chief of the French air staff, would protest sacrificing aircraft in order to relieve Poland, Gamelin had said that the promised air operations would depend on "a plan established in advance." Since no such plan existed when the war broke out, Gamelin was free to interpret France's commitment as he saw fit. As for ground-force operations, General Georges was to be in command of the entire Western front, and Gamelin had recommended to him that he prepare some offensive action but with emphasis on "limited objectives":

—in a first phase, to make contact with the German line of resistance

—in a second phase, to identify those parts of the German positions to be attacked subsequently, in correspondence with our capabilities

Though Gamelin also told Georges to prepare a larger follow-up offensive, his private resolve was to play it by ear and play very cautiously. In a note for himself, composed soon after his accord with the Poles, Gamelin wrote:

For my part, I was morally obliged to take action with the French army. On the one hand, if Germany attacked Poland with the bulk of its forces, I couldn't remain idle. (If you reason this way, you'll never have allies. Remember, this is war.) On the other hand, I could carry out a series of operations without risks, up to the Siegfried Line. Then we would see.[2]

Gamelin never supposed that Poland could hold off the German army indefinitely, but he had said on August 23 that Poland would put up "honorable resistance." He based this prediction in part on reports from a personal representative, General Félix Musse, who had been French military attaché in Warsaw a decade earlier. Musse had told him that conditions were much better than he expected, and that Polish war planning was very professional—almost French. The Deuxième Bureau had also advised him that the Polish armed forces had made marked progress in recent years. Hence, Gamelin expected and predicted that Germany would need three, possibly four, months for victory in the East. By then, winter would have arrived. The Western Allies would have at least until the spring of 1940 to determine how to act, in Gamelin's phrase, "in correspondence with our capabilities."[3]

On September 1, 1939, when Germany attacked Poland and Daladier ordered mobilization, Gamelin began to take the steps he had promised the Polish war minister. Given Vuillemin's insistence that France needed several more months to get ready for independent air operations, any air action to assist Poland depended on the British. Perhaps to his surprise, perhaps not, Gamelin found the RAF unwilling for the moment to undertake any attacks except against targets at sea. All he could pry from the British airmen—perhaps all he actually wanted—was affirmation of a commitment to send some fighters and bombers to France as soon as bases were prepared. When asked by Polish representatives "What about the promised air operations?" Gamelin answered that forward deployments of British and French aircraft forced Germany to keep some of its air forces in the West. On no evidence, but probably with confidence that Poland had no better information than he, Gamelin claimed that the Western Allies were tying down two-thirds of the Luftwaffe. When the Polish military attaché questioned this estimate, Gamelin became indignant and asked him to leave his office.[4]

Gamelin complained to Daladier that Britain's reluctance to provide air support for French ground operations handcuffed him from conducting even a limited offensive to relieve pressure on Poland. Not until France's mobilization was entering its fourth day could he send General Georges the order to set forces in motion, but he prodded him to act immediately: "If there are no shots fired, this would prove that we have done nothing, which is inadmissible." The prickly Georges jotted in the margin, "They should leave us in peace and have confidence in us." Ironically, Georges drew a similar response from General Gaston Prételat when he in turn pushed for quicker progress by forces at the front.[5]

The first units of Georges's armies began moving forward into German territory on September 7. Communiqués made the most of what these units were doing. "Our troops have made contact everywhere on our frontier between the Rhine and the Moselle," said one. Another boasted of capture of "the greater part of the Warndt Forest"; another of "furious fighting" in the vicinity of Lauterbourg, in the Saarland; yet another of a second offensive near the Luxembourg frontier and the repelling of a German counterattack. There were touches of truth in these bulletins, for French soldiers did run into mines and booby traps. One officer described part of the Warndt Forest as "a veritable volcano." Casualties—mostly wounded rather than dead— eventually numbered well over a thousand.[6] But in the end, French forces advanced only one to three miles into empty farmland. When the German army's chief supply officer, General Wagner, remarked that the communiqués were "unworthy of a great nation," the comment was echoed in France, where the economist Charles Rist noted: "The news from the front and the tone of the communiqués are exasperating to the officers. The feeling is that the current offensive is idiotic."[7]

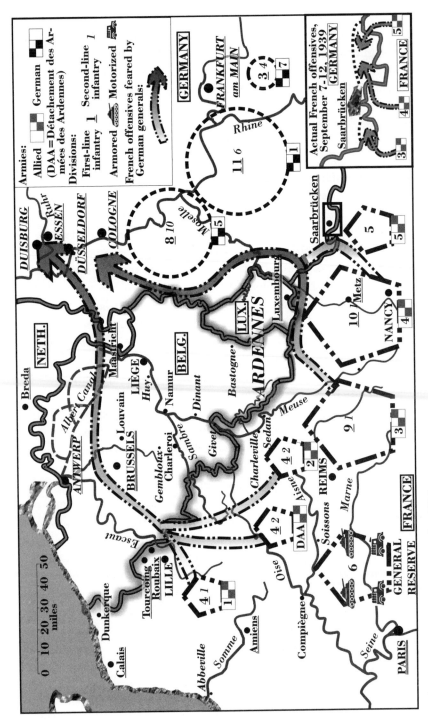

Armies:

⬛ Allied   ⬛ German

(DAA=Détachement des Ar-
mées des Ardennes)

Divisions:

1 First-line infantry
1 Second-line infantry
🚂 Armored   🚗 Motorized
French offensives feared by
German generals:

**Actual French offensives,
September 7-12, 1939**

The Western Front, Early September 1939

A number of people pressed Gamelin to get going on a large-scale offensive. Not surprisingly, Mandel was one of the first to do so, and Bonnet was another. Even though he passionately wanted no war at all, Bonnet now urged Gamelin to attack Germany so as to pull its forces away from Poland and ensure that a Polish front survived. General Pierre Héring, one of the army's most senior officers, now to be military governor of Paris, counseled him to open an immediate offensive even if it meant marching through neutral Belgium. Daladier's aide Jean Daridan heard that Gamelin's operations staff wanted serious action and thought their chief overly cautious. The Marquis de Villelume, going back and forth to Gamelin's and Georges's headquarters as liaison officer for the Quai d'Orsay, also heard this argument from operations officers, both in Paris and at the front. They talked eagerly of a frontal assault on Germany's Westwall or across Belgium.[8] It was widely expected among the public. Edmée Renaudin, the wife of a civil servant, living in the country with her five children, wrote in her diary, "We will undoubtedly attack across the Rhine."[9]

To those who urged bold action, Gamelin responded with excuses rather than arguments. He said to Mandel, "Not everything is in place." To Héring, he professed himself to be in favor of a strike through Belgium, which he couldn't do because of British objections. And he did in fact send Daladier a long memorandum saying that the best, perhaps only, route for an offensive would be via Belgium, since the German side of the border with France "has a very powerful system of fortifications," whereas Belgium offered a front twice as wide with more favorable terrain, fewer fortifications, and air bases from which to conduct operations against the German heartland. "Only through Belgium would we be able to provide Poland with assistance that would be powerful, definitely efficient, and relatively quick," he asserted.[10] But Gamelin did not end by recommending invasion of Belgium. He took it for granted that the Allies would respect Belgian neutrality. The purpose of his memorandum was probably to make it part of the record that the French government had considered an offensive in support of Poland but found it infeasible. Another purpose may have been to equip Daladier with arguments for later use with Belgium.

After 1940, it was to seem preposterous that France might ever have considered an actual large-scale offensive in 1939. Colonel Jacques Minart, Gamelin's aide, was to write in 1945, "The future historian will be stupefied at the optimism shown by those who carried out the mobilization. . . . Nothing more was required to instill in all of them a feeling of confidence in quick victory."[11] But the more we have learned about the actual military balance between Germany and the Western Allies in 1939, the less remarkable it seems that officers in Gamelin's and Georges's operations staffs should have advocated an early French offensive.

By September 6, the Maginot Line was fully manned. In addition to fortress troops, France had the equivalent of seventy-five divisions in position opposite Germany or along the borders of Luxembourg and Belgium. More than fifty of these were composed of regulars or Class A reserves, including infantrymen with fighting experience in North Africa. Two were mechanized divisions, seven were motorized, and there were two independent armored brigades.

In the mechanized divisions or armored brigades, or incorporated within infantry divisions, were more than thirty-two hundred tanks, some of which were the best in the world. One hundred and fifteen groups of the French air force were on full war footing. By prearrangement, ten squadrons of British bombers had deployed to French airfields. The Western Allies thus had formidable forces in position not only to defend France but to launch an attack.

The French general staff had an elaborate contingency plan for an attack aimed at overrunning the Siegfried Line. It was, of course, one of many such plans. Though Gamelin had shown some interest in it, most senior officers had looked upon its drafting as a theoretical exercise. Georges had scoffed at it; Villelume heard that Georges told his eager operations officers that he would resign rather than lead such an attack.[12] But the plan was in the files, ready to be executed.

As we have already seen, the German army had in the West at the time only thirty to forty makeshift divisions, composed mostly of second- and third-line troops with relatively little training. These divisions had no tanks, no motor transport, not much artillery, and not even an adequate supply of wagons and dray horses. General Leeb, their commander, rated German defenses on the Belgian border pathetic, and those opposite Luxembourg worse. He had no reserves of supplies or ammunition—none. Neither he nor the general who had been in charge of building the Siegfried Line deemed it more than a façade. Even though Hitler had given it high priority, the many demands created by his arms buildup had had the result of curtailing supplies for its construction. In practice, emphasis had gone to developing an air-defense zone between the border and the Ruhr, but that zone was, of course, temporarily empty because the German air force was mostly in Poland.[13] As the operations officers at General Georges's headquarters said to Villelume, the Siegfried Line was in almost no place proof against attack from the artillery and tanks of France's front-line units.

In 1965, the eminent (and usually prudent) German historian Andreas Hillgruber was to write: "A French attack against the weak German defensive front on the Siegfried Line . . . would, as far as it is humanly possible to judge, have led to a very quick military defeat of Germany and therefore to an end of the war." Four years later, Albert Merglen completed a doctoral thesis at the Sorbonne that analyzed in detail French and German forces on the Western front during the period of the German campaign in Poland. His conclusion was the same as Hillgruber's. Subsequently, in a published essay, he developed a plausible moment-by-moment scenario in which the German Army Group commanded by Leeb was routed, much as equivalent French armies were to be routed by German forces in 1940. In composing the scenario, he drew not only on rigorous training as a scholar but on many years of professional military experience, having turned historian after retiring as a major general in France's elite paratroop corps.[14]

Of course, the Hillgruber-Merglen thesis is fanciful. No serious historian would argue that General Gamelin could have successfully ordered an offensive against Germany in September 1939, even if he himself had been as sanguine as his and Georges's operations officers. He was confident of eventual victory. As time passed, British troops would arrive and the French army and air force and the RAF would all become progressively stronger as a result of the rearmament programs in progress. Meanwhile, Germany might collapse within, thus making sacrifice of French and British soldiers unnecessary. Why not wait? Even if Gamelin himself were not convinced by these arguments for delay, he faced near certainty that they would seem compelling to Daladier, who personally preferred to spill not a single drop of French blood, and who, in addition, feared that if serious fighting erupted the French legislature would want to exchange his government for one headed by a supposed strongman such as Reynaud or Pétain.

And even if Daladier's qualms could have been overcome, there would still have been potent resistance from general officers under Gamelin. Most of them, continuing to regard the Third Republic and the army as mutual enemies, distrusted civilian reservists and were certainly not willing to go into battle leading units that had just been mobilized. Because the economies of the 1930s had resulted in skimpy training for recruits, this reluctance had a basis in realism as well as in ideology. Army opponents of an offensive would have had strong allies in the air force and navy, for Vuillemin continued to belittle his own service's readiness and Darlan remained convinced that France would be better off conceding Central and Eastern Europe to Germany and concentrating on defending its empire against Britain.

With the British government strongly urging that France take no military action, it is almost impossible to invent a realistic political scenario that sets in motion the military scenario worked out by Merglen. But this does not undercut the argument that, had a French offensive occurred, it would have succeeded. The point that needs to be underlined again is that French decision-makers acted as they did not because they thought French forces inferior to German forces or likely to lose if a grand battle unfolded. The optimism described by Minart was pervasive. We shall see evidence of it repeatedly, even well into the Battle of France in 1940. Nor did the French government miss a great opportunity in September 1939 because it overestimated German strength. Notes written by Gamelin on September 5 show that he had a quite accurate estimate of German forces actually in the field—twenty to twenty-nine infantry divisions in the West; fifty-five in the East, including all armored and motorized forces; reserves and Landwehr being called up. He noted that, for the moment, France had an advantage of between three and four to one.[15] He decided to launch only a token offensive almost certainly because he had no doubt that France was eventually going to be victorious and had no reason to hurry decisive battles that events might render unnecessary.[16] Paradoxically and ironically, the French government may have forgone a chance to win, not lose, the war of 1939–40 not because of lack of confidence but because of overconfidence.

Had the war in Poland gone badly for Germany, Gamelin might have turned to thinking of an offensive as a *coup de grâce*. In fact, the war in Poland went better for Germany and worse for Poland than almost anyone had anticipated. From the very first hour, every truthful bulletin from Poland carried news of disaster. Germany's armies invaded Poland at daybreak on September 1. On the next day, when Daladier commenced conferring with colleagues about a declaration of war, his military aide spread out on the cabinet table a map showing German armies already holding the Polish Corridor and moving into Silesia.[17] By September 3, when France actually declared war, the maps showed German forces deep in Poland, both northwest and southwest of Warsaw; the Luftwaffe had destroyed Poland's small air force and ruined many of Poland's railway and highway bridges and other transport links.

Gamelin had set up for himself the equivalent of a field headquarters in the old Château de Vincennes, on the eastern rim of Paris. He could not establish it closer to the front because, by statute, he had to remain within call of a Comité de Guerre (Committee for War) composed of the president, prime minister, and key ministers and military chiefs. (See Appendix, pages 470–71, "Opposing Forces on the Western Front Around September 9, 1939.") But he made his headquarters Spartan, setting up a small staff in a barracks area, most of which was either windowless or looked out on the interior of an old moat. Gamelin's bedroom, writes Colonel Le Goyet, "a veritable monk's cell, contained nothing but a hospital bed, a very simple armoire, and, the only elements of comfort, a radiator and in a corner a bathtub." Villelume, who had to visit Vincennes often, recalled a first impression of a "sinister château, where the entryway reminds one a little of the Kremlin but even more, with its scrawny trees, of the Old Seraglio."[18]

At Vincennes, each subsequent day brought Gamelin news of additional German successes in Poland. Map markers had to be repositioned hourly to record the pace at which German tanks and motorized troop-carriers raced forward, with dive-bombers swooping down to clear their path. Markers representing Polish units had to be moved backward or often simply taken away, as observers reported units fragmenting or surrendering.

On September 9, with the rout of the Polish army already evident, Gamelin held an 8 A.M. meeting at Vincennes with officers of the army general staff. Since his own quarters were so spare, such conferences had to take place in a ceremonial room which a British officer described as "a medieval hall, on the walls of which hung a number of hideous and incongruous modern paintings."[19] Gamelin directed the staff officers to advise General Georges that Poland was near its end and to warn that Germany might in the near future turn against France "with the totality of its forces and perhaps those of Italy."[20]

On September 10, the end of France's first week of war, an attempt by Poland to mount a counteroffensive ended with the one remaining Polish army totally surrounded. On the next morning, Gamelin traveled to La Ferté-sous-Jouarre, the town thirty miles from Paris where General Georges had set up his field headquarters.

Three years Gamelin's junior, Georges presented himself as a bluff, pipe-smoking, no-nonsense soldier. Back in 1934, he had been with Foreign Minister Louis Barthou in Marseilles when Barthou was killed by a terrorist bomb, and the attack had wounded him, too: he had never recovered use of his left hand, which dangled in a cotton glove. Throughout the decade, he had been a voice of caution in the military establishment, questioning mechanization and other forms of innovation. When war came and he took up command of all French field forces in northeastern France, he rejected the idea of basing himself at Vincennes with Gamelin in part because it was located in a working-class area where "people profess the most subversive opinions."[21] At La Ferté he took over a grand residence, Les Bondons, which looked down on a largely medieval town through which the Jouarre River coursed. The glass doors of his conference room opened onto a large English lawn bordered by chestnut trees.

There Gamelin repeated his earlier warning. He even took pains to caution the conservative Georges against pushing any farther the token offensive into the Saarland. "Don't get your nose into the barbettes of the Boches," he said, referring to the turrets notched with gunposts that were features of fixed fortifications. "Instead, remain outside the range of their guns, so that the barbettes cannot serve the Germans as bases for a counterattack. Remember 1914. The Boches gave ground in order to draw [us] into a pocket that they had prepared."[22]

On September 17 came news that the Soviet army was moving into eastern Poland, effecting the partition provided for in secret clauses of the Nazi-Soviet pact. Though individual Polish units had fought well and continued to do so, there remained no semblance of a Polish front. General Lord Gort, newly designated as commander in chief of the British Expeditionary Force, flew to Paris to confer with Gamelin about the contingency of an immediate German turn against France.[23]

For more than a week, Gamelin had known that Germany was shifting forces to the West. (He did not know that these were the emergency redeployments Brauchitsch had ordered in response to General Leeb's warning that he could not otherwise hold off a French attack for even a day.) Unable to gauge the scale of these force transfers, he had no clear sense of how many divisions France might now face over and above the twenty to twenty-nine in place a fortnight earlier. Minart writes: "There was a great uncertainty at French Supreme Headquarters as to the quality of the German forces between the Moselle and the Rhine. Was the enemy facing us with active or reserve troops, or just with border guards? Were these troops organized differently? Did they have minefields and tank obstacles in place? Was their artillery in front of the Siegfried Line? Did they have armored vehicles?"[24] For the moment, neither the Deuxième Bureau nor the intelligence sections of French field forces had answers to any of these questions.

The possibility that Germany might be readying an early Western *Blitzkrieg* caused Gamelin and Georges to agree that they should not only halt the mini-offensive in the Saarland but give up its paltry gains, though they recognized the risk to morale, both among soldiers and at home, of announcing a pullback, having so loudly overstated this mini-offensive's scale and importance. Georges got into a staff car at La Ferté which, sirens screaming, carried him to the War Ministry building in Paris. (Sirens and high speed were routine for general officers' cars traveling to and from La Ferté.) There he met Gamelin, and the two of them walked up to Daladier's private office to tell him what they believed should be done. He approved, subject to the condition that there be no advance publicity. No civilian was to be told other than the president of the republic. Gamelin then gave Georges a personal and secret note suggesting but not ordering the pull-back: General Georges would thus bear responsibility for the actual order, but if there were recriminations, all three men could point fingers at one another.[25]

When the fact of the pullback became evident, a number of members of Parliament and newspaper editors expressed indignation, yet the noise quickly died down. Politicians and journalists found it uncomfortable to argue that more French soldiers should have died or been wounded. But the original sensitivity to possible criticism on the part of Daladier, Gamelin, and Georges, and the criticism itself, are significant reminders that wartime military decisions in France, tactical as well as strategic, were in some ways peacetime diplomatic decisions: political and military leaders bore responsibility for making them, but their range of choice was limited to options not likely to evoke strong resistance within elements of a pluralistic democracy.

Gamelin continued to look for signs that Germany might be planning to turn against France as soon as it finished off Poland. When General Gort visited him on September 17, he talked of little else. Since he wanted maximum effort from Britain, he might well have been overstating the case, but in his private journal, he wrote on the next day: "If Germany throws all its forces against us, the outcome of the war could be decided in one day with a single blow, and France is immediately at risk."[26] (There was no implicit pessimism in this note, merely a professional soldier's ingrained awareness of uncertainty—that, as Karl von Clausewitz had put it in *On War*, "there is no human affair which stands so constantly and so generally in close connection with chance as war.")

Reports from the Deuxième Bureau gave increasingly strong evidence that Germany was preparing an offensive. Maps of the Western front pinned up at the Château de Vincennes showed new concentrations of heavy artillery not far from the Luxembourg border, and motorized forces streaming into an area around Aachen that seemed a likely point of departure for an attack on Belgium.[27] In early October these maps began to include information from SR agents, signal intercepts, and aerial photography on moves being made in Germany as a result of Hitler's order for a prompt offensive. Earlier, Gamelin's staff had been able to pinpoint only eighteen German divisions along the Western front, though suspecting that the actual number could be twice as high.[28] By early October, they thought they could identify sixty to seventy German divisions, mostly between the Moselle and the Rhine, opposite Luxembourg and the Maginot Line.[29]

Georges and his chief of staff, General Henri Bineau, interpreted these German deployments as intended for defense, not offense. Though bridge-building on the Rhine and in the Saarland and the arrival of dive-bombers at bases in the Rhineland fitted the hypothesis of an impending attack on France, hurry-up work on additional tank barriers behind the Siegfried Line seemed to Georges and Bineau more consistent with a supposition that the Germans expected an Allied attack and were getting ready to defend themselves.[30] Estimating that not more than fifty German divisions were combat-ready, Bineau made light of the chance that Germany's generals might challenge what they presumably knew to be seventy-odd first-line French divisions. Germany might strike the Netherlands, Bineau thought, but not France or Belgium.[31] Colonel Georges Vialet, of Georges's operations staff, expressed equally strong doubts not only about German intentions but about the Deuxième Bureau's estimates. After a long visit, Villelume summarized in his diary what Vialet had said:

> The Germans will not take risk unless they can bring into play a technical surprise: bacteria, unknown gases, or very large tanks. It is estimated, he continued, that facing us are seventy divisions, including those on the Rhine or farther in the rear as a reserve. But we don't have anything precise on this subject. In reported groups of ten or twelve, often only a single one can be identified by its [division] number. Gauché does not have the stature for his task. If it were known who could replace him, he would be fired.[32]

But Gamelin credited the evidence Gauché gave him. His diary for October 5, a week after Poland's final capitulation, says, "The situation is evolving quickly; it is a matter of a few days."[33] On October 9, he heard Gauché predict that the Germans were likely to make a big push against

France on October 15. On at least two occasions, Gamelin summoned Rivet to get details about what SR agents were reporting. Via Brussels, Gamelin received Colonel Oster's warning of the directive Hitler issued on October 9 ordering a broad-front offensive against France.[34] The air force's intelligence arm advised him at about the same time that the Germans had fifteen bomber squadrons at Cologne being fitted out with heavy bombs specially designed for use against the Maginot Line.[35]

Taken all together, this intelligence seemed to Gamelin to create near certainty. He not only advised Daladier that an offensive against the Maginot Line was likely, but issued to all soldiers an Order of the Day saying: "Soldiers of France! A battle may begin at any moment on which again depends, as before in our history, the fate of the nation. The eyes of the country, those of the whole world, are on you. Lift up your hearts. Use your weapons well. Remember the Marne and Verdun!"[36]

Yet all that the German army did was to move back into the Saarland pastures that France had occupied in its token offensive and then abandoned after the collapse of Poland on September 27. Georges and Bineau thought this proved that Gamelin had been a victim of baseless fears, that there had never been any prospect of an immediate German attack. Gamelin, not surprisingly, presumed not that he had been wrong, but that the Germans had indeed planned an offensive and decided to call it off, perhaps because of almost continuous heavy rainfall.

He was more nearly right, but his conclusion accorded too well with some of his basic preconceptions. On September 27, the day of Warsaw's capitulation, General Édouard Réquin, commander of one of Georges's armies, recorded Gamelin's saying at Georges's headquarters:

> Hitler cannot remain inactive. He would lose prestige both within Germany and outside. He needs a victory. Therefore, he must do something before winter. . . . His only chance for immediate success is to invade Belgium and perhaps part of Holland. If he waits, he would give everyone the impression of a lack of confidence in his forces; he would allow us to put together a great army; and he would give us the time to reinforce our military base, in particular our air force. If he attacks now, I am hopeful he would be beaten. If he waits until spring, he definitely will be.[37]

This was the framework within which Gamelin placed reports from subordinates or from French intelligence services. When no attack came, he assumed the Germans had concluded that they were incapable of launching a successful attack.

This was, indeed, an accurate reading of how Germany's generals were thinking, but it is an interpretation of events that misses the truth about Hitler. Although the Deuxième Bureau received and passed on numerous reports of differences between Germany's generals and Hitler, Gauché told Gamelin, "Military decisions are made by Hitler and his entourage."[38] If Germany had planned an offensive and then called it off, it followed that Hitler, as well as his generals, had judged victory to be out of reach, or so Gamelin supposed. The result was that he became even more confident of Allied superiority and eventual Allied victory.

In November, Gamelin again saw indications of Germany's preparations for an offensive. Separately, the army and air-force intelligence bureaux sent him reports, said to be based on excellent sources, telling of high-level debates in Berlin that produced a decision against early attack in the West; but the SR intercepted a message from Himmler to a subordinate directing preparations for an early "decision in the West." Almost simultaneously, the Belgian ambassador in Berlin, Davignon, sent Brussels an urgent war warning. Again, the source was Colonel Oster of the Abwehr, via the Dutch and Belgian military attachés, who had passed on what he heard at second hand about the November 9 meeting at the Chancellory, where Hitler had stormed against Brauchitsch and Halder for their failure to carry out his order. Davignon said that other sources confirmed that a decision for an offensive had been made.[39]

Gamelin questioned Rivet about SR evidence but got no clear answers. As Rivet summarized it for his desk diary:

> The point of view of the SR [is] that the disposition and strength of the German forces in the West has not changed much. [There is] no movement into an attack mode with deployment of tanks. The German threat is being advertised, in order to enhance the peace offensive and to work on the neutrals. An offensive remains entirely possible, but it is not possible to know the intentions of the enemy.[40]

Only after another week did Rivet feel able to conclude that the alarm sounded through Brussels was probably false. Though he noted a continuing German buildup opposite the Netherlands, his diary entry for November 15 reads: "None of the intelligence coming from the legations and military attachés giving dates for the forthcoming German offensive seem to be confirmed. The SR has nothing to report."[41] Gauché meanwhile told Gamelin that he believed the danger of an attack to have lessened.[42] Around the Château de Vincennes, the whole episode seemed to confirm their earlier conclusion. Minart wrote, "In the final analysis, the French high command is inclined to interpret the passivity of the adversary as a favorable indication: wouldn't it have been in Germany's interest, in view of its economic difficulties, to move the war into a rhythm of decisive violence before the Allies could bring into play the immense resources at their disposal?"[43]

In mid-December, the Deuxième Bureau told Gamelin and the general staff that Germany would strike in the West only as an act of desperation. Hitler, it said, "does not 'think' of war in the classic manner" but counts on winning wars by subversion rather than by frontal battle. After defeating Poland, he had hoped to lure the Allies into another arranged peace, in which case France "could be out of the game forever. Politically, it would find it impossible to take up arms again." This tactic having failed, "the dominant thought of Hitler is to achieve conquest while avoiding a large-scale continental war," for he recognizes that

a war against France is by definition a war of slaughter. Whether it throws itself against the Maginot Line, or whether it tries to go around it by violating solemn pacts of neutrality, the German army cannot hope to conquer us without enormous human sacrifice. In this respect, such a war [would be] unpopular in Germany. With the risks stemming from the unpopularity of war, a serious defeat could have incalculable consequences. It could bring about the fall of the Nazi regime.

Hence, the Deuxième Bureau predicted, Hitler would wage a naval and air war against Britain. Believing the British to be materialists, he would count on them to quit the war once their pocketbooks suffered. Meanwhile, he would concentrate on propaganda and subversive activity aimed at dividing France from Britain, provoking class tension, strikes, and revolutionary movements, and encouraging a peace movement. The important front for 1940 would be the domestic front, concluded the Deuxième Bureau. There what would be needed would be "pitiless and relentless repression of all pro-German or communist activities" and "a persevering effort of counter-propaganda and education."[44]

CHAPTER TWENTY

"THE BORE WAR"

"In some quarters this war has already been named "The Bore War."
—*Diary of John Colville, assistant private secretary to prime ministers
Chamberlain and Churchill, September 28, 1939*

General Gamelin, believing as he did that Germany had decided on an offensive and then called it off because the odds were unfavorable, and believing also that time probably worked to the advantage of the Allies, set about preparing to win the war.

He had some basis for hope that the Allies would be victorious without ever going fully into battle. Just about everyone in authority in France or Britain was sure that Germany could not wage a long war. They reckoned that it was already short of iron ore, oil, and other key resources. They believed that an Allied blockade would starve the Germans as it had during the Great War. This belief was bolstered by the expectation that they would receive material support from the United States, and actions taken recently by the American government, though modest, seemed to justify this expectation. In early November 1939, for example, the U.S. Congress amended the 1937 Neutrality Act. Instead of forbidding sales of war materiel to any belligerent state, the act now permitted sales to belligerent states able to pay cash and to carry the materiel away in non-U.S. ships, which, of course, had to be ships permitted by the British navy to use the high seas.

In French and British cabinets and in an Anglo-French military liaison committee set up in September 1939, the dominant subject was the economic war. Ministers, senior officials, and senior military and naval officers tracked Germany's imports and exports, data on its industrial production and standards of living, and rumors about German morale. On average, they spent at least four hours on the economic war for every hour they spent on the possibility of major battles. (The fact that the proportion was very much the reverse on the German side had something to do both with Germany's success in 1940 and with German failures thereafter.)

The top-level emphasis on economic warfare naturally influenced priorities in intelligence collection. French intelligence services were reorganized in September 1939, with the SR detached to become an autonomous Cinquième Bureau. Although this new Cinquième Bureau, with its rich human- and signal-intelligence sources, continued to feed information to the Deuxième Bureau, it began to produce its own intelligence summaries, nearly all of which concerned economic conditions in Germany. It may have been this focus, with lessened attention to operational military forces, that caused Colonel Louis Rivet at the SR not to see signs of German preparations for an offensive in November. It may also have been a reason for the shortcomings in Gauché's capacity to identify enemy divisions (commented on by Colonel Vialet of General Georges's operations staff), for SR agents spent much of their energy gathering data on freight movements, factory inventories, and the lengths of lines at food stores.

The Cinquième and Deuxième Bureaux continually encouraged General Gamelin to believe that Germany might collapse all on its own. In early October, the air force's Deuxième Bureau reported:

> According to intelligence from good sources, the Hitler regime will continue to hold power until the spring of 1940 [and] then will be replaced by communism. . . . Certain categories of the German population (the aristocracy, general officers and other senior officers, industrialists, merchants, and peasants) are very much against the war and against Hitler, who [is seen as] leading the country into communism and anarchy.

The army's Deuxième Bureau sent in an almost identical report, citing State Secretary Weizsäcker by name as one of its sources.[1]

Gamelin clearly placed some faith in these predictions. "He thought that if nothing happened before the 10th of November we were comparatively safe this winter. Hitler would then be finished," he said in early October to General Sir Edmund Ironside, chief of the British army's Imperial General Staff.[2] And Gamelin was relatively cautious. Bineau and Georges assumed all along that Hitler and his generals would think it folly to launch an offensive. Léger said to the Italian ambassador, doubtless partly for effect but also partly in earnest, that Germany had had its one chance to attack France during the mobilization in September, and after that its military position had worsened. The German army could make minor advances into France only with huge losses of life and could not move against the Low Countries because it lacked the trained reserves needed for a war of movement. What German submarines and bombers could do against Britain would have little effect. Germany's cause, said Léger, was lost. At Georges's headquarters, Villelume heard a British general say, "The war is over. It is won." He also saw officers of Georges's operations staff working on peace terms and putting up on a wall a map that showed Germany broken up into five parts. At the very end of the year, Géneviève Tabouis would write in L'Oeuvre, "It seems to everyone indisputable that the Allies have won the war."[3]

When he was still expecting an early German offensive in the West, General Gamelin had speculated on its coming through the Ardennes Forest. Neither he nor any other French generals ever believed the Ardennes impassable, an area where Germany could not attack. After 1940, Pétain was reproached for having described the Ardennes Forest as "impenetrable." It was seldom remembered that he had added, "if special arrangements were made."[4] Nor was it understood in retrospect that Pétain's purpose was to resist too categorical a commitment to a defensive Maginot Line strategy. French politicians, especially from northeastern departments, wanted the Line extended so that all of France would be behind an iron wall. Daladier sometimes took this position, but professional soldiers, including Pétain and Gamelin, opposed it for two reasons. For some, the primary factor was economic. To extend the Maginot Line into the northeast, with its high water table, would be horrendously expensive, siphoning off all the funds that might otherwise go to troops or training or modernized equipment. For others, the primary objection was strategic: with an extended Maginot Line, France would have less flexibility in fixing the takeoff point for an offensive. Describing the Ardennes Forest as a natural bulwark helped to fend off proposals that underground rail lines, turrets, and the rest be built north and west of Longwy, where the Maginot Line now terminated. The characterization had plausibility, for the terrain was forbidding. An official manual warned British forces coming to France that, viewed from the French side, "the Ardennes appear as a black wall of for-

est rather than as a mountain range. Forests and peaty moors cover the surface whose shales and slates have weathered into stiff clay soils, often wa-
terlogged and boggy," and traversed by few roads.[5] But Gamelin and his
fellow generals were well aware that the Ardennes Forest had been a maneuver area for German armies in the Franco-Prussian War and the Great
War and for other armies in centuries past.

In May 1939, Gamelin had toured the Ardennes front and returned expressing serious concern about the weakness of French forces there, particularly their shortages of artillery and antitank weapons. In September, as
Ironside reported to another British general, Gamelin predicted that the
Germans would try to pin down French forces behind the Maginot Line,
then "attack across the western frontier of Luxembourg into the Ardennes,
sweeping south of the Meuse, which could be blocked, and from which no
Belgian attacks need be expected, against the whole length of the Franco-
Belgian frontier south of the Meuse to Namur, then across the Meuse and
south of the Sambre to Charleroi." He said that the German right might
"extend out to perhaps Valenciennes." Except for describing a maneuver
centered slightly farther north and with more of a hook shape than a sickle
shape, Gamelin could have been sketching the final version of Germany's
Plan Yellow. Ironside described him as "very calm" about this prospect,
commenting that the Germans had had more divisions in 1914 than they
had now and that the French defensive position was much stronger.[6]

What led Gamelin to discount an Ardennes scenario was his analysis of
the Polish war. Later, it would be said that France took no warning from this
first example of German *Blitzkrieg*: postwar memoirs cited officers and officials who simply sniffed that France was not Poland. This did occur, and
some Frenchmen discounted the Polish experience on the presumption that
the Poles were backward. Daladier called Poland's leaders "childlike."[7]
But evidence from the autumn of 1939, uncontaminated by knowledge of
later events, shows that French leaders, and British as well, gave very close
attention to the brief Polish war. Though they quite sensibly took note of
differences in terrain, training, doctrine, and such, they were, if anything,
too prone to see analogies between what had happened in Poland and what
might happen in the West.

Gauché's Deuxième Bureau had an important hand in framing French
understanding of the Polish war. Observers who returned from Poland prepared detailed reports. General Félix Musse, the former military attaché
who had been Gamelin's special representative in Warsaw; General Louis
Faury, once in secondment as director of the Polish War College, who had
headed an army mission to Warsaw in August; and General Jules Armen-

gaud, a former inspector general of the air force, who had headed a companion air mission, all had to explain why they had been wrong in predicting sustained Polish resistance to the German invasion. Perhaps not surprisingly, Musse and Faury, as ground-force officers, called attention in particular to the speed and effectiveness of German tanks and mobile infantry, and Armengaud, a flier, emphasized how the Luftwaffe had made it hard for the Poles to move or mass their own soldiers and horses. Gauché's aides took account of these reports and, in addition, interviewed and collected questionnaires from no fewer than six hundred men who had fought in Poland or watched the fighting there.

In October, Gauché published and distributed to all higher headquarters a pamphlet on the Polish campaign. It was circumspect, commenting that German operations in Poland "were in response to a particular strategic situation" and that on a Western front "operations would doubtless be of another sort." Nevertheless, it set forth seven respects in which, "on some parts of this front, the methods of the Polish campaign will again be applied":

1) Germany concentrated on defeating Poland's armed forces, passing up the temptation to seize Warsaw or other cities.

2) The Germans obtained air superiority from the very beginning, bombing railroads, military headquarters, and armaments factories, thus achieving "an almost complete paralysis of the Polish high command."

3) The Germans used autonomous formations of tanks in much the same way—to strike Polish communications lines and command centers.

4) In a second phase, tanks and mobile infantry combined to operate as much as fifty miles ahead of their advancing main infantry units.

5) Planes, tanks, and artillery were well coordinated.

6) The Germans had the advantage of a large intelligence network, chiefly composed of sympathetic ethnic minorities, that identified targets for bombing or tank attack.

7) The Germans battered Polish defense lines, taking advantage of the fact that the Polish army chose to fight at its borders instead of pulling back to prepared defensive positions.

Gauché later described this pamphlet as "without doubt the most important document that left the Deuxième Bureau in the course of the war." Since preparation for a war in the West was to be guided by a presumption that it would resemble the war in Poland, and since this pamphlet was the most readily available authoritative study of that war, he may have been right.[8]

Individuals differed in what they took to be the chief lessons of the Polish war. When Colonel de Gaulle said to General Georges that it confirmed his long-standing argument in favor of professionally manned armored divisions equipped for fast offensive operations, Georges chided him for downplaying the role of aviation. This was partly because Georges thought the Polish war confirmed his view that it had been a mistake to make the air force independent. He wrote in his diary:

> The war in Poland has demonstrated the advantages of employing the air force in liaison with the other arms. This being the case, we must get rid of compartmentation and make clear at each echelon the position of the air commander in relation to the ground commander. [There must be] a double subordination, [both] tactical and technical. Don't be afraid to say it. In essence, achieve unity of action if not of command. . . . Too many headquarters staffs . . . concentrate all powers in the hands of the chief.[9]

Gamelin was also inclined to note particularly the apparent lessons of the Polish war that jibed with what he had said earlier. During the 1930s, he had periodically prodded his more conservative colleagues to prepare for a war of movement, different from the static trench warfare of 1914–18. The Polish war seemed to him proof of the point. He directed Georges to "get the troops used to the idea that the battle can take a different form from that seen since the outbreak of hostilities: air attacks, use of gas, massive use of other means of destruction." Above all, the troops should be prepared to guard islands of resistance, not dispersing in the face of bombers and tanks but staying in place and preparing to counterattack as the enemy's main forces moved up behind the assault wave.[10] He also drew from the Polish experience a reinforcement for the doctrine of maintaining a continuous front and an accompanying inference that, to shelter against air attack, troops should move mainly by night.[11]

Across the Channel, Prime Minister Chamberlain saw in the Polish campaign evidence that the long-range bomber would be the war's decisive weapon. He wrote to his new Cabinet colleague, Winston Churchill:

> To my mind the lesson of the Polish campaign is the power of the Air force when it has obtained complete mastery in the air to paralyse

the operations of land forces . . . , and, as a result, it seems to me to be above all things vital that we should not allow ourselves to get into the same position vis à vis Germany as the unfortunate Poles. . . . Accordingly, as it seems to me, absolute priority ought to be given to our Air force, and the extent of our effort on land should be determined by our resources *after* we have provided for Air force extension.[12]

The fact that Georges, Gamelin, Chamberlain, and others drew different lessons from the Polish war is not surprising. Nor is it surprising that the most common conclusion was, I thought so all along! Human minds often work this way.[13] More significant was how much these various leaders agreed that a war in the West was likely in important respects to resemble the war in the East. True, the soldiers and statesmen in Paris and London would time and again hark back to supposed lessons from other events. Gamelin often drew analogies with the days of his service with Joffre. Georges would allude to the examples of Foch or Pétain. Churchill hardly let a day pass without recalling—and reminding others of—events when he had previously been First Lord of the Admiralty, from 1911 to 1915. But the influence of these more distant experiences, either as sources of precepts or as effective arguments, was greatly lessened by their agreement that the Polish war gave the best indications of what war would be like in the present day.

Three presumptions seemed to be accepted. The first was that any German offensive would take the form of a *Blitzkrieg*. *Time* magazine's coverage of the Polish war helped to give this word universal currency.[14] The French general staff issued instruction after instruction, nagging field commanders to work on antitank defense and prepare to deal with low-flying aircraft.

A second presumption was that Germany would make use of a "fifth column." The phrase had been popularized during the Spanish Civil War by the Soviet-backed Republicans, who had claimed that Franco and his Nationalists had attacked and taken Madrid by deploying five columns, four of which consisted of troops outside the city, the fifth of fascists planted behind Republican lines. In France, fascistlike organizations such as the Jeunesses Patriotes had long been suspected of being under Germany's direct influence. Communists had always been widely thought to be both plotters of revolution and tools of the Soviet Union. The Nazi-Soviet pact and the French Communist Party's wartime line, which decried the war against Germany as "imperialistic," made communists seem agents of the enemy.[15] When the SR separated from the Deuxième Bureau and became an autonomous Cinquième Bureau, one of its major components was a Section de Centralisation (SCR), charged with counterespionage. The general staff directed field commanders to give SCR officers every facility for sniffing out subversives.[16] Some of these officers were inclined to see subversion in any words complimentary to the Popular Front. After the war, one veteran, Lucien Rebatet, would write two volumes entitled, with no irony, *Memoirs of a Fascist*. Though the activities of SCR officers almost certainly created collection problems for the German Abwehr, their scrutiny of soldiers' letters and their interrogations of suspects irritated left-wing reservists and draftees, sowed suspicion, and did more harm than good.

Partly from fear of fifth columnists, partly from a supposition that Germany had efficient intelligence services, the army also took extreme precautions against enemy interception of communications. General Colson, now chief of staff for what was called the Army of the Interior (to distinguish it from Georges's Army of the Northeast), assumed personal responsibility for security in radio and telephone communications and made detailed arrangements for protecting ciphering equipment from being captured. One result was to make it difficult for Germany to learn much from signal intelligence, but another was to slow the installation of radios in tanks and other vehicles and to limit communication even among higher commands, let alone field units. Gamelin, at the Château de Vincennes, and Georges, thirty miles away at La Ferté-sous-Jouarre, sent each other written messages via courier rather than using telephone or radio.[17]

These two supposed lessons of the Polish war—to expect *Blitzkrieg* and to be wary of German spying—created some tension. The first counseled readiness for prompt action; the second blocked the communication necessary for prompt action. The result was to increase dependence on advance preparation. Since France's military forces had a tradition of top-down control, as the Germans had noted, partly because France's services were manned mostly by civilian reservists but run by professionals distrustful of civilians, advance preparation meant issuance of painstaking step-by-step instructions. From October 1939 on, memoranda to French field commanders from army or air-force headquarters prescribed with increasing precision what was to be done to make ready for an enemy attack and what was to happen, quarter-hour by quarter-hour, if attack came. The commanders had to fill out long questionnaires testifying that they were complying with these instructions. One officer on the staff of an army commander was reproached by General Gamelin himself for writing orders that were "too concise, hence incomplete."[18]

More important still, given the later consequences, was a third presumption based on the Polish experience—namely, that it was critical not to repeat Poland's mistake of trying to meet a *Blitzkrieg* head-on. Gamelin had long favored the principle of defense in depth, which had been one of his major reasons for resisting the enthusiasm of Daladier and others for extending the Maginot Line up into northeastern France. He thought it preferable in every respect for the front lines to be in the Low Countries, with northeastern France well to the rear. After studying the Polish campaign, he became dogmatic in insisting that, if there was active fighting in the West, the initial front should be as far forward as feasible.

By November 1939, Gamelin had come to think it highly likely that any German offensive would take more or less the route prescribed in Germany's pre-1914 Schlieffen Plan. German armies would wheel through Belgium and then cut toward Paris. (There was near consensus among analysts of the Great War that the German offensive of 1914 would have succeeded had it not been for last-minute redeployments that were inconsistent with the Schlieffen Plan.) Gamelin's earlier presumption that an attack might

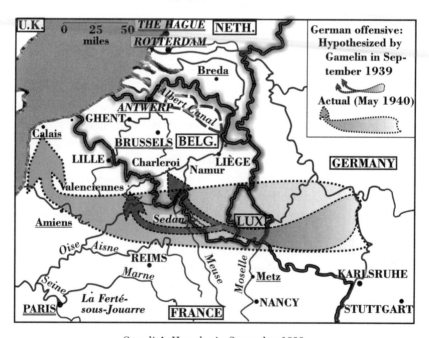

Gamelin's Hypothesis, September 1939

come through the Ardennes probably rested on Deuxième Bureau and SR reports that large numbers of German tanks had broken down in Poland and that Germany's armored divisions would be out of action until at least late October.[19] He had imagined men and horses filtering through the Ardennes as they had in the days before motor vehicles, but once the German army reconstituted its armored forces, the logical place for a *Blitzkrieg* on the Polish model seemed to be the coastal plain of Belgium. At the same meeting in which Gamelin sketched a possible German attack through the Ardennes, he said (according to notes by Ironside's aide, Colonel Roderick Macleod):

> The chief lesson to be learnt from the Polish campaign was the penetrative power of the speedy and hard-hitting German armoured formations and the close cooperation of their Air force. . . . Belgium was the more likely target because the Ardennes was not a good tank country and there were good defences behind Luxembourg. . . . The German attack would smash itself on the strong Allied defences, [and once the Germans were weakened, France] would start a counter-offensive. . . . Quite clearly and emphatically . . . there was only one place where the decisive battle could be fought and that was on the plains of Belgium.[20]

It exasperated Gamelin that Belgium could not be induced to enter into planning for joint action to deal with a German offensive. At a meeting with field commanders in late September, he reportedly exclaimed, "The two best auxiliaries of Hitler were the Russian and the Belgians."[21] He tried to precipitate staff talks by sending word to Brussels that France could not aid Belgium without prior planning. With his encouragement, Daladier used his roughest manner on a visiting Belgian political leader, saying to him: "The Belgian Government does not want to have contacts between headquarters. That's too bad. If Belgium is invaded, we will await the Germans on our border. Belgium will be destroyed." Daladier alleged that the British had said to him, " 'Since the Belgians refuse contacts between headquarters, when they are invaded we will drop bombs on their cities.' "[22]

General Gamelin nevertheless ordered continued preparation for moving into Belgium when and if Germany attacked. From his standpoint and that of other Allied planners, there seemed three possible lines of defense in Belgium. The first was the Escaut (or Scheldt) River, which crossed from France into Belgium not far from Lille, about seventy-five miles from the

North Sea coast, then ran through Tournai and Ghent and emptied into the North Sea about fifty miles west of the port of Antwerp. Deep, with steep banks above Ghent, then shallow and slow but usually wide as it meandered onward, the Escaut seemed to a military eye "a very wide ditch, very easy to defend," as General Bineau put it. Its chief liabilities were, first, that at some points its eastern bank had dominating cliffs that could serve the Germans as observation posts and sites for artillery; second and more important, that it was a line not very far away from France proper.[23]

A second possible line ran along the Dyle River, which rose in the Belgian Ardennes, trickled northward to the venerable university city of Louvain (or Leuwen), then bent sharply toward the west and merged with the Escaut, near its mouth, at Antwerp. Slow-moving at best and in many places narrow, the Dyle did not form a natural barrier comparable to the Escaut, less still to the wide, deep Meuse running through eastern Belgium. But the Dyle line had the advantage of covering much more of Belgium than the Escault line, including Brussels and its sprawling suburbs. If French and British forces took positions on the Dyle, they would have a significant part of the Belgian army beside them, and, precisely because the Dyle was not hard to cross, they could probably either receive retreating Belgian troops or, if the Belgians managed to hold a more distant line, reinforce them. If the Germans pushed the Belgians back and themselves crossed the Dyle, then the wooded highlands west of the river, a network of other small streams, and the built-up outskirts of Brussels would all provide good ground for a slow Allied retreat, draining German reserves of fuel and other supplies and thus setting the stage for the projected Allied counteroffensive.

The third line was the one the Belgians had prepared as their front line against Germany. It ran north and east of Antwerp along the deep, straight Albert Canal, then joined the Meuse just above Liège. Eben Emael, a fortress modeled on part of the Maginot Line, served as a hinge. Fortifications then followed the left bank of the river upstream toward France, with other strong points, especially at Huy, Namur, and Dinant. From Gamelin's standpoint, this was much the best of the three lines. French, British, and Belgian forces could act in coordination. They would be behind prepared defenses. They would be another eighty to a hundred miles farther away from French soil, with that much more space for maneuver warfare. But with no prior planning, perhaps even without some prior forward deployments, French and British troops would have a hard time getting there before a German breakthrough.

It was this that so vexed Gamelin. He was almost certain that the Germans would strike through Belgium. Believing that this should be as plain to the Belgians as it was to him, he struggled to comprehend why they refused to make preparations that seemed to him as much in their interest as in the interest of the Allies. He kept believing they would have to come to their senses.

Even when concerned by the collapse of Poland and the prospect of Germany's quickly turning against the West, Gamelin planned to move up to the line of the Escaut River. In an early communication to General Ironside, he said that he was considering the possibility of giving the British Expeditionary Force the assignment. Ironside protested that he thought it "absolutely impossible" for the BEF commander to be in the van, "leaving behind him only an area of forty kilometers separating him from the sea." Gamelin then conferred with Georges and with their most offensive-minded field commander, General Gaston Billotte. They agreed to Billotte's forming a First Army Group, which would take over the left of the front line. He would form a corps (ultimately XVI Corps), primarily of motorized infantry, place it on the left of the British, and give it the task of moving up to the Escaut. On the basis of this plan, Ironside withdrew his objection, and Gamelin issued a directive to Georges, telling him that if the Germans attacked he was to resist them along the French frontier, but "at the point where the Escaut joins Belgium (Maulde), we have in principle an interest

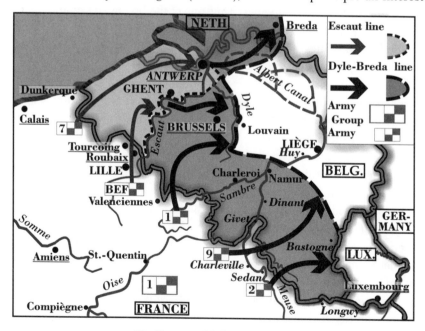

The Escaut and Dyle-Breda Plans

in setting up a first line of defense there, if only to receive the retreating Belgian army and meld it with our own in the area south of Ghent."[24]

Gamelin's exchanges with Ironside may have been manipulative. Ironside (who stood six foot four and inevitably was nicknamed "Tiny") had very much wanted to command the British Expeditionary Force. He spoke six languages, including French and Polish. But Leslie Hore-Belisha, the British war minister, believed that he would get along better with Ironside than with Gort and had therefore kept Ironside at home and sent Gort abroad. Gamelin had established a good relationship with Ironside before the war and knew his ambition (though to one of his staff officers Ironside had praised Gamelin as "a nice little man with a well-cut pair of breeches"). He may have calculated that he could buy a larger measure of cooperation from him by expanding the assignment given British ground forces. Also, he worried about leaving those forces on the left of Georges's armies. In one of the frequent moments when his mind went back to the Great War, he wrote in February 1940:

> Experience throughout the war of 1914–1918 has shown that it has always been necessary to maintain sizable French forces on the left flank of Belgian and British forces. Each time we stopped keeping them there, it became necessary, in crisis periods, to bring them back with the utmost urgency. Thus one of the first moves of Marshal Foch in 1918 was to move the army of General de Mitry to the left of the British armies.

Colonel Rocolle, a French military historian, comments: "Some would add with asperity that it is not advisable to put the British in a position where it is possible for them to evacuate to sea."[25]

As is evident in his directive to Georges, Gamelin's reasoning was political as well as military. He would observe several times later that, if French armies simply stood by while Belgium was conquered, there would be public outcry in both France and Britain.

Gamelin continued to believe and to argue that it would be better for everyone if the Allies went still farther into Belgium, if only the Belgian government would give some encouragement. In early November, he held a ruminative conference with Georges, Billotte, and several other army and air-force generals. The Dutch government had recently shown signs of fear lest Germany move against the Netherlands while leaving Belgium alone. This possibility had alarmed London, where it was easy to imagine Germany's doing this in order to set up air bases on the coast and to make

Britain the target of a major bombing campaign. No one saw just how the Allies could help the Netherlands if Belgium stayed neutral. But Gamelin and the other generals reviewed possible courses of action if an attack on the Netherlands prompted the Belgian government to change its stance. They agreed that in such an event French forces should not only take up positions on the bay shore west of Antwerp but also occupy the large islands on the other side of the bay, Walcheren and North Beveland. Furthermore, continue Gamelin's notes:

> Farther to the east, our front would be established on the Meuse, between Givet and Namur, while, according to the plan, French and British cavalry elements would advance in the direction of Brussels, between [the] Sambre and [the] Escaut.
>
> In a second phase, if the situation allowed, the Allied forces could move up to the line Antwerp-Louvain-Wavre-Namur, which would achieve a clear shortening of the front and would permit greater freedom [of movement] in the rear, in case of reaction by enemy air.[26]

Gamelin's thinking soon became bolder. When the Germans seemed once more to have called off a planned offensive, his confidence in his own forces and in ultimate Allied victory grew. Second, he thought that Belgian leaders might now be so nervous about the Germans they would be willing to engage in secret talks about cooperation. Third, during the first half of November, British military leaders did a complete turnabout. Whereas earlier they had seemed dubious even about the Escaut Plan, they now stressed the danger of a German move into the Netherlands and pressed for sending Allied forces much farther into the Low Countries. The crucial question was whether any cooperation could be expected from Belgium, where for the moment the border with France was as heavily guarded as the border with Germany.

As Daladier and Chamberlain had been the ultimate decision-makers in France and Britain before their nations went to war, so King Leopold III was the ultimate decision-maker in Belgium, and would remain such until May 1940, when Germany forced Belgium to become one of the Western Allies. In 1939, Leopold was thirty-seven years old. He had come abruptly to the throne in February 1934, when his father, King Albert, was killed in a rock-climbing accident. In the Europe of Hitler, Daladier, and Chamberlain, Leopold was an anachronism. His authority derived from birth and from the fact of Belgium's being so divided, linguistically and otherwise, that its domestic peace depended on having a royal arbiter with real power.

King Leopold understood only too well that his family ruled by default. Though Belgians could claim ancient roots, the Belgium of 1939 owed its existence to patchwork agreements of the 1830s designed primarily to assure both Britain and France that the terrain would not be a base of operations for the other. The long-serving French foreign minister, Prince Talleyrand, had said at the time, "There are no Belgians. There are only Flemings and Walloons." The saying retained some truth.

The Flemings, in the majority by about four to three, who predominated in the north, resented the economic and cultural dominion of the French-speaking Walloons, mostly in the south. After other solutions failed, the least unsatisfactory compromise proved to be linguistic division, with Flemish the official language in one region, French in the other, and the 20 percent of the population in and around Brussels compelled to see, if not use, both.

Since the linguistic divide did not parallel other splits among Belgians, there were battles among Flemings and among Walloons over state versus church schools, the relative rights of employers and workers, and other issues common to industrialized states. Even doctrinairely antimonarchist Belgians recognized the usefulness of a king who could dampen conflict and broker understandings. But the monarchy's usefulness—and its survival as an institution—depended on the king's appearing not to take sides.

Leopold's second year as monarch had seen the Rhineland crisis. After the Great War, Belgium had seemed to align with France, for Belgium and France engaged in military-staff conversations concerned with enforcement of the Versailles Treaty. Under the Locarno treaties, Belgium's independence and integrity had been guaranteed by France, Britain, Germany, and Italy. When Hitler's remilitarization of the Rhineland voided those treaties, the question arose whether Belgium would establish a new special relationship with France. There could not have been a worse moment for such a debate. Being dependent on export earnings, Belgium was one of the worst sufferers from the Great Depression, and communists and gangs imitating the Nazis were making Brussels look like Berlin in 1932.

Yet for King Leopold the moment was one of opportunity. Leopold worshipped his late father, who had tutored him as Lord Bute allegedly tutored

King George III, with the constant injunction to "be a king." As a school-boy, he had had to write at the top of every exercise, "It is necessary to put duty and honor above all else." His father had ordered his teachers to drill him in memorization, stress natural history over human history, and prevent his learning to hunt or to ride. (King Albert deemed gymnastics, tennis, and possibly fishing proper for his son.) Leopold believed that he had received an ideal education.[27] He said to his chief political adviser, Baron Robert Capelle, that the end of the Locarno system enabled him to carry out what he believed to have been his father's wishes. "My father said to me more than once," Capelle recalled Leopold saying, "[that] we need to do every-thing to avoid getting involved in a new war. If our fate is too intimately linked to that of a Great Power, we will not survive."[28] Paul-Henri Spaak, who served in cabinets under Leopold, told a pro-Allies deputy from Liège that he suspected King Albert had left behind a written testament, which Leopold was executing "with touching piety." He would say of Leopold af-ter the war, "He had only one concern: not to have men killed or cities de-stroyed."[29] As the great Belgian historian Jean Stengers writes, whereas Spaak and other practical politicians regarded neutrality as "a concrete program imposed by the situation that existed," it was for the king a policy that "responded to a deep inclination."[30]

By opting for and championing nonalignment—strict neutrality—Leo-pold could hope to gain support across the Belgian political spectrum. Though the socialists were cool toward the monarchy, their doctrinaire antimilitarism made them oppose any and all military entanglements. They would find it harder to attack a monarchy that was a symbol of neutrality. And since this was the period when Léon Blum's Popular Front was emerg-ing in France, a stand that seemed anti-French would be attractive to par-ties on the right. As the historian E. H. Kossmann comments, 1936 saw "a campaign of rare violence on the part of the Belgian right-wing Press which condemned the Franco-Russian Treaty and the Popular Front as a conspir-acy of Jews, Freemasons, and communists against the peaceful *third Reich.*"[31]

Many on the right and in the bureaucracy argued that a corollary of neu-trality had to be a strengthening of Belgium's military forces, both by extending the terms of service for draftees and by spending more on arma-ments. The socialists seemed adamantly opposed, but Leopold managed to talk them into not resisting these military measures. In return, he went in person to deliver an address to the cabinet, proposing a formal and uncom-promising declaration of neutrality. The cabinet voted unanimously on October 15, 1936, to endorse the policy and, on a motion from a socialist member, to have it published. Under the heading *"Goal of our policy: avoid war,"* King Leopold quoted his foreign minister as calling for "a policy 'exclusively and integrally Belgian.' " He declared, "This policy must be resolutely aimed at putting us outside the conflicts of our neighbors; it responds to our national ideal."[32] Circulated very widely, this document served thereafter as the touchstone for all Belgian decisions in international relations.

In 1939, neither King Leopold nor leaders in the various parliamentary factions saw any advantage in changing this policy. They had seen the rise among themselves of an imitator of Hitler—Léon Degrelle, head of the so-called Rexists. (Leopold, who had nothing in principle against authoritarianism, joked that Degrelle had "rex appeal."[33]) Mustering unusual unity, leaders in the older parties had combined in 1938 to defeat Degrelle in a municipal election, trouncing him so thoroughly as to eviscerate his party.[34] But there remained the potential for a surge of pro-Nazi feeling, or at least of anti-French and anti-British feeling, with someone else as leader.

Also, the continuing fragility of King Leopold's position was clear. In 1939, before the war commenced, the cabinet recommended that he name to the Flemish Academy of Medicine a Dr. Martens, who had collaborated with the Germans during their occupation of Belgium in 1914–18. Most leaders in Parliament were prepared to approve this action, which would be a sign of reconciliation at home and at the same time a gesture of good will toward Germany. The king could not bring himself to take the action, however. It smacked too much of repudiation of his father, who had been uncompromising toward collaborationists. Also, he thought the cabinet had no right to take the initiative in such a matter. The resultant furor showed that, if Leopold were not very careful, some other incident could put in question not only his own future but that of the monarchy.[35] And the criticism posed special danger to Leopold, for he was easily vulnerable to a charge of favoring the Western Allies. He had attended Eton and served briefly in a Belgian force trained in Britain during the Great War. By special arrangement, he had received military tutoring from a French officer. As Marshal Pétain liked to tell the story:

> After the war, King Albert made a surprise visit to me at my office in the rue St.-Dominique. He hadn't told me he was coming, and he arrived alone, in a taxi. The usher notified me that "there is a person

who claims to be the King of the Belgians and who is asking to see you." I went to see and there I was, indeed, in the presence of the king. He wanted to have the name of a French officer who could complete the education of his son, Prince Leopold. I designated Major Plée. I gather everyone was quite pleased.[36]

Given his background and the furor over Dr. Martens, Leopold had incentives to combat any and all doubts about his support for national neutrality. Another of his key advisers was General Raoul Van Overstraeten, a tall iron-backed artillerist with a Flemish father and a Walloon mother, who as an instructor in Belgium's War College had won a European-wide reputation as a military thinker. To a member of the Belgian Parliament, Spaak said privately of Van Overstraeten:

He is by far the most intelligent officer in the army. The misfortune is that he knows it.

When he comes to see me, he clicks his heels, makes a bow, and says to me: "Minister, the General Van Overstraeten is at your service." And, as he says it, he appears inwardly convinced of his overwhelming superiority to the minister for foreign affairs.

As another great Belgian historian, Jean Vanwelkenhuyzen, writes, it was Van Overstraeten's misfortune, and Belgium's, that he had not been born in a country with more scope for his talent and imperious will.[37] With the guidance of Van Overstraeten and Capelle, the king crafted a strategy intended, if possible, to prevent any fighting in Belgium, and even if this failed, to preserve the monarchy. This strategy involved not only declarations of neutrality but avoidance of any potentially embarrassing sub-rosa dealings with either side.

General Henri Denis, minister of defense, was a Walloon from the very Francophile city of Liège. Personally, he favored secret staff talks with the French and British to prepare for the possibility of a German attack, for professionally he recognized how difficult combined operations would be in the absence of such talks. But the king was adamant. In his view, as summarized by Capelle, Belgium had much to lose and nothing to gain: "In effect, it is in the interest of these states [France and Britain] to come to our help if we are attacked, [so] it is not necessary for us to pay for this guarantee."[38] Van Overstraeten, who had a similar view, toured general-staff headquarters every day, partly to ensure that no unauthorized contacts occurred.[39] He assumed that, as the king's military adviser, he was the supreme figure in Belgium's military establishment. One piece of evidence was that he drew up a defense plan for Liège, sent orders to the fortress commander, and merely provided file copies to the army chief of staff.[40]

Van Overstraeten also superintended measures to strengthen Belgium's defenses on all its frontiers, including that with France. The French air force's Deuxième Bureau cautioned the Allied high command that Belgian anti-aircraft units had orders to fire on any British planes that invaded Belgian air space.[41] From the beginning of the war, this militant Belgian neutrality had complicated French and British thinking about how to cope with a possible German offensive.

Belgians had, however, themselves become progressively more worried about the possibility of such an offensive. The Belgian army's Second Section, the equivalent of the French Deuxième Bureau, counted increasing numbers of German divisions along the frontiers of Belgium and the Netherlands and noted that more and more of them were motorized or armored and that more and more German aircraft were concentrating at nearby airfields. The Belgian mission in Berlin sent back worrisome reports, as, for example, that the German army was collecting maps of Belgium by the truckload. And, of course, the scare of mid-November 1939 obtained much of its fuel from warnings passed by Colonel Oster in the Abwehr to Major Sas in the Dutch Embassy, and thence to The Hague and Brussels, about Hitler's thunderous order for an early Western offensive.[42]

Belgians debated among themselves the question of what they should do if the Germans were to move only against the Netherlands. Though King Leopold's natural inclination was to think that Belgium could still remain neutral—accepting the new condition as Switzerland had accepted the German absorption of Austria—General Van Overstraeten said that, in his judgment, the situation would be intolerable. The Germans at Breda and the French at Maubeuge would each be a short distance from Brussels, a quarter-hour by air; and Belgium could not remain constantly ready for attack on either front. The king, he thought, was impressed by this reasoning.[43]

Several key cabinet ministers meanwhile concluded that Belgium had better concert measures with the Allies. Some were prepared even to send a military plenipotentiary to Paris. But Van Overstraeten easily persuaded them that the objective could be achieved without raising a domestic storm. He would instruct the Belgian military attaché in Paris, Colonel Maurice Delvoie, to make a secret approach to General Gamelin.[44]

This cautious Belgian move tipped Gamelin toward greater boldness in planning. On November 10, Colonel Delvoie visited him, saying he came in his capacity as an attaché, asking questions, not as a general-staff contact, but begging "absolute discretion" and then posing a question:

> If Belgium made an appeal to France and England, its guarantors, what forces could it count on for support on the Albert Canal:
> 1) in the first 48 hours
> 2) in the first four days.[45]

Gamelin responded imprecisely. He said that the Polish experience counseled maintaining a continuous front, sheltering against air attack, and thus moving mainly by night. French and British progress into Belgium, he cautioned, would be effectively at the pace of their foot soldiers, not their motorized or mechanized forces. He hoped they could reach the mouth of the Escaut, perhaps the line Antwerp-Lierre-Louvain-Wavre-Namur, perhaps even the Albert Canal, but everything would depend on prior arrangements and an early appeal from Belgium.[46] A few days later, Gamelin's chief of staff, Colonel Jean Petibon, came close to answering Delvoie's questions by saying that, since the nights were long and the Allies had plenty of motor transport, French and British forces might get to the Albert Canal in less than six days. Petibon, as Delvoie knew, had been with Gamelin since the 1920s and was thought always to express the opinions of his chief.[47]

Subsequently, Gamelin followed up by placing in Delvoie's hands a series of documents labeled "Suggestions." They outlined his own plan and recommended how Belgium should deploy its forces in order to coordinate action with Britain and France.[48] This plan was considerably different from that to which the Allies had been committed at the time of Delvoie's first visit, for in the meantime Gamelin had been engaged in delicate but intensive bargaining with the British government.

THE DYLE-BREDA PLAN

"The English have . . . such confidence in the French army that they are tempted to consider their military support as a gesture of solidarity rather than a vital necessity."
—*Ambassador Charles Corbin to Daladier, October 18, 1939*

From the beginning of September 1939, France had pressed Great Britain to make a maximum effort on the Western front. According to understandings reached before the war, the British government, as soon as war was declared, began to send to France advance elements of a four-division British Expeditionary Force (BEF), accompanied by a few squadrons of reconnaissance and fighter aircraft. Separately, several squadrons of British bombers were deployed to airfields in France. The movements were slow, partly because, for security against U-boats, the British troop-transports put in at Cherbourg, far from the front line. Gamelin and Vuillemin used the slowness of the British as one of their excuses for the pathetic pace and scale of France's mini-offensive in support of Poland, but official propaganda described the Allies as starting this war with the kind of cooperativeness that had developed between them only toward the end of the Great War.

In truth, when the two governments declared war, no one in either Paris or London had a clear notion of what was to happen next. Their threats to go to war had been intended to deter a war, not to bring one on. Apart from the two navies, which were ready to start sea patrols and a blockade, French and British armed forces had mobilization plans but little more.

On September 12, leaders of the two governments met. Reviving nomenclature from the Great War, they called themselves a Supreme War Council.[1] This first session was almost impromptu. Prime Minister Daladier had telephoned General Gamelin early in the morning to tell him that they were to fly to Abbeville for lunch with Prime Minister Chamberlain.

A hundred miles from Paris but only a dozen miles from the English Channel, Abbeville was an approximate midpoint. It was on the Somme, the river where France and Britain had stopped a German offensive in 1918 at the cost of hundreds of thousands of lives. It also happened to be the site where France and Britain had solemnized peace in 1514 through marriage of Louis XII to Mary Tudor. The talks took place in a shabby town hall. The subprefect invited Chamberlain to return for the fishing. Fingers crossed, Chamberlain said he surely would.

The primary purpose was to generate publicity showing the Allies cooperating and creating a false impression that they had some idea of what to do. Daladier had little to say other than that France hoped Britain would send over as many soldiers and airplanes as possible. Chamberlain wanted only to be reassured that France had no immediate intention of forcing a big battle on the Western front. The only exchange that Gamelin thought worth recording in his diary came when Daladier spoke to Chamberlain of his flight from Paris. He said that he had passed over unharvested fields and that he hoped men could be released from military service to bring in the crops. "The French peasant," he continued, "makes war as a patriot of good character. But in 1914 he was dismayed at the sight of fruit trees cut right down by the Germans, and he said to himself, 'These people are savages.'" Chamberlain, noted Gamelin, "looked at him and after a while added, 'They still are.'"[2]

Ten days later, on September 22, the Supreme War Council held a second session, this time in Britain. The final defeat of Poland was near, and the Allies needed to create a public appearance that they were prepared for having no Eastern front and for the possibility that Germany might open an offensive in the West.

The meeting took place at Hove, a place not far from Brighton, on the Channel coast, in what a Foreign Office official described as "an awful Victorian building, hung with Victorian pictures of dead Aldermen." To prevent premature publicity, the delegations were supposed to enter through a back door. The door proved to be locked. They had to troop around to the main entrance in front. Someone on the street recognized the British prime minister and exclaimed, "Chamberlain! Cor Blimey!" In no time, the mayor and other local dignitaries arrived to extend long-winded greetings. The delegations had to hear them out. After all, they were voters.[3]

Not much more happened at Hove than at Abbeville. Daladier pressed harder for British troops and planes. Chamberlain promised to make sympathetic presentations to his Cabinet and service chiefs and in turn spoke of the need for cooperation, recognizing that in practice the terms would be worked out by French and British military commanders. Two topics were broached that in time would consume enormous energy within both governments—the possibility of luring neutral Belgium into secret staff talks, and the possibility of creating a military front in the Balkans. But, again, an appearance of Allied harmony and activity was the paramount objective.

The pattern was now set for numerous Supreme War Council sessions, usually in Paris or London, in the next eight months. François Bédarida, the historian who has assembled and annotated the records of all these meetings, writes that they settled into a routine: "It was a sort of well-regulated ballet where one expected, as at the Opéra, that the tenors would occupy the foreground, but here the chorus consisted of silent figures." An admiral from that silent chorus described the typical proceeding as "a succession of alternating monologues."[4]

When it became evident that there would be no long-lasting Polish front, the French government became more exigent. Gamelin wrote to General Ironside on September 18, in English:

> If Germany operates against us with all its forces, it is the outcome of the war which is at stake at one blow, and it is France which is directly concerned. It is essential, then, that Great Britain assist us with all its resources: that is to say, apart from the operations of the B.E.F. and bomber aircraft, above all with fighter aircraft and A.A. [anti-aircraft] artillery.[5]

When he and Daladier met the British at Hove soon afterward, the British minute-taker noted that they "made strong appeals for the greatest and earliest support possible by British forces."[6]

The British government was of two minds regarding these French appeals. Chamberlain had had doubts all along about any continental commitments, and, having drawn from the Polish war the lesson that air power would be decisive, believed that Britain should therefore husband its aircraft to prepare for the great battle in the sky. His secretary of state for air,

Sir Kingsley Wood, believed similarly that British air power should be reserved primarily for defending Britain's industrial base. Though the RAF's senior officers were not so defense-minded as Chamberlain or Kingsley Wood, nor were they keen on obliging the French. Most of them objected in principle to having air forces support ground troops. In Chamberlain's War Cabinet, the chief arguments in favor of accommodating the French were more political than military and more sentimental than hardheaded. Churchill said, "I doubt whether the French would acquiesce in a division of effort which gave us the sea and air and left them to pay almost the whole blood-tax on land."[7]

The divisions within the British government and the preponderance of opinion in favor of home defense as opposed to continental commitments were exposed at inter-Allied conferences. At one, General Sir Hastings Ismay, secretary of the Committee of Imperial Defence, did his level best to reason his French counterparts into accepting the view that both Allies were better off if Britain kept its planes at home. The presumption was that the only reasons for committing British ground forces were political or sentimental. As French Ambassador Charles Corbin had reported from London in October 1939, "The English have . . . such confidence in the French army that they are tempted to consider their military support as a gesture of solidarity rather than a vital necessity."[8] And Churchill, after touring the Maginot Line, commented to friends at home that German troops visible across the frontier seemed "dead beat, or half starved, perhaps both," whereas the French fortress troops displayed "calm and resolute morale."[9] His friend and strong supporter Robert Boothby returned from a tour in October 1939 to write, "I came away filled with admiration for the strength and spirit of the French nation."[10] (Even after the German breakthroughs in May 1940, Churchill would protest that "he could not believe that the German army was as good as the French."[11])

The French were so exigent that in early September the British government decided in principle to build up the BEF to an eventual thirty-two divisions. At Churchill's insistence, the War Cabinet agreed that the actual total might ultimately be fifty-five divisions, but the French government was to be told only of the thirty-two-division goal. Ironside imparted this figure to Gamelin in October 1939, making plain that he was talking of 1941 and beyond. The outer limit for the BEF prior to mid-1940, he explained, would be fifteen divisions, with many of these short on equipment or training or both.[12]

General Gamelin and his colleagues were even more interested in arrangements regarding RAF units. The formal meetings of the Supreme War Council had yielded as a by-product agreement that military commanders should occasionally meet separately and that a delegation of French military officers should take up residence in London to participate in a standing inter-Allied military committee.

At the first full-dress conference that included generals from both the French air force and the RAF, Vuillemin said that the French air force was not yet equipped for daylight operations. If his Amiot 143s and Bloch 200s attempted to bomb advancing German forces, he said, the results would be "murderous in the extreme." The RAF repesentatives replied that, in the first place, the French exaggerated the qualitative differences between French and British bombers, and that, in the second place, Britain's bomber forces were not designed, trained, or suited for support of ground operations.[13]

Daladier intervened to move the question up to the prime ministers' level. In a long letter to Chamberlain, he stressed the "enormous disproportion" between the French and German air forces. He warned that the German government, through propaganda emphasizing its air superiority and the meagerness of Britain's air effort on the continent, could "put pressure on certain circles in France." Apologizing for the length and warmth of his letter, Daladier concluded, "Unless the first massive shock of the German army, which is counting on the effects of air superiority, is not broken with vigor, it will not be a long war."[14] (This was rhetoric aimed at helping Chamberlain prepare for a debate with his own armed services. There is no reason to suppose that Daladier actually imagined France's being defeated by Germany.)

This, and Daladier's sending to London as his personal representative the retired French air general (and tireless air-power publicist) Jules Armengaud, had some effect. British air officers thought Armengaud was an alarmist, for he attributed to the Luftwaffe a much wider numerical edge over the French air force than British air intelligence reckoned. Nevertheless, Marshal Sir Cyril Newall, chief of the British air staff, did go so far as to say that, if there were a great battle on the Western front, Britain would give France maximum air support. He declined to base any more aircraft in France, however, and he did not specify what kind of air support he had in mind.[15]

Inter-Allied conferences in October and November 1939 brought sharp debate about exactly what the RAF should do if the big battle were indeed to come. Gamelin wanted British fighter planes to protect French, British, and perhaps Belgian ground troops against German Stuka dive-bombers. He wanted British bombers to destroy bridges and rail lines and to harass advancing German columns. Newall and his adjutants were reluctant to part with fighters that might be needed to fend off German bombers attacking the British Isles. At home, the head of Fighter Command, Air Marshal Sir Hugh Dowding, would appeal loudly against any concession to the French. As an RAF historian writes: "To preserve and build up his Command for the great battle to come, Dowding looked neither to left nor to right: he scouted difficulties and opposed all competing claims, whether of Allies, sister services, or other Royal Air Force Commands. . . . A squadron lent might be—almost certainly would be—a squadron lost; and every distraction from the main task was playing the game of the enemy."[16] Moreover, though they did not confide the fact to their French counterparts, Newall and his colleagues were worried about the failure of British fighter-aircraft manufacturers to meet delivery deadlines. Hurricanes and Spitfires were both behind schedule.[17] As for bombers, they explained their view that, when the battle opened, perhaps even if the battle did not open, their proper role was to go for industrial plants in the Ruhr.[18]

This not only failed to meet Gamelin's wishes but alarmed him. He protested that, if the Allies bombed the Ruhr, Germany would retaliate against France's industrial centers, which neither the French air force nor its separate anti-aircraft command had the wherewithal to defend. As tactfully as possible, he said that the proposed British strategic operations would be the reverse of helpful. RAF officers went away shaking their heads over the French desire to waste strategic air power on "unprofitable objectives" such as advancing columns of German tanks.[19]

The German offensive of November that appeared to have been ordered, then called off, opened the way for Gamelin not only to begin exchanges with the Belgians but also to solve at least partially his problems with Britain. The key was the emergent possibility of Germany's moving against only the Netherlands. The locations of German armored and air concentrations lent plausibility to the hypothesis that this was Germany's plan, and the hypothesis gained force if one assumed that Hitler wanted to do something but had decided that an attack on Belgium would be too costly.

During and after the November scare, Gamelin pressed on the British an argument that, if France, Britain, and Belgium cooperated, they could not only fend off a German offensive against Belgium and France but also deny the Germans the Dutch coast. At a Supreme War Council meeting at Vincennes on November 9, General Georges proposed that, if Germany attacked the Netherlands and if Belgium responded by calling in the Allies, their first objective should be to seal the Escaut by occupying both its east bank and the islands in the river mouth; the second objective should be "the deepest penetration possible into Belgium, so as to move the air bases forward and thereby facilitate air attacks, first against enemy columns, and then industrial centers such as the Ruhr."[20]

Georges's formula had a magical effect. The RAF's leaders could accept a limited and temporary commitment to support ground forces if the ultimate goal related to a strategic air offensive—denying bases to the enemy and obtaining bases for themselves. General John Slessor, director of plans in the air staff and a dogmatic champion of strategic bombing, went away thinking that Georges was "a soldierly and impressive personality."[21] (He and his colleagues remained sniffish toward Gamelin, believing, rightly, that he thought of the bomber as a form of long-range field artillery.) Within days, RAF liaison officers were suggesting to French staff officers that additional squadrons of Gladiators, perhaps even Hurricanes, might be moved to France.[22]

Gamelin still felt misgivings about a commitment to plunge deep into Belgium—perhaps beyond, to the Dutch coast. The Deuxième Bureau had given him unencouraging reports about the Belgian army and defenses. Its assessment was that Belgium could not long hold the line of the Albert Canal and might not be able to hold the line of the Dyle long enough to be reinforced by the French and British, and that the Dutch would meanwhile buckle.[23] But the new planning link with Brussels, the brisk preparations made by the Belgian army during the November crisis, and the prospect of British air support all contributed to easing Gamelin's mind.

On November 14, at La Ferté, Gamelin committed himself provisionally to abandoning the Escaut Plan and adopting a new plan that called for *at least* an advance to the Dyle River. One of Georges's aides remembered Georges's objecting to a commitment to go beyond the Escaut, but, according to Captain François Huet, an aide to Gamelin, objections, if any, were made behind Gamelin's back. As Huet recalled it, the meeting adjourned and Gamelin walked out to the circular driveway in front of Les Bondons to get in his car. Huet stayed behind to gather up papers. It was then that he heard grumbling. At the car, he suggested that Gamelin might want to invite more discussion. Gamelin walked back into the house, asked if there were any further questions about the plan, heard none, and departed, thinking his aide had cried wolf.[24]

On the next day, Gamelin formalized the new plan in a Personal and Secret Instruction to Georges. "The goal to be sought would be to link up, by the shortest line possible, the national Belgian redoubt at Antwerp with our front on the Meuse and to be ready possibly to take in the Belgian forces." Those Belgian forces would be expected to hold the line from Ghent to Antwerp to Louvain. British forces would hold the Dyle below Louvain, covering the eastern approaches to Brussels. France's First and Ninth Armies would guard the remainder of the line to the French Meuse. "The Seventh Army, while fulfilling the mission given it regarding the mouth of the Escaut, would move to the rear and the left of the Belgian forces at Antwerp, ready to cover the left flank and linking up if possible with the Dutch."[25]

Though this was often referred to as the Dyle Plan, that is a misnomer. Gamelin's immediate concern was to establish a basis for cooperation with Belgium. If its twenty-two divisions could be added to his front line, he would be doubly confident of blunting a German attack on Belgian, not French, soil. As he understood it, the Belgian general staff intended to deploy those divisions along the Albert Canal to Liège and otherwise along the Meuse, and Gamelin had volunteered to provide support there—if Belgian forces could hold their positions for the four to eight days required for the arrival of French and British main forces. At a minimum, he would secure the line of the Dyle, behind which the Belgian army could regroup if compelled to give ground.

The new plan quickly acquired an additional dimension. Belgian forces would obviously need some bolstering around the northern approaches to Antwerp, where German invaders could outflank the Albert Canal, but Belgian military planners had no links with their Dutch counterparts. Both governments feared compromising their neutrality, and their relationship was in any case distant. Gamelin saw that, if he expanded the mission of the Seventh Army, he could address both Belgium's worries about the Antwerp flank and Britain's worries about German bombers taking off from Dutch bases. Instead of merely enjoining the commander of the Seventh Army to try to link the Belgians and the Dutch, he could direct that the army go farther, cross the Dutch frontier, and take a position shielding Breda and its environs.[26]

This time, General Georges did voice objections. He sent Gamelin a note saying that extension of the front to Holland was "very problematic to execute." Georges continued:

There is no doubt that our defensive maneuver in Belgium and Holland should be conducted carefully, so as not to allow the major part of our available forces to become engaged against a German action which could be merely a diversion. In case of a German attack in force launched in the center, against our front between the Meuse and the Moselle, we could find ourselves bereft of the necessary means for a riposte. It is therefore necessary, given this possibility, to act prudently.[27]

Though its language may seem prescient, Georges's letter did not disclose the real ground for his discontent. After all, it had been he who had called for "the deepest penetration possible into Belgium." And Gamelin noted in his journal that Georges had approved the idea of moving to Breda.[28] But Georges had since discovered that implementation of the concept might come at his expense. The King of the Belgians would not easily consent to be subordinate to a mere theater commander, and the British were likely to insist on parity with the Belgians. So General Georges might end up as merely commander of French forces, on a par with Leopold and Gort (and Gamelin probably as supreme commander).

Gamelin was clearly considering such a formula. Without inviting Georges, he held a long meeting with Billotte, the Army Group commander, to work out the new directive for the Seventh Army. At about the same time, he notified Georges of a planned reorganization: most of the general-staff personnel who had moved to La Ferté or its vicinity would be pulled back to a new site nearer Paris. Gamelin ended up locating it in a hillside château at Montry, about halfway between Vincennes and La Ferté. Georges grumbled that without his staff he would be "a fifth wheel,"[29] but in the end, he had no choice other than to yield and to accept his new title, commander of the Northeastern front. Georges had good reason for grousing about a change in war plan that entailed the downgrading of his own command.

In mid-January 1940 occurred the series of events remembered as the Mechelen incident, which we considered earlier because of its effects on German planning. Here it needs a closer look, for, on the Allied side, it soldered into place presumptions that would remain in the minds of decision-makers for the next three months.

During December 1939, in Brussels as in Paris, every week's intelligence bulletins had told of additions to the concentrations of German troops, tanks, and planes opposite the Netherlands and Belgium. King Leopold came more and more to think that a German invasion was likely. Though he continued to hope that Belgium could weather the war as another Switzerland, he concluded that he should hedge against the contrary. For the moment, France and Britain seemed inclined to conciliate Belgium. If Germany attacked and he called for their aid, the two Allied governments were likely to think of Belgium as being in their debt rather than the other way around. Now might therefore be a good time, Leopold thought, to ask for assurances that, if drawn into the war, Belgium would have a seat at any subsequent peace conference and would be able to keep its huge Congo colony.

Leopold suggested to Foreign Minister Spaak that an approach be made to the British government via Admiral Sir Roger Keyes, hero of a naval battle off Belgium during the Great War and an old friend of the royal family. But Spaak and the government were cool to broaching in any fashion the possibility of Belgium's entering the war.[30]

After Christmas and in early January 1940, Leopold saw signs again multiplying of an impending German attack. Count Galeazzo Ciano, Mussolini's foreign minister and son-in-law, usually reticent to the point of being inscrutable, began dropping word in Rome that Germany would soon march against the Low Countries.[31] Soon afterward came warnings from sources in Berlin, including the strongest to date from Ambassador Davignon, based again on word passed from Colonel Oster of the Abwehr via Sas, the Dutch military attaché, but also on a tip from his Swedish colleague. These sources all said that Hitler had picked January 15 as D-day. Davignon did not vouch for the precise date and, indeed, commented that the numbers of German soldiers in Berlin on furlough argued for a later date. Nevertheless, "People here . . . are expecting an offensive in the more or less short term."[32]

One other alarming sign was the increased number of German military planes reconnoitering eastern Belgium. They were taking advantage of Arctic temperatures that created unlimited visibility. But on January 9, temperatures rose, and fog settled over the Meuse Valley. In mid-morning on January 10, residents of Mechelen-sur-Meuse heard a low-flying plane. (This was not the cathedral city of Mechelen on the Dyle but a market town in Limbourg, only a few miles from the German and Dutch borders.) Farm families on the outskirts of town saw a small German Me-108 make a crash landing on a snow-covered meadow next to the river. Belgian soldiers on patrol sped to the scene, where they saw struggling from the wreckage two Luftwaffe officers—one the pilot, the other Major Hellmuth Reinberger, a paratroop officer based in Munster. Reinberger carried a portfolio of documents which he made a hasty effort to burn. The Belgian soldiers rescued some of the papers and packed the two officers off to Brussels for interrogation.[33]

As details emerged, it appeared that Major Reinberger had been ordered to Cologne to relay to the commander of the First Air Corps details of the new assignments for paratroops entailed in the most recent revision of Plan Yellow. He had planned to take the train, but at the officers' mess on the previous evening, Major Erich Hoenmanns, a reservist with experience as both a military and civilian pilot, offered him a ride by plane. Hoenmanns planned to fly to Cologne anyway, in order to take some laundry home to his wife. Reinberger accepted. Not long out of Munster, the plane began to misbehave. Hoenmanns, coming out of the clouds, believed himself over the Rhine, not the Belgian Meuse, and made an emergency landing. When he saw bowl-shaped helmets over blue uniforms instead of bell-shaped helmets over field-gray uniforms, he recognized his mistake. Major Reinberger tried to get rid of his documents but did not have time to finish.

In Brussels, army-intelligence officers cross-questioned the two Germans and scrutinized the documents. They also locked them up in a cell with a concealed microphone. After a time, they concluded that the documents were probably authentic. Van Overstraeten had decided this almost immediately, for experience as a staff officer told him that it would have required genius and extraordinary luck to concoct the incident for purposes of deception. Moreover, the contents of the documents jibed completely with what he had inferred from other sources. They indicated that the Germans did, indeed, intend to invade the Netherlands, but that this was to be one of two secondary offensives, the other a diversion aimed toward the Maginot Line. The main attack was to be across Belgium. The news was that it would run south of Liège-Huy-Namur fortifications, aiming then at a turn northwestward and a breakthrough on the plateau surrounding Gembloux. An entire division of paratroops was to drop just west of the Meuse, turn back, and seize the river crossings between Namur and Dinant. They were to hold them for quickly arriving armored and motorized forces. Unburned portions of the documents specified the areas where, because of these operations, the Luftwaffe was to refrain from any bombing, and commented also that ice would make an excellent surface for the drop.

Tension in Brussels rose when the Belgian mission in Berlin reported that the Germans knew of the plane crash and presumed that important documents had fallen into Allied hands. Van Overstraeten urgently summoned France's deputy military attaché in Brussels, Colonel Auguste Hautcoeur. (The senior attaché, General Edmond Laurent, had a reputation for indiscretion and was known not to be a favorite of Gamelin's. Hautcoeur had recently come to Brussels as Gamelin's personal liaison with Van Overstraeten, one of whose prize pupils he had been a few years earlier at the Belgian École de Guerre.[34]) He summarized the contents of the captured documents and urged Hautcoeur to go at once to Paris and inform Gamelin. Which Hautcoeur promptly did.

The story begins like one written by John Buchan, but its middle and end call to mind early Evelyn Waugh, perhaps even P. G. Wodehouse. At this juncture, King Leopold decided that he should act at once to obtain Allied guarantees for the future of Belgium and the Congo: he wanted to do so before asking French and British help to fend off a German attack, and time seemed to be running out. Without consulting anyone outside the royal household, he asked Admiral Keyes to fly over at once from England. Keyes did so. The king described the guarantees that he wanted from the Allies. Keyes then started for home.

By the time Keyes reached the airfield at Arras, in France, where his plane waited, the fog that had entrapped the German Me-108 at Mechelen-sur-Meuse had also arrived. Keyes's plane could not take off. Aware of the urgency of his mission, Keyes used the telephone. Since his only secure line ran to the Admiralty, Keyes rang up his presumptive chief, the First Lord of the Admiralty, Winston Churchill. He explained to Churchill why the king thought a German invasion imminent and described the assurances the king wanted. As often happens in telephone communication, what was heard differed from what was said.[35]

In common with others, Churchill presumed that the old Etonian on the throne of Belgium was wholeheartedly pro-Allies but constrained by the ministers in his government who were overly sensitive to Flemings. Churchill understood Keyes to be saying that the king desired Allied troops in Belgium right away, prior to any German attack, and inferred that Leopold needed political guarantees to help him justify this to his politicians.

Churchill at once called for a meeting of the War Cabinet. Since it was Sunday, Chamberlain was, of course, in the country. Admiral Chatfield, minister for coordination of defense, presided in his stead. Churchill and others argued that not a moment should be lost in seizing the new opportunity. But Chamberlain, reached by phone, questioned the desirability or need for hurried postwar commitments. (He tended to look with suspicion on any proposal that engaged Churchill's enthusiasm.) Hurrying back to London, he took the chair at a fuller, more formal meeting of the Cabinet. General Ironside, invited to be present, emphatically urged agreeing to the Belgian terms. A twelve-hour start on the Germans, he said, would allow the Allies to entrench themselves on the Antwerp-Namur line. Chamberlain persisted in voicing skepticism, surmising accurately that King Leopold did not intend for Allied troops to enter Belgium until after the Germans attacked.[36]

As was still usual, though less and less so, Chamberlain prevailed. Admiral Keyes was sent a formal text to communicate to Leopold. One can imagine the king's surprise when he read that the British government was "ready to accept the invitation of the Belgian government" to send their forces into Belgian territory and that, though the British government was not prepared to make commitments regarding the postwar settlement, it promised to do its best to protect the political and territorial integrity of Belgium and its colonies, provided that Belgium appealed for intervention "immediately." With an iciness matching that out of doors, King Leopold and Van Overstraeten told Keyes to say to London that the terms were "difficult to take into consideration."[37]

At Vincennes, on January 10–11, General Gamelin held a late-night meeting to discuss the intelligence brought from Brussels by Hautcoeur. Georges sped in from La Ferté, and General Doumenc, chief of staff in the new Land Forces headquarters, from Montry. General Jean Mendigal, Vuillemin's personal chief of staff, represented the air force. Though puzzled that Van Overstraeten had not given Hautcoeur photocopies of the documents, as well as by Rivet's report that SR sources had noted no unusual German military movements, Gamelin and the others accepted Van Overstraeten's judgment that the documents were genuine. They agreed that French forces should be put on alert to carry out the planned advance to the Dyle River, Antwerp, and Breda.[38]

On the night of January 13, while King Leopold was holding his first meeting with Admiral Keyes, his Foreign Ministry and military establishments were also reacting to the report from Berlin that the Mechelen incident might prompt Germany to strike at once. Spaak called in Paul Bargeton, who had been Massigli's predecessor as number two to Léger at the Quai d'Orsay and French ambassador in Brussels since 1937. As Bargeton telegraphed Paris in the wee hours of January 14, "He has asked me to let you know immediately that, according to the totality of intelligence in its possession this evening, the Belgian Government considers it probable that today, Sunday, there will be a German attack against Belgium starting in the morning."[39] The Belgian military attaché, Colonel Delvoie, had already visited Vincennes to pass to Gamelin word that "the attack is almost certain."[40]

As the sun rose on the morning of January 14, French lookouts discovered that, during the night, all barriers at crossings into Belgium had been removed and all guards withdrawn. That afternoon, Daladier heard from London about the supposed invitation issued by King Leopold through Admiral Keyes. He immediately told Gamelin. "The King has stated he is ready to call on us." Though Gamelin commented that heavy snow and below-zero temperatures seemed not propitious for a *Blitzkrieg*, he said, "we must seize the moment."[41]

Though Georges voiced some disquiet about actually moving French forces into Belgium at a time when ready air support was still meager, General Gamelin overrode his objections. Gamelin wrote later: "I replied . . . a little sharply: I have taken a position. I cannot go back on it. You have to know what you want. Otherwise you can't wage war."[42] Georges yielded, saying that he had only wanted acknowledgment that conditions were not perfect. Canceling all leaves, he sent an advance column of cavalry to Muno, a hamlet on the Senne River, just inside Belgian Luxembourg. During the night of January 14–15, lead elements of the Seventh and First Armies slithered or tramped through calf-high snow to the points where roads crossed from France into Belgium. But sunup on January 15 showed them that the barriers and guards were back in place.

What had happened was that the Belgian chief of staff, General Édouard Van den Bergen, had misunderstood Van Overstraeten. He had prepared a message to be flashed to higher Belgian commands and to the Belgian military attachés in Paris, London, and The Hague—"Imminent attack probable"—but Van Overstraeten had rewritten it to read: "Imminent attack virtually certain." Since the imperious military adviser to the king seldom disclosed the reasoning behind his actions, Van den Bergen, not understanding that Van Overstraeten intended to startle the heretofore phlegmatic Dutch into action, not to state his own assessment of risk, took the words literally and ordered measures appropriate for a war that was "virtually certain."[43] Clearing the border crossings was one of these. When Van Overstraeten learned what had been done, he was furious. He countermanded Van den Bergen's order and sent a message telling Belgium's border guards to prevent the entry of *any* foreign forces.[44]

Seeing the barriers go back up, General Gamelin, too, lost his temper. He dashed off a memorandum to Daladier:

At this moment, each hour lost can have grave consequences.

On the one hand, given the temperature, the troops are in a bad situation, not so much for the men, whom we have to shelter in the villages, as for the horses and perhaps above all the engines.

On the other hand, the enemy is certainly going to learn of our movements, if not by air [reconnaissance] then in any event by espionage. We are therefore losing what we could have gained by preempting, whether the enemy was already prepared to launch an offensive, or whether our forward movement stood a chance of surprising him. Given his capacity for air attack compared with ours, this is grave.

It is important, therefore, that the Belgian Government be made to face up to its responsibilities.[45]

A week earlier, Daladier had fallen from a horse, and was now confined to bed in his villa at Celle-St.-Cloud, on the opposite side of Paris from Vincennes. Gamelin, Léger, several other Foreign Ministry officials, and General Jules Decamp, Daladier's chief of staff in the Defense Ministry, came to his bedside. Then Daladier peremptorily summoned the Belgian ambassador. With as much dignity and sternness as a bedridden accident victim can muster, Daladier said to him: "As of this evening, France will be able to reinforce the Belgian army and apply the plan of cooperation envisaged," but the French troops could not long remain in place, and if the Belgian government did not immediately invite them in, they would return to their bases. "Moreover," said Daladier, "it could be impossible to repeat yesterday's maneuver for each serious alert. As a result, from now on the French troops will not leave their cantonments except at the moment that the German army will have effectively entered Belgium." It was then midafternoon. Daladier said that the Belgians had until 8 P.M. to act.[46]

As astonished by this ultimatum as by the rude communication sent from London via Admiral Keyes, King Leopold met hurriedly with Van Overstraeten and his chief ministers. At twenty minutes before eight, Spaak telephoned Paris to say that Belgium had never had any intention of inviting pre-emptive Allied military moves and that they were mystified as to why Daladier thought otherwise.[47] The French troops did return to their bases. Irritation and mystification lingered in all three capitals.

Major General Sir Richard Howard-Vyse of the British military mission in France described Gamelin and his entourage at Vincennes as "at the moment . . . like a deflated balloon."[48] In time, however, Gamelin gravitated to two conclusions. One was that King Leopold had wanted to call in the Allies but had once again been prevented from doing so by his government. Gamelin was probably influenced by members of the general staff whom he presumed to be expert on Belgium and who believed that the position of Leopold and the Belgian army were like theirs in France—monarchists pitted against republicans.[49] His second conclusion, based not only on the brief frontier opening but on evidence that Belgium's emergency deployments had conformed almost exactly to his "suggestions," was that Leopold and his generals were doing what they could to prepare for active cooperation along the lines of the Dyle-Breda Plan. It followed that, in spite of the embarrassing experience of mid-January, France and Britain should do their utmost to make eventual cooperation succeed.

Daladier also felt anger, but at least as much toward Gamelin as toward the Belgians. Since the SR or the Sûreté had a tap on the Belgian Embassy's telephone lines, he had been able to read a transcription of the Belgian ambassador's conversation with Spaak, and the Belgian foreign minister was clearly not pretending to astonishment: it appeared never to have entered his thoughts that French and British troops might be invited into Belgium prior to an actual German attack.[50]

The rebuff from Brussels was embarrassing to Daladier both personally and politically. Howard-Vyse heard rumors that he might be forced to turn the Ministry of War over to someone else.[51] Daladier held Gamelin responsible both for misjudging the Belgians and for misleading him. Jean Daridan later remembered Daladier's expressing doubt about Gamelin's whole plan. Why go to Antwerp-Wavre-Namur? he asked. Why was the Escaut line not good enough? Why did Gamelin not concentrate on fortifying the hinge between the terminus of the Maginot Line and the point where the Escaut crossed into Belgium? He thought he remembered Daladier's referring specifically to Sedan.[52]

The next phase of the war on the Allied side was to see much more intervention by Daladier and other civilian politicians on both sides of the Channel. And the comedy of errors surrounding the Mechelen incident contributed to this by making Belgium seem to Daladier an even more uncertain factor, and by causing him to doubt whether either General Gamelin or General Georges really knew what he was doing. At the same time, the incident steeled Gamelin and others in uniform against any changes in the presumptions underpinning their intention to meet a German attack by rapid movement into Belgium toward Breda and the Dyle River line.

It is worth a pause to note, however, that, as of January 1940, if General Gamelin's presumptions had been probed and tested, they would have seemed rock-solid. Van Overstraeten and Belgian military planners were following his "suggestions." The German documents retrieved at Mechelen-sur-Meuse indicated quite precisely how German operations would have proceeded had Hitler not reluctantly canceled his order for an offensive to commence on January 17. There would have been a messy situation in the Netherlands, for the Dutch planned to make a stand fifty miles east of Breda, expected French forces to back them up, yet had not communicated this expectation to anyone in France,[53] but elsewhere, Belgian, French, and British forces would have been in exactly the right positions to meet and check a German attack, especially given the aid they would have had from the weather.

Unhappily for the Allies, the realities of January changed. By May 1940, presumptions once valid were no longer so. But Allied leaders failed to discern the changes and adhered to their earlier presumptions, with the result that, in May, French, British, Belgian, and Dutch forces moved into positions that were almost the worst possible ones for coping with the revised plan of attack that the Germans had meanwhile devised. At the heart of the story of the Allies from January to May 1940 is a question similar to that which President John Kennedy posed for himself after the Bay of Pigs debacle. "How could I have been so stupid?" he asked. In those early months of 1940, how could exceptionally intelligent men like Daladier, Gamelin, Chamberlain, and Churchill have been so stupid?

DISTRACTIONS

"Depriving Germany of iron-ore imports . . . would bring about its rapid asphyxiation."
—French Ministry of Defense staff memorandum, January 15, 1940

The autumn of 1939 had been frustrating for Daladier. He had tried to form a national government, hoping that in wartime he would not have to continue formulating every act or decree like a pharmacist preparing a complicated prescription. With the goal of at least having his own Radical Socialist Party united behind him, he asked Herriot, his old mentor and rival, to replace Bonnet as foreign minister. But Herriot said he would serve only if the cabinet also included Marshal Pétain, and Pétain refused to serve with Herriot on the ground that Herriot's appointment as foreign minister would alienate Mussolini and Franco. Socialist leaders also refused to serve either with one another or without one another. Paul Faure, himself ineligible because a pacifist and unregenerately *munichois*, swore to oppose a cabinet that contained Léon Blum or any socialist on Blum's side. He reportedly said that, if Blum entered the government, "then all Israel with him! That would be war without end!"[1] Faure and Blum alike threatened to vote against a cabinet that included anyone from the right; Flandin and others linked to employers' groups vetoed inclusion of even a moderate trade-union leader. Exploring possibilities for recruiting a conservative Catholic, Daladier went so far as to offer a seat to Cardinal Verdier, Archbishop of Paris.[2] Nothing came of it.

After ten days and much press speculation, Daladier had to announce on September 14 that, after all, the war government would be much the same as the peace government. Bonnet would cease to be foreign minister but would not leave the cabinet: he would become minister of justice. (Rumor had it that Reynaud negotiated Bonnet's staying on, despite his *munichois* past, because Bonnet promised to amend the laws in order to make it easier for the Comtesse Hélène des Portes, Reynaud's mistress, to divorce her husband and become Madame Reynaud.) Daladier himself took over the Foreign Ministry, adding it to his war and defense portfolios, but continuing to work from the rue St.-Dominique. (As Élie Bois writes, he had "a superstitious horror of the Quai d'Orsay," because it reminded him of February 1934.[3]) A few minor posts changed hands. Jean Zay had already left the Ministry of Education to go to the front. (The parting gift from his Cabinet colleagues was, comfortingly, a Japanese hara-kiri sword.[4]) There would be two new ministries, one for blockade and one for armaments. The latter would be headed by Raoul Dautry, a hard-driving industrialist occasionally mentioned earlier as a possible head of government should the Third Republic become paralyzed by partisan bickering. That was all. "It was less a reshuffle than a papering over," observed one of Daladier's aides.[5] The satirical weekly *Le Canard enchaîné* said that the *cabinet de guerre* (war cabinet) had turned out to be a *"cabinet de naguère"* (roughly: "well-worn cabinet").[6]

Parliamentary and party politics continued much as usual. Although, with the government's power to rule by decree continuing until November, the legislature was in recess, factional leaders formed a "permanent delegation," composed of two deputies or senators from each of thirteen parties, to meet with the prime minister once a week. Committees of both the Chamber of Deputies and the Senate continued to meet and to take testimony from members of the government.[7] There and in the lobbies, *munichois* such as Flandin, Laval, Déat, and Faure could connive with Bonnet and de Monzie for a possible negotiated end to the war. (De Kérillis, one of the lone noncommunists to vote against the Munich accords, sided with them, saying, after Germany and the Soviet Union divided up Poland, "The war has lost its pretext."[8]) Bonnet continued to encourage the Italian government to offer mediation; de Monzie, still minister of public works, attempted to send peace feelers to Germany via Brussels.[9] The *antimunichois* were no less active, with Mandel, Reynaud, Navy Minister César Campinchi, and Deputy Foreign Minister Paul Champetier de Ribes encouraging friends on the "permanent delegation" or in Chamber or Senate committees to press the prime minister for a more vigorous war effort and for uncompromising refusal to discuss a negotiated peace.[10]

For hardly a moment was Daladier unaware of competitors hoping that he would stumble and open the way for an alternative government. Laval plotted continuously to create a coalition that would come to terms at least with Italy and perhaps with Germany.[11] Mandel said to anyone who would listen that Daladier lacked the spine to be a war leader. Dautry, though playing the simple businessman and not criticizing his chief, would hint to deputies, senators, and journalists that war was too important to be managed by politicians.

The front-runner—and eventual winner—among those seeking to displace Daladier was Reynaud. Six years older than Daladier, Reynaud had been trained as a lawyer and, like Daladier, entered the Chamber of Deputies soon after the Great War. Representing first a district in the high Pyrenees, then a blue-stocking faubourg of Paris, he had had fewer opportunities than Daladier to figure in cabinet combinations, but his lucid analyses of legal and financial issues had given him influence, especially in committees. Because of his championship of tight budgets and a stable currency and his criticism of the forty-hour law, financiers and industrialists had pronounced him "sound" and had continued to favor him despite his alliance with Mandel as an early *antimunichois*.

Less than five feet tall, with slightly slanted eyes and an almost expressionless face, Reynaud seemed always to be in hurry. He "screwed up his face like a monkey when he talked" and had an odd "habitual mannerism of moving his head about," said journalists.[12] Escorted by his tall, vivacious mistress, he was a familiar figure at fashionable dinner parties and in Parisian salons, where he would be seen "walking almost on tiptoe to appear taller, and with his hands in the arm-holes of his vest."[13] The editor of the *Petit Parisien*, Élie Bois, who preferred Daladier, compared Reynaud to the would-be strongman of the late 1920s and early 1930s, André Tardieu. Both were arrogant, he wrote, but "Tardieu made up for it by a personal dynamism, by something alive, gay, sensitive and human of which M. Paul Reynaud never had an ounce." Charles Pomaret, who served in cabinets alongside Reynaud, thought such assessments understandable but unfair. "We were close," wrote Pomaret. "I saw qualities few saw—tenderness, gentleness, timidity. In private, he lost the small-man arrogance."[14]

Politically, Daladier and Reynaud had been bound together ever since the dissolution of the Popular Front. Daladier had needed Reynaud's toughness and high standing in business circles in order to discipline the labor unions and muster the capital for rearmament. Reynaud had needed Daladier because he had neither the party base nor the political skills required to manage the legislature. As one of Reynaud's aides commented, the two men had created "a system," in which "Reynaud, judicious but dry and unpopular, would make the technical decisions, and Daladier, more accepted by the Chamber, would get them passed politically."[15]

Personally, the relationship between Daladier and Reynaud was never more than distant. The war turned it into hostility. Since Mandel was a Jew, Reynaud was the *antimunichois* in the cabinet with the best chance of displacing Daladier, and he passed up no opportunity to air the view that he was the man most qualified to be France's war leader.

That Daladier and Reynaud were neighbors and that their mistresses were old acquaintances only made matters worse. Daladier dealt with Belgian matters in January 1940 from a bed at Celle-St.-Cloud because, at the outset of the war, Count René Rivaud, a banker, had offered both him and Reynaud houses on his estate, La Châtaigneraie, as places of safety against the possibility of air raids on Paris. (Daladier's in-town residence was a modest flat near the Place de l'Étoile, from which he sometimes bicycled to work; Reynaud's was a luxurious townhouse very near the Palais Bourbon.) Both men accepted, Daladier taking the main dwelling, Reynaud the gatehouse. They themselves might have remained as much apart as in Paris, but they were accompanied to Celle St.-Cloud by their mistresses, who happened to be not only acquaintances but old social rivals. Daladier's mistress, the Marquise Jeanne de Crussol, and Reynaud's mistress, the Comtesse des Portes, had known each other since childhood, had come to Paris aspiring to lead salons, had succeeded, had established rival attachments, but continued to see each other. Des Portes was fiercely ambitious for Reynaud to become both her husband and prime minister. At every occasion, she put in words favoring her man and disparaging Daladier. Crussol kept track and reported it all syllable by syllable to Daladier.[16] Little wonder that Élie Bois observed between Daladier and Reynaud "a deep-seated physical and intellectual antipathy, so marked that, when they could possibly avoid it, they never spoke to one another."[17]

Despite his evident popularity among the public and his repeatedly proven ability to control the Chamber and Senate, Daladier was always aware of being politically vulnerable. Soon after the beginning of the war, he said to his friend William Bullitt, the American ambassador, that his government would probably not last three months.[18] Gamelin noted in his diary after a September conversation with Daladier: "He is worried about the internal situation. He is disturbed by letters and by what people say to him; he wants to convoke the Parliament, but he is afraid of being over-turned."[19] Reynaud's aide, Alfred Sauvy, had commented in September 1939, "The French are divided into two camps, those who do not want to make peace and those who do not want to make war." In Villelume's well-informed view, this condition gave Daladier good reason to be apprehensive, for, added together, those who reproached him for getting France into the war and those who reproached him for not conducting it more energetically made up a majority in both the Chamber and the Senate.[20]

One source of discomfort for Daladier was a changed relationship with General Gamelin. Before September 1939, Gamelin had been his deferential subordinate. Now, though no less punctiliously respectful, he was the man in charge. Key debates took place at Vincennes or La Ferté more often than in Daladier's offices, and Daladier would often be given notice of decisions rather than being allowed to make them.

Daladier made one attempt to assert his prerogative. In mid-September he wrote Gamelin, complaining that mobilization was pulling men away from jobs in defense industry and from fields needing harvesting. "A serious malaise has developed among the civilian population," he wrote. "The underlying cause is the uselessness of [military] dispositions made without any real national defense justification. . . . Rear echelons are bursting with officers who are well aware they have nothing to do." He cited Melun, west of Paris on the Seine River, where four officers occupied themselves censoring six weeklies.[21] Gamelin's reply put Daladier in his place. "We must . . . not forget that some people still have doubts about our will to conduct the war to the hilt," he wrote patronizingly; "it is important, therefore, to act in such a way that the measures that are taken are not interpreted as a hesitation or a slackening. In the grave hours that we are going through at present, we should think about the effort made by the country in the initial months of 1914 and the calm that everybody then displayed."[22]

Daladier received similar rebuffs every time he addressed Gamelin regarding the civilian economy's need for manpower. It seemed to make no impression on Gamelin that aircraft output had dropped sharply. When Dautry demanded 250,000 workers in order to meet armament-production targets for 1940, Daladier could not persuade Gamelin to part with them. The most he could get was the release of thirty-year-olds with children.[23]

In these circumstances, Daladier must have come close to tearing his thinning hair when, time after time, Gamelin rang alarm bells about an imminent German offensive, then reported that it had been called off. Aware of the Deuxième Bureau's record in getting things right about the Germans, Daladier did not necessarily think that the alarms had been false. Probably, he drew an inference similar to Gamelin's—that Hitler had backed off from an offensive because of a calculation that he could not win.

Unlike Gamelin, however, Daladier seems to have gone on to conclude that stalemate on the Western front was a permanent condition. When Parliament reconvened on November 30, he faced an accumulation of sharp questions about the inactivity of Allied military forces. To characterize what was going on, a writer in the right wing *Gringoire* had coined the phrase *"drôle de guerre"*—funny war. General Spears, in one of his many visits to France, heard that a German unit had put up a giant poster that could be read from French lines opposite. "Soldiers of the Northern Provinces," it said, "beware of the English. They are destroying your properties, eating your food, sleeping with your wives, raping your daughters." After a bit, the regiment on the French side, which happened to come from Gascony, put up its own poster, saying: *"On s'en fout, on est du midi.* ("Who gives a damn? We're from the south.") Well into the autumn, anyone touring the French-German border could see German soldiers insouciantly hanging laundry on riverside walls. The practice stopped only after German staff officers began to worry that the French could calculate numbers of German troops by counting undershirts.[24] Not surprisingly, Daladier began to cast about for alternative approaches to the war.

In December, Daladier began to see hope of, at one and the same time, achieving new harmony in his cabinet and the legislature, lifting public spirits, restoring his own political dominance (thus undoing Reynaud), and perhaps escaping from the war with the equivalent of victory, minimal loss of life, and no fighting at all on French soil. These visions came to Daladier because of news from the North of Europe. On November 30, the Soviet Union suddenly attacked Finland, seeking to seize by force border and coastal areas that the Finnish government had refused to cede peacefully. Over the next several weeks, bulletin after bulletin told of Finland's tiny army successfully holding off and beating back the much larger Soviet army. Footage of white-clad Finnish ski troops whizzing past slogging Soviet infantrymen highlighted newsreels in Parisian moviehouses.

Daladier's mind became seized with the following propositions:

• Since the League of Nations, in what amounted to its death rattle, had expelled the Soviet Union and declared it an aggressor, France and Britain had a warrant—indeed, a duty—to commit troops and planes to aid Finland.

• Though this would involve opening a second war—with the Soviet Union as well as Germany—not much would be risked, for the Soviet Union was already effectively a German ally, and its performance against Finland demonstrated that it was militarily of little account.

• Being at war with the Soviet Union as well as Germany would yield large net benefits for two reasons: the wider war would have enthusiastic support from those in France who feared Bolshevism as much as or more than Nazism and, as a result, were ambivalent about a war against Germany alone; and the Allies could make their economic war against Germany truly effective because they could attack the oilfields in the Caucasus, from which Germany was drawing fuel, and also, by going to Finland via Norway and Sweden, could cut off Germany from its major source of iron ore.

• Since the German economy was described by Allied intelligence services as under snapping strain, these actions by the Allies would force recognition in Berlin that the war was lost; German military men, officials, industrialists, and financiers, already disenchanted, would band together to remove Hitler and make peace, with no more shots fired or bombs dropped on the Western front.

To describe these propositions as forming a chain of reasoning would be to overstate both the solidity of each and their mutual coherence. But a reader, perhaps dizzied by the notion that anyone could have thought that the way to win a war against Germany was to start a war against Russia, should not forget that Daladier had shown himself for many years to be an astute political tactician and that he was no tyro in matters military. Each proposition had some plausibility. Each, separately, was believed to be true by one or another of Daladier's French or British colleagues. Churchill agreed with Daladier on almost all points.

Daladier certainly had good reason for believing that a war against Germany and the Soviet Union would be more popular in France than a war against Germany alone. Many in France had never forgotten or forgiven the Bolsheviks' abandonment of the Allies after the 1917 revolution. The actual or supposed doctrines of communism were abhorrent to the French bourgeoisie, and especially to the large Roman Catholic population. The Nazi-Soviet pact had seemed to validate the view that Moscow wanted only to see capitalists kill one another off. The French Communist Party's about-face maneuvers in response to dictates from Moscow reinforced the view pressed on Daladier by Deputy Prime Minister Chautemps that the party was a "permanent center of espionage" that should be destroyed, root and branch.[25] All these feelings contributed to gushing praise of valiant Finns, characterized by Charles Maurras in *Action Française* as defending the "Thermopylae of civilization."[26]

If French troops fought in Finland, Daladier was also entitled to believe, the public at home would feel not only that the troops were fighting in a good cause but, perhaps equally important, that at last they *were* fighting, not just waiting for a German attack. At an early point, General Decamp and others on Daladier's Defense Ministry staff had warned him of the "dissolving action" of a continuing *"drôle de guerre,"* possibly producing public demonstrations reminiscent of February 1934, but possibly leading to "a general enfeeblement more dangerous still."[27] The mood at the outset of the war was evident at the officer-candidate school where Michel Debré served as an instructor. "Things were simple," he writes. "Once more, Germany had attacked France. It was necessary to win. And the quality of our military chiefs gave confidence to everyone."[28] With winter arriving, Poland no longer in existence, and little happening on the Western front, French soldiers were reported to be asking out loud, "What the devil are we doing here?"[29] A young lieutenant in a cavalry regiment on the Luxembourg frontier, who had declared himself "delighted" to be going to the front, was writing home by February 1940: "Here, nothing. Absolutely nothing. The only distractions are eating and sleeping. The situation is 'desperately reassuring.' " Jean-Paul Sartre, the writer and philosopher, serving as a private in the army's weather corps behind the Maginot Line, had earlier commented on his comrades' eagerness for battle, but by mid-February was writing, "They're fed up. Most of them say: 'The collapse will come from within. On both sides.' "[30] This was not peculiar to France. As early as late September 1939, Chamberlain wrote his sister Ida, "This war twilight is trying people's nerves." In Cologne in late December, a German general-staff captain in the supply section of Army Group B headquarters wrote in his diary: "The discipline of the army gives cause for serious reflection. Officers who took part in the Great War compare the morale of the troops to that of the year 1917"—when some units were on the verge of mutiny.[31]

Some in Daladier's circle argued that it was Hitler's strategy to pin the Allies to the Western front. Aware of the odds against success, they said, Hitler had no intention of actually attacking. By constantly threatening to attack, then not doing so, he corroded morale among his opponents, meanwhile deterring them from undertaking military operations elsewhere that could enhance the effect of the blockade and bring about Germany's defeat. Léger and others at the Quai d'Orsay had been pressing ever since September for a second front in the Balkans, with a strong French-British contingent based at Salonika (Thessaloniki) providing the nucleus for an offensive to liberate Czechoslovakia and Poland, most of the manpower being provided by Turkey, Yugoslavia, and Romania.[32] By early December, Léger had Mandel and General Jules Bührer, chief of staff for Colonial Forces, as allies, and his counsel was reinforced by a stream of memoranda forwarded from Brussels by Ambassador Bargeton, one of the deans of the French diplomatic service.[33]

The Cinquième and Deuxième Bureaux were in total consensus about the frailty of Germany's economy. On the rare occasion when their views were challenged, they reacted indignantly and massively. Once, for example, Daladier reported hearing that the German population was not suffering and that conditions were considerably better than in 1914–18. The Cinquième Bureau shot back a nineteen-page single-spaced catalogue of German shortages, soon followed by a forty-page single-spaced supplement adding more details.[34]

Summaries of economic intelligence suggested to Daladier that Germany's greatest vulnerability was its dependence on iron-ore imports from Sweden. Before the war, Germany had obtained half of its iron ore from this source, primarily from mines around Gällivare, deep in the interior north.[35] In the Baltic's short summer season, the ore went to Germany via the Swedish port of Luleå; during the rest of the year, it traveled overland to go out through Narvik, in northwestern Norway. French and British intelligence services agreed that most of Germany's imported iron ore came by these routes and that Germany needed, over the first year of the war, to import nine million tons or would see a disastrous drop in steel output. The air-force Deuxième Bureau estimated that, as of October 1939, German iron stocks were already only 60 percent of normal. The British Ministry of Blockade identified iron ore as the resource that, if pinched off, could bring Germany to its knees by September 1940.[36]

In December, about three weeks after the beginning of the Soviet-Finnish war, a special SR report relayed to Daladier comments made in Switzerland by the industrialist Fritz Thyssen, who had just fled Germany (and who, in exile, would later publish a book entitled *I Paid Hitler*). "The supply of raw materials to Germany, particularly of iron ore, is so deficient, and its financial situation is so precarious, that one can predict with some precision the day when Germany will have to capitulate," he said. He explained his flight from Germany as a result of having tried to lay these unwelcome facts before Hitler and Göring. If Russia were to conquer Finland and continue into Sweden, Thyssen said, the flow of iron ore to Germany might continue. But if the Allies were to take the Swedish mines, "German resistance would be broken, perhaps without much loss of life, and in the space of several months."[37]

For Daladier, everything seemed to fit together. A war in behalf of Finland would win over restive right-wingers in the Chamber and Senate. Seeing something at last happening would buoy public morale (and silence Reynaud and Mandel). Waged against a Red Army already stumbling, it could hardly be a costly war. An important by-product would be a cut-off of ore shipments from Sweden to Germany, which, if Thyssen was right, would compel the Germans to sue for peace—Q.E.D. (almost).

Despite urgings from Léger and others, Daladier was not initially enthusiastic about a second front in the Balkans. (Gamelin's designation of Weygand as the commander in the area may have been a factor.) During the first stages of the Finnish war, however, while it still seemed likely that Finland would be overrun, he shifted stance.[38] At a meeting of the Supreme War Council at the Ministry of War in Paris on December 19, Daladier made a speech in favor of increasing the number of battlefronts. Plainly, he said, Germany had to look north or southeast or both for raw materials; hence, the Allies should act at once to bar German expansion in the direction of Romania. Enlisting Romania and Yugoslavia as allies, he further calculated, would add ninety divisions to the total forces arrayed against Germany. In addition, he urged that France and Britain take advantage of the League of Nations' resolution branding the Soviet Union an aggressor and give active aid to Finland.[39] He had already instructed the French ambassador in London to emphasize that "prolongation of Finnish resistance is of paramount interest to us." After the Supreme War Council meeting, Daladier told Bullitt that he believed Finland should be supported to the utmost and that France would prod Britain to join in aiding the Finns. American public sentiment, he knew, was strongly pro-Finnish. The famous American columnist Walter Lippmann, passing through Paris, had recently recommended that the Allies mount an attack against the Soviet Union, saying that, if they did not do something by summer, all chance of eventual U.S. support would disappear.[40]

Thus, as 1939 turned into 1940, Daladier became a crusader in behalf of Finland. Possibly he sensed a danger that Reynaud might take the initiative away from him, for Reynaud could not miss seeing the tide of sympathy for Finland running in Parliament and among the public. Learning that Reynaud was lunching in public with generals known to be advocates of action somewhere other than the Western front, including Giraud and Daladier's own Defense Ministry chief of staff, Decamp, Daladier began to fire off directives to Gamelin. On January 4, he ordered him to ready at least one brigade of mountain troops for dispatch to Finland. In the margin of a reminder, he penciled in a rude injunction not to procrastinate. Four days later, bedridden at Celle-St.-Cloud because of his riding accident, Daladier again used his pen as a goad, writing to Gamelin with emphasis, "I *insist* that everything be ready by the beginning of March."[41]

A friend who visited Daladier in late fall, well before his accident, had described him as "irritable and tired . . . overwhelmed by too many responsibilities. . . . He seemed stubborn, sometimes unreasonably so, and he spoke in a sour tone."[42] Lying about in bed or hobbling on crutches, Daladier became even more testy. His anger at Gamelin in the period of the Mechelen affair was one indication. Another was a rebuke to the British government for not getting on with its end of planning for an expedition to Finland. He directed the French ambassador in London to remind Foreign Minister Halifax of "the whole sweep of responsibilities we should take on if, because of a constantly temporizing and negative attitude, we neglect the possibilities offered of both a preventive and a positive action, in a theater of capital importance for the outcome of the war."[43]

Daladier's staff at the Ministry of Defense agreed with Léger that German threats of an offensive against the Low Countries were intended only to tie down Allied military forces that might be used effectively in other areas. This was the view of General Decamp and of Robert Coulondre, author of the "hold on, hold on, hold on" telegram, who, upon return from Berlin, had become chief diplomatic adviser in the ministry. By going to the aid of Finland, Decamp and Coulondre argued, the Allies could cut communications between Germany and the Swedish ore fields. Germany would have no choice but to fight to try to reopen the ore route. The Allies might succeed in holding Sweden. Even if they failed to do so, they could destroy the iron mines. "Depriving Germany of iron ore imports," said a Defense Ministry staff memorandum dated January 15, ". . . would bring about its rapid asphyxiation. . . . Whatever the risks encountered, the importance of the stake is such that it would appear opportune to undertake this action and devote to it a maximum effort."[44]

The Cinquième Bureau affirmed that Germany's economy was on the ropes. "Its economic situation reportedly is fast becoming critical," said its analysts. "From this point forward, the blockade should become really effective."[45] At the same time, warnings came from Helsinki that the Finns might not be able to hold out much longer without Western troops and planes.

Early in February, more or less back on his feet, Daladier attended another Supreme War Council meeting in Paris. In the interval, his key presumptions had all been reinforced. Admiral Darlan had written him: "If we accept, like the Germans, that any 'frontal' maneuver spells failure or excessive high cost, there is no other way to escape from the present stalemate except by a flanking or 'eccentric' maneuver." Darlan's own recommendations were (1) "attack where we can (Finland, Caucasus, Black Sea)" and (2) "deliberately open hostilities against the U.S.S.R."[46] Since Gamelin had forwarded the Darlan memorandum to Daladier without comment, the implication was that he would not actively dissent if Daladier chose to follow Darlan's advice. Moreover, Gamelin himself had proffered a plan which called for an Allied Expeditionary Force to land at Petsamo, in the far northeast of Finland, and march south.

During the Supreme War Council meeting, Daladier championed Gamelin's plan. In the course of discussion, however, he abandoned it in favor of an alternative sketched by British officers, under which the expeditionary force would land at Narvik, take the railroad that ran from there to Luleå, leave a garrison behind at the ore fields, and go on to Finland. This seemed to Daladier perfectly satisfactory, since it promised to accomplish all his goals. Moreover, Britain seemed prepared to put up most of the manpower and all the transport. Cadogan wrote after the meeting, "Everything agreed and merry as a marriage bell."[47]

Whether because the British representatives deliberately disguised some of their reservations, because Daladier's translator failed to note them, or simply because of wishful listening, Daladier carried away the impression that Britain had agreed to an expeditionary force of around fifty thousand men with a hundred supporting aircraft. He also had the impression that, although the British government thought it highly unlikely that Norway and Sweden would decline to cooperate, it intended that the force should land and proceed to Finland even in face of resistance from either or both. Another possibility is that Daladier chose to claim that he had so understood the British representatives, so that if a dispute became public Britain's public opinion would compel their government to do as he hoped.

Whatever the case, less than a week later, on February 10, Daladier went before a closed session of the Chamber of Deputies to declare that the Allies were about to send Finland enough men and airplanes so that it could continue to hold out against the Soviet Union. Herriot, burying old resentments, extolled Daladier, and the deputies gave the prime minister a unanimous ovation.[48] In the twenty years in which the Palais Bourbon had been the central theater of Daladier's career, he had seldom experienced such a moment of triumph. But it was his last.

The British government soon made it plain that it was not committed to any Scandinavian operation, let alone to one of the scale and character that Daladier had described in his speech. Chamberlain had agreed only to plan an operation, not necessarily to carry it out. If an expeditionary force landed, the British chiefs of staff envisioned one of around twelve thousand, not fifty thousand, and with fifty planes at most, not a hundred. Moreover, no matter what the pleas from Paris or Helsinki, the British contingent would not be ready to depart before mid-March.

Daladier was enraged. Even when talking with the ambassador from Fascist Italy, he let himself accuse the British of being afraid to fight the Russians.[49] He instructed Ambassador Corbin in London to go directly to Chamberlain and to "spare nothing, in this decisive moment, to obtain the agreement of the prime minister for an action which is so highly justified and on which in fact depends the very outcome of the war."[50] Talking with Corbin over the telephone (perhaps with a presumption that the British had it bugged), he said despairingly: "If we don't support the Finns, we will bind together Russia and the Reich. There is no question about it—they're making us draw back. If through our own fault nothing is done, I would just as soon throw in my hand."[51]

One reservation that Chamberlain had not emphasized during the Paris meeting had been any stipulation that the Allies not use Norwegian or Swedish territory or territorial waters without their consent, a point that he considered moot because, if they did not consent, "the world would cry shame upon them."[52] In fact, on March 4, the Norwegian and Swedish governments refused unambiguously to assist any operation for relief of Finland or to receive any Allied soldiers or ships. The British government promptly advised Paris that this put paid to all existing plans. If anything were to be done for Finland, it would be on a smaller scale, move directly through the open Baltic, and not occur until late April.

Daladier appealed against this decision but to no avail. He then went so far as to call in the Finnish ambassador and tell him that France would provide aid even if Norway and Sweden opposed and even if Britain was not yet ready to act. That was on March 11. A Finnish negotiating team was already in Moscow. On March 12, Daladier learned that the team had signed an agreement ending the war and essentially ceding to the Soviet Union the territory it had demanded earlier.

The surrender of Finland dissolved the temporary harmony in France.

In the government, the Parliament, and the press, supporters of Daladier denounced Great Britain. Critics renewed their calls for new men and new policies. Members of the Chamber not bold enough yet to beard Daladier himself summoned his acolyte, La Chambre, and grilled him about every reported shortcoming in air-force production.[53] Clare Boothe wrote home on March 10, "Clamor for more vigorous prosecution of the war must result in overthrow of Daladier although nobody here knows what anybody means by more vigorous prosecution." Prefects and other observers noted increased anti-British feeling. A British officer dining at the headquarters of the French Third Army heard officers opine that the Finns had been sold out by politicians paid with Moscow gold. French officers, he said, seemed even more hostile than British officers to "frocks"—civilian politicians.[54]

On March 18, Daladier announced that there would be no Northern offensive. On March 19, he appeared again before a closed session of the Chamber of Deputies. Gaston Bergery, a former Radical still close to Herriot, led an attack on the government, saying, "The men who were not able either to prevent or to prepare for the war are not qualified either to end it or to win it." Daladier called for a vote of confidence. It came at 2 A.M., with 239 deputies voting in his favor and only one against, but since three hundred deputies had abstained, the government no longer had a majority and Daladier had no choice but to resign.[55]

"The 'Bull of the Vaucluse,' " wrote Élie Bois, ". . . had received something more than darts this time. The toreador had planted the sword firmly between his ribs." Daladier's sometime naval aide Raphaël-Leygues named the toreador: "Reynaud finally succeeded in kicking Daladier when he was down. . . . He is a juggler, a city boy, a Parisian who thinks that France consists of the Faubourg St.-Germain representing the right in the country and Aubervilliers the left. . . . Reynaud, with his high cheekbones and his sharp voice . . . wants to have his victory!"[56]

It was an imperfect victory for Reynaud. Trying to form a cabinet that was completely his own, he learned how little leverage party leaders allowed any prime minister. He could not get a majority without support from the Radicals, and Daladier was still their leader. In the end, on March 21, after two days of negotiations, Reynaud proposed to the Chamber of Deputies a cabinet in which he would be prime minister and take over the Foreign Ministry but leave Daladier as both minister of defense and minister of war and retain most of the rest of Daladier's cabinet. Even with these concessions, Reynaud won confirmation by a margin of only one vote.

STUMBLES

" 'You have sat too long for any good you have been doing. Depart, I say, and
let us have done with you. In the name of God, go!' "
        —*Leo Amery in the House of Commons, May 9, 1940, quoting Oliver
        Cromwell and calling for the resignation of Prime Minister Chamberlain*

inland's capitulation and Reynaud's replacing Daladier as prime minister did not end discussion of possibly opening a second front against
Germany. Reynaud had criticized Daladier for indecisiveness and inaction. Even before the war, he had likened Daladier to King Louis XVI, de-
ferring to ministers who told him all was well and following no strategy "as
long as a certain number of taboos demanded by the political parties were
respected."[1] Against the earlier slogan of Daladier and Chamberlain that
time worked in favor of the Allies, Reynaud posed his own, soon quoted on
both sides of the Channel: "Time is neutral; it has to be annexed."[2] There
was no chance of his being less enterprising than his predecessor.

On March 28, not a week after becoming prime minister, Reynaud put
before the British government ambitious proposals for action. Actually,
Léger had formulated them for Daladier. Though Reynaud distrusted Léger
because of his closeness to Daladier, and eventually moved him out of the
center of his spiderweb, much as Bonnet had removed Massigli—by announcing that he would be posted to Washington—he nevertheless appropriated Léger's proposals, commas and all. The first was for an immediate effort
to cut off Germany's imports of Swedish iron ore. Occupy Narvik, Reynaud

urged; don't wait to form a large expeditionary force. The second was for prompt action in the Black Sea and Caucasus areas, "not only to limit the supply of oil to Germany but above all to paralyze the entire economy of the U.S.S.R. before the Reich succeeds in mobilizing it for its own purposes."[3]

Since Reynaud was on good terms with Churchill and with Sir Edward Spears, who was Churchill's chief expert on France, he probably knew he would have Churchill's backing for the first of his recommendations. At one time or another, Churchill had embraced or would embrace all the propositions that had captivated Daladier. He had thrilled to Finland's cause as much as any right-winger in the French Parliament and had seen Finland's success as proof of Soviet weakness. In a BBC broadcast (deplored by Chamberlain) he had said: "Everyone can see how Communism rots the soul of a nation; how it makes it abject and hungry in peace, and proves it base and abominable in war."[4] Within the British War Cabinet, he had been an early champion of going into Norway and Sweden, whatever their governments said. In mid-December 1939, in a memorandum to the War Cabinet, he had written:

We have right, and, indeed, are bound in duty, to abrogate for a space some of the Conventions of the very laws we seek to consolidate and reaffirm. Small nations must not tie our hands when we are fighting for their rights and freedom. The letter of the law must not in supreme emergency obstruct those who are charged with its protection and enforcement. . . . Humanity, rather than legality, must be our guide.[5]

Like Daladier, Churchill hoped for wondrous results from cutting off Germany's iron ore. "No other measure . . . ," he asserted in the same memorandum, "gives so good a chance of abridging the waste and destruction of the conflict, or of perhaps preventing the vast slaughters which will attend the grapple of the main armies." To Chamberlain, he wrote on Christmas Day: "The ironfields . . . may be the surest and shortest road to the end."[6] Though he claimed that it was his policy to try to avoid war with the Soviet Union, he argued for action in Scandinavia, whatever the risks. "If Germany is starved by want of iron ore," he wrote on the same day, "Russia could be no serious menace." In late March 1940, he recommended slipping British submarines into the Black Sea. "Two or three submarines would not only interrupt the Russian oil traffic in that sea," he said in Cabinet, "but would have a terrifying moral effect on Russia."[7]

Within Chamberlain's Cabinet, Churchill had been almost alone in seeing eye to eye with Daladier. For Chamberlain himself, the idea of a second war was horrifying. All he wanted was an honorable end to the war into which his colleagues had already dragged him. But he did see some appeal in the idea of cutting off Germany's iron ore. His Ministry of Economic Warfare had told him earlier that Germany could probably not survive the war for a year without Swedish iron ore, and Thyssen's testimony impressed him, as it had Daladier. He said to his Cabinet that stopping ore shipments might offer "a chance of dealing a mortal blow to Germany."[8] But Chamberlain wanted to act in concert with the Scandinavian states. When Norway and Sweden said "No!" he forced a Cabinet vote calling off the planned expedition. It was notice of this vote that so angered Daladier and contributed to his losing his premiership.

Churchill did not give up. He revived an alternative proposal, which was to lay mines across the sea approaches to Norway. After initially expressing doubts, Chamberlain adopted this idea. In addition to hurting Germany, he recognized, it could be helpful to France. Though Chamberlain had thought Daladier not a bad fellow for a Frenchman, he seems to have had no inkling that Daladier had domestic political problems. He did not like Reynaud. "His face has a foxy expression which causes me to wonder if his real name is not Renard instead of Reynaud," he wrote to his sister Hilda.[9] But he began to realize that Reynaud might be urging action in part because of pressure from the people who had voted down his predecessor. Even when questioning Churchill's mine-laying proposal, Chamberlain acknowledged that it might appease "the appetite of the public for spectacular operations."[10] A day later, on March 28, at a Supreme War Council meeting in London, he surprised the French representatives (and Churchill) by endorsing, as linked projects, not only mine-laying on the Norwegian coast but the RAF's cherished plan for bombing the Ruhr and another pet project of Churchill's—"Royal Marine" or "fluvial mines"— which involved air-dropping some ten thousand twenty-pound contact mines into German rivers and canals.[11]

Reynaud expressed gratitude to Chamberlain and rushed back to Paris, where he encouraged friends to praise him for getting more from Great Britain than Daladier had ever gotten. When he gathered his cabinet, however, Daladier, still minister of defense, made him regret his boast. He vetoed "Royal Marine" on the ground that Germany would retaliate, and vetoed any bombing of the Ruhr on the same ground. Gamelin and Vuillemin supported him. Their collective reasoning was summarized soon afterward in a letter from Daladier to Chamberlain, pointing out that French aircraft plants had only recently begun full-scale production; many were in vulnerable sites; and, because airfield construction was under way, many new planes were sitting in hangars waiting for runways. "The truth is that the French air force at this moment is like a snake that is changing its skin," he wrote. "Those who are in charge of the air force insist strongly that it has to be given time."[12] Reynaud's cabinet voted with Daladier and the military establishment. Since Chamberlain had presented his proposals as a package, everything was canceled. Reynaud's hands suddenly seemed embarrassingly empty.

Churchill traveled to Paris hoping to change Daladier's mind. He had no success. Concluding that stubbornness on the part of Britain would be profitless, he wired home a recommendation that the Norwegian operation proceed even if "Royal Marine" and a Ruhr-bombing campaign did not. (He may have heard the prediction being made by Mandel—that if Reynaud fell the successor cabinet would be headed by Herriot, with Laval as foreign minister and a negotiated peace with Germany as its platform.[13]) Chamberlain, convinced of the value of cutting German ore imports and more sensitive now to French politics, accepted this recommendation. The British War Cabinet agreed on April 5 to give Norway formal warning and, three days later, to commence sowing mines. The date, April 8, was selected specifically with an eye on Reynaud's domestic problems: in the

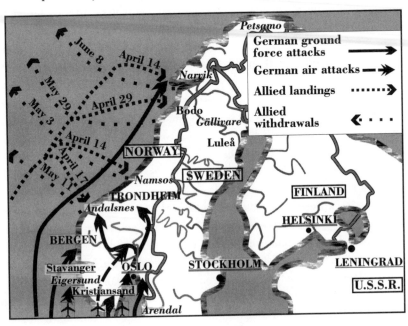

The Scandinavian Theater

Cabinet meeting, Oliver Stanley, the President of the Board of Trade, noted that it would help Reynaud avoid a vote of no confidence when the French Senate convened on April 9.[14]

Germany was expected to respond in some way, perhaps by trying to seize ports in Norway. If Norway then appealed for Allied help, the British and French governments wanted to be ready to act, so they resumed preparations for sending ground forces to Scandinavia. In fact, when British ships arrived on April 9 and began rolling mines into Norwegian coastal waters, German troops had already invaded Denmark, and German warships were crossing the Baltic with landing parties destined for Oslo, Arendal, Eigersund, Kristiansand, Stavanger, Bergen, Trondheim, and Narvik.

News subsequently reaching Paris and London was both confusing and disheartening. By April 11, the Germans had occupied Denmark, having encountered almost no opposition, and they quickly occupied their target cities and towns in Norway. The small Norwegian army retreated into the interior. The offsetting good news for France and Britain was that Norwegian coast artillery, together with the newly laid mines, and hastily dispatched elements of the Royal Navy had sunk three cruisers and ten destroyers, which represented a crippling loss for the German navy.

A hastily assembled expeditionary force, mostly British, set out for Norway a few days later. Four brigades, totaling about twelve thousand men, landed north and south of Trondheim, while other troops, in about the same number, went ashore north of Narvik. After two weeks of skirmishing, the Allied commanders in the Trondheim area concluded that their positions were hopeless and evacuated their troops by sea. The last ones embarked on May 3. At Narvik, by contrast, the Allied force joined the principal remnant of the Norwegian army, besieged the city, and drove the Germans out. By then, however, it was early June. Events in France eclipsed all else. Allied troops burned Narvik and shipped for home.

Though French and British intelligence services had occasionally given muffled warnings that German forces might be assembling for an operation in the Baltic Sea, Germany's invasion of Denmark and Norway came to leaders in the two governments as a complete surprise. When Prime Minister Reynaud learned of it late on April 9, he telephoned Gamelin, interrupting the general's dinner, only to find Gamelin as uninformed as he.[15] By emphasizing the ship sinkings and the quick landings by Allied troops,

Reynaud successfully fended off critics. The fact that the Allies were doing something seemed to quiet deputies and senators, who gave Reynaud a vote of confidence. The French press and public appeared to accept Reynaud's implicit argument—that France had galvanized the alliance into action, and that whatever failures occurred had been Britain's fault. Edmée Renaudin, the wife of a civil servant, made two entries in her diary for April 19. First: "A great English victory at Narvik." Second: "The news is good. German ships were sunk, the blockade is completed, and we are going to do a lot."[16]

The politician most damaged was Neville Chamberlain. His cancellation of the earlier expedition became common knowledge. Many in his own party had by now concluded that he was not the man to carry on the war. His appearances in the House of Commons brought increasingly weak applause. Newspapers that once supported him became critical, among them the *Daily Mail*, the *Telegraph*, and the *Express*. Whereas Reynaud could draw cheers in the Palais Bourbon by declaring that Germany had made a strategic blunder in invading Scandinavia, Chamberlain drew catcalls at Westminster when he alleged that "the balance of advantage" in Scandinavia rested with the Allies.

The Cabinet had agreed that there had to be a parliamentary debate on Norway, but it remained uncertain whether the Labour opposition would insist on a vote in the House of Commons testing confidence in the government. Though far from unanimously, the Labour leaders decided to do this. Chamberlain and David Margesson, the Conservative chief whip, calculated that it would be a victory if defections in their own party were few enough so that the government had a majority of a hundred or more. During two days of debate on May 7 and 8, Labour and Liberal leaders assailed Chamberlain; Lloyd George joined in, appealing to Chamberlain to resign. During the second day of debate came a famous moment when the hardline Tory Leo Amery concluded a speech by looking straight at Chamberlain and quoting Oliver Cromwell's words to the Long Parliament: "You have sat too long for any good you have been doing. Depart, I say, and let us have done with you. In the name of God, go!" Admiral Keyes, appearing in dress uniform with medals from shoulder to waist, declared that the prime minister had lost the confidence and respect of men in uniform.

The government won the vote of confidence in the House of Commons, but with a majority of only eighty-one. Chamberlain concluded that, at a minimum, he would have to form a government that included members of other parties. When Labour leaders said flatly that they would serve but not under him, he recognized that he had to do as Lloyd George and Amery had recommended. He talked with Halifax and Churchill, found Halifax dubious about trying to exercise leadership from the House of Lords, and regretfully settled on Churchill as his successor. Then, on the morning of May 10, came news that German armies had struck the Low Countries and France. Chamberlain thought for a moment that he should perhaps remain on the bridge during this moment of crisis. His friends said gently, "Better not." So, at this turning point, Chamberlain informed King George VI that he could not continue as prime minister, and the king summoned Churchill.

In France, meanwhile, Gamelin had coped with second-front fever by maintaining an appearance of open-mindedness. He had expected this fever. It had risen during the Great War, when public opinion became exasperated with the seeming stalemate on the Western front. Marshal Foch had championed starting one from Salonika, and he and others never ceased to argue that, if the front had been opened, France would have lost fewer men and won the war sooner. Anticipating that the proposal might rise again, Gamelin, during the August–September mobilization, had recalled to active duty Foch's disciple Weygand, and sent him to Syria to organize a force that might move to Salonika or that might back up Turkey or any Balkan nation that chose to resist Germany. (A memoir by Weygand's aide, then-major Pierre-André Bourget, describes how artfully Gamelin made to Weygand the case that Turkey's allegiance might be the key to victory in a war and that Weygand alone had the prestige to sway the Turkish government toward France.[17]) From Gamelin's standpoint, this arrangement had many advantages. For one, it removed Weygand from France and made it hard for him to kibitz. For another, because Daladier distrusted Weygand, it ensured that he would think twice before taking troops away from the Western front to bolster an adventure from Salonika.

In the early part of the war, Gamelin could pretend an interest in a possible Balkan theater without worrying that it would actually materialize. In a letter to General Ironside of mid-September 1939, he spoke of readiness to "galvanize the efforts" of Balkan states. Periodically, however, he reminded British generals—and his own prime minister—that no Balkan state had as yet asked for or offered a single soldier. At the September meetings of the Supreme War Council at Abbeville and Hove, he was gratified to hear Chamberlain voice misgivings about a Balkan front and question the wisdom of even the preliminary step of building up a force in or around Salonika. Chamberlain was concerned not to antagonize Italy.[18] Cadogan noted shrewdly in his diary: "P.M. threw gentle showers of cold water on [the Salonika proposal], and the French didn't seem entirely convinced by their own argument. It's moonshine to me."[19] Given also the fall of Poland and the succession of alerts on the Western front, British hesitancy temporarily removed Salonika and the Balkans from the operational agenda.

In December and January, however, Gamelin had to cope with revived interest in the Balkans, combined now with enthusiasm for intervention in Finland and perhaps war with the Soviet Union. General Weygand, theretofore kept busy by ministers and military men in Turkey and the Balkans who would talk with him grandly about cooperation and then do nothing, came to Paris to ginger up his own government. Arriving on December 3, just days after the Soviet invasion of Finland, he argued that, in view of Soviet and possibly German preoccupation with Northern Europe, opportunity was now at hand to organize the grand French-British-Turkish-Yugoslav-Romanian offensive toward Czechoslovakia and Poland.

Gamelin did not take issue with Weygand—that was not his way. Indeed, in meetings with a British military delegation running on, day after day, from January 29 to February 4, his representatives supported at least minimal action along the lines Weygand advocated. But it was quite evident that the British delegates remained dubious, preoccupied with Italy, and annoyed by Weygand's pretense to be supreme commander in an area where British interests outweighed those of France. Ironside, the British chief of staff, had written early in the war to the British commander in the Middle East theater: "Our strategy in the Middle East must be Imperial strategy and it is important that it should never be subordinated to French command."[20] Privately, the British chiefs of staff reckoned that a Salonika venture would require at least twenty French divisions, for which Britain would have to provide transport. The debates took time away from other matters, and Gamelin knew they were without likely consequence.[21]

Finland was a different matter, for Daladier's growing passion was matched or surpassed among leaders in both the Chamber of Deputies and the Senate. Moreover, reports from Britain told of speeches, sermons, and newspaper and magazine commentary that equated the cause of Finland with that of civilization. Knowing that he himself was being stigmatized as too defense-minded, Gamelin felt a need to be more forward about Finland than he was with regard to the Balkans. Hence, he developed his plan for sending an expeditionary force to Finland via Petsamo. In his memoirs, Gamelin confesses that his heart was not in this proposal, but, he explains,

"I didn't think I had the right, in this domain, to go against a decision of the government. The majority of the Parliament, and in particular the Senate, appeared to have resolutely taken a stand." Also, he notes, Weygand, well regarded in those quarters, had written, "I believe it is of capital importance to break the back of the U.S.S.R. in Finland . . . and elsewhere."[22] Given Chamberlain's determined opposition to war with the Soviet Union, Gamelin may have felt that he could propose this Petsamo expedition without much risk of its actually coming off. (Also, he could keep in the back of his mind the thought that, even if the politicians endorsed it, military planners might voice second thoughts when they noticed that it involved sending a fleet in winter to the skirt of the Arctic Ocean.[23]) Though his plan was soon dropped in favor of one that was theoretically more practicable, he was relieved to see the whole venture discarded when Chamberlain was unwilling to act against the wishes of Norway and Sweden.

After Reynaud replaced Daladier, Gamelin saw that the danger of troops' being diverted from the Western front to some second front had greatly increased. He coped with it by making himself even more open-minded. He submitted to the new prime minister a "Note on the Conduct of the War," which indicated, though not unambiguously, a willingness to consider operations in Scandinavia and also the bombing of Soviet oilfields. He made a point of showing this document to Villelume, known to be close to Reynaud and, indeed, ghostwriter for the speech that had won Reynaud his one-vote majority.[24] But in private, Gamelin and his staff remained cool toward all such projects. General Ironside noted in his diary hearing Gamelin comment of Reynaud's rhetoric and the parliamentary applause: "If they want to do something they must form an assault brigade from the deputies and start it off themselves."[25]

In the first meeting between General Gamelin and Prime Minister Reynaud after Germany invaded Denmark and attacked Norway, Gamelin told Reynaud that a French brigade had been poised to go to Scandinavia. Where was it? Reynaud inquired. In the Alps, the general replied. Why there? asked Reynaud. To prevent its detection by German spies, he explained. Reynaud observed acidly that the Germans had not seemed to fear having their forces detected by French spies.[26]

Both to Reynaud and before his own staff, Gamelin took the position that all the fault was Britain's. He insisted to Rivet that it had not been the SR's responsibility to predict German action in the Baltic: That duty lay with the British Secret Service. After Reynaud dressed him down, however, he quickly designated two brigades for immediate deployment to Norway and told General Georges that two or three divisions would be taken from the Western front to back them up. Catch *him* not energetically pursuing the war! Truthfully or not, Gamelin told Daladier he was thinking of resigning. Few things could have pleased Reynaud more.[27]

Throughout, even when proposing to take divisions away from Georges, Gamelin's constant objective was to maintain maximum forces on the Western front so as to meet and thwart a German offensive, which he deemed inevitable. In early January, when first encountering Daladier's enthusiasm for a new war with the Soviet Union, he sent him a long letter saying, "It certainly seems to be the case that the Germans, after having prepared a major offensive . . . hesitated, [but] the comparative equilibrium existing at present on our Northeastern front is in process of being altered to the advantage of our adversaries." Using Deuxième Bureau estimates akin to those he had used in prewar budget battles—making two and two add up to five or six—he asserted that the Germans would soon have two hundred divisions against 105 for France and Britain.[28]

He said then that Germany might move into Scandinavia but that, if so, it would be merely a prelude to an attack on the Western front. After Germany actually did attack Denmark and Norway, he said it again, warning Reynaud and Daladier that a German strike in the West might come as early as mid-April—that is, in less than a week.[29] His yielding to Reynaud and preparing to take whole divisions away from the Western front probably indicates his fear lest Reynaud replace him, perhaps with General Georges, whose judgment he now distrusted, or, worse yet, with Weygand, who seemed to think that southeastern Europe could become the main front. Gamelin himself never wavered from a belief that Hitler would eventually become desperate and would have to make a direct attack on France, and that the outcome of the war would be decided on the Western front. As Ironside wrote, Gamelin's eyes were "glued on the north-east frontier."[30]

One result of the running debate throughout early 1940 about possible offensives in Scandinavia or the Balkans or the Black Sea, and of Gamelin's preoccupation with preventing any drawdown of Allied forces on the Western front, was that no one in France or Britain had much time for reviewing the war plans developed in the autumn of 1939, or for asking whether their premises were still valid. That was unfortunate for Gamelin, for France, and perhaps for the world. The exact months when Gamelin's whole attention went to circumventing first Daladier, then Reynaud, were those in which Germany committed itself to the daring final version of Plan Yellow. The Deuxième Bureau and associated agencies collected many indications of this change, but no one noticed the warning flags.

INTELLIGENCE FAILURE

The experience of France and Britain in the spring of 1940 is a classic case of intelligence surprise. In retrospect, one can see scores of pieces of information available to both governments that indicated what Germany was planning. The French and British governments simply failed to pay attention.

Two other cases of intelligence surprise offer models of explanation of this one, both occurring soon afterward. One is Japan's attack on the American base at Pearl Harbor in December 1941; the other, on June 22 of the same year, is Hitler's sudden offensive against the Soviet Union. Roberta Wohlstetter, in her analysis of the first, concludes that Americans were bound to be taken by surprise. She uses the distinction made by students of communication between "signals" (genuine indications of what is going to happen) and "noise" (apparent signals that in fact suggest wrong conclusions). After the fact, it was easy to find warning signals, especially in secret Japanese communications that American cryptologists were reading. But, she makes plain, these genuine "signals" did not get through, in large part because there was so much surrounding "noise." Too many decrypted messages and too much other information supported inferences that the

Japanese intended to continue negotiations or, if they went to war, would attack only British and Dutch possessions in East Asia, not the distant American naval base in Hawaii.[1]

Barton Whaley's study of Hitler's invasion of the Soviet Union ("Operation Barbarossa") also concludes that the victim should not have been surprised. Stalin had received eighty-odd "signals" that Germany's attack was coming. German disinformation efforts had not generated enough "noise" to blanket them.[2] Whaley explains that Stalin chose to ignore these "signals" primarily because his paranoid mind suspected that they were planted by British intelligence with an eye to provoking a German-Soviet war.

In the Pearl Harbor case and other possibly parallel cases (as, in the 1990s, the Iraqi invasion of Kuwait, or the collapse of the Soviet Union), the diagnosis is that any "reasonable man of ordinary prudence," to borrow the lawyers' conceit, would likely have read the evidence wrongly. In the case of Operation Barbarossa (and, perhaps, the Middle East wars of 1967 and 1973, the fall of the Shah of Iran in 1979, and the debt crises of the 1980s and 1990s), the verdict runs the other way: the explanation for the surprise has to be sought within the minds of those who were caught off guard—in the blinkering effects of their prejudices, preconceptions, unprobed presumptions, or, as with Stalin, psychoses.

The surprise suffered by France and Britain in 1940 has more resemblance to Barbarossa than to Pearl Harbor.[3] Though there was a great deal of noise, there were many clear signals of Germany's plans. This is not to say that the French and British governments should have anticipated exactly what was to happen or when; there is nothing extraordinary in their having failed to perceive that the Germans shifted the main line of attack from the Low Countries to the Ardennes or turned its axis east to west instead of north to south. But the signals that this *might* be the case were abundant and distinct; it is simply astonishing that Allied leaders continued to discount such a contingency and made relatively few preparations for it.

The explanation, however, is different from that for Barbarossa or for other, similar surprises. This makes the case more instructive, for its moral is not simply: Don't have a paranoid dictator! The surprise experienced by French and British leaders in 1940, though due in part to individual failings, is traceable more to characteristics of their systems of collecting and analyzing intelligence and to their lack of system in relating this intelligence to their own decision-making. These procedural attributes of the two governments stand in sharp contrast to those of the German government, where more than anything else the system for mating intelligence and decision-making generated the final version of Plan Yellow. And it must be added that, in these respects, the United States and most other democracies today resemble France and Britain of 1940, not Germany.

Most writings about the 1940 surprise have missed this point, in large part because their authors have been taken in by veterans of the French intelligence services who claimed to have perceived what the Germans were going to do, sounded loud warnings, and been ignored by dull-witted generals and politicians. But little or no evidence dating from the period itself supports this claim. Some of the most frequently repeated and widely credited anecdotes in fact fall to pieces when tested against the surviving documentary record.

Several veterans of the Deuxième Bureau and the SR have written, for example, that their organizations predicted where and when Germany would attack; others have used this story to indict Daladier, Gamelin, or others. Gauché, in his postwar memoir, boasts of having told Gamelin, more than a week ahead of time, exactly what was to happen—"The SR . . . brought precious indications received from its stations, which had been on the alert for a long time"—and cites three reports from early and mid-April, particularly:

> May 1: The German army will attack between May 8 and 10 along the entire front, including the Maginot Line, the Sedan region, Belgium and Holland, and the north of France will be occupied in ten days and the rest of France in a month. . . . Of all the "intelligence regarding intentions" received, this was the one that was closest to the way the operation unfolded.[4]

Reynaud's postwar memoir, alleging that Daladier and Gamelin had created conditions that he could not remedy, amplifies this recollection and turns it into an accusation:

> On the morning of April 30, our military attaché in Bern learned from an accepted source that the Wehrmacht would go on the attack between May 8 and 10, with Sedan as the principal axis of the effort. He immediately advised the Deuxième Bureau at army headquarters, which straightaway transmitted this precious intelligence to the Supreme Headquarters. Gamelin remained deaf to these warnings.[5]

The truth is that the prediction "from an accepted source" originated with a Pole who was distantly associated with Göring. The *British* military attaché in Switzerland heard it and passed word to the French *air* attaché,

saying, however, that he believed the report to be purposely planted disinformation. The Frenchman so reported to Paris, and the head of the air
force's Deuxième Bureau included all the details and the disclaimer in the
intelligence summary that was routinely distributed to senior military officers and members of the government.[6] It was probably pure coincidence
that the Pole made an accurate prediction. No one in Paris or London had
any reason at the time to regard it as more than "noise." Nor did they.

The French and British intelligence services took care to pass on every
warning that came their way and to mention every even remotely plausible
contingency. The Deuxième Bureaux of the French army and air force
called attention to the possibility of a German offensive through Switzerland much more often than to that of an offensive through the Ardennes. To
chronicle all their warnings would tax the reader's patience too heavily, but
the following is a representative sample, all from 1940, with my editorial
notes in brackets:

• February 26, Deuxième Bureau (Air): A "new piece of intelligence considered more reliable than previous ones" predicts an early-March air attack on Britain accompanied by a ground offensive from the Saarland. [This
was presumably expected to skirt southern Luxembourg and try to cut in
behind the Maginot Line.]

• March 1, Deuxième Bureau and Deuxième Bureau (Air): An informant
who provided very good information before the war says there will be a
mid-March offensive against the Netherlands and Belgium accompanied by
air attacks on London and Paris and moves against Denmark, Norway, and
Sweden.

• March 6, British War Office and Deuxième Bureau: Reports of an impending offensive against Belgium seem doubtful, but indications of a possible offensive against the Netherlands alone deserve to be taken seriously.

• March 19, General Georges's headquarters: Villelume is told that three
independent sources say that Germany intends to attack the Maginot Line,
not the Netherlands or Belgium.

• April 13, Deuxième Bureau (Air): Reports from Switzerland predict an
imminent attack on the Netherlands, accompanied by a diversionary strike
against France.

• April 23, Gauché warns Gamelin of an impending German attack on the
Netherlands.

• April 30–May 1, [Gauché or Rivet] advises Gamelin that a "very good
source" forecasts a German offensive against the Low Countries within a day
or two, and Petibon passes an urgent warning to the Belgian military attaché.

• May 10 [the day of the German attack], the SR learns that yesterday Oster told Sas that the offensive would take place on May 10.[7]

It is hard to see how such a potpourri of largely unevaluated warnings could have been of much use to operations planners, commanders, or other decision-makers. At the same time, it is striking how little use Allied intelligence officers made of the rich information reaching them about debates in Berlin. Time after time, memoranda from the Deuxième Bureaux or the British joint intelligence committee referred to evidence of disputes between Hitler and his generals. Some of it was wildly distorted—as, for example, rumors in November 1939 that Hitler intended to resolve these disputes by making Beck president of Germany and Halder war minister[8]—but not a line in any of these memoranda addressed the questions "Why?" or "What is really going on?"

As the reader already knows, conflict between Hitler and his generals shaped German strategy. Hitler's passionate desire for an early offensive and the generals' fears of military disaster created the dialectic from which emerged the plan that the Germans put into effect in May 1940. Of course, the exact nature, timing, and outcome of the struggle could not be known to or inferred by intelligence officers in Paris or London. Surely, however, it did not need genius to suppose that the struggle *might*—I stress *might*— produce something other than a simple "go" or "no go" verdict on some replica of the Schlieffen Plan.

The closest approach that French and British intelligence officers made to interpreting what they were told about conflicts in the German government came in an exchange among themselves. In late January 1940, the British-French liaison committee that had been functioning in London ever since the first Supreme War Council meeting produced an agreed document which asserted that no hypothesis could be ruled out, because "the personal influence of the Führer, with whom the final decision rests, makes it impossible to assign to each, as logic demands, its appropriate degree of probability."[9] This was actually more the view of the French participants than of the British. At a meeting of the same committee in early March, the British members reported that the British chiefs of staff did not agree that German strategy would be determined by Hitler's whims. "Our view . . . ," they said, "is that Germany's military policy is far more likely to be based on strategical considerations than it was before the war."[10] This premise contributed to the conclusion by the British chiefs of staff that a German naval and air offensive against Britain was more likely than a ground offensive against the Low Countries and France.

As the reader is aware, no question offered better entrée into understanding both German decision-making and its outcomes. Would the determining appreciation be Hitler's? Would it be that of military professionals? Would it be some compromise? Alas, the exchange ended with the British stating their dissent. Surviving records show no indication that anyone ever explored differences between these contrasting presumptions.

French and British intelligence services did no better in pulling together estimates of total forces on the enemy side. The practices of peacetime continued into the war. In France, the Deuxième Bureaux made their own calculations, then gave Gamelin figures open to a variety of interpretations; he then made two and two add up to three or less, or five or more, depending on his purposes. With regard to ground forces, the British generally deferred to him.

In January 1940, Gauché's Deuxiùme Bureau estimated—exclusively for the use of British intelligence officers—that Germany had fifty-six divisions that could be used for a Western offensive, six of them being armored divisions. Another forty divisions were being equipped and trained and could eventually be front-line units. Fifty more consisted of older men, less well armed, likely to be employed only for defensive missions. Hence, the potential German offensive force totaled ninety-six divisions. At the end of March, again for their own purposes, the air-force Deuxième Bureau and Colonel Louis Baril, the chief intelligence officer at Georges's headquarters, agreed that the number of German divisions that could be used in a Western offensive now totaled fifty-seven, eight of them armored. They reckoned at fifty the number of divisions that might eventually become front-line forces. The estimated total had thus risen to 107.[11]

As before the war, the data supplied to Gamelin and other senior officers permitted them to cite larger numbers. Thus Gamelin told Daladier in January 1940 that the Germans had 135 divisions, soon to become two hundred.[12] French representatives in inter-Allied committees spoke of Germany having 170–75 divisions.[13] After Reynaud came to power, talking of energetic warfare possibly elsewhere than on the Western front, he was told by Gamelin and others that the Germans had 190 divisions. Indeed, in mid-April, Gamelin worked the figure up to 205, though conceding that only 190 were battleworthy.[14] The reality came close to the intelligence services' in-house estimates: the Germans would attack in May 1940 with 112 divisions, ten of them armored.[15]

French and British intelligence services also carried over from peacetime their habit of distributing exaggerated estimates of German strength in vehicles and aircraft. Here they sometimes deceived themselves as well as the recipients of their reports. Although they tracked with some accuracy the numbers of German armored divisions, they supposed the existence of many tank battalions brigaded with infantry divisions. This resulted probably from projection. Gauché and his colleagues knew of Guderian's argument that all armor should be concentrated in independent divisions. The Deuxième Bureau had translated *Achtung Panzer!* and given it wide distribution. But the French army had been slow to form armored divisions, because senior officers saw so many good reasons for keeping tanks and infantry together. Gauché and other intelligence officers may have presumed that many German senior officers thought similarly and may have doubted that the Germans would adopt Guderian's doctrine wholesale. Perhaps they simply thought that, even if it were the case, it would not be believed. Too many of France's senior officers had spent too much time combating the comparable doctrine when it was expounded in France by Charles de Gaulle. Hence, the Deuxième Bureau credited the Germans with the equivalent of six to eight additional armored divisions scattered in with infantry.

The French and British overestimation of the number of German armored units was a minor error compared with their overestimation of the tanks at the disposal of the German high command. At some point in the past, the Deuxième Bureau had settled on a supposition that each German tank battalion had about a hundred tanks; since an armored division had four tank battalions, this meant four hundred tanks per division. As radio intercepts, agent reports, and occasional prisoner interrogations made possible identification of armored divisions and other units that might have tanks, analysts simply multiplied.

Thus, at the beginning of April 1940, the Anglo-French liaison committee distributed an estimate that the Germans had 5,800 tanks—4,000 of them Panzer Is and Panzer IIs, the remaining 1,800 medium Panzer IIIs, with heavy Panzer IVs beginning to come on line.[16] These figures were lower than those the Deuxième Bureau preferred. (With their own army farther along in forming armored divisions, the British committee members questioned some identifications of armored battalions associated with infantry divisions.) Gauché and Colonel Baril, Georges's chief intelligence officer, told Gamelin and Georges that, in their view, the Germans certainly had 7,000 tanks and might have as many as 10,000.[17] In fact, almost all German tanks were assigned to armored divisions, and a typical German armored division had between 200 and 250 tanks, so the actual total as of May 1940 was a little more than 2,400.

The French and British intelligence services similarly overestimated German air strength. As with tanks, the error resulted partly from adopting a wrong base number, then multiplying. In this case, the erroneous base number was not of planes per squadron or anything comparable but, rather, of planes produced. The British, again more conservative than the French, calculated that Germany's output of military aircraft had been about 700 a month at the outbreak of the war, had risen to almost 1,000 a month by early 1940, and had a theoretical limit of 2,400 a month. Largely from this baseline, the Anglo-French liaison committee, in its April 1, 1940, report, attributed close to 4,500 first-line aircraft to Germany, with more than 7,500 in reserve—a total strength of 12,000. The figures that Vuillemin presented to Reynaud, Daladier, Gamelin, and Georges were higher—5,700 first-line planes, 8,500 in reserve, thus more than 14,000. In reality, on May 10, 1940, the Luftwaffe possessed about 3,400 bombers and fighters with perhaps another 2,000 planes ready for reconnaissance or troop-transport missions.[18]

In wartime as in peacetime, the estimates of German force levels that the French and British intelligence services recorded had little or no bearing on judgments about fighting a war. The major function of these estimates was to fortify rhetoric. Supposed gross numbers of German divisions or tanks or airplanes did occasionally come into play in debates about grand strategy. High numbers helped Gamelin make his case for not stripping forces from the Western front. But, as in peacetime, they were mainly used in debates about budgets.

Had there been any serious Allied analysis of what and how the Germans were thinking, comparable to the analyses that Liss made at Zossen about French and British thinking, these overestimates of gross German force levels could have been a handicap. A key problem for General Halder and the German general staff was how to distribute across the entire Western front a finite number of armored and motorized divisions and ground-support air squadrons. Clever minds in the Deuxième Bureau or Cinquième Bureau or the British joint intelligence committee (and there were some) could perhaps have arrived at useful conclusions had they worked at trying to understand Halder's problem and tried empathetically to imagine the arguments that German planners might possibly be exchanging. Had anyone had this assignment, these wildly wrong gross estimates of German forces could have interfered with accurate inferences. But the experiment was never even run.

To describe how French and British intelligence agencies assessed their evidence about German strategy and overall German capabilities is to tell a sad story of wasted opportunity and large-scale error. When one turns, as we do next, to their record in reading German operational intentions, the story becomes tragic. There is scarcely a grain of truth in the postwar claim that Allied intelligence officers perceived those intentions, alerted the higher commands, and were ignored. The fact is that they neither noticed the significance of the information they were accumulating nor assisted others to understand it.

Allied intelligence services were at their very worst in providing what intelligence professionals call "I&W"—indications and warning. The extraordinary, even unique, sources they had which gave them potential insight into high-level German decision-making had lost much of their value by the spring of 1940. Although these sources had told the Allies accurately of Hitler's orders for a Western offensive, the fact that the event repeatedly failed to occur made recipients of the information increasingly wary. The Dutch army's chief of intelligence told Sas that he was going to remove him from Berlin. When Sas asked what was to happen regarding the pipeline to Oster, his boss responded, "What do you want me to do with all your dates?" Sas said later to a Belgian historian, "He didn't believe any of it. The game of the Germans seemed very clear to him. Every time there was an alert in Holland, their agents only had to open their eyes and make a report to Berlin. At this rate, Dutch intentions would soon be an open book for Brauchitsch!"[19]

The security restrictions that Hitler imposed after the Mechelen incident made it hard even for highly placed individuals like Oster to learn what was being planned. And as the time for the offensive approached, the Germans took pains to plant false warnings. (The Pole in Switzerland was almost certainly doing that. He would probably have been more astonished than anyone else to learn that, when he said an offensive would start on May 10 and succeed in a matter of weeks, he was speaking the truth.)

At the beginning of May, the Allies lost their best source regarding German air operations. In January 1940, Major Bertrand's Section D of the Cinquième Bureau had begun to break messages encrypted by the German Enigma machines. The original work of duplicating the machines had been done by Poland's intelligence service, and the Poles had come to Paris in

September 1939 with everything they could remove from Poland. At a château not far from Vincennes and another not far from Georges's headquarters, Bertrand had brought the Poles together with his own cryptologists and with others from Britain's Government Code and Cipher School. Although the first messages whose codes were broken belonged to the German army, Bertrand's people and an increasingly active team in Britain concentrated on Luftwaffe traffic, because most of it came via radio as opposed to land line and therefore there was more of it. By early March, Rivet was exclaiming in his diary about the quality of information being obtained. By late April, it was abundant. Then, on May 1, the Germans changed the indicators for the keys to all messages except those in the Norwegian theater. Decryption did not recommence until late in the month, by which time the Battle of France was well under way.[20] Had this not been the case, communications intercepts might have shown what was going on clearly enough so that officers in Allied intelligence service could sound an alarm. But probably not even then.

For, even without highly placed agents and without Enigma decryption, French and British intelligence officers had ample reason for saying that an offensive was highly likely, that it became more likely with each day of good weather, and that one spearhead was likely to strike through Luxembourg and the Belgian and French Ardennes. They even had reasons for hazarding the guess that the latter would be the primary spearhead. One cannot look back through their daily and weekly reports—which rested primarily on routine radio interception and aerial reconnaissance—without becoming amazed that this was not done. The "signals" were clear and abundant. The "noise" was minimal.

Let us recall that it was between the middle of February and the end of March that Hitler and the German high command definitely settled on the sickle-cut plan. General Halder had already shifted significant forces from Bock's Army Group B to Rundstedt's Army Group A: that is, from the Dutch-Belgian theater to the Luxembourg-Ardennes theater. But the decision to make Bock's offensive diversionary and Rundstedt's primary, instead of the other way around, resulted from war games and conferences with Army Group commanders and chiefs of staff that continued into mid-March and beyond.

French and British intelligence services had evidence about these German deployments. The following highlights of regular or special intelligence reports are, of course, selective, but they were not a few "signals" amid thunderous "noise":

• On March 13, the Deuxième Bureau (Air) noted that bridging equipment was being assembled in Germany opposite the border of Luxembourg. Two days later, it commented on an increase in the number of tanks deployed opposite southern Belgium and northern Luxembourg. On March 15, British army intelligence identified four armored divisions as in or moving into the Eifel, which was the part of the Ardennes forest on the German side of the border, and a new armored division forming there. These divisions were thus in position to move either into central or southern Belgium or into Luxembourg. At about the same time, the Deuxième Bureau (Air) and the French air attaché in Copenhagen commented on new aircraft in the neighborhood of Koblenz, headquarters of Rundstedt's Army Group A (with, however, many dummy aircraft on the runways).

• On April 5, British army intelligence spotted buried telephone cables between the Koblenz area on the Moselle River and *southeastern* Luxembourg. Munitions depots were also sighted on the right bank of the Moselle, opposite the town of Remich, in the same part of Luxembourg. Between April 10 and April 12, Gauché reported signs of troop movements opposite Remich and the presence of a new, as yet unidentified German armored division at Trier, on the Moselle, parallel with central Luxembourg. On April 12, the Deuxième Bureau (Air) pinpointed several new air groups near Koblenz, and the Luxembourg government advised Paris of concern about a buildup of troops and of river-crossing gear on the German side of the German-Luxembourg border. On the very same day, British army intelligence commented on the many new bridges over the Moselle and the lower Rhine, some designed to carry very heavy loads.

• On April 21, the Deuxième Bureau (Air) summarized the results of aerial reconnaissance: there were now four to five German divisions on the border of the Netherlands, thirty to thirty-four in the Eifel, twenty-three to twenty-seven between Luxembourg and the Rhine, and sixteen to nineteen just to the south, in Baden and Württemberg. Though no commentary was offered, anyone acquainted with the terrain should have recognized that the divisions in the Eifel and those between Luxembourg and the Rhine could, on short notice, be concentrated in an offensive against central Belgium or, still more easily, in an offensive via Luxembourg; if the latter, the attacking force could be buttressed by divisions from Baden and Württemburg. Moreover, on the commonsense assumption that tanks and motor vehicles have to keep to roads when navigating dense stands of trees, it should have been a reasonable surmise that armored and motorized forces in the southern Eifel were positioned as they were so that they could use the road network running through Luxembourg, Belgian Luxembourg, and the Belgian and French Ardennes.

• On April 30, British GHQ intelligence noted a large number of supply depots now on the frontiers of Belgium and Luxembourg; on a nineteen-kilometer front in the latter area, there were sixteen. Nowhere else, even on much more extended fronts, were there more than eight or nine depots, the report observed, and two of the sixteen depots on the Luxembourg frontier were for fuel. Not a line, however, suggested that Germany might be preparing to move vehicles such as tanks across Luxembourg to the Ardennes.

Of course, the evidence was not glassy clear. Aerial reconnaissance also noted some buildup of troops and air forces opposite the Netherlands, and exercises by paratroops in areas near the Netherlands and northern and central Belgium. Intensive aerial reconnaissance on May 7, 8, and 9 spotted no unusual movements of troops or vehicles or railroad cars anywhere on the Western front. But one would think that there had been enough prior reportage so that a "reasonable man of ordinary prudence" would have said: You know, there might be a major attack across Luxembourg. Hadn't we better take precautions?[21]

In Belgium and Switzerland, where military-intelligence services were keeping track of both German and Allied deployments, this possibility does seem to have come to mind. Based on evidence collected by the Second Division of the Belgian general staff, General Van Overstraeten warned Gamelin that Germany might launch an offensive with its axis "more or less from Bastogne to Mézières,"[22] the evidence at the time being chiefly the heavy reinforcement of Rundstedt's Army Group A. This antedated the final German decision to give this front the *Schwerpunkt*, and Van Overstraeten himself would later think that the Netherlands and Belgium were the most likely focus for a German attack. Still, his warning shows that the inference seemed plausible, even before it was firm reality.

Colonel Eddy Bauer of the Swiss general staff asserts that what was coming was apparent to him and his colleagues in Bern. Like Halder looking at the *Kuhhaut* at Zossen, Swiss officers could see the weakness of the French line guarding the Ardennes. They saw the same concentrations on the German side that were noted in French and British intelligence reports. They saw all but three of Germany's armored divisions on a line south of Liège. In their view, it seemed reasonable to expect that Germany would strike where the French were most weak. "Should one have supposed," he writes scornfully, "that the offensive, which was expected very shortly,

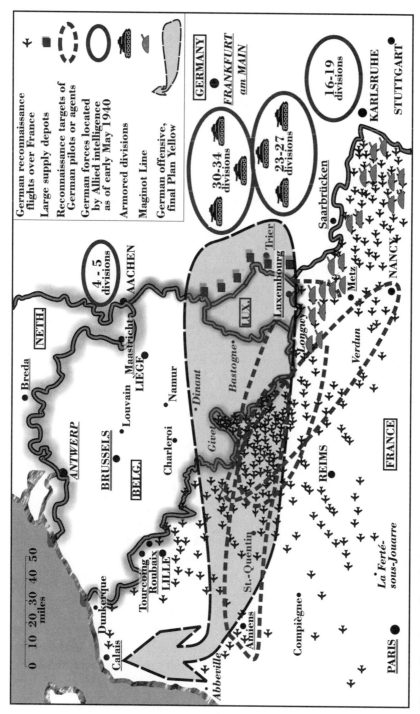

Warning Signs Ignored by Allied Intelligence, April–May 1940

would begin by a curious, tight maneuver, aimed at gathering around Aix-la-Chapelle [Aachen] an enormous mass of vehicles which together would have made up a column of 1,000 kilometers?"[23]

Even if reports on German deployments did not prompt speculation that the Germans might be thinking of an offensive via Luxembourg, such speculation should have been stirred by reports about what German intelligence agencies were up to.

Prior to April, the Allies saw very little German aerial reconnaissance. In November 1939, it may be recalled, Göring had halted all one-plane reconnaissance flights because of Luftwaffe losses in dogfights. He relaxed this restriction only when it became urgent to collect information relevant to the projected spring offensive.

Then, on April 5, a Dornier 17 reconnaissance plane was shot down near Sedan. The German pilot, closely interrogated over a period of days, finally confessed that he had secret orders to photograph the quadrangle between Merzig, just over the Saarland border from Luxembourg, to Metz, to Charleville, to Bastogne. (The center of this quadrangle is Sedan.) On April 12, the SR learned, probably from one of its double agents, that the Abwehr station in Hamburg had assigned one of its best operatives to do a ground-level survey of the area from Sedan to Charleville-Mézières to St.-Quentin to Amiens. According to Colonel Paillole (who sometimes, unfortunately, overdramatizes), the agent was to note obstacles, check the load-bearing of bridges and any gasoline supplies—all suggesting that he was looking for tank routes.

On April 14, the Deuxième Bureau (Air) reported that there was German aerial reconnaissance going on from Nancy, well behind the Maginot Line, to Charleville-Mézières. On April 17, Captain Archen, the SR station chief in Luxembourg, drawing on reports from Clervaux and elsewhere, cautioned Paris that an extraordinary number of German "tourists" were arriving in Luxembourg. On April 23, several German reconnaissance planes overflew the triangle Givet-Vervins-Mézières, northwest and west by north from Sedan. This was repeated on May 2, May 6, and May 9. Meanwhile, on May 4, forty German reconnaissance planes passed over the Pas-de-Calais. Of course, there were other flights, including some over the heart of the Maginot Line, and a few on the border of Switzerland. But anyone counting up German reconnaissance flights would have had to conclude that the center of Luftwaffe interest was very much the same area that the Abwehr agent was commissioned to examine—that from the Ardennes Forest through Sedan to the Channel coast.[24]

Intelligence on German deployments and intelligence targets did not establish unquestionably that the Germans intended an attack across Luxembourg, through the Ardennes, and thence west by north through Sedan and Charleville-Mézières. But it seems almost incredible that General Gamelin and others in the Allied high command were not concerned that the Ardennes area—essentially the border of Belgian Luxembourg, running from Longwy at the northern terminus of the Maginot Line to Sedan, on the Meuse—had the thinnest coverage of any portion of the front.

THE REASONS WHY

Given the information reaching French and British intelligence services, their prewar record for accurately predicting Hitler's moves, and their detection in 1939 and early 1940 of all Hitler's orders for a Western offensive, why did Gauché or Rivet or their counterparts in London not at least prod the generals—Gamelin, Georges, Ironside, Gort—and their operations officers to reconsider the presumption that an actual German attack would concentrate in the Netherlands and central Belgium? Although there are answers at many levels, three in overlapping categories concern individuals, organization, doctrine, and culture.

Individuals. Part of an answer in this category was given by Colonel Vialet when he said in October 1939 that Lieutenant-Colonel Gauché was not up to his job as France's chief intelligence officer. Gauché's own views were, to put it blandly, uncomplicated. In an early meeting with a British counterpart, Gauché aired his opinion that Nazism and communism were indistinguishable, that only Hitler's personal force had thus far kept them separate, and that the moment Hitler disappeared Germany and the Soviet Union would fuse. As for Italy and Spain, Gauché regarded them as the natural allies of France.[1] Presumably, he was the person chiefly responsible for the December 1939 estimate that Hitler would fear a "war of slaughter" on the Western front and would not risk it; therefore, France should concentrate on rooting out domestic subversives.

Gauché's limitations were recognized not only at Georges's headquarters but at Gamelin's. General Louis Koeltz, one of Colson's deputies, had been Gauché's predecessor as head of the Deuxième Bureau and was a genuine expert on Germany. After the war, he wrote a good book trying to explain how the Germans developed their plan of campaign for the war against France. Sometime in 1939, Gamelin gave him the assignment of acting as chief liaison with foreign officers, especially with the British, and Koeltz told them candidly that Gamelin lacked confidence in the Deuxième Bureau.[2]

In January 1940, when Gamelin effected his complicated reorganization plan, one reason was dissatisfaction with the Deuxième Bureau. He complained to an aide that, since the outbreak of the war, Gauché had expanded his staff from sixteen officers to seventy-five.[3] Apparently, Gamelin did not think that the army was getting proportional benefit.

One consequence of the reorganization was to create a new Deuxième Bureau for the Land Forces, headed by Gauché's former deputy, Lieutenant Colonel Joseph Martin-Gallevier de Mierry. We know almost nothing about Mierry, but the quality of his mind is suggested by a report signed by him, dated May 18, 1940, eight days after the German attack. It interprets the attack as an act of desperation resulting from the pressure of the Allied blockade and comments smugly that, in actuality, the Germans have made their situation worse, for they will no longer be able to obtain imports via the Netherlands and Belgium.[4]

Organization. Even if men of genius had manned the Deuxième Bureau, the structure of the French military establishment might have frustrated efforts to analyze intelligence and make it useful.

From the beginning, staff elements were physically separate from one another. Colson and some of the prewar general staff remained at the rue St. Dominique, in what was now called the headquarters of the Army of the Interior; another general staff took form in châteaux and other buildings in and around Meaux, thirty-five miles from Paris.

Gauché took over a large country house at almost the point where the Paris road entered La Ferté-sous-Jouarre. It was thus at the opposite end of the town from General Georges's headquarters at Les Bondons. Called the Château de Condé, it had fifty-five rooms furnished in Directoire style, full of frescoes and Italian oil paintings. Gauché appropriated as his office the bedroom of the owner and allowed her to visit it only under double guard. Trees were cut down so that the grounds could be illuminated by searchlights and covered by machine guns. The area gradually became, as one of Gauché's subordinates recalls, "an immense tapestry decorated with electric wires," for Bertrand's cryptographers were housed in a different château, on the other side of the Jouarre River; other elements of the Deuxième Bureau were elsewhere in the vicinity; and the Cinquième Bureau had its own châteaux. The air-force Deuxième Bureau had moved with General Vuillemin to a command post at St.-Jean-les-Deux-Jumeaux, a hamlet between Georges's headquarters and Meaux.[5]

The Deuxième and Cinquième Bureaux answered to Gamelin, Colson, and Georges. Paillole says that officers of both organizations found the dispersal of headquarters irksome and confusing. The SR, he writes, did not know "to which saint it should bow." Officers had to travel frequently to Les Bondons, Vincennes, and Colson's offices in the rue St.-Dominique. This was more efficient, recalls one, because it meant that they wrote less. But it became burdensome after the January reorganization, for Montry had to be included in the itinerary, and written reports required signatures from at least two headquarters.[6]

The structure—or lack of it—baffled British liaison officers. A major and a brigadier who dealt directly with Gauché strongly advised their superiors not to press for formal arrangements. Anything that was regularized, they said, would be too complicated to work. At a level above them, there was a formal agreement, as a result of which General Howard-Vyse could not talk with General Dentz without going through General Jamet. Best leave matters alone.[7] Even as to the highest-level command arrangements, there was ambiguity. Spears records a conversation with Gamelin in a deep-vaulted corridor at Vincennes. He asked him who would give orders to the British Expeditionary Force. "Looking at me keenly, he answered in his pleasant, pink satin voice: 'Mais, le Général Georges!' then, a light having shown for a moment at the back of his eyes, as it does when you look through the back of a camera and press the release, he added: 'And of course I give General Georges his instructions.' "[8]

Gamelin probably had many reasons for the January changes, which made more complex an organization that was already byzantine. His public explanation—that he wanted a clearer separation between the Land Forces command and Georges's theater command—seems inadequate. Another probable factor was the growing rivalry between the two. In late September, André Pironneau, editor of Kérillis's daily, *L'Époque*, told Gamelin that a right-wing cabal was trying to unseat him and get Georges appointed in his place. As early as October 1939, Petibon took note of Georges's lunching with Reynaud and surmised that the general was playing politics. By the turn of the year, common gossip had it that the officer corps wanted Georges in place of Gamelin, and there was no question that Georges was the favorite of the English.[9]

Another possibility is that General Gamelin intended the headquarters at Montry to be the nucleus for a field command of his own. Since he supposed (wrongly, as it turned out) that King Leopold would not allow his forces to come under a mere theater commander, he had already thought of acting operationally as supreme commander. In March 1940, he was to set his personal staff thinking about where and how he might set up a forward command post. His one stipulation was that it not be at La Ferté-sous-Jouarre.[10]

Whatever the reasons, Gamelin's reorganization of January 1940 had the effect of complicating even further the processes of examining intelligence, selecting material to go to the high command, and getting it circulated.

Doctrine. Gauché insisted that the Deuxième Bureau's officers think of themselves as members of a priesthood. After the war, he wrote:

> The officer of the Deuxième Bureau, much more than his comrades on the general staff, is, in his work, free of all external influence and enjoys complete intellectual independence. It is thus that, in the synthesis . . . which he presents to the high command, the chief of the Deuxième Bureau is guided by only one concern: the truth—whether or not it will be agreeable to learn. This truth he presents completely, as he sees it, and, in the conclusions to which it leads him he can hide nothing and attenuate nothing. There is no doubt that this independence confers on the person who accepts it a *personal responsibility* for which it not possible elsewhere to find the equivalent.[11]

Gauché also prescribed for intelligence officers a kind of scholastic exactitude. In the same postwar book, he argued that the methodology of intelligence analysis "derives from the rigorous application of a certain number of principles . . .":

> First of all, knowledge of an enemy is an objective, concrete notion, based solely on the ascertainment of positive, precise, and verified facts. Whoever works in intelligence can never depart from contact with realities and must avoid being led by intuition or excessive imagination.[12]

Gauché commented scornfully on those who would go to a commander with just one item of intelligence. The intelligence officer, he argued, must present to the commander, "in a *single synthesis*, immediately usable, all intelligence received regarding the enemy that could determine or modify his decision." He advocated "patient objectivity, based on study of actual information, controlled and analyzed, which will permit us progressively to reduce the number of hypotheses originally developed. . . . The ideal which ought to be pursued, but which will never be attained, is to be able to reject all hypotheses save one."[13]

In his postwar book, Gauché singled out as an example of poor work some reports filed in 1938–39 by General Henri-Antoine Didelet, then France's military attaché in Berlin. Didelet questioned whether German military forces were as ready for war as the Deuxième Bureau customarily said. If Hitler was not crazy, Didelet said, he would probably wait at least two or three years before forcing a war. This outraged Gauché. Didelet was making a subjective evaluation and saying that facts could be discounted. He was trying to read Hitler's mind. Gauché could not tell Didelet what he thought of such reasoning at the time, for Didelet had two stars on his sleeve and Gauché had only four stripes. But he could tell Chief of Staff Colson what he thought, and he did; Colson sent Didelet a private letter cautioning him "against the tendency to deem a fact that which can only be a hypothesis."[14]

With all its remarkable resources, the Deuxième Bureau conceived itself as essentially a conduit for data. Generals and ministers were expected to develop from the bare facts their own estimates of what was happening that might matter in decisions as to what was to be done.

Culture. Weaknesses in personnel and organization accounted in part for the poor performance of the French intelligence services, but cultural factors were probably more important than any others. In the French military establishment, intelligence officers were comparatively isolated. This was partly their own choice. Once in the Deuxième Bureau or the SR, men tended to stay there and not to return to troop duty. They then compensated for not having as much field experience as their contemporaries by emphasizing how arcane their work was, which only increased the barriers to communication between them and the officers who were preparing plans and conducting operations. Reflecting on intelligence officers he had observed at various headquarters, Marc Bloch commented, in *Strange Defeat,* that they "live in a world haunted by the spirit of secrecy. Not that the formal code of good manners is not . . . scrupulously observed. The fact remains, however, that a system of watertight compartments is universal in the higher reaches of the Army. Nowhere have I found them less penetrable than at the very top."[15]

Though many officers of the Deuxième Bureau and the SR rose to high rank, duty in intelligence had much lower status than duty as an operations officer or an actual commander. Henri Navarre, who eventually became a four-star general and a victim of France's war in Vietnam, explained in his memoir that he served in the SR from 1935 to 1940 because he had just completed a tour commanding a cavalry squadron in Morocco, wanted to stay in Paris on account of a girl, and asked help from a relative who was a deputy chief of the general staff. After a few days, the relative called to tell him that the best he could do was an assignment in the SR: "He seemed almost ashamed to make me that offer. The SR was, in fact, regarded in high military spheres as a second-rate organization, almost beneath the dignity of an officer brevetted to the general staff."[16]

Gauché and Rivet had direct access to General Gamelin and were occasionally summoned by him and asked questions, but they were clearly expected to offer reports and opinions only with regard to what the enemy was doing or appeared likely to do in the immediate future. At unit levels, intelligence officers functioned as scouts. (That is effectively what Daladier had been in the Great War.) They delivered information without necessarily taking responsibility for anything except an estimate of a particular report's reliability. As was evident in their failing to comment on the pattern in German aerial reconnaissance, they did not, as a rule, compare new information with earlier information. Bloch testified in *Strange Defeat* that in his own experience intelligence bulletins would arrive "without any attempt being made to stress the relationship between them. By studying them closely, one often came to realize that they were mutually contradictory, or that, having first underlined one particular group of facts as offering results rich in possibilities, a later issue would gaily relegate these same facts to oblivion without a word of warning or explanation."[17] And such performance was characteristic at the highest levels.

As far as one can tell, French intelligence officers were rarely if ever asked to explain what the Germans had done or to speculate about German thinking. Gamelin said repeatedly that Germany's move into Scandinavia was preliminary to an offensive in the West. Soon he was saying that if Italy entered the war that would be a sure sign that the Western offensive was coming. Did he base these assertions on intelligence regarding Germany? Did he test them with anyone more knowledgeable than he about Hitler's

Reich? There is no sign of it. Certainly, there is no evidence of any kind to suggest that he looked to Gauché or Rivet for such expertise. In his memoirs, he does pay tribute to the SR and the Deuxième Bureau: "Their product was what one could logically and reasonably expect. My understanding is that they perfectly well oriented us as to the efforts and possibilities, as well as the probable solutions, of our adversaries."[18] He is, however, praising success in predicting Hitler's prewar moves and what he supposed to be precise order of battle data. He was not complimenting the intelligence agencies' analyses of German processes or plans, because he had not asked for such analyses or received them. He was saying, in effect, that they had done well as scouts.

No senior officer had the duty of assimilating intelligence and relating it to operational planning. The French general staff had no one doing what, on the German side, was done by Tippelskirch and earlier by Stülpnagel. Overseeing the Deuxième Bureau was but one of many functions of one of the deputy chiefs of staff, and not of high priority. Koeltz, who obviously had the background for it, appears neither to have had much to do with his former Deuxième Bureau colleagues nor to have worked in operational planning. He served essentially as emissary to the British for Gamelin and Georges (and eventually Doumenc).

One consequence was that, as far as one can tell, neither the French general staff nor Georges's theater staff had anyone thinking hard and knowledgeably about what might be going on among their counterparts on the other side of the front. At neither Vincennes nor Meaux nor La Ferté nor Montry does there seem to have been a *Kuhhaut* like the one Liss maintained at Zossen and that Halder and his colleagues periodically studied. Maps that matched Allied and German deployments must have been on walls or tables in the operations bureaux at those headquarters, where markers for German units can only have been put in place on the basis of reports from the Deuxième Bureaux. Yet no one from the Deuxième Bureaux seems to have been involved in studying these maps, as Liss and his colleagues were obliged to do at Zossen.

Though some French intelligence officers might have come upon the knowledge by chance, information as to French and British deployments did not routinely go their way. And, in the ordinary course of events, operations officers would not have disclosed to intelligence officers even the outlines of highly secret plans. Thus, it is possible, even probable, that Gauché, Rivet, and other intelligence officers could not have recognized the significance of the data they accumulated regarding German deployments and German intelligence collection. The system would have left this up to operations officers.

One piece of reminiscence argues the contrary. Paillole writes that, upon learning that an Abwehr agent had been commissioned to survey roads, bridges, and gasoline supplies on the Sedan-Charleville-Amiens route, he and Rivet decided to alert the high command. His account is quite circumstantial. He says that they first went to Petibon, at Vincennes, who told them Gamelin was in London, meeting with the British. He promised to pass their news on to Gamelin, but urged them to go immediately to see General Georges. He would telephone to say they were coming:

> At La Ferté-sous-Jouarre, we were received by Colonel Navereau, chief of the operations bureau of the headquarters of the Northeastern front. He was a polytechnician, forty-five years old, serious, courteous, and calm. His huge office was covered with intelligence maps. While Rivet spoke, he observed us silently. He took several puffs on his pipe.
>
> "It's curious," he said. "What you are reporting to us, and I respect its value, is in contradiction with other intelligence that leads us to think that the main German effort will take place higher up, through Holland and northern Belgium."
>
> General Georges joined us. Affable, simple, with a keen eye behind his thick glasses, he studied at length with Navereau the hypothesis of an offensive through the Ardennes toward Sedan. He thanked us and left without stating any conclusions.

Paillole adds that he saw Georges in Algiers in 1943, that Georges remembered the meeting clearly, and that he expressed regret at having ignored the information from the SR and at having gone on presuming that the German attack would come in the North.[19]

In this case, there is no rebutting evidence comparable to that for the much-touted warning via Switzerland. Nor, however, is there any supporting evidence. Paillole dates the events in mid-April, which is the period when the Germans would have been seeking information about conditions along the projected route of attack. But neither Gamelin's diary nor Georges's nor Rivet's contains any entries for April that could be construed as recording these events. Their diaries do, however, indicate something going on a month earlier.

On March 7, the military attaché in Brussels had warned that Germany planned to launch a Western offensive in mid-March. This stirred some alarm at Georges's headquarters. Rivet attended a meeting there, at La Ferté, on March 9, and on March 12 noted in his diary: "Some movements and reinforcements in the rear areas behind the German front makes us apprehensive about offensive preparations. (In the North, across from Holland, in the center of the Eifel, where three or four armored divisions seem to be concentrated.)" Three days later, Daladier commented on hearing talk of a possible German offensive in mid-March that "would exceed in scope anything that was seen in 1914–1918." On March 19, Rivet's diary says: "Summoned by General Gamelin concerning important intelligence to be conveyed to him."

Gamelin's diary shows that Rivet was received by Petibon at nine that morning.[20]

That's it. We do not know what anyone said. What seems to me most likely is that Paillole, writing a quarter-century later and knowing what had happened in 1940, remembered the report about the Abwehr agent and was sure that he and Rivet must have perceived its significance at the time. He also recalled Rivet's having had urgent meetings with Georges, Petibon, and Gamelin, and memory tricked him into making everything into a single story.

I doubt that events could have gone as Paillole describes them in part because it seems unlikely that either he or Rivet would have known enough about existing operational plans to have been aware that these plans did not already anticipate an Ardennes offensive. But if Paillole's story were perfectly true, it would serve only as an exception that proved the rule. Not a single surviving written report from the SR or the army and air-force Deuxième Bureaux or British GHQ intelligence contains any commentary on how the items of intelligence they catalogued might bear on the Allies' planning.

One is entitled to fault Allied intelligence officers for making mistakes in estimates of enemy-force levels, and for failing to connect one day's reportage with reportage from previous days. It is hard to explain why none of their documents commented on the increasing concentration of German armored forces south of Liège or made the point made in retrospect by Colonel Bauer about how hard it would have been for these masses of tanks and vehicles to take roads north, then west, through the choke point at Aachen. But it has to be said, in extenuation, that it is hard for intelligence officers ever to do their jobs well if they do not know who is making decisions in their own government or what those decisions are about.

THE DAM BREAKS

E ven if the individuals had all been first-rate, if France's command and staff system had been well organized, and if the organizational culture had been less constraining for intelligence officers, alarms might still not have been heard, for, in April and early May 1940, the French government and high command were even more distracted than they had been during the preceding winter.

On April 3, Gamelin and Daladier arrived at Reynaud's offices in the Quai d'Orsay for a meeting of the Comité de Guerre. To their surprise, they found General Weygand present. With the evident approval of the prime minister, Weygand made a plea for sending more forces to the Mediterranean to prepare for opening a Balkan front. Gamelin's diary says, "Daladier was furious."[1]

Just at this time, General Gamelin thought he saw a new opportunity to solidify France's relationship with Belgium. According to French representatives in Brussels, members of the Belgian government who had previously insisted on maintaining neutrality were now alarmed. They saw what seemed an ominous German buildup on the Dutch and Belgian frontiers. Also, they had from their mission in Berlin a precise warning of impending German military moves.

With the Abwehr getting urgent requests from the German army's general staff for information relevant to the sickle-cut plan, Colonel Oster had begun to sense what was up, and as an officer in the armed-forces high command, he saw at first hand Germany's planning for the war in Scandinavia. He had not had any news for Major Sas for some time, but now he had a lot. Sas passed it on to the Belgians, as a result of which Brussels was told that a Western offensive was due at almost any time but that meanwhile an offensive would be launched against Denmark and Norway. (Colonel Goethals, in the Belgian Embassy in Berlin, supplemented this with a message based on information from an American source that the German offensive in the West would have two *Schwerpunkten,* one on the line of Aachen, the other south of Trier.)[2]

The French ambassador in Brussels reported that Foreign Minister Spaak was now willing to talk about inviting intervention by the Allies.[3] In Gamelin, this report awakened the hope that King Leopold, who he still supposed was strongly pro-Allies, could now do what, as Gamelin imagined it, he had wanted to do earlier but been prevented from doing by his cabinet. Then, when Prime Minister Reynaud interrupted his dinner on April 9 with news of the German moves into Scandinavia, Gamelin seems to have thought, first, that this was a prelude to a Western offensive, as he had predicted, and, second, that it would trigger the hoped-for action by King Leopold.

The next day's meeting of the Comité de Guerre almost brought a fight. Admiral Darlan proposed responding to the German attack on Scandinavia by proceeding at once to enter Belgium, to carry out Churchill's river-mining scheme, and to launch limited attacks on the Northeastern front. Gamelin seconded the move into Belgium, but Reynaud objected that, as he understood it, the Germans had superiority in both air power and manpower. (It was a reasonable inference that he was most concerned lest a move into Belgium doom chances for detaching forces from the Western front for the campaign in Norway or for Balkan operations.) Gamelin repeated what he had said, and Georges, who was also present, agreed. Daladier supported the two generals. The outcome was a decision to sound out the Belgians on their willingness to let Allied troops enter their country.[4]

What ensued was as frustrating for the French as what had happened in January, and almost as farcical. After the Comité de Guerre meeting, Reynaud, Daladier, and Darlan flew to London for a session of the Supreme War Council, hurriedly called to discuss the German action in Scandinavia. Gamelin did not accompany them. Though most of the discussion necessarily concerned Scandinavia, Reynaud was obliged by the presence of Daladier and Darlan to raise the matter of Belgium. He again emphasized his own doubts, based on a presumption that, if the Germans reacted, they would have more planes and men to throw into Belgium. Daladier weighed in with an assertion that action was urgent. Chamberlain and the other British delegates agreed that both governments "should make strong representations to the Belgian government, insisting firmly that the Allies be invited to enter Belgian territory without awaiting a German attack on Belgium."[5]

The French and British ambassadors in Brussels asked urgently for a meeting with Foreign Minister Spaak. He saw them at midnight on April 10. After hearing them out, Spaak said that he himself was less apprehensive than earlier and expressed surprise that the ambassadors seemed to have no more evidence than he of an impending German attack. He went on nevertheless to inquire just how far into Belgium the Allies wanted to come. Did they really intend to go as far as the Albert Canal? he asked.

Gamelin had stayed in Paris instead of going to London so that he could prepare for the move into Belgium. He backed up the démarche of the ambassadors through communications to Colonel Hautcoeur, still his personal representative in Brussels, with injunctions that his messages be passed on to "the person to whom you regularly speak"—meaning General Van Overstraeten. To Spaak's question, he gave a guarded answer: "If the Belgian government calls upon the Allies as guarantors, he would do his utmost to get to the Albert Canal and the Meuse; and he believes that there would be a good chance of arriving there." To the Belgian military attaché in Paris, he amplified this: "You, who are a soldier, know that in a war, when there is an enemy of the cut of the German, one cannot give a guarantee of attaining the goal one seeks, at least not straightaway."[6] Gamelin's cautious language may have been meant chiefly to egg on the Belgians into agreeing to early Allied intervention. In part, however, it may have been a candid confession of uncertainty.

Meanwhile, as he had in January, Gamelin directed Georges to move forces toward the Belgian frontier. Georges did so. But in Brussels the king's ministers met and unanimously agreed to advise him against yielding to the Allies. Because they learned that some Paris newspapers were speculating about an Allied move into Belgium, the prime minister's office made a radio announcement affirming the government's "intention to to persevere firmly with the policy of independence and neutrality."[7] Van Overstraeten, taking his daily stroll through the general-staff headquarters, saw map markers indicating the advance of General Georges's French troops. At once, he ordered troop movements signaling again Belgium's determination to resist invasion from any direction. He told Hautcoeur that Belgium remained resolved "to refuse any preventive appeal."[8]

Gamelin, in the end, had to direct Georges to pull his troops back. The chief result was to stiffen the Allied resolve to try to reach the Albert Canal. The most that Gamelin obtained was a secret promise from the Belgian minister of war that, if Germany attacked, Belgium would immediately ask for Allied aid. In his memoirs, Gamelin writes, "I confess that, with this, I had one weight less on my heart."[9] Right.

The question whether troops would be taken from the Western front to fight in Norway or to go to the Balkans had only gone into abeyance. Now that an immediate move into Belgium seemed not in the cards, Prime Minister Reynaud renewed his call for more energetic warfare elsewhere. And he seemed to have a new ally. British officials, previously on Gamelin's side in opposing any Salonika expedition, suddenly indicated a possible interest, provided the purpose were preparation to aid Yugoslavia against attack by Italy. Therotofore, Weygand had had support in Britain only from the British Middle East–theater commander, General Sir Archibald Wavell, and Wavell had complained that hardly anyone would even listen to him. Now, suddenly, his views appeared to be influential.[10] Reynaud asked the Comité de Guerre to consider how to answer this question if it were raised formally.

Behind this was a growing conviction in the British government that Britain rather than France would be the primary target of Germany's next offensive. As one result, the British chiefs of staff increasingly thought of British forces based in France as wasted assets. They had originally thought of pulling them away to Norway. The decision to give up all positions except Narvik made this moot. The temptation remained to use them somewhere, and this inspired the inquiries that Reynaud elevated to the level of the Comité de Guerre.

Not having recovered from his embarrassing setback in Belgium in March, Gamelin now had to cope with a new and seemingly more dangerous Balkan-front proposal. Shadowing it, moreover, was a new proposal for action in the Caucasus. The proposal was not, properly speaking, new: the staff officers who had been set to work earlier had finally begun to come up with a plan. So it was more like a corpse sitting up because of rigor mortis. Reynaud, however, threatened to give it new life. He instructed the French ambassador in London to nag the British about their end, which had drifted off to corners of the air staff and a headquarters in Egypt. With help from Léger, he pushed arguments for such an operation on his war cabinet and in a secret session of the Chamber of Deputies.[11]

At the Comité de Guerre, Gamelin questioned whether France should say yes to the British about helping the Yugoslavs. He maintained that the Yugoslav army, with twenty divisions, could probably hold its own against the Italian army so long as Germany stayed out. He also pointed out that the only Allied forces that could readily reach Yugoslavia were Weygand's three divisions in Syria. He conceded that, if the Yugoslavs put up no resistance, Romania and Greece were likely to fall as well. Darlan and Bührer, the commander of Colonial Forces, argued that France should do whatever the British asked. Daladier summed up the dilemma: to do nothing would be to reward aggression; to agree to do something could divert forces away from the main theater. The outcome was an agreement to pursue discussions with the British but not, as yet, to take a position. Since the British were themselves still undecided, there the issue hung. It was finally resolved in early May, when the British notified Paris that they had decided not to try to aid Yugoslavia. Daladier applauded, saying the Allies could not afford another Norway.[12]

Regarding the Caucasus, the scheme prepared by the staff officers called for an air strike on Soviet oil wells and refineries. This engaged the enthusiasm of General Vuillemin, who sent officers to the Balkans to make preparations. (According to the British air attaché, they were "received with terror" in Bucharest.) Here, too, Gamelin resisted. Belgium and the Netherlands, he argued, "remain what is important for the air forces." Fortunately, from his standpoint, further analysis by other staff officers revealed that air bases in the area were not adequate for the scale of operation proposed. Reynaud, who had been under the misconception that the operation could be carried out right away if only orders were given, lost his enthusiasm.[13] So did Vuillemin. The Comité de Guerre agreed to set aside money for constructing new airfields in Greece and Romania. For the time being, there would be no drawdown of French air forces committed to the Western front. Gamelin wrote in his memoirs, with emphasis, "This is a relief for me."[14] This time, he surely meant it.

Regarding British air forces, two difficult problems arose during April and early May. The first developed from the British presumption that the British

Isles would be Germany's primary target. If that were to prove true, they asked, would General Vuillemin send French fighters to aid in Britain's air defense? Without consulting Gamelin, Vuillemin said he didn't think so. Gamelin's efforts to soothe the resultant British indignation did not meet with complete success. Though it might have occurred in any case, it became all the more likely that the British would prepare to pull their planes out of France.[15]

The second problem, made more acute by the first, was a revival of British insistence that, if the Germans launched a Western offensive, even against the Netherlands alone, the first Allied response should include bombing the Ruhr. Vuillemin remained opposed. By his reckoning, Germany had enough fighters to ward off bombers and the Allies did not. Gamelin urged instead that such an attack on the Ruhr simply be postponed. There was a chance, he said, that, if the Allies showed restraint, the Germans would do likewise. If the Germans held off bombing roads and railways in Belgium, the Allies would have an easier time getting to the Albert Canal and the lower Meuse, where, he pointed out, they would then have bases for a much more punishing bombing campaign.

Meeting with Vuillemin and Gamelin, Air Chief Marshal Sir Arthur Barratt disagreed. Since the beginning of the year, he had been in charge of all British air operations in France. He asserted that the British air staff had certain knowledge that Germany planned an initial offensive against the Netherlands alone, to be followed by "an offensive on a very large scale against England." He added, "The date for this second phase is already fixed."[16] The British air staff was probably a victim partly of German disinformation, partly of the fact that interception of Luftwaffe signals worked best in the area where the German Air Army was preparing to support operations in the Netherlands.

Given that the British seemed adamant, that there was reason to fear the RAF's pulling fighters out of France, and that Reynaud tended to side with the British in order to strengthen his hand against Daladier and his own cabinet, Gamelin concluded that he could not continue to hold out regarding the Ruhr. At a meeting of the Supreme War Council in Paris on April 22–23, Reynaud announced that the French government agreed that bombing of Germany's key industrial targets in the Ruhr could commence the moment the Germans launched an attack anywhere in the West. He also agreed that, in event of a German attack on the Netherlands alone, the Allies should not necessarily await an invitation from the Belgians to march across Belgium.[17] Though Gamelin was not displeased with the latter decision, his agreeing to almost all items on the British agenda probably reflected a judgment that opposition would be fruitless. Even more, however, it evidenced his concern lest the British pare back their air and ground forces on the Western front. Though he accepted it as not out of the question that the Germans might move only against the Netherlands, he continued to think it much more likely that they would strike in force across the Low Countries toward northeastern France and that, as he said in a Comité de Guerre meeting on May 4, "it will be the great battle that will begin, and it is in the northeast that it will have to be won."[18]

In these circumstances Gamelin found himself challenged by Georges to reconsider the Dyle-Breda Plan developed the previous autumn. In mid-April, while the abortive discussions with the Belgians were in progress, Georges sent him a memorandum, followed up by a face-to-face meeting. Georges proposed scaling back the projected response to a German attack. He had talked with Giraud, whose army was to make the dash toward Breda, and both of them had concluded that it would be a risky operation. In Georges's view, it would be better to cancel not only this move but all or most of the planned move of French troops into Belgium. He could then deploy twelve more French divisions to hold the line when the Germans reached the French frontier. If he had to keep to the current plan, said Georges, he would be unable to release more forces for the campaign in Norway or, as he believed desirable, to deploy forces to the Swiss and Italian frontiers. "The Northeastern front," he wrote, "no longer disposes of a single division to cope with the unexpected."[19]

What lay behind Georges's representations to Gamelin is not easy to reconstruct. The only lines in his memorandum that suggest the influence of recent intelligence were those noting that troops might be needed on the Swiss or Italian frontier or to fend off a direct attack on the Maginot Line. If he had any concern about a possible German strike through the Ardennes to Sedan, Charleville, and Amiens, he covered it by his reference to "the unexpected."

Gamelin probably saw and heard little other than a reassertion of the conservative position that Georges had taken when the Dyle-Breda Plan first took form. From time to time since, Georges had repeated his arguments against striking for Breda, seeking to keep Giraud's Seventh Army close at hand. Gamelin had consistently rejected his proposals. Georges's arguments about being unable otherwise to spare troops for Norway or other fronts, Gamelin could easily have read as intended to please Reynaud. Gamelin could equally easily have noted that the effect of the proposed strategy would be to confirm Georges as field commander for all Allied forces in the theater, for, if the Allies did not advance far into Belgium, the amour propre of Leopold, as commander of Belgian forces, would no longer have to be taken into account.

But what must have struck Gamelin most forcibly was that the effect just of canceling the Breda move, let alone of canceling any move deep into Belgium, would be a flaming quarrel with the British, and he must have assumed that Georges knew this as well as he. He thus had some warrant for thinking that Georges's proposals were not serious but were intended only to improve his prospects for being chosen by Reynaud as successor generalissimo. Gamelin might well have taken wry comfort, then, in hearing not long afterward Reynaud's reported statement that "there are two 'able' soldiers, Weygand and Giraud—'as for Georges, he is worth no more than Gamelin.' "[20]

Of course, in retrospect, one can say that the Allies missed an opportunity here. Had Georges's recommendations been adopted, Allied forces would have been better positioned to respond to Germany's actual offensive. But the most important point to be made is an echo of the one repeated earlier. As far as we can tell, Georges simply outlined a more cautious action option. Implicit was a shade of difference in estimates of what was important, with Georges not only risk-averse but having different personal stakes from Gamelin's. But he made no effort to show that his assessments of Germany's intentions differed in any way from Gamelin's, even though a mountain of reports from intelligence agencies could have been piled up to show that conditions were probably different from what they had been when the original Dyle-Breda Plan was developed and adopted. Georges's arguments have been cited as evidence of his being wiser than Gamelin. I think the stronger conclusion is that both of them, and their colleagues, were contemptuous of intelligence and of the inductive reasoning processes for which intelligence is food.

Another opportunity for re-examining the Dyle-Breda Plan had arisen in March, when members of the army committee of the Chamber of Deputies had toured the front and issued a report commenting sharply on the weakness of defenses around Sedan. Its chief author was Pierre Taittinger, a veteran right-winger continually critical of both Daladier and Gamelin. With help from the army commander in the area, General Charles

Huntziger, the operations section of the general staff prepared a response saying that the deputies were misinformed and that the sector needed no significant reinforcement. There is no indication that the report prompted thought about its substance, either at Huntziger's headquarters, or at Montry or Vincennes. It was seen as a political nuisance, not something to be taken seriously.[21]

A last, sad confrontation before the commencement of the Battle of France occurred at the Quai d'Orsay on May 8. Prime Minister Reynaud had decided much earlier that he wanted to be rid of General Gamelin. Just after discovering that Gamelin was as surprised as he by Germany's invasion of Denmark and Norway, he had been heard to say, "I have had enough. I would be a criminal if I left at the head of the French army that nerveless man, that philosopher!"[22] Daladier had defended Gamelin repeatedly and successfully, but by the second week in May, Reynaud had come to the view that he could not succeed in extracting France from the *drôle de guerre* unless he were rid of both Daladier and Gamelin. Encouraged both by frustrated advocates of a more energetic war effort such as Mandel and Dautry—and also by others, such as his mistress and his *chef de cabinet*, Paul Baudouin, who hoped for some deal to end the war—Reynaud decided to stage a showdown.

In late March, Reynaud had contracted the flu. Keeping nevertheless to a frantic schedule, he began to have complications—chest congestion and intermittent fevers. On May 8, he issued a sudden call for a cabinet meeting on the following day. "[He] arrived," writes Élie Bois, "with a bulky file the contents of which it took him two hours to read. Many of his colleagues had not seen him for a fortnight. They found him much altered, thinner, feverish of eye, unsteady of voice. He had, however, been toned up to the greatest possible extent. His usual doctor, recalled from the army, had doped him to the full."

The file Reynaud read aloud offered a point-by-point indictment of General Gamelin, particularly on a charge of not anticipating Germany's move into Scandinavia and not showing sufficient diligence in managing the Allied campaign there. Daladier seemed to Deputy Prime Minister Chautemps to be listening "disdainfully," and when Reynaud finished, Daladier asked for the floor. He said that Gamelin might have faults but, in the particular case of the Scandinavian expedition, deserved "nothing but praise." He continued, "If he is guilty, then I am." He tendered his own resignation. A long silence followed. Reynaud, "white-faced, . . . slowly closed his file and said emphatically: 'As I cannot make my point of view prevail, I am no longer Head of the Government.' "[23] Afterward, he called on President Lebrun at the Élysée Palace and announced that he intended to go to the Chamber of Deputies and try to form another cabinet without Daladier.

Hence, on the following morning, when Germany's attack commenced, France was technically without a government.

PART FIVE

THE WAR—A PARABLE?

BATTLE!

"Both matters are important; but if the *battle* is lost . . . !"
—*General Gamelin, when criticized by Jean Fabry for*
planning for a grand battle rather than a prolonged war

A round 1 A.M. on May 10, a duty officer at the Cinquième Bureau at
Meaux telephoned his counterpart at Vincennes. He relayed a report
from Captain Archen, the SR station chief in Luxembourg, that Germans in that country had received word to assemble before dawn, bringing
guns; he also relayed reports from other SR posts about much noise on the
German side of the Dutch, Belgian, and Luxembourg borders. Awakened,
General Gamelin said the reports did not justify an alert. He went back to
sleep. Colonel Olivier Poydenot, of his staff, informed General Georges's
headquarters at La Ferté, where a call to Billotte's First Army Group
headquarters at Soissons drew the answer "So far . . . nothing unusual."
Georges was allowed to sleep undisturbed. So was Doumenc at Montry.

Shortly before dawn, spotters on the border radioed that formations of
German bombers were crossing into France. At 4:45 A.M., sirens blared at
Vincennes, and soon afterward in all parts of Paris. An SR officer spending
the night in the capital with his family recalled later:

The sun rose in a light, clear sky. My wife and my sister, who had
been in Paris for a few days, and I had our elbows on our balcony.

We would have savored the pleasure and freshness of this radiant spring dawn. Everyone in the street, like ourselves, was at the windows, laughing and chatting, eyes looking upward. A few explosions reverberated. Two or three little airplanes pranced very high up, shining in the first rays. Little white flakes came into being behind them. "Well, that must be Fritz! It's the first time we've seen him." Never has an alert been more enjoyable.[1]

When he arrived at the Cinquième Bureau offices at Meaux, the officer found that his colleagues, too far away to have heard the sirens and apparently unaffected by the reports from their own agents, did not know anything had happened.

Ever since 5:30 A.M., however, airwaves and telephone lines at all French operational commands had chattered reports of attacks on airfields, supply depots, railheads, and random targets such as the central market in the city of Nancy. In later mythology, the Germans were said in their initial raids to have crippled an already frail French air force. Not true at all. The Dutch and Belgian air forces suffered—the Dutch losing half of their planes, the Belgians about a quarter, with total losses for both above a hun-

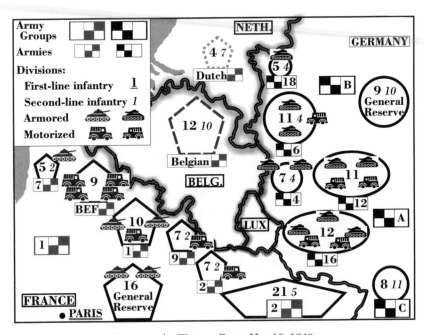

Forces on the Western Front, May 10, 1940

dred. But few of the losses were on the ground. By air action and anti-aircraft fire, the Dutch and Belgians brought down 230 German planes, including most of Germany's troop-transport aircraft. In France, end-of-day reports counted only four French planes destroyed on the ground and thirty damaged but repairable—this out of 879 fighters and bombers deemed ready for battle. The RAF lost six planes and had twelve others put out of action, out of 384 fighters and bombers deployed that day in France. Forty-four enemy planes had been downed. Not a single airfield in France had been rendered unusable.[2]

A few minutes after 6 A.M., the Dutch government asked for aid from the Allies to cope with a larger-scale German invasion. Clare Boothe, who was in Brussels, remembered being awakened, going to the window of her bedroom in the U.S. Embassy,

and as I stood there in my nightgown watching a lovely red gold dawn behind the black trees across the park, about twenty planes, very high up, came over in formation. Their bellies gleamed in the gold and red sunrise. Then I heard a thin long, long whistle and a terrible round *bam!* The whistle was from the bomb that pierced the roof of a three-storeyed house across the square, and the *bam* was the glut and vomit of glass and wood and stone that was hurled into the little green park before me.[3]

With anguish, King Leopold recognized that Belgium was not to be another Switzerland, and at 6:50 A.M., the Belgian government finally invited French and British troops to enter the country.

As soon as he saw the Belgian request for assistance, Gamelin telephoned Georges. "It's the Dyle maneuver?" asked Georges immediately. "Since the Belgians have appealed to us, do you see how we can do anything else?" Gamelin asked in response. "Clearly not," said Georges.

Gamelin again issued an order of the day:

The attack that we have foreseen since last October has opened this morning.

Germany is waging against us a war to the death. The proper responses are, for France and all its allies: courage, energy, confidence.

He wanted to add: "As Marshal Pétain said, twenty-four years ago, *'Nous les aurons'* [We will get them]." Daladier vetoed the addition, perhaps because of rumors that Reynaud was thinking of replacing him with Pétain.[4]

Captain Beaufre, who arrived at Vincennes from Montry while Gamelin was preparing for breakfast, remembered afterward: "Gamelin was striding up and down the corridor in his fort, humming, with a pleased and martial air which I had never seen before."[5] Villelume, who visited Vincennes later in the morning, heard Gamelin say that he had always expected this attack. The officers on his staff, wrote Villelume, were "loudly triumphant. They saw in the event condemnation of the Norwegian affair. 'See how the general was right to attach no importance to anything except the Northeastern front!'" Colonel Minart, who was with Gamelin at Vincennes, wrote in sour retrospect:

> His face showed no apparent emotion, no inner doubt. The commander in chief preserved that supple calm and that slightly sugary affability that had contributed so much to give him [his] seductive charm. . . . The general, while not hiding the extreme gravity of the moment, remained optimistic. He was waiting for the battle.[6]

Across France, reactions resembled Gamelin's. As mentioned earlier, General André Corap, commander of the Ninth Army, exulted: "This is the moment that we have waited for," and his chief of staff said much the same. In bistros around Paris, veterans of the Great War celebrated, saying that the Germans would break their teeth against the Maginot Line.[7] A Danish journalist who was in Paris on May 10 recalls that the city was "bubbling with enthusiasm. On the streets and cafés, in the press and on the radio, there was jubilation over the blunder that Germany had just committed."[8]

As of May 10, France and Britain had approximately one hundred divisions on the Northeastern front. Though General Georges was in overall command, the entire Belgian border area came under Billotte as commander of the First Army Group. (Another Army Group was behind the Maginot Line, and a third opposite Italy.) Billotte's Group included, from the Channel coast to Longwy, at the northern edge of the Maginot Line, four French armies—the Seventh, First, Ninth, and Second; in between the Seventh and the First was effectively a fifth army, the British Expeditionary Force.

According to the Dyle Plan, now made up of inches-thick volumes of instructions specific to each headquarters, Giraud's Seventh Army was to head up the Channel coast and go past Antwerp, across the Albert Canal, and to Breda in the Netherlands. Giraud had seven divisions, mostly motorized, one of which was a light mechanized division (DLM) roughly equivalent to a two-thirds-strength German Panzer division.

The BEF, on Giraud's right, under General Gort, was to hurry in the direction of Brussels and take up positions on the Dyle River south and east of it, leaving the capital's defense to Belgian forces. Nine divisions strong, all at least partially motorized, the BEF included also an armored brigade with almost as many tanks as a DLM.

General Georges Blanchard's First Army was to make a shorter journey and link up with the BEF on the upper Dyle. Its ten divisions were then to cover thirty miles down to the city of Namur, where an old fortress overlooked the confluence of the Sambre and the Meuse rivers. Near the First Army front was the small industrial town of Gembloux. On all the planners' maps at Vincennes, Montry, La Ferté, and First Army Group headquarters, Gembloux was highlighted, for it was the center of a narrow, open plain which not only seemed topographically ideal for the Germans to execute a wheeling maneuver in the model of the Schlieffen Plan but had been singled out by them for the brunt of the offensive in the operation plan captured at Mechelen-sur-Meuse back in January. Three of Blanchard's divisions were fully motorized. Five were partially motorized infantry divisions. All eight were crack units. The other two divisions in Blanchard's army were the two DLMs of the Corps of Cavalry commanded by General René Prioux. Because of concern about "the Gembloux gap," the two DLMs were to race beyond the Dyle and prepare to fend off any possible German attack.

From Namur south, General André Corap's Ninth Army was to guard the Belgian and French Meuse. It had nine divisions and a little more. One was motorized infantry, two were light cavalry divisions (DLCs), each with a brigade of tanks and a brigade of horse cavalry together with a regiment of artillery.

General Charles Huntziger's Second Army covered the rest of the front to the northern end of the Maginot Line. Its left-hand boundary was the point where the Bar River, scarcely more than a creek, trickles into the French Meuse, about halfway between Charleville-Mézières and Sedan. From there west, the Second Army front ran along the border of the French Ardennes. Two of its divisions were DLC's. None was motorized.

The best French units were either regulars, Class A reserves, or North African or Moroccan divisions. The troops in these units were comparatively young and had recent training and, in some cases, combat experience in the colonies. Most such units were under the command of either Giraud or Blanchard, for it was assumed that the southern Netherlands and the Belgian plain would be the principal battlegrounds. Corap's Ninth Army and Huntziger's Second Army each had two divisions of Class B reserves, with men who were older than average and had less recent training, and with officers and noncommissioned officers who were also reservists with limited experience. Many of the Class B units had obsolete equipment: their antitank guns were old 37-mm.'s that didn't have the power to stop a Panzer IV. The Class B 55th Infantry Division, which guarded Sedan, had only one modern 25-mm. antitank gun, and it lacked a gunsight.[9]

Man for man overall, French and German forces were not mismatched. Most of the units in General Leeb's Army Group C and many rear-echelon infantry divisions under Generals Bock and Rundstedt had men with no more time in service and weaponry no more modern than in the French Class B divisions. All sixteen divisions in the French general reserve were first-line units. This was true of only nine of the nineteen divisions in Germany's general reserve. The French were prepared for extended warfare; the Germans were playing Vabanquespiel. Yet as the German and Allied plans worked themselves out, the best French soldiers would be in the wrong places, and the worst-prepared French soldiers would face the best that the Germans had.

The disparity between France's worst and Germany's best had, moreover, widened during the long "bore war." On both sides, commanders of first-line units had used those months for intensive training. German staff officers had sought out terrain similar to that which they expected in Belgium or France and used it for exercises. The Sixth Panzer Division practiced river crossings in a part of the Lahn River Valley, not far from the North Sea, which resembled the division's target area at Monthermé on the Meuse. The Twelfth Infantry Division, which was scheduled to cross south of Dinant, Belgium, just above the French border, used picture postcards to design an exercise area with all the contours of that segment of the Meuse Valley,[10] General Giraud likewise put units of his Seventh Army through exacting maneuvers in wetland similar to that beyond Antwerp, and Prioux staged simulated engagements of his mechanized divisions on ground as much as possible like that around the Gembloux gap.[11]

Neither Corap nor Huntziger, however, thought it worthwhile to expend such effort on divisions that were expected to fulfill essentially defensive functions, least of all on those in Class B. Both generals did send units to rear areas for spells of training. When the German offensive opened, the front line of Huntziger's Second Army was thin because the 55th Infantry, a Class B division, was in a rear area for a three-week refresher course. Its regiments puffed in, weary from a three-day forty-mile march, just in time to take positions opposite two German Panzer divisions.

General Corap complained incessantly to Billotte, Georges, and Gamelin about the condition of his troops. Though fat, lethargic, and approaching retirement, he had a reputation for caring about his men and for being comparatively supportive of reservists and draftees. He came from a poor family, had been a scholarship student at St.-Cyr, and had spent most of his career in the colonies. He asked for more uniforms and stores and newer rifles and guns. He protested that his Ninth Army did not have enough men or adequate equipment for its mission. He said he wanted to give his men more training, which they badly needed, but it was hard to do so in face of demands for the routine patrolling of a fifty-mile front. Corap, however, found it hard to get attention. He was viewed askance by Gamelin and his coterie because he had been Weygand's chief of staff, but he was also viewed askance by most of the Weygand clique because of his social origin.

General Huntziger could have lodged similar complaints but did not. Small, trim, precise, and self-controlled, he was one of the French army's intellectuals, had the rare distinction of enjoying approval from both Gamelin and Georges, and was widely thought in line eventually to succeed Gamelin—perhaps soon, if Gamelin retired and Georges were passed over. He had been assigned the Second Army command back in the days when the French high command's chief concern was that Germany might attempt to come in behind the Maginot Line. In that event, the area between the northern end of the Line and the Bar River would have been the crucial theater of combat. From Huntziger's standpoint, it was his bad luck that, in light of lessons of the Polish war, expectations changed, the Dyle-Breda concept supervened, the Second Army lost importance, and he found himself assigned large numbers of inexperienced reservists.

Huntziger and some of his subordinate commanders were among the army officers who were least appreciative of reservists and draftees. General Pierre-Paul-Charles Grandsard, a corps commander, remembered the infantrymen of the Second Army as fat and slow, the artillerymen as old and poorly trained. General Edmond Ruby, a senior staff officer, commented that the Second Army's cavalry units were slightly better than average because "the least desirable elements among formations of reservists carefully avoided this branch, which was deemed aristocratic." Like Corap, Huntziger considered his force inadequate for its mission, but, unlike

Corap, he did not make representations to generals above him. He simply made a note for the record that, with a fifty-mile front to cover, he could not both construct defensive works and train troops, and he therefore decided to emphasize the former.[12]

Huntziger had put his men to work digging holes and filling them in. The thin line of fixed defenses north of the Maginot Line consisted of pill-boxes—*maisons fortes* (literally, "strong houses"). At mobilization in 1939, the Second Army had had approximately five pillboxes per mile of front; Huntziger resolved to have about twelve per mile. He probably calculated that the area would then at least have concrete works from which real soldiers could fight if the Ardennes ever became a battleground. But the actual result was that Huntziger faced the German army's onslaught in 1940 commanding men who were practiced more in use of a pick and shovel than in that of a rifle or an artillery piece.

One further difference in the area that was soon to be the center of the Battle of France lay in the comparative autonomy of the French Ninth and Second Armies. Because the Great War had seen many instances when Allied field commanders misunderstood one another, the postwar French army organized a Higher Council of War—located in the portion of the War Ministry building in Paris fronting on the Boulevard des Invalides—to ensure that all prospective high-level commanders would be intimately acquainted with one another. The war minister was nominally its chairman, the senior officer of the army and generalissimo-designate was vice-chairman. On one gabled top floor, each general ticketed for a major wartime command had a suite of offices for himself and his prospective staff. Through regular meetings of the council and through day-to-day interaction, the generals were expected to develop mutual understanding.

In practice, the reverse happened. The council's operations validated an old army saying about officer-contemporaries, which Bloch quoted in *Strange Defeat*: "If they are lieutenants, they are friends; if captains, comrades; if majors, colleagues; if colonels, rivals; if generals, enemies."[13] The commanders-to-be and their staff officers divided into cliques. General Ruby, who officed there with Huntziger, wrote that each group "lived as if in a hothouse confined in its own little cell," each an enemy of the others.[14] Whether true for Giraud and Blanchard, it is hard to say. But Corap and Huntziger left headquarters for their field commands barely on speaking terms. Even in crises, communications would go not from one army's staff to the other but instead through Billotte's headquarters or Georges's and back down again.

Even the best French and British troops deployed slowly. Those inches-thick compilations of directives took time to read, let alone to execute. Prioux has commented on the "enormous dossiers" that had accumulated with "the piling up of corrections, additions, annexes, appendices, etc."[15] Each individual motorized or mechanized unit in the Seventh and First Armies had specific orders regarding speeds for vehicles, distances to be maintained, and formalities to be observed in each Belgian jurisdiction en route. Had these orders been strictly observed, commented one staff officer after the war, the rate of progress of the Seventh Army could not have exceeded ten miles a day.[16] It was 10 A.M. on May 10 before lead units of that army could set out. Since doctrine based on the Polish war called for infantry to move mainly at night, it was late afternoon before the bulk of Giraud's army moved. Though Prioux's mechanized divisions had begun to cross into Belgium around noon, Gamelin, who had asked Georges for his timetable, was told that the rest of Blanchard's First Army would not follow before 9:30 A.M. on May 11, nor the British Expeditionary Force until around 1 P.M. on the same day.

During the first day, it appeared that German forces were making an all-out effort to conquer the Netherlands. Their first large operation had been to bomb Dutch airfields. Using paratroops as well as armor and infantry, they also assaulted bridges across the Maas/Meuse River (the former its name in the Netherlands and Flemish Belgium, the latter in French-speaking Belgium and in France). That seemed to portend, as expected, a drive into central Belgium more or less along the lines of the operation sketched in the documents captured at Mechelen-sur-Meuse. At Vincennes, the day was so clear and sunny as to brighten even casemates where light seldom penetrated. Colonel Minart writes, "It was hard to have a first judgment on events. In general, the impression was favorable."[17]

In an echo of earlier debates, General Billotte asked if cooperating air forces could attack major communication links and power lines even if the targets were near built-up localities. General Marcel Têtu, the French air-force theater commander (counterpart to Georges), said "No," and directed that only actual enemy forces on open roads be attacked. Otherwise, he feared, German planes might retaliate against built-up sites in France. Air Chief Marshal Barratt, for the RAF, had already scheduled raids near built-up areas. He apologized, said he couldn't call off the raids, but promised not to do it again. (If he had had his way, no British planes would have been used in any operation in direct support of ground forces. Had General Vuillemin had his way, the same would have been true for the French air force. RAF officers regarded the mission as "prostitution of the air force," and Vuillemin had just reaffirmed his official line that it was justified only "exceptionally."[18])

On May 11, early bulletins reaching Vincennes told of Belgian troops falling back from the Albert Canal and German tanks being sighted west of Maastricht, beyond the canal. Telephone communication with Liège had ceased. No one could tell what was going on in northern and eastern Belgium. At noon, Gamelin learned that Billotte had reported to Georges: "I possess only confused reports on the situation west of Maastricht, [which] do not imply that there is reason to give up sending the mass of our forces to the Dyle, but they should get there as quickly as possible."[19] Deciding to forgo the safety of night movement, Billotte announced that he would try to get Blanchard's three motorized infantry divisions in place behind the Dyle before nightfall. Worried lest the Allied line become too thinly stretched, Gamelin cautioned Georges and Billotte that Giraud should not succumb to the temptation of going beyond Breda.[20] Then, in view of reports that Belgian troops were falling back and that Giraud's and Blanchard's armies were not yet in place, he and Georges lifted Têtu's prohibition of the previous day: French and British air commanders were told to destroy bridges across the Maas/Meuse no matter how many houses or buildings were nearby.

During this second day of real warfare, Gamelin and Georges had what was probably their last real opportunity to rearrange Allied deployments. When Captain Paul-Alfred Métivier, an intelligence officer on Prioux's staff, arrived at Gembloux, he expected to find extensive lines of Cointet barriers—huge linked triangular or X-shaped spikes—fixed in the ground. None did he see. "Where are the Cointet?" he asked. Maybe six miles to the east, around Perwez, he was told.

After bumping over a narrow dirt road and the cobblestones of intervening villages, Métivier reached Perwez, where he found the Cointet, but not in place. They had just been moved up, and they were only piles of spikes, not antitank obstacles. In agitation, Métivier went to the one-room post office and, despite the rules governing communication security, used its public telephone to call Prioux and Army Group headquarters, now at Caudry, a few miles south of the Belgian border. This was between 2 and 3 P.M.

When Prioux received Métivier's call from Perwez, he was also hearing reports that German troops had crossed the Albert Canal and Belgian infantry was in retreat. A premise of the Dyle-Breda Plan had been that Belgian forces would hold their advanced line for four days. They seemed not to have held it for much more than twenty-four hours. At about 3 P.M. on May 11, Prioux sent Blanchard a *colombogramme chiffrée*—an enciphered message via carrier pigeon. In it, he asked if the Allies should not halt their advance toward the Dyle and take up positions instead on the Escaut line.

Gamelin had meanwhile driven to Georges's headquarters at La Ferté, arriving in early afternoon, at about the time when Prioux's pigeon departed. He had deliberately stayed away on May 10, he says in his memoirs, because, "if I had been in Georges's place, I would have been humiliated and offended to see the arrival of the commander in chief of all land forces."[21] A day's delay satisfied Gamelin's sense of propriety. But he was at Les Bondons with Georges when General Blanchard reported Prioux's proposal, saying that neither he nor Billotte agreed with it. Georges recorded in his diary and presumably said to Gamelin, "Billotte judges that this is no longer possible: the Ninth Army is at the Belgian Meuse, the English on the Dyle. I am in agreement. We should hasten to get to the Dyle."[22] Georges and Gamelin accepted Billotte's judgment without, it appears, much more than a moment's thought. Regardless of Belgian dispositions, Gamelin directed, Allied forces should move up to the line running from Antwerp through Namur. Prioux's mechanized divisions should carry out their mission of going beyond the Dyle to provide a screen for the First Army as it took up positions along the river and in front of the Gembloux gap. Gamelin added, "All aircraft should be used to retard the German columns."[23]

That night, Billotte visited Prioux. A contemporary of Georges's and thus in his mid-sixties, like Georges he projected the image of a warrior. No one would have said of him, as more than one person said of Gamelin, that he should have been a prefect or a bishop.[24] Full-faced, robust, with a decisive air but also a ready smile, he had had a brilliant record at St.-Cyr and the War College but had by choice spent most of his career commanding troops in the colonies. "A great thruster and a most determined commander," commented General Sir Philip Neame, one of Gort's senior staff officers.[25] Prioux, a prim, precise martinet but a hero to his men—"our great-hearted leader," Marc Bloch called him[26]—had a comparable background. Their exchange resembled ones that would take place in the same area a little more than four years later between two generals similar in appearance and temperament—Dwight Eisenhower and Bernard Law Mont-

gomery. Billotte asked Prioux jokingly if the Germans had scared him. Un-
amused, Prioux restated his doubts. Billotte said to him emphatically that
it was too late for a change in plan: "We have to play it out to the end."
Prioux was not convinced, but he acquiesced. The last chance thus disappeared for the French high command to rearrange forces before discovering
the true German plan.

When Gamelin's headquarters asked General Laurent, the French military attaché in Brussels, to inquire about the missing Cointet barrier, Laurent eventually explained that General Van Overstraeten had decided to set
up two lines of Cointet, not one, and he was sure he had communicated his
intention to the French high command. (He had in fact done so, and there
was a record of this at Georges's headquarters dating from mid-March, but
no one there had taken note or bothered to tell Blanchard or Prioux.)[27] The
forward line was to run through Perwez but was unfortunately not yet in
place. Nor was the rear line around Gembloux. Its spikes and buttresses
were mostly in railroad cars.

Gamelin and Georges saw other signs that Belgian actions were not
meshing with theirs. In the Belgian Ardennes, the elite Belgian Chasseurs
Ardennnais had demolished bridges and blown up sections of strategic
roads so as to block or delay a German invasion. They had done this with
skill and dispatch, even in the process fighting off an advance party of General Guderian's Panzers. But then they had packed up and left to join Belgian forces grouping around Namur, well to the north. Their commanders
believed that the French knew what they intended to do. This might have
been true, for General Laurent had been told more than once, and had
passed word back to Paris, and the message had registered with a few officers. But it had not registered with General Corap or his staff, who were
counting on the Chasseurs Ardennais to reinforce the generally weak Ninth
Army.[28]

Another evidence of persisting misunderstanding appeared when the
British Expeditionary Force arrived at the Belgian border and was told that
it could not cross without a written permit. The commander of the British
advance party responded by driving a truck through the border barrier.[29]

Gamelin tried yet again to straighten out links with Brussels. He asked
if the Chasseurs Ardennais could not be placed under Corap's command,
which drew the stiff answer that the Constitution did not permit Belgian
troops to be under any command except King Leopold's. A Belgian official
historian explains that the Belgian general staff feared a French propensity
to "vassalize" its allies.[30] Gamelin then proposed that King Leopold allow

General Georges to "coordinate" French, British, and Belgian operations. Indignant about the missing Cointet barrier and the withdrawal of the Chasseurs Ardennais, Georges told Gamelin that he was being much too tactful: he should demand that Leopold agree to take orders from Billotte. Georges then resolved to go himself the next day—May 12—to Belgium to adjust matters. The theater commander was thus to be absent from his headquarters for the entire third day of the war, just to deal with a matter of protocol.

On May 12, Gamelin, at Vincennes, received bulletins mostly conforming to his expectations. Germany appeared indeed to be attempting in the Netherlands and northern Belgium a *Blitzkrieg* comparable to the one it had waged earlier in Poland. The effort in the Netherlands was on a large enough scale to justify the earlier British supposition that a primary German objective was to obtain bases for air attacks against the British Isles. Almost all Germany's elite paratroops were committed in operations to seize Dutch airfields, to get a lodgment in Rotterdam, and to take bridges over key rivers. At least one German armored division was in motion, in advance of the infantry, crossing the northern Netherlands toward the cities that faced the sea.

In Belgium, the German attack seemed also to be on a large scale, and it was making significant headway. Belgian troops had successfully destroyed the Meuse bridges at Maastricht, so German vehicles and troops were piling up on the German side of the river. But the holdup promised to be brief, for German troops, once in full occupation of the city, could easily lay down temporary bridges. Belgian plans had called for blocking any German progress beyond Maastricht by destroying the three bridges that crossed the Albert Canal just west of the city, and keeping the canal impassable by pinning down any advancing German troops with guns from Fort Eben Emael.

The pride of Belgium's fortress system, completed in 1935, Eben Emael had been built into one of the steep cliffs created when the canalway was dynamited.[31] Triangular in shape, more than half a mile long on its canal and inland faces, and almost that wide on the face that looked northward, with thirty miles of rooms and corridors and a complex internal railway system, it was a Maginot Line unto itself. The great guns projecting from its turrets could in theory blast to dust any German troops or vehicles arriving to try to rebuild any of the bridges or otherwise cross the canal.

To the dismay of Generals Gamelin, Georges, and Van Overstraeten, news had arrived on May 11 that glider-borne German troops had landed on the roof of Eben Emael, where there were no defenses. By rappelling down the faces of the fortress and throwing grenades through gunports, the Germans had disabled the fortress's guns after only one canal bridge had been destroyed. Once German forces could cross the river at Maastricht, they would thus have two bridges over which to stream across the Albert Canal. A Belgian infantry division had moved forward to try to dislodge the German soldiers from the roof of Eben Emael. By May 12, however, it appeared that enough German tanks and troops had arrived to block them. Gamelin learned that the Belgian commander had decided to pull back altogether from the Albert Canal and Van Overstraeten had confirmed his decision. (In fact, though Van Overstraeten had planned this pullback well in advance, he not only had feared communicating his intention to the French but had kept it secret from everyone except a few officers in the Belgian army.)[32]

The better news for Gamelin was that these Belgian troops were pulling back in good order, bringing their artillery with them, and that the Maastricht area was the only part of Belgium where German forces were gaining ground. Liège had not been attacked after all: its telephone lines had simply gone down. Giraud's Seventh Army, the BEF, and Blanchard's First Army seemed to be getting into position, even though they had had to accelerate their timetables. And daylight movement had cost them nothing, for Luftwaffe harassment had been minimal. Villelume commented to Gamelin that it looked as if the Germans *wanted* Allied forces to get deep into Belgium. Almost no one else thought so. French air-force and RAF officers were sure that their successes on the first day of the war had made Göring loath to risk losing any more German planes.[33]

General Georges meanwhile dealt with the Belgians. Again, a predominantly tragic story is touched with comedy. Having himself driven to Belgium, he stopped at Caudry to pick up Billotte. There he saw a civilian dressed in plus fours and gaiters. Who was it? Daladier! "Where are you going?" Daladier asked. "To Belgium," Georges replied. "I'll go with you," said the minister of national defense. Apparently, Daladier had learned that Reynaud planned to visit King Leopold. Not to be upstaged, he had decided to beat him there. General Pownall also joined the party, representing Gort.

At the Château de Casteau, thirty miles south of Brussels and ten miles in from the French border, King Leopold and General Van Overstraeten awaited the Allied delegation. They were surprised to see emerge from the caravan in the courtyard not only Georges, Billotte, and a British officer but also someone apparently come to play golf. When they recognized the unexpected guest, they, of course, pretended to welcome him. After the pleasantries, Georges got down to business by asserting that Gamelin was determined to fight on the line from Antwerp along the Dyle to the Meuse, and that Billotte should have command over all forces on that line, including the Belgian army as well as the BEF. Aware that the loss of Eben Emael and the consequent retreat from the Albert Canal left them in a poor position to bargain, the king and Van Overstraeten agreed, insisting only that Belgium have its own sector of the line, just as the BEF did. Georges said that this could be worked out. The French and British visitors then left, Pownall noting that the king "seemed pretty dazed."[34]

In fact, Leopold's principal reaction had been disappointment. He commented to Van Overstraeten that neither Georges nor Billotte resembled Joffre or Foch as his father had described these heroes for him. It seems not have entered his thoughts that he had just entertained men in their sixties who had not slept much for the past two days and who had just completed a long, uncomfortable, and dangerous automobile journey for no purpose other than to appease his amour propre. As far as Georges, Billotte, and Pownall knew at the time, however, everything was going as expected except for the rapidity of the collapse of Dutch and Belgian forward defenses. They had every reason to anticipate that when they reached their home bases the maps maintained by planners would show a strongly held Allied line more or less where the Dyle-Breda Plan prescribed.

General Georges did not get back to La Ferté until the morning of May 13. Gamelin was already there, accompanied by Doumenc and Vuillemin. What brought them was primarily belief that the coming day would see the beginning of the great battle for Belgium and that they should all be in one place so as to provide strategic direction to their front-line commanders. German tanks and infantry were reported to be only about ten miles from the Dyle, on a line from Diest to St.-Trond to Hannut to Huy, headed for collision with the forces of Blanchard and Prioux guarding the Gembloux gap. Air attacks on the advancing German columns had proved ineffective. Twenty-four British Blenheim bombers trying to destroy the Albert Canal bridges adjacent to Eben Emael had come in level at four thousand feet. The squadron commander remembered afterward "a tornado of fire . . . from the ground." The "whole earth seemed to be erupting," he writes. "The sky was filled with hundreds of black puffs intermingled with the flash of bursting shells and the criss-cross pathways of the tracer. Every few seconds my aircraft shook as if struck by flying splinters."[35] Though French pilots flying Breguet 693s had practiced low-level bombing all through the winter and could spot German tanks by the big orange or red spots painted on their hoods to prevent their own planes from bombing them, they found the tanks accompanied by armored cars capable of delivering heavy, well-aimed anti-aircraft fire. Of the twenty-four planes in the British squadron, only fifteen returned to base, and all of those had suffered severe damage. Of eleven planes in one French bomber group, only two returned to base.

Neither Têtu nor Barratt had ever been enthusiastic about using bombers to attack tanks. At RAF headquarters, Marshal Portal held that the mission was "fundamentally unsound, and . . . if . . . persisted in . . . likely to have disastrous consequences on the future of the war in the air." And the commander of fighter forces on the front, General Astier de la Vigerie, was reluctant to provide bombers with fighter cover, for he wanted the planes available to counter German bombers when the Luftwaffe began to attack strategic targets. Têtu and Barratt announced that Allied forces in Belgium would thenceforth have to do without significant air support.[36]

After this notice, Gamelin and Georges had to assume that German forces would have an edge in the air during the great battle for Belgium. But Allied forces would have much stronger artillery support, and historically big guns had decided the outcome of major battles. Gamelin showed every sign of continuing to be confident. At the same time, he could never forget Clausewitz's dictum about the role of chance in war. Once, earlier, when chided by war minister Jean Fabry for seeming to focus on preparing for a battle rather than for a long war, Gamelin had responded, "Both matters are important; but if the *battle* is lost . . . !"[37] He went to La Ferté on May 13 in expectation of seeing the *battle* won.

Gamelin, Georges, and the other generals gathered at Les Bondons were not unaware that another battle might be developing in the sectors of the French line assigned to Corap and Huntziger. On May 11, the air force's Deuxième Bureau had reported, "The principal enemy effort seems to concern the region between Maastricht and Nijmegen; a reasonably violent secondary effort is in progress west of Luxembourg."[38] At noon on May 12, the air force's Deuxième Bureau had reported large numbers of tanks and other vehicles crossing from Luxembourg into the Belgian Ardennes. Since they seemed to be moving in a northeasterly direction, they could be presumed to be heading toward Namur to reinforce the drive against the Gembloux gap. At the end of the day on May 12, however, additional reconnaissance flights, supplemented by intelligence from prisoner interrogations, had produced a new report, warning that the Germans could possibly be conducting a second major offensive. The air-force Deuxième Bureau said: "Very strong enemy pressure is being exerted in the direction of Sedan (two armored divisions and six [other] first-line divisions have been identified). The enemy has crossed the Semois River at Bouillon and has reached Gironne (five kilometers northeast of Sedan). Enemy air has shown itself particularly active both in supporting enemy troops and in massive attacks on Allied columns."[39] These were omens of what was actually in progress as German forces executed the final version of Plan Yellow. Their significance was not yet apparent, however, to Gamelin or to the other Allied commanders.

"HITCH" AT SEDAN

"There has been a rather serious hitch at Sedan."
—*Colonel Henri Lacaille, chief of staff of the French Second Army,*
reporting to headquarters, Allied Forces, Northeastern front, May 13, 1940

On May 13, reports from Belgium appeared to tell of the great battle that Gamelin awaited. Over the two Albert Canal bridges west of Maastricht that the Germans had captured along with Eben Emael, a German armored corps commanded by General Erich Hoepner had crossed into Belgium, moving in the general direction of Gembloux. Behind the Dyle, paralleling railroad tracks that ran through Gembloux from Brussels to Namur, General Blanchard, commander of the First Army, was positioning six of France's best divisions. Three were motorized infantry; three were experienced North African infantry. In addition, as a result of the Château de Casteau agreement, Blanchard had under his command Belgium's Chasseurs Ardennais at Namur.

Between the gathering line of infantry and the oncoming German armored corps, Blanchard positioned Prioux's two light mechanized divisions. The general area of deployment was one that deserved the name appropriated by the state of Kentucky—a dark and bloody ground. Just to the First Army's left was Waterloo. Just behind Prioux's forward position was Ramillies, the scene in 1706 of one of the Duke of Marlborough's costly victories. Prioux's mission was to beat back any German attack so as to give Blanchard until the end of May 14 to get all his infantry divisions into place with their accompanying artillery.

Each of Prioux's light mechanized divisions had three regiments of tanks, one regiment of armored cars carrying machine guns and powerful 25-mm. cannon, one regiment of motorized field artillery, and a regiment of dragoons. The latter, writes a veteran, were

omnipresent on the battlefields of Flanders; whenever a portion of the front was hard-pressed, a platoon or a section would be rushed to the spot. One could see them riding single-file, on powerful motor-cycles and sidecars, never under fifty miles per hour, along the narrow, winding country roads, Bren guns poised for action, men oblivious to bombs or shells. With their vizorless steel helmets and goggles, they had the appearance of beings from another world.[1]

The line that Prioux hoped to hold lay along the bank of the Dyle, about fifteen miles forward of the railroad tracks where Blanchard was stationing his infantry. The left terminus of his line was the old Flemish market town of Tienen (Tirlemont to the French). Its right terminus, twenty-five miles away, was Huy, one of the historic fortress towns on the Meuse.

On May 12, lead elements of General Hoepner's armored corps assailed the center of Prioux's line. Heavy firing from both sides went on from 9 A.M. until afternoon, with tanks, guns, and motorcylists from Prioux's Third Light Mechanized Division thronging the tiny hamlet of Crehen. Though reckoning that Hoepner's losses were heavier, Prioux decided that too many of his vehicles were being disabled, and he pulled his division back, hoping the Germans would move in behind and that he could mount a counter-attack, taking advantage of exterior maneuver ground, as Hoepner had done when attacking him. Hoepner, however, did not take the bait. Crehen was left empty and desolate, with nearly every house having at least one big shell hole in its roof or walls.

During the night of May 12–13, Prioux's Second and Third Light Mechanized Divisions fought off German efforts to run the left flank of his line. At dawn, the German effort slackened. The morning of May 13 was then quiet. About 11 A.M., a German observation plane appeared overhead, after which, writes Prioux, "the battle lighted up all the front, from Tirlemont to Huy"[2] All the rest of the day, Prioux's divisions dealt with German attacks, some on the left, some on the right. The most ferocious, however, came in the center, particularly around the small town of Hannut.

Inevitably, given the decisions made by Barratt and Têtu, the air belonged to the Germans. Prioux appealed regularly for air support but received none. Hoepner, by contrast, had the better part of a German air corps running observation and bombing missions for him. He did not have the whole corps, for some of its planes had gone south to support Group Kleist, but the impression on the French side was of incessant strafing and bombing. Yet Prioux had equivalent preponderance in artillery, and his 75s and 105s and antitank cannon continually sought out German positions or moving German tanks. One veteran of Hoepner's corps remembered thinking afterward that the shelling had resembled the worst of the Great War. French artillery, he wrote, had created a "volcano of fire."[3]

Primarily, the battle pitted tanks against tanks. Maneuvering in and around the town and the level fields separating it from adjacent towns and villages, Prioux's Somuas and Hotchkiss H-39s fired their 47-mm. and 37-mm. guns against the 13-mm. to 30-mm. armor of Hoepner's Panzers. The Panzers in return fired 20-mm. to 75-mm. shells at the 45-mm. to 55-mm. armored sides of the French tanks. If the shell was heavy enough and the armor light enough and the hit right on, any tank on either side could be reduced to scrap iron or set ablaze. It was the first large-scale tank-on-tank battle in the history of warfare. It was also the most intense tank confrontation of the entire war of 1939–40.

On May 14, Prioux pulled back from the Tirlemont-Hannut-Huy line. A Cointet barrier had meanwhile been assembled to run through Perwez, and

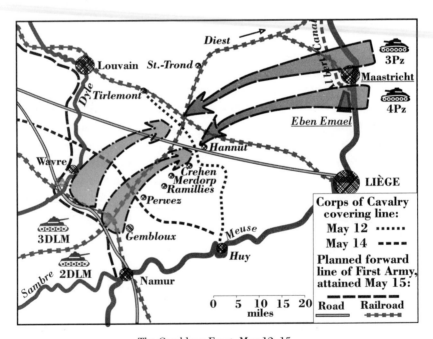

The Gembloux Front, May 12–15

Prioux's corps sheltered behind it. Hoepner, after regrouping, launched a new series of attacks. Though his force managed at one point to disrupt the Cointet chain and get in behind the French line, the German tanks were driven back. Prioux's second line held as firmly as the first.

On May 15, Prioux's whole corps left the field of battle. His men were exhausted, and he needed to replace both vehicles and guns. He was not, however, executing a forced retreat. His mission had been to provide a screen for the assembly of Blanchard's main forces, and his orders authorized him to back off as soon as those forces were in place. He had continued to fight for a half-day beyond the time when he was supposed to withdraw. Blanchard finally insisted that he give over, go back behind the main line, and refit his divisions to be part of the First Army's general reserve.

The whole battle, remembered as the battle of Hannut, was a clear victory for the French. At the time, this was the impression of most participants on both sides. Prioux and his subordinate commanders misjudged the size and strength of Hoepner's force: Prioux thought he saw two hundred German tanks at one point when he actually faced not more than forty, and one of his staff officers thought the Panzer IV was a seventy-six-ton tank when in truth it weighed in at only twenty tons, exactly equivalent to the French Somua.[4] Still, Prioux and his officers were certain that, though their divisions had suffered very heavy losses, the German losses had been heavier. And they were right. After-action reports from the two sides show that Prioux's two divisions lost 105 tanks while Hoepner's two divisions lost 160, and the numbers of severely damaged tanks were proportional.[5]

The sense of Germany's having been outmatched in battle is apparent both in contemporaneous German records and in later writings by participants. German commanders were initially critical of Prioux for staying in position instead of coming out to fight in the open. One regiment's diary characterized the French forces as "leaderless, aimless, badly commanded, and tactically inferior." By May 14, however, an afternoon report of the brigade to which that regiment belonged was acknowledging that the French had inflicted "heavy losses" and warning that prolongation of the battle could be "suicide." A veteran of the division (the Fourth Panzer) wrote after the war, "It . . . appeared that every disabled French tank was replaced by two new ones." Hermann Zimmermann, a German battle historian, concludes that, if Blanchard had not pulled Prioux's divisions to the rear and if Prioux had kept up his pressure on Hoepner, the whole German front in Belgium might have crumpled.[6]

If Belgium had been the main theater of war, as Gamelin and the French high command supposed it to be, and as it would have been had the

German offensive been launched earlier, the battle of Hannut could probably be taken as indicating how the war as a whole might have gone. And it was not the only such index. In another, smaller encounter, armored units of Giraud's army approaching Breda bested elements of the German Ninth Panzer Division, with Giraud losing five out of eighty tanks while the Ninth Panzer lost a hundred out of 150.[7] Later, at Arras, even though the war was by then all but lost, a small British force temporarily routed a Panzer division. Of course, if Belgium had been the central battleground, German forces there would have been stronger, for they would have included most of Rundstedt's Army Group A. But good German soldiers would have been fighting good French soldiers, and the French would have been the better equipped, for everyone conceded that the Panzer IVs were outclassed by Somuas, and the Panzer Is and Panzer IIs outclassed not only by Hotchkisses but by almost any French or British tank. As a German officer wrote later, in a simple duel with a French Char B or a Somua, the best Panzer had almost no chance of success.[8] It is hardly wild to extract from events in Belgium in the first few days of fighting a surmise that, if the war had been fought where the French expected it to be fought, it would have gone much more as they expected it to go. The optimism with which Gamelin and others greeted the German offensive could well have been justified.

Unfortunately for France, the main theater turned out to be the Ardennes, where the defending forces were not the armies of Blanchard and Giraud but those of Corap and Huntziger.

Corap's assignment was to set up a defense line in the Ardennes Forest several miles east of the Meuse River. The theory was that, if an attack occurred in that area, his forces would stall its progress and gradually back up to the Meuse, where reinforcements would meanwhile have arrived, either from other armies or from the general reserve. No one imagined that Corap's Ninth Army could by itself hold off a German onslaught—not Gamelin, not Georges, not Billotte, least of all Corap himself. The Ninth Army was *supposed* to retreat if its sector turned hot.

Corap's continual pleading for more men and better equipment came from a well-founded estimate that, if an attack did occur on his front, the forces he had were inadequate for the kind of deliberate, delaying-action retreat that would give time for summoning up reserves. Gamelin, Georges, and Billotte disregarded his appeals because they all thought the chances small of a major German attack on the Ninth Army front. They could conjure up an image of a secondary German offensive aimed at encircling the Maginot Line, but that would run through Huntziger's zone, not Corap's. The picture of a large German force emerging from the Ardennes Forest below Namur and well north of the Maginot Line did not come easily to the mind of any senior French officer—certainly not the picture of a force with armored divisions in the van. That was a pity, for which intelligence analysis more like that on the German side might have provided a remedy.

On May 10, after sharing congratulations that the German offensive had at last commenced and agreeing that Allied victory was certain, General Corap and his chief of staff, Colonel Olivier Thierry d'Argenlieu, had issued orders to move toward the designated defense line. On the left, the Fifth Motorized Infantry Division would occupy both banks of the Meuse below Namur. Its particular responsibility would be to guard and, if necessary, destroy the bridges over the Meuse at Yvoir, Anhée, and adjacent points. On this division's edge and south of it would be the Fourth Light Cavalry Division (DLC). The center of the army line was to be held by another DLC, the First. The right of the line would be the responsibility of the Third Brigade of Spahis.

Each DLC had a regiment of artillery, a brigade of horse cavalry, and a mechanized brigade, the latter with one regiment of light tanks and one regiment of dragoons. In a cavalry division (in contrast to one of Prioux's mechanized divisions), the dragoons traveled mostly by armored car, not by motorcycle. All in all, each DLC had about fifty tanks, predominantly AMRs with about the same armament as Panzer IIs. The Spahi brigade consisted of North African cavalrymen. One of its regiments came from Algeria, the other from Morocco. Though all tough, experienced horsemen, they were more used to fighting in the desert than in a forest.

Corap's forces moved out slowly from their bases. Long months of inactivity, broken by what appeared to have been false alarms, had dulled their readiness. It was 5 P.M. on May 10 before Corap could advise Billotte and Georges that all his forward units were at the Meuse. He said that he planned to let them rest until 11 A.M. on the following day before sending them farther. In mild reproof, Georges told him they should get going sooner. As a result, Corap had his cavalrymen awakened and on the move again by 2 A.M. on May 11.

During May 10, Corap had had two unpleasant surprises. One was the discovery that the Belgian Chasseurs Ardennais were not to become reinforcements for his frail front line but instead had disappeared toward Namur. The second, a harbinger that should have attracted more notice at Billotte's headquarters and at La Ferté and Vincennes, was unexpectedly early contact with unexpectedly strong enemy units.

Corap's forward commanders were at least as dismayed as he was at the departure of the Belgians. The experience of the Chasseurs themselves seemed to prove that they should stay in place, for it was they who had actually waged the first battles in the Ardennes. At Martelange, just across the Belgian border from Luxembourg, one company of Chasseurs had been set upon at 9 A.M. on May 10 by German motorized infantry. The mission of destroying the bridge over the Sûre had already been completed. Digging into a hillside, the Belgians had nevertheless opened fire on the Germans and kept them off for almost two hours. When it appeared that they might be overrun, they had taken off toward Namur. At Bodange, not far from Martelange, another company of Chasseurs had seen German motorized infantry accompanied by actual tanks. Better positioned than the Chasseurs at Martelange, they had held the Germans at bay all afternoon before they, too, withdrew. One lieutenant colonel from Corap's army became so indignant that the Chasseurs were deserting a field of battle that he threatened to shoot a Belgian major if he did not order his motorcycle troops to remain where they were. He had to be restrained, say Belgian records, by others "less excited."[9]

On May 11, it was the turn of Corap's Fourth DLC to encounter advancing Germans. At the village of Marche, its machine-gunners exchanged fire

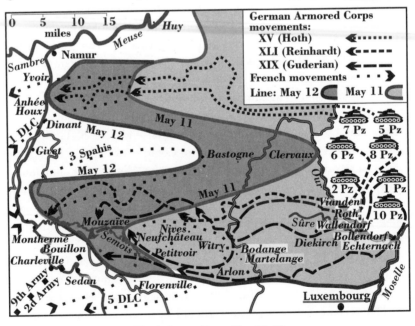

The Ardennes Front, May 11–12

with German machine-gunners. The exchange was a standoff. Meanwhile, however, on the division's right, Colonel Olivier Marc, commanding the Spahi brigade, was told that neighboring elements of Huntziger's Second Army had come under very heavy attack and were pulling back at least to the upper Semois River, perhaps to the Meuse.

Schooled to believe in the crucial importance of a continuous front, Marc, all the division commanders, and Corap and his staff worried lest Huntziger's forces withdraw and leave an opening for an enemy end run to their army's rear. Marc asked permission to retreat. Corap granted it. To protect his own continuous front, he ordered that both of his DLCs also move back, even though the Fourth had had only the equivalent of a skirmish and the First had seen no enemy at all. By 7 P.M. on May 11, the Ninth Army front line ran along the sinuous Semois River, which flowed into the Meuse at Monthermé. Neither at the army's headquarters nor along the front line, however, was there yet any sense of things being amiss. A lieutenant in one of Corap's cavalry regiments wrote home on May 11: "Everything is going well—everything is going indeed well."[10]

Though not a wide river, the Semois had features that made it potentially a strong defensive line for France. The banks were steep. Willows, birch trees, and poplars grew thickly on both sides, down to the water's edge. Gunners concealed among these trees could fire almost point-blank at enemy soldiers trying to cross the river. From Corap's standpoint, however, the Semois could serve as a defensive line only if its upper reaches were firmly held by units of Huntziger's army. Otherwise, his men might find the enemy at their back.

On May 12, the Spahi brigade reported that it still had no contact with elements of Huntziger's army. Marc said he had been told that its Fifth DLC, which was supposed to be on his right, had been heavily attacked, had tried to make a stand along the Semois, but had found the pressure too great and had retreated to the Meuse. Around midnight, moreover, his own brigade's Moroccan regiment had been surprised and outflanked by German tanks that had crossed the Semois at the village of Mouzaïve. At 2 A.M., Marc informed Corap that he intended to take his entire brigade back across the Meuse. At 8 A.M., Corap ordered the two DLCs to follow suit. By nightfall on May 12, the Ninth Army had thus given up all ground east of the Meuse. From Yvoir down to Monthermé, they had destroyed every bridge across the river.

Despite all his complaints about the weaknesses of his army, Corap was confident that it could hold the line of the Meuse. The German forces seen east of the river were obviously fast troops running ahead of a slowly advancing main body. Until the bulk of their infantry and artillery slogged up, he believed, they could not even try to force a crossing of the wide, swift-running Meuse. If they eventually assembled the wherewithal for such an effort, he would surely be reinforced from the general reserve.

In the early hours of May 13, Corap had the shock of learning that German tanks were *already* on his side of the Meuse. Though the French and Belgians had in fact efficiently demolished every bridge, at the riverside village of Houx, just south of Yvoir and Anhée, a sluice ran from the right bank to a small island, and a weir connected the island with the left bank. The sluice and weir had been left intact partly because they served a mill on the island and partly out of concern lest their destruction lower the water level so much that a portion of the river would be fordable.

Somehow, during the night, German soldiers had managed to use the sluice and weir to mask their crossing of the river. Though two of Corap's best divisions guarded the east bank of the river, their commanders had posted lookouts on the heights but not on the riverbank. When day arrived, the French discovered that the Germans had developed a beachhead, to which tanks were soon being ferried. By late morning, German tanks were roving behind the lines of the Fifth Motorized Infantry. That division's commander and his corps commanders were calling up reserve tanks and artillery. A serious battle was in progress on the ground east of the Meuse that Corap had supposed to be safe.[11]

Huntziger's army had a mission different from Corap's. The actual orders to him from Billotte and Georges were vague. As one of his staff officers writes, they were "a product of the habitual editorial complexity of very specialized general-staff officers and the abuse, from the highest level of command, of 'if possible' and 'if necessary,' as well as assignments with a double or triple option indicated by 'in the event that . . . in the event that.' "[12] But Huntziger and all his staff officers and subordinate commanders thought the highest priority for the Second Army was to protect against a German effort to come around behind the Maginot Line. That preoccupation dictated both Huntziger's initial deployments and his tactical decisions after battle commenced.

Huntziger's army had one corps composed of two light cavalry divisions, the Second and the Fifth, a cavalry brigade, and two corps of infantry. One of the latter, X Corps, under General Grandsard, was assigned to hold the Sedan sector—the portion of the Second Army front that ran from the junction with Corap's Ninth Army to the eastern outskirts of Sedan. XVIII Corps, on its right, had the rest of the line, known (from a village near its center) as the Mouzon sector. Because the Mouzon sector guarded the approach to the Maginot Line, XVIII Corps had the army's best infantry divisions, while X Corps had the comparative dregs. Though X Corps had one good North African division, it included both of the army's Class B units, the 55th and 71st Infantry.

On May 10, Huntziger, like Corap, had sent his light cavalry divisions to take up positions a few miles east of the Meuse, the Fifth on the left, the Second on the right. At about 5 P.M., forward elements of the Second DLC spotted large numbers of German vehicles approaching from the east. The division commander formed a line of light tanks but quickly concluded they were in danger of being outgunned. Moreover, irregular fire from the cannon of tanks was making the horses in his division and in the cavalry brigade skittish. He ordered a retreat to the Semois. The appearance of a reserve squadron of slightly heavier French tanks enabled him to halt there, but he advised Huntziger that his position was precarious.

On the morning of May 11, Huntziger learned that his other DLC, the Fifth, had suffered a hard hit from a German force consisting mostly of tanks. The aerial-reconnaissance unit attached to his headquarters had told him the evening before that they had seen no German tanks; then, in a 7:30 A.M. report on May 11, it described very heavy road traffic headed west across Luxembourg but was not specific about the type of traffic. At noon, it identified thirty of the vehicles as tanks, now well into Belgium. That afternoon, Huntziger was told that interrogation of German soldiers captured by the Second DLC revealed that no fewer than three German armored divisions were proceeding through the Ardennes.[13]

Huntziger's immediate thought was that the tanks were headed toward the Maginot Line. Just to the right of the Mouzon sector was the boundary between Billotte's First Army Group and General Gaston Prételat's Second Army Group. Since late morning on May 10, Prételat had been coping with a large-scale German infantry attack against the lightly fortified town of Longwy, which lay just outside the northern tip of the Maginot Line. Huntziger, though familiar with the arguments of Guderian and de Gaulle, adhered to the orthodox view that tanks ordinarily backed up infantry rather than the other way around. He thought it logical to assume that the German tanks coming through the Ardennes had the mission of supporting the infantry at Longwy. It followed also that Germany must be complementing the drive in Belgium with a major secondary effort to cut behind the Maginot Line. His front could therefore be the major front that he had expected it to be when he accepted the Second Army command.

Taking this to be the case, Huntziger pulled back his entire force. If the German tanks were headed for Longwy, they would not try to cross the Semois but would simply follow the winding road south along its bank. There was no point, therefore, in his stationing troops along the river to block a crossing. Instead, he ordered his light cavalry divisions to return to the left side of the Meuse to form a reserve. He posted infantry from both X Corps and XVIII Corps to the pillboxes lining the right side of the Meuse. Unfortunately, many of the new pillboxes were still under construction and lacked doors or roofs or both. And many of the older ones were inaccessible because assignments to them had been a form of punishment: the troops garrisoning them had therefore been called back to be replaced by better-disciplined soldiers, but many of the departing men had locked the doors and taken the keys away. Huntziger soon decided to abandon the pillboxes entirely and, as Corap was doing simultaneously, to destroy all bridges across the Meuse. This involved abandoning most of the city of Sedan, since most of its twenty-odd thousand people lived or worked around the giant fifteenth-century fortress on the right bank. Huntziger positioned the Class B 55th and 71st Infantry Divisions opposite Sedan. He detached X Corps's North African division to reinforce the Mouzon sector.

At 3 P.M. on May 12, Huntziger signaled La Ferté that he wanted strong reinforcements to repel a prospective German attack. With Georges in Belgium, General Roton, Georges's chief of staff, was in charge. Roton, too, had been schooled to assume that German forces might try to come around the flank of the Maginot Line, and he respected Huntziger's judgment. Possibly, too, he was glad of an opportunity to oblige a man who might before long head the army. On his own initiative, he ordered that three of the strongest elements in the general reserve proceed immediately to join Huntziger's Second Army: the Third Armored, Third Motorized, and Fourteenth Infantry Divisions. The armored division had just been put together. The infantry division was a crack unit commanded by Weygand's former aide and reputed Svengali, General Jean de Lattre de Tassigny.

Having learned of Huntziger's request for reinforcements and Roton's response, Gamelin and Georges on the morning of May 13 were keeping their eyes out not only for the great battle in Belgium but for a possible second, if lesser, great battle against German forces debouching from the Ardennes and attempting to cut behind the Maginot Line.

Around midday, they began for the first time to see bulletins at odds with all their expectations. At noontime, they learned of the German feat at Houx and of the fact that French infantrymen were battling German tanks on the left bank of the Meuse, twelve miles south of Namur and more than forty miles north of Sedan. Reports from Corap's headquarters, corroborated by aerial reconnaissance, meanwhile indicated that the tanks at Houx were part of a two-division Panzer corps. Puzzlingly, this corps seemed neither to be headed northward toward the Gembloux gap, as would have been predicted from the war plan captured at Mechelen-sur-Meuse in January, nor to be turning south toward the Maginot Line. Instead, it seemed to be going due west. Why?

By midafternoon, with no further news from Corap, Gamelin placed a telephone call directly to Corap's chief of staff, d'Argenlieu. From an aristocratic family (brother of Admiral Georges Thierry d'Argenlieu, who would later misrule French Indochina), a former professor at the War College and former commander of the French army's very best regiment, the 151st Infantry, d'Argenlieu was known for his imperturbability. He displayed this quality here, saying to Gamelin simply, "The incident at Houx is in hand."

Communications from Huntziger's sector were less soothing. Most of the reinforcements ordered up by Roton had not arrived. And at the very end of the day, a message came from Huntziger's chief of staff, Colonel Henri Lacaille, a gifted artillerist well known to Gamelin, that said: "There has been a rather serious hitch [pépin] at Sedan." German forces, he reported, had succeeded in seizing ground on the left bank of the Meuse in the neighborhood of the town. Via pontoon bridges and ferries, tanks and troops had come across. But Lacaille minimized the significance of the German success, saying reassuringly that the Third Armored and Third Motorized Divisions were expected soon. Roton reported separately that the crack Fourteenth Infantry was due to arrive at Sedan by rail on the morrow. Huntziger himself remained confident. When told that fifty German infantrymen had established a beachhead on his side of the river, he said, "That makes that many prisoners."

Showing more anxiety than Huntziger, Georges and Billotte joined in asking Têtu and Barratt to make an all-out dawn air attack on the pontoon bridges and ferry routes at Sedan. Billotte said to them, "Victory or defeat rides on those bridges." At a quarter to midnight, Georges signaled Gamelin, "Here we are calm."[14]

Only on May 14 did Gamelin, Georges, and other French and British leaders realize how completely they had been deceived regarding German strategy. Gamelin, who had been scheduled to remain in Paris for a morning
meeting of the Comité de Guerre, arranged for the meeting to be postponed
so that he could rejoin Georges at La Ferté. Hardly had his staff car pulled
into the circular driveway at Les Bondons and its siren been stilled when a
code clerk put before him and Georges an alarming message from Corap:
his Ninth Army had not succeeded, after all, in stanching the flow of German tanks through Houx, and they were now crossing at more than one
place and creating havoc behind Ninth Army lines.

A second piece of bad news popped out from between the lines of a
message from Huntziger that was intended to add fresh reassurance. Sum-
marizing his reports of the previous night, Georges's headquarters had
signaled Vincennes: "The breach at Sedan has been contained and a counterattack with strong formations was carried out at 4:30 A.M." But
Huntziger's morning report said that the counterattack had not yet taken
place. Though he asserted, "We have the situation in hand," he mentioned
an engagement with German tanks at Bulson. It took only a flashing glance
at a map to identify Bulson as a sad little hilltop village more than three
miles south of Sedan. Then, just before noon, a truly dismaying message
followed. Huntziger's Fifth Light Cavalry Division appeared to have disin-
tegrated. Huntziger's headquarters reported "panic" in that division and
something close to it in the 71st Infantry Division at Sedan.

Hard upon this bulletin came news of worsening conditions on Corap's
front. Nothing came from Corap himself or from d'Argenlieu. As it turned
out, they were themselves going from division to division trying to find out
what was going on. But the headquarters of Blanchard's First Army passed
on a rumor that panic had developed in elements of the Ninth Army around
Dinant. And "no one knows exactly what is going on."

At nightfall, the message receivers at La Ferté learned that Huntziger's
counteroffensive had still not taken place. Lacaille reported laconically
that it had been postponed "for technical reasons." A blow fell from yet another quarter when, just before 8 P.M., the Dutch army surrendered, with
Queen Wilhelmina flying off to take refuge in Britain.

At every level, France's commanders tried to display brave faces and to
act energetically. Georges shifted the First Armored Division from Blanchard's First Army to Corap's Ninth, expressing hope that, with it, Corap

would be able to turn the Germans back. Georges also exchanged sharp words with Huntziger, saying to him over the phone that he had been given the Third Armored in order to stage a counterattack and he was expected to use it. But everyone recognized now that the war was going badly. At Vincennes, writes Minart, the Meuse crossings "seemed incomprehensible, inexplicable," save that there must have been "grave errors of execution."[15]

Georges put in a late-night call to Doumenc, asking him to come to La Ferté from Montry. He arrived around 3 A.M., bringing Beaufre with him. As Beaufre wrote later, he and Doumenc found Georges and other officers gathered around the huge map table in the large salon left of the entryway, which served as a sanctum for the operations staff. "The atmosphere is that of a family keeping vigil over a dead member. Georges rises briskly and comes up to Doumenc. He is terribly pale. 'Our front has been pushed in at Sedan! There have been some failures [*défaillances*]. . . .' He falls into an armchair and a sob silences him."[16] An anonymous author claiming to have been a British staff officer in France alleges that at Billotte's headquarters, at about the same time, several French officers were also weeping.[17]

Prime Minister Reynaud, still feverish, had sent Winston Churchill an urgent message when the first bad news arrived, saying, prematurely, that the Germans had broken through at Sedan. Misinterpreting the German objective, he went on to say that Paris was in danger. At the time, he believed he was overstating, but he had just learned from General Vuillemin that the French air force had asked Britain for additional fighters and Britain had refused to send them, citing need to defend the British homeland. Reynaud's objective was to arm Churchill, whom he believed sympathetic to the French request, for an effort to reverse the vote in his own War Cabinet.

Afterward, Reynaud learned that he had not exaggerated. Early on the morning of May 15, he put in a telephone call to London. Churchill, awakened from sleep and probably with a little customary morning-after muzziness, heard Reynaud say in English: "We have been defeated!" After a moment of silence, Reynaud repeated: "We are beaten; we have lost the battle." As Churchill himself recalled, he began, with some hope of calming the Frenchman, to muse aloud about dark days in 1918 that had been successfully weathered. This tactic failing, Churchill said he would come to Paris to see for himself.[18]

What had happened did not quite justify the phrase later used as a book title by Paul-Émile Caton: a war lost in four days. But it was close.

PLAN YELLOW PLAYS OUT

"No one knows exactly what is going on."
—*Headquarters, French First Army, to headquarters,*
Northeastern front, May 13, 1940

What had hit the French was a German war plan executed so successfully as to be almost beyond belief. "It is a miracle, a decided miracle!" Hitler said after the Sedan breakthrough.[1] Guderian, who trusted his guiding star more than did almost any other general, recalled pausing at Donchery, observing the tanks that had crossed the Meuse River, and using to himself the same word: "The success of our attack struck me as almost a miracle."

German operations had hardly gone like clockwork. Hitler had hoped that the Dutch would buckle as the Danes had—inviting German occupation in order to avoid the futile loss of lives. Paratroops descending on The Hague had contingency plans for a ceremonial handover parade. According to unproven rumor, one plane carried their commander's horse—just in case.

The Dutch reaction was the reverse of what Hitler hoped, and it infuriated him. In Rotterdam, early risers walking along the waterfront saw seaplanes come down on each side of the two long bridges that cross to an island opposite and thence to Breda and beyond. Since the planes were coming in from the west, the observers assumed them to be British; when small rubber boats filled with soldiers emerged, dockers tossed out lines and extended poles to help them out of the water. Once recognizing the uniforms as German, they pushed the soldiers back in and cried alarm. Policemen came, cleared the enemy from the quayside, and set up defenses.

Dutch reservists uncloseted their uniforms and mustered with such equipment as they had. A mock-up of the defense of Rotterdam in the city's Marinier Museum shows an officer with a 1915 pistol and a corporal with an 1895 rifle. Even so, the city's defenders managed to destroy both the regular bridge and the railroad bridge, which left the German troops marooned on the island, able only to fire machine guns across several hundred yards of water.

In Amsterdam and The Hague, Dutch troops succeeded in recapturing airfields and hemming German paratroopers into pockets.[2] But continued Dutch resistance clearly depended on the arrival of reinforcements. The long causeway at Moerdijk, twenty miles to the south of Rotterdam, was left undestroyed in hope that a French army might reach Breda and keep going.

In the sickle-cut concept, General Bock's attack in the Netherlands and northern Belgium was the equivalent of a toreador's waving a cape to attract a bull. Rundstedt's Army Group A would then be the sword piercing the bull's side.[3] The Germans expected the Allies to detect the ruse and regroup, turning their armies back to cope with the thrust through the Ardennes. For that reason, the German backup plan, in case the Dutch did not submit peacefully, called for smashing all Dutch resistance within two days so that Bock could shift his forces south to bolster Army Group A. For Bock, therefore, the top priorities were motion and speed. On May 10 and 11, he was to give an impression of delivering the brunt of the German offensive. By May 12, he was to be letting up and rerouting trucks and tanks toward the upper Belgian Meuse.

As of May 10, the northernmost of Bock's two armies was the Eighteenth, under General Georg von Küchler. Equipped to get quickly to the Dutch heartland on the coast and to batter down any opposing forces in the way, it was to send one corps overland toward Amsterdam and a second toward Rotterdam. The commander of this corps was none other than General Rudolf Schmidt, the brother of the French SR's favorite agent, "H.E." In the lead was the Ninth Panzer division and motorized infantry. Had Bock's plan worked, these lead elements would have blocked reinforcements coming to the Netherlands from the south and would, by late on May 11 or early on May 12, have entered Rotterdam to reinforce the German paratroops inside the city.

The efficiency of the Rotterdamers in dealing with the German landing parties and destroying their own bridges disrupted General Bock's timetable. Though the rapidity with which his tanks and motorized infantry reached the Moerdijk estuary did deter General Giraud from sending troops beyond Breda, Bock saw May 13 end with his tanks and troop carriers simply piling up across a wide stretch of water from Rotterdam, and the engagement between Giraud's armored brigade and elements of the Ninth Panzer, which cost Küchler a hundred tanks, augured ill for simply trying to win by battering Allied lines.

On the night of May 13–14, the German commanders on the scene agreed to give the Dutch an ultimatum and, if it was rejected, to have the Luftwaffe bomb out the city as it had bombed out Warsaw in September 1939. Faced with this threat and seeing no further hope of French or British reinforcement, the Dutch government decided to capitulate. Notification reached the German ground-force commanders, however, after a hundred Heinkel 111s of the German 54th Bomber Squadron were already in the air, and on the afternoon of May 14, more than thirteen hundred hundred-pound and five-hundred-pound bombs exploded in Rotterdam, demolishing most houses and shops on the waterfront, killing nine hundred, and wounding thousands more. Though this bombing outraged and embittered the Dutch, the government did not retract its order that troops lay down their arms.[4]

Bock could now begin arranging for troop transfers to the south. Two days had been lost from the optimal timetable, one day from the supposed minimal one. If the Allied awakening and turnaround had not come so slowly, the extra time contributed by Rotterdam's sacrifice might have interfered with the "miracle" in progress on the Meuse.

In Belgium, Bock's other army, the Sixth, under General Reichenau, came closer to completing its mission on time. Reichenau had five corps, the fastest of which was Hoepner's. It was this corps that, despite destruction of the bridges in Maastricht, succeeded in reaching the two still-intact bridges over the Albert Canal in time to salvage the effort of the glider-borne troops holding the roof of Fort Eben Emael. The glider attack had been thoughtfully planned. Since German contractors and workers had helped to build the fortress, the Abwehr had been able to supply a complete set of its specifications to General Kurt Student, the commander of all German paratroops. The landing force had known therefore that there were no defenses on the roof, and they carried rappelling equipment of just the right lengths to permit their reaching the gunports on its sides. But, as always in war, something had gone wrong. The commander of the landing force and a number of his men had dropped in the wrong places and had to crawl through woods to reach the fort. The whole operation was left to a sergeant and a remnant of what had only been an eighty-five-man force to begin with. Even so, they had accomplished their mission, with only fifty-five dead as against 435 on the Belgian side.[5] The arrival of Hoepner's tanks then turned back the Belgian infantry division on its way to retake the fortress.

Hoepner now commenced the drive across Belgium that ended in his confrontation with Prioux's cavalry corps at Hannut on May 13 and 14. The infantry and horse-cavalry units in his train were left well behind and found the going hard. One horse-tender remembered, "Corpses were everywhere. . . . The stench . . . filled our nostrils with a sickening odour. Our horses . . . were constantly shying away from it." When he and his comrades encountered even light French tanks, their experience was similar to that of Corap's and Huntziger's troops. "All the horses were screaming," he writes, "my eyes were burning and I was half blinded," and he ran away.[6] Up ahead, Hoepner's corps suffered heavy losses. His two divisions had had between them 623 tanks: the Third Panzer Division, with 280 tanks, had been above standard complement; the Fourth Panzer, with 343, had had the largest complement in the armored force. Together, the two divisions had more than a quarter of *all* German tanks, though only 20 percent were Panzer IIIs or IVs. In the battles around Hannut, Prioux's mechanized divisions destroyed 160 and severely damaged more than two hundred others. Since most of those destroyed or damaged were Panzer Is and Panzer IIs, the net effect on German offensive capabilities was not as great as it might have seemed, but the accompanying loss of trained men and the drain on Germany's meager stores of ammunition and fuel put paid to any prospect of Reichenau's sending reinforcements to Rundstedt's Army Group A. The net effect for Plan Yellow was nevertheless a gain, because the effort and sacrifice by Hoepner's Panzer divisions did much to keep alive the Allied illusion that Belgium was the central theater of the war.

In any case, the shortfall in reinforcements was more than made up by the extraordinary good luck experienced by Rundstedt's field commanders.

On the first day, May 10, it had been far from clear that the final version of Plan Yellow was going to work. The cape-waving by Bock had clearly attracted the bull. It remained to be seen whether Rundstedt could get the sword out of its scabbard in time for a crippling thrust. Halder spent the first day of the war as much in the dark about the Allies as they were about the Germans. He prodded Tippelskirch and Liss to find out whether the Allies were in fact moving into Belgium or were holding fast. Because of the slowness of Allied deployments and the disinclination of the French to use radio or telephone, Tippelskirch lacked clear information. He could tell Brauchitsch and Halder only that Allied mobile forces seemed to be bunching along the Belgian border. Not until the next day could he begin to report with confidence that Allied forces were actually moving into Belgium. And not until May 12 could he state with conviction that the most mobile Allied army, Giraud's Seventh, was hurrying toward northern Belgium and the Netherlands. On that day, moreover, Tippelskirch was able to add the glad news that Liss and Roenne had made a major mistake in their estimate of Allied order of battle. In the Belgian and French Ardennes, Rundstedt's Army Group A would not run into Blanchard's French First Army with Prioux's cavalry corps. Blanchard's army and the British Expeditionary Force were both headed toward central Belgium. Rundstedt's forces would instead encounter the weaker Ninth Army under Corap.[7]

Success depended on Group Kleist's five Panzer divisions' getting across the Meuse River in France before Allied generals saw what was going on and pulled their armies back from Belgium. After late April's war games at Koblenz, General Hans Reinhardt, who was to be one of Kleist's corps commanders, had warned of possible traffic jams. The Group was going to have to cross Luxembourg and the Belgian and French Ardennes following four narrow, winding roads. His and Guderian's corps would put on those roads 1,222 tanks, 545 other tracked vehicles, and 39,333 troop-carrying trucks and cars. General Kurt Zeitzler, chief of staff of the Group's backup motorized infantry corps, a skilled logistician who would later be Halder's successor as army chief of staff, had developed a scheme for keeping all these machines fueled and supplied. Trucks would go ahead of the columns and drop cans of gasoline and boxes of rations at exactly the points where the tanks and other vehicles could be expected to be running low on fuel. But Reinhardt predicted that the columns would get in each other's way and have trouble keeping pace.

Group Kleist experienced just the problems that Reinhardt had foreseen. At first light on May 10, German forces had seized almost every bridge that crossed the Moselle, Sûre, and Our Rivers from Germany into Luxembourg and southern Belgium. Most of the bridges were taken by infantry units accompanied by horse-drawn carts with treks of a week or more ahead of them before they reached France. That was the case at Vormeldange, where the German lieutenant and his twenty men overpowered the Luxembourg border guards.

The tanks and vehicle-borne infantry of Group Kleist used four bridges in the center of the Army Group A front. Guderian's XIX Corps led. He and his staff accompanied the First Panzer Division, crossing the Sûre at Wallendorf, then turning and following a road that meandered, the river to its right and steep slopes to its left thick with poplars, sycamores, and spruce. His Second Panzer Division, which crossed at Roth, followed a road that was north of the river but was governed also by its twists and turns. His third Panzer Division, the Tenth, came over at Bollendorf, to the south, where a largely unimproved road wound directly westward. His motorized infantry crossed at Echternach, still farther to the south, to take a similar road. Strung out sufficiently to reduce risk of rear-end collisions, each division occupied at least two miles of roadway. Though they occasionally came to plateaux where tanks could fan out, there was always another stretch of forest ahead, where travel could only be single-file.

The two Panzer divisions in Reinhardt's XLI Corps sat all day on the Luxembourg border, waiting to move in behind Guderian's divisions. Trucks carrying troops and supplies tried to get ahead of them. Reinhardt himself had to jump on a motorcycle and weave to the head of the line. Only the sight of his general officer's insignia and the sound of his angry voice moved other vehicles to the sides of the road so that his tanks could roll through. Meanwhile, Guderian's trailing units had lagged enough to get snarled with trucks and tanks coming up behind them. By May, as Karl-Heinz Frieser writes in *Blitzkrieg-Legende,* the approaches to the Belgian and French Ardennes witnessed "the greatest traffic jam known up to that date in Europe."[8]

At any moment during daylight on May 10, 11, or 12, well-aimed Allied bombs could have sent Group Kleist scattering and clogged its advance. In openings between areas of forest, the slow-moving German tanks would have made easy targets. Where the roadside trees were spreading oaks or sycamores, spring leaves provided protective canopies. Where they were trunk-hugging spruce or pine, the single-file tanks could have been spotted, hit, disabled, and turned into corks bottling up vehicles behind them.

The weather was perfect for such attacks—clear, almost cloudless, and with only light winds. Though the Luftwaffe sent over an occasional Me-109 or Me-110 to ward off Allied observation planes, nearly all German aircraft were committed to covering Bock's movements into the Netherlands and northern Belgium and helping to create the appearance that this was the focus of the German offensive. Colonel Kielmansegg, operations officer for the First Panzer Division, recalls his thoughts when pausing at Diekirch, a major road junction in northern Luxembourg and a famous brewery town: "Again and again I look with anxious eyes at the beaming blue sky; for what a target the division offers as long as it is compelled to progress by moving slowly forward along a single road. But not once does one French observation plane appear." Though Kielmansegg does not mention it, he and others probably drew comfort from a mistaken claim by Luftwaffe headquarters that large numbers of Allied aircraft had been destroyed on the ground during the first day's bombing. An officer of an accompanying motorized infantry division recalls how the spirits of his troops lifted when two British planes flew over and dropped bombs that were both duds and one of the planes was shot down. This, he says, got rid of all their "*Fliegerangst*"—fear of planes.[9]

Several Allied planes passed over the long columns of tanks and trucks winding through the Ardennes. Their reports were too few, however, to excite interest at any French or British headquarters. Têtu, Barratt, and General François Astier de la Vigerie, who commanded the bomber and fighter forces supporting Billotte's armies on the Northeastern front, could all see that the Luftwaffe was heavily engaged in the Netherlands and northern Belgium. For them and other airmen, it defied reason to suppose that aircraft would be risked in support of ground operations in a secondary theater.

One of many moments when the Battle of France might have taken a different turn had occurred late on May 11, when Colonel Henri Alias, who commanded an air-reconnaissance group, telephoned the chief intelligence officer of Corap's Ninth Army to report that large numbers of tanks seemed to be headed its way. Alias recalls sensing over the phone that his news was being received with skepticism if not incredulity, and, indeed, there is no evidence that the intelligence officer even relayed the report to General Corap, let alone that he gave it any emphasis. When questioned after the war, the intelligence officer protested: "To say that I would not have accepted the reports that had been furnished me by Colonel Alias would be to misunderstand the technique of the Deuxième Bureau." One infers that Alias's report fell victim to the Deuxième Bureau doctrine preached by Gauché. The hypothesis it suggested did not merit communication to the commander in the absence of other evidence establishing its credibility.[10] From the Allied standpoint, perhaps from that of humanity, this was a pity.

Traffic jams were not the only problem besetting Group Kleist. Aware of how hard it would be to meet the timetable, General Guderian had turned to the Luftwaffe for help in securing bridges and other points where there was risk of his tanks' being delayed. Because of the concentration of air action in the north, paratroops or comparable forces were not available. Göring, however, came up with a substitute.

The Luftwaffe had a large fleet of Fi-156s—Fieseler Storchs. These planes could carry troops and needed only a ninety-foot clearing in which to land and a 250-foot stretch from which to take off. Göring offered Guderian their use. The hitch was that each plane could carry only two men, lightly equipped. But Guderian took what he could get. Hence, a hundred Fieseler Storchs were to deliver infantrymen to spots on his projected route where there was danger that the Belgians or French would destroy bridges or roadways. In two flights, they could land four hundred men. The operation was code-named NiWi, for the two villages that were its principal targets—Nives and Witry, in Belgian Luxembourg. The troops joked that the letters stood for *nichts wissen* (know nothing).

The Storchs set down the first ten men in exactly the right place. The second five-plane flight lost its way. Succeeding flights saw the second flight, not the first, and followed it. In the end, the Storchs scattered four hundred men over a ten-kilometer area mostly well south of where intended. In yet another instance of good luck for the Germans and bad luck for the Allies, the four hundred men turned out to be just west of Martelange and Bodange, the sites where Belgian Chasseurs Ardennais temporarily held up Guderian's advance parties. The men were therefore in just the right locations to block advancing units of the French Ninth Army that might have taken over from the Belgians. French scouts had the double surprise of finding the Chasseurs gone and their places taken by what appeared to be German paratroops. Those who thought of looking farther afield seem to have been turned back by a "Road Closed" sign put in place by enterprising members of the NiWi expedition. Guderian's Panzers ended the day exactly where their timetable called for them to be, but hardly because their progress had gone according to plan.

On May 12, Allied fighters and bombers did begin to appear overhead. They were few, for the air forces of both sides remained mostly committed in the north. Moreover, the Allied planes did not range far beyond their own lines and never targeted the traffic still jammed up between the German border and the middle of the Ardennes. But one French bomber pilot, if a little more lucky, might have affected the whole course of the war. He released bombs at Bouillon, a small Belgian town eleven miles north of Sedan, where an eleventh-century château occupies a height on one side of a bend in the Semois River and hotels on the heights opposite have an enchanting view of both the château and the houses and shops clustered around its walls.

At the outset of the war, General Huntziger had visited Bouillon to ask that the mayor designate a hotel for use as a troop hospital. The mayor had said no: Bouillon was a resort city, and hotel rooms had to be reserved for tourists. When the First Panzer Division rolled into town, General Guderian was not as polite as Huntziger had been. He did not call on the mayor. He simply seized for his own use one of the city's best-situated hotels, the Panorama, and set up a temporary command post in a parlor at the rear of its ground floor. Above a fireplace in the parlor was mounted the stuffed head of a giant Ardennes boar. Guderian was standing by the fireplace when the French pilot's bomb hit a munitions truck on the hotel's frontage road. The explosion threw Guderian to the floor. The boar's head flew off the fireplace. Unluckily for France, it missed Guderian's skull by inches. (Though little of the old hotel survives in the Panorama of today, the boar's head is still on display.)

As forces from Army Group A neared the French border, they began to experience the benefits of being part of a large first-line force pitted against a smaller second-line force. To the right of Group Kleist and acting in coordination with it were two armored divisions belonging to General Hans-Günther von Kluge's Fourth Army. One, the Fifth Panzer, was under General Max von Hartlieb; the other, the Seventh, under General Erwin Rommel.

Though Rommel was to acquire lasting fame as a commander of armored forces, he was at this time quite new to the job. His immediately prior post had been as chief of the small staff serving Hitler's command train, the *Amerika*. His Great War experience had been primarily in leading behind-the-lines commandos, particularly in Romania. Since Hitler had taken a liking to him, Rommel had asked for command of an armored division and been given one despite his lack of apparent qualifications. But he turned out to have a genius for handling tanks in a totally unorthodox way—as if they were commando elements. In contrast to Guderian, who believed in hammering one spot with all the tanks he could focus on it, Rommel favored slash-and-thrust tactics.

From his experience in Romania, he had drawn the moral that troops should always advance with guns ablaze. By now, he had built this into a broader rule. As he wrote his wife on the day before the offensive opened:

The day goes to the side that is the first to plaster its opponent with fire. . . . Motorcyclists at the head of a column must keep their machine guns at the ready and open fire the instant an enemy shot is heard. . . . When the exact position of the enemy is unknown, . . . the fire must simply be sprayed over enemy-held territory. . . . Even indiscriminate machine-gun fire and 20 mm. anti-tank fire into a wood in which enemy anti-tank guns have installed themselves is so effective that in most cases the enemy is completely unable to get into action or else gives up his position.[11]

Rommel applied this rule when sighting what turned out to be regiments from the Fourth Light Cavalry Division fanning out to form the left wing of the French Ninth Army. His tactic worked. It was the sight of Rommel's motorcyclists riding toward them, machine guns chattering, with Panzer IIIs and Panzer IVs coming up behind, that caused the French commander to conclude he would be outgunned, even if his men took positions in the escarpments and ravines of the Semois River.[12] His report to Corap, accompanied by the Spahi brigade commander's report of seeing no sign of Huntziger's Second Army, led to Corap's decision to pull all his forces back to the Meuse.

Able to cross the Semois unopposed, the two German armored divisions reached the Meuse by dusk on May 12. An advance party almost succeeded in capturing the bridge at Yvoir. Demolition charges had been placed under the bridge's pilings by a Belgian engineer unit, but when the lieutenant commanding the unit pushed the plunger on the activator, nothing happened. A wire had come loose. German troops were actually on the eastern side of the bridge, under fire from French troops on the western side, when the Belgian lieutenant jumped into the water, swam out, and managed to touch off the charges by hand before being killed by German gunfire.

With the bridges gone, the broad river looked impassable. One German soldier recalls looking across and seeing massive stone towers and houses with thick walls, all of them suitable sites for riflemen or machine-gunners. From grottoes among the trees on the steep slopes above, the enemy could train guns on the whole eastern bank, and heavy artillery fired from positions behind the slopes. The heights above the river, the soldier writes, seemed like "fire-spitting mountains."[13]

During the night, German scouts crept along the riverbank. They came upon the point about halfway between Yvoir and Dinant where the river divides around the little island of Houx. There they spotted the weir and sluice that had been left intact. In the moonlight, their field glasses detected no defenders right at the site. They concluded (rightly) that French observation posts might be well up the wooded slope above the sluice. The same veteran remembers seeing infantrymen attached to Hartlieb's Fifth Panzer "jump from tree to tree, seeking any cover, even the most unlikely, with soft, catlike movements along the broad green strip which lies open like a gift box along the river."[14]

German soldiers bunched up on the island, unseen from the French posts up above. Just as day began to break, they marched across the sluice. One account describes them as goose-stepping. French rifles and machine guns immediately opened fire, and French artillery took aim at Germans on the eastern bank. The attack was bloody. A sergeant reported: "Dead lie in the water. Wounded hang on to the doors of the sluice. They cry for help, but no one can help them."[15] Enough German soldiers made their way across, however, to begin overpowering defenders on the western bank. Because much of Corap's infantry was coming up on the original slow schedule, the French defenses proved thin. By the end of the day on May 13, infantry from the Fifth Panzer and from Rommel's Seventh Panzer had fanned out into an area almost three miles deep beyond the Houx sluice.

Behind the infantry screen, engineers attached to the two Panzer divisions rigged rafts and rubber boats to ferry tanks and other vehicles across. The appearance of the first of these tanks west of the Meuse River was the event that startled both Georges and Gamelin and set Gamelin telephoning directly to Corap's chief of staff to find out what was up. The reassuring answer that d'Argenlieu gave him was based on the fact that the tanks west of the Meuse were still few and that the French cavalry and infantry commanders in the area were as yet unaware of the extent of the German infantry's penetration. Neither the field commanders nor Corap's staff would begin to understand what had happened until late on May 13, by which time the Meuse was threatened or had been breached all the way upriver to Sedan.

Reinhardt's corps was to the left of the one that included Hartlieb's and Rommel's divisions. As Reinhardt had foretold, traffic snarls had continued to keep his corps well behind timetable. Even after he broke his Panzer battalions free from the foot soldiers and wagons that got in their way in Luxembourg, he had to reckon with a narrow road that followed almost all the loops of the Semois, nearly always requiring single-file progress between a clifflike riverbank on one side and steep forested slopes on the other. His tanks were continually climbing or going down inclines that strained even the engines of his Panzer IIIs and Panzer IVs. Moreover,

Reinhardt's lead units encountered Belgian and French troops that were much more tenacious and much more inclined to take advantage of natural blinds and overlooks than those that had scuttled before Rommel to his north and Guderian to his south.

Not until dark on May 12 did Reinhardt's tanks arrive at the rocky heights, a thousand feet high, that look down on Monthermé, where the Semois flows into the Meuse and makes a sharp bend around the picturesque old town.[16] Reinhardt had no chance of surprise. Even if his infantrymen had led the way, practicing flawless concealment, they would have been spotted by hikers or farmers taking advantage of the balmy May weather. The road his tanks had to take curled two miles down from the heights, much of it visible from below. French troops were sure to have destroyed the bridge and probably to have dug in to defend the river. (A plaque on the restored bridge, testifying to the valor of the 42nd Colonial Machine-Gun Brigade, is one of the few monuments to an engagement by the French Ninth Army in 1939–40.) Reinhardt planned to assemble as much power as possible on his side of the destroyed bridge and try to force a crossing.

By the end of day on May 13, he was still weaving tanks and infantry into the shelter of the fifteenth-century fortified church and surrounding houses and schools that backed up against the river just around from the remains of the bridge. Having seen the mile-long column of tanks come down from the heights, the French commander became desperate enough to resort to an open radio to appeal to the Ninth Army headquarters for reinforcements. He, like Gamelin and Georges at La Ferté, could get no answer, for Corap and his staff were in the field trying themselves to ascertain what was happening around Houx and whether the whole Army Group line had been breached as a result of the "hitch" at Sedan.

Guderian's force had arrived in good time opposite Sedan in part because of its continuing run of luck. Halder had shared with Rundstedt, and Rundstedt with Kleist and Guderian, the glad news brought by Tippelskirch that the opposition around Sedan would come from Huntziger's Second Army instead of Blanchard's First. But the situation maps supplied from Foreign Armies West at Zossen did not indicate clearly the location of French-army area boundaries.

Chance, however, brought Guderian's Second Panzer Division to the boundary between the Ninth Army and the Second. There Corap's Spahis had already pulled back because of their failure to make contact with elements of Huntziger's army. One of Huntziger's two light cavalry divisions, the Fifth, had actually been on its way but had moved slowly (without, of course, anyone's informing Corap). When its lead regiment arrived, it was its commander's turn to become alarmed at the absence of any neighboring force. Now, at last, a message went from the First Army to the Ninth Army: Where are the Spahis? "The Spahis will do what they can," was the ambiguous message that came in reply.

Nervous already, the regimental commander suddenly saw in front of him, rumbling toward the Belgian town of Neufchâteau, German motorcyclists and an armored command car. His own regiment consisted mostly of horse cavalry. At the first exchange of fire, the French horses began to bolt. A youngster on a farm near Petitvoir, a little over a mile west of Neufchâteau, reported afterward hearing galloping horses and seeing, from a window, riderless horses trailing their harnesses, helmets rolling along the road, and men running and crying with fright. What had set this off was the sight, behind the motorcyclists and command car, of a Panzer IV rearing up over a hilltop.[17]

The retreat of the regiment, together with reports of the Germans' infantry assault on Longwy at the head of the Maginot Line, prompted the subsequent reactions that moved the front line of the French Second Army back to the string of pillboxes and then, when these proved untenable, to the west bank of the Meuse. From Neufchâteau to the river, Guderian's divisions advanced almost unopposed. By the evening of May 12, they were present in force at Sedan.

On the opposite bank, French forces seemed to be entrenched in depth. All the bridges had been blown up. The inhabited part of the city had emptied. Kielmansegg, the operations officer of the First Panzer Division, writes that it was "completely dead and still. Not a dog or a cat did I see on the streets."[18] The French-held left bank bristled with gun turrets and the snouts of artillery pieces and machine guns all the way to the Marfée Heights, almost a mile away.

One reason for comparative insouciance on the part of the French was their assumption that the Germans could not even attempt to force a crossing of the Meuse at Sedan without strong artillery support, and General Guderian himself was very conscious of lacking artillery. The heaviest guns on his tanks were the 75-mm. cannon on Panzer IVs, and not many of them. Panzer Is had only machine guns; Panzer IIs, 20-mm. cannon; and Panzer IIIs, 37-mm. cannon. Only the 37-mm. and 75-mm. guns could penetrate French pillboxes, and then only with direct hits. It took 88-mm. and 105-mm. cannon to take a pillbox out with a glancing hit.

Guderian boarded a Fieseler Storch and flew to the rear to consult with Kleist. Since the cape-and-sword maneuver seemed still to be working and the Allies had not yet shifted any significant force southward, Guderian proposed that they postpone their attack on Sedan for a day. This would allow some artillery to arrive. It would also give his sleepless men a few hours' rest (and himself—shaken up by the blast at Bouillon).

Kleist said no. He had already yielded to Guderian's insistence that the attack be at Sedan rather than, as Kleist preferred, at Flize, seven miles downstream. He had also had to swallow Guderian's near insubordination in deploying the Tenth Panzer Division. Kleist had told him to use it to protect his left flank, but Guderian had moved most of the division straight toward Sedan, diverting only a few of its elements to flank defense. Having himself taken the position that the armored group should not concern itself unduly with flank defense, Kleist had reason to believe that his demands on Guderian had been minimal. This time, Kleist would not bend.[19]

All the night long of May 12–13, tanks and other vehicles moved back and forth on the German-held side of the Meuse. Many ran with headlights. They made no effort to be quiet. Guderian had in his entire corps a total of 141 big guns. He gathered them all along the portion of the river he had assigned to the First Panzer Division.[20]

The Meuse flows into Sedan from the south-southeast, passing a railroad freight complex at Wadelincourt, then, paralleled by railroad tracks, through and past the town. Less than a half-mile after it emerges from the town, the river splits. Part of it turns north, then south again, forming a bend with the shape of half a paper clip, before it rejoins the main river. The half-mile-wide flatland enclosed between the two segments of the river is the Presqu'île d'Iges. The river then runs almost due west, with the village of Donchery on its right bank.

Guderian's plans called for infantry to move around the Presqu'île d'Iges and attempt a crossing about where the two parts of the Meuse come back together, using Donchery as a launching point. If the infantry succeeded in establishing a bridgehead across from Donchery, engineers would lay a pontoon bridge for tanks of the Second Panzer Division. Guderian's plans also called for the Tenth Panzer to try to cross on the other side of Sedan, at Wadelincourt, where, similarly, infantry were supposed to establish a bridgehead so that a pontoon bridge could be laid. Lastly, the First Panzer, with all the artillery laying barrages before it, was to make its assault in between the other two, focusing on the point where the river first splits to create the Presqu'île d'Iges. The elite Grossdeutschland infantry regiment would lead.

Artillery fire was to begin soon after daylight. All three efforts to seize ground on the other side of the river were to come in late afternoon. The operational orders that Guderian issued to division commanders were, word for word, those he had used in his last war game at Koblenz. The only change was in the hour prescribed for the infantry units to attack—4 P.M. instead of 10 A.M.

In spite of Kleist's refusal to allow any delay, he and everyone else at the upper level of the army recognized the problems that existed because of Guderian's lack of artillery. Halder had included air-force officers in a mid-March war game at Zossen. Afterward, they had explained to Göring and Air Force Chief of Staff Jeschonnek that the new version of Plan Yellow, in part because of shortage of artillery, would depend on "strongest support from the Luftwaffe."[21] As a result, Sperrle, the commander of the Third Air Fleet, had agreed to commit to the mission every plane he could muster.

Operational command of the air-support force went to General Bruno Loerzer of II Air Corps, but the force included units from three other corps, one of which came from Kesselring's Second Air Fleet. Known as the "Close Support Corps," it had just been helping to rescue Hoepner at Hannut. Its commander, General Wolfram Count von Richthofen, cousin and flying rival of the famous "Red Baron" of the Great War, had led German air forces participating on Franco's side in the Spanish Civil War.[22] All in all, Loerzer's force included six hundred standard bombers (Heinkel 111s, Dornier 17s, and Junker 88s) and 250 Stukas (Junker 87s), designed for dive-bombing. Loerzer also had 620 Me-109 and Me-110 fighters for cover.

Beginning at 8 A.M. on May 13, flights of Loerzer's bombers attacked fortified places along the river. Exactly at noon, Richthofen's Stukas commenced laying bombs from a low altitude on gun emplacements guarding the sites where Guderian's infantry hoped to make their crossings. Formations of roughly forty planes each would circle a mile overhead. Two or three planes at a time would swoop down. In the last forty minutes before 4 P.M., Stukas and heavier bombers alternated. At 4 P.M., they moved their line of attack back from the river, aiming at any and all French forces moving up to counter the German infantry crossings.

There had never before been such a rain of fire from the air. Rarely afterward would there ever be comparably concentrated bombardment from the air. It resembled the drenching artillery fire in some of the big battles of

the Great War, which had caused men in trenches on both sides to go insane. The actual damage was meager. Though parts of the landscape were
transformed so that, even today, they resemble areas around Verdun and
other cratered battlefields of the Great War, not many French gun emplacements suffered direct hits. Even though a number of pillboxes were
incomplete, and in particular lacked steel roofing, few were put out of commission. Not many French soldiers were killed or wounded. Making a count
afterward, the physician of one French infantry regiment that lost many
men found only one to have been wounded, and none killed, by a Stuka
bomb.[23]

The psychological effects of the sustained bombardment were, however,
horrendous. No one who lived through that day at Sedan ever forgot the
nerve-shattering effect of hour after hour filled with the whine of Stukas,
the usually futile pop-pop-pop of anti-aircraft guns, blast on blast of bombs,
the thud and clatter of collapsing stonework and showering gravel, and the
brief, awful intervals of silence. A lieutenant at a battalion headquarters on
the Marfée Heights wrote afterward that, when the first bombs came,
"everyone tightened his back, gasping, teeth clenched. The earth shook,
seemed to part. These were five terrible minutes." When the bombing
paused, "we breathed; we looked around, almost joyfully." Then bombs
came again and again and again. In the end, he said, "we were there, immobile, silent, backs bent, shrunken into ourselves, mouths open so as not
to have the eardrums burst."[24]

The whole performance—of Guderian's guns and Loerzer's planes—almost failed. Even with such preparation, most of the German troops that
tried to get across the river had to fall back. Infantry trying to get to
Wadelincourt for Schall's Tenth Panzer Division had eighty-one of their
ninety-six rubber boats shot out from under them. But, eventually, the Germans succeeded. Men from all three of Guderian's Panzer divisions managed to gain footholds on the left bank of the river. By night, men from the
Grossdeutschland Regiment laid a pontoon bridge. It extended across from
a factory called L'Espérance at Gaulier, on the western edge of Sedan. It
was rated as capable of carrying sixteen-ton loads. Guderian made it carry
double weight, even though, had it collapsed, it would have been hard to
replace, given the amount of bridging equipment his divisions had already
used in Luxembourg and Belgium. By daylight on May 14, tanks of the
First Panzer Division were flowing across the river.

All day May 14, it remained touch and go whether the footholds could
be held. Têtu and Barratt responded to Billotte's appeal by ordering

bombers to attack the pontoon bridge. Têtu committed every plane at hand, including obsolete models standing by to be replaced. Barratt, moved also by Billotte's assertion that the war could turn on destruction of that bridge, ordered in more than a hundred of his Battles and Blenheims.

The scene from the ground is described by Kielmansegg:

> The summer landscape with the sleepy river running through it, with the light-green meadows bordered by the darker summits of heights over the river, arched over by a blue sky, filled with the noise of war. For hours, the dull impact of bombs, the fast rat-rat of machine guns, the different sounds of various calibers of anti-aircraft guns, mixed with the drone of aircraft motors and the rumble of the division constantly traveling over the bridge.[25]

The Allied air attack failed to stop the movement of the tanks. The German forces were well equipped with anti-aircraft guns. German fighter planes occasionally made successful forays even though, on this occasion, French fighter planes were present in force to protect the bombers. Air-staff dogma that bombers should provide their own defenses gave way in the face

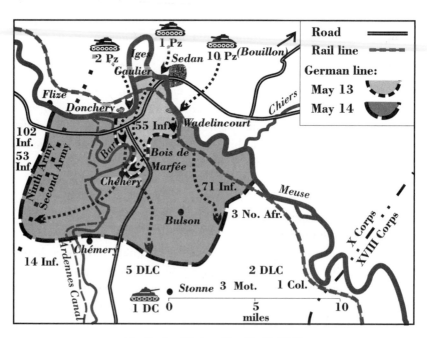

The Battle of Sedan, May 13–14, 1940

of insistence by Gamelin and Georges that nothing be left undone to stem the German advance.[26] Kielmansegg recalled seeing eleven Allied planes shot down in the short time during which he himself was being ferried across the river. But it was more the fault of the Allies than the Germans that the air mission failed. Their bombing was inaccurate. Smoke from ground firing made it hard for pilots to see their targets or to tell what they had hit. The records of the French air force accuse the British pilots of having flown their missions quickly, hit-or-miss, and having bombed or fired at almost as many French soldiers as German. Also, it has to be said, the 250-pound bombs in use on both sides were not powerful enough for the mission of destroying a well-constructed bridge. Later operations analysis concluded that this required bombs weighing two hundred *tons.*[27] The Gaulier bridge, being temporary, could probably have been made useless by several direct hits, but, again, luck was with the Germans, not the Allies.

The uninterrupted stream of German tanks across the Meuse induced effects that, when reported to Billotte's headquarters at Caudry and to La Ferté, caused French generals to sob and led Reynaud soon afterward to phone Churchill and say that France was beaten. In rear areas behind Sedan, men thought they saw German tanks. Though there were none as yet, these men began to run, shouting to others that tanks were right behind them. Panic spread. Artillerymen abandoned their guns. Officers, even combat veterans, deserted their command posts.

Yet the panic affected only a few units. Most of even the Class B divisions remained in place, firing at the Germans as they advanced. Nevertheless, the emptying of pockets in the lines of the French 55th and 71st Infantry Divisions, and especially the slackening of fire from their divisional artillery, meant that German forces found it easier to consolidate their positions beyond the river.

The arrival of the German tanks was not in itself decisive. The men who had panicked were soon channeled to rear areas. The rest followed orders to take up new positions behind Sedan. Many of them fought with new determination because they were ashamed of the few who had fled. The commander of one French tank unit writes, "The morale of the unit was *splendid.* Each person occupied himself with his weapons; confidence was complete; the spectacle of the disorder on the road had 'puffed up' the men who thought that they had nothing in common with that lot and that, with them, the Germans would have to reckon with something very different.'[28] The Third Armored Division, promised to Huntziger earlier by Roton, began to arrive. Its commander had two battalions of Hotchkiss H-39s ready.

More than a match for Panzer Is or Panzer IIs, these tanks gave Huntziger some capacity for counterattack.

The crossing of the Meuse River had been costly for the Germans. The entry in the war diary of the First Panzer Division at nightfall on May 14 says, "Heavy casualties and losses in personnel and materiel. Many officers have been killed or wounded. Only a quarter of the tanks can still be counted on to be combat ready." Hermann Balck, an officer in one of Guderian's elite infantry regiments and an often decorated veteran of the Great War, recalls having concluded around that time that his men were "really at the end of their resources." He had received permission to rest them for two hours. Then word came from Chéhery, a village south of Sedan, that a German unit was under heavy attack. So Balck roused his troops and quick-marched them to the scene—just in time. "In a matter of minutes," he writes, "the French tanks would have overrun us." He and his men helped hold off the French until German tank reinforcements arrived.[29] General Georges Brocard, the commander of the Third Armored, on his side, had already urged Huntziger to let him give his troops some rest. Hoping that more reinforcements would arrive quickly, Huntziger and his subordinate commanders pulled their forces back. In a postwar analysis of the fighting at Sedan, the German general Hermann Hoth, who commanded the armored corps that included Rommel's division, wrote of this engagement that the French units had acted audaciously, threatening the whole flank of Guderian's corps, but that, "in adjourning their counterattack, the French lost a favorable opportunity: that counterattack, conducted resolutely, would have been able to turn defeat into victory."[30]

Balck, though probably overstating the centrality of his own role, believed that the outcome at Sedan remained in the balance until at least May 15. He tells of marching his men to Bouvellemont, a village west of Sedan that had to be cleared if Guderian's divisions were to begin to move toward the Channel. On the way, at La Horgne, they encountered the Third Spahi regiment, whose colonel had pulled it back from the Ninth Army front on May 11 because of absence of contact with any unit from the Second Army. The Third Spahis proved that it had not been lack of spirit that had guided their move. "I have fought against many enemies in both wars and always at the focal points [*Brennpunkte*]," Balck writes. "Seldom has anyone fought as outstandingly."

After overcoming the Spahis, Balck continues, his men mutinied against continuing on to Bouvellemont. They were unmoved by his saying that not to do so would "give away the victory." So he stood up, turned toward La Horgne, and began to walk there by himself. After he had gone fifty to a hundred yards, his men rose and filed in behind him. (Anyone familiar with William Wyler's film *The Big Country* may recall Major Terrill [Charles Bickford] setting out for the confrontation with the head of the Hannessey clan [Burl Ives]. The music at La Horgne could even have been Jerome Moross's score.) Together, they took the town, but, again, Balck tosses in a tribute to French soldiers. If the defenders had been de Lattre's Fourteenth Infantry, he writes, the outcome would have been different.

Though Balck may have exaggerated the significance of the action at Bouvellemont, he is probably right that engagements on May 15 still held the possibility of reversing Guderian's success. His forces found themselves hard-pressed at a number of points south of Sedan. One was the hilltop at Bulson, where the defenders were hopelessly outmatched. But the most important was Stonne, the highest of the hilltops and the one from which, at least in the imagination of French soldiers arriving fresh from the general reserve, the Germans could have been rolled back to the other side of the Meuse.

Bulson, Stonne, and sites near Stonne are among the few places in France, other than Monthermé, where the war of 1939–40 is memorialized. At Stonne, there is an inlaid map showing where engagements were fought in the area from May 14 until France's capitulation in June. It says, accurately, that Stonne and the surrounding area, defended by the Third Motorized Infantry Division and the Third Armored Division, changed hands seventeen times and, when finally occupied in German hands, was "a cemetery of tanks."

But Huntziger never succeeded in gathering his forces for a coordinated counteroffensive. At Sedan, in contrast to Hannut, German tanks outnumbered French, and the proportion of Panzer IIIs and Panzer IVs was high. When the area around Stonne was clear enough for General Guderian's armored command car to wend its way up to the height, he and his staff looked out for miles to the west and to the south. He invited his staff's advice as to whether he should concentrate on continuing to battle the remnants of Huntziger's army or begin a drive toward the Channel. He was known for the motto *"Klotzen, nicht Kleckern,"* which Alistair Horne translates as "Wallop them; don't tap them." A First Panzer staff officer, probably grinning, quoted the motto back to him. Guderian ordered that some detachments remain behind but that the bulk of his corps start racing west.[31]

CHAPTER THIRTY

FRANCE FALLS

"We were through the Maginot Line! It was hardly conceivable."
—*Diary of General Erwin Rommel, May 17, 1940*

The rest of the story of the Battle of France can be abbreviated. German infantry continued to batter Longwy. When the town was finally evacuated, German troops moved against Fermont, the northernmost *gros ouvrage* of the Maginot Line. With firebombs, they turned the underground tunnel into a crematorium for more than a hundred French fortress troops. It was news of this that temporarily brought General Georges back to the view that Germany's main aim was to encircle the Maginot Line, and this caused him to detach troops to the area and refrain from ordering fortress troops to move to the Meuse Valley.

Though the Tenth Panzer Division continued to be occupied in fighting off the French around Sedan, General Guderian's other two divisions, the First and Second Panzer, were by nightfall on May 15 almost thirty miles west of Sedan.

Reinhardt's corps, once having broken through at Monthermé, also headed west. His Eighth Panzer Division went straight through Charleville-Mézières, most of whose residents had already packed up and left; the area was unguarded because so much of Corap's Ninth Army had been summoned north by commanders trying to stop the rush of German tanks across makeshift bridges at Houx and nearby. Reinhardt's Sixth Panzer Division, fanning out across open fields, was by the end of May 15 at Montcornet, on the Serre River forty miles due west of Sedan. His tanks overran infantry units from a new Sixth Army that Georges was trying to pull together under General Robert-Auguste Touchon.

Hoth's corps made comparable speed. When Rommel's division arrived at Flavion, a crossroads village ten miles west of Dinant, he happened on the French First Armored Division. Like the Third Armored, which had participated in the counteroffensive at Stonne and then retreated, the First Armored had been in existence only a few months. Its commander, General Marie-Germain-Christian Bruneau, had originally been ordered to reinforce Prioux at Gembloux, but en route he had received urgent orders to make an about-face and join up with the Ninth Army. Partly because of this change, most of his artillery was behind him. So were his fuel trucks. When Rommel's tanks came rolling down toward his division along the dirt roadway from Yvoir, Bruneau's Char B tanks were waiting to gas up. Rommel, of course, started firing at once.

Although Bruneau's heavy tanks were proof against Rommel's cannon, his light tanks were not. And his tank crews could not communicate with one another, since the batteries had run down in many of the tanks that had radios. Rommel's gunners soon found vulnerable spots even on the thickly armored Chars B. When Rommel saw tanks of his sister division, the Fifth Panzer, coming down the road, he broke off action and continued westward, while the Fifth Panzer finished the demolition of Bruneau's division. By morning, it had no more than twenty tanks left out of an original 170.

On May 16 and 17, the maps at French headquarters at Vincennes and La Ferté showed the Germans bounding west. It was now clear that the infantry action near the Maginot Line had been at most an effort to hold French fortress troops in place. It was also clear that the German tanks were not leading a procession toward Paris. At last the French could see the outline of the German sickle-cut plan. The capture of a German staff car, with a copy of Guderian's plans inside, provided confirmation: the Germans were headed toward the English Channel.

Though Billotte had been slow to give up the presumption that Belgium was the main theater and the Gembloux gap the likely site of decisive battles, he had taken seriously the setbacks of both the Ninth and Second Armies. Early on May 15, he had telephoned Georges to say that he intended to relieve Corap and to give Giraud command of the Ninth Army, which he would reinforce not only with the First Armored Division but also with some units from his own prior command, the Seventh Army. Georges's diary for that day records his telephone call to Corap, expressing almost tearful sorrow that, after forty-six years of friendship, he had to deliver such a message. By the end of the day, having begun to recognize where the crucial battles were taking place, Billotte decided to order a pullback in Belgium to the line of the Escaut, and told Blanchard at once. For some reason, he waited until 5 A.M. the next day before notifying Gort, and until 10 A.M. before telling the Belgians. Perhaps he wanted some rest before facing the indignation of King Leopold and Van Overstraeten.

During May 16–17, Rommel crossed from Belgium to France, moving against a line of light fortifications shown on German maps as an extension of the Maginot Line. He shot into the market town of Avesnes-sur-Helpe, blasting lines of light French tanks parked on each side of the main street. Then he made a successful night assault on one of the French forts and, by the early morning of May 17, was well west of the Sambre River. He wrote exultantly in his diary: "We were through the Maginot Line! It was hardly conceivable."[1]

During May 17, officers at French headquarters noticed with relief that they were no longer having constantly to reposition the markers for German

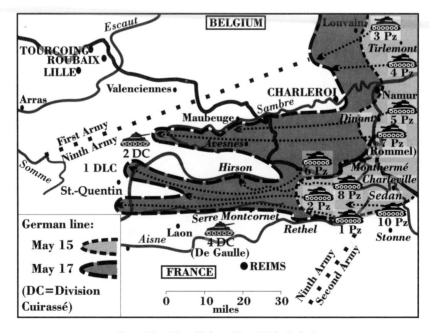

From May 15 to Hitler's First "Halt Order"

Panzer divisions on their maps. By the end of the day, the maps seemed to show that French forces were holding a line just behind the Sambre and Oise Rivers and a large rectangular salient east of them, which separated Rommel's Seventh Panzer Division from Kempf's Sixth.

The salient was nominally held by General Julien Martin's XI Corps, a remnant from Corap's Ninth Army composed of two Class A divisions. But the XI Corps had already begun to disintegrate, though the extent of its disarray was not yet known, even to Giraud, let alone Billotte, Georges, or Gamelin. Meanwhile, the newly formed French Fourth Armored Division, under Colonel Charles de Gaulle, attacked some of Guderian's tanks at Montcornet. Though de Gaulle eventually had to withdraw, he retained most of his force and left behind a number of German dead and wounded.

The apparent pause in the German offensive on May 17 lifted spirits on the Allied side. De Gaulle was sure that his action at Montcornet had turned the tide. Gamelin asked Vuillemin for air reconnaissance over the rear of the German Panzer units, and the results confirmed his suspicion: German supply lines were stretched thin, and masses of infantry were only beginning to form to straggle in behind them. Gamelin then suggested to Georges, and discussed with staff officers in Paris, a possible counteroffensive, aimed at pinching off and surrounding the Panzer formations. Billotte, thinking along similar lines, ordered Prioux to take position so as to strike across Rommel's rear and link up with Martin's infantry corps.

In fact, the Germans' decision to rein in their offensive was made at Montcornet but before de Gaulle's attack, not on account of it. Very early on May 17, a Fieseler Storch had brought General Kleist to the town. Kleist had ordered Guderian to meet him there at 7 A.M. Instead of offering Guderian congratulations, he told him in emphatic terms that the offensive was to stop immediately. Guderian protested. Kleist repeated his order. Guderian said, "I resign!" Kleist replied with the German equivalent of "O.K." and announced that General Rudolf Veiel, the commander of the Second Panzer Division, would henceforth command XIX Corps. Then Kleist reboarded his plane and returned to Germany.

The storm quickly abated, as storms around Guderian usually did. Kluge, commander of the Fourth Army, appealed to Rundstedt, who asked Kleist and Guderian to reconsider. They did, and Guderian resumed his former command. Yet, for the time being, the stop order remained in effect.

Guderian and his partisans blamed Kleist—holding him to be an old fogey who didn't understand armored warfare—for the puzzling order. Like other old fogeys, they thought, he worried about exposed flanks and tightly stretched supply lines. In Guderian's view, "Open flanks are the best things

Panzer troops can have; the longer they are, the better." The whole objective, he argued, was to get the enemy off balance. "So long as we ourselves remain in motion, so long must the enemy be in motion and is kept from getting into position to act."[2] Kleist, he thought, failed completely to comprehend this logic.

This was unjust. True, Kleist did worry about the exposed flanks of his armored group, but he trusted his field commanders, and Guderian especially. When he flew to Montcornet, he went not on his own but as an agent of General Rundstedt, who really was an old fogey, from Guderian's point of view, and who had become daily more concerned about how far ahead Kleist's armored formations were running of the infantry, artillery, and supply train that followed them. Late on May 15, an entry in the war diary of Rundstedt's Army Group said:

> For the first time there arises a question whether it may be necessary to halt the motorized forces before they cross the Oise. In this connection, the commander [Rundstedt] emphasizes that the enemy must not under any circumstances have even a localized success on the Aisne or—later—in the vicinity of Laon. It would affect the whole operation injuriously, for it would indicate a marked "interruption" in the tempo of our motorized forces.[3]

But Rundstedt, whose style as a commander was either to give subordinates free rein or precipitately to fire them, might not have given in to his fears and ordered a pause in the offensive had he not been prompted to do so from the very highest level—by Hitler himself. Rundstedt had had his staff prepare a stop order and had told his army commanders, including Kleist, that it might be issued. Then, apparently, he received a telephone call from Hitler's armed-forces high command directing him to issue the order.

Rundstedt's war diary does not record the telephone call, but it was remembered after the war by a number of officers at both ends—at the armed-forces high command and at Rundstedt's headquarters, now at Bastogne. And the Army Group A war diary does record Hitler's emphatic endorsement of the order. On May 17, indeed, he visited Bastogne, and

> underlined especially the significance that the south flank has, not only for the operations of the army as a whole but also politically and psychologically. Under no circumstances should there be at this

moment a counterattack from any location, for that could give fateful encouragement not only to the military but above all to the political leaders of our enemies. So, for the moment, what is decisive is not a rapid push to the Channel coast but, much more, the rapid establishment of completely reliable defense preparations on the Aisne, in the area of Laon, and, later, on the Somme.[4]

Though Hitler did not specify his concerns, it is not hard to infer what they were. He knew that the cape-and-sword maneuver had succeeded and that the bull was wounded, but he also knew that a wounded animal was not a dead animal. He had been confidently scornful of a France governed by Daladier and a Britain governed by Chamberlain, but he felt less assurance about a France under Reynaud and particularly a Britain under Churchill. He had remarked in October 1939, when Churchill was only First Lord of the Admiralty, that he would rather have Churchill out of the Cabinet than sink two British warships.[5] Moreover, Hitler believed that Mussolini was on the verge of declaring war on France and Britain, and he continued to attach high value to having Italy as an active ally.

Earlier, Hitler had been at odds with his generals because he wanted them—for political reasons—to take military risks. Now he wanted them—for political reasons—not to take military risks. General Halder was as outraged as he had been in the autumn of 1939, when Hitler bade him conduct an offensive that he regarded as potentially suicidal. His intelligence chief, Tippelskirch, disputed categorically the proposition that the broken French Ninth Army could threaten the German advance with a counterattack. And Halder's own diary says: "The Führer insists that the main threat is from the south. (I see no threat at all at present!). . . . The Führer is terribly nervous. Frightened by his own success, he is afraid to take any chance and so would rather pull the rein on us."[6]

During the night of May 17–18, in virtual defiance of Hitler, Halder induced General Brauchitsch, as commander in chief, to order a resumption of the offensive. Then, during the morning of May 18, Halder visited Hitler and made with uncustomary vehemence the argument that fear for the southern flank of Group Kleist was baseless. His contempt for Hitler's judgment was as ill-concealed as Beck's had been during the prewar crises over Czechoslovakia. His diary records Hitler's vexed acquiescence in what he had made a fait accompli: "The Führer unaccountably keeps worrying about the south flank. He rages and screams that we are on the best way to ruin the whole campaign and that we are leading up to a defeat. . . . This is the subject of a most unpleasant discussion." A 6 P.M. entry on the same day says: "The right thing is being done after all, but in an atmosphere of bad feeling."[7]

At daybreak on May 18, Rommel and the other Panzer commanders had resumed their drive toward the Channel. French staff officers at Vincennes, Montry, and La Ferté had to go back to moving markers on their maps. In Belgium, taking advantage of Billotte's withdrawal to the Escaut, Hoepner's XVI Corps, from Army Group B, drove through the Gembloux gap and was following the Sambre in the wake of Hoth's XXV Corps, led by Rommel's Seventh Panzers. By the end of day on May 20, the map markers showed German tanks less than fifty miles from Calais and Boulogne. The Second Panzer was at Abbeville, and a detachment of its motorized infantry had actually reached the sea at the mouth of the Somme; the First Panzer was not far behind, at Amiens. General Giraud, trying to show himself to his front-line troops, failed to find them but did find elements of the Sixth Panzer, who took him prisoner.

Despite this resumption of the German drive on May 18, General Gamelin continued to press Georges and Billotte for a counteroffensive aimed at cutting in behind the Panzer formations. On the morning of May 19, he was driven to La Ferté, where Doumenc and Vuillemin were already present, and urged that Billotte throw all his forces, British and Belgian and French, against the rear of Hoth's Panzer corps, and do so before Army Group B's Panzer corps penetrated far beyond the Gembloux gap. Meanwhile, Huntziger was to be ordered to pull together all his Second Army, including what remained of the armored, motorized, and infantry divisions sent him earlier as reinforcements, and aim for Charleville-Mézières. "It is all a question of hours," Gamelin said.[8]

This "suggestion" to General Georges was to be Gamelin's last. Though Reynaud had desisted from trying to fire Gamelin on May 10, he had not ceased wanting to do so. The brief halt in the German offensive on May 17 stimulated him to act: he summoned Weygand from the Levant.[9] After a long, dangerous flight, Weygand reached Paris late in the morning of May 19. Once he had visited headquarters at Vincennes and listened to an exposition of Gamelin's counteroffensive plan, he asked permission to visit Georges at La Ferté. He had already commented that Gamelin seemed not to be Reynaud's favorite—a polite way of telling Gamelin that he was about to be replaced, and that his own request for permission to go to La Ferté was pro forma. Not long afterward, from the Quai d'Orsay, Reynaud announced that Weygand would replace Gamelin as generalissimo and that he himself would trade places with Daladier, taking over the Ministry of Defense.

The old-line French military establishment was delighted. General Jamet, who remained chief of staff at the Ministry of Defense, had always thought Gamelin was "a pusher, a creature of politics. His name was no longer pronounced without doubling up the first syllable: Gagamelin. Weygand by contrast was of the pure blood, with the soul of Foch."[10]

Still, part of Gamelin's planned counteroffensive took place and, for a brief moment, held promise of success. Elements of the BEF moved through Arras and engaged the lead columns of Rommel's Seventh Panzer Division. The British Matilda was even more heavily armored than the French Char B, and the short-barrel 75 of a Panzer IV could only dent its 80-mm. side. As the Matildas kept moving forward, with infantry sheltered behind them, Rommel called in Stukas. As Guderian had done at Sedan, he tilted 88-mm. anti-aircraft guns to fire at ground level. With a direct hit,

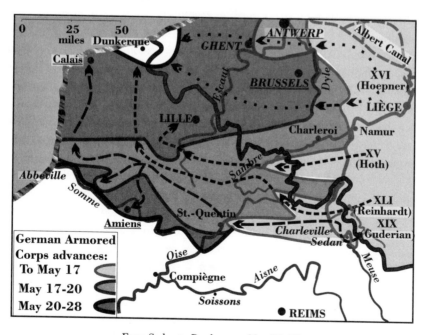

From Sedan to Dunkerque, May 17–28

one of these guns could knock out a Matilda. But the British advance nevertheless continued.

The German side experienced a little of what the French had experienced around Sedan. Infantrymen panicked. Artillerists deserted their guns. Only by showing himself in a staff car and going from unit to unit to shout orders and encouragement did Rommel stave off a rout. By the end of the day, his forces had succeeded in destroying a number of British tanks and compelling the British to pull back, but his losses had been heavy, and a number of his men remained trapped behind the British line. (One German infantry officer spent the night underneath a bed with two British officers snoring above him.) Though the actual Allied force had consisted of only four British battalions with divisional artillery and a small supporting contingent from one of Prioux's DLMs, Rommel believed himself to have fought off an attack by five Allied divisions. He so reported to Kluge and Rundstedt.[11]

This brief counteroffensive at Arras was almost the last twitch on the Allied side. Though General Weygand's own thoughts ran parallel to Gamelin's, he did not want to give commands until after he had consulted with field commanders. He did, however, send a message to General Prételat, who was in charge of all troops behind the Maginot Line, urging him to "turn General Huntziger toward a resolutely aggressive posture," and Prételat responded by assigning Huntziger some additional troops.[12] But Weygand, believing it necessary to confer in person with Billotte and the Belgian leaders, took an adventurous flight that ended him up at Ypres, near the western tip of Belgium, scene of some of the most grisly fighting of the Great War. Billotte was there to meet him, as were not only Leopold and Van Overstraeten but also a number of Belgian ministers (who claimed the king had tried to prevent their coming). The outcome was confused. As a Belgian military historian writes: "There was much talking; energetic and high-sounding phrases were uttered, but they could not take the place of clear and precise instructions."[13] Neither Gort nor Blanchard had arrived, but Billotte committed them to an offensive that either or both, if present, would have characterized as unrealistic. Leopold agreed to have Belgians fill in behind the BEF but not to take part in any offensive. After an even more hazardous journey, partly by sea, Weygand returned to Paris apparently under the illusion that something like Gamelin's two-pronged counteroffensive would soon occur. Billotte was in an automobile accident on his trip back to his headquarters; he went into a coma and, after two days, died. Therefore, everything went on hold until Blanchard took his place, while Prioux became commander of the First Army. By this time, almost no hope remained of mounting successful actions on the model of the Arras counteroffensive.

On May 19, General Gort had told Billotte that he planned to evacuate the BEF by sea. (The Royal Navy had already begun to assemble a fleet of transports.) He believed then that the French First Army had gone the way of the Ninth Army and that the BEF sector of Belgium was totally vulnerable. When he learned that he was wrong and that Blanchard's army remained largely intact, he went back to discussing combined action with France and Belgium: the counteroffensive at Arras indicated Britain's continued willingness to commit its troops to the common cause. Then and for a time afterward, Ironside championed what was called "the Weygand plan." So did Churchill, who found Weygand "brisk, buoyant, incisive." Yet all of Gort's movement orders carried the BEF toward Dunkerque, the projected base for evacuation.

By May 23, the British chiefs of staff agreed formally that the war in France had to be considered lost. Indeed, they advised the government that, without an all-out commitment from the United States to support the Allies with economic aid, "we do not think we could continue the war with any chance of success."[14] By May 26, Churchill had decided to order that evacuation proceed. Gort disengaged the BEF from what remained of a front at Arras—which left naked the left flank of Prioux's First Army. Even with this abrupt action, and with orders that his force proceed to the port as fast as was safely possible, Gort and Ironside anticipated that no more than thirty thousand men would be able to escape from France and that nearly all their equipment would remain behind.

Again, however, this time to their amazement, Allied staff officers saw the markers on their maps staying in place. The reason, though they did not know it, was exactly the same as on May 17: Hitler had once more ordered that the Panzer divisions stop moving forward.

This time, it is more clear that the order originated with General Rundstedt. He took alarm from the British counteroffensive at Arras, especially given Rommel's estimate that it involved five divisions. Sodenstern, his chief of staff, feared exactly the kind of maneuver Gamelin and Weygand had outlined—an attack on the rear of the Panzer formations "from north and south." And Kleist cautioned both Kluge and Rundstedt that his divisions had been on the move for two weeks and that half his tanks were out of commission. "If the enemy attacks in great strength," he wrote, "I have to observe that the Panzer divisions are little equipped for defense." Kluge suggested that the Panzer commanders be told to let supporting forces catch up before they moved forward. During the night of May 23–24, Rundstedt issued such a "catch-up" order.

General Halder, who was in constant touch with Tippelskirch and Liss, saw no reason to believe the Allies had the capability for a serious counteroffensive any longer. As early as May 21, Foreign Armies West had alerted him that the British intended to attempt evacuation via Dunkerque.[15] Their maps showed Guderian's First Panzer, with a supporting Hitler Life Guard regiment, only ten miles from the port, and Reinhardt's entire Panzer corps not much farther away. So he reacted as angrily to the new stop order as he had to that of May 17. He exclaimed in his diary: "The left wing, consisting of armored and motorized forces, which has no enemy in front of it, will be stopped dead in its tracks—on direct orders from the Führer!"

When Hoepner's corps began moving from Belgium toward France, Halder had effected a reorganization, designating all the Panzer formations and associated motorized infantry as the "Schnelle Truppen"—Fast Forces. He had put the new organization under Kluge, commander of the Fourth Army. Seeing Rundstedt's "catch-up" order, he decided that the quickest remedy was to transfer the Fast Forces from Rundstedt's command to

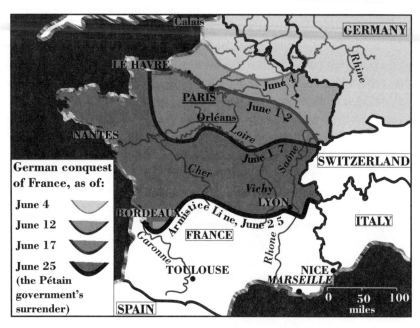

The Last Weeks of the Third Republic

Bock's, for he knew that Bock had been critical of the earlier stop order and, if given the Fast Forces, would want to achieve with them something rivaling what Rundstedt had achieved.

Halder's attempted finesse failed. Rundstedt objected and complained to Hitler. Hitler declared that he shared Rundstedt's concerns "fully and completely," and formally issued a new stop order. In addition, he made Halder the victim of his own ruse: he put the Fast Forces firmly back under Rundstedt's control but directed that Bock's Army Group B have responsibility for dealing with Dunkerque. This meant that the assignment went to divisions of foot soldiers, most of whom were at least fifty miles away, with the remaining elements of the Belgian army and the French Seventh Army in their path.

Why Hitler issued this stop order remains almost as puzzling as why, eighteen months later, after the Japanese bombed Pearl Harbor in December 1941, he chose to declare war on the United States. He had heard Göring boast that the Luftwaffe could take care of the BEF all by itself, and he may have wanted to give Göring an opportunity to make good on this boast. Or, conversely, he or Göring or both may have had some back-of-the-mind thought about sparing the BEF so as to encourage the British to dump Churchill and make peace. Most likely, as military historian Karl-Heinz Frieser argues, Hitler wanted primarily to assert his dominance over the army. Halder had said during the winter to a couple of the officers plotting to get rid of the Führer that they should hope the army had a big victory in the West, for then the generals might be able to assert themselves against Hitler. Very likely, the same thought occurred to Hitler himself. He already had the propaganda apparatus working to describe the German victory in the West as *his* victory, not the army's. A message broadcast to all German troops, for example, said: "Behind the battle of annihilation of May 1940 stands in lone greatness the name of the Führer."[16]

In any case, the stop order worked greatly to the benefit of the Allies. As of May 28, the Royal Navy had been able to evacuate from Dunkerque fewer than 10,000 men. With the grace period resulting from Hitler's stop order, the BEF completed beach work that made it possible to remove almost 50,000 more men on May 29 and increasing numbers thereafter. All told, almost 340,000 men (123,000 of them French) and more than 85,000 vehicles safely reached ships or boats that transported them to the British Isles.

When summoning Weygand from the Levant and naming him to succeed Gamelin, Reynaud had also brought Marshal Pétain into the government as deputy premier. Reynaud talked passionately of France's fighting Germany to the death. So did Weygand, for a time. But along with the maps that showed more and more of France in German hands, the departure of British forces and King Leopold's announcement on May 28 that Belgium was surrendering made their rhetoric seem unrealistic.

French divisions continued to fight, often valiantly, but the retreat continued. Marc Bloch remembers spending an hour with Blanchard at the Army Group headquarters he had set up near Lille. "During all that time, he sat in tragic immobility, saying nothing, doing nothing, but just gazing at the map spread on the table between us, as though hoping to find on it the decision which he was incapable of taking."[17] The government moved from Paris to Tours to Bordeaux. Reynaud's cabinet debated endlessly the question of whether to leave France, perhaps for North Africa. Several of Reynaud's advisers, including his chief of cabinet, Paul Baudouin, and his mistress, Hélène des Portes, urged him to seek an armistice with the Germans. He became increasingly distraught. On June 14, he sent a message to President Roosevelt saying that France could not continue to fight unless the United States declared an intention to enter the war "in the very near future." After Roosevelt predictably replied in the negative, Reynaud resigned. Pétain became prime minister.

Pétain was known as a conservative, but better known as a hero of the Great War. He had been often mentioned as a possible strongman. Even among those who thought they knew him, few were aware how much he detested the Third Republic and secular liberalism in all its forms. Though France's defeat on the battlefield dismayed him, he saw it both as proof of the "moral weakness" of the Third Republic and as offering an opportunity to purge the nation's political and social system. Discouraging discussion in the cabinet of possibly carrying on the war from North Africa, he inquired cautiously what Germany's terms for peace would be. Like German leaders at the end of the Great War, he ended up accepting a *Diktat*. The terms set by Hitler were incorporated in a document presented to a French delegation at the exact spot where a comparable document had been presented to a German delegation in November 1918—in a railroad car at Compiègne.[18] One of the signers for France was General Huntziger.

Not long after, German forces paraded victoriously on the Champs-Élysées, while Hitler watched approvingly. He had always wanted to see

Paris, he said, and he took time to visit a few tourist sites, then returned to Berlin. He said to Captain Engel that he now understood why so many artists loved the city.[19] Perhaps if he had gone there instead of Vienna when he aspired to be an artist, this whole story would never have occurred.

CONCLUSION: WHY? AND WHAT CAN BE LEARNED?

France capitulated in 1940 because its armies were defeated in battle. Many writers on the fall of France do not accept this simple-seeming assertion, for they portray France's defeats on the battlefield as the last gasps by a nation already doomed. I think such an interpretation is wrong. Perhaps if things had been different in the "hollow years," France's capitulation might not have been so abrupt, or more French leaders might have chosen to continue to fight the war from a French base in North Africa, or fewer might have toadied to their Nazi conquerors. But, absent defeats in battle in May 1940, France was in no more danger of moral collapse than Britain, it seems to me, and in less danger than Germany.

In the battles on the Meuse on May 13–14, it is true, a number of French soldiers panicked and ran. But on occasion, German soldiers also panicked. The elite infantry attached to Rommel's Seventh Panzer Division almost did so before the Houx crossing and actually did so at Arras.[1] Yet panic was rare in the German armies on the Western front in the spring of 1940, whereas it became common in the French Ninth and Second Armies. The reason was that these two French armies contained the dross of French soldiery and were carelessly commanded from army level on down. German armies in Army Group C ("Leeb's museum"), which were similarly composed though better led, might well have behaved similarly if French mechanized and armored divisions had come storming into their sector of the front. What happened in the battles around Houx, Monthermé, and Sedan in mid-May 1940 was indicative of the condition of particular French military units, not of the French national soul.

In many battles of that month, French soldiers fought well and still lost. One reason was that the German soldiers had better field commanders. Giraud, Prioux, and de Gaulle and Gort's corps commanders, General Sir John Dill and General Sir Alan Brooke, were probably the equal of most German generals, but none was a match for Guderian or Rommel. At the other end of the spectrum, the German army—thinned because of Versailles restraints—had fewer generals like Désiré-Louis Sivot, commander of XLII Corps (Class B infantry), described by a superior as "always a little behind time and . . . desperately slow of mind."[2]

In fast-moving battles, German units had the advantage of good communications. True, their radio and field-telephone transmissions could be intercepted and deciphered, but usually too late to make a difference.[3] French units suffered because security consciousness limited their use of radios and forced them to depend on couriers, who were slower. The list of such tactical-level differences could go on and on, with most items being plusses for the Germans and minuses for the French.

At a higher level, the German army may have had more up-to-date military doctrine. This is a matter of dispute, particularly since Guderian's doctrine about tank warfare was neither fully understood nor fully approved by his commanders, and Rommel's idiosyncratic doctrine was at odds with it. Still, German generals, even German colonels and majors, certainly felt freer to try new approaches and tactics than did their counterparts in the French army or the BEF.[4]

France was handicapped by having been the victor in the Great War. Like the United States entering the Vietnam War or the "post–Cold War world," or like an extremely profitable corporation in the 1980s such as General Motors or IBM, France had an almost religious faith in the principles that it believed to have been keys to its past success. But in application, many of these principles proved unsuitable to conditions of 1939–40. As one minor example, the French army had learned in the Great War to rotate companies and battalions assigned to the front lines, which helped to offset the demoralizing effects of long service in the trenches. Practiced by the infantry divisions defending Sedan in May 1940, however, it resulted in troops and their commanders not knowing who was supposed to be to their right or left.

It is also certainly the case that Germany benefited from fighting alone as Germany, whereas France fought in an alliance, in which the whole was often a great deal less than the sum of the parts. France and Britain might well have been better off had Belgium been an ally of Germany. (Italy's declaration of war on France and Britain on June 10, 1940, thus becoming Germany's ally, was not to work to Germany's advantage. Churchill was alleged to have said spitefully, "It's only fair. They were on our side in the last war.") In air operations, Germany and the Allied powers were closely matched, but one major liability on the Allied side was that the French air force and RAF had to cooperate and often didn't. Individual French and British flying units did well. Between May 10 and May 15, one French fighter squadron downed fifteen German planes with no losses of its own. But neither French nor British commanders relished assigning fighters to escort bombers, and commanders of bomber squadrons dodged or passed the buck for ground-support missions of which they disapproved in principle, often citing lack of fighter cover as a reason.[5]

These and many other factors, some as technical as the turning radius in tank turrets, help to explain why German forces had an edge in particular battles. Indeed, a case can be made that French and British forces won battles only when they had a wide superiority over the enemy. When Prioux's light mechanized divisions turned back Hoepner's Panzer divisions at Hannut, they had 415 heavy tanks (Somuas and Hotchkiss H-39s) against only 125 Panzer IIIs and IVs. At Arras, when the British had forty tanks and were attacking motorized infantry with none, they were the most successful.[6]

In May 1940, then, France and its allies may have been destined to do less well on the battlefield than would have been predicted on the basis of their advantages in numbers and quality of equipment. But this argument is not so easy to make for September 1939, when Germany lacked many of the soldiers and much of the equipment it would have by the spring of 1940. It is still less easy to make for September 1938, when Germany had almost no divisions as well trained or well outfitted as those of Czechoslovakia, let alone of France.[7]

But even if France was likely to lose engagements in May–June 1940, it was not doomed to lose the entire war, and certainly not in a matter of weeks. (Again, my choice of words implies a disputable interpretation. Many people prefer de Gaulle's phrase "the *Battle* of France" as signifying that the actions of May 1940 were merely an episode in a war that France eventually won. I think it is more accurate to say that France lost a war in 1940, then later took part in another war that ended differently.)

The scale and suddenness of Germany's victory has to be explained primarily, I believe, as a result of the surprise achieved under the final version of Plan Yellow. If German forces had concentrated their attack across the Belgian plain, as they would have done had Hitler insisted on giving a "go" signal in January 1940 or earlier, they might well have made inroads against the Allied armies under Georges and Billotte. But first-line German units would have been up against first-line Allied units. So the most likely outcome would have been a duel of forces in fixed positions not unlike that of the Great War, and, though both France and Germany would have had trouble sustaining such a war, Germany would probably have faced more difficulties sooner, not only because of resource shortages, but because of weaker morale among its civilian population and military and political elites.

By concentrating their main attack in the Ardennes and catching French forces unaware, the German commanders gained a temporary three-to-two advantage in numbers of divisions and an even greater advantage in tanks; moreover, they were pitting their very best units against units on the French side, many of which were mediocre. It is less a wonder that the Germans broke through at Houx, Monthermé, and Sedan than that their successes were (in the phrase coined by the Duke of Wellington to describe his victory over Napoleon at Waterloo) damned close-run things. Guderian, Rommel, and the other German generals termed their accomplishments miraculous, or "hardly conceivable," because they could scarcely credit the good luck that left their pontoon bridges intact despite Allied bombing and shelling, or the fact that, as at Stonne, French commanders failed to press an advantage when the outcome of the whole campaign seemed at issue.

After Group Kleist broke across the Meuse River and began racing westward, there remained possibilities for the Allies to regroup, launch a counteroffensive, and keep the war going. Defeat for France was not inevitable by the fifth day of the German offensive or even the tenth. As of May 19, when Prime Minister Reynaud replaced Gamelin with Weygand, the Allies still had, on paper, forces enough for a counteroffensive, and the best Allied units remained eager to fight. On May 20, de Lattre de Tassigny wrote his wife that his Fourteenth Infantry Division "shows magnificent endurance and ardor."[8] And though he thought it unlikely, Tippelskirch calculated for Halder that the Allies had thirty, possibly thirty-two divisions to throw into a counteroffensive.[9] The halt orders that interrupted the German armored offensive on May 17–18 and again on May 24–26 were issued in part because General Rundstedt, unlike Tippelskirch, feared the Allies would do what they seemed capable of doing.[10] By May 28, with Dunkerque and Belgium's capitulation, France's defeat probably had become inevitable—but not much sooner.

It is very hard to compose a scenario that would end with Germany so quickly victorious if the Allies had anticipated—even as one possibility among several—a major fast-moving German offensive through the Ardennes. It is even hard to compose such a scenario if Gamelin, Georges, and other Allied commanders had recognized what the Germans were doing soon after the Ardennes offensive commenced. Of possible "what if?" games, one of the most engaging starts by imagining that Generals Blanchard, Billotte, Georges, and Gamelin on May 11 accept General Prioux's recommendation to stop the Allied advance into Belgium on the line of the Escaut River. Another starts if one imagines Allied commanders noticing the horrendous traffic jams in Luxembourg and southern Belgium on May 11 or 12 and ordering in squadrons of bombers.

Germany's strange victory of 1940 traces back, above all, to the German general staff's having been right in presuming that the French high command would (a) dispatch nearly all first-line forces to Belgium, (b) not recognize for several days that this had been a mistake, and (c) have great difficulty adjusting to and coping with the newly discovered reality. And note that the surprise Germany achieved in 1940 differed in its duration from the surprises at Operation Barbarossa and Pearl Harbor. The Soviet Union and the United States knew immediately that they had been fooled. French and British leaders needed *four* days to discover it.

To end the story, here is a summary of some conclusions and some possible lessons. Many of the conclusions concur with those in other works about the Battle of France, while others do not. Several involve conjecture about what might have happened if one condition or another had been different. I have already indulged in such conjecture. Though many historians raise eyebrows at counterfactual speculation, I think it integral to any historical reconstruction. When a historian of the French Revolution describes the system of taxation under the *ancien régime,* or a historian of the American Civil War describes African-American slavery, he or she implies that, absent those phenomena, the Revolution or the Civil War would not have occurred how and when it did. I simply choose here to say explicitly that, if condition X had not obtained, the actual events would probably not have gone as they did, and condition Y seems to me the more likely of possible alternative outcomes.

One obvious conclusion to draw is that Hitler understood the French and British governments better than those governments understood his. He foresaw that they would not resort to war to oppose Germany's expansion at the expense of Austria and Czechoslovakia, despite the resultant injury to their interests and despite their quantitative military superiority. The reasons for his better understanding included the fact that he focused on political leaders and public opinion rather than on apparent national interests or capabilities; and the companion fact that his assessments of those governments were not negotiated assessments. He would explicitly state not only his predictions regarding France and Britain but the reasoning behind them, then fight against and overcome competing assessments, such as those of Beck and Weizsäcker.

The most remarkable characteristic of decision-making in Nazi Germany from 1937 to 1940 was that its starting point was usually an exposition by Hitler of what he believed to be going on, why he thought it was important, and what he proposed to do about it. He did not always disclose every consideration in his mind. Discussing Czechoslovakia with military men and diplomats, for example, he did not mention pressure of time due to uncertainty about how long he could depend on Konrad Henlein, leader of the Germans in Czechoslovakia's Sudetenland. But as a rule, he was extraordinarily open in acknowledging his priorities and stating his assumptions. Recall Sir John Wheeler-Bennett's comment: "Except in cases where he had pledged his word, Hitler always meant what he said."[11] This then opened the possibility for counterargumentation.

A second conclusion is that understanding of Hitler's aims and policies was clouded in Paris, London, and other Western capitals by a general inability to believe that any national leader might actually *want* another Great War; a desire and need to push away the very possibility of such a war, given the intensity of public antipathy to the prospect; and a need to negotiate, within pluralistic parliamentary systems, agreed appreciations concerning Germany and other nations.

Important figures in the French government rarely knew what Prime

Minister Daladier believed or intended to do until, at the last moment, he would explain why he had only one alternative. For example, this was how he disclosed to his cabinet in September 1938 his conclusion that France had to follow Britain and sacrifice Czechoslovakia, by which time, for practical purposes, it was too late for anyone to question the basic rationale—to ask whether he was right that Britain would refuse to follow France into a war, or whether the air-power balance really was as unfavorable as he said, or, if so, whether that made much difference. (General Gamelin did not think so.) The same was true in 1939, in the meandering meetings that led to France's following Britain into war with little discussion of why the Allies were supposed to back Poland when they had no intention of giving Poland serious assistance. And, in the winter of 1939–40, Daladier surprised almost all his colleagues and advisers by bringing forth his scheme for going to war with the Soviet Union as well as with Germany.

Decision-makers in France and Britain were consistently *reticent*: they hoarded information and opinions. Partly because they did not expose their presumptions and thus invite challenge, they adopted and adhered to the suppositions about reality that suited their individual *convenience*—which enabled them to believe that they had to do what they needed to do in order either to remain in office or to accomplish what they wanted to accomplish.[12] Thus, Daladier in 1938 appropriated Vuillemin's perception that the air-power balance was badly tilted against France and that this necessarily prevented France from acting militarily against Germany. In 1939, with no better evidence, he was prepared to believe the contrary when it appeared that the French public would not tolerate further concessions to Hitler. In the winter of 1939–40, he and Chamberlain both seized upon and credited Thyssen's testimony that Germany could be defeated just by cutting off German imports of iron ore from Sweden. They were prepared to embrace almost any belief supporting a supposition that the war could be won without throwing soldiers into battles like those of the Great War.

Third, Hitler eventually erred. He supposed that when Germany attacked Poland, the Western powers would once again shrink from war. He made this miscalculation because, though he paid close attention to political trends in France and Britain, he assumed that past behavior provided the best index to political leaders' future behavior, and he attached too much weight to foreign press commentary that suited his own wishes. As a result, he missed perceiving a strong change in French and British public opinion, which, by mid-1939, was crying "Enough!" so loudly that neither Daladier nor Chamberlain could resist.

Fourth, if the Western powers had chosen to do so, they could probably have defeated Germany militarily not only in 1938, when Czechoslovakia would have been an ally, but in 1939, during Germany's four-week war in Poland. At that time, German forces in the West were so weak that French armies alone, though perhaps needing British air support, could have seized the Ruhr Valley industrial basin and, as a result, forced Germany either to capitulate or to wage a long, losing war of attrition.

Fifth, France did not take the offensive against Germany in 1939 because French leaders wanted to be sure that, if lives were lost in battle, some would be British, because French and British leaders hoped an economic blockade would force Germany's surrender without the necessity for bloody battles, and, crucially, because French and British leaders were sure of Allied military superiority and confident of their ultimate victory—whether through strangulation of the German economy or through battles precipitated by a desperate Germany. The whole story behind Germany's surprise success from 1938 through 1940 is understandable only if one recognizes that, until that awful revelatory night of May 14–15, 1940, no French or British leader—*not one*—suspected for a moment that France might decisively lose a war.

A sixth point to remember is that, in September 1939, when Hitler demanded of his officers that they plan an immediate offensive against France, his generals thought it insane. They debated the possibility of a coup but concluded that Hitler was too popular and that their own soldiers would rebel.

Seventh, with Hitler continually setting dates for an attack on France, then postponing action, the German general staff developed versions of a plan, Plan Yellow, all of which called for concentrated strikes across the Belgian plain. In January 1940, Hitler was on the verge of launching such an offensive when bad weather closed in and, coincidentally, the Allies obtained portions of the plan as a result of the forced landing of a German plane at Mechelen-sur-Meuse in Belgium. If the offensive had commenced then or earlier, with its spearheads all in Belgium or the Netherlands, German forces would have run against first-line French and British forces which—though German units might have fought better than French or British units—would probably have checked them, even thrown them back, simply because they had more and better tanks and a huge advantage in artillery and munitions.

Then, during the winter of 1939–40, the German general staff came up with a daring—indeed, reckless—plan for feigning an attack on Belgium and the Netherlands while actually centering an offensive in the Ardennes Forest with the goal of having German tank divisions cut a swathe from the Meuse River to the coast of the English Channel. The concept had many authors, including Generals Guderian, Manstein, Rundstedt, and Halder and Hitler himself. (This final version of Plan Yellow is commonly called the Manstein Plan because Manstein and his friends assiduously advertised his claim to authorship. In fact, Manstein's contribution was no more important than that of many others.) Absolutely key to its development was the work of General Tippelskirch, chief of army intelligence, and Lieutenant Colonel Liss and his associates in Tippelskirch's foreign-armies branch. With certification from Tippelskirch, an experienced troop commander, Liss played the Allied generalissimo in war games, testing the concept of an offensive with its central spearhead in the Ardennes. Having for many years studied French and British training and doctrine, Liss had come to a view similar to that articulated by Hitler, namely that "to operate and to act quickly . . . does not come easily either to the systematic French or to the ponderous English." In the war games, Liss acted according to his understanding of French and British patterns and routines, making little provision for the possibility of surprise and responding slowly when actually surprised.[13] Trusting Liss's judgment, and Tippelskirch's, regarding the probable behavior of French and British commanders, Halder, the chief of staff, began to think that an Ardennes offensive might possibly succeed. Though he and all other German generals continued to the last moment to consider the chances of defeat greater than the chances of success, he developed the plan and put it into effect in May 1940. It is hard to imagine his having done so without the encouragement given by his intelligence analysts' estimates of likely French and British behavior. Intelligence analysis was an integral part of German operational planning: without it, the odds against Germany's adopting anything like the final version of Plan Yellow would have been at least two to one.

Eighth, the French high command developed the Dyle-Breda Plan partly for military reasons but even more for political ones. Their military logic rested on the premise that Germany's best strategy would involve a drive across the Belgian plain—which remained valid until the development of the final version of Plan Yellow. The political logic arose from the French government's need to assure Britain that France took seriously the danger of Germany's acquiring bomber bases in the Netherlands and the Meuse/Maas estuary, and also to hearten the Belgian and Dutch governments. Because it would have been so difficult politically to back away from the plan, its military premise became an article of faith, not to be re-examined. Also, the nine-month period that saw little active fighting (the *drôle de guerre*, "bore war," "phoney war," or *Sitzkrieg*) ignited demands for Allied offensives somewhere other than the Western front, with strong movements in Paris and London in favor of opening fronts in Scandinavia or the Balkans, perhaps even starting a new war with the then neutral but German-leaning Soviet Union. General Gamelin could not compromise the Dyle-Breda Plan without risk that the Western front would be denuded of forces because of adventures undertaken elsewhere.

Ninth, although the intelligence *sources* of the French Deuxième Bureau and even of the British Secret Service were better than those of any part of Germany's fractionated intelligence community, intelligence *analysis* in France and Britain had much less connection than in Germany with either planning or decision-making. French and British intelligence services delivered data to the desks of operations officers much as if dropping off a daily newspaper or a strip of ticker tape. The planners' presumptions about Germany, about allies, and about prospective allies such as Belgium were undoubtedly influenced by bits of information passed on by the intelligence services, but, in contrast to Germany at the general-staff level, intelligence officers were not invited to comment on those presumptions. They were isolated, partly by their own choice, but with the result that, if they had been invited to comment, they would have been unable to identify weak points (as, for example, an expectation that Germany would stick with the plan for a strike through central Belgium despite its having been betrayed by the Mechelen documents).

Allied intelligence services performed abominably, even in carrying out the limited function of delivering data to planners and commanders. They continued into wartime the peacetime, budget-driven practice of overestimating the numbers of German troops, guns, tanks, and aircraft. (Persistent later claims by Deuxième Bureau veterans to have warned of the German offensive but been ignored find no confirmation in contemporaneous evidence—*none*.) The daily and weekly intelligence reports delivered to French and British senior officers offered largely unevaluated items of information supporting almost any imaginable hypothesis about Germany's intentions. (An oft-cited intelligence report from Switzerland predicting a German attack in early May through the Ardennes turns out to have been forwarded to Paris earmarked as German disinformation, which it probably was.) There were fewer items suggesting an Ardennes offensive than ones suggesting an offensive through Switzerland or into southeastern Europe.

Worse, Allied intelligence services failed even to notice, let alone to high-light, patterns in German behavior peculiarly consistent with the hypothesis of an attack through the Ardennes, notably their special concentrations of supplies and communications equipment on the border with Luxembourg and their persistent aerial reconnaissance over an area centering in Sedan and Charleville-Mézières. The intelligence failures symbolized by Pearl Harbor and Barbarossa pale by comparison.

In the end, of course, the men at the top of the French and British governments were responsible for not demanding better of their intelligence services. The fact that Germany could achieve such a complete surprise is, more than anything else, evidence that in Germany, in 1937–40, even with Hitler as leader, the processes of executive judgment worked better than in France or Britain. Or, to put it the other way around, however much more civilized their judgments of values and objectives, leaders in France and Britain exhibited much less common sense in appraising their circumstances and deciding what to do.

This is obviously not to say that the Germans showed greater wisdom—far from it. The basic values that governed German choices were Hitler's—mad cravings to gain land and glory, to exterminate Jews, to enjoy a killing war. But neither do I mean to say only that Germany succeeded while France failed. German *processes* of executive judgment—the ways in which the German government decided how to act—worked better than did those in the French and British governments, a truth Marc Bloch touched on when he commented in *Strange Defeat* that the German victory had been a "triumph of intellect" and observed in a letter to his sometime collaborator, Lucien Febvre, that the victory owed much to Hitler's "methodical opportunism."[14]

At any time or place, executive judgment involves answering three sets of questions: "What is going on?"; "So what?" (or "What difference does it make?"); and "What is to be done?" The better the process of executive judgment, the more it involves asking the questions again and again, not in set order, and testing the results until one finds a satisfactory answer to the third question—what to do (which may be, of course, to do nothing).[15]

The tests for "what is going on" include distinguishing what is actually known from what is presumed to be true, then probing the strength and reliability of the presumptions. The tests for action choices also have additional questions: "Exactly what is to be done?" ("*What* to do?" becomes "What to *do*?") "How will success or failure be recognizable?" "Why is the particular action under consideration likely to lead to success so conceived?" In other words, "What is the theory of the case?"

In the German government in 1937–40, these questions were asked, re-asked, and re-asked, but in the French and British governments they were hardly asked at all. French and British political and military leaders— Churchill not excepted—answered for themselves the question, "What is going on?" The almost inevitable answer was based on those pieces of information most consistent with their preconceptions. They did not test or even identify critical presumptions. They believed what they needed to believe in order to do what they thought either desirable or expedient. General Bock had it right when, after learning that Group Kleist had crossed the Meuse River, he wrote in his war diary: "The French seem really to have lost all common sense! Otherwise they could and would have stopped us."[16]

Even with their failures in executive judgment, French and British leaders might have been able to halt or at least check the German offensive had it not been for extraordinary, almost incredible good luck on the German side and bad luck on theirs. Of course, it is in some degree true that human beings make their own luck. The great golfer Jack Nicklaus once observed that, the more he practiced, the luckier he became. But the underlying principle accounts for only part of what befell German and French commanders in May 1940. At numerous moments during the critical first days of the German offensive, as German commanders noted either at the time or in retrospect, a very slight difference could have caused a particular engagement to become a defeat rather than a victory. Even after large numbers of German tanks had crossed the Meuse, the Allies might have had a chance of conducting an effective counteroffensive. General Prioux, no mean judge, was confident of its success even as of May 19.[17] But by that time, Belgian refugees clogged the roads that would have been needed for redeploying motorized and mechanized forces, and French transport services, which had performed efficiently in moving troops into Belgium, were disoriented because they had no detailed plans for moving them out.[18] In any case, if there had been a chance of success, it was lost when Prime Minister Reynaud chose just that moment to substitute General Weygand for General Gamelin, because Weygand needed two days to settle in before proceeding with an operation of which Gamelin had said, "It is all a question of hours."

The defeat of France by Germany in May–June 1940 was not, then, foreordained. As late as mid-May, events could have turned in such a way that later historians would have been explaining why Germany launched an offensive that failed. Even though the "hollow years," deficiencies in French military doctrine, training, and communications, and sclerosis in the military establishment all contributed to the magnitude of France's collapse after its defeats in battle, none of these factors made the defeats inevitable. Had German armies suffered serious setbacks, as could easily have happened, Nazi Germany might have imploded. If so, historians would cite as causes the "frightening demoralization" among the German populace (noted by one representative of Fascist Italy), the Wehrmacht's shortcomings in training and equipment, and a combination of recklessness and pessimism on the part of German generals.[19]

In sum, the essential thread in the story of Germany's victory over France hangs on the imaginativeness of German war planning and the corresponding lack of imaginativeness on the Allied side. Hitler and his generals perceived that the weakness of their otherwise powerful enemies resided in habits and routines that made their reaction times slow. They developed a plan that capitalized on this weakness. French and British leaders made no effort to understand how or why German thinking might differ from theirs. They neglected to prepare for the possibility of surprise, and, as German analysts and planners predicted, they could not react promptly once events began to be at odds with expectations. Mercifully for humankind, the German advantage did not persist. After the "miracle" in France, Hitler became so sure of his own genius that he ceased to test his judgments against those of others, and his generals virtually ceased to challenge him. His conduct of the Battle of Britain, his invasion of the Soviet Union, and his subsequent declaration of war on the United States were, to say the least, ill-considered. But up through the victory over France in 1940, the story contrasts the exercise on the German side of some common sense and the failure on the Allied side to exercise any common sense.

If these are the elements of the story, what are its morals? All great stories teach lessons. All too often, unfortunately, lessons taken from history are put in the form of precepts. (Don't appease dictators. Don't get into Vietnam-like wars.) But much more useful are lessons that take the form of questions or suggestions. (This happened once. Is there a chance that something of the sort might happen again? If not, why not?)[20] Hence I offer the following propositions:

The best assessments of other governments may be those made by political leaders rather than by officials or supposed experts who are factually more knowledgeable. The actions of the other governments, after all, result from decisions by its political leaders, and though they doubtless reflect calculations about national interest and national capabilities, they have to be decisions that will be accepted by the individuals or groups from whom the political leaders derive their authority to make decisions. This may be a mass public, as in Hitler's case. It may be factional leaders in political parties and in Parliament, as with Daladier. It may be factions within one party, as was true for Chamberlain. It may be a complex network of elected representatives and special interests, as for any president of the United States. It may be a cloistered minority, such as that surviving Stalin's purges. Politicians within one system may fail completely to comprehend those within another system. Chamberlain could assess Hitler as a man with whom one could do business; Roosevelt and, for a time, his successor, Harry Truman, could view Stalin as good old "Uncle Joe." Potentially, though, politicians have special capacities for understanding other politicians.

In all modern nations, career government officers concerned with foreign affairs deplore the tendency of presidents or ministers to arrive at their own assessments of foreign governments, heavily influenced as they are by personal interaction with foreign leaders. (Though Cadogan was hardly a typical careerist, his attitude toward politicians was not unique. "Silly bladders!" he wrote of them in his diary. "Self-advertising, irresponsible nincompoops . . . They embody everything that my training has taught me to eschew—ambition, prejudice, dishonesty, self-seeking, light-hearted irresponsibility, black-hearted mendacity."[21]) Journalists and scholars with claims to expertise join in deprecating politicians' judging other governments for themselves. But Hitler's comparative success in anticipating how France and Britain would behave, and Daladier's insight, as early as April 1938, that Hitler's ambitions were greater than Napoleon's, may serve as reminders that politicians are not always mistaken when guided by their own tacit knowledge of how politicians as a breed think and act.[22]

Politicians, officials, and foreign-area experts all run a risk of mistakenly supposing that what another government did in the past is a good indication of what it will do in the future. Sometimes it is, but sometimes it is not. Politicians may be the least vulnerable to surprise if a change in behavior by another government accompanies a change in political leadership, for they understand that national interests are in some sense social constructions defined by political leaders according in part to their domestic political needs. (In peacetime, this is even more true of military capabilities, which are second-order constructions, imagined to be comparatively small or large depending on the imagined force-levels of potential enemies. In wartime, of course, capabilities become subject to the test of battle.) But they, too, can be taken by surprise if the political leadership in another nation remains the same while the attitudes or opinions among the constituencies to which they answer significantly change. Hitler's not expecting the French and British declarations of war in September 1939 is an illustration. This suggests the possible usefulness—even for politicians, let alone for officials or experts—of asking frequently whether the political dynamics of yesterday are working in the same way today.[23]

Past success can easily create overconfidence, too. Though this point is so obvious as to be banal, it deserves inclusion here because history offers few more stark examples than that of France in 1940. As an American writing in the decade of the Gulf War and the Kosovo affair, I cannot resist noting that French leaders and the French public believed before May 1940 that France, as a result of having learned the lessons of the Great War, had mastered the keys to victory in any future war. Advanced technology, manifest in the Maginot Line and the Somua and Char B tank, would ensure military success with minimum loss of life. If battle were absolutely necessary, economy of life could be ensured by emphasizing what would now be called "force protection." The example of France in 1940 is one of many suggesting that rules of conduct derived from past success deserve particularly close scrutiny.

The achievement of Tippelskirch and his intelligence analysts illustrates the added value of asking questions about other governments' habits and routines. Politicians, diplomats, journalists, and academic experts almost always focus on the probable decisions or policies of other governments, but don't spend much time asking *how* another government arrives at decisions or implements them. In the German planning for the campaign of 1940, answers to such "how" questions were at least as important as the answers to questions about French or British intentions. A similar point has been made by the political scientist Alexander George, who asserts: "Even when warning systems provide information on an adversary's intentions that is *plentiful, relatively consistent* and *free of noise*, its proper interpretation requires a theory of the actor's behavioral style."[24]

Governments may profit from integrating intelligence analysis with policy-planning and decision-making, even though there are obvious risks. Intelligence analysts can easily lose their detachment and mortgage their expertise to advocacy of one course of action as against others. But the German example of the analysts' helping to prepare the final version of Plan

Yellow argues powerfully that the benefits can exceed the risks, and the irrelevancy of French intelligence analysis at the same time supports the point. Perhaps a key to gaining the benefits while hedging the risks is in the example of General Tippelskirch, who mediated between the analysts and the general staff, bringing to bear his authority not only as an intelligence officer but as someone potentially qualified for high command. In the United States of the Cold War era, the two directors of central intelligence (DCIs) generally conceded to have been most effective were General Walter Bedell Smith, a career army officer, and John McCone, a utilities executive who had previously managed U.S. nuclear-energy programs. The integration of analysis and decision-making can be accomplished by men and women who bring to the question "What is going on?" successful past experience in answering questions about what is to be done.

Even though comparatively democratic nations have usually prevailed in contests with autocratic nations (as, obviously, in the Second World War and the Cold War), the fact remains that in such contests democracies suffer handicaps. Their leaders, like those of France and Britain in 1938–40, have to expend much of their energy watching and responding to domestic constituencies. Because their decisions are usually products of intensive bargaining, they are apt to behave like the French and British leaders described in this book—with reticence among themselves and with reliance on convenience when framing perceptions of the world around them. Autocrats, even when paranoid about competitors at home, are freer to focus on those abroad. This was true to an extraordinary degree for Hitler because of the strength of support for him within the Nazi Party and among the German populace. It was France's fate to be the center of his interest at a time when his megalomania was tempered by operational common sense. It was the good fortune of Britain, the Soviet Union, the United States, and the world that his success in the contest with France caused him to abandon the decision-making procedures that had contributed to that success. Britain in particular benefited from the fact that the sense of emergency created by the fall of France caused its people to tolerate a government that behaved like an autocracy, with Churchill as prime minister disregarding domestic constituencies, concentrating exclusively on the war, and employing procedures remarkably like Hitler's earlier ones: that is, exposing his presumptions in monologues and memoranda and allowing advisers to quarrel with them.

This is said only to underline the primary moral that emerges from the story of Germany and France in 1938–40: the importance of operational common sense. In the management of conflict, the key differences between the German government and the French and British governments up through mid-1940 were procedural. In the German government, the question "What is going on?" was repeatedly re-examined in light of changing answers to the questions "So what?" and "What is to be done?" In the French and British governments prior to June 1940, this did not occur. Leaders did not state their presumptions or expose them to debate. They made choices and then either blinkered themselves against questions or invented answers to the question "What is going on?" in order to fortify their preferred answers to the question "What is to be done?" The first was the case with Gamelin, when failing to review the premises of the Dyle-Breda Plan, the second with Daladier, when he became an advocate of winning the war with Germany by going to war with the Soviet Union, and with Reynaud and Churchill, when they championed opening new theaters of war in Scandinavia or the Balkans.

To conclude with a question that is almost a precept, I borrow from Oliver Cromwell, Britain's Lord Protector when the Puritans held control during the civil war of the seventeenth century. However dimly remembered, the story of Germany's defeat of France in 1940 ought to bring to mind Cromwell's injunction in 1650 to the General Assembly of the Church of Scotland: "I beseech you, in the bowels of Christ, think it possible you may be mistaken."

APPENDIX:
TABLES AND CHARTS

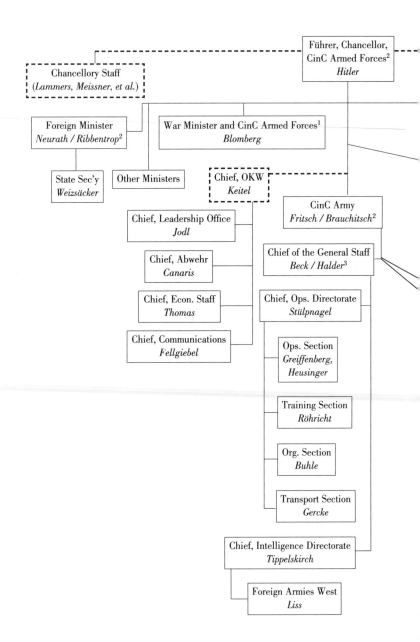

THE GERMAN HIGH COMMAND, 1938-40

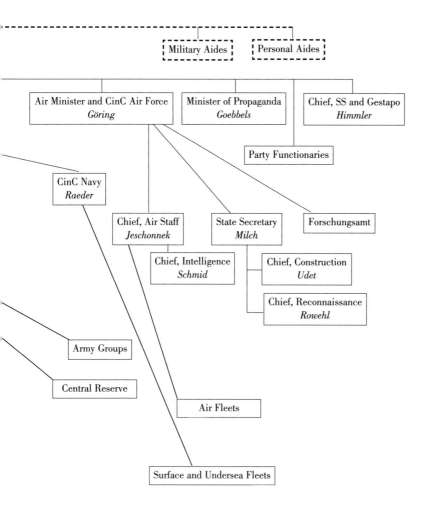

| Military Aides | Personal Aides |

| Air Minister and CinC Air Force | Minister of Propaganda | Chief, SS and Gestapo |
| *Göring* | *Goebbels* | *Himmler* |

Party Functionaries

CinC Navy
Raeder

| Chief, Air Staff | State Secretary | Forschungsamt |
| *Jeschonnek* | *Milch* | |

| Chief, Intelligence | Chief, Construction |
| *Schmid* | *Udet* |

Chief, Reconnaissance
Rowehl

Army Groups

Central Reserve

Air Fleets

Surface and Undersea Fleets

[1] Until Feb. 1938
[2] After Feb. 1938
[3] After Aug. 1938

FRANCE

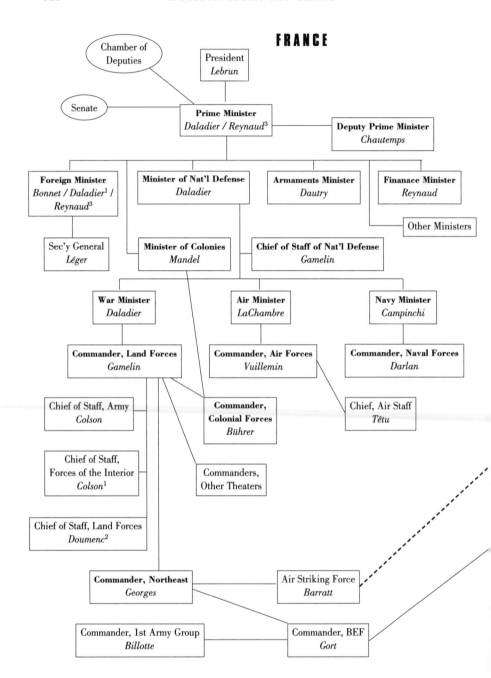

ALLIED COMMAND STRUCTURES, 1938-40

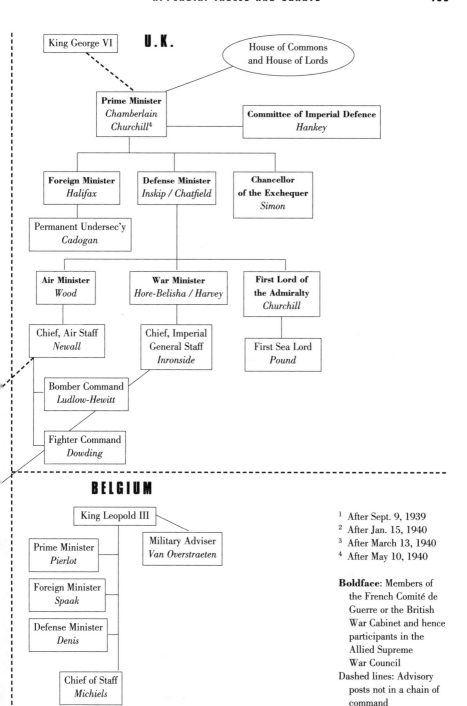

U.K.

King George VI

House of Commons and House of Lords

Prime Minister
Chamberlain
Churchill[4]

Committee of Imperial Defence
Hankey

Foreign Minister
Halifax

Defense Minister
Inskip / Chatfield

Chancellor
of the Exchequer
Simon

Permanent Undersec'y
Cadogan

Air Minister
Wood

War Minister
Hore-Belisha / Harvey

First Lord of
the Admiralty
Churchill

Chief, Air Staff
Newall

Chief, Imperial
General Staff
Ironside

First Sea Lord
Pound

Bomber Command
Ludlow-Hewitt

Fighter Command
Dowding

BELGIUM

King Leopold III

Prime Minister
Pierlot

Military Adviser
Van Overstraeten

Foreign Minister
Spaak

Defense Minister
Denis

Chief of Staff
Michiels

[1] After Sept. 9, 1939
[2] After Jan. 15, 1940
[3] After March 13, 1940
[4] After May 10, 1940

Boldface: Members of
the French Comité de
Guerre or the British
War Cabinet and hence
participants in the
Allied Supreme
War Council
Dashed lines: Advisory
posts not in a chain of
command

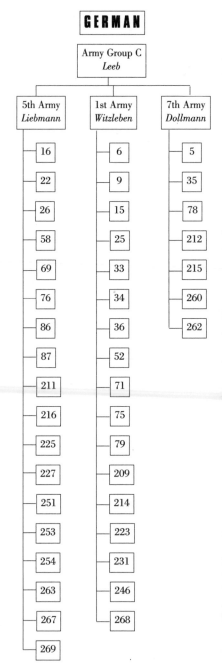

**OPPOSING FORCES ON THE WESTERN FRONT
AROUND SEPTEMBER 9, 1939**

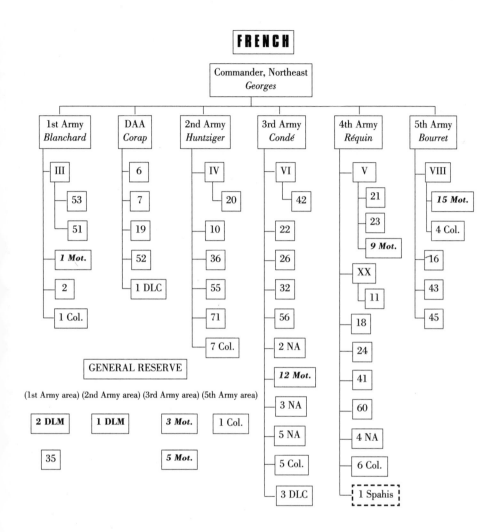

FRENCH

Commander, Northeast
Georges

| 1st Army *Blanchard* | DAA *Corap* | 2nd Army *Huntziger* | 3rd Army *Condé* | 4th Army *Réquin* | 5th Army *Bourret* |

1st Army *Blanchard*: III — 53 — 51 — *1 Mot.* — 2 — 1 Col.

DAA *Corap*: 6 — 7 — 19 — 52 — 1 DLC

2nd Army *Huntziger*: IV — 20 — 10 — 36 — 55 — 71 — 7 Col.

3rd Army *Condé*: VI — 42 — 22 — 26 — 32 — 56 — 2 NA — *12 Mot.* — 3 NA — 5 NA — 5 Col. — 3 DLC

4th Army *Réquin*: V — 21 — 23 — *9 Mot.* — XX — 11 — 18 — 24 — 41 — 60 — 4 NA — 6 Col. — 1 Spahis

5th Army *Bourret*: VIII — *15 Mot.* — 4 Col. — 16 — 43 — 45

GENERAL RESERVE

(1st Army area) (2nd Army area) (3rd Army area) (5th Army area)

2 DLM   **1 DLM**   *3 Mot.*   1 Col.

35   *5 Mot.*

Boldface: Armored units
Boldface italic: Motorized units
Italic: Second- or third-line infantry
Dashed-line boxes: Brigades
(All other units are divisions)
Col. = Colonial
DAA = Détachement des Armées des Ardennes
DLC = Light Cavalry Division
DLM = Light Mechanized
F = Fortress
NA = North African

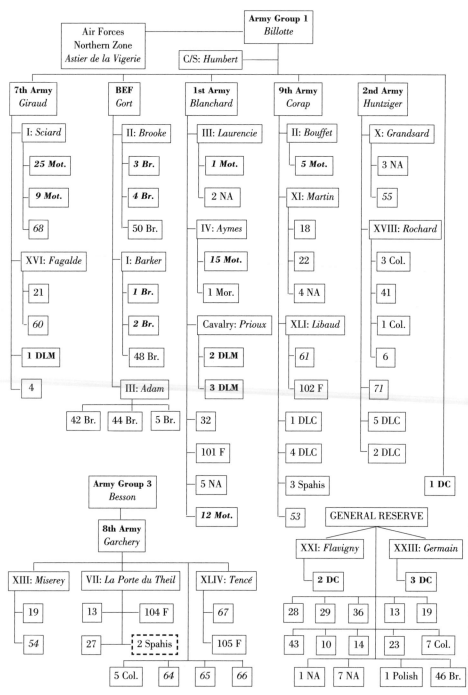

ALLIED ORDER OF BATTLE, MAY 10, 1940

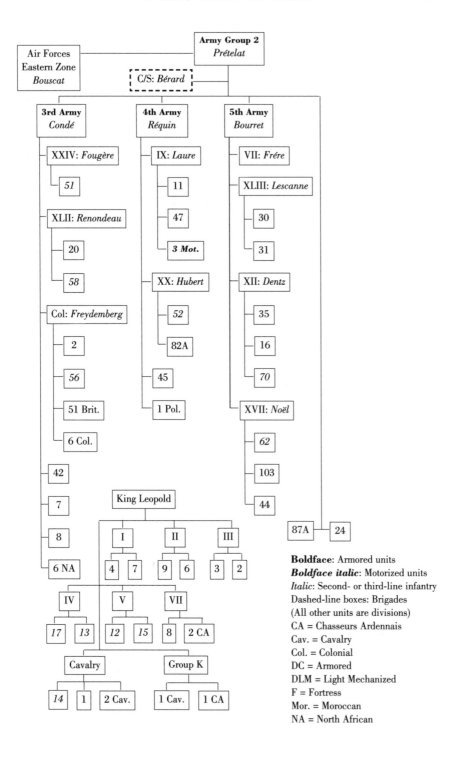

Army Group 2
Prételat

Air Forces
Eastern Zone
Bouscat

C/S: *Bérard*

3rd Army
Condé

XXIV: *Fougère*
- *51*

XLII: *Renondeau*
- 20
- *58*

Col: *Freydemberg*
- 2
- *56*
- 51 Brit.
- 6 Col.

42
7
8
6 NA

4th Army
Réquin

IX: *Laure*
- 11
- 47
- *3 Mot.*

XX: *Hubert*
- 52
- 82A
- 45
- 1 Pol.

5th Army
Bourret

VII: *Frére*

XLIII: *Lescanne*
- 30
- 31

XII: *Dentz*
- 35
- 16
- *70*

XVII: *Noël*
- *62*
- 103
- 44

87A — 24

King Leopold

I	II	III
4 7	9 6	3 2

IV	V	VII
17 *13*	12 15	8 2 CA

Cavalry
- *14* 1 2 Cav.

Group K
- 1 Cav. 1 CA

Boldface: Armored units
Boldface italic: Motorized units
Italic: Second- or third-line infantry
Dashed-line boxes: Brigades
(All other units are divisions)
CA = Chasseurs Ardennais
Cav. = Cavalry
Col. = Colonial
DC = Armored
DLM = Light Mechanized
F = Fortress
Mor. = Moroccan
NA = North African

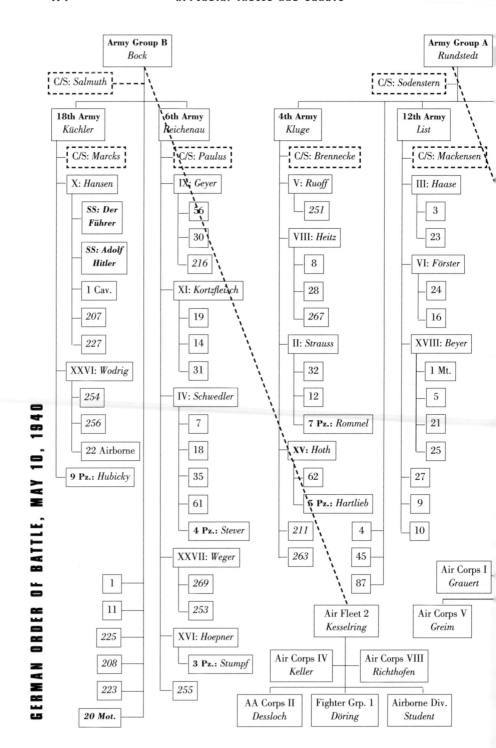

GERMAN ORDER OF BATTLE, MAY 10, 1940

| Army Group B | | | |
| Bock | | | |

C/S: Salmuth

| 18th Army | 6th Army | 4th Army | 12th Army |
| Küchler | Reichenau | Kluge | List |

| C/S: Marcks | C/S: Paulus | C/S: Brennecke | C/S: Mackensen |

X: Hansen   IX: Geyer   V: Ruoff   III: Haase

SS: Der Führer — 56 — 251 — 3

SS: Adolf Hitler — 30 — VIII: Heitz — 23

1 Cav. — 216 — 8 — VI: Förster

207 — XI: Kortzfleisch — 28 — 24

227 — 19 — 267 — 16

XXVI: Wodrig — 14 — II: Strauss — XVIII: Beyer

254 — 31 — 32 — 1 Mt.

256 — IV: Schwedler — 12 — 5

22 Airborne — 7 — 7 Pz.: Rommel — 21

9 Pz.: Hubicky — 18 — XV: Hoth — 25

35 — 62 — 27

61 — 5 Pz.: Hartlieb — 9

4 Pz.: Stever — 211 — 4 — 10

XXVII: Weger — 263 — 45

1 — 269 — 87 — Air Corps I / Grauert

11 — 253 — Air Fleet 2 / Kesselring — Air Corps V / Greim

225 — XVI: Hoepner

208 — 3 Pz.: Stumpf — Air Corps IV / Keller — Air Corps VIII / Richthofen

223 — 255

20 Mot. — AA Corps II / Dessloch — Fighter Grp. 1 / Döring — Airborne Div. / Student

| Army Group A |
| Rundstedt |

C/S: Sodenstern

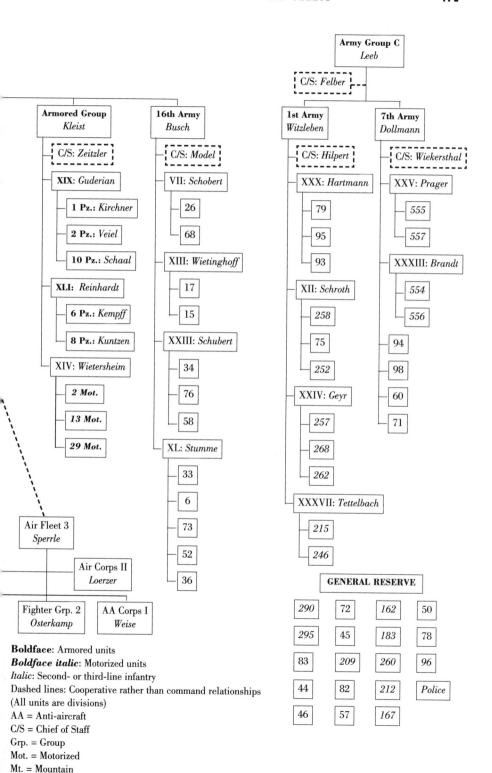

Army Group C
Leeb

C/S: *Felber*

| **Armored Group** *Kleist* | **16th Army** *Busch* | **1st Army** *Witzleben* | **7th Army** *Dollmann* |

C/S: *Zeitzler* — C/S: *Model* — C/S: *Hilpert* — C/S: *Wiekersthal*

XIX: *Guderian* — VII: *Schobert* — XXX: *Hartmann* — XXV: *Prager*

1 Pz.: *Kirchner* — 26 — 79 — 555

2 Pz.: *Veiel* — 68 — 95 — 557

10 Pz.: *Schaal* — XIII: *Wietinghoff* — 93 — XXXIII: *Brandt*

XLI: *Reinhardt* — 17 — XII: *Schroth* — 554

6 Pz.: *Kempff* — 15 — 258 — 556

8 Pz.: *Kuntzen* — XXIII: *Schubert* — 75 — 94

XIV: *Wietersheim* — 34 — 252 — 98

2 Mot. — 76 — XXIV: *Geyr* — 60

13 Mot. — 58 — 257 — 71

29 Mot. — XL: *Stumme* — 268

33 — 262

6 — XXXVII: *Tettelbach*

Air Fleet 3
Sperrle — 73 — 215

52 — 246

Air Corps II
Loerzer — 36

GENERAL RESERVE

| Fighter Grp. 2 *Osterkamp* | AA Corps I *Weise* |

290	72	162	50
295	45	183	78
83	209	260	96
44	82	212	Police
46	57	167	

Boldface: Armored units
Boldface italic: Motorized units
Italic: Second- or third-line infantry
Dashed lines: Cooperative rather than command relationships
(All units are divisions)
AA = Anti-aircraft
C/S = Chief of Staff
Grp. = Group
Mot. = Motorized
Mt. = Mountain
Pz. = Panzer

OPPOSING FORCES ON THE GROUND IN EUROPE, SEPTEMBER 1939

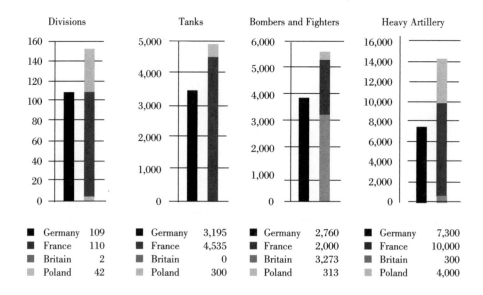

	Divisions		Tanks		Bombers and Fighters		Heavy Artillery
■ Germany	109	■ Germany	3,195	■ Germany	2,760	■ Germany	7,300
■ France	110	■ France	4,535	■ France	2,000	■ France	10,000
■ Britain	2	■ Britain	0	■ Britain	3,273	■ Britain	300
■ Poland	42	■ Poland	300	■ Poland	313	■ Poland	4,000

OPPOSING FORCES ON THE WESTERN FRONT, SEPTEMBER 1939

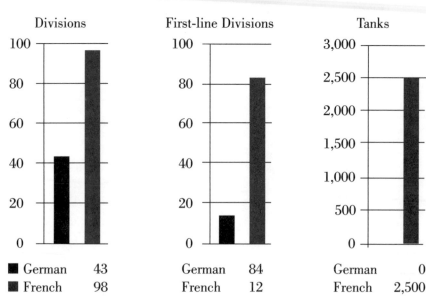

	Divisions		First-line Divisions		Tanks
■ German	43	German	84	German	0
■ French	98	French	12	French	2,500

OVERALL BALANCE OF FORCES, MAY 10, 1940

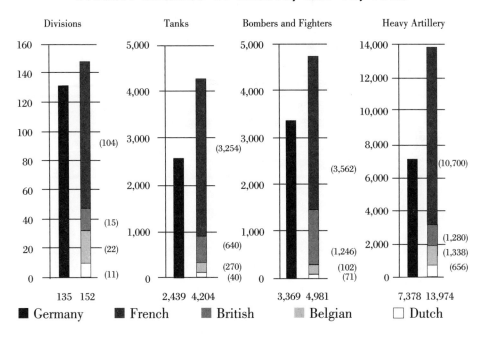

| Divisions | Tanks | Bombers and Fighters | Heavy Artillery |

■ Germany   ■ French   ■ British   ▨ Belgian   ☐ Dutch

GROUND-FORCE DIVISIONS ON THE WESTERN FRONT, MAY 10, 1940

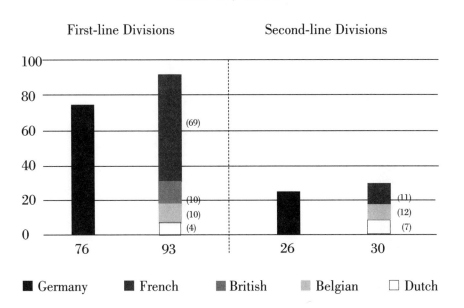

First-line Divisions   Second-line Divisions

■ Germany   ■ French   ■ British   ▨ Belgian   ☐ Dutch

TANKS DEPLOYED, MAY 10, 1940

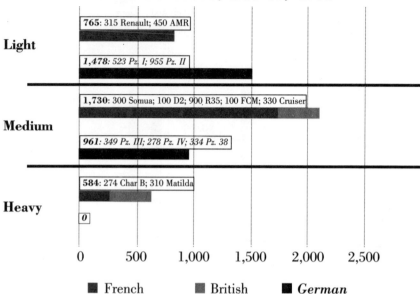

Light

765: 315 Renault; 450 AMR

1,478: 523 Pz. I; 955 Pz. II

Medium

1,730: 300 Somua; 100 D2; 900 R35; 100 FCM; 330 Cruiser

961: 349 Pz. III; 278 Pz. IV; 334 Pz. 38

Heavy

584: 274 Char B; 310 Matilda

0

0   500   1,000   1,500   2,000   2,500

■ French   ■ British   ■ *German*

TANK TYPES (FRENCH, BRITISH, *GERMAN*)

	Weight (tons)	Speed (mph)	Armor	Armament (n x n mm cannon / n machine guns)
Heavy				
Char B1	32	17	60 mm	1 x 75, 1 x 47 / 2
Matilda II	27	15	78 mm	2 x 40 / 2
Medium				
Somua S-35	20	23	56 mm	1 x 47 / 1
D2	20	20	40 mm	1 x 47 / 1
R35	10	13	45 mm	1 x 37 / 1
FCM-36	12	15	40 mm	1 x 37 / 1
Cruiser Mk III	15	30	38 mm	1 x 40 / 1
Panzer III	20	20	30 mm	1 x 37 / 2
Panzer IV	20	25	30 mm	1 x 75 (short barrel) / 2
Panzer 38(t)	10	20	25 mm	1 x 37 / 2
Light				
Renault FT	7.4	20	22 mm	1 x 37 / 1
AMR	7	20	13 mm	0 / 2
Panzer I	6	22	13 mm	0 / 2
Panzer II	8	25	14.5 mm	1 x 20 / 1

BOMBERS AND FIGHTERS ON THE WESTERN FRONT, MAY 10, 1940

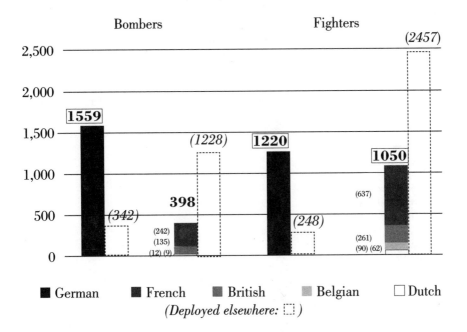

Bombers   Fighters

■ German   ■ French   ■ British   ■ Belgian   □ Dutch

(Deployed elsewhere: ▫)

AIRCRAFT TYPES

	Engines	Speed (mph)	Ceiling (feet)	Range (nautical miles)	Armament (machine guns)	Bombs (lbs.)
Bombers						
French						
Amiot 143	2	185	26,000	1,200	3	3,500
Bloch 175	2	340	36,000	1,000	4	900
Bloch 310	2	210	32,500	1,050	2	3,750
Glenn Martin 167	2	285	35,000	1,300	3	1,750
Lioré-Olivier 451	2	300	30,000	1,800	2 + 1 x 20 mm	3,300
Potez 63-11	2	265	33,000	1,000	1 + 2 x 20 mm	700
British						
Armstrong "Whitley" III	2	210	18,000	1,250	5	7,000
Bristol "Blenheim"	2	300	27,000	1,450	2	10,000
Fairey "Battle"	1	250	23,500	1,000	2	1,000
Handley Page "Hampden"	2	265	19,000	1,750	5	750
Vickers "Wellington"	2	260	18,000	2,500	6	4,400
German						
Dornier DO 17	2	250	28,000	1,500	6	4,400
Heinkel HE 111	1	240	26,000	400	3	1,100
Junkers JU 87 ("Stuka")	1	225	26,000	1,000	3	1,100
Junkers JU 88	2	280	26,250	1,000	3	4,000
Fighters						
French						
Bloch 152	1	320	10,000	400	2 + 2 x 20 mm	
Curtiss "Hawk" 75	1	310	10,000	835	4	
Dewoitine 520	1	330	36,000	620	4 + 1 x 20 mm	
Morane Saulnier MS 406	1	300	31,000	500	2 + 1 x 20 mm	
British						
Hawker "Hurricane"	1	350	34,000	480	8	
Supermarine "Spitfire"	1	370	34,000	500	8	
German						
Messerschmidt ME 109	1	350	34,500	360	2 + 2 x 20 mm	
Messerschmidt ME 110	2	320	29,500	570	4 + 2 x 20 mm	

NOTES

INTRODUCTION

1. French and British reactions to the German offensive are detailed later. On Schneider, Archen, and events of May 9–10 in Luxembourg, see Archen, *Missions spéciales*; Bruge, *Juin 1940*, pp. 104–21; Koch-Kent, *10 mai 1940 en Luxembourg*, pp. 11–12, 64–67; Haupt, *Sieg ohne Lorbeer*, pp. 9–11.

2. Radio address announcing the armistices with Germany and Italy, Pétain, *Actes*, p. 454.

3. Bodinier, "Gamelin"; Faber du Faur, *Macht und Ohnmacht*, p. 115. Stolfi, "Equipment for Victory," which is a summary of Stolfi, "Reality and Myth," the first significant recalculation of the 1940 balance of forces. The most recent and thorough recalculation appears in Frieser, *Blitzkrieg-Legende*. David Markowitz, when a doctoral candidate in computer sciences at Harvard, worked out for me some simulations of the Battle of France. He tested portions on a high-powered U.S. Army tactical simulation system. It always took active human intervention to prevent the Allies from winning. The proposition is validated in computer-game simulations, in which the German side has to be given an arbitrary force advantage in order to permit an outcome resembling actuality. An example is Big Three, a computer game first issued by SJD Enterprises of New York in 1991.

4. Entry for April 18, 1939, in Zay, *Carnets secrets*, pp. 57–58; Gunnar Andreassen, quoted in Heimsoeth, *Zusammenbruch*, p. 342. On the mood of France in the mid-1930s, see especially Weber, *Hollow Years*. On the changes in 1938–39, see especially Rémond, ed., *Édouard Daladier*, and Rémond, ed., *La France et les Français*.

5. Diary entry for Nov. 23, 1939, in Simoni, *Berlino, ambasciata d'Italia*, p. 27.

6. Halder to his wife, May 11, 1940, in Schall-Riaucour, *Aufstand und Gehorsam*, p. 151. On Corap and his chief of staff, see Paillat, *Désastre*, 5:157–158. For a description of Gamelin, see Beaufre, *Drame*, p. 180.

7. Christienne, *Histoire de l'aviation militaire française*, p. 373; Astier de la Vigerie, *Le Ciel n'était pas vide*, p. 75.

8. Bloch, *Strange Defeat*, pp. 136–37.

9. May, ed., *Knowing One's Enemies*, pp. 512–19.

10. For me, Frieser's *Blitzkrieg-Legende* leads the works focused mainly on Germany, though in some respects it is only a complement to older or broader works such as Jacobsen, *Fall Gelb*; Weinberg, *Foreign Policy of Hitler's Germany*; and Müller, *Heer und Hitler*. Crémieux-Brilhac, *Français de l'an 40*; Paillat, *Désastre*; and Rocolle, *Guerre de 1940*, stand out among works that focus on France, though, again, they are complementary to works such as Adamthwaite, *France and the Coming of*

the Second World War; Duroselle, Décadence and Abîme; Heimsoeth, Zusammenbruch; Mysyrowicz, Autopsie; Weber, Hollow Years; and Young, France and the
Origins of the Second World War. Horne's To Lose a Battle is an almost matchless
battle narrative, as good on German operations as on French, but, regarding politics and strategy, chiefly concerned with France. The qualification "almost" is because Deighton, Blitzkrieg, comes close to being a match. Parker, Struggle for
Survival, Weinberg, World at Arms, and other general histories of the Second
World War set that war in its larger context. Two thoughtful general studies of the
war in 1939–40 are Lukacs, The Last European War, and Williams, Ides of May.

11. Kahn, Hitler's Spies, cannot be rivaled. Based on many interviews as well as on extensive archival research, it is a work of permanent value, but is entirely about
Germany's intelligence services, not about their use by Hitler's government.
Porch, French Secret Services, is the outstanding book for the French side but covers a long period, not just that of the war. It does not supersede Robert J. Young,
"French Military Intelligence and Nazi Germany," in May, Knowing One's Enemies, pp. 271–309.

CHAPTER ONE: ORDERS

1. Life, Jan. 30, 1939, p. 16; Speer, Inside the Third Reich, p. 113.
2. Mustache: Schroeder, Er war mein Chef, pp. 71–72. Speaking style: Domarus, ed.,
Hitler: Speeches, 1:65–66.
3. Entry for Sept. 27, 1939, in Halder Diary. The official OKW note on the meeting,
in OKW KTB, 1:951, lists as being in attendance only Brauchitsch, Göring,
Raeder, and General Wilhelm Keitel, chief of the small staff that Hitler maintained as commander in chief of the armed forces. It says Hitler did not explain the
order he was issuing. Jacobsen, Fall Gelb, pp. 268–69, n. 2, reports that in
the 1950s Captain Gerhard Engel, an army aide to Hitler, confirmed to him that
the meeting included only the commanders in chief. In testimony during the
Nuremberg trials, Halder referred to a decisive "short conference at the end of
September" (U.S. v Leeb, 10:856). Halder's notes, however, not only summarize a
meeting that could hardly have occupied less than an hour; they also give, as indicated in the text here, a generous exposition of Hitler's logic. In n. 1 to the Halder
diary entry, Jacobsen reports that Halder told him in 1961 that these were steno-
graphic notes that he had taken during the meeting. Also, the then air-force adjutant writes in his memoirs that also present were the air-force chief of staff,
Colonel Hans Jeschonnek; Keitel's number two, Colonel Alfred Jodl; and Göring's
aide, General Karl Bodenschatz: Below, Als Hitlers Adjutant, p. 210. Since the official OKW note speaks of an "afternoon" meeting but Halder's notes are headed
"5 P.M.," it is possible that there were two meetings—a brief one for just the commanders and another soon after, with chiefs of staff invited in. A footnote to the
OKW notes says that Brauchitsch and Raeder were taken entirely by surprise. All
later quotations from Hitler's remarks on September 27 come from the entry in the
Halder Diary.
4. Leeb to Brauchitsch, Sept. 2, 1939, in Jacobsen, ed., Dokumente zur Vorgeschichte,
doc. 22. In addition to the brief authoritative account of the German war against
Poland appearing in vol. 1 of Deist, Germany in the Second World War, see the

older, more extensive narratives: Jars, *Campagne de Pologne*, Kennedy, *The German Campaign in Poland*, and Vormann, *Feldzug 1939 in Polen*.

5. Below, *Als Hitlers Adjutant*, p. 210; diary, Sept. 7, 1939, in Wagner, ed., *Generalquartiermeister*, p. 131.

6. Walther Hubatsch (later an eminent historian), interviewed in 1955, in Jacobsen, *Fall Gelb*, p. 268, n. 33.

7. Entry for Sept. 7, 1939, in *Halder Diary*; OKH directive, Sept. 19, 1939, in Jacobsen, ed., *Dokumente zur Vorgeschichte*, doc. 9.

8. "Organisationsstudie '1950,'" May 2, 1938, NARS Film T 971, reel 36; "Planstudie 1939" [not otherwise dated but c. May 1938], ibid., reel 17 Luftwaffe Führungstab Ia, memo, Sept. 23, 1939, ibid., reel 50. See also Deist, Maier, et al., *Germany and the Second World War*, 2:31–59; Völker, *Deutsche Luftwaffe*, pp. 159–65; Homze, *Arming the Luftwaffe*, pp. 241–44.

9. Conference, Sept. 23, 1939, in *Lagevorträge*, pp. 24–26.

10. Liss, *Westfront*, pp. 82–84, describes "Zeppelin," as does Jodl, *Jenseits des Endes*, p. 27. Photographs and plans can be found in Kampe, *Underground Military Command Bunkers*.

11. Entry for Sept. 28, 1939, in *Halder Diary*. See Appendix, pp. 466–67, on the organization of the German high command.

12. Entry for Sept. 29–30, 1939, ibid.; FHW, "Operationsmöglichkeiten der Westheere," Sept. 30, 1939, NARS Film T 78, reel 454. On the Stülpnagel memo of Sept. 25, 1939, see Jacobsen, *Fall Gelb*, p. 10; Bücheler, *Stülpnagel*, pp. 164–67.

13. Note, Sept. 29, 1939, in Engel, *Heeresadjutant*, pp. 60–61; entry for Sept. 29, 1939, in *Rosenberg Tagebuch*, pp. 81–82.

14. Entries for Sept. 30, Oct. 3, 1939, in *Halder Diary*.

15. Testimony by Admiral Schniewind, in U.S. v. Leeb, 10:876.

16. Entries for Oct. 3–4, 8, 1939, in *Halder Diary*; Hillgruber, *Hitlers Strategie*, p. 38, n. 51.

17. On Brauchitsch: entry for Oct. 3, 1939, in *Halder Diary*. On junior officers: Heusinger, *Befehl im Widerstreit*, pp. 69–71.

18. Bethell, *War Hitler Won*, advances the arresting argument that Hitler's terms should not have seemed unacceptable in the West and that the Allies, led by Chamberlain, passed up an opportunity to preserve peace. The book foreshadows some of the argumentation in Charmley's sensational *Chamberlain and the Lost Peace*.

19. Entry for Oct. 10, 1939, in *Halder Diary*. On the composition of the memorandum: *TMWC*, 38: doc. L-52; *TMWC*, 15:412; Jacobsen, *Fall Gelb*, p. 271. The original is in the Institut für Völkerecht in Göttingen. Hitler's "million men" comment appears in entry for October 17, 1939, *Weizsäcker Papiere*, p. 180.

20. Entries for Sept. 28, Sept. 30, Oct. 14, 1939, in *Halder Diary*.

21. On the evolution of Prussia/Germany as an army with a state, nothing else in English, and not much in any other language, matches Craig, *Politics of the Prussian Army*, but see also Taylor, *Sword and Swastika* (by a postwar war-crimes prosecutor) and Wheeler-Bennett, *Nemesis of Power*.

22. Frederick, quoted by Eric Robson in *The New Cambridge Modern History*, vol. 7 (Cambridge: Cambridge University Press, 1957), p. 181. On Seydlitz at Kunersdorf, some traces of the evolving legend are a 1797 pamphlet by General Christian

Friedrich von Blanckenburg, an 1837 sketch of Seydlitz by a General Bismarck, an official history of Kunersdorf published in 1859 by General von Stiele, a life of Seydlitz published by Varnhagen von Ense around 1870, a general-staff officer's essay on Seydlitz and his significance for the cavalry published in 1874, and a biography of Seydlitz published in 1882 by an anonymous "German cavalry officer." See Klaus Christian Richter, *Friedrich Wilhelm von Seydlitz, ein preussicher Reitergeneral und seine Zeit* (Osnabrück: Biblio-Verlag, 1996).

23. F. N. Maude, *The Leipzig Campaign, 1813* (New York: Macmillan, 1908), pp. 18–19.

24. Heinrich von Treitschke, *German History in the Nineteenth Century* (7 vols.; New York: Macmillan, 1915–19), 1:491–92. The historiography is elegantly summarized in Walter Elze, *Der Streit um Tauroggen* (Breslau: F. Hirt, 1926).

25. See Reginald H. Phelps, "Aus den Groener Dokumenten," *Deutsche Rundschau,* 76 (1950).

26. Hans von Seeckt, *Gedanken eines Soldaten* (Berlin: Verlag für Kulturpolitik, 1929), pp. 92–93; Ernst R. Huber, *Heer und Staat in der deutsche Geschichte* (Hamburg: Hanseatische Verlagsanstalt, 1938), p. 443.

CHAPTER TWO: HONEYMOON

1. Bracher, Sauer, and Schulz, *Machtergreifung,* pp. 710–11, 718–19. The text of Hitler's talk is in Vogelsang, "Neue Dokumente," translated in Noakes, *Nazism,* 3:628–29. The room where Hitler spoke is in a surviving part of the old War Ministry building in Berlin, which is now the Museum of the German Resistance. In the very same room, General Ludwig Beck killed himself after the failure of the July 20, 1944, attempt on Hitler's life.

2. Kershaw, *Hitler,* pp. 505–17. There are graphic eyewitness descriptions in Noakes, *Nazism,* 1:178–81. See also Fallois, *Kalkül und Illusion.*

3. Deutsch, *Hitler and His Generals,* p. 18.

4. Müller, *Heer und Hitler,* pp. 158–59.

5. O'Neill, *The German Army and the Nazi Party,* pp. 68–72, 97–99.

6. Wheeler-Bennett, *Nemesis of Power,* p. 295.

7. Bracher, Sauer, and Shulz, *Machtergreifung,* p. 714.

8. Müller, whose sermons drew analogies between Nazis and early Christians, made converts also among young officers who were both conservatives and romantics. Among them were Henning von Tresckow and Claus Schenck Count von Stauffenberg, who in 1944 would be key figures in the effort to murder Hitler.

9. O'Neill, *The German Army and the Nazi Party,* p. 138; Faber du Faur, *Macht und Ohnmacht,* p. 159.

10. Höhne, *Order of the Death's Head,* p. 100; Röhricht, *Pflicht und Gewesen,* pp. 42–44.

11. Blomberg: Wheeler-Bennett, *Nemesis of Power,* p. 325. Reichenau: Kershaw, *Hitler,* p. 521.

12. O'Neill, *The German Army and the Nazi Party,* p. 138.

13. Hossbach, *Zwischen Wehrmacht und Hitler,* p. 20.

14. Müller, *Heer und Hitler,* pp. 130–39. O'Neill, *The German Army and the Nazi Party,* pp. 19–22, points out the similarities between the oath to Hitler and the oaths standard in the British and American armed forces. Müller, one of the fore-

most historians of army-party relations, argues convincingly that Blomberg and Reichenau saw the oath primarily as a device for strengthening the position of the army in relation to the Nazi Party. Blomberg shared Reichenau's hope of making the army the primary pillar of state, not just one of two. With regard to the oath, Blomberg was later to write, "We swore an oath of loyalty to Hitler as the leader of the German people, not as leader of the Nazi Party. No one realized that our oath would become a pact of fealty to the Nazi Party." (Manuscript memoir by Blomberg quoted in Erfurth, *Deutschen Generalstabes*, pp. 164–65. Müller, *Heer und Hitler*, p. 135, n. 291, says this part of the manuscript memoir has disappeared from the archives, but he accepts it as genuine.)

15. See Bracher, Funke, and Jacobsen, *Nationalsozialistische Diktatur*; Schoenbaum, *Hitler's Social Revolution*; and the review of literature in Thomas Saunders, "Nazism and Social Revolution," in Martel, ed., *Modern Germany Reconsidered*, pp. 159–77. On the slower erosion of the independence of the diplomatic service, see Seabury, *Wilhelmstrasse*; Sasse, "Problem" (which is essentially a commentary on Seabury); and especially Jacobsen, *Nationalsozialistische Aussenpolitik*. Döscher, *Auswärtige Amt*, is a careful study of Nazification in the diplomatic service. Dahrendorf, *Society and Democracy*, p. 296, comments regretfully that the Nazis aroused unprecedented public engagement on the part of people previously apolitical.

16. The most authoritative account of Beck's career, and the source of the key documents showing his appreciations, is Müller, *Beck*, which almost completely supplants Foerster, *Ein General*. The best account in English is Reynolds, *Treason Was No Crime*. On the general staff, see Craig, *Politics of the Prussian Army*, but also Görlitz, *History of the German General Staff*, Model, *Deutsche Generalstabsoffizier*, and Millotat, *Understanding the Prussian-German General Staff System*.

17. Deutsch, *Hitler and His Generals*, p. 31.

18. Reynolds, *Treason Was No Crime*, p. 56.

19. Ibid., p. 64.

20. The best account is in Kindermann, *Hitler's Defeat in Austria*.

21. *Punch*, Aug. 8, 1934, p. 155; *Review of Reviews*, Aug. 1934, p. 59.

22. Reynolds, *Treason Was No Crime*, pp. 95–96.

23. Shore, "Hitler, Intelligence and the Rhine."

24. Reynolds, *Treason Was No Crime*, p. 107; Hossbach, *Zwischen Wehrmacht und Hitler*, p. 97.

25. Churchill, *Second World War*, 1:194.

26. Deutsch, *Hitler and His Generals*, p. 38.

27. Müller, *Beck*, pp. 298–99, adds to Deutsch, *Hitler and His Generals*, pp. 97–98. See also Schuker, "France and the Remilitarization of the Rhineland."

28. Deutsch, *Hitler and His Generals*, p. 148; Hossbach, *Zwischen Wehrmacht und Hitler*, p. 11; Engel, *Heeresadjutant*, pp. 24–25.

CHAPTER THREE: RIFTS

1. *TMWC*, 34:735.

2. Ibid., 34:doc. C-175.

3. Fritsch memo, Aug. 1937, in *Keitel*, pp. 123–42.

4. See Wilhelm Deist's chapter on the arming of the various services in Deist et al.,

Germany and the Second World War, 1:373–540. Thomas, *Geschichte der deutschen Wehr- und Rüstungswirtschaft,* is an authoritative account by the former head of the war economics branch of the armed-forces high command. Bernhardt, *Deutsche Aufrüstung,* is a thoughtful account of the rationales underpinning German rearmament and the understanding or misunderstanding of them in France and Britain. Geyer, *Aufrüstung,* gives a complex but persuasive account of how the rearmament program was interwoven with the rest of the Nazi revolution. On air-force plans and programs, Baumbach, *Zu spät* and Irving, *Rise and Fall of the Luftwaffe,* were early postwar studies; the latter focused on Erhard Milch, the architect of the Luftwaffe building program. Völker, *Deutsche Luftwaffe,* is an encyclopedic work put together in the 1960s. Suchenwirth, *Development of the German Air Force,* draws on Völker's data, as do Killen, *Luftwaffe,* Herbert Mason, *Rise of the Luftwaffe,* and Homze, *Arming the Luftwaffe.* Murray, *Strategy for Defeat,* concentrates on German air-force doctrine. Corum, *The Luftwaffe,* the most recent study, takes issue with the widely accepted view, developed in Murray's book, that the Luftwaffe was designed more as a tactical than a strategic force. Heinkel, *Stürmisches Leben,* gives a description from the standpoint of a bomber designer and builder. On navy programs, see Dülffer, *Weimar, Hitler, und die Marine,* but also Salewski, *Deutsche Seekriegsleitung,* which provides more information about navy doctrine.

5. See Hillgruber, *Hitlers Strategie,* pp. 29ff.
6. The official English translation is in *DGFP,* 1:29ff., the German original in *TMWC,* 25:doc. 386-PS. A slightly more polished English translation is in Noakes, *Nazism,* 3:680–87. The literature disputing and then successfully re-establishing the authenticity of this document is summarized in Meinck, *Hitler und die deutsche Aufrüstung,* pp. 173ff.; 276, n. 4; and in Smith, "Die Überlieferung des Hossbach-Niederschrift." The latest, most careful analysis is in Wright and Stafford, "Hitler and the Hossbach Memorandum."
7. In his memoir, however, Hossbach accepts the war-crimes trials' characterization of the November meeting. He writes of it as marking "a radical change of course in foreign policy" (Hossbach, *Zwischen Wehrmacht und Hitler,* p. 163). There has been lively controversy over the question whether or to what extent Hitler was forced to turn to territorial conquest because the alternative was to scale back not only rearmament but the delivery of loaves and fishes to the admiring German multitudes. See Mason, Kaiser, and Overy, "Debate."
8. Hossbach, *Zwischen Wehrmacht und Hitler,* p. 191.
9. Göring: *TMWC,* 9:344–45. Raeder: ibid., 14:34–37; Raeder, *My Life,* pp. 267–68.
10. Kielmansegg, *Fritschprozess,* p. 34, has a sample of Fritsch's letters from Egypt.
11. Hossbach, *Zwischen Wehrmacht und Hitler,* p. 191.
12. Müller, *Beck,* pp. 498–501.
13. The fullest account in English is in Deutsch, *Hitler and His Generals.* The most up-to-date account is Janssen and Tobias, *Sturz der Generale,* which complements but does not replace Foertsch, *Schuld und Verhängnis.*
14. O'Neill, *The German Army and the Nazi Party,* p. 150, notes the coincidence of the Soviet and British purges.
15. Entries for Jan. 28–Feb. 2, 1938, in Goebbels, *Tagebücher.*
16. Entry for Jan. 28, 1938, ibid.
17. Wiedeman, *Der Mann der Feldherr werden wollte,* p. 113.

18. Rintelen, *Mussolini als Bundesgenosse*, p. 94. Mueller, *Forgotten Field Marshal*, is a mildly sympathetic biography of Keitel. Scheurig, *Jodl*, is a biography of his chief deputy, who, like Albert Speer, possessed both intelligence and sensitivity and yet was drawn to Hitler and captivated by him. Warlimont, *Inside Hitler's Headquarters*, and Greiner, "OKW," give some sense of how the new OKW functioned. Schott, *Wehrmachfführungstab*, is a detailed analysis.

19. Entry for Feb. 1, 1938, in Goebbels, *Tagebücher.*

20. Faber du Faur, *Macht und Ohnmacht*, p. 161.

21. Curt Siewert, who served under Brauchitsch and who tried to defend him against criticism, conceded that Brauchitsch should have seen acceptance of the gift, combined with failure to insist on exoneration of Fritsch, as compromising, at least in the eyes of many fellow officers (Siewert, *Schuldig?*, pp. 85–87).

22. Entry of July 6, 1934, in Dodd, *Diary*, p. 120; Fromm, *Blood and Banquets*, pp. 180–81.

23. Jacobsen, *Nationalsozialistische Aussenpolitik*, pp. 28–36. On Neurath: Heineman, *Neurath.* On Ribbentrop: Michalka, *Ribbentrop*; English, Weitz, *Hitler's Diplomat.* Bollmus, *Amt Rosenberg*, explains how little competition Ribbentrop faced. Blasius, *Für Grossdeutschland*, and Thielenhaus, *Zwischen Anpassung und Widerstand*, describe how professional diplomats responded to the changes.

24. Spears, *Assignment to Catastrophe*, 1:25. Jules Romains, *Sept mystères*, pp. 200–1, however, credits Ribbentrop with more than passable command of French.

25. *Weizsäcker Papiere*, p. 60.

CHAPTER FOUR: CONFLICT

1. Domarus, ed., *Hitler: Speeches*, 2:944–51; Weinberg, *Foreign Policy of Hitler's Germany*, 1:279ff.

2. Report on Hitler-Halifax conversations, Nov. 22, 1937, in *DGFP*, 1:doc. 33; Welczek to Neurath, Nov. 27, 1937, ibid., doc. 46; Mackensen, memo, Sept. 20, 1937, ibid, doc. 252.

3. Papen, memo, Dec. 16, 1937, ibid., doc. 80.

4. Pauley, *Hitler and the Forgotten Nazis*, p. 168. The literature on German-Austrian relations in the 1930s was already large, then virtually doubled during or soon after the fortieth anniversary of the *Anschluss* in 1978 and doubled again after the fiftieth anniversary in 1988. Of early accounts, one that retains pungency is Gedye, *Betrayal in Central Europe.* Korber, *Night over Vienna*, is another eyewitness account, though published much later. See also essays in Kreissler, ed., *Fünfzig Jahre danach.* Reichhold, *Kampf um Österreich*, describes Austrian resistance. Rosar, *Deutsche Gemeinschaft*, is a study of Arthur Seyss-Inquardt, a leading Austrian Nazi; Liebmann, *Theodor Innitzer*, is one of the cardinal who welcomed the Nazis to Vienna. Luza, *Austro-German Relations*, and Schmidl, *März 38*, focus on German policy; Franz Müller, *Ein "Rechtskatholik,"* focuses on the then–German ambassador, Franz von Papen. Arnberger, *"Anschluss" 1938*, is a documentary collection. The best analyses of the event are the essays by Jagschitz, Kindermann, and Weinberg in Stourzh and Zaar, eds., *Österreich, Deutschland und die Mächte*, pp. 61–74, and Weinberg's additional essay, *Der gewaltsame Anschluss.*

5. Pauley, *Hitler and the Forgotten Nazis*, p. 170.

6. Rosar, *Deutsche Gemeinschaft*, pp. 103–4, 136–37, 142.

7. Friedrich Rainier, speech, March 11, 1942, in *TMWC*, 34:doc. 4005-PS.
8. Pauley, *Hitler and the Forgotten Nazis*, p. 187.
9. Weinberg, *Foreign Policy of Hitler's Germany*, 2:288–89.
10. Meissner, *Staatsekretär*, p. 449; Berndt, *Meilensteine*, pp. 191–93; Domarus, ed., *Hitler: Speeches*, 1:807–8.
11. Some historians, it should be noted, believe that the evidence shows Göring to have been the prime mover regarding Austria, with Hitler merely following his lead. The narrative here accepts Weinberg's view that Hitler was always in control. See Kube, *Pour le mérite und Hakenkreuz*, and the exchanges between Hans Mommsen and Weinberg in Stourzh and Zaar, eds., *Österreich, Deutschland und die Mächte*, pp. 98–107.
12. The records are in *TMWC*, 31:354–69. See Brook-Shepherd, *Anschluss*, pp. 26–30.
13. Jodl testimony, in *TMWC*, 15:356.
14. Ibid.
15. Weinberg, *Foreign Policy of Hitler's Germany*, 2:83.
16. IMT, *Nazi Conspiracy and Aggression*, 6:docs. C-102, C-103.
17. *TMWC*, 31:354–69.
18. Weizsäcker, *Memoirs*, p. 122; Göring testimony, in *TMWC*, 9:196; phone conversations cited in *TMWC*, 31:354–69; Weinberg, *Foreign Policy of Hitler's Germany*, 2:299.
19. See Brügel, *Tschechen und Deutsche*; Král, ed., *Deutschen*; Smelser, *Sudeten Problem*; Theisinger, *Sudetendeutschen*; and Komjathy and Stockwell, *German Minorities*.
20. Weinberg, *Foreign Policy of Hitler's Germany*, 1:109.
21. *DGFP* [C], 2:doc. 180; Jacobsen, *Nationalsozialistische Aussenpolitik*, pp. 441–43; Faber du Faur, *Macht und Ohnmacht*, p. 244.
22. *DGFP*, 2:doc. 107.
23. Domarus, ed., *Hitler: Speeches*, 1:850; Steinert, *Hitler*, pp. 367–71.
24. Keitel to Ribbentrop, March 7, 1938, in *DGFP*, 2:doc. 66.
25. *Keitel*, p. 63.
26. *DGFP*, 2:doc. 133.
27. Domarus, ed., *Hitler: Speeches*, 1:855–56.
28. Weizsäcker, *Memoirs*, p. 130.
29. There is some hilarious detail in a chapter entitled "The Meeting of the Two Corporals" in Anfuso, *Roma, Berlino, Salò*, pp. 39–77.
30. Domarus, ed., *Hitler: Speeches*, 1:856–63.
31. *Hungarian Documents*, 2:doc. 180.
32. *DGFP*, 2:doc. 175.
33. See Bramsted, *Goebbels*, pp. 124–42; Martens, *Zum Beispiel*, pp. 38–40.
34. Andrew, *Her Majesty's Secret Service*, pp. 392–93.
35. *DGFP*, 2:doc. 186.
36. Ibid., 2:doc. 221.
37. Weinberg, *Foreign Policy of Hitler's Germany*, 2:337–41, 366–71, details his reasons for quarreling with Watt, "Hitler's Visit to Rome." Dülffer, *Weimar*, pp. 550–52, lends support to Watt's view, arguing that the effect of the May Crisis was to end Hitler's hope of separating Great Britain from France.

CHAPTER FIVE: CLASHES

1. The text is in Müller, *Beck*, pp. 502–12.
2. Müller, *Heer und Hitler*, p. 305.
3. Engel, *Heeresadjutant*, pp. 24–25.
4. Below, *Als Hitlers Adjutant*, pp. 28–31; Schroeder, *Er war mein Chef*, p. 47.
5. Müller, *Beck*, pp. 512–20.
6. Ibid., pp. 521–28.
7. Though Beck's memo was dated May 29, a note on the front said that it was read to Brauchitsch on May 30, and the wording of the final paragraphs suggests that they may have been added after Beck saw the May 30 directive announcing Hitler's intention "to smash Czechoslovakia by military action in the near future."
8. Beck to Brauchitsch, June 3, 1938, in Müller, *Beck*, pp. 528–37.
9. Engel, *Heeresadjutant*, p. 24.
10. Halder to Beck, June 13, 1938, in BA-MA, N 28/3.
11. General Strategic Directive, June 18, 1938, in *DGFP*, 2:doc. 282.
12. "Factors Affecting the Situation," July 7, 1938, ibid.
13. Conference at Luftwaffe headquarters, May 5, 1938, NARS Film T 971, reel 15; chief of staff of the Luftwaffe, memo, Aug. 12, 1939, ibid., reel 17; Luftwaffe Kommando 2, memo, Aug. 12, 1939, ibid., reel 36.
14. Göring speech, July 8, 1938, in *TMWC*, 38:412–19. See Weinberg, *Foreign Policy of Hitler's Germany*, 2:387.
15. Beck to Brauchitsch, July 15, July 16, 1938, and memorandum of conversation, July 16, 1938, in Müller, *Beck*, pp. 537–54.
16. Memorandum of conversation, July 19, 1938, ibid., pp. 554–56.
17. Engel, *Heeresadjutant*, p. 26; Weinberg, *Foreign Policy of Hitler's Germany*, 2:408–9; entry for July 25, 1938, in Goebbels, *Tagebücher*.
18. Müller, *Heer und Hitler*, pp. 335–36; Reynolds, *Treason Was No Crime*, pp. 162–64.
19. Engel, *Heeresadjutant*, pp. 27–28.
20. Entry for Aug. 10, 1938, in Jodl diary, in *TMWC*, 28:374; O'Neill, *The German Army and the Nazi Party*, p. 223; Reynolds, *Treason Was No Crime*, p. 166; Müller, Heer und Hitler, p. 338.
21. Engel, *Heeresadjutant*, p. 32.
22. Förster, *Befestigungswesen*, p. 118. See also Gross, *Westwall*.
23. Reynolds, *Treason Was No Crime*, pp. 164–68; Müller, *Beck*, pp. 245, 309–11.

CHAPTER SIX: WAR!

1. *Weizsäcker Papiere*, pp. 123, 131.
2. Diary entry for May 22, 1938, ibid., p. 128; Weizsäcker to Ribbentrop, June 8, 1938, ibid., pp. 129–30, and in *DGFP*, 2:doc. 259 (misdated June 20, 1938).
3. Weizsäcker, memo, July 12, 1938, in *DGFP*, 2:doc. 288.
4. Weizsäcker, memo, July 21, 1938, ibid., doc. 304.
5. Weizsäcker, memo, Aug. 19, 1938, ibid., doc. 374; diary entry for Aug. 22, 1938, in *Weizsäcker Papiere*, p. 137.
6. Diary entries for Aug. 22, 23, 1938, in *Weizsäcker Papiere*, pp. 137–38; Blasius, *Für Grossdeutschland*, p. 56.

7. Diary entry for Aug. 28, 1938, in *Weizsäcker Papiere*, p. 139.
8. Weizsäcker to Ribbentrop, Aug. 30, 1938, in *DGFP*, 2:doc. 409; Weizsäcker to Ribbentrop, Sept. 8, 1939, in *Weizsäcker Papiere*, pp. 142–43.
9. Diary entry for May 22, 1938, in *Weizsäcker Papiere*, p. 128.
10. Diary entry for Sept. 7–10, 1938, ibid., p. 142; Henderson to Halifax, Sept. 10, 1938, in *DBFP*, 2:doc. 823.
11. Entry for Sept. 1, 1939, in Burckhardt diary, cited in Blasius, *Für Grossdeutschland*, p. 58.
12. Schmidt, *Statist*, p. 93; Weizsäcker, *Memoirs*, p. 151. In a voluminous and often contradictory literature on the negotiations commencing at Berchtesgaden and concluding at Munich, the best starting points are Weinberg, *Foreign Policy of Hitler's Germany*, and Parker, *Chamberlain*. Rönnefarth, *Sudetenkrise*, and Celovsky, *Münchener Abkommen*, nevertheless retain reference value.
13. Kordt to Weizsäcker, Sept. 21, 1939, in *DGFP*, 2:doc. 554.
14. Kordt, *Nicht aus den Akten*, p. 265.
15. Entry for July 25, 1938, in Goebbels, *Tagebücher*; memo, Oct. 9, 1939, in *Weizsäcker Papiere*, p. 145.
16. Letter, Dec. 17, 1938, in *Weizsäcker Papiere*, p. 146.
17. Teske, *Silbernen Spiegel*, p. 59. See also diary entry for Feb. 1, 1939, in *Weizsäcker Papiere*, p. 149.
18. Diary entry for Sept. 15, 1938, in *Weizsäcker Papiere*, p. 143.
19. Ibid.; directive, Dec. 17, 1938, in *U.S. v. Leeb*, 10:615–16.
20. Speech, Jan. 18, 1939, in Domarus, ed., *Hitler: Speeches*, 2:1427–28.
21. Speech, Jan. 26, 1939, ibid., p. 1435.
22. Speech, Feb. 10, 1939, ibid., p. 1468; Weinberg, *Foreign Policy of Hitler's Germany*, 2:515; Thies, *Architekt*, pp. 79–80, 112–20.
23. Kordt, *Wahn und Wirklichkeit*, p. 144.
24. Müller, *Heer und Hitler*, pp. 390–91.
25. Directive, April 11, 1939, in *DGFP*, 2:doc. 185.
26. Notes on speech of May 23, 1939, *U.S. v. Leeb*, 10:671–79. See also Müller, *Heer und Hitler*, p. 397.
27. Manstein, *Lost Victories*, p. 22.
28. Müller, *Heer und Hitler*, p. 392, n. 73.
29. Below, *Als Hitlers Adjutant*, pp. 148–49.
30. Engel, *Heeresadjutant*, p. 26; Leach, "Halder," p. 104.
31. Halder to Beck, Aug. 6, 1934, in Hartmann, *Halder*, p. 44.
32. Blumentritt, "Thoughts of a Former Soldier," p. 71.
33. Engel, *Heeresadjutant*, pp. 17, 35.
34. See Deutsch, *Hitler and His Generals*, pp. 401–6; Leach, "Halder," pp. 104–5; Müller, "Witzleben, Stülpnagel, and Speidel," pp. 49–51; Weizsäcker, *Memoirs*, p. 142. In his several writings about Halder, Ueberschär assembles all the relevant evidence.
35. Hartmann, *Halder*, pp. 69, 71, 74.
36. Gisevius, *To the Bitter End*, p. 166; *Hassell Diaries*, p. 64.
37. Entry for Aug. 22, 1939, in *Halder Diary*; entry for Aug. 22, 1939, in Groscurth, *Tagabücher*, p. 179 (which reproduces Admiral Canaris's notes); Warlimont, *Inside Hitler's Headquarters*, p. 25; *Keitel*, p. 87. See Müller, *Heer und Hitler*, p. 411.
38. Engel, *Heeresadjutant*, p. 58.

39. Müller, *Heer und Hitler*, p. 411; *Vollmacht des Gewissens*, pp. 377–78.
40. Diary entry for July 21, 1939, in *Weizsäcker Papiere*, pp. 155–56.
41. Diary entry for Aug. 13, 1939, ibid., p. 158.
42. Diary entry for Aug. 23, 1939, ibid., pp. 159–60.
43. Diary entry for Aug. 25, 1939, ibid., pp. 160–61.
44. Diary entry for Aug. 28, 1939, ibid., pp. 161–62.
45. Diary entry for Aug. 29, 1939, ibid., p. 162.
46. Entry for Sept. 7, 1939, in Wagner, ed., *Generalquartiermeister*, p. 131.

CHAPTER SEVEN: HITLER

1. Hitler made this remark to Hans Frank; see Kershaw, *Hitler*, p. 240. The putsch is described in Kershaw, pp. 191–219; this book provides much the best account of Hitler's early life. Other good biographies of Hitler include those by Bullock, Fest, Maser, and Steinert. The older biography by Schramm still retains value, largely because Schramm, an eminent medieval historian, was attached to Hitler's head-quarters during the war. The literature on Hitler is so large, diverse, and controversial that thoughtful books have been devoted just to analyzing these differences. Two such are Kershaw, *The "Hitler Myth,"* and Masur, *The Hitler of History.* On Hitler's thinking, Jäckel, *Hitler's Weltanschauung*, is a penetrating essay. Jäckel, *Frankreich in Hitlers Europa*, Knipping, "Frankreich," and Henke, *England in Hitlers politischen Kalkul*, treat his views on the Western powers. Binion, *Hitler Among the Germans*, Clemens, *Herr Hitler in Germany*, Peukert, *Inside Nazi Germany*, and Steinert, *Hitler's War and the Germans* and "Deutsche im Krieg," all deal, marvel at, but do not completely explain his popularity among and hold on the German populace. *Deutschland-Berichte* contains many dispatches from members of the Socialist underground reporting criticism of the Nazi Party but little or none of the Führer. Comparable evidence appears in Kopka, *Meldungen aus Münster*, and, for Bavaria, is analyzed in Kershaw, *Popular Opinion and Political Dissent.*
2. See P. Vidal de la Blache and L. Gallois, eds., *Géographie universelle*, vol. IV, Emm. de Martonne, *Europe Centrale*, pt. 2 (Paris: Armand Colin, 1931), pp. 478–80; *Das Waldviertel: Zeitschrift des Waldviertler Heimatbundes für Heimatkunde und Heimatpflege des Waldviertels und der Wachau* (a semischolarly magazine that has been published at Krems since 1961).
3. The quotations below come from Hitler, *Mein Kampf*, pp. 35–45.
4. The exact level of Hitler's poverty during his time in Vienna remains unclear. Most long-standing issues about this period of Hitler's life are resolved in Hamann, *Hitlers Wien.*
5. Bullock, *Hitler*, p. 50. The photograph is reproduced in Toland, *Hitler: The Pictorial Documentary of His Life*, no. 27.
6. Hitler, *Mein Kampf*, p. 213.
7. Ibid., p. 266.
8. Bullock, *Hitler*, pp. 115–16.
9. Kershaw, *Hitler*, p. 125. Pauley, *From Prejudice to Persecution*, deals with Austrian anti-Semitism.
10. Wheeler-Bennett, *Nemesis of Power*, p. 461.
11. Hitler, *Mein Kampf*, p. 137.

12. Ibid., pp. 107–8, 850.
13. Gunther, *Inside Europe*, p. 39.
14. Bullock, *Hitler*, p. 162; Gunther, *Inside Europe*, p. 66. See Orlow, *Nazi Party*, and the analysis in Turner, *Hitler's Thirty Days to Power*.
15. Hitler, *Mein Kampf*, p. 45.
16. Kershaw, *Hitler*, pp. 117–21, summarizes evidence that Hitler initially served the social-democratic republic before becoming its enemy.
17. Though Hitler later claimed to have been one of the first seven members of the party, he was actually member number 555 (ibid., p. 127).
18. Hitler, *Mein Kampf*, p. 492.
19. Ibid., pp. 511–13.
20. Ibid., pp. 234, 239. Zitelmann, *Hitler: Selbstverständnis*, makes a persuasive case that Hitler modeled himself on Mussolini.
21. Bullock, *Hitler*, p. 76.
22. Hitler, *Mein Kampf*, p. 475.
23. Domarus, ed., *Hitler: Speeches*, 1:64.
24. Ibid., pp. 60–71.
25. Schroeder, *Er war mein Chef*, p. 70.
26. Hitler, *Mein Kampf*, p. 313.
27. Heineman, *Hitler's First Foreign Minister*, p. 134; Engel, *Heeresadjutant*, pp. 46–47. Faber du Faur, *Macht und Ohnmacht*, p. 200, suggests that Hossbach contributed to Hitler's disdain for military attachés, for Hossbach himself thought them a *"quantité négligeable."*
28. Dodd, *Through Embassy Eyes*, pp. 258–59.
29. Dietrich, *12 Jahre*, pp. 154–55; Jacobsen, *Nationalsozialistische Aussenpolitik*, pp. 324–27, 348–50.
30. See Guikovaty, *Les Extravagantes Soeurs Mitford*.
31. Paine, *German Military Intelligence*, p. 37; NARS Film T-77, roll 932, contains reports from OKW Amt Ausland Abwehr.
32. Walter Peipe deposition, in Sept. 23, 1945, "Forschungsamt." Kahn, *Codebreakers*, is the standard general work on cryptology.
33. "Detailed Interrogation Report," Sept. 6, 1945, in "Forschungsamt," says that some records of telephone conversations between Germans went on blue paper, which was usually used for transcripts of radio broadcasts, and that these were known as "blue friends." But there is no other testimony to this effect.
34. Gellermann, *. . . und lauschten für Hitler*, pp. 82–83.
35. Ibid., pp. 88–96; Speer, *Inside the Third Reich*, pp. 146–50.
36. Gellermann, *. . . und lauschten für Hitler*, pp. 67–69.
37. See the file of reports on British policy from Munich to the outbreak of war, ibid., pp. 219–68, also in David Irving, *Das Reich hört mit*, pp. 172–246, and (with less annotation) *Breach of Security*.
38. Gellermann *. . . und lauschten für Hitler*, p. 137.
39. One of Hitler's adjutants thought that the Forschungsamt intercepts tended to indicate that France and Britain *would* fight for Poland and that Hitler therefore dismissed its "pessimistic material." Julius Schaub is so quoted in Ulrich Kittel, "RLM-Forschungsamt," in Irving, *Das Reich hort mit*, p. 24. See D. C. Watt's introduction to Irving, *Breach of Security*, p. 39.

40. See Jervis, *Perception and Misperception*; Steinbruner, *Cybernetic Theory*.
41. Frank, *Im Angesicht des Galgens*, pp. 380, 396–97; entry for Oct. 3, 1939, in *Halder Diary*.
42. Birchall, *The Storm Breaks*, p. 49.
43. Entries for Oct. 16, 19, 1937, in Goebbels, *Tagebücher*.
44. See entries for Jan. 21, 22, 1936, Sept. 5, 8, 14, 15, Nov. 2, 1937, July 28, 1938, ibid. See Manvell and Fraenkel, *Goebbels*, Bramsted, *Goebbels and National Socialist Propaganda*; and the sketch of Goebbels in Peuschel, *Männer um Hitler*.
45. Gunther, *Inside Europe*, p. 66. Overy, *Goering*, is the best biography, but see also those by Manvell and Fraenkel, Paul, Stefan Martens, and Kube and the sketch of Göring in Peuschel, *Männer um Hitler*.
46. *Preussisches Staatshandbuch . . . für das Jahr 1939*, 1:7–14, 105; Fromm, *Blood and Banquets*, pp. 113, 86.
47. Fromm, *Blood and Banquets*, pp. 244, 239; Bérard, *Un Ambassadeur se souvient*, 1:226–28.
48. Manvell and Fraenkel, *Göring*, p. 31.
49. Steinhoff, Pechel, and Showalter, *Voices from the Third Reich*, pp. 80–81; Deichmann, *Chef im Hintergrund*, p. 95.
50. Rieckhoff, *Trump oder Bluff*, pp. 149–150; Feuchter, *Geschichte des Luftkriegs*, p. 113; Boog, *Deutsche Luftwaffenführung*, p. 96.

CHAPTER EIGHT: DALADIER

1. Du Réau, *Daladier*, p. 30. See also Lapaquellerie, *Daladier*, which is by someone who knew him and, most important, was written before the events of 1940.
2. Simone, *J'Accuse*, p. 150. On the party: Larmour, *French Radical Party*; Nordmann, *Histoire des Radicaux*; Berstein, *Parti radical*. On Daladier's mentor, Herriot, see the biography by Soulié.
3. Girault, "Impact of the Economic Situation," p. 211. See Julian Jackson, *Politics of Depression*.
4. Albert, "Presse française," p. 511.
5. See Chavardès, *Le 6 février*.
6. See Colton, *Blum*, Julian Jackson, *Popular Front*, and studies of the French Socialist Party by Gombin and Lefranc.
7. Du Réau, *Daladier*, pp. 81–86. Cot, *Le Procès*, is a polemical defense of the Popular Front. Skidmore, *Pierre Cot*, seconds its arguments. On Cot's possible Soviet tie: Andrew and Gordievsky, *KGB*, pp. 446–47.
8. Young, *In Command*, is the best overall survey of French defense policy, but important points about the logic of the Maginot Line are made in Hughes, *To the Maginot Line*; Doughty, *Seeds of Disaster*; Kier, *Imagining War*; Kiesling, *Arming Against Hitler*; and Kemp, *Maginot Line*. Bruge, *Ligne Maginot*, is a detailed work by an enthusiast. Tournoux, *Haut-Commandement*, explains the military logic. Olivier Koch, *Ligne Maginot*, give a detailed description of one *petit ouvrage*.
9. Amery, *Political Life*, 3:335.
10. *Darlan Lettres*, pp. 66–68ff.; Armengaud, *Batailles*, pp. 37ff.; Doughty, "De Gaulle's Concept."
11. Kiesling, *Arming Against Hitler*, gives a splendid analysis of deficiencies in

French army training during the early and mid-1930s. The quotation from Sartre is on p. 62.

12. Hoff, *Programmes d'armement*, pp. 178–79.
13. Alexander, "Gamelin and the Defence of France," pp. 78–79.
14. Kiesling, *Arming Against Hitler*, p. 30.
15. Loustaunau-Lacau, *Mémoires*, p. 103 See also Chapman, *State Capitalism*, pp. 154–56.
16. U.S. military attaché report, March 7, 1938, U.S. military intelligence reports, reel 6.
17. Chapman, *State Capitalism*, pp. 154–56, has a good survey of air-force building programs. See also Boudot, "Problèmes du financement"; Boussard, *Problème de défense nationale*; and Wieland, *Zur Problematik der französischen Militärpolitik*. Young provides a summary, wryly entitled "Preparations for Defeat."
18. Montigny, *Défaite*, p. 234.
19. Du Réau, *Daladier*, p. 221.
20. Daridan, *Chemin*, p. 43.
21. Leeds, *These Rule France*, p. 88.

CHAPTER NINE: GAMELIN

1. The best and most up-to-date biographical study is Alexander, *Republic in Danger*. But this does not entirely displace Le Goyet, *Mystère Gamelin*, which is by an author with experienced feel for the Ministry of War.
2. De Gaulle, *Mémoires de guerre: L'Appel*, p. 30.
3. Blumentritt, *Rundstedt*, pp. 64–65; Messenger, *Rundstedt*, p. 109; Reynolds, *Treason Was No Crime*, p. 114. Beck's June 5, 1937, report on an extended trip to Paris is full of admiration for Gamelin (Beck, *Studien*, pp. 295–302). See Alexander, *Republic in Danger*, pp. 394–95, for other evidence on Gamelin's contemporaneous reputation.
4. Gamelin, *Servir*, 2:445. One indication of the extent of monarchism within the army is the testimony by one of Charles de Gaulle's War College classmates that de Gaulle said to him, "As for me, by family tradition, I could not be anything but a monarchist" (Laffargue, *Fantassin*, p. 130).
5. Poydenot, "Vu du PC de Vincennes," pp. 168–70.
6. Gen. Erich Kühlenthal, quoted in Beaumont-Nesbitt to the War Office, March 11, 1937, in Alexander, *Republic in Danger*, p. 32; Jordan, *Popular Front*, p. 53. Girardet, *Société militaire*, provides a wonderful sense of the world of the French army officer.
7. Loustaunau-Lacau, *Mémoires*, p. 92.
8. De Lattre, *Jean de Lattre, mon mari*, 1:66–67.
9. Gamelin, *Servir*, 3:522; Alexander, *Republic in Danger*, p. 39; Bankwitz, *Weygand*, p. 119. See also records of the CSG in 1 N 22, SHAT, and Duvignac, *Armée motoriseé*.
10. Gamelin, *Servir,* 2:89–92; Alexander, *Republic in Danger*, pp. 97–99. Tournoux, *Histoire secrète*, argues that Bourret's concern was justified.
11. Session of Feb. 9, 1938, quoted in Alexander, "Maurice Gamelin and the Defence of France," p. 64.

12. Entry for Sept. 25, 1939, in Villelume, *Journal*, pp. 42–43.
13. Bois, *Truth*, p. 96.
14. Le Goyet, *Mystère Gamelin*, pp. 227–28.
15. Porch, *French Secret Services*, is the broadest study. The best one focused on the 1930s is Young, "French Military Intelligence and Nazi Germany." Details on the organization of the Deuxième Bureau can be found in a manuscript with that title in 7 N 2523, SHAT. A number of Deuxième Bureau files removed by the Germans were found in Berlin by the Soviets when they occupied the capital after the Second World War, but these were mostly counterintelligence files of no use here. See Gusev and Bazov, "Frantsuska voennaya razvedka," and Maksimenka, "Arkhivy."
16. Warusfel, "Organisation du contre-espionnage français."
17. Dutailly, *Problèmes*, p. 35. Dentz would in fact have a longer career. When France was collapsing in June 1940, General Weygand made him governor of Paris on a presumption that he could use the resources of army intelligence and counterintelligence, and the Vichy regime put him in command of Syria. But none of this was anticipated earlier (Groussard, *Chemins secrets*, p. 13).
18. Strong, *Men of Intelligence*, p. 37.
19. Paillole, *Homme des services secrets*, pp. 78–80; Paillole, *Notre Espion*, pp. 16–17; Paillole, *Services spéciaux*, p. 24; Conte, *1er janvier*, p. 145.
20. Allard, *Responsables*, p. 210; Dutailly, *Problèmes*, pp. 277–78; Simiot, *De Lattre*, pp. 131–32; du Réau, *Daladier*, pp. 221–22. Gamelin, *Servir*, 2:92, says Bourret hoped to gain control of the SR.
21. Paillole, *Notre Espion*, is primarily about "H.E."
22. Ibid., pp. 85–87.
23. Ibid., p. 90.
24. Ibid.; Paillole, *Services spéciaux*, pp. 92–93; Faligot, *Markus*, p. 38.
25. In addition to accounts in memoirs, there is an "as-told-to" book: Koch-Kent, *Doudot*.
26. Paillole, *Services spéciaux*, p. 149.
27. Bézy, *SR Air*, pp. 13, 19–22; Hinsley et al., *British Intelligence*, 1:496–99.
28. Accart, *On s'est battu*, pp. 93–99; Paillole, *Notre Espion*, p. 70; Paillole, *Services spéciaux*, p. 161; Allard, *Responsables*, p. 210. See also Paquier, *Aviation de renseignement*.
29. See Porch, "French Intelligence and the Fall of France."
30. Zimmer, *Septennat policier*, pp. 220–22; Sarraz-Bourret, *Témoignage*, pp. 16–18; Allard, *Responsables*, p. 210.
31. Jackson, "French Military Intelligence and Czechoslovakia," p. 84.
32. This is painstakingly detailed in Castellan, *Réarmement clandestin*.
33. Dutailly, *Problèmes*, p. 77.
34. Ibid., pp. 77–78.
35. Ibid., p. 36.
36. Quoted in du Réau, *Daladier*, p. 198.
37. Dutailly, *Problèmes*, p. 46; Young, "French Military Intelligence," p. 146; Buffotot, "French High Command," p. 550.
38. Le Goyet, *Mystère Gamelin*, p. 66.

CHAPTER TEN: CROSS-CURRENTS

1. Navarre et al., *Service de Renseignements*, p. 78; Armengaud, *Batailles*, p. 27, quoting a conversation with Gamelin of Jan. 10, 1936; Clauzel to Laval, Jan. 10, 1936, in *DDF*, 1:doc. 27; Paillole, *Notre Espion*, p. 16; Renondeau to Fabry, Jan. 15, 1936, in *DDF*, 1:doc. 63; Maurin to Flandin, Feb. 12, 1936, in *DDF*, 1:doc. 170; note from general staff of army, Feb. 18, 1936, in *DDF*, 1:doc. 202; Déat to Pietri, March 2, 1936, in *DDF*, 1:doc. 269.
2. *Le Canard enchaîné* quoted in Kupferman, *Laval*, p. 172; Duroselle, *Décadence*, pp. 170–71. See also Dreyfus, "Pacifisme en France (1930–1940)"; Vaïsse, "Pazifismus."
3. Déat, quoted in Kupferman, *Laval*, p. 172. Schuker, "France and the Remilitarization of the Rhineland," p. 328, notes that Déat's memoir, written in 1944 and never published, is the most nearly contemporaneous comment by a member of the government, and no prewar evidence concerning *any* member of the government indicates serious thought of a military response to the German action.
4. Entries for March 6, 9–10, April 22, 1936, in Schweisguth diary, cited in Young, *In Command of France*, pp. 121–23; 283, n. 70. On the limited role of the air staff, see Christienne, "L'Armée de l'air et la crise du 7 mars 1936."
5. Dutailly, *Problèmes*, p. 78; Müller-Hillebrand, *Das Heer*, 1:25, 59–60.
6. Paillole, *Notre Espion*, pp. 108–10.
7. Rivet diary, Nov. 12, 1937.
8. CPDN, minutes, Dec. 12, 1937, in *DDF* 7:doc. 325.
9. Lamarle to Delbos, Jan. 19, 1938, ibid., 8:doc. 10; reports from Vienna of various dates in early 1938, ibid.; Paillole, *Notre Espion*, p. 122; Stehlin, *Témoignage*, pp. 75–76.
10. See Bullitt's letter, Aug. 29, 1939, in *Bullitt*, p. 361; testimony in *Français et britanniques*, pp. 158–59.
11. The corrective to the gossip is Crouy-Chanel, *Léger*, pp. 109–12. The quotations are from Chauvel, *Commentaires*, p. 44; Crouy-Chanel, *Léger*, p. 53; Leeds, *These Rule France*, p. 342.
12. Adamthwaite, *France and the Coming of the Second World War*, p. 255.
13. Quoted in Parker, *Chamberlain*, p. 63.
14. Girault, "Impact of the Economic Situation," offers an even-handed analysis of this much-disputed topic.
15. Delbos to Corbin, Feb. 17, 1938, in *DDF*, 9:doc. 190.
16. Du Réau, *Daladier*, p. 210.
17. François-Poncet's reportage can be sampled in his *Souvenirs*. On his reputation: Davignon, *Souvenirs*, p. 13. Crouy-Chanel, *Léger*, p. 30, comments acidly of François-Poncet: "His correspondence was not as concise as his bons mots. The pouch from Berlin brought each time long reports which weighed down desks without great profit from the very much diluted information that they contained."
18. Letter, Jan. 21, 1933, in du Réau, *Daladier*, p. 15.
19. Crouy-Chanel, *Léger*, pp. 118–19, 149.

CHAPTER ELEVEN: TO MUNICH

1. Vallette and Bouillon, *Munich*, p. 32.
2. Paillole, *Services spéciaux*, p. 149.

3. DDF, 9:doc. 121.
4. Quoted in Vallette and Bouillon, *Munich*, p. 144. Ingram, *Politics of Dissent*, is a good study of French pacifism.
5. Lacaze, *Opinion publique*, pp. 279, 365–67.
6. Vallette and Bouillon, *Munich*, pp. 27–28.
7. Daladier testimony, in *Événements . . . : Tém.*, 1D:33. The whole subject is exhaustively reviewed in Lacaze, *Opinion publique*, pp. 353–402.
8. Werth, *France and Munich*, p. 71; Simone, *J'Accuse*, pp. 33–34. Adamthwaite, *France and the Coming of the Second World War*, makes Bonnet a far more understandable and sympathetic character than does most earlier writing, in which he figures simply as one of France's chief "gravediggers." Everything in this and other chapters that concerns French politics and diplomacy owes more to Adamthwaite's book than any specific notes can acknowledge.
9. Bois, *Truth*, p. 61.
10. Boothe, *Europe in the Spring*, pp. 102–3; Favreau, *Mandel*, pp. 341–44. See also the biographies of Mandel by Wormser and Sherwood.
11. See Ferris, "Indulged in Too Little?"
12. Deuxième Bureau, "Grand Rapport: Allemagne," July 12, 1938, 7 N 2290, SHAT; Deuxième Bureau, "Compte rendu," Aug. 25, 1938, in *DDF*, 10:doc. 458; Deuxième Bureau, "Compte rendu," Aug. 27, 1938, in 7 N 2523, SHAT; Deuxième Bureau, "Bulletin des renseignements," Aug. 30, 1938, in *DDF*, 10:doc. 506; Gauché, *Deuxième Bureau*, p. 70; Paillole, *Services spéciaux*, p. 107; Weinberg, *Foreign Policy of Hitler's Germany*, 2:394.
13. Du Réau, *Daladier*, p. 260.
14. Dutailly, *Problèmes*, pp. 61–62.
15. Buffotot, "Perception du rearmement allemand," p. 176; Facon, "Visite du Général Vuillemin en Allemagne." See also Teyssier, "Vuillemin"; Jackson, "Perception de la puissance aérienne allemande'; Young, "The Use and Abuse of Fear."
16. Lapaquellerie, *Daladier*, pp. 130–31; Cox, *Countdown*, p. 190.
17. *DDF*, 11:doc. 273.
18. Du Réau, *Daladier*, p. 258.
19. Zay, *Carnets*, pp. 4–5.
20. Du Réau, *Daladier*, pp. 264–65.
21. Raphaël-Leygues, *Chronique*, p. 114; du Réau, *Daladier*, p. 221.
22. Phipps to Halifax, Sept. 21, 1938, in *DBFP*, 2:doc. 1012.
23. Gauché, *Deuxième Bureau*, pp. 71–72, 141–43. Gauché says that he presented this report on September 27. I have not found the original.
24. Du Réau, *Daladier*, p. 275.
25. *Dalton Diary*, p. 249.
26. Raphaël-Leygues, *Chroniques*, pp. 118–19. See Lacaze, *France et Munich*.

CHAPTER TWELVE: CHAMBERLAIN

1. The most thorough and judicious studies of Chamberlain's prewar policies are Parker, *Chamberlain and Appeasement*, and the relevant portions of Watt, *How War Came*. McDonough, *Chamberlain, Appeasement*, pp. 1–12, provides an excellent review of the literature. Early postwar writings were unqualifiedly critical of

Chamberlain. Churchill, *The Gathering Storm* (vol. 1 of *The Second World War*); Namier, *Diplomatic Prelude*; and Wheeler-Bennett, *Munich*, stand out. Once British archives began to open, David Dilks led a movement to revise this assessment, pointing out the extent to which the documentary record showed Chamberlain to have had a relatively limited range of options and to have accompanied his diplomatic efforts with an increasingly vigorous program of rearmament. (See Dilks entries in the Bibliography.) Middlemas, *Diplomacy of Illusion*, argues that the archives do not in any way exculpate Chamberlain. Fuchser, *Neville Chamberlain and Appeasement*, though similarly critical, argues that Chamberlain's decisions were made almost inevitable by his fixed beliefs regarding the lessons of the First World War and the interwar years. John Charmley has replied to all the critics of Chamberlain in *Chamberlain and the Lost Peace*. Going far beyond Dilks, Charmley argues that Chamberlain's appeasement was actually the most wise and prudent course of action open to Britain. In *Churchill's Grand Alliance*, Charmley has gone on to argue that Churchill's uncompromising policy toward Hitler cost Britain its power and influence in the world. The latest polemics against Chamberlain revive a left-wing argument of the late 1930s. Liebowitz, *The Chamberlain-Hitler Deal*, and Liebowitz and Finkel, *The Chamberlain-Hitler Collusion*, allege that Chamberlain's diplomacy aimed entirely at building an anti-Soviet coalition. On the atmosphere surrounding Chamberlain and his Cabinet, see Cowling, *Impact of Hitler*; Gannon, *British Press and Germany*; Schmidt, "Domestic Background."

2. See Cockett, *Twilight of Truth*, and especially Adamthwaite, "The British Government and the Media."

3. On Chamberlain's influence over the news media, see McDonough, *Chamberlain, Appeasement*, pp. 114–30; Cockett, *Twilight of Truth*.

4. Churchill, memorandum, Oct. 25, 1939, in *Churchill War Papers*, 1:239.

5. Sir Arthur Salter, quoted in Addison, *Road to 1945*, pp. 29–30.

6. Margesson, quoted in Addison, p. 61; entries for Jan. 24 and Feb. 2, 1940, in Colville, *Fringes of Power*, pp. 74, 79; Amery, *My Political Life*, 3:225.

7. Oct. 21, 1933, NC 2/24a, Chamberlain Papers.

8. See Wark, *Ultimate Enemy*, pp. 17–32; Bond, *British Military Policy*, pp. 191–214. See also Powers, *Strategy Without Slide Rule*.

9. *Economist*, quoted in Macleod, *Chamberlain*, p. 258; Chamberlain speech of April 1938, quoted in same, p. 208.

10. Entry for May 22, 1936, in Jones, *Diary*; Gilbert, *Churchill*, 5:741.

11. The appointment was damned by Churchill's friends, one of whom described it as the worst since the Roman Emperor Caligula made his horse a consul. Greenwood, " 'Caligula's Horse,' " offers a balanced assessment of Inskip, making a case that he was a reasonable choice to occupy a difficult post.

12. Parker, *Chamberlain and Appeasement*, p. 277.

13. Chamberlain, note, June 20, 1934, quoted in Wark, *Ultimate Enemy*, p. 40. See, in general, Shay, *British Rearmament*, and Peden, The *Treasury and British Rearmament*. On the air force, see the official history, Penrose, *British Aviation*, and Hyde, *British Air Policy*. On the navy, see two works sanctioned by the Admiralty: Roskill, *Naval Policy*, and Marder, *Dardanelles to Oran*.

14. Except where indicated, the paragraphs below derive from Wark, *Ultimate Enemy*, pp. 35–79, or Murray, "Appeasement and Intelligence."

15. Winterbotham, *Ultra Spy*, pp. 151–54, gives a firsthand account of confrontation between himself, representing the SIS, and the air staff.
16. Corum, *Luftwaffe*, pp. 228–33, contends that the chief officers in the Luftwaffe, though with backgrounds in ground forces, would have been prepared to continue an emphasis on strategic bombing, but that Jeschonnek, the young pilot who became service chief of staff, supported Milch in preparing primarily for a ground *Blitzkrieg*.
17. Chiefs of Staff memorandum, March 28, 1938, CAB 53/37.
18. Speech, Nov. 26, 1937, quoted in Feiling, *Chamberlain*, p. 333.
19. Newton to Halifax, March 15, 1938, in *DBFP*, 1:doc. 86. See Zorach, "British View of the Czechs."
20. Cabinet meeting minutes, March 22, 1938, CAB 23/93; Phipps to Halifax, Sept. 24, 1938, in *DBFP*, 2:doc. 1076. Asked by Cadogan for clarification, Phipps said that the war party consisted mainly of Communists (Phipps to Halifax, Sept. 26, 1938, in *DBFP*, 2:doc. 1099).
21. Foreign Policy Committee minutes, Sept. 24, 1938, CAB 27/646; Cabinet meeting minutes, Sept. 24, 1938, CAB 23/95. Middlemas, *Diplomacy of Illusion*, pp. 370–80, quotes the discussions at length.
22. Middlemas, *Diplomacy of Illusion*, pp. 370–71.
23. Halifax's account of the visit can be pieced together from excerpts in his own *Fulness of Days*, pp. 183–91, and from Birkenhead, *Halifax*, pp. 367–74. Schwoerer, "Lord Halifax's Visit to Germany," offers full details but overstates the significance of the event. Before his first visit to London, Daladier asked Léger for a memo on Halifax's bad influence on Chamberlain. Léger responded that such comments should not be put on paper. (Du Réau, *Daladier*, p. 222, based on an interview with Étienne Crouy-Chanel.) The best study of Halifax is Roberts, "*Holy Fox*."
24. Halifax to British delegation, Godesberg, Sept. 23, 1938, in *DBFP*, 2:doc. 1058.
25. Cadogan to Eden, May 13, 1936, in *Cadogan Diaries*, p. 13, is good evidence of his enthusiasm for appeasement. "Awful rubbish": entry for April 29, 1938, ibid., p. 73.
26. Entry for Sept. 25, 1938, ibid., p. 105.

CHAPTER THIRTEEN: ENOUGH!
1. Bellstedt, "*Apaisement*" *oder Krieg*, pp. 148–50; Adamthwaite, *France and the Coming of the Second World War*, p. 149; Coulondre, *De Staline à Hitler*, p. 198. Bellstedt's book is an elaborate account of Bonnet's negotiating effort.
2. Report, Oct. 11, 1938, in U.S. Military Intelligence Reports: France, reel 6. In his diary for Oct. 14, 1938, Daladier's naval aide, Raphaël-Leygues, wrote, "Anti-Semitic conversation everywhere" (Raphaël-Leygues, *Chronique*, p. 121).
3. Duroselle, *Décadence*, pp. 387–89, offers a careful review of the evidence.
4. See his dispatches of Jan. 26, 1939, Feb. 8, 1939, and Feb. 23, 1939, in *DDF*, 13:doc. 432, 14:doc. 80, and 14:doc. 190.
5. Deuxième Bureau report, Nov. 30, 1938, in *DDF*, 12:doc. 461; Deuxième Bureau reports, Dec. 22, 1938, Dec. 23, 1938, 7 N 2523, SHAT.
6. Gamelin to Vuillemin and Darlan, Oct. 12, 1938, in *DDF*, 12:doc. 86.

7. Vuillemin to Gamelin, Oct. 25, 1938, ibid., doc. 213.

8. Gamelin to Daladier, Oct. 26, 1938, ibid., doc. 225.

9. Gamelin to Daladier, Dec. 3, 1938, Fonds Gamelin, 1 K 224, SHAT.

10. CPDN meeting, Dec. 5, 1938, in *DDF*, 13:doc. 37; Gamelin, *Servir*, 2:371; Daladier Senate testimony, Dec. 14, 1938, quoted in Frankenstein, *Financement du réarmement*, p. 76; Bourret, quoted in Coulondre, *De Staline à Hitler*, p. 198. See Bodinier, "Gamelin, les fortifications, et les chars."

11. Gamelin to Daladier, Dec. 19, 1938, 5 N 579, SHAT; Gamelin to Daladier, Dec. 27, 1938, in *DDF*, 13:doc. 234. The text of the Deuxième Bureau report of Dec. 19, 1938, appears in Gauché, *Deuxième Bureau*, pp. 82–83. Le Goyet, *"Coup de Prague,"* p. 55, surmises that the source was Canaris. Paillole, *Notre Espion*, p. 140, suggests that it was General Schmidt, quoted to the SR by his brother, "H.E." But there is no German record of a meeting of the period involving field commanders.

12. Janet Flanner, *New Yorker*, Jan. 12, 1939, in Flanner, *Paris Was Yesterday*, p. 197.

13. See Duroselle, *Décadence*, pp. 389–96.

14. Bonnet to Campinchi, Jan. 13, 1939, in *DDF*, 13:doc. 363; Deuxième Bureau report, Jan. 25, 1939, ibid., doc. 423; Chiefs of Staff memorandum 830, Jan. 25, 1939, CAB 53/44. On the French-British army conspiracy, see entry for Nov. 14, 1938, *Pownall Diaries*, pp. 169–70. On Oster and the Dutch military attaché, see Vanwelkenhuyzen, *Avertissements*.

15. Montbas (Chargé, Berlin) to Bonnet, Dec. 5, 1938, in *DDF*, 14:doc. 34; Montbas to Bonnet, Dec. 6, 1938, ibid., doc. 42; Deuxième Bureau report, Dec. 23, 1938, 7 N 2523, SHAT; Didelet, report, Jan. 10, 1939, in *DDF*, 13:doc. 334; Deuxième Bureau report, Feb. 1, 1939, in *DDF*, 14:doc. 6.

16. The claims are in Gauché, *Deuxième Bureau* p. 85; Paillole, *Services spéciaux*, p. 115; Paillole, *Notre Espion*, p. 143; and Navarre et al., *Service de Renseignements*, p. 80. Coulondre and his air attaché, Paul Stehlin, were told repeatedly, from early February on, by Colonel Bodenschatz of the Luftwaffe, what Hitler intended regarding Czechoslovakia, but they did not make much of this information in their reports to Paris (Coulondre, *De Staline à Hitler*, pp. 240, 252–53; Stehlin, *Témoignage*, p. 136). But, although Rivet's diary for March 12, 1939, says that the action was foreseen in February, it records the action's having been specified (*précisée*) only on March 6, and the earliest discoverable contemporaneous document broadcasting a warning is a Deuxième Bureau report of March 10, 7 N 2524, SHAT.

17. Dutailly, *Problèmes*, pp. 77–79; Deuxième Bureau report, Feb. 21, 1939, 7 N 2516, SHAT.

18. Hoff, *Programmes d'armement*, p. 216; du Réau, *Daladier*, pp. 315–16.

19. Du Réau, *Daladier*, p. 312.

20. Entry for March 17, 1939, in Zay, *Carnets secrets*, pp. 46–47; Sauvy, *De Paul Reynaud à Charles de Gaulle*, pp. 107–8.

21. Zimmer, *Septennat policier*, pp. 79–80.

22. Phipps to Halifax, Sept. 24, 1938, in *DBFP*, 2:doc. 1076; Phipps to Halifax, Sept. 26, 1938 (two messages), ibid., docs. 1106, 1119.

23. Saint-Exupéry, quoted in du Réau, *Daladier*, p. 255; Werth, *France and Munich*, p. 308; Welczek to Ribbentrop, Oct. 31, 1938, in *DGFP*, 4:doc. 344.

24. Montherlant, *Équinoxe de septembre*; Vallette and Bouillon, *Munich*, p. 224; Lacaze, *Opinion publique*, pp. 90, 300, 362–64. Some of the arguments of these "realists" appear in their books, though with undue stress on those that seemed prescient in light of France's defeat in 1940: Paul-Boncour, *Entre deux guerres*; Géraud (Pertinax), *Gravediggers*; Tabouis, *They Call Me Cassandra* and *Vingt ans*.

25. Quoted in Vallette and Bouillon, *Munich*, p. 201. See Lacaze, *Opinion publique*, pp. 472–74, which describes the struggle within the editorial board of *Temps présent*. Cointet-Labrousse, "Syndicat National," describes the torment within one union. Christophe, *Catholiques*, describes crosscurrents within the confession.

26. Lacaze, *Opinion publique*, pp. 323–27, 342–44.

27. Bois, *Truth*, p. 193.

28. Berstein, *Parti radical*, 1:550–60; Lacaze, *Opinion publique*, pp. 375–79; Nordmann, *Histoire des Radicaux*, pp. 282–84.

29. Quoted in Vallette and Bouillon, *Munich*, p. 144.

30. Lefranc, *Mouvement socialiste*, 2:367–70; Lacaze, *Opinion publique*, pp. 393–401. See Taubert, *Französische Linke*.

31. Vallette and Bouillon, *Munich*, p. 239.

32. Churchill, *Second World War*, 1:327–28.

33. Chamberlain letter, Oct. 2, 1938, quoted in Feiling, *Chamberlain*, p. 375.

34. Cabinet meeting minutes, Oct. 3, 1938, CAB 23/95.

35. Letter to Hilda Chamberlain, March 27, 1938, NC 18/1/1043, Chamberlain Papers. On the rearmament program, see Shay, *British Rearmament*; Peden, *Treasury and British Rearmament*; Höbelt, *Britische Appeasementpolitik*.

36. Letter, NC 18/1/1089, Chamberlain Papers.

37. House of Commons Debates, March 15, 1939, quoted in Newman, *March 1939*, p. 100.

38. Birkenhead, *Halifax*, p. 432; entry for March 16, 1939, in *Cadogan Diaries*, p. 157; entry for March 16, 1939, in *Harvey Diaries*, p. 262.

39. Feiling, *Chamberlain*, pp. 400–1; Cabinet meeting minutes, March 18, 1939, CAB 23/98. The evidence used by Halifax is analyzed in Newman, *March 1939*, pp. 107–120, and Watt, "British Intelligence."

40. Entry for April 3, 1939, in *Pownall Diaries*, p. 197.

41. Hankey to Phipps, April 4, 1939, quoted in Douglas, *Advent of War*, p. 9.

42. Cabinet meeting minutes, March 30, 1938, CAB 23/98; Chief of Staff memorandum 872, April 3, 1939, CAB 53/47.

43. Letter, April 9, 1939, NC 18/1/1093, Chamberlain Papers.

44. Deuxième Bureau report, April 8, 1939, in *DDF*, 15:doc. 308; Gauché to Lelong, April 9, 1939, 7 N 3439, SHAT; Bonnet to Corbin, April 12, 1939, in *DDF*, 15:doc. 354. See also Jackson, "France and the Guarantee to Roumania."

45. Corbin to Bonnet, April 12, 1939, in *DDF*, 15:doc. 358, reports the initial adverse British reaction, as does an entry for the same date in *Cadogan Diaries*, p. 173. An entry for April 13, 1939, in *Cadogan Diaries* characterizes the arguments for the guarantee as "unanswerable." Corbin to Bonnet, April 14, 1939, in *DDF*, 15:doc. 402, reports British explanations for concurrence. Quotation: Cabinet meeting minutes, March 20, 1939, CAB 23/98.

46. Kordt, *Wahn und Wirklichkeit*, p. 144.

CHAPTER FOURTEEN: ACCEPTING WAR

1. Letter, July 23, 1939, NC 18/1/1108, Chamberlain Papers.
2. Record of Anglo-French conversations, April 28–29, 1938, *DBFP*, 1:doc. 164 (p. 217).
3. Phipps to Halifax, April 19, 1939, *DBFP* 4:doc. 218; entry for April 21, 1939, in *Cadogan Diaries*, p. 176.
4. Chamberlain to Ida Chamberlain, March 26, 1939, NC 18/1/1091, Chamberlain Papers.
5. Parker, *Chamberlain and Appeasement*, p. 207. See Dennis, *Decision by Default*.
6. Direction politique to British Embassy, April 24, 1939, in *DDF*, 15:doc. 482.
7. Parker, *Chamberlain and Appeasement*, p. 328.
8. Chamberlain to Ida Chamberlain, March 26, 1939, NC 18/1/1091, Chamberlain Papers.
9. Quoted in Douglas, *Advent of War*, p. 9.
10. Minutes of Franco-British conversations, July 13, 1939, in *DDF*, 17:doc. 198; entry for July 17, 1939, in *Doumenc Papiers*, pp. 36–37. Buffotot, "French High Command," and Jordan, "Cut-Price War," may be right, however, that Gamelin was less interested in what the Soviets might actually do than in simply having another Eastern ally. See Vaïsse, "Perception de la puissance soviétique."
11. Chiefs-of-staff meeting, May 16, 1939, CAB 53. See also Herndon, "British Perceptions." On the admiral's qualities: Watt, *How War Came*, pp. 452–54.
12. Letter, July 23, 1939, NC 118/1/1108, Chamberlain Papers.
13. Stehlin, *Témoignage*, p. 144; Gauché, *Deuxième Bureau*, p. 98; Deuxième Bureau report, May 10, 1939, 7 N 2516, SHAT; Cabinet meeting minutes, May 24, 1939, CAB 23; Coulondre to Bonnet, May 8, 1939, in *DDF*, 16:doc. 105; League of Nations Bureau of the Foreign Ministry, June 30, 1939, in *DDF*, 17:doc. 56; Chamberlain to Hilda Chamberlain, May 21, 1939, NC 118/1/1100, Chamberlain Papers.
14. Foreign Office memorandum, May 22, 1939, in *DBFP*, 5:doc. 589.
15. Deuxième Bureau reports, April 5, 11, 20, 1939, May 4, 1939, 7 N 2524, 7 N 2516, 7 N 2525, 7 N 2516, SHAT.
16. Deuxième Bureau report, May 3, 1939, in *DDF*, 16:doc. 26; Deuxième Bureau reports, May 4, 10, 1939, 7 N 2516, SHAT; Coulondre to Bonnet, May 11, 1939, in *DDF*, 16:doc. 148. Paillole, *Notre Espion*, p. 146, attributes the latter information to "H.E." Though it seems unlikely that "H.E." would have been described as "an uncontrolled source," this may have been an instance in which the actual source was his brother, the general, for this was more or less the plan actually carried out by the German army in September.
17. Rivet diary, June 9, 1939.
18. Deuxième Bureau reports, June 14 (two reports), June 26, July 22, Aug. 2, 1939, 7 N 2516, 7 N 2524, SHAT.
19. Gauché, *Deuxième Bureau*, pp. 99–101.
20. Rebatet, *Mémoires d'un fasciste*, 1:163.
21. Entry for Aug. 22, 1939, in Zay, *Carnets secrets*, pp. 60–64.
22. Ibid.; memorandum on dinner at the U.S. Embassy, Aug. 22, 1939, in *DDF*, 18:doc. 258. Much is added to Zay, *Carnets secrets* and *Souvenirs*, and de Monzie, *Ci-devant*, by the biographies: Ruby, *Zay*, and Planté, *Grand Seigneur*.

23. CPDN meeting, Aug. 23, 1939, in *DDF*, 18:doc. 324. Gamelin's protestations are in Gamelin, *Servir*, 1:23–43.
24. Coulondre, *De Staline à Hitler*, p. 291.
25. Coulondre to Bonnet, Aug. 29, 1939, in *DDF*, 19:doc. 180; Coulondre to Bonnet, Aug. 30, 1939, ibid., doc. 235; Coulondre, *De Staline à Hitler*, pp. 297–304; Stehlin, *Témoignage*, pp. 176–77; Adamthwaite, *France and the Coming of the Second World War*, p. 153.
26. Coulondre to Daladier, Aug. 30, 1939, in *DDF*, 19:doc. 235; Chauvel, *Commentaires*, p. 59.
27. Entry for Aug. 31, 1939, in Bonnet diary, in *DDF*, 19:addenda 1; Bonnet, *Quai d'Orsay*, pp. 259–60; Clapier, memorandum, Sept. 1, 1939, in *DDF*, 19:doc. 351.
28. Chamberlain to Hilda Chamberlain, July 2, 1939, NC 18/1/1105, Chamberlain Papers.
29. Chamberlain to Ida Chamberlain, July 23, 1939, NC 18/1/1108, ibid.
30. See Parker, *Chamberlain and Appeasement*, pp. 336–42; Watt, *How War Came*, pp. 590–95; Chamberlain to Ida Chamberlain, Sept. 10, 1939, NC 18/1/1116, Chamberlain Papers.
31. Hore-Belisha to Halifax, Aug. 30, 1939, quoted in Wark, *Ultimate Enemy*, p. 120.32.
32. Christian de Lavarenne, a future *inspecteur des finances*, quoted in Weber, *Hollow Years*, pp. 247–48; Debré, *Trois Républiques*, 1:159.
33. Frankenstein, "Decline of France," p. 239.
34. Doise and Vaïsse, *Outil militaire*, comment on how, at various periods, French military leaders could swing from near panic to complacency. Nicole Jordan's *Popular Front*, "Cut-Price War," and "Maurice Gamelin" evoke brilliantly the near panic of the mid-1930s, when Gamelin and his colleagues appeared to question how France would fare in a war with even a relatively weak Germany. She did not see the sharp shift that occurred soon after the period on which she concentrated her documentary research.
35. Gauché, *Deuxième Bureau*, pp. 103–4. Italics in original.
36. Du Réau, *Daladier*, pp. 251–52, 264–65.
37. Deuxième Bureau reports, Jan. 15, Feb. 26, June 14, June 19, 1939, 7 N 2515, 7 N 2516, 7 N 2524, SHAT.
38. Financial Attaché, Washington, to Bonnet, Feb. 26, 1939, in *DDF*, 14:doc. 165; La Chambre to Bonnet, March 1939, ibid., 15:doc. 223; entry for Aug. 22, 1939, in Zay, *Carnets secrets*, pp. 60–64; Vuillemin to La Chambre, Aug. 26, 1939, in *Evénements . . . : Rap.*, 2:331–32; La Chambre to Daladier, Aug. 26, 1939, in *DDF*, 19:doc. 51. See also Chapman, *State Capitalism*, pp. 158–60, 201–7.
39. "Le Problème militaire français," Jan. 1939, 7 N 2695, SHAT.
40. See CPDN minutes, April 9, 1939, in *DDF*, 15:doc. 316; Gamelin, *Servir*, 2:403.
41. École Militaire, "La Problème stratégique," April 15, 1939, 7 N 2524, SHAT.
42. De Lattre, *Jean de Lattre, mon mari*, 1:122. See also Jacomet, *Armement de la France*, p. 289; Bankwitz, *Weygand*, p. 147.
43. Bonnet, *Fin d'une Europe*, p. 258. Sanson, *Les 14 juli*, provides context.
44. Amouroux, *Français sous l'Occupation*, 1:79.
45. DiNardo, *Mechanized Juggernaut*, pp. 21–26.

46. Jacobsen, *Fall Gelb*, pp. 10, 19.
47. Entry for Nov. 9, 1939, in Tippelskirch diary; Göring directive, Nov. 24, 1939, NARS Film T 971, reel 50; entry for Nov. 27, 1939, in *Halder Diary*.
48. See Reynolds, "Churchill and the British 'Decision.' "
49. *L'Oeuvre*, May 4, 1939, quoted in Albert, "Presse française," p. 567.
50. Phipps to Halifax, May 5, 1939, in *DBFP*, 5:doc. 384.
51. Benteli and Jeancolas, "Cinéma français," gives an overview. What appears here is mostly taken from that essay and Jeancolas's more detailed *15 Ans* Martin, *Golden Age of French Cinema*; Garçon, *De Blum à Pétain*; or Guillaume-Grimaud, *Cinéma du Front Populaire*.
52. One example is Carné's *Quai des brumes*, described in the subsequent text. It was certainly taken as a pacifist film. A Vichy official went so far as to single it out as a factor in causing France's defeat. But Carné and his backers had had no hesitation about originally seeking financing in Germany. They seem to have been somewhat surprised when Goebbels pronounced the treatment "unwholesome." It was released in France after serious vetting by censors, who insisted, among other things, that the hero treat his uniform with respect—fold it on a chair instead of dropping it on the floor. And Jean Renoir, after seeing rushes, pronounced the film "fascist." See Carné, *Vie à belles dents*, pp. 93–117.
53. Guillaume-Grimaud, *Cinéma du Front Populaire*, pp. 93–113, gives a detailed history of *La Marseillaise*. One can argue that this ambivalence was foreshadowed in *Grand Illusion*, for some viewers of that film must have thought its high point the dining-hall scene, where Jean Gabin as Lieutenant Maréchal announces that the French have recaptured Douaumont, and the French prisoners stand up and break into their national anthem.
54. Sesonske, *Jean Renoir*, pp. 380ff.
55. Crémieux-Brilhac, "Opinion publique française, pp. 7–8. The two songs had actually been current earlier, sung by Marie Dubas (Crosland, *Piaf*, pp. 52–54). That probably makes it more significant that Piaf made them hits in 1939.
56. Entry for April 18, 1939, in Zay, *Carnets secrets*, pp. 57–58; Aragon, quoted in Bédarida, *Stratégie secrète*, p. 53.
57. Lamoureux, quoted in Crémieux-Brilhac, *Français de l'an 40*, 1:143; Lazareff, *Deadline*, p. 245.

CHAPTER FIFTEEN: NOW FRANCE?

1. Letter, Oct. 11, 1939, in Wagner, *Generalquartiermeister*, p. 141.
2. Höhne, *Canaris*, p. 213.
3. Entry for Sept. 2, 1938, in Groscurth, *Tagebücher*, p. 111.
4. Müller, "German Military Opposition."
5. For obvious reasons, the resistance to Hitler has been one of the most studied aspects of Third Reich history. The role of military officers in the resistance has been a particular focus of study, and their names have been commemorated: the old Bendlerstrasse in Berlin was renamed Stauffenbergstrasse, and the remnants of the onetime War Ministry and OKW headquarters now comprise a resistance museum with room after room full of the memorabilia of officers connected with the July 20, 1944, plot against Hitler's life. Though the specifics of that plot now seem fairly clear, the earlier history of the military's role in the resistance remains murky. On

civilian participants in the early resistance, consult Gisevius, *To the Bitter End,* and Ritter, *Goerdeler.* On the resistance as a whole, see Schellendorf, *Secret War;* Kosthorst, "Deutsche Opposition"; Hoffmann, *Widerstand;* Kettenacker, ed., "*Das Andere Deutschland*"; Walle, *Aufstand des Gewissens* and *Vollmacht des Gewissens.* On the military specifically, Klaus-Jürgen Müller, "German Military Opposition," is a careful survey; Scheurig, *Henning von Tresckow,* Ueberschär, "Generaloberst Halder" and "Ansätze und Hindernisse," and Thun-Hohenstein, *Der Verschwörer* (about Oster) tend to make cases for individuals.

6. Weizsäcker, *Memoirs,* p. 143.
7. Reynolds, *Treason Was No Crime,* p. 209.
8. Meehan, *Unnecessary War,* pp. 191–206, details Goerdeler's proposals, explains why they were necessary if the Germans who executed a coup were to win public support in Germany, and expresses indignation that the British government did not go along with him.
9. Leeb to OKH, Oct. 11, 1939, in Jacobsen, *Dokumente zur Vorgeschichte,* doc. 24; Oct. 11, 1939, NARS Film T 311, reel 198; Jacobsen, *Fall Gelb,* pp. 26, 272.
10. Entry for Oct. 17, 1939, in *Halder Diary;* Hitler directive no. 7, Oct. 18, 1939, in *DGFP,* 7:doc. 276; entry for Oct. 22, 1939, in *Halder Diary.*
11. Jacobsen, *Fall Gelb,* pp. 34–36; Commander, Führungsstab Ia, "Feindlage," Oct. 24, 1939, NARS Film T 971, reel 50.
12. Bracher, Sauer, and Schulz, *Nationalsozialistische Machtergreifung,* p. 365.
13. Entry for Oct. 25, 1939, in *Halder Diary;* Jacobsen, *Fall Gelb,* p. 40.
14. Entry for Oct. 27, 1939, in *Halder Diary.*
15. Entry for Nov. 2, 1939, in Groscurth, *Tagebücher,* pp. 223–24.
16. Schall-Riaucour, *Aufstand und Gehorsam,* p. 230; Reynolds, *Treason Was No Crime,* p. 195.
17. See Müller, *Heer und Hitler,* pp. 442, 466–70.
18. Leeb to Brauchitsch, Oct. 31, 1939, in Jacobsen, *Fall Gelb,* p. 45.
19. Entries for Nov. 2, Nov. 3, 1939, in *Halder Diary;* KTB, AGB, Nov. 2, 1939, NARS Film T 311, reel 198; KTB, AGA, Nov. 3, 1939, in NARS Film T 311, reel 236; Cooper, *German Army,* p. 184.
20. Entry for Nov. 3, 1939, in *Halder Diary;* entries for Nov. 2, Nov. 5, 1939, in Tippelskirch diary. Wagner, the supply chief, wrote his wife that he had been much impressed by those with whom Brauchitsch and Halder had spoken. He thought they had shown "much will and great ability and high sense of responsibility" (Nov. 3, 1939, in Wagner, *Generalquartiermeister,* p. 147). Choltitz, *Soldat unter Soldaten,* pp. 58–59, the memoir of a paratroop-battalion commander who landed in the Netherlands in May 1940, says that he and other junior officers had misgivings then about violating Dutch neutrality.
21. Entries for Nov. 3, Nov. 4, 1939, in Groscurth, *Tagebücher,* pp. 223–24.
22. Engel, *Heeresadjutant,* pp. 19–20; Domarus, ed., *Hitler: Speeches,* 1:881.
23. Heusinger, *Befehl im Widerstreit,* pp. 72–76.
24. Jacobsen, *Fall Gelb,* p. 47.
25. Entry for Nov. 5, 1939, in Groscurth, *Tagebücher,* pp. 224–25; Engel, *Heeresadjutant,* pp. 66–67.
26. Entry for Nov. 5, 1939, in *Halder Diary;* Jacobsen, Fall *Gelb,*p. 47.
27. Entry for Nov. 5, 1939, in Groscurth, *Tagebücher,* pp. 224–25.
28. Entry for Nov. 6, 1939, in Tippelskirch diary.

29. Entry for Nov. 7, 1939, in *Halder Diary*.
30. Entry for Nov. 8, 1939, in Goebbels, *Tagebücher*; entry for Nov. 8, 1939, in *Halder Diary*.
31. Jacobsen, *Fall Gelb*, p. 50; Müller, *Heer und Hitler*, pp. 542–43.
32. Entry for Nov. 10, 1939, in *Halder Diary*; Müller, *Heer und Hitler*, pp. 513, n. 56; 544–46.
33. Müller, *Heer und Hitler*, p. 542.
34. Jacobsen, *Fall Gelb*, pp. 49–50, 52; KTB, AGB, Nov. 13, 1939, NARS Film T 311, reel 198.
35. KTB, AGB, Dec. 12, 1939, NARS Film T 311, reel 198.
36. OKW Directive, Dec. 28, 1939, in Jacobsen, ed., *Dokumente zur Vorgeschichte*, doc. 5.
37. Jacobsen, *Fall Gelb*, pp. 59–64.
38. Ibid., p. 64.
39. Entry for Jan. 22, 1940, in *Goebbels, Tagebücher*.
40. Entry for Jan. 10, 1940, in *Halder Diary*; AGB, KTB, Jan. 12, 1940, NARS Film T 311, reel 198.
41. Entry for Jan. 18, 1940, in *Halder Diary*.
42. KTB, AGA, Nov. 9, 1939, NARS Film T 311, reel 236, notes OKH request for daily weather forecasts. Halder testimony: *U.S. v. Leeb*, 10:860; entry for Oct. 4, 1939, in *Halder Diary*.
43. Vanwelkenhuyzen, *Avertissements*, passim.
44. Entries for Oct. 21, 1939, Jan. 6, 1940, in Bock, *Zwischen Pflicht und Verweigerung*, pp. 66–67, 87–88; entry for Jan. 10, 1940, in *Halder Diary*; Jacobsen, *Fall Gelb*, p. 51.

CHAPTER SIXTEEN: NOT DEFEAT?

1. Rundstedt, AGA Operation Orders for Fall Gelb, Oct. 30, 1939, NARS Film T 311, reel 43.
2. Blumentritt, "Critique of 'The German Campaign in the West' "; Manstein, *Lost Victories*, pp. 67–127; Heusinger interview with Manstein, *Nie ausser Dienst*, pp. 35–44; Blumentritt, *Rundstedt*, pp. 59–66; Manstein and Ruchs, *Manstein*, pp. 135–43.
3. Macksey, *Guderian*, p. 58, noting that this did not necessarily mean at the time that Hitler had any grasp of Guderian's ideas on possible uses of tanks. On the development of German tanks and tank doctrine, see Oswald, *Kraftfahrzeuge und Panzer*, and Stoves, *Die gepanzerten und motorisierten deutschen Grossverbände*. On the general development of armored forces and armor doctrine in Germany, see Nehring, *Geschichte der deutscher Panzerwaffen*; Menke, "Militärtheoretische Überlegungen"; and Steiger, *Panzertaktik*. On Guderian, see his own *Achtung! Panzer*, *Panzer-Marsch!*, and Plettenberg, *Guderian*; Bradley, *Guderian*; Scheibert, *Das war Guderian*; Walde, *Guderian*; Macksey, *Guderian*.
4. Müller, *Beck*, pp. 208–12; Reynolds, *Treason Was No Crime*, pp. 154–55. Partisans of Beck were later to attribute to him the concept of combined air-armor operations, but close students of German military texts argue that, if it had a parent other than Guderian, it was Seeckt, not Beck. See Citino, *Evolution of Blitzkrieg Tactics*; Corum, *Roots of Blitzkrieg*

5. Faber du Faur, *Macht und Ohnmacht*, p. 161.
6. Below, *Als Hitlers Adjutant*, pp. 40–41; Engel, *Heeresadjutant*, p. 24.
7. Revised directive for Fall Grün, May 30, 1938, in *DGFP*, 2:doc. 221; Below, *Als Hitlers Adjutant*, pp. 120–21; Keitel, p. 69.
8. Frieser, *Blitzkrieg-Legende*, pp. 22–24.
9. Halder to Leeb, Oct. 7, 1939, NARS Film T 311, reel 41. The rest of the list ran: "(3) Attack against fixed fortifications, (4) Battle in villages and forests, (5) River crossing, (6) Night-breakthrough and follow-up battles, (7) Security for marches and layovers, (8) Special weapons traning for individual units and individual soldiers."
10. Entry for Oct. 25, 1939, in Bock's private diary, in Jacobsen, *Fall Gelb*, p. 39. Jablonsky, "Paradox of Duality," makes a persuasive argument that Hitler had developed over the whole course of his career a very keen sense for ingrained weaknesses in his enemies.
11. Entry for Oct. 28, 1939, in *Halder Diary*; entry for Oct. 30, 1939, in *Jodl Diary*. Greiner, *OKW*, p. 94, argues that Hitler took this from Army Group A, and there is no question that Rundstedt, on this same date, laid out as a contingent operation for his Twelfth Army a "move across the Meuse at Fumay-Sedan in the direction of Laon" (Rundstedt directive, Oct. 30, 1939, NARS Film T 311, reel 43). But Jacobsen, *Dokumente*, doc. 36, explains why it is not likely that Hitler had seen this document. Hitler's later urging of an attack toward Sedan: Jacobsen, *Fall Gelb*, p. 52; entries for Nov. 5, 9, 1939, in *Halder Diary*; entry for Nov. 11, 1939 in Bock diary; OKH directive to Army Groups A and B, Nov. 11, 1939, in Jacobsen, ed., *Dokumente zur Vorgeschichte*, doc. 12.
12. OKW Directive No. 8, in Jacobsen, ed., *Dokumente zur Vorgeschichte*, doc. 4; Engel, *Heeresadjutant*, p. 69.
13. Entry for Feb. 13, 1940, in *Jodl Diary*. On Manstein's maneuvers, see Manstein, *Lost Victories*, pp. 115–18; Engel, *Heeresadjutant*, pp. 73–74, Jacobsen, *Fall Gelb*, pp. 69–80.
14. Entry for Jan. 9, 1940, in *Halder Diary*.
15. Manstein, *Lost Victories*, p. 107; Jacobsen, *Fall Gelb*, pp. 69–70; Manstein, memorandum, Nov. 21, 1939, in Jacobsen, ed., *Dokumente*, doc. 35; KTB, AGA Nov. 27, 1939, in NARS Film T 311, reel 236.
16. Rosinksi, *German Army*, pp. 187–88.
17. Manstein, memorandum, Nov. 21, 1939, NARS Film T 311, reel 236; Rundstedt to Brauchitsch, Nov. 30, 1939, in Jacobsen, ed. *Dokumente zur Vorgeschichte*, doc. 36; Manstein to Halder, Dec. 6, 1939, AGA, KTB, Dec. 6, 1939, NARS Film T 311, reel 236; memorandum by Manstein, Dec. 18, 1939, in Jacobsen, *Dokumente zur Vorgeschichte*, doc. 37.
18. Entries for Dec 13, 21, 27, 1939, in *Halder Diary*; Rundstedt to Brauchitsch, Jan. 12, 1940, in Jacobsen, *Dokumente zur Vorgeschichte*, doc. 38; Engel, *Heeresadjutant*, pp. 73–74; Below, *Als Hitlers Adjutant*, pp. 222–23; Manstein, *Lost Victories*, pp. 112–21; Guderian, *Panzer Leader*, pp. 90–91; Jacobsen, *Fall Gelb*, pp. 77–82.
19. Liss, *Westfront*, p. 104.
20. Diary entry for Jan. 6, 1940, in Meier-Welcker, *Aufzeichnungen*, p. 46.
21. Frieser, *Blitzkrieg-Legende*, pp. 111–12.

CHAPTER SEVENTEEN: INTELLIGENCE

1. This chapter draws very heavily on Kahn, *Hitler's Spies*. The reader can assume that any statement not attributed to a different source derives from Kahn's book.
2. Gellermann, . . . *und lauschten für Hitler*, p. 61.
3. Peipe deposition, in "Forschungsamt."
4. See Bonatz, *Seekrieg im Aether*; Boelcke, " 'Sechaus.' "
5. What is said here about army communications goes beyond Kahn but on the basis of the same source Kahn cites: Praun, "German Radio Intelligence."
6. Müller, *Heer und Hitler*, p. 522. See also Wildhagen, *Fellgiebel*.
7. Praun, "German Radio Intelligence," pp. 21–22.
8. AGC to FHW, Feb. 11, 1940, NARS Film T 311, reel 43.
9. FHW report, April 8, 1940, NARS Film T 78, reel 449; FHW report, May 12, 1940, ibid.
10. Brammer, *Spionageabwehr*. Some glimpses of Abwehr routines and procedures can be obtained from sensational and generally unreliable books about particular individuals and operations, e.g.: Ritter, *Decknahme Dr. Rantzau*; Norden, *Salon Kitty*; Ruland, *Spionin für Deutschland*; Joesten, *Im Dienste des Misstrauens*; Loeff, *Spionage*.
11. Mader, *Hitlers Spionagegenerale*, p. 317.
12. Ibid., pp. 78–79.
13. Reile, *Geheime Westfront*, p. 78.
14. See Tippelskirch, "Intelligence Division," and the various writings by Liss.
15. Boog, *Deutsche Luftwaffenführung*, p. 96.
16. See Erfurth, *Deutschen Generalstabes*.
17. Strong, *Men of Intelligence*, p. 88.
18. Schall-Riaucour, *Aufstand und Gehorsam*, p. 230.
19. On Liss, in addition to his own *Westfront* and associated articles, see Strong, *Men of Intelligence*, pp. 70–72. The makeup of Foreign Armies West and the dates of rank of officers in it: Podzun, ed., *Deutsche Heer*, p. 15. Liss was only a major when made head of the section. His promotion to lieutenant colonel came soon after. It is worth noting that pre-World War II ranks tended to be lower than postwar ranks, and also that the German rank system differed from the British and American. Though *Oberst* translates best as "colonel," a German *Oberst* could have assignments that, in Britain or the United States, would have gone to a brigadier. Similarly, an *Oberstleutnant*, which translates as "lieutenant colonel," could have assignments appropriate in foreign armies to a colonel. See O'Neill, *The German Army and the Nazi Party*, pp. i–ii and app. E.
20. Strong, *Men of Intelligence*, pp. 70–71.
21. Strik-Strikfeldt, *Against Stalin and Hitler*, p. 61; Kahn, *Hitler's Spies*, p. 424; Jacobsen, *"Spiegelbild einer Verschwörung,"* 1:456.
22. U.S. War Dept., MID, *German Military Intelligence*, pp. 273–80.
23. Kielmansegg, *Panzer*, pp. 97–98.
24. Schellendorf, *Duties of the General Staff*, pp. 514–15.
25. Liss, *Westfront*, p. 19.
26. FHW, "Grosses Orientierungsheft Frankreich," May 10, 1938, NARS Film T 78, reel 444.
27. FHW, "Der französische Generalstab und die höhere Führerausbildung," June 1, 1938, NARS Film T 78, reel 444.

28. FHW, "Erfahrungen der Abteilung Fremde Heere West in der Spannungszeit September 1938," vol. 1, "Französisches Heer," Jan. 1, 1939, in NARS Film T 78, reel 454.
29. Liss, *Westfront,* p. 67; Tippelskirch to Geyr von Schweppenburg, May 3, 1938, in Müller, *Beck,* p. 504, n. 6.
30. Entry for Aug. 21, 1938, in *Halder Diary.*
31. Liss, *Westfront,* p. 83; entries for Aug. 27, Aug. 30, Sept. 1, Sept. 4, 1939, in *Halder Diary.*
32. Reynolds, *Treason Was No Crime,* p. 187.
33. Groscurth, *Tagebücher,* p. 202.
34. Entry for Oct. 5, 1939, ibid., p. 212.
35. Liss, *Westfront,* p. 90.
36. Entry for Sept. 27, 1939, in *Halder Diary.*

CHAPTER EIGHTEEN: GAMBLE
1. Entries for Nov. 2, Nov. 6, Nov. 10, 1939, in Tippelskirch diary.
2. Liss, *Westfront,* p. 88.
3. Tippelskirch, "Westfeldzug," 1:76; Liss, *Westfront,* p. 97. Entry for Oct. 30, 1939, in Tippelskirch diary, notes that most of the October keys had been broken.
4. Liss, *Westfront,* pp. 96–97.
5. Jacobsen, *Fall Gelb,* p. 275, n. 22, reporting a conversation with Liss in 1956.
6. FHW, "Französischen Kriegswehrmacht 1939," Oct. 15, 1939, NARS Film T 78, reel 444.
7. FHW, "Kräfteübersicht der Westfront," Oct. 20, 1939, NARS Film T 78, reel 452.
8. FHW, "Das belgische Kriegsheer," Oct. 28, 1939, NARS Film T 78, reel 444.
9. FHW, "Lagebericht," Nov. 28, 1939, NARS Film T 78, reel 449.
10. FHW, "Mögliche Kräftverteilung der Westmächte für eine Operation in Belgien," Oct. 18, 1939, NARS Film T 78, reel 444; entry for Nov. 8, 1939, in Tippelskirch diary; FHW, "Lagebericht," Nov. 16, Nov. 20, Nov. 23, Dec. 4, Dec. 6, 1939, NARS Film T 78, reel 449.
11. Hofmann, "War Games."
12. Heusinger to Tippelskirch, June 2, 1956, in Tippelskirch, "Westfront," 1:236–37.
13. Halder, "Grundlagen für die Lage Rot," Dec. 15, 1939, NARS Film T 78, Reel 454.
14. Liss, *Westfront,* pp. 106–7.
15. Tippelskirch, "Westfront," 1:237–38.
16. Ibid., 1:66.
17. OKW Weisung, Dec. 28, 1939, in Jacobsen, ed., *Dokumente,* doc. 5; entries for Jan. 1, Jan. 10, 1940, in *Halder Diary;* Brauchitsch to Rundstedt, Jan. 16, 1940, in Jacobsen, *Dokumente zur Vorgeschichte,* doc. 16.
18. Entry for Feb. 13, 1940, in *Jodl Diary.*
19. AGB, KTB, Dec. 28, 1939, NARS Film T 311, reel 198.
20. FHW, "Lagebericht," Dec. 28, 1939, NARS Film T 78, reel 449; Liss, *Westfront,* pp. 107, 120.
21. AGB KTB Jan. 22, 1940, NARS Film T 311, reel 198.
22. Entry for Feb. 7, 1940, in *Halder Diary;* Guderian, *Panzer General,* p. 91; Bradley, *Wenck,* pp. 139–40.

23. Entry for Feb. 14, 1940, in *Halder Diary*.
24. Entry for Feb. 16, 1940, ibid.
25. AGB, KTB, Feb. 17, 1940, NARS Film T 311, reel 198.
26. Entries for Feb. 21, Feb. 24, 1940; in *Halder Diary*; Sodenstern to Rundstedt, Feb. 22, 1940, in Frieser, *Blitzkrieg-Legende*, p. 113.
27. Sodenstern to Halder, March 5, 1940, in Frieser, *Blitzkrieg-Legende*, pp. 113–14. As evidence of Sodenstern's worshipful attitude toward Hitler, see his "Wesen des Soldatentums."
28. Faber du Faur, *Macht und Ohnmacht*, p. 209.
29. Liss, *Westfront*, p. 122.
30. Halder to Rundstedt, March 12, 1940; AGA, KTB NARS Film T 311, reel 237; Heusinger, *Befehl im Widerstreit*, p. 86.
31. AGB, KTB, March 31, 1940, NARS Film T 311, reel 198; entries for Feb. 14, Apr. 3, 1940, in Meier-Welcker, *Aufzeichnungen*, pp. 50–51, 55.
32. Kielmansegg interview, cited in Frieser, *Blitzkrieg-Legende*, p. 136.
33. See Scheurig, *Kleist*.
34. Charisius, "Zur Rolle von Spionage und Diversion"; Lahousen diary, part of which appears in Wighton, *They Spied on England*.
35. The best account of the planning and the operation is Ottmer, *Weserübung*, but see also Hubatsch, *Weserübung*; Gemzell, *Raeder, Hitler and Skandinavien*; and the thoughtful analysis of the operation's logic in Claasen, "Blood and Iron."
36. Entry for March 27, 1940, in *Halder Diary*.
37. Entries for April 25, May 1, 1940, in Goebbels, *Tagebücher*.
38. Entry for March 17, 1940, in *Halder Diary*.
39. Entry for April 14, 1940, ibid.
40. Entry for April 5, 1940, in Meier-Welcker, *Aufzeichungen*, pp. 55–56.

CHAPTER NINETEEN: WAR BUT NOT WAR

1. Conversations between General Kasprzycki and General Gamelin, May 19, 1939, in *DDF*, 16:doc. 233.
2. Gamelin directive, May 31, 1939, cited in Dutailly, *Problèmes*, p. 110; Gamelin private notes, May 21, 1939, ibid., p. 67.
3. Reports by Musse, July 19, July 26, 1939, in *DDF*, 17:docs. 241, 319; Beaufre to Doumenc, Aug. 19, 1939, *Papiers Doumenc*, p. 92; Deuxième Bureau reports, Jan. 30, Feb. 22, May 3, June 19, 1939, in *DDF*, 13:doc. 462, 14:doc. 76:16, doc:26; and 7 N 2524, SHAT; Gamelin statement in "Conversations militaires france-britanniques," July 13, 1939, CSDN files, carton 136, SHAT. See Turlotte, "L'Alliance polonaise."
4. Gamelin, *Servir*, 3:50; entry for Sept. 2, 1939, in Villelume, *Journal*, p. 19. The sad story of French and British relations with their Polish ally can be followed in the memoirs of the Polish ambassador in Paris and the French ambassador in Warsaw: Lukasiewicz, *Memoirs*; Noël, *Ambassade à Varsovie*. Cienciala, *Poland and the Western Powers*, provides a chronicle based on early documentary publications; Prazmowska, *Britain, Poland and the Eastern Front*, is based on later-released British archives. On the limited cooperation permitted by Vuillemin, see Vivier, "L'Aviation française en Pologne."

5. Paillat, *Désastre*, 4(2): 179–80; Prételat, *Destin tragique*, pp. 58–59.
6. Réquin, *Combats pour l'honneur*. Estimates of casualties vary. For one on the high side, see Gunsburg, *Divided and Conquered*, p. 91; for lower ones, Rocolle, *Guerre de 1940*, 1:260, and Bruge, *Ligne Maginot*, pp. 1:61–62.
7. Diary entry for Sept. 7, 1939, in Wagner, *Generalquartiermeister*, p. 131; Rist, *Saison gatée*, p. 37.
8. Favreau, *Mandel*, p. 215; Bonnet, *Quai d'Orsay*, p. 272; Paillat, *Désastre*, 4(2):215–16; Daridan, *Chemin*, pp. 145–46; Villelume, *Journal*, p. 36.
9. Entry for Sept. 4, 1939, in Renaudin, *Sans fleur*, p. 44.
10. Gamelin to Daladier, Sept. 1, 1939, in *DDF*, 19:doc. 353.
11. Minart, *P.C. Vincennes*, 1:57.
12. Prételat, *Destin tragique*, pp. 13–14, 49–50; Dutailly, *Problèmes*, pp. 97–104; Delmas, "Exercices du Conseil Supérieur de la Guerre"; Navarre, *Temps de vérité*, pp. 71–72; entry for Sept. 10, 1939, in Villelume, *Journal*, p. 28.
13. Expert firsthand testimony on the flimsiness of the Westwall is in Förster, *Befestigungswesen*, pp. 45–50, and Mellenthin, *Panzerschlachten*, pp. 15–17.
14. Hillgruber, *Hitlers Strategie*, p. 34; Merglen, "Forces allemandes." Merglen's counterfactual scenario is outlined in his *Vérité historique*. A book overarguing the counterfactual case is Kimche, *Unfought Battle*.
15. Gamelin, journal de marche, Sept. 5, Sept. 8, 1939, Fonds Gamelin, 1 K 224, SHAT.
16. Jordan, "Cut-Price War," emphasizes the high priority that Gamelin always attached to avoiding loss of French lives. Geyer, "Crisis of Military Leadership," makes the interesting argument that Gamelin and Beck were alike in this respect and that a combination of aversion to casualties and fear of the social upheaval that might attend serious warfare made both men unconsciously prefer defeat to costly victory. Posen, *Sources of Military Doctrine*, explains how military doctrine was shaped by the sense of vulnerability created by demographic and geographic realities. See also Kier, *Imagining War*, pp. 49–54.
17. Zay, *Carnets secrets*, pp. 85–86.
18. Dutailly, *Problèmes*, p. 34; Vial, "Organisation"; Le Goyet, *Mystère Gamelin*, p. 227; entry for Sept. 3, 1939, in Villelume, *Journal*, pp. 20–21. See also Verzat, "À propos du P.C. Gamelin."
19. Kennedy, *Business of War*, p. 43.
20. Gamelin, journal de marche, Sept. 9, 1939, Fonds Gamelin, 1 K 224, SHAT.
21. Georges to Gamelin, Dec. 8, 1939, Fonds Gamelin, ibid. In this letter, Georges says he is repeating views that he expressed in September.
22. Gamelin, journal de marche, Sept. 11, 1939, Fonds Gamelin, ibid.
23. *Ironside Diaries*, pp. 107–8; *Cadogan Diaries*, pp. 216–17; Paillat, *Désastre*, 4(2):241.
24. Minart, *P.C. Vincennes*, 1:22.
25. Gamelin, *Servir*, 3:84–85.
26. Gamelin, journal de marche, Sept. 18, 1939, Fonds Gamelin, 1 K 224, SHAT.
27. Roton, *Années cruciales*, p. 76.
28. Gamelin, *Servir*, 3:69; Minart, *P.C. Vincennes*, 1:34.
29. Gamelin, journal de marche, Oct. 9, Oct. 13, 1939, Fonds Gamelin, 1 K 224, SHAT.

30. Entries for Oct. 10, Oct. 11–13, Rivet diary.
31. Entry for Oct. 2, 1939, in Villelume, *Journal*, p. 49.
32. Entry for Oct. 15, 1939, ibid., p. 68.
33. Gamelin, journal de marche, Oct. 5, 1939, Fonds Gamelin, 1 K 224, SHAT.
34. Alexander, *Republic in Danger*, p. 329, citing files of the Belgian military attaché in Paris.
35. Deuxième Bureau (Air) report, Oct. 14, 1939, 1 D 23, SHAA. Attributed to "a usually reliable source," this may well have come from signal intercepts.
36. Gamelin, *Servir*, 3:92.
37. Entry for Sept. 27, 1939, in Réquin diary, quoted in Paillat, *Désastre*, 4(2): 185–86.
38. Gauché, report, Oct. 27, 1939, 7 N 2516, SHAT.
39. Davignon to Spaak, Nov. 7, 1939 in *DDB*, 5:doc. 185; Bargeton to Daladier, Nov. 7, 1939, Bruxelles, carton 344, MAE; Gauché, *Deuxième Bureau*, p. 193; Paillole, *Services speciaux*, p. 184.
40. Rivet diary, Nov. 7, 1939, partly quoted in Paillole, *Notre Espion*, pp. 170–71.
41. Rivet diary, Nov. 15, 1939, partly quoted in Paillole, p. 171.
42. Gamelin, journal de marche, Nov. 15, 1939, Fonds Gamelin, 1 K 224, SHAT.
43. Minart, *P.C. Vincennes*, 2:10.
44. Deuxième Bureau, "Note sur le conception allemande de la Guerre de propagande," Dec. 15, 1939, 7 N 2526, SHAT.

CHAPTER TWENTY: "THE BORE WAR"

1. Deuxième Bureau (Air) report, Oct. 6, 1939, 1 D 23 SHAA; Deuxième Bureau report, Oct. 8, 1939, 7 N 2517, SHAT.
2. Ironside to Wavell, Oct. 10, 1939, WO 106/1684.
3. Guariglia to Ciano, Nov. 18, 1939, in *DDI* [9], 2:doc. 262; entry for Nov. 22, 1939, in Villelume, *Journal*, pp. 102–3; Daridan, *Chemin*, p. 170.
4. Gamelin, *Servir*, 2:128.
5. N.I.D., *France*, p. 54.
6. Notes on remarks by Gamelin, May 12, 1939, 7 N 3716, SHAT; Ironside to Wavell, Oct. 10, 1939, WO 106/1684.
7. Navarre et al., *Service de Renseignements*, pp. 72–73; Armengaud, *Bataille*, pp. 171–72; Gamelin, journal de marche, October 11, 1939, Fonds Gamelin, 1 K 224, SHAT.
8. Deuxième Bureau, "La Campagne de Pologne," Oct. 1939, 7 N 2517, SHAT; Armengaud, *Bataille*, p. 140; Facon, "Leçons de la campagne de Pologne"; Le Goyet, *Mystère Gamelin*, pp. 236–39; Paillat, *Désastre*, 4(2):164; Gauché, *Deuxième Bureau*, p. 167.
9. Entry for Sept. 18, 1939, in Paillat, *Désastre*, 4(2):166.
10. Gamelin, *Servir*, 1:245–47.
11. Delvoie, report, Nov. 10, 1939, in *Relations militaires Franco-belges*, pp. 152–53.
12. Chamberlain to Churchill, Sept. 16, 1939, in *Churchill War Papers*, 1:100–101.
13. For abundant examples, see Kahneman, Slovik, and Tversky, eds., *Judgment Under Uncertainty*.
14. Frieser, *Blitzkrieg-Legende*, pp. 5–6.

15. Report from the British mission in Paris, Oct. 7, 1939, AIR 40/2033.
16. Daladier memoranda, Oct. 3, Nov. 14, Dec. 15, 1939, 7 N 2572, SHAT; Cinquième Bureau memorandum, Nov. 16, 1939, ibid.; Gamelin, *Servir*, 3:263; Navarre et al., *Service de Renseignements*, p. 95; Paillole, *Services spéciaux*, p. 164.
17. Colson to Troisième Bureau, Oct. 23, 1939 (two messages), 7 N 4043, SHAT; "Reflections on Organization," July 12, 1940, Fonds Georges, 1 N 47, SHAT; Paillat, *Désastre*, 4(2):132–33.
18. Guillaume, *Homme de guerre*, p. 85. See files of correspondence between the Troisième Bureau and division commanders in 7 N 4043, SHAT.
19. For references to the extensive Deuxième Bureau data on conditions in German armored forces, see Alexander, "Fall of France," p. 18.
20. *Ironside Diaries*, pp. 117–118.
21. Réquin diary, Sept. 27, 1939, cited in Paillat, *Désastre*, 5:185–86.
22. Capelle, *Roi Léopold*, pp. 161–62.
23. Mendigal, report on commanders' meeting, Sept. 30, 1939, 1 D 34, SHAA; Rocolle, *Guerre de 1940*, 1:351. See also N.I.D., *Belgium*.
24. Gamelin to Ironside, Sept. 18, 1939, WO 106/1653; Lelong dispatch, Sept. 19, 1939. 7 N 2817, SHAT; journal de guerre, Sept. 23, 1939, in Fonds Georges, 1 N 47, SHAT; Gamelin, personal instruction no. 6, Sept. 30, 1939, in Gamelin, *Servir*, 3:82–83.
25. Rocolle, *Guerre de 1940*, 1:282–83. On Ironside, see, in addition, Wark, "Ironside." Ironside's comment about Gamelin is recorded in Kennedy, *Business of War*, p. 20. On Hore-Belisha's reasoning about the appointments, see de Guingand, *Operation Victory*, p. 23.
26. Gamelin to Georges, Nov. 5, 1939, in Gamelin, *Servir*, 3:140–41.
27. Dumont, *Léopold III*, pp. 11–12; Polderman, *Léopold III*, p. 28; Cammaerts, *Prisoner at Laeken*, pp. 54–56.
28. Capelle, *Roi Léopold*, p. 30. Leopold's other close political advisers were the great literary critic Paul deMan and Louis Frédéricq, the chief intermediary between the king and cabinets (Giscard d'Estaing, *Léopold III*, pp. 26–28).
29. Unnamed Belgian deputy quoted in Consul General, Liège, to Bargeton, March 1, 1940, Bruxelles, carton 337, MAE; Giscard d'Estaing, *Léopold III*, p. 28.
30. Stengers, *Léopold III*, p. 17. See also Zuylen, *Mains libres*, pp. 363–71.
31. Kossmann, *Low Countries*, p. 591.
32. *DDB*, 4:doc. 128. See Spaak, *Combats inachevés*, and Van Overstraeten, *Au service de la Belgique*; Willequet, *Spaak*; Kieft, *Belgium's Return to Neutrality*; Van Langenhove, *La Belgique*. As Vanwelkenhuyzen's *Neutralité armée* points out in detail, there are many inconsistencies between Van Overstraeten's early *Albert I–Léopold III* and later *Au service de la Belgique*, not all of which resolve in favor of the second. Anyone using these extremely important source volumes should study Vanwelkenhuyzen's critique.
33. Giscard d'Estaing, *Léopold III*, p. 22.
34. See Jaspar, *Souvenirs*.
35. Capelle, *Roi Léopold*, pp. 89–91; Pirenne, "Attitude de Léopold III de 1936 à la Liberation," p. 27; Dumont, *Léopold III*, pp. 118–28.
36. Capelle, *Roi Léopold*, p. 143.
37. Unnamed deputy from Liège, quoted in Consul General, Liège, to Bargeton, March

30, 1940, Bruxelles, carton 337, MAE; Vanwelkenhuyzen, *Neutralité armée*, p. 93.

38. Capelle, *Roi Léopold*, p. 112.

39. Vanwelkenhuyzen, *Avertissements*, pp. 294–95. There was some liaison between the Belgian Secret Service and the French SR, but even that was limited (Verhoeyen, " 'Honorables Correspondants' "), and the British Secret Service became extremely cautious after November 9, 1939, when three of its agents based in the Netherlands were lured into an Abwehr trap at Venlo on the Dutch-German border. See Best, *The Venlo Incident*; Kessler, *Betrayal at Venlo*; Hinsley, *British Intelligence*, 1:57.

40. Vanwelkenhuyzen, *Neutralité armée*, pp. 34–35.

41. Deuxième Bureau (Air) report, Oct. 19, 1939, 1 D 23, SHAA.

42. Van Overstraeten, *Au service de la Belgique*, p. 134.

43. Ibid., pp. 361–62.

44. Marnay, "Politique militaire de la Belgique," p. 27.

45. Delvoie, report, Nov. 10, 1939, in *Relations militaires Franco-belges*, pp. 152–53.

46. Ibid.

47. Delvoie, report, Nov. 11, 1939, ibid., pp. 153–54. On Petibon: Col. William Fraser to Phipps, Sept. 28, 1938, in *DBFP*, 2:doc. 1199.

48. "Suggestions," Nov. 19, Dec. 1, Dec. 3, 1939, in *Relations militaires Franco-belges*, pp. 158–60. See, in addition to works cited earlier, Wullus-Rudiger, *Défense de la Belgique*, an anti-French polemic published in 1940, and Langenhove's cooler critique of Belgium's allies, *La Belgique et ses garants*.

CHAPTER TWENTY-ONE: THE DYLE-BREDA PLAN

1. Bédarida, *Stratégie secrète*, is the definitive compilation of French records of meetings of this council.

2. Gamelin, journal de marche, Sept. 12, 1939, Fonds Gamelin, 1 K 224, SHAT.

3. Entry for Sept. 22, 1939, in *Cadogan Diaries*, p. 218.

4. Bédarida, *Stratégie secrète*, pp. 32–33.

5. Gamelin to Ironside, Sept. 18, 1939, WO 106/1653.

6. Minutes of meeting at War Office, Sept. 20, 1939, WO 106/1776.

7. Churchill to Chamberlain, Sept. 18, 1939, in *Churchill War Papers*, 1:111–12.

8. Corbin to Daladier, Oct. 18, 1939, 3 DA 2/3, Archives Édouard Daladier.

9. Entry for Aug. 25, 1939, in *Crawford Papers*, p. 602.

10. James, *Boothby*, p. 237.

11. Minutes of Supreme War Council, May 3, 1940, Papiers 40, Hoppenot, vol. 1, MAE.

12. War Cabinet, Land Forces Committee, Sept. 7, 1939, in *Churchill War Papers*, 1:43–45; Churchill to Chamberlain, Sept. 18, 1939, ibid., pp. 111–12; Churchill to Chamberlain, Oct. 1, 1939, ibid., pp. 188–89; Butler, *Grand Strategy*, 2:32; notes on meeting at Gamelin's headquarters, Nov. 19, 1939, WO 106/1701.

13. Mendigal, notes on Anglo-French commanders' meeting, Sept. 30, 1939, 1 D 34, SHAA.

14. Daladier to Chamberlain, Oct. 1, 1939, Papiers 40, Fouques-Duparc, vol. 35, MAE.

15. Armengaud, *Batailles*, p. 180; Gunsburg, *Divided and Conquered*, pp. 111–12.

16. Richards and Saunders, *Royal Air Force*, 1:62–63.

17. Ritchie, *Industry and Air Power*, p. 85.

18. Newall to Gamelin, Nov. 2, 1939, 1 D 34, SHAA; Gamelin, *Servir*, 3:144.

19. Webster and Frankland, *Strategic Bombing*, 1:136–37; Gamelin–Air Vice Marshal Evill, Oct. 25, 1939, 1 D 34, SHAA [also in WO 106/1684]; Gamelin, *Servir*, 3:144; Gunsburg, *Divided and Conquered*, pp. 126–27; Slessor, *Central Blue*, pp. 230–34.

20. Gamelin, *Servir*, 3:141–43.

21. Slessor, *Central Blue*, p. 251.

22. Rozoy to Vuillemin, Nov. 12, Nov. 14, 1939, 1 D 34, SHAA.

23. Deuxième Bureau, "Bulletin de Renseignements," Sept. 14, 1939, 7 N 2524, SHAT; Deuxième Bureau (Air), "Bulletin de Renseignements," Oct. 11, 1939, 1 D 23, SHAA; Report from Deuxième Bureau, Section Allemande, Oct. 14, 1939, 40, Daladier, vol. 5, MAE; memo from British Military Mission, Oct. 29, 1939, in WO 106/1654, Roton, "Note on the Military Situation of Belgium," Oct. 31, 1939, 1 D 31, SHAA.

24. Rocolle, *Guerre de 1940*, 1:283, 351.

25. *Relations militaires Franco-belges*, pp. 155–56.

26. Roton, *Années cruciales*, p. 97; Gamelin, "Follow-up Suggestions," Dec. 3, 1939, in *Relations militaires Franco-belges*, pp. 159–60.

27. Georges to Gamelin, Dec. 5, 1939, in Minart, *P.C. Vincennes*, 2:103.

28. Gamelin, journal de marche, Nov. 24, 1939, Fonds Gamelin, 1 K 224, SHAT.

29. Georges to Gamelin, Dec. 11, 1939, Fonds Gamelin, ibid.

30. Van Overstraeten, *Au service de la Belgique*, p. 457.

31. *Relations militaires Franco-belges*, p. 102.

32. Davignon to Spaak, Jan. 4, 1940, in *DDB*, 5:doc. 109.

33. Most details here and elsewhere in the next few pages come from Van Overstraeten, *Au service de la Belgique*, pp. 169–207, as amended and corrected by Vanwelkenhuyzen, *Avertissements*, pp. 64–83, and Jacobsen, *Fall Gelb*, pp. 93–99.

34. Rocolle, *Guerre de 1940*, 1:350–51.

35. *Relations militaires Franco-belges*, p. 107; Churchill, *Second World War*, 1:612; *Churchill War Papers*, 1:638–40.

36. Bond, *Britain, France and Belgium*, pp. 38–39.

37. *Relations militaires Franco-belges*, pp. 109–10.

38. *Evénements . . .: Tém.*, 1D: 72; Gamelin, *Servir*, 3:155; Minart, *P.C. Vincennes*, 2:120; Roton, *Années cruciales*, p. 98. Memoirs from members of the SR indicate that they never saw the actual documents (Paillole, *Services spéciaux*, p. 184; Navarre et al., *Service de Renseignements*, p. 100). The account by Gauché, *Deuxième Bureau*, p. 199, indicates that he did see them. Apparently, Van Overstraeten gave Hautcoeur only a summary. This was consistent with his habit of secrecy. Also, he may have preferred that the French not learn of the apparent southward shift of the German *Schwerpunkt*, given that he was still seeking from them a commitment to rush to the Albert Canal. According to a Swiss intelligence officer, photocopies were transmitted to Paris a few days later via Laurent. The same Swiss officer says that the French were also given transcripts of the conversations between the two Germans collected by the hidden listening device. (Bauer, *Guerre des blindés*, pp. 88–89.)

39. *Relations militaires Franco-belges*, pp. 104–5; Minart, *P.C. Vincennes*, 2:123–24.
40. *Relations militaires Franco-belges*, p. 104.
41. Gamelin, *Servir*, 3:157.
42. Ibid., pp. 157–58.
43. Vanwelkenhuyzen, *Avertissements*, p. 79.
44. *Relations militaires Franco-belges*, pp. 108, 112–13.
45. Gamelin, *Servir*, 3:159.
46. Le Tellier to Spaak, Jan. 15, 1940, in *DDB*, 5:doc. 214; *Relations militaires Franco-belges*, p. 111.
47. *Relations militaires Franco-belges*, p. 112.
48. Howard-Vyse, report, Jan. 16, 1940, WO 106/1655.
49. Alexander, "In Lieu of Alliance," p. 415.
50. Vanwelkenhuyzen, *Avertissements*, p. 104.
51. Howard-Vyse, report, Jan. 16, 1940, WO 106/1655.
52. Daridan, *Chemin*, pp. 178–79.
53. *Relations militaires Franco-belges*, pp. 114–16.

CHAPTER TWENTY-TWO: DISTRACTIONS

1. Crémieux-Brilhac, *Français de l'an 40*, 1:150.
2. Desgranges, *Journal*, p. 318.
3. Bois, *Truth*, p. 98.
4. Zay, *Carnets secrets*, p. 84.
5. Daridan, *Chemin*, p. 148.
6 Rossi-Landi, *Drôle de guerre*, p. 30, n. 10.
7. Crémieux-Brilhac, *Français de l'an 40*, 1:205–6.
8. Fabre-Luce, *Journal*, p. 134.
9. Guariglia to Ciano, Sept. 23, 1939, in *DDI*, 1:doc. 395; Crémieux-Brilhac, *Français de l'an 40*, 1:154–55; Planté, *Grand Seigneur*, pp. 278–79.
10. Bois, *Truth*, pp. 122–23; Crémieux-Brilhac, *Français de l'an 40*, 1:157–62.
11. Kupferman, *Laval*, pp. 210–11.
12. Leeds, *These Rule France*, pp. 207; Bois, *Truth*, p. 217.
13. Lazareff, *Deadline*, p. 110.
14. Bois, *Truth*, pp. 217–18; Pomaret, *Dernier Témoin*, pp. 88–89.
15. Sauvy, *Histoire économique*, pp. 92–93. See also Michel Debré's testimony in Rémond, ed., *Daladier*, pp. 189–94, and the affectionate memoir by Reyaud's daughter: Demey, *Paul Reynaud*.
16. Germain, *Grandes Favorites*, pp. 232–34.
17. Bois, *Truth*, p. 132.
18. Bullitt to Roosevelt, Sept. 16, 1939, in Bullitt, *For the President*, p. 373.
19. Gamelin, journal de marche, Sept. 19, 1939, Fonds Gamelin, 1 K 224, SHAT.
20. Savvy, *De Paul Reynaud à Charles de Gaulle*, p. 99; entry for Sept. 24, 1939, in Villelume, *Journal*, pp. 41–42. Veteran Senator Jules Jeanneney said this to Daladier himself: Jeanneney, *Journal*, pp. 14–16.
21. Daladier to Gamelin, Sept. 16, 1939, Papiers 40, Daladier 4, MAE.
22. Gamelin to Daladier, Sept. 17, 1939, ibid.
23. Baudouï, *Dautry*, pp. 200–201. Chapman, *State Capitalism*, pp. 215–16, docu-

ments the decline in aircraft production.

24. Spears, *Assignment to Catastrophe*, 1:69; Teske, *Silbernen Spiegel*, pp. 65–66.
25. Chautemps to Daladier, Dec. 19, 1939, 3 DA 6/6, Archives Édouard Daladier.
26. Quoted in Bédarida, "France, Britain and the Nordic Countries," p. 11.
27. CSDN note, Sept. 28, 1939, 2 N 224, SHAT.
28. Debrè, *Trois Républiques*, 1:172.
29. Howard-Vyse, report, Jan. 8, 1940, WO 208/619.
30. Letters, Sept. 3, 1939, Feb. 12, 1940, in Fonvieille-Alquier, *Français*, pp. 453, 455; entry for Feb. 18, 1940, in Sartre, *War Diaries*, pp. 207–8.
31. Chamberlain to Ida Chamberlain, Sept. 23, 1939, NC 18/1/1122, in Chamberlain Papers; entry for Dec. 27, 1939, in Meier-Welcker, *Aufzeichnungen*, p. 42.
32. Note de direction politique, "Constitution d'un front d'Orient," Sept. 20, 1939, Papiers 40, Daladier 4, MAE; Dejean memo, Sept. 26, 1939, Dejean, PA 288, MAE.
33. Entry for Dec. 5, 1939, in Villelume, *Journal*, p. 121; anonymous memoranda, Feb. 28, March 22, 1940, Bruxelles, carton 331, MAE.
34. Daladier-Secy CSDN, March 13, 1940, 2 N 153, SHAT; Cinquième Bureau, summaries of reports on the war economy, March 15, 1940, April 2, 1940, 7 N 2572, 7 N 2574, SHAT.
35. The basic studies are Kersaudy, *Stratèges et Norvege*; Munch-Petersen, *Strategy of Phoney War*; a collection of articles in *Scandinavian Journal of History*, nos. 1 and 2, 1979, by François Bédarida and David Dilks, among others; and Parker, "Britain, France, and Scandinavia."
36. Medlicott, *Economic Blockade* pp. 180–81; Cinquième Bureau report, Oct. 5, 1939, 7 N 2572, SHAT; Deuxième Bureau (Air), "Bulletin de Renseignements," Oct. 14, 1939, 1 D 23, SHAA; Service Économique et Financier, report to Minister of Blockade, Dec. 15, 1940, 2 N 52, SHAT.
37. Daladier to Minister of Blockade, Dec. 21, 1939, 2 N 153, SHAT. See also Arnal, "Campagne de Norvège."
38. The basic work on diplomacy of the Winter War is Nevakivi, *Appeal That Was Never Made*. See also the official campaign history, Derry, *Campaign in Norway*, and the official history of British-Norwegian relations published later, which has more political detail: Salmon, "British Strategy in Norway." Moulton, *Norwegian Campaign*, and Harvey, *Scandinavian Misadventure*, are popular histories containing some details lacking in the official accounts. Holst, "Surprise, Signals and Reaction," is a careful scholarly analysis focused on possible lessons applicable to NATO Cold War planning regarding Europe's northern flank.
39. Supreme War Council, minutes Dec. 19, 1939, in Bédarida, *Stratégie secrète*, pp. 202–7.
40. Bullitt to Roosevelt, Dec. 19, 1939, in Bullitt, *For the President*, p. 395; Fabre-Luce, *Journal*, pp. 288–89. See Sobel, *Origins of Interventionism*.
41. Daladier, handwritten notes, Jan. 4, 8, 1940, 3 DA 6/6, Archives Édouard Daladier. On Daladier's knowledge of Reynaud's maneuvers: Lazareff, *Deadline*, pp. 263–264.
42. Desgranges, *Journal*, p. 334.
43. Daladier to Corbin, Jan. 16, 1940, 3 DA 6/7, Archives Édouard Daladier.
44. CSDN memorandum, Jan. 15, 1940, 2 N 224, SHAT.
45. Cinquième Bureau, summary of economic intelligence, Feb. 2, 1940, 7 N 2572,

SHAT. On actual economic conditions in Germany, which were not yet as parlous as French and British analysts supposed, see Overy, *War and Economy.*

46. Darlan, memorandum, Jan. 22, 1940, in *Lettres et Notes de Darlan,* pp. 143–44, Darlan to Gamelin, Jan. 23, 1940, ibid., pp. 144-45, copy in 496 AP/22, Archives Édouard Daladier.
47. Entry for Feb. 5, 1940, in *Cadogan Diaries,* p. 253.
48. Entry for Feb. 10, 1940, in Desgranges, *Journal,* p. 348.
49. Guariglia to Ciano, Feb. 14, 1940, DDI [9], 3:doc. 305.
50. Daladier to Corbin, March 4, 1940, 3 DA 7/4, Archives Édouard Daladier.
51. Daladier, memo, March 1, 1940, ibid.; see Parker, "Britain, France, and Scandinavia," p. 379.
52. Chamberlain to Ida Chamberlain, Jan. 27, 1940, NC 18/1/1140, Chamberlain Papers.
53. Chapman, *State Capitalism,* p. 222.
54. Informal report from a British liaison officer with the French III Corps, quoted in Watt, "Le Moral," p. 207.
55. Pernot, *Journal,* p. 46.
56. Fabre-Luce, *Journal,* pp. 251–52; Bois, *Truth,* 187; Raphaël-Leygues, *Chronique,* p. 155.

CHAPTER TWENTY-THREE: STUMBLES

1. Michel Debré, in Rémond, ed., *Daladier,* p. 196.
2. Minister of Blockade to Secretary, CSDN, Feb. 4, 1940, 2 N 153, SHAT.
3. Bédarida, *Stratégie secrète,* pp. 289–91, analyzes the composition and transmission of Reynaud to Chamberlain, March 25, 1940. See Richardson, "French Plans for Allied Attacks on the Caucasus Oil Fields," and Mourélos, *Fictions et réalités.* Kaiser, *Economic Diplomacy,* makes clear the extent to which France and Britain had exaggerated German interest in the Balkans throughout the 1930s. On the actual level of German dependence on Romanian oil, see Marguerat, *Le IIIe Reich et le pétrole roumain.*
4. BBC broadcast, Jan. 20, 1940, quoted in Gilbert, *Churchill,* 6:136–37.
5. Churchill, War Cabinet paper, Dec. 16, 1939, in *Churchill War Papers,* p. 524.
6. Churchill to Chamberlain, Dec. 25, 1939, ibid., p. 564.
7. Churchill, memorandum, Dec. 25, 1939, ibid., p. 569; War Cabinet minutes, March 27, 1940, ibid., p. 921.
8. War Cabinet, confidential annex, Dec. 22, 1939, in *Churchill War Papers,* 1:555.
9. Chamberlain to Hilda Chamberlain, March 30, 1940, NC 18/1/1145, Chamberlain Papers.
10. War Cabinet meeting minutes, March 27, 1940, CAB 65.
11. "Royal Marine": see *Churchill War Papers,* pp. 502–4, 647–50.
12. Daladier to Chamberlain, April 5, 1940, 496 AP/22, Archives Édouard Daladier.
13. Rossi-Landi, *Drôle de guerre,* pp. 62–63.
14. War Cabinet meeting minutes, April 3, 1940, CAB 65.
15. As examples of muffled warnings: Deuxième Bureau note, Jan. 11, 1940, in Gauché, *Deuxième Bureau,* pp. 196–98; Military Attaché, Madrid, to Deuxième Bureau, 7 N 4044, SHAT; SR agent report, Feb. 25, 1940, cited in Navarre et al., *Service de Renseignements,* p. 109; entry for Feb. 27, 1940 (referring to a report

from the military attaché in Copenhagen), in Villelume, *Journal*, p. 212; British GHQ bulletin, April 5, 1940, 1 D 25, SHAA; summary of SR and attaché reports, April 5–6, 1940, in Gauché, *Deuxième Bureau*, p. 206, also in Minart, *P.C. Vincennes*, 2:191–92; Deuxième Bureau (Air), summary of intelligence, April 9, 1940, 1 D 24, SHAA. On the surprise: Reynaud, *Au Coeur de la mêlée*, p. 387; Villelume, *Journal*, p. 261; confirmed by Gamelin, journal de marche, April 8, 1940, Fonds Gamelin, 1 K 224, SHAT.

16. Renaudin, *Sans fleur*, p. 79.
17. Bourget, *De Beyrouth à Bordeaux*, pp. 1–5.
18. Gamelin to Ironside, Sept. 18, 1939, WO 106; Gamelin, journal de marche, Sept. 19, 1939, Fonds Gamelin, 1 K 224, SHAT; Gamelin, *Servir*, 3:111; Supreme War Council sessions, Sept. 12, Sept. 22, 1939, in Bédarida, *Stratégie secrète*, pp. 97–100, 124–30. The fullest discussion, mostly from British records, is in Barker, *British Policy in South-East Europe*.
19. Entry for Sept. 22, 1939, in *Cadogan Diaries*, p. 218.
20. Ironside to Wavell, Sept. 11, 1939, in Connell, *Wavell*, p. 216.
21. Voluminous records are in CAB 85; PRO; Allied Military Committee, "Policy in the Balkans," Jan. 29–Feb. 4, 1940, CAB 84. See also Barker, *British Policy in South-East Europe*, pp. 15–17.
22. Gamelin, *Servir*, 3:199.
23. Darlan's biographers comment, "The ignorance of the Admiralty regarding the Arctic theater was stupefying" (Coutau-Bégarie and Huan, *Darlan*, p. 197).
24. Gamelin, "Note on the Conduct of the War," March 16, 1940, in Reynaud, *Au Coeur de la mêlée*, pp. 370–71; entry for March 17, 1940, in Villelume, *Journal*, p. 238.
25. Ironside diary, March 24, 1940, cited in Alexander, "Gamelin and the Defeat of France," p. 127.
26. Entry for April 9, 1940, in Villelume, *Journal*, p. 262.
27. Gamelin, *Servir*, 3:301, 336; Roton, *Années cruciales*, p. 107.
28. Gamelin to Daladier, Jan. 7, 1940, Fonds Gamelin, 1 K 224, SHAT (partly in Gamelin, *Servir*, 3:155).
29. Minart, *P.C. Vincennes*, 2:139–41.
30. Ibid., pp. 10, 157; entry for Dec. 30, 1939, in *Ironside Diaries*, p. 191. Alexander, "Fall of France," pp. 28–29, offers further evidence of Gamelin's intentness on keeping his job: he began to talk with allies among newspaper publishers and leaders of parliamentary factions.

CHAPTER TWENTY-FOUR: INTELLIGENCE FAILURE

1. Wohlstetter, *Pearl Harbor*. Kahn, "The United States Views Germany and Japan in 1941," amends Wohlstetter importantly by emphasizing preconceptions that blinded readers to the significance of some of the intercepted messages, and procedures that prevented the messages from being analyzed in sequence and context. See also Kaiser, "Conspiracy or Cock-up?"
2. Whaley, Codeword BARBAROSSA. Important context and an addition to Whaley's tally of "signals" appears in Erickson, "Threat Identification." See also contributions by Hinsley and Volkogonov in Erickson and Dilks, *Barbarossa*.
3. The only study of the war of 1940 faintly comparable to Wohlstetter, *Pearl Harbor*,

or Whaley, *BARBAROSSA,* is Brauch, "Sedan, 1940," which has never been translated, even into French, and which has been little read. George, "Warning and Response," amplified in Levite, *Intelligence and Strategic Surprises* (by one of
George's students), and Betts, in various articles and books, have been the leaders
in developing prescriptions based on past experience. They make relatively infre-
quent reference to events of 1940. Daniel and Herbig, *Strategic Military Deception,* surveys a large number of theories and case studies, all from Barbarossa
forward. The same is true of Hybel, *Logic of Surprise.* Knorr, "Strategic Surprise,"
deals with the German attack on Denmark and Norway and with the Ardennes offensive, but briefly and only descriptively. Handel, "Problem of Strategic Surprise," and Kam, *Surprise Attack,* are the only analytic works on the subject that
take serious account of these surprises, but they, too, are dominated by Pearl Harbor, Barbarossa, and like events of later date. The literature reflects the Cold War
preoccupation with a nuclear bolt-from-the-blue. Mearsheimer, *Conventional Deterrence,* deals extensively and thoughtfully with the German offensive against
France but is not focused on anticipation or detection of surprise attack.

4. Gauché, *Deuxième Bureau,* p. 211. The same message is quoted in Navarre et al.,
   Service de Renseignements, p. 74.
5. Reynaud, *Au Coeur de la mêlée,* p. 422.
6. Deuxième Bureau (Air), "Bulletin de Renseignements," May 6, 1940, 1 D 24,
   SHAA.
7. Deuxième Bureau (Air), "Bulletin de Renseignements," Feb. 26, 1940, ibid.;
   Deuxième Bureau (Air), "Bulletin de Renseignements," March 1, 1940, ibid.;
   Gauché, *Deuxième Bureau,* p. 205; memorandum on meeting at the War Office,
   March 6, 1940, WO 106; entry for March 19, 1940, in Villelume, *Journal,* p. 240;
   Deuxième Bureau (Air), "Bulletin de Renseignements," April 12, 1940, 1 D 24,
   SHAA; Gamelin, journal de marche, April 23, 1940, Fonds Gamelin, 1 K 224,
   SHAT; Gamelin, journal de marche, April 30, 1940, 1 K 224, SHAT; Military Attaché, Paris, to Brussels, May 1, 1940, in Vanwelkenhuyzen, *Avertissements,* p.
   238.
8. Entry for Nov. 25, 1939, in Villelume, *Journal,* p. 105.
9. Anglo-French Committee, report, Jan. 22, 1940, CAB 85.
10. Anglo-French Committee, report, March 6, 1940, ibid.
11. Deuxième Bureau answers to questions from British Joint Intelligence Committee,
    Jan. 16, 1940, 2 N 55, SHAT; Deuxième Bureau (Air), memorandum, March 30,
    1940, 1 D 24, SHAA.
12. Gamelin to Daladier, Jan. 7, 1940, Fonds Gamelin, 1 K 224, SHAT.
13. Anglo-French Liaison Committee meeting, Jan. 22, 1940, CAB 85.
14. Comité de Guerre, minutes, April 16, 1940, 2 N 26, SHAT.
15. Deist, *Germany and the Second World War,* 2:279; Frieser, *Blitzkrieg-Legende,* pp.
    41–65. My numbers, which differ slightly from Deist's and Frieser's, are based on
    a combination of Müller-Hillebrand, *Das Heer,* and maps in NARS Film T 78, reel
    449. But, as Deist observes, no numbers are certain. They should all be allowed a
    range of error of at least plus or minus 5 percent.
16. Anglo-French Committee, report, April 1, 1940, CAB 85.
17. Gauché, *Deuxième Bureau,* pp. 189–90; Daladier testimony, in *Événements . . . :
    Tém.,* ID: 22.

18. "Study of the German Aircraft Industry," Jan. 1940, 2 N 237, SHAT; Anglo-French Committee, report, April 1, 1940, CAB 85; Vuillemin to Gamelin, April 1940, 1 D 33, SHAA.
19. Vanwelkenhuyzen, *Avertissements*, p. 61.
20. Bertrand, *Enigma*, pp. 70–86; Hinsley et al., *British Intelligence*, 1:108–9, 487–95; Rivet diary, March 12, 1940; Paillole, *Notre Espion*, pp. 182–83. Literature arguing about relative credit for breaking Enigma includes Bloch, "Contribution française"; Garlinski, *Enigma War*; Kozaczuk, *Enigma*; Stengers, "Enigma"; and Woytak, *On the Border*.
21. These various reports are all in 1 D 24, 1 D 25, and 1 D 26, SHAA, or 7 N 2157, SHAT.
22. Van Overstraeten, *Au service de la Belgique*, 1:211–12.
23. Bauer, *Guerre des blindés*, 1:86–87.
24. These sightings and reports of pilot interrogations are all in daily bulletins from the Deuxième Bureau (Air), 1 D 24, SHAA. Paillole's account is in *Service speciaux*, pp. 185–86.

CHAPTER TWENTY-FIVE: THE REASONS WHY

1. Brigadier Swayne to GHQ, Sept. 29, 1939, WO 106/1653.
2. Howard-Vyse, report, Feb. 3, 1940, WO 106/1655.
3. Roton, *Années cruciales*, pp. 118–20.
4. Deuxième Bureau weekly report, May 18, 1940, 7 N 2517, SHAT.
5. Allard, *Responsables*, pp. 211–13; Sarraz-Bourret, *Témoignage*, pp. 14–18.
6. Paillole, *Services spéciaux*, pp. 163–64; author interview with Paillole.
7. Memo for the record, Oct. 1, 1939, WO 106/1653.
8. Spears, *Assignment to Catastrophe*, 1:75.
9. Gamelin, journal de marche, Sept. 26, 1939, Fonds Gamelin, 1 K 225; entry for Oct. 3, 1939, in Villehume, *Journal*, p. 53; Desgranges, *Journal*, p. 343; *Ironside Diaries*, p. 90; Daridan, *Chemin*, pp. 149–50; Fabry, *De la Place de la Concorde*, p. 222.
10. Gamelin, journal de marche, March 5, 1940, 1 K 224, SHAT.
11. Gauché, *Deuxième Bureau*, pp. 21–22.
12. Ibid., p. 12.
13. Ibid.
14. Ibid., pp. 96–97. Some of the original memoranda are in *DDF*, 13:docs. 103 (Dec. 12, 1938), 334 (Jan. 10, 1939), and 335 (Jan. 17, 1939), and 15:doc. 351 (April 11, 1939).
15. Bloch, *Strange Defeat*, p. 98.
16. Navarre, *Temps de vérités*, p. 41. Alexander, "Did the Deuxième Bureau Work?," contends that the low status of intelligence service in France has been exaggerated but does not deny that intelligence officers tended to be isolated bureaucratically if not necessarily socially.
17. Bloch, *Strange Defeat*, p. 86. Similar testimony is in Lerecouvreux, *Huit Mois*, pp. 94–95.
18. Gamelin, *Servir*, 2:194–95.
19. Paillole, *Services spéciaux*, pp. 185–86.

20. Deuxième Bureau (Air), "Bulletin des Renseignements," March 8, 1940, 1 D 24, SHAA; Rivet diary, March 12 and March 19, 1940; Gamelin, journal de marche, March 19, 1940; Fonds Gamelin, 1 K 224, SHAT.

CHAPTER TWENTY-SIX: THE DAM BREAKS

1. Gamelin, journal de marche, April 3, 1940, Fonds Gamelin, 1 K 224, SHAT.
2. Vanwelkenhuyzen, *Avertissements*, pp. 134–35.
3. Bargeton to Reynaud, April 6, 1940, Bruxelles, carton 345, MAE.
4. Reynaud and Gamelin, notes on the meeting of the Comité de Guerre, April 9, 1940, in Bédarida, *Stratégie secrète*, pp. 366–68. The original of the former, in 2 N 26, SHAT, has a marginal note by Gamelin complaining that an official record was made of the French government's discussing possible violation of the territory of a neutral.
5. Supreme War Council, minutes, April 9, 1940, in Bédarida, *Stratégie secrète*, pp. 383–91.
6. Gamelin to Hautcoeur, April 11, 1940 (two messages), in *Relations militaires Franco-belges*, pp. 127–28; Delvoie, report, April 11, 1940, ibid., p. 128.
7. Ibid., pp. 126–27.
8. Van Overstraeten, *Au service de la Belgique*, 1:550–52.
9. Gamelin, *Servir*, 3:350.
10. Connell, *Wavell*, pp. 219–26.
11. Bédarida, *Stratégie secèrte*, pp. 405–6.
12. Comité de Guerre, minutes, May 4, 1940, 2 N 26, SHAT.
13. As Bédarida, *Stratégie secrète*, pp. 405–6, points out, Reynaud's claim in *Au coeur de la mêlée*, p. 371, to have turned away from the Baku project before the Supreme War Council meeting of April 22–23, is belied by the minutes of the meeting. He appears not to have internalized until after that meeting the fact that the project could not materialize for months, if not years. The minutes of the Comité de Guerre for April 26, 2 N 26, SHAT, provide the earliest documentary evidence of his cooling toward the project.
14. Comité de Guerre, minutes, April 16, 1940, 2 N 26, SHAT; Bédarida, *Stratégie secrète*, pp. 405–6; Barker, *British Policy in South-East Europe*, p. 17; Bührer, *Aux heures tragiques*, pp. 140–42, Comité de Guerre, minutes, April 26, 1940, 2 N 26, SHAT; Gamelin, *Servir*, 3:362–63.
15. Anglo-French Liaison Committee, minutes, April 10, 15, 1940, CAB 85, PRO.
16. Meeting of the French chiefs of staff with Air Chief Marshal Barratt, April 15, 1940, 1 D 34, SHAA.
17. Supreme War Council meeting, April 22–23, 1940, in Bédarida, *Stratégie secrète*, pp. 437–44, 471–72.
18. Comité de Guerre, minutes, May 4, 1940, 2 N 26, SHAT. On his entertaining the Netherlands-only hypothesis: Gamelin, journal de marche, April 18, 23, 1940, 1 K 224, SHAT; Gamelin to Daladier, April 21, 1940, in Gamelin, *Servir*, 3:360.
19. Georges to Gamelin, April 14, 1940, in Gamelin, *Servir*, 3:340. Though Gamelin writes in his memoirs as if this were Georges's only memorandum on the subject, it clearly was not. It was headed "No. 1084 3/op." Gamelin's response of April 15, ibid., pp. 343–44, deals with points not explicit, not even clearly implicit, in the

printed memorandum by Georges. Moreover, it says that it is a response to "No. 1086–3/O.P." In his diary entry for April 20, Villelume (*Journal*, p. 284) attributes to Georges the additional points to which Gamelin referred in his response. On conversations between Georges and Giraud, see Lyet, *Bataille de France*, pp. 28–29.

20. Gamelin, journal de marche, May 10, 1940, 1 K 224, SHAT.
21. The report is in *Événements . . . : Tém.*, 2:359–60. According to Reynaud, *Au coeur de la mêlée*, p. 132, Huntziger, who was minister of war in Pétain's Vichy regime, tried to destroy the letter he had sent to the general staff à propos of the report but was prevented from doing so by conscientious archivists. General-staff notes for a reply, dated March 23, 1940, are in 7 N 4045, SHAT. See Alexander, "Prophet Without Honour?"
22. Entry for April 12, 1940, Baudouin, *Neuf Mois au gouvernement*, p. 63.
23. Bois, *Truth*, pp. 261–63; Chautemps, *Cahiers*, pp. 69–71.

CHAPTER TWENTY-SEVEN: BATTLE!

1. Rebatet, *Mémoires d'un fasciste*, 1:369.
2. D'Astier de la Vigerie, *Le Ciel n'était pas vide*, pp. 83–84; Deuxième Bureau (Air), "Bulletin des Renseignements," May 10, 1940, 1 D 24, SHAA; Ellis, *War in France and Flanders*, p. 37. These figures jibe with the global picture drawn in Buffotot and Ogier, "L'Armée de l'Air Française," which calculates that the French air force lost 410 planes during the entire six weeks of war, just about half destroyed by anti-aircraft fire.
3. Boothe, *Europe in the Spring*, p. 223.
4. Gamelin forgot the editing and included the Pétain line in his version of the order of the day in his memoirs (Gamelin, *Servir*, 3:390).
5. Beaufre, *Drame*, p. 180.
6. Villelume, *Journal*, p. 330; Minart, *P.C. Vincennes*, 2:101.
7. Paillat, *Désastre*, 5:157–58; Fontaine, *Last to Leave*, pp. 3–5.
8. Gunnar Andreassen, quoted in Heimsoeth, *Zusammenbruch*, p. 342.
9. Vidalenc, "Divisions de série 'B.' "
10. Paul, *Brennpunkte*, p. 56; Teske, *Bewegungskrieg*, p. 16.
11. Lerecouvreux, *Armée Giraud*, pp. 20–21; Prioux, *Souvenirs*, p. 25.
12. Grandsard, *10e Corps*, p. 47; Ruby, *Sedan*, p. 71.
13. Bloch, *Strange Defeat*, p. 96.
14. Ruby, *Sedan*, pp. 17–19.
15. Prioux, *Souvenirs*, p. 40.
16. Lerecouvreux, *Armée Giraud*, pp. 85–93.
17. Minart, *P.C. Vincennes*, 2:108.
18. Kennedy, *Business of War*, p. 7; Robineau, "Conduite de la guerre aérienne," p. 106. See Vivier, "Douhétisme français"; Harvey, "Armée de l'air"; Young, "Strategic Dream."
19. Paillat, *Désastre*, 5:98.
20. Ibid., p. 100.
21. Gamelin, *Servir*, 3:390.
22. Paillat, *Désastre*, 5:100.

23. Ibid., pp. 100–101.
24. Bois, *Truth*, p. 96, says Mandel spoke of Gamelin as a prefect; Pomaret, *Dernier Témoin*, pp. 35–36, quotes himself as having said Gamelin should have been a prefect and Daladier as having responded, "Or a bishop!"
25. Neame, *Playing*, pp. 248–49.
26. Bloch, *Strange Defeat*, p. 16.
27. The Belgian instruction to lay down two lines of Cointet, one through Perwez, is noted in Northeastern Front General Staff, "Note sur la situation en Belgique," March 19, 1940, 1 D 31, SHAA.
28. Vanwelkenhuyzen, *Neutralité armée*, pp. 111–13. See also Rollot, "Rapports Franco-belges."
29. Ellis, *War in France and Flanders*, p. 36.
30. De Fabribeckers, *Campagne*, p. 164.
31. See Mrazek, *Fall of Eben Emael*; Sprengling, "How Eben Emael Was Taken."
32. Vanwelkenhuyzen, *Neutralité armée*, pp. 101–10.
33. Villelume, *Journal*, p. 332; Deuxième Bureau (Air), noon report, May 12, 1940, 1 D 24, SHAA; Headquarters, BAAF, daily intelligence summary, May 12, 1940, 1 D 25, SHAA.
34. *Pownall Diaries*, pp. 311–12.
35. Embry, *Mission Completed*, p. 146.
36. Chambes, *Équipages*, pp. 60–97. Portal to Newall, May 8, 1940, in Richards, *Portal*, p. 147; d'Astier de la Vigerie, *Le ciel n'était pas vide*, pp. 75–78. On the condition of the French air force, see, in addition to Buffotot and Ogier's "L'Armée de l'Air" and Christienne's *Histoire de l'aviation militaire française*, Paquier, *Forces aériennes françaises*; Paquier, *L'Aviation de bombardement*; Seive, *L'Aviation d'assaut*; Salesse, *L'Aviation de chasse*; Kirkland, "French Air Force" and "French Air Strength"; Kennett, "German Air Superiority." On the management of the air campaign, see Robineau, "Conduite de la guerre aérienne"; Fridenson, *La France et le Grande Bretagne*; Richards and Saunders, *Royal Air Force*, 1; and, at a grander comparative level, Boog, *Conduct of the Air War*, and Overy, *Air War* and *Air Power*. Sormail, "Haut Commandement aérien," contains Vuillemin's retrospective complaints as of July 1940. Two memoirs, Goddard, *Skies to Dunkirk*, and Joubert de la Ferté, *Fated Sky*, give abundant evidence of the noncooperative attitudes common among senior British air officers.
37. Alexander, "Gamelin and the Defence of France," p. 56.
38. Deuxième Bureau (Air), "Renseignements Généraux," May 11, 1940, 1 D 24 SHAA.
39. Deuxième Bureau (Air), noon report, May 12, 1940, 1 D 24, SHAA; Deuxième Bureau (Air), "Bulletin des Renseignements," May 12, 1940, ibid.

CHAPTER TWENTY-EIGHT: "HITCH" AT SEDAN

1. Framery, "Campaign of Flanders," pp. 635–36.
2. Prioux, *Souvenirs*, p. 74.
3. Jungenfeld, "German Panzers," p. 775.
4. Prioux, *Souvenirs*, p. 74; Framery, "Campaign of Flanders," pp. 767.
5. Delater, *Avec la 3e D.L.M.*, p. 234; Frieser, *Blitzkrieg-Legende*, p. 302. See also Gunsburg, "Battle of the Belgian Plain, and Bücheler, "Panzerschlacht."

6. Frieser, *Blitzkrieg-Legende*, p. 306; Jungenfeld, "German Panzers," p. 775; Zimmermann, *Griff ins Ungewisse*.
7. Lerecouvreux, *Armée Giraud*, 247–56.
8. Steiger, *Panzertaktik*, p. 98.
9. Rocolle, *Guerre de 1940*, 2:19; de Fabribeckers, *Campagne*, p. 165.
10. Fonvieille-Alquier, *Français*, p. 456.
11. Doumenc, *Neuvième Armée*, and Le Goyet, "IIe Corps d'Armée," provide high-level views. The many articles by Bikar in *RBHM* trace events unit by unit.
12. Lyet, "À propos de Sedan," p. 92.
13. Marill, "Perception de la menace allemande," pp. 88–91.
14. Ruby, *Sedan*, p. 144; Georges to Gamelin, 11:45 P.M., May 13, 1940, Rocolle, *Guerre de 1940*, 2:68.
15. Minart, *P.C. Vincennes*, 2:145.
16. Beaufre, *Drame*, p. 183. Georges's papers include a memorandum dated May 14, 1940, overstating (as would French survivors for decades afterward) the extent to which events had been out of the leaders' control: "Enormous numerical superiority in aircraft and tanks [had] a moral effect on the troops, [and they] panicked. Our notion concerning the value of breaks [*coupures*], particularly the Meuse, has been contradicted by facts.... The Boches passed the rivers and destroyed bridges with unexpected speed. On top of that, there have been failures and grave negligence." I believe the date is not that of the document but, rather, that of the date whose events Georges was trying to explain.
17. Gunsburg, *Divided and Conquered*, p. 194.
18. Churchill, *Second World War*, 2:42.

CHAPTER TWENTY-NINE: PLAN YELLOW PLAYS OUT

1. Frieser, *Blitzkrieg-Legende*, p. 2. Rottgart, "Deutsche Panzertruppe," provides an overview as of May 10, 1940. Plato, *5. Panzerdivision*, Manteuffel, *7. Panzerdivision*, and Scheibert, *Gespensterdivision*, are the semi-official histories of the two divisions in the Fourth Army, and Rommel, the commander of the "Gespensterdivision," has, of course, been the subject of several biographies by, among others, Koch, Lewin, and Macksey. There is a lively history of one regiment in the Fifth Panzer Division, the Fifteenth: Schrodek, *Ihr Glaube*. Zeitzler, "Panzer-Gruppe v. Kleist," provides an extraordinarily clinical view of the the Group's logistical problems. Horst Adalbert Koch, *Flak*, and Kurowski and Tornau, *Sturmartillerie*, supply details on anti-aircraft protection and on the materiel that Group Kleist lacked—heavy artillery. Spaeter, *Geschichte des Panzerkorps Grossdeutschland*, offers an overview of Guderian's operations; Neumann, *4. Panzerdivision*, of one of Hoepner's divisions. Reinhardt, "Im Schatten Guderians," gives a commander's impressions of operations of X Corps. Oswald, *Kraftfahrzeuge*, is the best source of information about particular tanks or other armored vehicles.
2. Choltitz, *Soldat unter Soldaten*, pp. 60–72, is a firsthand account by a German paratroop-battalion commander.
3. Liddell Hart, *German Generals Talk*, p. 117.
4. A careful account, stressing that it was not an intentional terror-bombing attack, is Boog, "Operationen der Luftwaffe." For the war in Netherlands as a whole, see Van Kleffens, *Juggernaut*, and De Jong, *Het Koninkrigk*.

5. Melzer, *Albert-Kanal und Eben-Emael*, p. 132; Götzel, *Student*, pp. 120ff.
6. Kuhnert, *Will We See Tomorrow?* pp. 30–33.
7. Entry for May 10–12, 1940, *Halder Diary*; Liss, *Westfront*, pp. 142–52; FHW, situation report, May 12, 1940, NARS Film T 78, reel 449.
8. Frieser, *Blitzkrieg-Legende*, p. 135.
9. Kielmansegg, *Panzer*, p. 103; AGA, KTB, May 11, 1940; NARS Film T 311, reel 236; Teske, *Bewegungskrieg*, p. 22.
10. Paillat, *Désastre*, 5:166, n. 24.
11. Rommel, *Attacks*, p. 132; *Rommel Papers*, p. 7.
12. Bikar, "4e Division Légére."
13. *Kampferlebnisse*, p. 23.
14. Ibid., p. 24.
15. Quoted in Frieser, *Blitzkrieg-Legende*, p. 285.
16. Maassen, *Über die Maas*, is a firsthand account.
17. Berben and Iselin, *Panzers passent la Meuse*, p. 106.
18. Kielmansegg, *Panzer*, p. 115.
19. See Steiger, *Panzertaktik*, pp. 47–49.
20. See Rothbrust, *Guderian's XIXth Panzer Corps*.
21. Memorandum, "War Game at OKH," March 18–19, 1940, NARS Film T 971, reel 1.
22. Killen, *Luftwaffe*, p. 93.
23. Accart, *On s'est battu*, pp. 115–16.
24. Berben and Iselin, *Panzers passent la Meuse*, pp. 199–200.
25. Kielmansegg, *Panzer*, p 116.
26. Embry, *Mission Completed*, p. 148.
27. Laubier, "Bombardement"; Ellis, *War in France and Flanders*, p. 30.
28. Lyet, "À propos de Sedan," p. 129.
29. Doughty, "Almost a Miracle," p. 51; Balck, *Ordnung*, pp. 272–73.
30. Hoth, "Schicksal," p. 377. Doughty, *Breaking Point*, develops at length evidence that the battle was very close.
31. Horne, *To Lose a Battle*, pp. 374–76.

CHAPTER THIRTY: FRANCE FALLS

1. Horne, *To Lose a Battle*, p. 464.
2. Zentner, *Frankreichfeldzug*, p. 93.
3. AGA, KTB, May 15, 1940, in Frieser, *Blitzkrieg-Legende*, p. 320.
4. AGA, KTB, May 17, 1940, ibid., p. 321.
5. Entry for Oct. 20, 1939, in Goebbels, *Tagebücher*.
6. Entry for May 17, 1940, in Tippelskirch diary; entry for May 17, 1940, in *Halder Diary*.
7. Entry for May 18, 1940, in *Halder Diary*. See Meier-Welcker, "Erlebnisse," on reactions to the stop order at Fourth Army headquarters.
8. Ellis, *War in France and Flanders*, p. 114.
9. Though it seems almost too malicious to be true, Élie Bois claims to have heard Reynaud's mistress, Hélène des Portes, urge that he act lest Gamelin get credit for a French victory (Bois, *Truth*, p. 271).

10. Jamet, *Carnets*, p. 95. On Weygand, see, in addition to his own writings, Bourget, *De Beyrouth à Bordeaux*; books by Édouard and Jacques Weygand; Bankwitz, *Maxime Weygand*; and Destremau, *Weygand*.

11. Scheibert, *Gespensterdivision*, p. 36. On the battle at Arras, see, in addition to Ellis, *War in France and Flanders*, Rogers, "Arras," and particularly Bond, "Arras," a splendid analysis.

12. Prételat, *Destin tragique*, pp. 155–56.

13. Gillet, "Conférence d'Ypres."

14. Chief of Staff, minutes, May 23, 1940, CAB 84. See also Bell, *A Certain Eventuality*; Gates, *End of the Affair*.

15. Liss, *Westfront*, p. 190.

16. Bartov, *Hitler's Army*, p. 123.

17. Bloch, *Strange Defeat*, p. 28. Also on the armistice, see, among other works: Giraudoux, *Armistice*; Lottmann, *Fall of Paris*; Lassaigne, *Vérité sur juin 1940*; Leca, *Rupture de 1940*. Of recent studies of Pétain, Ferro, *Pétain*, is the most nuanced; Pedroncini, *Pétain*, is the most detailed. The Pétain government's prosecution of the Third Republic at Riom is detailed in, among other works, Michel, *Procès de Riom*; Pottecher, *Procès de la défaite*; Mazé, *Grandes journées*.

18. To earlier writings on the first part of World War II, the reflective historian John Lukacs has recently added *Five Days in London*, making a strong case that Churchill barely prevented Halifax from persuading the British Cabinet to make approaches to Berlin that could have resulted in Britain's joining Pétain's armistice bid.

19. Entry for June 26, 1940, in Engel, *Heeresadjutant*, pp. 83–84.

CONCLUSION: WHY? AND WHAT CAN BE LEARNED?

1. Horne, *To Lose a Battle*, pp. 566–67.

2. Rocolle, *Guerre de 1940*, 2:36.

3. Herman, *Intelligence and Power*, by a thoughtful veteran of the British signal-intelligence service, analyzes brilliantly the inherent trade-offs between efficiency and security in communications.

4. The most thoughtful analyses of shortcomings in French doctrine are in the works of Doughty, especially *Seeds of Disaster* and *Breaking Point*, and in Posen, *Sources of Military Doctrine*. But see also the questions about their arguments posed in Kiesling, *Arming Against Hitler*.

5. Gisclon, *Cinquième Quart d'heure*, p. 83; Chambes, *Équipages*, pp. 56–58; Christienne, *Aviation militaire*, p. 374; Richards, *Portal*, pp. 147–50; Robineau, "Conduite de la guerre aérienne"; Seive, *Aviation d'assault*, pp. 121–25. The extent to which alliance relationships magnify what Clausewitz described as "friction" in warfare is shown in exquisite detail in Gunsburg, *Divided and Conquered*.

6. Frieser, *Blitzkrieg-Legende*, pp. 302, 344–47.

7. See Murray, *Change in the European Balance*, for 1938; Merglen, "Forces allemandes," for 1939.

8. De Lattre, *Jean de Lattre, mon mari*, 1:155.

9. Entry for May 19, 1940, in Tippelskirch diary.

10. Goutard, *1940*, argues persuasively that the counteroffensive could have suc-

ceeded, or at least made serious headway, had it been carried out when Gamelin ordered it.

11. Wheeler-Bennett, *Nemesis of Power*, p. 461.

12. The role of reticence and convenience in shaping governmental thinking is developed in beautiful detail in Neustadt, *Alliance Politics*. Lebow, *Between Peace and War*, and Stein, "Building Politics into Psychology," invoke somewhat the same concept as "motivated misperception." Vertzberger, *The World in Their Minds*, p. 345, describes decision-makers as "cognitive misers."

13. Jacobsen, *Fall Gelb*, p. 39. One of the most careful analyses of France's military defeat concludes that the fundamental reasons were exactly those pinpointed ahead of time by Liss and Foreign Armies West analysts (Cohen and Gooch, *Military Misfortunes*, pp. 197–230).

14. Bloch, *Strange Defeat*, p. 36; Bloch to Febvre, July 26, 1942, in Fink, *Marc Bloch*, p. 240.

15. The framework outlined here will be immediately recognized by anyone familiar with Vickers, *Art of Judgment*. The characterization of an appropriate outcome will also be recognized by the larger population familiar with the concept of "satisficing" developed by Vickers's friend and sometime collaborator, Nobelist Herbert Simon, initially in *Administrative Behavior*. The tests suggested for reality estimates are elaborated in Neustadt and May, *Thinking in Time*, the tests for action choices in Zelikow, "Foreign Policy Engineering."

16. Entry for May 13, 1940, in Bock, *Zwischen Pflicht and Verweigerung*, p. 123.

17. Gillet, "La Percée allemande," p. 94.

18. *Manoeuvre*, pp. 34–40.

19. Diary entry for Nov. 23, 1939, in Simoni, *Berlino, ambasciata d'Italia*, p. 27.

20. This point is made at length in May, *"Lessons" of the Past*, and Neustadt and May, *Thinking in Time*.

21. *Cadogan Diaries*, p. 18.

22. The concept of "tacit knowledge" is developed at length in Polanyi, *Personal Knowledge*.

23. This proposition, though put somewhat differently, is elaborated in Ben-Zwi, "Hindsight and Foresight," and "Intention, Capability and Surprise," and in Vertzberger, *The World in Their Minds*.

24. George, "Warning and Response," p. 19.

BIBLIOGRAPHY

ABBREVIATIONS
AG: Army Group (AGA—Army Group A, etc.)
BA-MA: Bundesarchiv-Militärarchiv, Freiburg im Bresgau
FHS: *French Historical Studies*
FHW: Fremde Heere West—the Foreign Armies West section of the intelligence
         directorate of the German general staff
IMT: International Military Tribunal
INS: *Intelligence and National Security*
JCH: *Journal of Contemporary History*
JMH: *Journal of Modern History*
JSS: *Journal of Strategic Studies*
KTB: *Kriegstagebuch*—war diary (of a division, army, army group, etc.)
MAE: Ministère des Affaires Étrangères (Foreign Ministry), France
MGM: *Militärgeschichtliche Mitteilungen*
NARS: (U.S.) National Archives and Records Service, Washington, D.C.
OKH: Oberkommando des Heeres—the German army high command
OKL: Oberkommando der Luftwaffe—the German air force high command
OKM: Oberkommando der Marine—the German navy high command
OKW: Oberkommando des Wehrmachts—the German armed-forces high com-
         mand
RHA: *Revue historique des Armées*
RBHM: *Revue belge d'histoire militaire*
RG: Record Group at NARS
RHDGM: *Revue d'histoire de la deuxième guerre mondiale*
SHAA: Service Historique de l'Armée de l'Air, Château de Vincennes, Paris
SHAT: Service Historique de l'Armée de Terre, Château de Vincennes, Paris
VfZ: *Viertel Jahreshefte für Zeitgeschichte*

(See also abbreviations under "Published Documents," below)

ARCHIVES AND MANUSCRIPTS
BRITAIN (all in the Public Record Office [PRO] at Kew, unless otherwise noted)
Admiralty records:
   ADM 223: Records of the Director of Naval Intelligence
Air Ministry records:
   Air 8: Air Staff records
   Air 40: Air Intelligence Directorate records

Cabinet records:
CAB 23: Minutes and Conclusions of the Cabinet
CAB 24: Cabinet memoranda
CAB 27: Proceedings of Cabinet committees
CAB 50: Reports of the British Chiefs of Staff Committee
CAB 53: Proceedings of the Chiefs of Staff Committee
CAB 65: War Cabinet Conclusions
CAB 66–68: War Cabinet Memoranda
CAB 69: Defence Committee (Operations)
CAB 84: Records of the British Chiefs of Staff Committee
CAB 85: Records of Anglo-French Coordinating Committees
CAB 99: Minutes of the Supreme War Council
Foreign Office records:
FO 371: general correspondence
Prime Minister's records:
PREM 3
Private papers:
Chamberlain Papers, Birmingham University Library
Churchill Papers, Churchill College, Cambridge University
War Office records:
WO 106: Intelligence Summaries
WO 120: Records of the Director of Military Intelligence
WO 208: Reports of Liaison Missions in France

FRANCE
Air Force:
SHAA
Army:
SHAT
Foreign Ministry:
MAE archives stored in Paris and at Nantes: post records filed by post (e.g., Bruxelles, Londres) and carton number; office file collections filed by number and name of collecting official (e.g., Daladier, Dejean, Hoppenot)
Private Papers:
Daladier Papers: Archives Édouard Daladier, Fondation Nationale des Sciences Politiques, Paris
Rivet diary: manuscript in the possession of Colonel Paul Paillole, La Queue les Yvelines

GERMANY (cited by NARS film series where available)
Air Force:
NARS Film T 321 (records of the OKL)
NARS Film T 971 (the von Rohden collection of Luftwaffe records)
Armed Forces High Command:
NARS Film T 77 (records of the OKW)

Army:
  NARS Film T 78 (records of the OKH)
  NARS Film T 311 (records of German Army Group headquarters)
Navy:
  NARS Film T 608 (records of the OKM)
Special Collections:
  Ludwig Beck Papers, BA-MA
  Lahousen diary: desk diary of Erwin Lahousen, BA-MA
  Tippelskirch diary: desk diary of General Kurt von Tippelskirch, chief of intelligence in the German army general staff, BA-MA

UNITED STATES
Blumentritt, Günther, "Critique of 'The German Campaign in the West,'" Historical Division, Headquarters, U.S. Army, Europe, Manuscript P-208, NARS RG 338.
———, "The German Campaign in the West," vols. 2 and 3, ibid.
———, "Thoughts of a Former Soldier on Strategy, Politics and Psychology of the 1939–1945 War," Manuscript B-647, ibid.
"Forschungsamt," Counter Intelligence Corps, Headquarters, U.S. Army, Europe, NARS, RG 338.
Halder, Franz, "Operational Basis for the First Phase of the French Campaign in 1940," Historical Division, Headquarters, U.S. Army, Europe, Manuscript P-151, ibid.
Hofmann, Rudolf, "War Games," Manuscript P-094, ibid.
Praun, Albert, "German Radio Intelligence," Manuscript P-038, ibid.
Tippelskirch, Kurt von, "The German Campaign in the West," Manuscript P-208, ibid.
———, "Intelligence in Foreign Armies," Manuscript P-041h, ibid.
———, et al., "Organization and Working Methods of the Intelligence Division of the German General Staff," Manuscript P-041i, ibid.
U.S. Military Intelligence Reports: France, 1919–1941, ed. Dale Reynolds (Frederick, Md.: University Publications of America microfilm, 1985).
U.S. Military Intelligence Reports: Germany, 1919–1941, ed. Dale Reynolds (Frederick, Md.: University Publications of America microfilm, 1983).

PUBLISHED DOCUMENTS
Actes et documents du Saint Siège, 11 vols. (Vatican: Libreria Editrice Vaticana, 1965–81).
Annuaire officiel des officers de l'Armée Active (Paris: Ministère de Guerre, annual).
Baynes, Norman H., ed., The Speeches of Adolf Hitler (2 vols.; New York: Howard Fertig, 1969).
Bédarida, François, ed., Stratégie secrète de la drôle de guerre: La Conseil supréme interalliée, septembre 1939–avril 1940 (Paris: Presses de la Fondation Nationale des Sciences Politiques, 1979).
Boberach, Heinz, ed., Meldungen aus dem Reich 1938–1945: Die geheimen Lageberichte des Sicherheitsdienstes der SS (17 vols.; Herrsching; Pawlak, 1984).
Bullitt: For the President, Personal and Secret: Correspondence Between Franklin D. Roosevelt and William C. Bullitt, ed. Orville H. Bullitt (Boston: Houghton Mifflin, 1972).
The Churchill War Papers, vol. 1: At the Admiralty, September 1939–May 1940, ed. Martin Gilbert (New York: W. W. Norton, 1993).

DBFP: Documents on British Foreign Policy; 1919–1939, ed. E. L. Woodward and Rohan Butler, 3rd ser., 9 vols. (London: HMSO, 1949–55).

DDB: Ministry of Foreign Affairs, Belgium, *Documents diplomatiques belges, 1920–1940*, 4 vols. (Brussels: Ministry of Foreign Affairs, 1964–66).

DDF: Ministère des Affaires Étrangères, Commission de Publication des Documents Relatifs aux Origines de la Guerre, *Documents diplomatiques français*, 2nd ser., vols. 1–19 (Paris: Imprimerie Nationale, 1972–86).

DDI: Ministerio degli Affari Esteri, Commissione per la Publicazione dei Documenti Diplomatici, *I documenti diplomatici italiani*, 8th ser., *1935–1939*, 13 vols. (Rome: Libreria dello Stato, 1953–91); 9th ser., *1939–1943*, vols. 1–5 (Rome Libreria dello Stato, 1954–65).

Deutschland-Berichte der Sozialdemokratischen Partei Deutschlands, 1934–1940, 7 vols. Frankfurt am Main: Petra Nettelbeck, 1980).

DGFP: United States Department of State, *Documents on German Foreign Policy, 1918–1945*, ser. D, *1937–1945*, vols. 1–9 (Washington, D.C.: Government Printing Office, 1949–56).

DGFP [C]: United States Department of State, *Documents on German Foreign Policy, 1918–1945*, ser. C, *1933–1937*, vols. 1–6 (Washington, D.C.: Government Printing Office, 1957–83).

Domarus, Max, ed., *Hitler—Reden und Proklamationen*, 2 vols. (Munich: Schmidt, 1963); trans. Mary Fran Gilbert, *Hitler: Speeches and Proclamations, 1932–1945*, 4 vols. (Wauconda, Ill.: Bolchazy-Carducci, 1990–98).

Événements . . .: Rap.: Assemblé Nationale, *Les Événements survenus en France de 1933 à 1945: Rapport de M. Charles Serre, député au nom de la Commission d'Enquête Parlementaire*, 2 vols. (Paris: Presses Universitaires, 1947).

Événements . . .: Tém.: Assemblé Nationale, *Les Événements survenues en France de 1933 à 1945; Témoignages et documents recueillies par la Commission d'Enquête Parlementaire*, 9 vols. (Paris: Presses Universitaires, 1947).

Geheimakten des französischen Generalstabes, ed. Ministry of Foreign Affairs (Berlin: Deutsche Verlag, 1940).

Geheimen Tageberichte der deutschen Wehrmachtführung im Zweiten Weltkrieg, 1939–1945, ed. Kurt Mehner, 12 vols. (Osnabrück: Biblio 1984–   ).

Hitler, Adolf, *Mein Kampf*, 2 vols. (Munich: Franz Eher, 1925–1926); trans. Ralph Manheim (Boston: Houghton Mifflin, 1943).

————, *Tischgespräche im Führerhauptquartier* (Stuttgart: Seewald, 1976); trans. Norman Cameron and R. H. Stevens, *Hitler's Table Talk, 1941–1944* (New York: Oxford University Press, 1988).

Hitlers Weisungen für die Kriegsführung, 1939–1945: Dokumente des OKW, ed. Walther Hubatsch (Frankfurt am Main: Bernard & Graefe, 1962); trans. H. R. Trevor-Roper, *Hitler's War Directives, 1939–1945* (London: Sidgwick and Jackson, 1964).

Hitlers zweites Buch: Ein Dokument aus dem Jahr 1928, ed. Gerhard L. Weinberg (Stuttgart: Deutsche Verlags-Anstalt, 1961); trans. Salvatore Attenario, *Hitler's Secret Book* (New York: Grove Press, 1962).

Hungarian Documents: Zsigmond László, Diplomáciai Iratok Magyarország Kölpolitikájához, 1936–1945, 4 vols. (Budapest: Akadémiai Kiadó, 1962); see also Kerekes below.

IMT; International Military Tribunal, *Nazi Conspiracy and Aggression*, 8 vols. (Washington, D.C.: Government Printing Office, 1946).

Irving, David, *Breach of Security: The German Secret Intelligence File on Events Leading to the Second World War* (London: William Kimber, 1968). *Das Reich hört mit: Görings "Forschungsamt": Der geheimste Nachrichtendienst des Dritten Reiches* (Kiel: Arndt, 1989) is an extended, annotated version of the same book.

Jacobsen, Hans-Adolf, ed., *Dokumente zur Vorgeschichte des Westfeldzuges, 1939–1940* (Berlin: Musterschmidt, 1956).

———, ed., *Dokumente zum Westfeldzug* (Göttingen: Musterschmidt, 1960).

———, ed., *1939–45: Der Zweite Weltkrieg in Chronik und Dokumenten* (Darmstadt: Wehr und Wissen Verlagsgesellschaft, 1961).

Kerekes, Lajos, ed., *Allianz Hitler-Horthy-Mussolini: Dokumente zur ungarischen Aussenpolitik (1933–1944)* (Budapest: Akadémiai Kiadó, 1966).

Lagevorträge: Gerhard Wagner, ed., *Lagevorträge des Oberbefehlshabers der Kriegsmarine vor Hitler, 1939–1945* (Munich: J. F. Lehmann, 1972).

OKW KTB: Kriegstagebuch des Oberkommandos der Wehrmacht (Wehrmachtführungsstab), ed. Hans-Adolf Jacobsen, 5 vols. (Frankfurt am Main: Bernard & Graefe, 1965).

Soviet Documents: Soviet Peace Efforts on the Eve of World War II, ed. A. A. Gromyko et al. (Moscow: Progress Publishers, 1973).

TMWC: International Military Tribunal, *Trials of the Major War Criminals*, 42 vols. (Nuremberg: International Military Tribunal, 1947–49).

U.S. v. Leeb: International Military Tribunal, *Nuremberg Military Tribunals* (Washington, D.C.: Government Printing Office, 1951).

Vogelsang, Thilo, "Neue Dokumente zur Geschichte der Reichswehr, 1930–1933," *VfZ*, Oct. 1954, pp. 434–35.

Young, A. P., *The "X" Documents*, ed. Sidney Aster (London: André Deutsch, 1974).

MEMOIRS AND DIARIES

Accart, Gen. Jean, *On s'est battu dans le ciel* (Paris: Arthaud, 1942).

Anfuso, Filippo, *Roma, Berlino, Salò, 1936–1945* (n.p.: Garzanti, 1950).

Alanbrooke Papers: Bryant, Arthur, *The Turn of the Tide, 1939–1943: The Diaries of Field Marshal Alanbrooke* (London: Collins, 1957).

Alphand, Hervé, *L'étonnement d'être: Journal, 1939–1973* (Paris: Fayard, 1977).

Amery, Leo, *My Political Life*, 3 vols. (London: Hutchinson, 1953–1956).

Archen, Lt. Col., *Missions speciales au Luxembourg* (Paris: Éditions France-Empire, 1969).

Armengaud, J., *Batailles politiques et militaires sur l'Europe: Témoignages, 1932–1940* (Paris: Éditions du Myrte, 1948).

Astier de la Vigerie, *Le ciel n'était pas vide:* 1940 (Paris: Julliard, 1952).

Bailby, Léon, *Souvenirs* (Paris: Plon, 1951).

Balck, Hermann, *Ordnung in Chaos: Erinnerungen 1893–1948* (Osnabrück: Biblio-Verlag, 1980).

Barbey, Bernard, *Von Hauptquartier zu Hauptquartier: Mein Tagebuch als Verbindungsoffizier zur französischen Armee, 1939/40* (Frauenfeld: Huber, 1967).

Bardoux, Jacques, *Journal d'un témoin de la troisième, 1 septembre 1939–15 juillet 1940* (Paris: Fayard, 1957).

Barlone, D., *A French Officer's Diary* (Cambridge: Cambridge University Press, 1942).

Baudouin, Paul, *Neuf mois au gouvernement, avril–décembre 1940* (Paris: Éditions de la Table Ronde, 1948); trans. Sir Charles Petrie, *The Private Diaries (March 1940 to January 1941)* (London: Eyre and Spottiswoode, 1948).

Beaufre, Gen. André, *La Drame de 1940* (Paris: Plon, 1965): abridged and trans. Desmond Flower, *1940: The Fall of France* (London: Cassell, 1965).

Beauvior, Simone de, *Journal de guerre, septembre 1939–janvier 1941* (Paris: Gallimard, 1990).

Bekker, Cajus, *Angriffshöhe 4000: Ein Kriegstagebuch der deutschen Luftwaffe* (Oldenburg: G. Stalling, 1964); trans and ed. Frank Ziegler, *The Luftwaffe War Diaries* (Garden City, N.Y.: Doubleday, 1968).

Bélin, René, *Du secretariat de la C.G.T. au gouvernement de Vichy: Mémoires, 1933–1942* (Paris: Albatros, 1978).

Below, Nicolaus von, *Als Hitlers Adjutant 1937–45* (Mainz: Hase und Koehler, 1980).

Bérard, Armand, *Un ambassadeur se souvient*, vol. 1:, *Au temps du danger allemand* (Paris: Plon, 1976).

Berndt, Alfred-Ingemar, *Meilensteine des Dritten Reiches: Erlebnischilderungen grosser Tage* (Munich: Zentralverlag der NSDAP, 1939).

Bertin-Boussu, Gen., *La 3è division d'infanterie motorisée, 1939–1940* (Aurillac: n.p., n.d.)

Bertrand, Gustave, *Enigma, ou la plus grande enigme de la guerre 1939–1945* (Paris: Plon, 1973).

Béthouart, Marie-Émile, *Cinq années d'espérance: Mémoires de guerre, 1939–1945* (Paris: Plon, 1968).

Birchall, Frederick T., *The Storm Breaks, A Panorama of Europe and the Forces That Have Wrecked Its Peace* (New York: The Viking Press, 1940).

Bloch, *Strange Defeat*: Marc Bloch, *Étrange défaite: Temoignage écrit en 1940* (Paris: Société des Éditions Franc-tireurs, 1946); trans. Gerard Hopkins, *Strange Defeat: A Statement of Evidence Written in 1940* (London: Oxford University Press, 1949).

Blumentritt, Günther, *Von Rundstedt, the Soldier and the Man* (London: Odham's, 1952).

Boberach, Heinz, ed., *Meldungen aus dem Reich 1938–1945: Die geheimen Lageberichte des Sicherheitsdienstes der SS*, 17 vols. (Herrsching: Pawlak, 1984).

Bock, Fedor von, *Zwischen Pflicht und Verweigerung: Das Kriegstagebuch*, ed. Klaus Gerbet (Munich: Herbig, 1995).

Bois, Elie-Joseph, *Le malheur de la France* (London: Hachette, 1941); trans. N. Scarlyn Wilson, *Truth on the Tragedy of France* (London: Hodder and Stoughton, 1941).

Bonnet, Georges, *De Munich à la Guerre* (Paris: Plon, 1967).

———, *Défense de la Paix*, 2 vols. (Geneva: Cheval Ailé, 1948).

Bonotaux, Lt. Col., et al., "Avec la 3è D.I.M. à Stonne," *RHA*, no. 2, 1950, pp. 47–50.

Boothe, Clare, *Europe in the Spring* (New York: Alfred A. Knopf, 1940).

Bor, Peter, *Gespräche mit Halder* (Wiesbaden: Limes, 1950).

Bourget, Pierre-André, *De Beyrouth à Bordeaux. La guerre de 1939–1940 vue du P. C. Weygand* (Paris: Berger-Levrault, 1946).

Bourret, Victor, *La tragédie de l'armée française* (Paris: Table Ronde, 1947).

Brasillach, Robert, *Une génération dans l'orage: Mémoires, notre avant-guerre; journal d'un homme occupé* (Paris: Plon, 1941).

Brinon, Fernand de, *Mémoires* (Paris: L.L.C., 1949).

Bryher, Winifred Ellerman, *The Days of Mars: A Memoir, 1940–1946* (New York: Harcourt Brace Jovanovich, 1972).

Bührer, Jules (as General * * * *), *Aux heures tragiques de l'Empire, 1938–1941* (Paris: Office Colonial d'Édition, 1947).

Butler, Lord, *The Art of Memory: Friends in Perspective* (London: Hodder and Stoughton, 1982).

Cadogan Diaries: Cadogan, Alexander, *Diaries 1938–1945*, ed. David Dilks (London: Cassell, 1971).

Capelle, Robert, *Dix Huit Ans auprès du roi Léopold* (Paris: Fayard, 1970).

Carné, Marcel, *La Vie à belles dents: Souvenirs* (Paris: Jean-Pierre Ollivier, 1975).

Chambes, René, *Équipages dans la fournaise 1940* (Paris: Flammarion, 1945).

Chambrun, René Aldebart, Comte de, *I Saw France Fall* (New York: William Morrow, 1940).

Chatfield, Lord, Admiral of the Fleet, *The Navy and Defence*, vol. 2, *It Might Happen Again* (London: Heinemann, 1947).

Chautemps, Camille, *Cahiers secrets de l'armistice, 1939–1940* (Paris: Plon, 1963).

Chauvel, Jean, *Commentaires* (Paris: Fayard, 1971).

Choltitz, Dietrich von, *Soldat unter Soldaten* (Zürich: Europa, 1951).

Ciano, Galeazzo, *Diario*, 2 vols. (Milan: Rizzoli, 1946); trans. ed. Hugh Gibson, *The Ciano Diaries, 1939–1943* (Garden City, N.Y.: Doubleday, 1946).

———, *Diario 1937–1938* (Bologna: Cappelli, 1948); trans. Andreas Mayor, *Ciano's Hidden Diary, 1937–1938* (New York: E. P. Dutton, 1953).

Colonel X, *La Ligne Maginot, bouclier de la France* (Paris Nouvelles Éditions Excelsior, 1939).

Colville, John R., *Fringes of Power: 10 Downing Street Diaries, 1939–1955* (New York: W. W. Norton, 1985).

Cot, Pierre, Le Procès de la république, 2 vols. (New York: Éditions de la Maison Française, 1944).

Coulondre, Robert, *De Staline à Hitler: Souvenirs de deux ambassades: 1936–1939* (Paris: Hachette, 1950).

Crawford Papers: Crawford, Earl of, *The Crawford Papers: The Journals of David Lindsay. Twenty-seventh Earl of Crawford and Tenth Earl of Balcarres, 1871–1940, During the Years 1892 to 1940*, ed. John Vincent (Manchester: Manchester University Press, 1984).

Crouy-Chanel, Étienne, *Alexis Léger, l'autre visage de Saint-John Perse* (Paris: Jean Picollec, 1989).

Dalton Diary: The Political Diary of Hugh Dalton, 1918–40, 1945–60, ed. Ben Pimlott (London: Jonathan Cape, 1986).

Daridan, Jean, *Le Chemin de la défaite* (Paris: Plon, 1980).

Darlan Lettres: Lettres et notes de l'Amiral Darlan, ed. Hervé Coutau-Bégarie (Paris: Economica, 1992).

Davignon, Vicomte Jacques, *Berlin 1936–1940: Souvenirs d'une mission* (Brussels: Éditions Universitaires, n.d.).

Debré. Michel, *Trois Républiques pour une France: Mémoires*, 3 vols. (Paris: Albin Michel, 1984).

de Gaulle, Charles, *Lettres, notes et carnets 1919–juin 1940* (Paris: Plon, 1980).

————, *Mémoires de guerre: L'Appel, 1940–1942* (Paris: Cercle du Bibliophile, n.d.).

Deichmann, Paul, *Der Chef im Hintergrund: Ein Leben als Soldat von der preussischen Armee bis zur Bundeswehr* (Oldenburg: Stalling, 1979).

Delater, G., *Avec la 3e D.L.M. et le Corps de Cavalerie: Belgique-Flandre-Dunkerque-Seine-Loire, le janvier–25 juillet 1940* (Grenoble: B. Arthaud, 1946).

Demey, Evelyne, *Paul Reynaud, mon père* (Paris: Plon, 1980).

Desgranges, Jean-Marie, *Journal d'un prêtre député (1936–1940)* (Paris: La Palatine, 1960).

Dietrich, Otto, *12 Jahre mit Hitler* (Munich: Isar, 1955).

Dodd, Martha, *Through Embassy Eyes* (New York: Harcourt Brace, 1939).

Dodd, William E., *Ambassador Dodd's Diary, 1933–1938*, ed. William E. Dodd, Jr., and Martha Dodd (New York: Harcourt Brace, 1941).

Dönitz, Karl, *Zehn Jahre und zwanzig Tage* (Bonn: Atheneum, 1958); trans. R. H. Stevens, *Memoirs* (Annapolis: Naval Institute Press, 1990).

Doumenc, Joseph, *Dunkerque et la campagne de Flandre* (Grenoble: B. Arthaud, 1947).

————, *Histoire de la Neuvième Armée* (Grenoble: B. Arthaud, 1945).

Doumenc Papiers: Les papiers secret du Général Doumenc: Un Autre Regard sur 39–40, ed. François Delpla (Paris: Olivier Orban, 1992).

Duff Cooper, Alfred, *Old Men Forget* (London: Rupert Hart-Davis, 1954).

Durtel, Jean, *Les Coulisses de la politique: Une Femme témoigne, 1932–1942* (Paris: Nouvelles Éditions Latines, 1966).

Eden, Anthony (Earl of Avon), *Facing the Dictators* (London: Cassell, 1962).

Engel, *Heeresadjutant:* Hildegard von Kotze, ed., *Heeresadjutant bei Hitler. 1938–1943: Aufzeichnungen des Majors Engel* (Stuttgart: Deutsche Verlags-Anstalt, 1974).

Faber du Faur, Moriz von, *Macht und Ohnmacht: Erinnerungen eines alten Offiziers* (Stuttgart: Hans E. Günther, 1953).

Fabre-Luce, Alfred, *Journal* (Paris: Imprimerie J.E.P., 1941).

Fabry, Jean, *De la Place de la Concorde au cours de l'intendance, février 1934–juin 1940* (Paris: Éditions de France, 1942).

Felsenhardt, Robert, *1939–40 avec le 18e Corps d'Armée* (Paris: Editions la Tête de Feuilles, 1973).

Flandin, Pierre-Étienne, *Politique française, 1919–1940* (Paris: Éditions Nouvelles, 1947).

Flanner, Janet [Genêt], *Paris Was Yesterday, 1925–1939* (New York: The Viking Press, 1972).

Fontaine, Peter, *Last to Leave Paris* (London: Chaterson, 1941).

Förster, Otto-Wilhelm, *Das Befestigungswesen: Rückblick und Ausschau* (Neckargemünd: Kurt Vowinckel, 1960).

Framery, Capt. Leo, "Campaign of Flanders, 1940," *Field Artillery Journal*, Sept. 1941, pp. 634–42; Oct. 1941, pp. 762–68; Nov. 1941, pp. 886–94; Dec. 1941, pp. 978–84.

François-Poncet, André, *Souvenirs d'une ambassade à Berlin, septembre 1931–octobre 1938* (Paris: Flammarion, 1946); trans. Jacques LeClercq, *The Fateful Years: Memoirs of a French Ambassador in Berlin, 1931–38* (London: Victor Gollanz, 1949).

Frank, Hans, *Im Angesicht des Galgens: Deutung Hitlers seiner Zeit auf Grund eigener Erlebnisse und Erkenntnisse* (Munich: Friedrich Alfred Beck, 1953).

Fromm, Bella, *Blood and Banquets: A Berlin Social Diary* (New York: Harper Bros., 1942).

Galland, Adolf, *Die Ersten und die Letzten* (Darmstadt: F. Schneekluth, 1953); trans. Mervyn Savill, *The First and the Last: The Rise and Fall of the German Fighter Forces* (New York: Henry Holt, 1954).

Gamelin, Maurice-Gustave, *Servir*, 3 vols. (Paris: Plon, 1946–1947).

Gauché, Maurice-Henri, *Le Deuxième Bureau au Travail (1935–1940)* (Paris: Amiot-Dumont, 1953).

———, "Role et travail du 2e Bureau," *Revue militaire suisse* (1967), 1–14.

Genébrier, Roger, *La France entre en guerre: Le Témoignage du chef de cabinet de Daladier* (Paris: Philippine, 1982).

Géraud, André [Pertinax], *Les Fossoyeurs: Défaite militaire de la France, armistice, contre-révolution*, rev. ed., 2 vols. (New York: Éditions de la Maison Française, 1944); trans., *The Gravediggers of France* (Garden City, N.Y.: Doubleday, 1944).

Geyr von Schweppenburg, Leo, Freiherr, *Erinnerungen eines Militärattachés, London 1933–1937* (Stuttgart: Deutsche Verlags-Anstalt, 1949); trans., *The Critical Years* (London: Wingate, 1952).

Giraud, Henri, *La 29e D.I. et le 141e R.I.A. au feu* (Marseilles: M. Leconte, 1941).

Giraudoux, Jean, *Armistice à Bordeaux* (Monaco: Éditions du Rocher, 1945).

Gisevius, Hans Bernd, *Bis zum bitteren Ende: Vom Reichstagsbrand bis zum 20. juli 1944* (Zürich: Fretz & Wasmuth, 1946; trans. Richard and Clara Winston, *To the Bitter End* (Boston: Houghton Mifflin, 1947).

Goddard, Victor, *Skies to Dunkirk: A Personal Memoir* (London: William Kimber, 1982).

Goebbels, *Tagebücher: Die Tagebücher von Joseph Goebbels, Sämtliche Fragmente*, ed. Elke Fröhlich, pt. 1, *Aufzeichnungen 1924–1941*, vols. 3–4 (Munich: K. G. Saur, 1987).

Göring, Hermann, *Aus Görings Schreibtisch: Ein Dokumentenfund*, ed. T. R. Emessen (Berlin: Dietz, 1990; orig. 1947).

———, *Germany Reborn* (London: Elkin Mathews and Marrot, 1934).

Grandsard, C., *Le 10e Corps d'armée dans la bataille 1939–1940: Sedan, Amiens, de la Seine è la Dordogne* (Paris: Berger-Levrault, 1949).

Groscurth, Helmuth, *Tagebücher eines Abwehroffizier: 1938–40* (Stuttgart: Deutsche Verlags-Anstalt, 1970).

Guderian, Heinz, *Achtung Panzer! Die Entwicklung der Panzerwaffe, ihre Kampftaktik und ihre operativen Möglichkeiten* (Stuttgart: Deutsche Verlags-Anstalt, 1938).

———, *Erinnerungen eines Soldatens* (Heidelberg: K. Vowinckel, 1951); trans. Constantine Fitzgibbon, *Panzer Leader* (London: Michael Joseph, 1952).

———, *Panzer-Marsch! Aus dem Nachlass des Schöpfers der deutschen Panzerwaffe*, ed. O. Munzel (Munich: Schild, 1956).

Guingand, Francis de, *Operation Victory* (London: Hodder and Stoughton, 1947).

Halder, Franz, *Hitler als Feldherr* (Munich: Münchener Dom Verlag, 1949); trans. Paul Findley, *Hitler as War Lord* (New York: G. P. Putnam, 1950).

Halder Diary: Franz Halder, *Kriegstagebuch: Tägliche Aufzeichnungen des Chefs des Generalstabes des Heeres, 1939–1942*, vol. 1, *Vom Polenfeldzug bis zum Ende der Westoffensive* (14.8.1939–30.6.1940), ed. Hans-Adolf Jacobsen (Stuttgart: W. Kohlhammer, 1962); partial trans. Arnold Lissance, *The Halder Diaries: The Private War Journals of Colonel General Franz Halder* (Nuremberg: Chief of Counsel for War Crimes, Office of Military Government for Germany, 1948).

Halifax, Earl of, *Fulness of Days* (London: Collins, 1957).

Harris, Sir Arthur, *Bomber Offensive* (London: Collins, 1947).

Harvey Diaries: Harvey, Oliver, *The Diplomatic Diaries of Oliver Harvey, 1937–1940,* ed. John Harvey (London: Collins, 1970).

Hassell Diaries: Hassell, Ulrich von, *Die Hassell Tagebücher 1938–1944: Aufzeichnungen von Andern Deutschland,* ed. Freiherr Hiller von Gaertringen and Klaus Peter Reiss (Berlin: Siedler, n.d.); trans., *The Von Hassell Diaries, 1938–44* (Garden City, N.Y.: Doubleday, 1947).

Hedin, Sven, *German Diary, 1935–1942,* trans. Joan Bulman (Dublin: Euphorion Books, 1951).

Heinkel, Ernst, *Stürmisches Leben* (Stuttgart: Mindus-Verlag, 1953).

Hencke, Andor, *Augenzeuge einer Tragödie: Diplomatenjahre in Prag 1936–1939* (Munich: Fides Verlagsgesellschaft, 1977).

Henderson, Nevile, *Failure of a Mission* (New York: G. P. Putnam, 1940).

Herriot, Édouard, *Études et témoignages* (Paris: Publications de la Sorbonne, 1975).

Heusinger, Adolf, *Befehl im Widerstreit: Schicksalstunde der deutschen Armee* (Tübingen: Rainer Wunderlich, 1950).

Hoare, Sir Samuel (Viscount Templewood), *Nine Troubled Years* (London: Collins, 1954).

Hore-Belisha Papers: The Private Papers of Hore-Belisha, ed. R. J. Minney (Garden City, N.Y.: Doubleday, 1961).

Hossbach, Friedrich, *Zwischen Wehrmacht und Hitler, 1934–1938,* 2nd rev. ed. (Göttingen: Vandenhoeck & Rupprecht, 1965).

Hoth, Hermann, "Mansteins Operationsplan für den Westfeldzug 1940 und die Aufmarschanweisung des O.K.H. vom 27.2.40," *Wehrkunde,* no. 3, 1958, pp. 127–30.

———, "Das Schicksal der französischen Panzerwaffe im i. Teil des Westfeldzuges 1940," *Wehrkunde,* no. 7, 1958, 367–77.

Ironside Diaries: Ironside, Edmund, *Time Unguarded: The Ironside Diaries, 1937–1940,* ed. R. Macleod and D. Kelly (London: Constable, 1963).

Ismay, Lord, *Memoirs* (London: Heinemann, 1960).

Jacomet, Robert, *L'Armement de la France; 1936–1939* (Paris: Éditions de la Jeunesse, 1945).

Jamet, Claude, *Carnets de Déroute* (Paris: F. Sorlot, 1962).

Jaspar, Marcel-Henri, *Souvenirs sans retouche,* 2 vols. (Paris: Fayard, 1968).

Jeanneney, Jules, *Journal politique, septembre 1939–juillet 1942,* ed. Jean-Noël Jeanneney (Paris: Armand Colin, 1972).

Jodl Diary: "Das dienstliche Tagebuch des Chefs des Wehrmachtführungsamtes im Oberkommando der Wehrmacht für die Zeit vom 13. Okt. 1939 bis zum 30. Jan. 1940," ed. Walther Hubatsch, *Die Welt als Geschichte,* 12 (1952), pp. 274–87; (1953), pp. 58–71.

Jodl, Luise, *Jenseits des Endes: Leben und Sterben des Generaloberst Alfred Jodl* (Vienna: Fritz Molden, 1976).

John, Otto, *Twice Through the Lines: The Autobiography of Otto John* (London: Macmillan, 1972).

Jones, Thomas, *A Diary with Letters, 1931–1940* (Oxford: Oxford University Press, 1954).

Joubert de la Ferté, Air Marshal Sir Philip, *The Fated Sky* (London: Hutchinson, 1952).

Jouhaud, Gen. Edmond, *La Vie est un combat* (Paris: Fayard, 1974).

Jünger, Ernst, *Gärten und Strassen: Aus dem Tagebüchern von 1939 und 1940* (Berlin: E. S. Mittler, 1942).

Kampferlebnisse aus dem Kriege an der Westfront 1940: Nach Schilderungen von Front-käpfern, ed. Kriegswissenschaftliche Abteilung, Generalstab des Heeres (Berlin: E. S. Mittler, 1941).

Keitel: Walter Görlitz, ed., *Generalfeldmarschall Keitel, Verbrecher oder Offizier?: Erinnerungen, Briefe, Dokumente des Chefs OKW* (Göttingen: Musterschmidt, 1961); trans. Wilhelm Keitel, *Memoirs* (New York: Stein and Day, 1966).

Kennedy, *Business of War: The Business of War: The War Narrative of Major General Sir John Kennedy,* ed. Sir Bernard Fergusson (London: Hutchinson, 1957).

Kérillis, Henri de, *Français, voici la vérité!* (New York: Éditions de la Maison Française, 1942).

Kesselring, Albert, *Soldat bis zum letzten Tag* (Bonn: Athenäum, 1953); trans. Lynton Hudson, *The Memoirs of Field Marshal Kesselring* (London: William Kimber, 1953).

Keyes, Roger, *Outrageous Fortune: The Tragedy of Leopold III of the Belgians, 1901–1941* (London: Secker and Warburg, 1984).

Keyes Papers, The, ed. Paul Halpern, vol. 3 (London: Allen and Unwin, 1981).

Kielmansegg, Johann Adolf, Graf, *Panzer zwischen Warschau und Atlantik* (Berlin: Verlag "Die Wehrmacht," 1941).

Kordt, Erich, *Nicht aus den Akten: Wilhelmstrasse in Frieden und Krieg* (Stuttgart: Union Deutsche Verlagsgesellschaft, 1950).

————, *Wahn und Wirklichkeit,* 2nd ed. (Stuttgart: Union Deutsche Verlagsgesellschaft, 1948).

Kosak, Georges, *Belgique et France 1940, avec la compagnie de génie des 4e D.L.C. et de 7e D.L.M.* (Grenoble: B. Arthaud, 1946).

Kuhnert, Max, *Will We See Tomorrow? A German Cavalryman at War, 1939–1942* (London: Leo Cooper, 1993).

Laffargue, André, *Fantassin de Gascogne: De mon jardin à la Marne et au Danube* (Paris: Flammarion, 1962).

Lahousen Diary: Charles Weighton and Gunther Peis, eds., *Hitler's Spies and Saboteurs: Based on the German Secret Service War Diary of General Lahousen* (New York: Henry Holt, 1958).

Lazareff, Pierre, *Dernier Édition* (New York: Brentano's, 1942); trans. David Partridge, *Deadline: The Behind-the-Scenes Story of the Last Decade in France* (New York: Random House, 1942).

Lebrun, Albert, *Témoignage* (Paris: Plon, 1945).

Leeb, Wilhelm Ritter von, *Tagebuchaufzeichnungen und Lagebeurteilungen aus zwei Weltkriegen,* ed. Georg Meyer (Stuttgart: Deutsche Verlags-Anstalt, 1976).

Lémery, Henry, *D'une république à l'autre: Souvenirs de la mêlée politique, 1894–1944* (Paris: Table Ronde, 1964).

Lerecouvreux, Marcel, *L'Armée Giraud en Hollande* (Paris: Nouvelles Éditions Latines, 1951).

————, Huit Mois d'attente, un mois de guerre (Paris: Charles-Lavauzelle, 1946).

Liddell Hart, Basil H., *The German Generals Talk* (New York: William Morrow, 1948).

————, *Memoirs,* vol. 2 (London: Cassell, 1965).

———— et al., eds., *The Rommel Papers* (New York: Harcourt Brace, 1953).

Liebling, A. J., *The Road Back to Paris* (New York: Paragon House, 1989).

Linge, Heinz, *Bis zum Untergang: Als Chef des persönlichen Dienstes bei Hitler* (Berlin: Herbig, 1980).

Lipski, *Memoirs: Diplomat in Berlin, 1933–1939: Papers and Memoirs of Józef Lipski, Ambassador of Poland*, ed. Waclaw Jedrzejewicz (New York: Columbia University Press, 1968).

Liss, Ulrich, "Die deutsche Westoffensive 1940 vom Blickpunkt des Ic.," *Wehrwissenschaftliche Rundschau*, 1958, pp. 208–19.

——, "Dünkirchen, gesehen mit den Augen des Ic.," *Wehrwissenschaftliche Rundschau*, 1958, pp. 325–40.

——, "Der entscheidende Wert richtiger Feindbeurteilung," *Wehrkunde*, 1959, pp. 584–92, 638–44.

——, "Erfahrungen im Feindnachrichtendienst aus drei Armeen," *Wehrkunde*, 1961, pp. 576–79.

——, "Erfahrungen und Gedanken zum Ic-Wesen," *Wehrwissenschaftliche Rundschau*, 1957, pp. 616–27.

——, "Die Tätigkeit des französischen 2. Bureau im Westfeldzug 1939/40," *Wehrwissenschaftliche Rundschau*, 1960, pp. 267–78.

——, *Westfront 1939/40: Erinnerungen des Feindarbeiters im O.K.H.* (Neckargemünd: Kurt Vowinckel, 1959).

Lossberg, Bernhard, *Im Wehrmachtführungsstab* (Hamburg: Nölke, 1949).

Loustaunau-Lacau, *Mémoires d'un Français rebelle* (Paris: Robert Laffont, 1948).

Lüdecke, Kurt G. W., *I Knew Hitler* (New York: Scribner, 1938).

Lukasiewicz, *Memoirs: Diplomat in Paris, 1936–1939: Memoirs of Juliusz Lukasiewicz, Ambassador of Poland*, ed. Waclaw Jedrzejewicz (New York: Columbia University Press, 1970).

Lyet, Pierre, "La Bataille de Belgique et du nord (la campagne 1939–1940)," *RHA*, no. 2, 1946, pp. 41–75; no. 3, 59–91.

——, *La Bataille de France (mai–juin 1940)* (Paris: Payot, 1947).

——, "Mitrailleurs malgache à Monthermé mai 1940," *RHA*, no. 4, 1963, pp. 130–32.

——, "À propos de Sedan 1940," *RHA*, no. 4, 1962, pp. 89–130.

Maassen, Heinz, *Über die Maas: Die Erzwingung des Übergangs bei Monthermé* (Düsseldorf: Völkischer Verlag, 1941).

Mader, Julius, *Hitlers Spionagegenerale sagen aus* (Berlin: Verlag der Nation, 1970).

——, *Nicht länger Geheim* (Berlin: Deutsche Militärverlag, 1969).

Manstein, Erich von, *Aus einem Soldatenleben, 1887–1939* (Bonn: Athenäum, 1958).

——, *Verlorene Siege* (Bonn: Athenäum, 1955); trans. Anthony G. Powell, *Lost Victories* (London: Methuen, 1958).

Manstein, Rüdiger von, and Theodor Ruchs, *Manstein, Soldat im 20. Jahrhundert: Militärisch-politische Nachlasse* (Munich: Bernard & Graefe, 1981).

Manteuffel, Hasso von., ed., *Die 7. Panzer-Division im Zweiten Weltkrieg: Einsatz und Kampf der "Gespenster-Division" 1939–1945* (Friedberg: Podzun-Pallas, 1986).

Maurin, Gen. Jean Louis, *L'armée moderne* (Paris: Flammarion, 1938).

Meier-Welcker, Hans, *Aufzeichnungen eines Generalstabsoffiziers 1939–1942* (Freiburg: Rombach, 1982).

——, "Der Entschluss zum Anhalten der deutschen Panzertruppen in Flandern 1940," *VfZ*, no. 2, 1954, pp. 274–90.

————, "Erlebnisse beim Oberkommando der 4. Armee während der Kämpfe zwischen Maas und Sambre am 15. und 16. Mai," *Militärwissenschaftliche Rundschau,* no. 2, 1941, pp. 132–39.

Meissner, Otto, *Staatsekretär unter Ebert-Hindenburg-Hitler: Der Schicksalsweg des deutschen Volkes von 1918–1945, wie ich ihn erlebte* (Hamburg: Hoffmann & Campe, 1950).

Mellenthin, Friedrich Wilhelm von, *Schach dem Schicksal: Ein deutscher Generalstabsoffizier berichtet von seiner Herkunft, seinem Einsatz im Zweiten Weltkrieg und seinem breuflichen Neubeginn nach dem Kriege* (Osnabrück: Biblio, 1988).

Michiels, Lt. Gen. Oscar, *Dix-Huit Jours de guerre en Belgique* (Paris: Berger-Levrault, 1947).

Minart, Jacques, *Le Drame du désarmement français (ses aspects politiques et techniques), 1918–1939* (Paris: Le Nef de Paris, 1959).

————, *P.C. Vincennes: Secteur 4,* 2 vols. (Paris: Berger-Levrault, 1945).

Montgomery, Field Marshal Viscount, *Memoirs* (London: Collins, 1958).

Montigny, Jean, *Le Complot contre la paix (1935–1939)* (Paris: Table Ronde, 1966).

————, *Heures tragiques de 1940: La Défaite* (Paris: Grasset, 1941).

Monzie, Anatole de, *Ci-devant* (Paris: Flammarion, 1941).

Moravec, Frantisek, *Master of Spies: The Memoirs of General Frantisek Moravec* (London: The Bodley Head, 1975).

Mousset, P., *Quand le temps travaillait pour nous: Récits* (Paris: B. Grasset, 1946).

Navarre, Henri, et al., *Le Service de Renseignements, 1871–1944* (Paris: Plon, 1978).

————, *Temps de vérités* (Paris: Plon, 1979).

Neame, Sir Philip, *Playing with Strife* (London: Harrap, 1947).

Nicolson, Harold, *Diaries and Letters,* ed. Nigel Nicolson, 3 vols. (London: Collins, 1966–68).

Nizan, Paul, *Chronique de septembre* (Paris: Gallimard, 1978).

Noël, Léon, *Une Ambassade à Varsovie, 1935–1939: L Aggression allemande contre la Pologne* (Paris: Flammarion, 1946).

————, *Un Témoignage: Le Diktat de Rethondes et l'armistice franco-italien de juin 1940* (Paris: Flammarion, 1945).

Nordmann, Léon-Maurice, *Journal, 1938–1941* (Paris: J. Cahen Salvador, 1993).

Paillole, Paul, *L'Homme des services secrets: Entretiens avec Alain-Gilles Minella* (Paris: Julliard, 1995).

————, *Notre Espion chez Hitler* (Paris: Robert Laffont, 1985).

————, "Le Recueil des renseignements sur l'adversaire allemand pendant la 'drôle de guerre,' 1er septembre 1939–juin 1940," in *La France et l'Allemagne en guerre,* pp. 69–87.

————, *Services spéciaux 1935–1945* (Paris: Robert Laffont, 1975).

"Panzers Across the Meuse," *The Field Artillery Journal,* April 1941, pp. 195–203.

Paul-Boncour, Joseph, *Entre deux guerres* (Paris: Plon, 1945).

Pernot, Georges, *Journal de guerre, 1940–1941,* vol. 124 of *Annales Littéraires de l'Université de Besançon* (Paris: Les Belles Lettres, 1971).

Pertinax (see Géraud).

Pétain, Philippe, *Actes et Écrits,* ed. Jacques Isorni (Paris: Flammarion, 1974).

Pomaret, Charles, *Le Dernier Témoin: Fin d'une guerre, fin d'une république, juin et juillet 1940* (Paris: Presses de la Cité, 1968).

5 6 5 5 5 6 5 6 5 5 5 5 5 5 65 6 6 5 5 5 5 5 5 5 5 5 5 5 5 5 5 5 5 5 5 5 5 5 5 6 6 6 6 6 6 6 6 6 6 6 6 6 6 6 6 6 6 6 6 6

Pownall Diaries: Chief of Staff: The Diaries of Lieutenant-General Sir Henry Pownall, ed. Brian Bond (London: Leo Cooper, 1972).

Poydenot, Olivier, "Vu du PC de Vincennes: Quelques Aspects de la campagne 1939–1940," *Revue des Deux Mondes,* Jan. 15, 1968, pp. 166–85.

Prételat, General André Gaston, *Le Destin tragique de la ligne Maginot* (Paris: Berger-Levrault, 1950).

Price, G. Ward, *I Know These Dictators* (New York: Henry Holt, 1938).

Prioux, René Jacques, *Souvenirs de guerre, 1939–1943* (Paris: Flammarion, 1947).

Raeder, Erich, *Mein Leben,* 2 vols. (Tübingen: F. Schlichtenmayer, 1956–57); trans. Henry W. Drexel, *My Life* (Annapolis, Md.: United States Naval Institute, 1960).

Raphaël-Leygues, Jacques, *Chronique des années incertaines, 1935–1945* (Paris: France-Empire, 1977).

Rauschning, Hermann, *The Voice of Destruction* (New York: G. P. Putnam, 1940).

Rebatet, Lucien, *Les Mémoires d'un fasciste,* vol. 1, *Les Décombres, 1938–1940* (Paris: Fauvert, 1976).

Reile, Oscar, *Der deutsche Geheimdienst im II. Weltkrieg,* 2 vols. (Augsburg: Weltbild, 1990).

———, *Geheime Westfront: Die Abwehr, 1935–1945* (Munich: Welsermühl, 1962).

Reinhardt, Hans, "Im Schatten Guderians: das XXXXI Pz.-Korps und seine Nöte bei dem Vorgehen gegen und über die Maas vom 10. bis 16. Mai 1940," *Wehrkunde,* no. 10, 1954, pp. 333–41.

Renaudin, Edmée, *Sans fleur au fusil* (Paris: Stock, 1979).

Requin, Édouard, *Combats pour l'honneur (1939–1940)* (Paris: Charles-Lavauzelle, 1946).

———, *D'une guerre à l'autre, 1919–1939* (Paris: Charles-Lavauzelle, 1949).

Revol, Joseph-Fortuné, *Chroniques de guerre (1939–1945)* (Paris: Charles-Lavauzelle, 1945).

Reynaud, Paul, *Au Coeur de la mêlée* (Paris: Flammarion, 1951); trans. James D. Lambert, *In the Midst of the Fight* (New York: Simon & Schuster, 1955).

———, *La France a sauvé l'Europe,* 2 vols. (Paris: Flammarion, 1947).

Ribbentrop, Joachim, *Zwischen London und Moskau: Erinnerungen und letzte Aufzeichnungen* (Leoni am Starnbergersee: Drüffel, 1953); trans. Oliver Watson, *Memoirs* (London: Weidenfeld and Nicolson, 1954).

Rieckhoff, H. J., *Trump oder Bluff: 12 Jahre deutsche Luftwaffe* (Geneva: Interavia, 1945).

Rintelen, Enno von, *Mussolini als Bundesgenosse: Erinnerungen des deutschen Militärattachés in Rom, 1936–1943* (Tübingen: Rainer Wunderlich, 1951).

Rist, Charles, *Une Saison gatée: Journal de la guerre et de l'occupation (1939–1945)* (Paris: Fayard, 1983).

Ritter, Nikolaus, *Decknahme Dr. Rantzau: Die Aufzeichungen des Nikolaus Ritter, Offizier im Geheimen Nachrichtdienst* (Hamburg: Hoffman und Campe, 1972).

Rivet, Louis, "Abwehr et Gestapo en France pendant la guerre," *RHDGM,* no. 1, 1950, pp. 28–50.

Röhricht, Edgar, *Pflicht und Gewesen: Erinnerungen eines deutschen Generals, 1932–1944* (Stuttgart: W. Kohlhammer, 1956).

Romains, Jules, *Sept Mystères du destin de l'Europe* (New York: Éditions de la Maison Française, 1940); trans. Germaine Brée, *Seven Mysteries of Europe* (New York: Alfred A. Knopf, 1940).

Rommel, Erwin, *Infanterie greift an: Erlebnis und Erfahrung* (Potsdam: L. Voggenreiter, 1944); trans., *Infantry Attacks* (Vienna, Va.: Athena Press, 1979).
————, *Krieg ohne Hass*, ed. Lucie-Marie Rommel and Lt. Gen. Fritz Bayerlein (Heidenheim: Heidenheimer Zeitung, 1950).
Rommel Papers: Rommel, Erwin, *The Rommel Papers*, ed. Basil H. Liddell Hart (New York: Harcourt Brace, 1953).
Rosenberg Tagebuch: Hans-Günther Seraphim, ed., *Das politische Tagebuch Alfred Rosenbergs 1934/35 und 1939/40* (Berlin: Musterschmidt, 1955).
Roton, Gen. G., *Années cruciales: La Course aux armements (1933–1939), la campagne (1939–1940)* (Paris: Charles-Lavauzelle, 1947).
Ruby, Edmond, *Sedan: Terre d'Épreuve: Avec la IIème Armée, Mai–Juin 1940* (Paris: Flammarion, 1948).
Rueff, Jacques, *De l'aube au crépuscule: Autobiographie* (Paris: Plon, 1977).
Sadoul, Georges, *Journal de guerre, 1939–40* (Paris: Les Éditeurs Français Réunis, 1977).
Sarraz-Bourret, Marius, *Témoignage d'un silencieux: G.Q.G., 2e Bureau, Turin, Vichy* (Paris: Self, 1948).
Sartre, Jean-Paul, *Les Carnets de la drôle de guerre (novembre 1939–mars 1940)* (Paris: Gallimard, 1983); trans. Quintin Hoare, *War Diaries: Notebooks from a Phoney War, November 1939–March 1940* (London: Verso, 1984).
Sauvy, Alfred, *De Paul Reynaud à Charles de Gaulle: Scènes, tableaux et souvenirs* (n.p.: Casterman, 1972).
Schall-Riaucour, Heidemarie Gräfin, *Aufstand und Gehorsam: Offizierstum und Generalstab im Umbruch—Leben und Wirken von Generaloberst Franz Halder, Generalstabschef 1938–1942* (Wiesbaden: Limes, 1972).
Schellenberg, Walther, *The Labyrinth: Memoirs* (New York: Harper, 1956).
Schmidt, Paul, *Statist auf diplomatischer Bühne, 1923–1945: Erlebnisse des Chefdolmetschers im Auswärtigen Amt mit den Staatsmännern Europas* (Bonn: Athenäum, 1954); abridged, trans., and ed. R. H. C. Steed: *Hitler's Interpreter* (New York: Macmillan, 1951).
Schroeder, Christa, *Er war mein Chef: Aus dem Nachlass der Sekretärin von Adolf Hitler*, ed. Anton Joachimsthaler (Munich: Langen-Müller, 1985).
Schwerin von Krosigk, Count Lutz, *Es geschah in Deutschland: Menschenbilder unseres Jahrhunderts* (Tübingen: Rainer Wunderlich, 1951).
Seive, Gen. Fleury, *L'Aviation d'assaut dans la bataille de 1940* (Paris: Berger-Levrault, 1948).
Seydoux, François, *Mémoires d'outre-Rhin* (Paris: Grasset, 1975).
Shirer, William L., *Berlin Diary: The Journal of a Foreign Correspondent, 1934–1941* (New York: Alfred A. Knopf, 1941).
————, *End of a Berlin Diary* (New York: Alfred A. Knopf, 1947).
Simon, Viscount, *Retrospect: The Memoirs of The Rt. Hon. Viscount Simon* (London: Hutchinson, 1952).
Simone, André, *J'accuse: The Men Who Betrayed France* (New York: Dial, 1940).
Simoni, Leonardo, *Berlino, ambasciata d'Italia, 1939–1943* (Rome: Migliaresi, 1946).
Slessor, Sir John, *The Central Blue* (London: Cassell, 1956).
Smith, Truman, *Berlin Alert: The Memoirs and Reports of Truman Smith*, ed. Robert Hessen (Stanford, Calif.: Hoover Institution Press, 1984).

Sodenstern, Georg von, "Vom Wesen des Soldatentums," *Militärwissenschaftliche Rundschau*, 1939, pp. 42–60.

Soltikow, Michael Graf von, *Ich war mittendrin: Meine Jahre bei Canaris* (Vienna: Paul Neff, 1980).

Sonnleithner, Franz von, *Als Diplomat im Führerhauptquartier: Aus dem Nachlass* (Munich: Langen Müller, 1989).

Spaak, Paul-Henri, *Combats inachevés* (Paris: Fayard, 1969); trans. Henry Fox, *The Continuing Battle: Memoirs of a European 1936–1966* (Boston: Little, Brown, 1971).

Spears, Edward L., *Assignment to Catastrophe*, 2 vols. (London: Heinemann, 1954).

Speer, Albert, *Inside the Third Reich: Memoirs* (New York: Macmillan, 1970).

Staff Officer of a Division, "A Diary of Events in France and Belgium," *Army Quarterly*, April 1941, pp. 112–21.

Stehlin, Paul, *Témoignage Pour l'histoire* (Paris: Robert Laffont, 1964).

Steinhoff, Johannes, Peter Pechel, and Dennis Showalter, *Voices from the Third Reich* (Washington, D.C.: Regnery Gateway, 1989).

Strik-Strikfeldt, Wilfried, *Against Stalin and Hitler: Memoir of the Russian Liberation Movement, 1941–1945* (London: Macmillan, 1970).

Strang, Lord, *Home and Abroad* (London: André Deutsch, 1956).

Strong, Gen. Sir Kenneth, *Intelligence at the Top: Recollections of an Intelligence Officer* (London: Cassell, 1968).

Sweet-Excott, B., *Baker Street Irregular* (London: Methuen, 1965).

Swinton, Philip Cunliffe-Lister, Earl of, *Sixty Years of Power* (London: Hutchinson, 1966).

Tabouis, Geneviève, *They Call Me Cassandra* (New York: Scribner, 1942).

———, *Vingt Ans de "suspense" diplomatique* (Paris: Albin Michel, 1958).

Teske, Hermann, *Bewegungskrieg: Führungsprobleme einer Infanterie-Division im Westfeldzug 1940* (Heidelberg: Kurt Vowinckel, 1955).

———, *Die silbernen Spiegel: Generalstabsdienst unter der Lupe* (Heidelberg: Kurt Vowinckel, 1952).

Van Overstraeten, Raoul François Casimir, *Albert I–Léopold III: Vingt Ans de politique militaire belge, 1920–1940* (Bruges: Desclée de Brouwer, 1946).

———, *Au service de la Belgique*, vol. 1, *Dans l'Étau* (Paris: Plon, 1960).

Vassiltchikov, Marie, *Berlin Diaries, 1940–1945* (New York: Alfred A. Knopf, 1987).

Vauhnik, Vladimir, *Memoiren eines Militärattachés: Mein Kampf mit dem Fingerspitzengefühl Hitlers* (Klagenfurt: Hermagorasbruderschaft, 1967).

Villelume, Paul de, *Journal d'une Défaite: Août 1939–Juin 1940* (Paris: Fayard, 1976).

Wagner, Elisabeth, ed., *Der Generalquartiermeister: Briefe und Tagebuchaufzeichnungen des Generalquartiermeisters des Heeres General der Artillerie Eduard Wagner* (Munich: Günter Olzog, 1963).

Wanty, Gen. Émile, "La Défense des Ardennes en 1940," *RHDGM*, April 1961, pp. 1–16.

———, "Improvisation de la liaison belgo-britannique du 10 mai au 18 mai 1904," *RHDGM*, Jan. 1964, pp. 29–50.

Warlimont, Walter, *Im Hauptquartier der deutschen Wehrmacht* (Frankfurt am Main: Bernard & Graefe, 1962); trans. R. H. Barry, *Inside Hitler's Headquarters, 1939–1945* (London: Weidenfeld and Nicolson, 1964).

Weizsäcker, Ernst von, *Erinnerungen* (Munich: P. List, 1950); trans. John Andrews, *Memoirs* (London: Victor Gollancz, 1951).
Weizsäcker Papiere: Leonidas E. Hill, ed., *Die Weizsäcker-Papiere, 1933–1950* (n.p.: Propyläen n.d.).
Westphal, Siegfried, *Erinnerungen* (Mainz: von Hase & Kohler, 1975).
———, *Heer im Fesseln* (Bonn: Athenäum, 1950); trans. *The German Army in the West* (London: Cassell, 1951).
Weygand, Édouard, *Un non lieu en Haute Cour* (Paris: René Hergué, 1974).
Weygand, Jacques, *Weygand, mon père* (Paris: Flammarion, 1947); trans. J. H. F. McEwen, *The Role of General Weygand: Conversations with His Son* (London: Eyre & Spottiswoode, 1948).
Weygand, Maxime, *En lisant les mémoires du Général de Gaulle* (Paris: Flammarion, 1955).
———, *Mémoires*, 3 vols. (Paris: Flammarion, 1950); trans. E. W. Dickes, *Memoirs: Recalled to Serve* (London: Heinemann, 1952).
Wiedeman, Fritz, *Der Mann der Feldherr werden wollte: Erlebnisse und Erfahrungen des vorgesetzten Hitlers im 1. Weltkrieg und seines späteren persönlichen Adjutanten* (Dortmund: Blickbild, 1964).
Winterbotham, F. W., *The Nazi Connection* (New York: Harper and Row, 1978).
———, *The Ultra Secret* (New York: Harper and Row, 1974).
———, *The Ultra Spy* (New York: Harper and Row, 1989).
Zay, Jean, *Carnets secrets*, ed. Philippe Henriot (Paris: Éditions de France, 1942).
———, *Souvenirs et solitudes* (Paris: Julliard, 1946).
Zeitzler, Kurt, "Die Panzer-Gruppe v. Kleist im West-Feldzug 1940," *Wehrkunde*, no. 4, 1959, pp. 182–88; no. 5, pp. 239–45; no. 6, pp. 293–98; no. 7, pp. 366–72.
Zimmermann, Hermann, *Der Griff ins Ungewisse: Die ersten Kriegstage 1940 beim XVI Panzerkorps um die Dylestellung, 10–17 Mai* (Neckargemünd: Kurt Vowinckel, 1964).
Zoller, Albert, *Hitler privat: Erlebnisbericht seiner Geheimsekretärin* (Düsseldorf: Droste, 1949).

OTHER WORKS CONSULTED
Abransky C., ed., *Essays in Honour of E. H. Carr* (Hamden, Conn.: Archon Books, 1974).
Absolon, Rudolf, *Die Wehrmacht im Dritten Reich*, vol. 4, *5 Feb 1938 bis 31 Aug 1939* (Boppard am Rhein: Boldt, 1979).
Adams, Jack, *The Doomed Expedition: The Norwegian Campaign 1940* (London: Leo Cooper, 1989).
Adamthwaite, Anthony, "The British Government and the Media, 1937–1938," *JCH*, no. 2, 1983, pp. 281–97.
———, *France and the Coming of the Second World War, 1936–1939* (London: Frank Cass, 1977).
———, "France and the Coming of War," in Mommsen and Kettenacker, eds., *Fascist Challenge*, pp. 146–257.
———, "French Military Intelligence and the Coming of War, 1935–1939," in Andrew and Noakes, eds., *Intelligence and International Relations*, pp. 191–208.

Addington, Larry, *The Blitzkrieg Era and the German General Staff, 1865–1941* (New Brunswick, N.J.: Rutgers University Press, 1971).

Addison, Paul, *The Road to 1945: British Politics and the Second World War* (London: Jonathan Cape, 1975).

Albert, Pierre, "La Presse française de 1871 à 1940," part 3 of vol. 3 of Bellanger, Godechot, Guiral, and Terrou, eds., *Histoire générale de la presse.*

Alexander, Donald, "Repercussions of the Breda Variant," *FHS*, Spring 1974, pp. 459–88.

Alexander, Martin S., "Did the Deuxième Bureau Work? The Role of Intelligence in French Defence Policy and Strategy, 1919–1939," *INS*, no. 2, 1991, pp. 292–333.

——, "The Fall of France, 1940," *JSS*, no. 1, 1990, pp. 10–44.

——, "In Lieu of Alliance: The French General Staff's Secret Cooperation with Neutral Belgium, 1936–1940," *JSS*, no. 4, 1991, pp. 413–27.

——, "Maurice Gamelin and the Defeat of France," in Bond, ed., *Fallen Stars*, pp. 107–40.

——, "Maurice Gamelin and the Defence of France," Ph.D. thesis, Oxford University, 1982.

——, "Prophet Without Honour? The French High Command and Pierre Taittinger's Report on the Ardennes Defences, March 1940," *War and Society*, no. 1, 1986, pp. 52–77.

——, *The Republic in Danger: General Maurice Gamelin and the Politics of French Defence, 1933–1940* (Cambridge: Cambridge University Press, 1992).

Allard, Paul, *Les Journées pathétiques de la guerre* (Paris: Éditions de France, 1941).

——, *Quai d'Orsay* (Paris: Éditions de France, 1938).

——, *Les Responsables du désastre* (Paris: Éditions de France, 1941).

Allison, Graham T., and Philip. D. Zelikow, *Essence of Decision: Explaining the Cuban Missile Crisis*, 2nd ed. (New York: Longman, 1999).

Amouroux, Henri, *La Grande Histoire des Français sous l'Occupation*, 10 vols. (Paris: Robert Laffont, 1976–93).

Andrew, Christopher, *Her Majesty's Secret Service: The Making of the British Intelligence Community* (New York: The Viking Press, 1986).

——, and David Dilks, eds., *The Missing Dimension: Governments and Intelligence Communities in the Twentieth Century* (London: Macmillan, 1984).

——, and Oleg Gordievsky, *KGB: The Inside Story of Its Foreign Operations from Lenin to Gorbachev* (New York: HarperCollins, 1990).

——, and Jeremy Noakes, eds., *Intelligence and International Relations, 1900–1945* (Exeter: University of Exeter Press, 1987).

Angot, Eugène, and René de Lavergne, *Le Général Vuillemin* (Paris: Palatine, 1965).

(Les) Armées françaises pendant la Seconde Guerre Mondiale, Actes du Colloque International de Mai 1985 (Paris: Atelier, 1986).

Arnal, P., "À propos de la campagne de Norvège: Fritz Thyssen et la route de fer," *Revue d'histoire diplomatique*, April–June 1962, pp. 147–57.

Arnberger, Heinz, *"Anschluss" 1938: Eine Dokumentation* (Vienna: Österreichischer Bundesverlag, 1988).

Aron, Robert, *Léopold III ou le choix impossible* (Paris: Plon, 1977).

Aspinall-Oglander, C., *Roger Keyes* (London: Hogarth Press, 1951).

Assmann, Kurt, *Deutsche Schicksaljahre* (Wiesbaden: Brockhaus, 1950).

Aster, Sidney, " 'Guilty Men': The Case of Neville Chamberlain," in Boyce and Robertson, eds., *Paths to War*, pp. 233–68.

——, *1939: The Making of the Second World War* (London: André Deutsch, 1973).

Ausems, André, "The Netherlands Military Intelligence Summaries 1939–40 and the Defeat in the Blitzkrieg of May 1940," *Military Affairs*, Oct. 1986, pp. 190–99.

Azéma, Jean-Pierre, *1940, l'année terrible* (Paris: Éditions du Seuil, 1990).

Bankwitz, Philip Charles Farwell, *Maxime Weygand and Civil-Military Relations in Modern France* (Cambridge, Mass.: Harvard University Press, 1967).

Barker, Arthur James, *Dunkirk: The Great Escape* (London: Dent, 1977).

Barker, Elisabeth, *British Policy in South-East Europe in the Second World War* (London: Macmillan, 1976).

Barnett, Corelli, *The Collapse of British Power* (London: Eyre Methuen, 1972).

——, *Engage the Enemy More Closely: The Royal Navy in the Second World War* (London: Hodder and Stoughton, 1991).

——, ed., *Hitler's Generals* (London: Weidenfeld and Nicolson, 1989).

——, ed., *Old Battles and New Defences* (London: Brassey's, 1986).

Bartel, Heinrich, *Frankreich und die Sowjetunion 1938–1940* (Stuttgart: Steiner, 1986).

Bartov, Omer, *Hitler's Army: Soldiers, Nazis, and War in the Third Reich* (New York: Oxford University Press, 1991).

Bartz, K., *The Downfall of the German Secret Service* (London: William Kimber, 1956).

Baudouï, Remi, *Raoul Dautry, 1880–1951: La Technocrate de la république* (Paris: Éditions Balland, 1992).

Bauer, Eddy, *La Guerre des blindés*, 2 vols. (Lausanne: Payot, 1962).

Baumbach, Werner, *Zu spät: Aufstieg und Untergang der deutschen Luftwaffe* (Munich: R. Pflaum, 1950).

Baumont, Maurice, "The Rhineland Crisis: 7 March 1936," in Waites, ed., *Troubled Neighbors*, pp. 158–69.

Bédarida, François, "France, Britain and the Nordic Countries," *Scandinavian Journal of History*, no. 2, 1977, pp. 7–27.

——, "La 'Gouvernante anglaise,' " in Rémond, ed., *Daladier*, pp. 228–42.

Beesly, Patrick, *Very Special Admiral: The Life of Admiral J. H. Godfrey* (London: Hamish Hamilton, 1980).

——, *Very Special Intelligence: The Story of the Admiralty's Operational Intelligence Centre, 1939–1945* (London: Hamish Hamilton, 1977).

Bell, P. M. H., *A Certain Eventuality* (n.p.: Saxon House, 1974).

Bellanger, Claude, Jacques Godechot, Pierre Guiral, and Fernand Terrou, eds., *Histoire générale de la presse française*, 5 vols. (Paris: Presses Universitaires, 1972).

Bellstedt, Hans F., *"Apaisement" oder Krieg: Frankreichs Aussenminister Georges Bonnet und die deutsch-französische Erklärung von 6. Dezember 1938*, vol. 37, in Deutschen Historischen Institut Paris, *Pariser Historische Studien* (Bonn: Bouvier, 1993).

Bénoist-Mechin, Jean Jacques, *Soixante Jours qui ébranlèrent l'Occident, 10 mai–10 juillet 1940*, 3 vols. (Paris: A. Michel, 1956–62); trans. and abridged by Peter Wiles, *Sixty Days That Shook the West* (New York: G. P. Putnam, 1963).

Benteli, Marianne, Daniel Jay, and Jean-Pierre Jeancolas, "Le Cinéma français: Thèmes et public," in Rémond, ed., *La France et les Français*, pp. 27–42.

Benz, Wolfgang, et al., eds., *Miscellanea: Festschrift für Helmut Krausnick zum 75. Geburtstag* (Stuttgart: Deutsche Verlags-Anstalt, 1980).

Ben-Zwi, Abraham, "Hindsight and Foresight: A Conceptual Framework for the Analysis of Surprise Attacks," *World Politics*, no. 3, 1976, pp. 381–98.

———, "Intention, Capability and Surprise: A Comparative Analysis," *JSS*, no. 4, 1990, pp. 19–40.

Berben, Paul, and Bernard Iselin, *Les Panzers passent la Meuse, 13 mai 1940* (Paris: Robert Laffont, 1967).

Bernhardt, Walter, *Die deutsche Aufrüstung 1934–1939: Militärische und politische Konzeptionen und ihre Einschätzung durch die Alliierten* (Frankfurt am Main: Bernard & Graefe, 1969).

Berstein, Serge, *Édouard Herriot, ou, La République en personne* (Paris: Presses de la Fondation Nationale des Sciences Politiques, 1985).

———, *Histoire du parti radical*, 2 vols. (Paris: Presses de la Fondation Nationale des Sciences Politiques, 1980–82).

———, *Le 6 février 1934* (Paris: Gallimard, 1975).

Berteil, Louis, *L'Armée de Weygand* (Paris: Albatros, 1975).

Best, S. Payne, *The Venlo Incident* (London: Hutchinson, n.d.).

Bethell, Nicholas, *The War Hitler Won: September 1939* (London: Allen Lane, 1972).

Betts, Richard, "Analysis, War, and Decision: Why Intelligence Failures Are Inevitable," *World Politics*, Oct. 1978, pp. 61–89.

———, *Surprise Attack: Lessons for Defense Planning* (Washington, D.C.: Brookings Institution, 1982).

———, "Surprise Despite Warning: Why Sudden Attacks Succeed," *Political Science Quarterly*, Winter 1980, pp. 551–72.

Bézy, Jean, *Le SR Air* (Paris: France-Empire, 1979).

Bialer, Uri, "Elite Opinion and Defence Policy: Air Power Advocacy and British Rearmament during the 1930s," *British Journal of International Studies*, 1980, pp. 32–51.

———, *The Shadow of the Bomber: The Fear of Air Attack and British Politics 1932–1939* (London: Royal Historical Society, 1980).

Bidlingmaier, G., "Die Grundlagen für die Zusammenarbeit Luftwaffe/Kriegsmarine und ihre Erprobung in den ersten Kriegsmonaten," in Arbeitskreis für Wehrforschung, *Beiträge zur Wehrforschung*, 1964, pp. 73–112.

———, "10 mai 1940—'Hedderich' et 'Niwi': Les Deux Opérations allemandes aéroportées sur petits avions Fieseler 'Storch,'" *RBHM*, 1973–74, pp. 411–34, 591–622, 699–723; 1975–76, pp. 48–78, 123–56.

Bikar, A., "La Campagne de mai 1940 en Belgique: La 4e Division Légère de Cavalerie française à l'est de la Meuse, les 10, 11 et 12 mai 1940," *RBHM*, 1983–84, pp. 519–50, 627–51.

———, "La 3e Brigade de Spahis dans nos Ardennes, les 10, 11 et 12 mai," *RBHM*, 1985–86, pp. 387–402.

———, "Les Événements dans le sud de la province de Luxembourg: Le Repli des chasseurs ardennais le 10 mai et la 2e Division Légère de Cavalerie française (2e DLC) les 1-, 11 et 12 mai," *RBHM*, 1987–88, pp. 437–74, 537–73, 613–48.

———, "Le 5e Division légère de cavalerie française en Ardenne, de 10 à 12 mai," *RBHM*, 1989–90, pp. 476–508, 589–613, 691–714.

Binion, Rudolph, *Hitler Among the Germans* (New York: Elsevier, 1976).

Birkenhead, Earl of, *Halifax: The Life of Lord Halifax* (London: Hamish Hamilton, 1965).

Blasius, Rainer A., *Für Grossdeutschland—gegen den Krieg* (Cologne: Böhlau, 1981).

———, "Weizsäcker contra Ribbentrop: 'München' statt des grossen Krieges," in Knipping and Müller, *Machtbewusstsein*, pp. 93–118.

Bloch, Gilbert, "La Contribution française à la reconstitution et au décryptement de l'enigma militaire allemande en 1931–1932," *RHA*, no. 4, 1985, pp. 17–25.

Bodinier, Capt. Gilbert, "Gamelin, les fortifications et les chars à travers les rapports de l'E.M.A. (1935–1939)," *RHA*, no. 4, 1979, pp. 125–44.

Boelcke, Willi A., "Das 'Seehaus' in Berlin-Wannsee: Zur Geschichte des deutschen 'Monitoring-Service während des zweiten Weltkrieges," *Jahrbuch fur die Geschichte Mittel- und Ostdeutschlands*, 1974, pp. 231–69.

Bollmus, R., *Das Amt Rosenberg und seine Gegner* (Stuttgart: Deutsche Verlags-Anstalt, 1970).

Bonatz, Heinz, *Seekrieg im Aether: Die Leistungen der Marine-Funkaufklärung 1939–1945* (Herford: Mittler, 1981).

Bond, Brian, "Arras 21 May 1940: A Case Study in Counter-Stroke," in Barnett, ed., *Old Battles and New Defences*, pp. 61–84.

———, *Britain, France and Belgium, 1939–1940*, new ed. (London: Brassey's, 1990).

———, *British Military Policy Between the Two World Wars* (London: Oxford University Press, 1980).

———, ed., *Fallen Stars: Eleven Studies of Twentieth Century Military Disasters* (London: Brassey's, 1991).

Boog, Horst, *Die deutsche Luftwaffenführung, 1939–1945* (Stuttgart: Deutsche Verlags-Anstalt, 1982).

———, "Die Operationen der Luftwaffe gegen die Niederlande vom 10. bis 15. Mai 1940," in Ottmer and Ostertag, eds., *Ausgewählte Operationen*, pp. 347–67.

———, ed., *The Conduct of the Air War in the Second World War: An International Comparison* (New York: Oxford University Press, 1992).

Boudot, François, "Sur les problèmes du financement de la défense nationale, 1936–1940," *RHDGM*, 1971, pp. 49–72.

Boussard, Dominique, *Un Problème de défense nationale: L'aéronautique militaire au Parlement, 1928–1940* (Vincennes: Service Historique de l'Armée d'Air, 1983).

Boyce, Robert, and Esmonde M. Robertson, eds., *Paths to War: New Essays on the Origins of the Second World War* (New York: St. Martin's Press, 1989).

Bracher, Karl Dietrich, Manfred Funke, and Hans-Adolf Jacobsen, eds., *Nationalsozialistische Diktatur 1933–1945: Eine Bilanz* (Bonn: Schriftenreihe der Bundeszentrale für politische Bildung, vol. 192, 1983).

———, Wolfgang Sauer, and Gerhard Schulz, *Die nationalsozialistische Machtergreifung* (Cologne: Westdeutscher Verlag, 1960).

Braddick, Henderson B., *Germany, Czechoslovakia, and the "Grand Alliance" in the May Crisis, 1938* (Denver: University of Denver Press, 1969).

Bradley, Dermot, *Generaloberst Heinz Guderian und die Entstehungsgeschichte des modernen Blitzkrieges* (Osnabrück: Biblio-Verlag, 1978).

———, *Walther Wenck, General der Panzertruppe* (Osnabrück: Biblio-Verlag, 1981).

Brammer, Uwe, *Spionageabwehr und "Geheimer Meldedienst": Die Abwehrstelle im Wehrkreis X Hamburg, 1935–1945* (Freiburg: Rombach, 1989).

Bramsted, Ernest K., *Goebbels and National Socialist Propaganda, 1925–1945* (East Lansing: Michigan State University Press, 1965).

Brauch, Gerhard, "Sedan, 1940: Deuxième Bureau und strategische Überraschungen," *MGM*, no. 2, 1967, pp. 15–92.

Braunschweig, Pierre T., *Geheimer Draht nach Berlin: Die Nachrichtenlinie Masson-Schellenberg und der schweizerische Nachrichtendienst im Zweiten Weltkrieg* (Zürich: Verlag Neue Zürcher Zeitung, 1989).

Brook-Shepherd, Gordon, *Anschluss* (London: Macmillan, 1963).

Bruge, Robert, *Historie de la Ligne Maginot*, 4 vols. (Paris: Fayard, 1973–80).

Brügel, Johann W., *Tschechen und Deutsche*, 1918–1938 (Munich: Nymphenburger Verlagshandlung, 1967).

Buchbender, Ortwin, and Reinhard Hauschild, *Geheimsender gegen Frankreich: Die Täuschungsoperation "Radio Humanité" 1940* (Herford: Mittler, 1984).

Bücheler, Heinrich, *Carl-Heinrich von Stülpnagel, Soldat-Philosoph-Verschwörer: Biographie* (Berlin: Ullstein, 1989).

Bücheler, Heinrich, "Die Panzerschlacht von Hannut: Pfingsten 1940," *Kampftruppen*, no. 3, 1980, pp. 125–27.

Buchheit, Gert, *Ludwig Beck, ein preussischer General* (Munich: List, 1964).

——, *Spionage in Zweiten Weltkrieg* (Augsburg: VPD, 1975).

Buckmaster, M., *They Fought Alone: The Story of British Agents in France* (London: Oldhams, 1958).

Buffotot, Patrice, "The French High Command and the Franco-Soviet Alliance, 1933–1939," *JSS*, 1982, pp. 546–60.

——, *Histoire de l'Armée de l'Air,. 1939-1945* (Paris: Défense Éditions, 1980).

—— "La Perception du réarmement allemand par les organismes de renseignement français de 1936 à 1939," *RHA*, no. 3, 1979, pp. 173–84.

——, "Le Réarmement aérien allemand et l'approche de la guerre vus par le IIe bureau air français (1936–1939), "in Hildebrand and Werner, eds., *Deutschland und Frankreich*, pp. 249–324.

——, and Jacques Ogier, "L'Armée de l'Air Francaise dans la campagne de France (10 mai–25 juin 1940)," *RHA*, no. 3, 1975, pp. 88–117.

Bullock, Alan, *Hitler: A Study in Tyranny*, rev. ed. (New York: Harper and Row, 1962).

Butler, Ewan, *Amateur Agent* (London: Harrap, 1963).

——, *Mason-Mac: The Life of Lieutenant General Sir Noel Mason-Macfarlane: A Biography* (London: Macmillan, 1972).

Butler, J.R.M., *Grand Strategy*, vol. 2 (London: HMSO, 1957).

Butterworth, Susan B., "Daladier and the Munich Crisis: A Reappraisal, " *JCH*, 1974, pp. 194–215.

Cairns, John C., "March 7, 1936, Again: The View from Paris," in Gatzke, ed., *European Diplomacy*, pp. 172–92.

——, "Some Recent Historians and the Strange Defeat of 1940," *JMH*, 1974, pp. 60–81.

Cammaerts, Émile, *The Prisoner at Laeken: King Leopold, Legend and Fact* (London: Cresset, 1941).

Cartier, Raymond, *La Seconde Guerre mondiale*, 2 vols. (Paris: Larousse "Paris Match," 1965–66).

Castellan, Georges, *Le Réarmement clandestin du Reich, 1930–1935* (Paris: Plon, 1954).

Caton, Paul-Émile, *Une Guerre perdue en quatre jours*, 2 vols. (Blainville sur Mer: L'Amitié par le Livre, 1969–74).

Cave Brown, Anthony, *"C": The Secret Life of Sir Stewart Menzies, Spymaster to Winston Churchill* (New York: Macmillan, 1987).

Ceadel, Martin, "A Pro-War Peace Movement? The British Movement for Collective Security," in Vaïsse, ed., *Le Pacifisme en Europe*, pp. 167–92.

Celovsky, Boris, *Das Münchener Abkommen von 1938* (Stuttgart: Deutsche Verlags-Anstalt, 1958).

Chapman, Herrick, *State Capitalism and Working-Class Radicalism in the French Aircraft Industry* (Berkeley: University of California Press, 1991).

Chapon, Ch., "L'Armée de terre française, le 2 septembre 1939 et le 9 mai 1940," *RHA*, no. 4, 1979, pp. 164–92.

Charisius, A., "Zur Rolle von Spionage und Diversion in den Blitzkriegplanen des deutschen Generalstabes," *Zeitschrift für Militärpolitik*, 1962, pp. 1367–79.

Charmley, John, *Chamberlain and the Lost Peace* (Chicago: Ivan R. Dee, 1989).

———, *Churchill's Grand Alliance* (New York: Harcourt Brace, 1995).

Chavardès, Maurice, *Le 6 février: La République en danger* (Paris: Calmann Lévy, 1966).

Christienne, Gen. Charles, "L'Armée d'air française de mars 1936 à septembre 1939," in Hildebrand and Werner, eds., *Deutschland und Frankreich*, pp. 215–48.

———, "L'Armée de l'air française et la crise du 7 mars 1936," in SHAA, *Recueil d'articles et études, 1976–1978*, pp. 45–68.

———, *Histoire de l'aviation militaire française* (Paris: Charles-Lavauzelle, 1980).

Christophe, Paul, *1939–1940: Les Catholiques devant la guerre* (Paris: Éditions Ouvrières, 1989).

Churchill, Randolph, and Martin Gilbert, *Winston S. Churchill*, 8 vols. (London: Macmillan, 1966–85).

Churchill, Winston S., *The Second World War*, 6 vols. (Boston: Houghton Mifflin, 1948–54).

Cienciala, Anna M., *Poland and the Western Powers, 1938–1939* (London: Routledge and Kegan Paul, 1968).

Citino, Robert M., *Evolution of Blitzkrieg Tactics: Germany Defends Itself Against Poland, 1918–1933* (New York: Greenwood Press, 1987).

Claasen, Adam, "Blood and Iron, and *der Geist des Atlantiks*: Assessing Hitler's Decision to Invade Norway," *JSS*, no. 3, 1997, pp. 71–96.

Clemens, Detlev, *Herr Hitler in Germany: Wahrnehmung und Deutungen des Nationalsozialismus in Grossbritannien 1920 bis 1939* (Göttingen: Vandenhoeck & Ruprecht, 1996).

Cockett, Richard, *Twilight of Truth: Chamberlain, Appeasement and the Manipulation of the Press* (New York: St. Martin's Press, 1989).

Cohen, Eliot, and John Gooch, *Military Misfortunes: The Anatomy of Failure in War* (New York: Free Press, 1990).

Cointet-Labrousse, Michèle, "Le Syndicat National des Instituteurs, le pacifisme et l'Allemagne (1937–1939)," in *Relations Franco-allemandes*, pp. 137–50.

Collier, Basil, *Hidden Weapons: Allied Secret or Undercover Services in World War II* (London: Hamish Hamilton, 1982).

Colton, Joel G., *Leon Blum: Humanist in Politics* (Durham, N.C.: Duke University Press, 1987).

Colville, John R., *Man of Valour: The Life of Field Marshal the Viscount Gort* (London: Collins 1972).

Colvin, Ian, *The Chamberlain Cabinet* (London: Victor Gollancz, 1971).
————, *Vansittart in Office* (London: Victor Gollancz, 1965).
Compton, James V., *The Swastika and the Eagle: Hitler, the United States, and the Origins of World War II* (Boston: Houghton Mifflin, 1967).
Connell, John, *Wavell, Scholar and Soldier* (London: Collins, 1964).
Conte, Arthur, *Le 1er janvier 1940* (Paris: Plon, 1977).
Cooper, Matthew, *The German Army, 1933–1945: Its Political and Military Failure* (New York: Stein and Day, 1978).
Corum, James S., *The Luftwaffe: Creating the Operational Air War, 1918–1940* (Lawrence: University Press of Kansas, 1997).
————, *The Roots of Blitzkrieg: Hans von Seeckt and German Military Reform* (Lawrence: University Press of Kansas, 1992).
Coutau-Bégarie, Hervé, and Claude Huan, *Darlan* (Paris: Fayard, 1989).
Cowling, Maurice, *The Impact of Hitler: British Politics and British Policy, 1933–1940* (Cambridge: Cambridge University Press, 1975).
Cox, Geoffrey, *Countdown to War: A Personal Memoir of Europe, 1938–1940* (London: William Kimber, 1988).
Craig, Gordon A., *The Politics of the Prussian Army, 1640–1945* (Oxford: Clarendon Press, 1955).
Crémieux-Brilhac, Jean-Louis, *Les Français de l'an 40*, 2 vols. (Paris: Robert Laffont, 1990).
————, "L'Opinion publique française," in *Français et britanniques dans la drôle de guerre*, pp. 1–50.
Creveld, Martin van, *Fighting Power: German and U.S. Army Performance, 1939–1945* (Westport, Conn.: Greenwood, 1982).
Crosland, Margaret, *Piaf* (New York: G. P. Putnam, 1985).
Dahrendorf, Ralf, *Gesellschaft und Demokratie in Deutschland* (Munich: R. Piper, 1965); trans., *Society and Democracy in Germany* (Garden City, N.Y.: Doubleday, 1967).
Darcy, Robert, *Oraison funèbre pour la vieille armée* (Paris: Boivin, 1946).
Deacon, Richard, *The French Secret Service* (London: Grafton, 1990).
Deberles, Kleber, *1940, la terrible année*, 2nd ed. (Auchel: I.T.J.F., 1980).
Deighton, Len, *Blitzkrieg: From the Rise of Hitler to the Fall of Dunkirk* (London: Jonathan Cape, 1979).
Deist, Wilhelm, Klaus Maier, et al., *Das Deutsche Reich und der Zweite Weltkrieg*, vols. 1–2 (Stuttgart: Deutsche Verlags-Anstalt, 1979), trans. P. S. Falla, Dean S. McMurry, and Ewald Osers, *Germany and the Second World War*, vols. 1–2 (Oxford: Clarendon Press, 1990–91).
De Jong, L., *Het Koninkrijk der Nederlanden in de Tweede Wereldoorlog*, vols. 1–2 (S-Gravenhage: Martinus Nijhoff, 1969–70).
Delmas, Jean, "Les Exercices du Conseil Supérieur de la Guerre, 1936–37 and 1937–38," *RHA*, no. 4, 1979, pp. 29–56.
————, Paul Devautour, and Eric Lefèvre, *Mai-juin 1940: Les Combattants de l'honneur* (Paris: Copernic, 1980).
Dennis, Peter, *Decision by Default: Peacetime Conscription and British Defense, 1919–1939* (Durham, N.C.: Duke University Press, 1972).
Derry, T. K., *The Campaign in Norway* (London: HMSO, 1952).
Destremau, Bernard, *Weygand* (Paris: Perrin, 1989).

Detweiler, Donald S., et al., eds., *World War II German Military Studies*, 24 vols. (New York: Garland, 1979).

Deutsch, Harold, C. *The Conspiracy Against Hitler in the Twilight War* (Minneapolis: University of Minnesota Press, 1968).

————, *Hitler and His Generals: The Hidden Crisis, January–June 1938* (Minneapolis: University of Minnesota Press, 1974).

Dietrich, Richard, and Gerhard Oestreich, eds., *Forschungen zu Staat und Verfassung: Festgabe für Fritz Hartung* (Berlin: Duncker & Humblot, 1958).

Dilks, David, "Flashes of Intelligence: The Foreign Office, the SIS and Security before the Second World War," in Andrew and Dilks, eds., *Missing Dimension*, pp. 101–25.

————, "Great Britain and Scandinavia in the Phoney War," *Scandinavian Journal of History*, no. 2, 1977; pp. 29–51.

————, "Intelligence and Appeasement," in Dilks, ed., *Retreat from Power*, 1:139–69.

————, *Neville Chamberlain*, vol. 1, *Pioneering and Reform, 1869–1929* (Cambridge: Cambridge University Press, 1984).

————, "The Twilight War and the Fall of France: Chamberlain and Churchill in 1940," in Dilks, ed., *Retreat from Power*, 2:36–65.

————, "The Unnecessary War? Military Advice on Foreign Policy in Great Britain, 1931–1939," in Preston, ed., *General Staffs*, pp. 98–132.

————, " 'We must hope for the best and prepare for the worst': The Prime Minister, the Cabinet and Hitler's Germany, 1937–1939," *Proceedings of the British Academy*, 73 (1987), pp. 309–352.

————, ed., *Retreat from Power*, 2 vols. (London: Macmillan, 1981).

DiNardo, R. L., *Mechanized Juggernaut or Military Anachronism? Horses and the German Army of World War II* (New York: Greenwood, 1991).

Doise, Jean, and Maurice Vaïsse, *Diplomatie et outil militaire, 1871–1968* (Paris: Imprimerie Nationale, 1987).

Donald, Daniel C., and Katherine L. Herbig, eds., *Strategic Military Deception* (New York: Pergamon 1982).

Döscher, Hans-Jürgen, *Das Auswärtige Amt im Dritten Reich: Diplomatie im Schatten der "Endlösung"* (Berlin: Siedler, n.d.).

Doughty, Robert Allan, "Almost a Miracle," *Quarterly Journal of Military History*, Spring 1990, pp. 42–53.

————, *The Breaking Point: Sedan and the Fall of France* (Hamden, Conn.: Archon Books, 1990).

————, "De Gaulle's Concept of a Mobile Professional Army: Genesis of French Defeat?," *Parameters*, no. 4, 1974, pp. 23–34.

————, "The Enigma of French Armored Doctrine, 1940," *Armor*, Sept.–Oct. 1974, pp. 39–44.

————, "French Antitank Doctrine, 1940: The Antidote that Failed," *Military Review*, no. 5, 1976, pp. 36–48.

————, *The Seeds of Disaster: The Development of French Army Doctrine. 1919–1939* (Hamden, Conn.: Archon Books, 1985).

Douglas, Roy, *The Advent of War, 1939–40* (London: Macmillan, 1978).

————, *In the Year of Munich* (London: Macmillan, 1977).

Draper, Theodore, *The Six Weeks War: 10th May–25th June* (New York: The Viking Press, 1944).

Dreyfus, François-Georges, "Le Pacifisme en France (1930–1940)," in Vaïsse, ed., *Le Pacifisme en Europe*, pp. 137–144.

Dülffer, Jost, "Der Beginn des Krieges 1939: Hitler, die innere Krise und das Mächtesystem," in Bracher, Funke, and Jacobsen, eds., *Nationalsozialistische Diktatur*, pp. 317–44.

————, *Weimar, Hitler, und die Marine: Reichspolitik und Flottenbau 1920 bis 1945* (Düsseldorf: Droste, 1973).

————, "Zum 'Decision-Making Process' in der deutschen Aussenpolitik 1933–1939," in Funke, *Hitler, Deutschland, und die Mächte*, pp. 186–204.

Dumont, Georges H., *Léopold III, roi des belges* (Paris: Charles Dessart, 1944).

Dunbabin, John, "The British Military Establishment and the Policy of Appeasement," in Mommsen and Kettenacker, eds., *Fascist Challenge*, pp. 174–96.

Duroselle, Jean-Baptiste, *L'Abîme (1939–1945)* (Paris: Imprimerie Nationale, 1982).

————, *La Décadence (1932–1939)* (Paris: Imprimerie Nationale, 1979).

Dutailly, Henry, *Les problèmes de l'armée de terre française (1935–1939)* (Paris: Imprimerie Nationale, 1980).

Dutton, David, *Simon: A Political Biography of Sir John Simon* (London: Aurum Press, 1992).

Duvignac, André, *Histoire de l'armée motorisée* (Paris: Imprimerie Nationale, 1948).

Ellis, L. F., *The War in France and Flanders, 1939–1940* (London: HMSO, 1953).

Embry, Basil, *Mission Completed* (London: Methuen, 1957).

Emmerson, James T., *The Rhineland Crisis, 7 March 1936: A Study in Multicultural Diplomacy* (Ames: University of Iowa Press, 1977).

Eppler, John W., *Geheimagent in Zweiten Weltkrieg* (Preussisch Oltendorf: K. W. Schülz, 1974).

Erasmus, J., *Der geheime Nachrichtendienst*, 2nd ed. (Göttingen: Musterschmidt, 1955).

Erfurth, Waldemar, *Die Geschichte des deutschen Generalstabes von 1918 bis 1945* (Göttingen: Musterschmidt, 1957).

Erickson, John, "Threat Identification and Strategic Appraisal by the Soviet Union, 1930–1941," in May, ed., *Knowing One's Enemies*, pp. 375–423.

Evron, Yair, ed., *International Violence: Terrorism, Surprise, and Control* (Jerusalem: Hebrew University of Jerusalem, 1979).

de Fabribeckers, Édouard, *La Campagne de l'Armée belgique en 1940*, 2nd ed. (Brussels: Rossel, 1978).

Facon, Patrick, "Chasseurs et bombardiers dans la bataille," *Historia Spécial*, no. 5, 1990, pp. 34–40.

————, "Le Haut Commandement aérien français et la crise de Munich," *RHA*, no. 3, 1983, pp. 10–17.

————, "Le Haut Commandement aérien français et le problème du réarmement 1938–1939: Une Approche technique et industrielle," *RHA*, no. 3, 1989, pp. 91–101.

————, "Les Leçons de la campagne de Pologne vues par l'état-major aérien français: Le Rapport du colonel Bergeret, aide-major général des forces aériennes (19 septembre 1939)," *RHA*, no. 4, 1985, pp. 103–8.

————, "Le Plan V, 1938–1939," *RHA*, no. 4, 1979, pp. 102–24.

————, "La Visite du Général Vuillemin en Allemagne (16–21 août 1938)," *RHA*, no. 2, 1982, pp. 111–21.

Faligot, Roger, *Markus: Espion allemand* (Paris: Temps Actuels, 1986).

Fallois, Immo von, *Kalkül und Illusion: Der Machtkampf zwischen Reichswehr und SA während des Röhm-Krise 1934* (Berlin: Duncker & Humboldt, 1994).

Fanning, William J., Jr., "The Origins of the Term 'Blitzkrieg': Another View," *JMH*, no. 2, 1997, pp. 283–302.

Favreau, Bertrand, *Georges Mandel, ou la passion de la République* (Paris: Fayard, 1996).

Feiling, Keith, *The Life of Neville Chamberlain* (New York: Macmillan, 1946).

Fernez, A., *Les Coulisses de l'espionnage* (Antwerp: Gerard, 1965).

Ferris, John R., "Indulged in Too Little? Vansittart, Intelligence and Appeasement," *Diplomacy and Statecraft*, no. 1, 1995, pp. 122–75.

Ferro, Marc, *Pétain* (Paris: Fayard, 1987).

Fest, Joachim C., *The Face of the Third Reich: Portraits of the Nazi Leadership* (New York: Pantheon, 1970).

Fest, Joachim C., *Hitler*, trans. Richard and Clara Winston (New York: Vintage, 1975).

Feuchter, Georg W., *Geschichte des Luftkriegs: Entwicklung und Zukunft* (Bonn: Athenäum, 1954).

Fink, Carole, *Marc Bloch: A Life in History* (Cambridge: Cambridge University Press, 1989).

Foerster, Wolfgang, *Ein General kämpft gegen den Krieg* (Munich: Münchener Dom, 1949).

Foertsch, Hermann, *Schuld und Verhängnis: Die Fritsch-Krise* (Stuttgart: Deutsche Verlags-Anstalt, 1951).

Fonvieille-Alquier, François, *Les Français dans la drôle de guerre, 39–40* (Paris: Robert Laffont, 1971).

Ford, Harold P., *Estimative Intelligence: The Purposes and Problems of Intelligence Estimating* (Washington, D.C.: Defense Intelligence College, 1993).

Forstmeier, Friedrich, *Kriegswirtschaft und Rüstung: 1939–1945* (Düsseldorf: Droste, 1977).

———, and Hans-Erich Volkmann, eds., *Wirtschaft und Rüstung am Vorabend des Zweiten Weltkrieges* (Düsseldorf: Militärgeschichtliches Forschungsamt, 1975).

Forty, George, and John Duncan, *The Fall of France: Disaster in the West, 1939–1940* (Tunbridge Wells: Nutshell, 1980).

Fournier, Nicolas, *Dossier E: Comme espionage* (Paris: Moreau, 1978).

Fox, d'Ornano, "La Percée des Ardennes," *RHDGM*, June 1953, pp. 77–118.

Français et britanniques dans la drôle de guerre, ed. Comité d'Histoire de la Deuxième Guerre Mondiale (Paris: Centre Nationale de la Recherche Scientifique, 1979).

(La) France et l'Allemagne en guerre, septembre 1939–novembre 1942, ed. Claude Carlier and Stefan Martens, Actes du XXVème Colloques Franco-Allemand, Wiesbaden 17–19 mars 1988 (Paris: n.p., 1990).

Frankenstein, Robert, "The Decline of France and French Appeasement Policies, 1936–9," in Mommsen and Kettenacker, eds., *Fascist Challenge*, pp. 236–45.

———, *Le Financement du réarmement de la France* (Paris: Sorbonne, 1978).

Fridenson, Patrick, *La France et la Grand Bretagne face aux problèmes aériens 1935–mai 1940* (Vincennes: Service Historique de l'Armée de l'Air, 1976).

Frieser, *Blitzkrieg-Legende*: Militärgeschichtliches Forschungsamt, *Operationen des Zweiten Weltkrieges*, vol. 2, Karl-Heinz Frieser, *Blitzkrieg-Legende: Der Westfeldzug 1940*, 2nd ed. (Munich: R. Oldenbourg, 1996).

Fuchser, Larry William, *Neville Chamberlain and Appeasement: A Study in the Politics of History* (New York: W. W. Norton, 1982).

Funke, Manfred, *Hitler, Deutschland und die Mächte* (Düsseldorf: Droste, 1976).

———, "7 März 1936: Fallstudie zum aussenpolitischen Führungstil Hitlers," in Michalka, ed., *Nationalsozialistische Aussenpolitik*, pp. 277–324.

Gackenholz, Hermann, "Reichskanzlei, 5 November 1937," in Dietrich and Oestreich, eds., *Forschungen zu Staat und Verfassung*.

Galante, Pierre, *Operation Valkyrie: The German Generals' Plot Against Hitler* (New York: Harper and Row, 1981).

Gallo, Max, *Et ce fût la défaite de 40: La Cinquième Colonne* (Paris: Perrin, 1970).

Gannon, Franklin Reid, *The British Press and Germany, 1936–1939* (Oxford: Clarendon Press, 1971).

Garçon, François, *De Blum à Pétain: Cinéma et société française (1936–1944)* (Paris: Éditions du Cerf, 1984).

Garder, Michel, *La Guerre secrète des services spéciaux français (1935–1945)* (Paris: Plon, 1967).

Garlinksi, Josef, *The Enigma War* (New York: Scribner, 1980).

Gates, Eleanor M., *End of the Affair: The Collapse of the Anglo-French Alliance* (London: George Allen and Unwin, 1981).

Gatzke, Hans, ed., *European Diplomacy Between the Two Wars, 1919–1939* (Chicago: Quadrangle, 1972).

Gedye, G.E.R., *Betrayal in Central Europe: Austria and Czechoslovakia, the Fallen* (New York: Harper, 1939).

Gelb, Norman, *Dunkirk: The Complete Story of the First Step in the Defeat of Hitler* (New York: William Morrow, 1989).

Gellermann, Günther W., *. . . und lauschten für Hitler: Geheime Reichsache: Die Abhörzentralen des Dritten Reiches* (Bonn: Bernard & Graefe, 1991).

Gemzell, Carl-Axel, *Raeder, Hitler und Skandinavien: Der Kampf für einen maritimen Operationsplan* (Lund: C.W.K. Gleerup, 1965).

George, Alexander L., *Presidential Decisionmaking in Foreign Policy: The Effective Use of Information and Advice* (Boulder, Colo.: Westview Press, 1980).

———, "Warning and Response: Theory and Practice," in Evron, ed., *International Violence*, pp. 12–24.

———, and Richard Smoke, *Deterrence in American Foreign Policy: Theory and Practice* (New York: Columbia University Press, 1974).

George, Margaret, *The Warped Vision: British Foreign Policy, 1933–1939* (Pittsburgh: University of Pittsburgh Press, 1966).

Germain, André, *Les Grandes Favorites, 1815–1940: L'Amour et la politique* (Paris: Sun., n.d.).

Geyer, Michael, *Aufrüstung oder Sicherheit: Deutsche Reichswehr in die Krise der Machtpolitik, 1924–1936* (Wiesbaden: Steiner, 1980).

———, "The Crisis of Military Leadership in the 1930s," *JSS*, no. 4, 1991, pp. 448–62.

———, *Deutsche Rüstungspolitik, 1860–1980* (Frankfurt am Main: Suhrkamp, 1984).

———, "National Socialist Germany: The Politics of Information," in May, ed., *Knowing One's Enemies*, pp. 310–46.

Gilbert, Martin, *Churchill:* (see Churchill, Randolph, and *Churchill War Papers*).

———, *The Second World War* (New York: Henry Holt, 1989).

Gillet, E., "La Conférence d'Ypres le 21 mai 1940," *RBHM*, 1992, pp. 271–300.

———, "La Percée allemande en mai 1940 et la contre-attaque d'Arras," *RBHM*, 1992, pp. 593–619.

Gillet, Marcel, *De Blum à Daladier: Le Nord et Pas-de-Calais, 1936–1939* (Lille: Presses Universitaires de Lille, 1980).

Girardet, Raoul, *La Société militaire dans la France contemporaine* (Paris: Plon, 1953).

Girault, René, "The Impact of the Economic Situation on the Foreign Policy of France, 1936–39," in Mommsen and Kettenacker, eds., *Fascist Challenge*, pp. 209–26.

Giscard d'Estaing, Antoine, *Léopold III, un roi dans la tourmente* (Brussels: Éditions Racine, 1996).

Gisclon, Jean, *Le Cinquième Quart d'heure* (Paris: Éditions France-Empire, 1965).

Giuliano, Gérard, et al., *Les Ardennais dans la tourmente* (Charleville-Mézières: Éditions Terres Ardennaises, 1990).

Glover, Michael, *The Fight for the Channel Ports, Calais to Brest 1940: A Study in Confusion* (London: Leo Cooper, 1985).

Gombin, Richard, *Les Socialistes et la guerre: La S.F.I.O. et la politique étrangère française entre les deux guerres mondiales* (Paris: Mouton, 1970).

Görlitz, Walther, *Deutsche Generalstab: Geschichte und Gestalt* (Frankfurt am Main: Verlag der Frankfurter Hefte, 1950); trans. Brian Battershaw, *History of the German General Staff* (New York: Praeger, 1953).

Götzel, Hermann, *Generaloberst Kurt Student und seine Fallschirmjäger: Die Erinnerungen des Generaloberst Kurt Student* (Friedberg: Podzun-Pallas, 1980).

Gounelle, Claude, *Sedan, mai 1940* (Paris: Presses de la Cité, 1965).

Goutard, Adolphe, *1940: La Guerre des occasions perdus* (Paris: Hachette, 1956): trans. A.R.P. Burgess, *The Battle of France, 1940* (London: Frederick Muller, 1958).

Graml, Hermann, *Europas Weg in den Krieg: Hitler und die Mächte 1939* (Munich: Oldenbourg, 1990).

Grasser, Kurt, and Jürgen Stahlmann, *Westwall Maginot-Linie Atlantikwall: Bunkerund Festungsbau 1930–1945* (Leoni am Starnberger See: Druffel-Verlag, 1983).

Greenwood, Sean, " 'Caligula's Horse' Revisited: Sir Thomas Inskip as Minister for the Coordination of Defence, 1936–1939," *JSS*, no. 2, 1994, pp. 17–38.

Groehler, Olaf, *Geschichte des Luftkriegs, 1910 bis 1970* (Berlin: Militärverlag der Deutschen Demokratischen Republik, 1975).

———, "Die Wehrmachtstudie 1936/37," *Revue internationale d'histoire militaire*, 1989, pp. 207–25.

Gross, Manfred, *Der Westwall* (Köln: Rheinland, 1982).

Groussard, Georges-André, *Chemins secrets* (Mulhouse: Bader-Dufour, 1948).

Guillaume, Gen. Augustin, *Homme de guerre* (Paris: France-Empire, 1977).

Guillaume-Grimaud, Geneviève, *Le Cinéma du Front Populaire* (Paris: Lherminier, 1986).

Guikovaty, Emile, *Les Extravagantes Soeurs Mitford* (Paris: Grasset, 1983).

Gunsburg, Jeffrey, "The Battle of the Belgian Plain, 12–14 May 1940: The First Great Tank Battle," *Journal of Military History*, no. 2, 1992, pp. 207–44.

———, *Divided and Conquered: The French High Command and the Defeat of the West* (Westport, Conn.: Greenwood, 1979).

Gunther, John, *Inside Europe* (New York: Harper, 1938).

Gusev, B, and L. Bazov, "Frantsuska voennaya razvedka i ogrotsa fashistskoi agressii protiv Frantsii," *Voenno-istoricheskii Zhurnal*, no. 12, 1966, pp. 21–31.

Hagen, W., *Die geheime Front: Organisation, Personen und Aktionen des deutschen Geheimdienstes*, 2nd ed. (Leipzig: Nibelungen, 1950).

Hamann, Brigitte, *Hitlers Wien: Lehrjahre eines Diktators*, 2nd ed. (Munich: R. Piper, 1996); trans. Thomas Thornton, *Hitler's Vienna: A Dictator's Apprenticeship* (Oxford: Oxford University Press, 1998).

Hamilton, Nigel, *Monty: The Making of a General, 1887–1942* (London: Hamish Hamilton, 1981).

Handel, Michael, "The Problem of Strategic Surprise," *JSS*, no. 3, 1984, pp. 229–81.

———, ed., *Intelligence and Military Operations* (London: Frank Cass, 1990).

Harris, J. P., "British Military Intelligence and the Rise of German Mechanized Forces, 1929–1940," *INS*, no. 2, 1991, pp. 395–417.

Harris, Kenneth, *Attlee* (London: Weidenfeld and Nicolson, 1982).

Hartmann, Christian, *Halder, Generalstabschef Hitlers, 1938–1942* (Paderborn: Ferdinand Schöningh, 1991).

Harvey, A. D., "The French Armée de l'Air in May–June 1940: A Failure in Conception," *JCH*, no. 4, 1990, pp 447–65.

Harvey, Maurice, *Scandinavian Misadventure: The Campaign in Norway* (Tunbridge Wells: Spellmount, 1990).

Haupt, Werner, *Sieg ohne Lorbeer: Der Westfeldzug 1940* (Preetz, Holstein: E. Geerdes, 1965).

Hawes, Brigadier L. A., " 'D'accord': The Story of the 'W' Plan, the Move of Our Forces to France in 1939," *Army Quarterly*, July 1971, pp. 445–56.

Heimsoeth, Hans-Jürgen, *Der Zusammenbruch der Dritten Französischen Republik: Frankreich während der "Drôle de Guerre" 1939/40* (Bonn: Bouvier, 1990).

Heineman, John Louis, *Hitler's First Foreign Minister: Constantin Freiherr von Neurath, Diplomat and Statesman* (Berkeley: University of California Press, 1979).

Henke, Josef, *England in Hitlers politischen Kalkul* (Boppard am Rhein: Boldt, 1973).

Herman, Michael, *Intelligence Power in Peace and War* (New York: Cambridge University Press, 1996).

Herndon, James S., "British Perceptions of Soviet Military Capability, 1935–9," in Mommsen and Kettenacker, eds., *Fascist Challenge*, pp. 297–322.

Hildebrand, Klaus, Jürgen Schmädeke, and Klaus Zermak, *1939: An der Schwelle zur Weltkrieg* (Berlin: Walter de Gruyter, 1990).

———, and Karl-Ferdinand Werner, eds., *Deutschland und Frankreich, 1936–1939*, vol. 10 of Deutschen Historischen Institut Paris, *Beihefte der Francia* (Munich: Artemis, 1981).

Hill, Christopher, *Cabinet Decisions on Foreign Policy: The British Experience, October 1938–June 1941* (Cambridge: Cambridge University Press, 1991).

Hillgruber, Andreas, *Hitlers Strategie: Politik und Kriegführung 1940–1941* (Frankfurt am Main: Bernard & Graefe, 1965).

———, *Die Zerstörung Europas: Beiträge zur Weltkriegsepoche 1914 bis 1945* (Frankfurt am Main: Propyläen, 1988).

Hinsley, F. H., et al., *British Intelligence in the Second World War: Its Influence on Strategy and Operations*, 4 vols. (London: HMSO, 1979–90).

Höbelt, Lothar, *Die britische Appeasementpolitik: Entspannung und Nachrüstung, 1937–1939* (Vienna: Österreichischer Bundesverlag, 1983).

Hoch, Anton, and Hermann Weiss, "Die Erinnerungen des Generalobersten Wilhelm Adam," in Benz et al., eds., *Miscellanea*, pp. 32–62.

Hoff, Pierre, *Les Programmes d'armement de 1919 à 1939* (Paris: Service Historique de l'Armée de Terre, 1982).

Hoffmann, Peter, *Widerstand—Staatsreich—Attentat: Der Kampf der Opposition gegen Hitler* (Munich: R. Piper, 1969).

Hohnadel, Alain, and Michel Truttmann, *Guide de la Ligne Maginot: Des Ardennes au Rhin, dans les Alpes* (Bayeux: Heimdal, 1988).

Höhne, Heinz, *Canaris, Porträt im Zwielicht* (Munich: Bertelsmann, 1976); trans. J. Maxwell Brownjohn, *Canaris. Hitler's Master Spy* (New York: Doubleday, 1979).

———, *Der Krieg im Dunkeln: Macht und Einfluss des deutschen und preussischen Geheimdienstes* (Munich: Bertelsmann, 1985).

———, *Der Orden unter dem Totenkopf* (Gütersloh: Sigbert Mohn, 1867); trans. Richard Barry, *The Order of the Death's Head: The Story of Hitler's S.S.* (London: Secker and Warburg, 1969).

Holst, Johan Jorgen, "Surprise, Signals and Reaction: The Attack on Norway, April 9, 1940—Some Observations," *Cooperation and Conflict*, no. 2, 1966, pp. 31–45.

Homer, F.X.J., and Larry D. Wilcox, eds., *Germany and Europe in the Era of the Two World Wars: Essays in Honor of Oron James Hale* (Charlottesville: University Press of Virginia, 1986).

Homze, Edward L., *Arming the Luftwaffe: The Reich Air Ministry and the German Aircraft Industry, 1919–1939* (Lincoln: University of Nebraska Press, 1976).

Horne, Alistair, *The French Army and Politics, 1870–1970* (London: Macmillan, 1984).

———, *To Lose a Battle, France 1940* (New York: The Viking Press, 1969).

Howard, Anthony, *RAB: The Life of R. A. Butler* (London: Jonathan Cape, 1987).

Howard, Michael, "British Military Preparations for the Second World War," in Dilks, ed., *Retreat from Power*, 1:102–17.

———, *The Continental Commitment* (London: Maurice Temple Smith, 1972).

Huard, Paul, *Le Colonel de Gaulle et ses blindés: Laon 15–20 mai 1940* (Paris: Plon, 1980).

Hubatsch, Walther, *Weserübung: Die deutsche Besetzung von Dänemark und Norwegen* (Göttingen: Musterschmidt, 1960).

Hughes, Judith M., *To the Maginot Line: The Politics of French Military Preparation in the 1920's* (Cambridge, Mass.: Harvard University Press, 1971).

Huvelin, Paul, "Sedan, Mai 1940: L'Armée française coupée en deux," *Historia*, May 1990, pp. 50–60.

Hybel, Alex Roberto, *The Logic of Surprise in International Conflict* (Lexington, Mass.: Lexington Books, 1986).

Hyde, H. Montgomery, *British Air Policy Between the Wars, 1918–1939* (London: Heinemann, 1976).

Ingram, Norman, *The Politics of Dissent: Pacifism in France, 1919–1939* (New York: Oxford University Press, 1991).

Irving, David, *Hitler's War* (New York: The Viking Press, 1977).

———, *The Rise and Fall of the Luftwaffe: The Life of Luftwaffe Marshal Erhard Milch* (London: Weidenfeld and Nicolson, 1973).

Jablonsky, David, "The Paradox of Duality: Adolf Hitler and the Concept of Military Surprise," *INS*, no. 3, 1988, pp. 55–117.

Jäckel, Eberhard, *Frankreich in Hitlers Europa* (Stuttgart: Deutsche Verlags-Anstalt, 1966).

———, *Hitler's Weltanschauung* (Tübingen: R. Wunderlich, 1969); trans. Herbert

Arnold, *Hitler's Weltanschauung* (Cambridge, Mass.: Harvard University Press, 1981).

Jackson, Julian, *The Politics of Depression in France, 1932–1936* (Cambridge: Cambridge University Press, 1985).

————, *The Popular Front in France Defending Democracy, 1934–38* (Cambridge: Cambridge University Press, 1988).

Jackson, Peter, "France and the Guarantee to Roumania, April 1939," *INS*, no. 2, 1995, pp. 242–72.

————, "French Military Intelligence and Czechoslovakia, 1938," *Diplomacy and Statecraft*, no. 1, 1994, pp. 81–106.

————, "La Perception de la puissance aérienne allemande et son influence sur la politique extérieure française pendant les crises internationales de 1938 à 1939," *RHA*, no. 4, 1994, pp. 76–87.

Jacobsen, Hans-Adolf, *Dünkirchen: Ein Beitrag zur Geschichte des Westfeldzuges* (Neckargemünd: Kurt Vowinckel, 1958).

————, "L'Erreur du commandement allemand devant Dunkerque," *RHA*, no. 3, 1958, pp. 63–74.

————, *Fall Gelb: Der Kampf um den deutschen Operationsplan zur Westoffensive 1940* (Wiesbaden: Franz Steiner, 1957).

————, *Nationalsozialistische Aussenpolitik 1933–1938* (Frankfurt am Main: Alfred Metzner, 1968).

————, *"Spiegelbild einer Verschwörung": Die Opposition gegen Hitler und der Staatsreich vom 20. Juli 1944 in der SD-Berichterstattung, Geheime Dokumente aus dem ehemaligen Reichssicherheitshauptamt*, 2 vols. (Stuttgart: Seewald, 1984).

————, and Jürgen Rohwer, *Decisive Battles of World War II: The German View* (London: André Deutsch, 1965).

————, and Jürgen Rohwer, "Planungen und Operationen der deutschen Kriegsmarine im Zusammenhang mit dem Fall 'Gelb,' " *Marinerundschau*, no. 2, 1960, pp. 65–78.

Jagschitz, Gerhard, "Die österreichischen Nationalsozialisten," in Stourzh and Zaar, eds., *Österreich Deutschland und die Mächte*, pp. 229–70.

James, Robert Rhodes, *Bob Boothby: A Portrait* (London: Hodder and Stoughton, 1991).

Janssen, Karl-Heinz, and Fritz Tobias, *Der Sturz der Generale: Hitler und die Blomberg-Fritsch-Krise 1938* (Munich: C. H. Beck, 1994).

Jars, Robert, *La Campagne de Pologne* (Paris: Payot, 1949).

Jeancolas, Jean-Pierre, *15 Ans d'années trente: Le Cinéma des Français, 1929–1944* (Paris: Stock/Cinéma, 1983).

Jeanneney, Jean-Noël, *L'Argent caché: Milieux d'affaires et pouvoirs politiques dans la France du 20e siècle* (Paris: Fayard, 1981).

————, *François de Wendel en république: L'Argent et le pouvoir, 1914–1940* (Paris: Éditions du Seuil, 1976).

Jervis, Robert, *Perception and Misperception in International Politics* (Princeton, N.J.: Princeton University Press, 1976).

Joesten, J., *Im Dienste des Misstrauens: Das Geschäft mit Spionage und Abwehr* (Munich: Ruetten & Loening, 1964).

Jordan, Nicole, "The Cut-Price War on the Peripheries: The French General Staff, the

Rhineland and Czechoslovakia," in Boyce and Robertson, eds., *Paths to War*, pp. 128–66.

———, "Maurice Gamelin, Italy and the Eastern Alliances," *JSS*, 1991, pp. 428–41.

———, *The Popular Front and Central Europe: The Dilemmas of French Impotence, 1918–1940* (Cambridge: Cambridge University Press, 1992).

Jungenfeld, Capt. Ernst von, "German Panzers vs. French Light Mechanized Divisions," *Field Artillery Journal*, Oct. 1941, pp. 772–75.

Kahn, David, *The Codebreakers: The Story of Secret Writing* (London: Weidenfeld and Nicolson, 1967).

———, *Hitler's Spies: German Military Intelligence in World War II* (New York: Macmillan, 1978).

———, "The United States Views Germany and Japan in 1941," in May, ed., *Knowing One's Enemies*, pp. 476–501.

Kahneman, Daniel, Paul Slovic, and Amos Tversky, eds., *Judgment Under Uncertainty: Heuristics and Biases* (New York: Cambridge University Press, 1982).

Kaiser, David, "Conspiracy or Cock-up? Pearl Harbor Revisited," *INS*, April 1994, pp. 354–72.

———, *Economic Diplomacy and the Origins of the Second World War* (Princeton, N.J.: Princeton University Press, 1980).

———, (coauthor) (see Mason, Tim).

Kam, Ephraim, *Surprise Attack: The Victim's Perspective* (Cambridge, Mass.: Harvard University Press, 1988).

Kampe, Hans George, *Underground Military Command Bunkers of Zossen, Germany: Construction History and Use by the Wehrmacht and the Soviet Army 1937–1994* (Atglen, Pa.: Schiffer Military/Aviation History, 1996).

Kemp, A., *The Maginot Line: Myth and Reality* (New York: Military Heritage Press, 1988).

Kennedy, Robert M., *The German Campaign in Poland* (Washington, D.C.: U.S. Department of the Army, 1956).

Kennett, Lee, "German Air Superiority in the Westfeldzug, 1940," in Homer and Wilcox, eds., *Germany and Europe*, pp. 141–56.

Kersaudy, François, *Stratèges et Norvège, 1940: Les Jeux de la guerre et du hasard* (Paris: Hachette, 1977); trans. *Norway 1940* (London: Collins, 1990).

Kershaw, Ian, *Hitler, 1889–1936: Hubris* (London: Allen Lane, 1998).

———, *The "Hitler Myth": Image and Reality in the Third Reich* (Oxford: Oxford University Press, 1987).

———, *Popular Opinion and Political Dissent in the Third Reich, Bavaria 1933–1945* (Oxford: Oxford University Press, 1983).

Kessler, Leo, *Betrayal at Venlo: The Secret Story of Appeasement and Treachery, 1939–1945* (London: Leo Cooper, 1991).

Kettenacker, Lothar, ed., *Das "Andere Deutschland" im Zweiten Weltkrieg* (Stuttgart: Ernst Klett, 1977).

Kieft, David O., *Belgium's Return to Neutrality: An Essay in the Frustration of Small Power Diplomacy* (Oxford: Clarendon Press, 1972).

Kielmansegg, Johann Adolf Graf, *Der Fritschprozess 1938: Ablauf und Hintergründe* (Hamburg: Hoffmann & Campe, 1949).

Kier, Elizabeth, *Imagining War: French and British Military Doctrine Between the Wars* (Princeton, N.J.: Princeton University Press, 1997).

Kiersch, Gerhard, et al., *Berliner Alltag im Dritten Reich* (Düsseldorf: Droste, 1981).

Kiesling, Eugenia C., *Arming Against Hitler: France and the Limits of Military Planning* (Lawrence: University of Kansas Press, 1996).

Killen, John, *The Luftwaffe: A History* (London: Muller, 1967).

Kimche, Jon, *Spying for Peace: General Guisan and Swiss Neutrality*, 2nd ed. (London: Weidenfeld and Nicolson, 1962).

————, *The Unfought Battle* (London: Weidenfeld and Nicolson, 1968).

Kindermann, Gottfried-Karl, "Der Feindcharakter Österreichs in der Perzeption des Dritten Reiches," in Stourzh and Zaar, eds., *Österreich, Deutschland und die Mächte*, pp. 75–96.

————, *Hitlers Niederlage in Österreich* (Hamburg: Hoffmann & Campe, 1984); trans. Sonia Brough and David Taylor, *Hitler's Defeat in Austria, 1933–1934: Europe's First Containment of Nazi Expansionism* (London: C. Hurst, 1988).

Kirkland, Faris Russell, "The French Air Force in 1940: Was It Defeated by the Luftwaffe or by Politics?," *Air University Review*, no. 6, 1985, pp. 101–18.

————, "French Air Strength in May 1940," *Air Power History*, no. 1, 1993, pp. 22–34.

Klefisch, Peter, *Das Dritte Reich und Belgien, 1933–1939* (Frankfurt am Main: Peter Lang, 1988).

Knipping, Franz, "Frankreich in Hitlers Aussenpolitik 1933–1939," in Funke, ed., *Hitler, Deutschland, und die Mächte*, pp. 612–27.

————, and Klaus-Jürgen Müller, eds., *Machtbewusstsein in Deutschland am Vorabend des Zweiten Weltkrieges* (Paderborn: Ferdinand Schöningh, 1984).

Knorr, Klaus, "Strategic Surprise in Four European Wars," in Knorr and Morgan, *Strategic Military Surprise*, pp. 9–42.

————, and Patrick Morgan, *Strategic Military Surprise: Incentives and Opportunities* (New Brunswick, N.J.: Transaction Books, 1983).

Koch, Horst Adalbert, *Flak: Die Geschichte der deutschen Flakartillerie und der Einsatz der Luftwaffenhelfer* (Bad Nauheim: Podzun, 1965).

Koch, Lutz, *Rommel, der "Wustenfuchs"* (Bielefeld: W. Goldmann, 1978).

Koch, Olivier, *Ligne Maginot: Le Petit Ouvrage de Rohrbach* (Sarreguemines: L'Imprimerie Sarregueminoise, 1995).

Koch-Kent, Henri, *10 mai 1940 en Luxembourg* (Luxemburg: n.p., 1971).

————, *Doudot, figure légendaire du contre-espionage français* (Tournai: Castermann, 1976).

Koeltz, Louis, *Comment s'est joué notre destin* (Paris: Hachette, 1957).

Komjathy, Anthony, and Rebecca Stockwell, *German Minorities and the Third Reich* (New York: Holmes and Meier, 1980).

Korber, Lili, *Night over Vienna* (Riverside, Calif.: Ariadne Press, 1990).

Kossmann, E. H., *The Low Countries, 1780–1940* (Oxford: Clarendon Press, 1978).

Kosthorst, Erich, "Die deutsche Opposition gegen Hitler zwischen Polen und Frankreichfeldzug," in Kosthorst, *Zeitgeschichte*, pp. 23–46.

————, *Zeitgeschichte und Zeitperspektive* (Paderborn: Ferdinand Schöningh, 1981).

Kozaczuk, Wladyslaw, *Enigma: How the German Cipher Machine Was Broken and How It Was Read by the Allies in World War II* (Frederick, Md.: University Publications of America, 1984).

Král, Václav, ed., *Die Deutschen in der Tschechoslowakei, 1933–1947* (Prague: Ceskoslovenské Akademie, 1964).

Kreissler, Felix, ed., *Fünfzig Jahre danach—Der "Anschluss" von innen und aussen gesehen* (Vienna: Europavg, 1989).

Krop, Pascal, *Les Secrets de l'espionnage français, de 1870 à nos jours* (Paris: J. C. Lattès, 1993).

Kube, Alfred, *Pour le mérite und Hakenkreuz: Hermann Göring im Dritten Reich* (Munich: R. Oldenbourg, 1986).

Kuhn, Axel, *Hitlers aussenpolitisches Programm* (Stuttgart: Klett, 1971).

Kupferman, Fred, *Laval* (Paris: Balland, 1987).

Kuropka, Joachim, *Meldungen aus Münster 1924–1944* (Münster: Regensberg, 1992).

Kurowski, Franz, and Gottfried Tornau, *Sturmartillerie, 1939–1945* (Stuttgart: Motorbuch, 1977).

Kurz, Hans Rudolf, *Nachrichten Zentrum Schweig* (Frauenfeld: Horst, 1972).

Lacaze, Yvon, *La France et Munich: Étude d'un processus decisionnel en matière de relations internationales* (Bern, New York: Peter Lang, 1992).

———, *L'Opinion publique française et la crise de Munich* (Paris: Peter Lang, 1991).

Lakowski, Richard, "Berlin als Sitz der Wehrmachtfuhrung und Zentrum der militärischen Vorbereitung des zweiten Weltkrieges," *Militärgeschichte*, no. 4, 1987, pp. 335–37.

Lammers, Donald M., *Explaining Munich: The Search for Motive in British Policy* (Stanford: Hoover Institution, 1966).

———, "Fascism, Communism, and the Foreign Office, 1937–1939," *JCH*, no. 3, 1971, pp. 66–86.

———, "From Whitehall After Munich: The Foreign Office and the Future Course of British Policy," *Historical Journal*, Dec. 1973, pp. 831–56.

Langenhove, Fernand van, *La Belgique et ses garants: L'Été 1940* (Brussels: Palais des Académie, 1972).

Langhorne, Richard, ed., *Diplomacy and Intelligence During the Second World War* (Cambridge: Cambridge University Press, 1985).

Lapaquellerie, Yvon, *Édouard Daladier* (Paris: Flammarion, 1940).

Larmour, Peter J., *The French Radical Party in the 1930s* (Stanford: Stanford University Press, 1964).

Lassaigne, Jacques, *La Vérité sur juin 1940* (Algiers: Imprimerie Pfister, 1943).

Laubier, Philippe de, "Le Bombardement français sur la Meuse: Le 14 mai 1940," *RHA*, no. 3, 1985, pp. 96–109.

Leach, Barry A., "Halder," in Barnett, eds., *Hitler's Generals*.

Lebow, Richard Ned, *Between Peace and War: The Nature of International Crisis* (Baltimore: Johns Hopkins University Press, 1981).

Leca, Dominique, *La Rupture de 1940* (Paris: Fayard, 1978).

Lecuir, Jean, *La France et la Grande-Bretagne face aux problèmes aériens, 1935-mai 1940* (Paris: Service Historique de l'Armée d'Air, 1976).

Lee, Bradford, "Strategy, Arms, and the Collapse of France, 1930–1940," in Langhorne, ed., *Diplomacy and Intelligence*, pp. 43–67.

Leeds, Stanton B., *These Rule France* (New York: Bobbs-Merrill, 1940).

Lefranc, Georges, *Le Front populaire: 1934–1938* (Paris: Presses Universitaires de Frances, 1978).

———, *Histoire du Front populaire, 1934–1938* (Paris: Payot, 1974).

———, *Le Mouvement socialiste sous la Troisieme République*, vol. 2, *De 1920 à 1940* (Paris: Payot, 1977).

Le Goyet, Pierre, "Contre-attaques manquées: Sedan 13–15 mai 1940," *RHA*, no. 4, 1962, pp. 110–30.

————, "L'Engagement de la 2e division cuirasée française," *RHA*, no. 1, 1964, pp. 147–67.

————, *Munich: "Un traquenard"?* (Paris: Éditions France-Empire, 1988).

————, *Le Mystère Gamelin* (Paris: Presses de la Cité, n.d.).

————, Le 11e Corps d'armée dans la bataille de la Meuse, 10–15 mai 1940," *RHA*, no. 2, 1962, pp. 83–94.

————, "La Percée de Sedan (10–15 mai 1940)," *RHDGM*, no. 59, 1965, pp. 25–52.

————, *15 Mars 1939: Le Premier "Coup de Prague"* (Paris: France-Empire, 1989).

Leverkuehn, P., *Der geheime Nachrichtendienst der deutschen Wehrmacht*, 2nd ed. (Frankfurt am Main: Bernard & Graefe, 1957).

Levite, Ariel, *Intelligence and Strategic Surprises* (New York: Columbia University Press, 1987).

Lewin, Ronald, *Rommel* (London: B. T. Batsford, 1968).

Liebmann, Maximilian, *Theodor Innitzer und der Anschluss: Österreichs Kirche 1938* (Graz: Styria, 1988).

Liebowitz, Clement, *The Chamberlain-Hitler Deal* (Edmondton, Alberta: Duval, 1993).

————, and Alvin Finkel, *The Chamberlain-Hitler Collusion* (Halifax, Nova Scotia: James Lorimer, 1997).

Loeff, W., *Spionage, aus den Papieren eines Abwehr-Offiziers* (Stuttgart: Riegler, 1950).

Lottman, Herbert R., *The Fall of Paris, June 1940* (New York: HarperCollins, 1992).

Low, Alfred D., *The Anschluss Movement, 1931–1938, and the Great Powers* (New York: Columbia University Press, 1985).

Lukacs, John. *Five Days in London: May 1940* (New Haven: Yale University Press, 1999).

————, *The Hitler of History* (New York: Alfred A. Knopf, 1997).

————, *The Last European War (September 1939-December 1941)* (New York: Anchor Press, 1976).

Luza, Radomir, *Austro-German Relations in the Anschluss Era* (Princeton, N.J.: Princeton University Press, 1975).

Macksey, Kenneth J., *Guderian, Panzer General* (London: MacDonald, 1975).

————, *Kesselring: The Making of the Luftwaffe* (London: B. T. Batsford, 1978).

————, *Rommel, Battles and Campaigns* (London: Arms and Armour, 1979).

Macleod, Iain, *Neville Chamberlain* (London: Frederick Muller, 1961).

Macmillan, Captain Norman, *The Royal Air Force in the World War*, vols. 1–2 (London: Harrap, 1942–44).

Macready, Sir Gordon, *In the Wake of the Great* (London: Clowes, 1965).

Maier, Klaus (see Deist, Wilhelm).

Makela, Jukha L., *Im Rücken des Feindes: Der finnische Nachrichtendienst im Krieg* (Frauenfeld: Huber, 1967).

Maksimenka, E., "Arkhivy frantsuzkoi razvedki skryvali na Leningradskoe shosse," *Izvestiya*, Oct. 9, 1991.

(La) Manoeuvre pour la bataille: Les Transports pendant la guerre 1939–1940 (Paris: Charles-Lavauzelle, 1941).

Manvell, Roger, *Heinrich Himmler* (New York: G. P. Putnam, 1965).

————, and Heinrich Fraenkel, *Doctor Goebbels*, 2nd ed. (London: New English Library, 1968).

————, and Heinrich Fraenkel, *Hermann Göring*, rev. ed. (London: New English Library, 1968).

Marabini, Jean, *La Vie quotidienne à Berlin sous Hitler* (Paris: Hachette, 1985).

Marder, F. J., *From the Dardanelles to Oran* (Oxford: Oxford University Press, 1974).

Marguerat, P., *Le IIIe Reich et le pétrole roumain 1938–1940* (Leiden: A. W. Sijthoff, 1977).

Marill, Jean Marc, "La Perception de la menace allemande dans les Ardennes," in Vaïsse, ed., *Ardennes*, pp. 83–92.

Marin, Louis, "Gouvernement et commandement (mai–juin 1940)," *RHDGM*, Oct. 1952, pp. 1–28; Jan. 1953, pp. 1–14.

Marnay, Philippe [pseudonym for Jean Vanwelkenhuyzen], "La Politique militaire de la Belgique en 1939–1940," *Revue générale belge*, May 1960.

Martel, Gordon, ed., *Modern Germany Reconsidered, 1870–1945* (London: Routledge, 1992).

Martens, Erika, *Zum Beispiel "Das Reich"* (Cologne: Wissenschaft und Politik, 1972).

Martens, Stefan, *"Erster Paladin des Führers" und "zweiter Mann im Reich"* (Paderborn: Ferdinand Schöningh, 1985).

Martin, John W., *The Golden Age of French Cinema, 1929–1939* (Boston: Twayne, 1983).

Maser, Werner, *Hitler*, trans. Peter and Betty Ross (London: Allen Lane, 1973).

Mason, Herbert, *The Rise of the Luftwaffe: Forging the Secret German Air Weapon, 1918–1940* (New York: Dial, 1973).

Mason, Tim, David Kaiser and R. J. Overy, "Debate: Germany, 'Domestic Crisis,' and War in 1939," *Past and Present*, 1989, pp. 200–40.

Masson, Philippe, "La Marine française en 1939–1940," *RHA*, no. 4, 1979, pp. 57–70.

Matt, Alphons, *Zwischen allen Fronten: Die Zweite Weltkrieg aus der Sicht des Büros Ha* (Frauenfeld: Huber, 1969).

May, Ernest R., *"Lessons" of the Past: The Use and Misuse of History in American Foreign Policy* (New York: Oxford University Press, 1973).

————, ed., *Knowing One's Enemies: Intelligence Assessment Before the Two World Wars* (Princeton, N.J.: Princeton University Press, 1984).

Mazé, Pierre, *Les Grandes Journées du procès du Riom* (Paris: La Jeune Parque, 1945).

McDonough, Frank, *Neville Chamberlain, Appeasement, and the British Road to War* (Manchester: Manchester University Press, 1998).

Mearsheimer, John J., *Conventional Deterrence* (Ithaca, N.Y.: Cornell University Press, 1984).

Meehan, Patricia, *The Unnecessary War: Whitehall and the German Resistance to Hitler* (London: Sinclair-Stevenson, 1992).

Mehringer, Helmut, *Frankreichs Öffentliche Meinung* (Berlin: Junker & Dunnhaupt, 1940).

Meinck, Gerhard, *Hitler und die deutsche Aufrüstung, 1933–1937* (Wiesbaden: Franz Steiner, 1959).

Mellenthin, F. W. von, *Panzerschlachten: Eine Studie über den Einsatz von Panzerverbänden im Zweiten Weltkrieg* (Neckargemünd: Kurt Vowinckel, 1963).

Melzer, Walther, *Albert-Kanal und Eben-Emael* (Heidelberg: Kurt Vowinckel, 1957).

Menke, Erich, "Militärtheoretische Überlegungen im deutschen Generalstab vor dem zweiten Weltkrieg über den Einsatz von Panzern," *Revue internationale d'histoire militaire*, 1989, no. 71, pp. 151–63.

Merglen, Albert, "Les Forces allemandes sur le front de l'Ouest en septembre 1939," Ph.D. thesis, Sorbonne, 1969.

——, *La Vérité historique: Drames et aventures de la seconde guerre mondiale* (Paris: La Pensée Universelle, 1985).

Messenger, Charles, *The Last Prussian: A Biography of Field Marshal Gerd von Rundstedt* (London: Brassey's, 1991).

Michalka, Wolfgang, "Conflicts Within the German Leadership on the Objectives and Tactics of German Foreign Policy, 1933–9," in Mommsen and Kettenacker, eds., *Fascist Challenge*, pp. 48–60.

——, *Ribbentrop und die deutsche Weltpolitik, 1933–1940* (Munich: Fink, 1980).

Michel, Henri, *La Défaite de la France (septembre 1939–juin 1940)* (Paris: Presses Universitaires, 1980).

——, *La Drôle de guerre* (Paris: Hachette, 1971).

——, *Le Procès de Riom: Le Procès du Front Populaire et la défaite de 1940* (Paris: Albin Michel, 1979).

——, et al., "La Campagne de France (mai–juin 1940)," *RHDGM*, June 1953, pp. 1–163.

——, ed., *Nationalsozialistische Aussenpolitik* (Darmstadt: Wissenschaftliche Buchgesellschaft, 1978).

Middlemas, Keith, *Diplomacy of Illusion: The British Government and Germany, 1937–1939* (London: Weidenfeld and Nicolson, 1972).

Millotat, Christian O. E., *Understanding the Prussian-German General Staff System* (Carlisle, Pa.: The Strategic Studies Institute, 1992).

Model, Hansgeorg, *Der deutsche Generalstabsoffizier: Seine Auswahl und Ausbildung in Reichswehr, Wehrmacht und Bundeswehr* (Frankfurt am Main: Bernard & Graefe, 1968).

Mommsen, Wolfgang J., and Lothar Kettenacker, eds., *The Fascist Challenge and the Policy of Appeasement* (London: Allen and Unwin, 1983).

Moulton, J. L., *The Norwegian Campaign* (London: Eyre and Spottiswoode, 1966).

Mourélos, Yannis G., *Fictions et réalités: La France, la Grèce et la stratégie des opérations périphériques dans le sud-est européen (1939–1940)* (Thessaloniki: Institute for Balkan Studies, 1990).

Mrazek, James E., *Prelude to Dunkirk: The Fall of Eben Emael* (London: Hale, 1972).

Mueller, Gene, *The Forgotten Field Marshal: Wilhelm Keitel* (Durham, N.C.: Moore, 1979).

Müller, Franz, *Ein "Rechtskatholik" zwischen Kreuz und Hakenkreuz: Franz von Papen als Sonderbevollmachtiger Hitlers in Wien 1934–1938* (New York: Peter Lang, 1990).

Müller, Klaus-Jürgen, *Armee, Politik und Gesellschaft in Deutschland, 1933–1945* (Paderborn: Ferdinand Schöningh, 1979); trans., *The Army, Politics, and Society in Germany, 1933–45* (Manchester: Manchester University Press, 1987).

——, *General Ludwig Beck: Studien und Dokumente zur politisch-militärischen Vorstellungswelt und Tätigkeit des Generalstabschefs des deutschen Heeres 1933–1938* (Boppard am Rhein: Boldt, 1980).

——, "The German Military Opposition Before the Second World War," in Mommsen and Kettenacker, eds., *Fascist Challenge*, pp. 61–78.

——, *Das Heer und Hitler* (Stuttgart: Deutsche Verlags-Anstalt, 1969).

——, "Witzleben, Stülpnagel, and Speidel," in Barnett, ed., *Hitler's Generals*.

Müller-Hillebrand, Burkhart, *Das Heer*, 3 vols. (Frankfurt am Main: E. S. Mittler und Sohn, 1956).

Munch-Petersen, Thomas, *The Strategy of Phoney War: Britain, Sweden and the Iron Ore Question* (Stockholm: Militärhistoriska, 1981).

Murray, Williamson, "Appeasement and Intelligence," *INS*, no. 4, 1987, pp. 47–66.

———, *The Change in the European Balance of Power, 1938–1939: The Path to Ruin* (Princeton, N.J.: Princeton University Press, 1984).

———, *German Military Effectiveness* (Baltimore: Nautical and Aviation Publishing, 1992).

———, "Munich, 1938: The Military Confrontation," *JSS*, 1979, pp. 282–302.

———, "Net Assessment in Nazi Germany," in Murray and Millett, eds., *Calculations*, pp. 60–96.

———, *Strategy for Defeat: The Luftwaffe 1933–1945* (Maxwell Air Force Base, Ala.: Air University Press, 1983).

———, and Allan R. Millett, eds., *Calculations: Net Assessment and the Coming of World War II* (New York: Free Press, 1992).

———, and Allan R. Millett, eds., *Military Effectiveness*, 3 vols. (Boston: Allen and Unwin, 1987–88).

Mysyrowicz, Ladislas, *Autopsie d'une défaite: Origines de l'effondrement militaire française de 1940* (Lausanne: L'Age d'Homme, 1973).

Namier, Lewis, *Diplomatic Prelude, 1938–1939* (London: Macmillan, 1948).

Nehring, Walther K., *Die Geschichte der deutschen Panzerwaffen, 1916–1945* (Augsburg: Weltbild, 1995).

Neumann Joachim, *Die 4, Panzerdivision 1938–1943* (Bonn: privately printed, 1985).

Neustadt, Richard E., *Alliance Politics* (New York: Columbia University Press, 1970).

Neustadt, Richard E., and Ernest R. May, *Thinking in Time: Uses of History for Decisionmakers* (New York: Free Press, 1986).

Nevakivi, Jukka, *The Appeal That Was Never Made: The Allies, Scandinavia and the Finnish Winter War, 1939–1940* (Montreal: McGill-Queen's University Press, 1976).

Newman, Simon, *March 1939: The British Guarantee to Poland* (Oxford: Clarendon Press, 1976).

N.I.D. (Great Britain, Naval Intelligence Division), *Belgium* (London: Admiralty, 1944).

———, *France*, vol. 1, *Physical Geography* (n.p., n.d.).

Nie ausser Dienst: Zum achtzigsten Geburtstag von Generalfeldmarschall Erich von Manstein (Cologne: Markus, 1967).

Niedhart, Gottfried, ed., *Kriegsbeginn 1939: Entfesselung oder Ausbruch des zweiten Weltkriegs?* (Darmstadt: Wissenschaftliche Buchgesellschaft, 1976).

Norden, Peter, *Salon Kitty: Report einer Geheimen Reichssache* (Wiesbaden: Limes, 1976).

Nordmann, Jean-Thomas, *Histoire des Radicaux, 1820–1973* (Paris: Table Ronde, 1974).

O'Neill, Robert J., *The German Army and the Nazi Party* (London: Cassell, 1966).

Orlow, Dietrich, *The History of the Nazi Party*, 2 vols. (Pittsburgh: University of Pittsburgh Press, 1969–73).

Oswald, Werner, *Kraftfahrzeuge und Panzer der Reichswehr, Wehrmacht and Bundeswehr* (Stuttgart: Motorbuch, 1970).

Ottmer, Hans-Martin, *Weserübung: Der deutsche Angriff auf Dänemark und Norwegen in April 1940* (Munich: R. Oldenbourg, 1994).

———, and Heige Ostertag, eds., *Ausgewählte Operationen und ihre militärhistorischen Grundlagen* (Bonn: E. S. Mittler and Son, 1993).

Ovendale, Ritchie, *"Appeasement" and the English Speaking World* (Cardiff: University of Wales Press, 1975).

Overy, R. J., *Air Power, Armies, and the War in the West, 1940* (Boulder, Colo.: U.S. Air Force Academy, 1990).

————, *The Air War, 1939–1945* (London: Europa, 1980).

————, *Goering, the "Iron Man"* (London: Routledge & Kegan Paul, 1984).

————, *War and Economy in the Third Reich* (Oxford: Clarendon Press, 1994).

————, (see Mason, Tim).

Padfield, Peter, *Himmler, Reichsführer SS* (New York: Henry Holt, 1990).

Paget, Reginald T., *Manstein, His Campaigns and His Trial* (London: Collins, 1951).

Paillat, *Désastre*, 4(2): Claude Paillat, *Les Dossiers secrets de la France contemporaine*, vol. 4, pt. 2, *Le Désastre de 1940: La Guerre immobile, avril 1939–mai 1940* (Paris: Robert Laffont, 1984).

Paillat, *Désastre*, 5: Claude Paillat, *Les Dossiers secrets de la France contemporaine*, vol. 5, *Le Désastre de 1940: La Guerre éclair, 10 mai–24 juin 1940* (Paris: Robert Laffont, 1985).

Paine, Lauran, *German Military Intelligence in World War II: The Abwehr* (New York: Stein and Day, 1984).

Paoli, Col. François-André, *L'Armée française de 1919 à 1939*, vol. 2, *La Fin des illusions, 1930–1935* (Paris: Imprimerie Nationale, n.d.).

Paquier, Gen. Pierre, *L'Aviation de bombardement française en 1939–1940* (Paris: Berger-Levrault, 1948).

————, *L'Aviation de renseignement française en 1939–1940* (Paris: Berger-Levrault, 1947).

————, *Les Forces aériennes françaises de 1939–1945* (Paris: Berger-Levrault, 1949).

Parker, R.A.C., "Britain, France, and Scandinavia, 1939–1940," *History*, Oct. 1976, pp. 369–87.

————, *Chamberlain and Appeasement: The Coming of the Second World War* (New York: St. Martin's Press, 1993).

————, *Struggle for Survival: The History of the Second World War* (New York: Oxford University Press, 1990).

Paul, Wolfgang, *Brennpunkte: Die Geschichte der 6. Panzerdivision* (Krefeld: Albert Hoentges and Son, 1971).

————, *Wer war Hermann Göring? Biographie* (Esslingen: Bechtle, 1983).

Pauley, Bruce F., *From Prejudice to Persecution: A History of Austrian Anti-Semitism* (Chapel Hill: University of North Carolina Press, 1992).

————, *Hitler and the Forgotten Nazis: A History of Austrian National Socialism* (Chapel Hill: University of North Carolina Press, 1981).

Peden, G. C., "A Matter of Timing: The Economic Background to British Foreign Policy, 1937–1939," *History*, no. 1, 1984, pp. 19–22.

————, *The Treasury and British Rearmament, 1932–1939* (Edinburgh: Scottish Academic Press, 1979).

Pedroncini, Guy, *Pétain, le Soldat, 1856–1940* (Paris: Perrin, 1998).

Penrose, Harald, *British Aviation: The Ominous Skies, 1935–1939* (London: HMSO, 1980).

Péri, Gabriel, *Gabriel Péri, un grand Français: Une Vie de combat pour la paix et la sécurité de la France* (Paris: Éditions Sociales, 1947).

Pernot, François, "L'Armée d'Air face aux crises des années trente: Une Étude du moral," *RHA*, no. 4, 1990, pp. 116–27.

Perrett, Bryan, *A History of Blitzkrieg* (London: Robert Hale, 1983).

Peskett, S. John, *Strange Intelligence: From Dunkirk to Nuremberg* (London: Robert Hale, 1981).

Peukert, Detlev J. K., *Inside Nazi Germany: Conformity, Opposition, and Racism in Everyday Life* (New Haven, Conn.: Yale University Press, 1982).

Peuschel, Harald, *Die Männer um Hitler: Braune Biographien, Martin Bormann, Joseph Goebbels, Hermann Göring, Reinhard Heydrich, Heinrich Himmler und andere* (Düsseldorf: Droste, 1982).

Piekalkiewicz, Janusz, *Ziel Paris: Der Westfeldzug 1940* (Munich: Herbig, 1986).

Pimlott, *Hugh Dalton* (London: Jonathan Cape, 1985).

Planté, Louis, *Un Grand Seigneur de la politique: Anatole de Monzie* (Paris: R. Clavreuil, 1955).

Plato, Anton Detlev von, *Die Geschichte der 5. Panzerdivision 1938–1945* (Lüchow: Gemeinschaft der angehörigen des ehemaligen 5. Panzerdivision, 1978).

Plettenberg, Malte, *Guderian: Hintergründe eines deutschen Schicksals 1918–1945* (Düsseldorf: ABZ, 1950).

Podzun, H. H., ed., *Das deutsche Heer 1939: Gliederung, Standorte, Stellenbesetzung und Verzeichnis sämtlicher Offiziere am 3.1.1939* (Bad Nauheim: n.p., 1953).

Polanyi, Michael, *Personal Knowledge: Towards a Post-Critical Philosophy* (London: Routledge, 1958).

Polderman, Fabrice, *Léopold III et le destin de la Belgique* (Rio de Janeiro: Atlantica, 1943).

Porch, Douglas, "French Intelligence and the Fall of France, 1930–1940," *INS*, no. 1, 1989, pp. 28–58.

———, *French Secret Services: From the Dreyfus Affair to the Gulf War* (New York: Farrar, Straus and Giroux, 1995).

———, "French Spies and Counter-Spies," *INS*, Jan. 1987, pp. 191–95.

———, "Why Did France Fall?," *Quarterly Journal of Military History*, Spring 1990, pp. 30–41.

Posen, Barry, *The Sources of Military Doctrine: France, Britain, and Germany Between the World Wars* (Ithaca, N.Y.: Cornell University Press, 1984).

Pottecher, Frédéric, *Le Procès de la défaite, Riom* (Paris: Fayard, 1989).

Powers, Barry, *Strategy Without Slide Rule: British Air Strategy, 1914–1939* (London: Croom Helm, 1976).

Prazmowska, A., *Britain, Poland and the Eastern Front, 1939* (Cambridge: Cambridge University Press, 1987).

Preston, Adrian, ed., *General Staffs and Diplomacy Before the Second World War* (London: Croom Helm, 1978).

Puy-Montbrun, Déodat du, *Les Armes des espions* (Paris: Ballard, 1972).

Raïssac, Guy, *Un Soldat dans la tourmente* (Paris: Albin Michel, 1963).

du Réau, Élisabeth, *Édouard Daladier* (Paris: Fayard, 1993).

———, "La France devant l'entrée en guerre et les premiers développements de la drôle de guerre: Une Politique attentiste," in *La France et l'Allemagne en guerre*, ed. Carlier and Martens, pp. 23–43.

Reichhold, Ludwig, *Kampf um Österreich: Die Vaterländische Front und ihr Widerstand gegen den Anschluss 1933–1938, eine Dokumentation* (Vienna: Österreichischer Bundesverlag, 1984).

Relations Franco-allemandes, 1933–1939, Actes du Colloque, Strasbourg, Oct. 7–10, 1975 (Paris: Éditions du Centre National de la Recherche Scientifique, 1976).

Relations Franco-brittaniques: Comité d'Histoire de la 2ème Guerre Mondiale, *Les Relations Franco-britanniques de 1935 à 1939* (Paris: Centre National de la Recherche Scientifique, 1975).

Relations militaires Franco-belges de mars 1936 au 10 mai 1940, Travaux d'un Colloque d'Historiens Belges et Français (Paris: Éditions du Centre National de la Recherche Scientifique, 1968).

Rémond, René, ed., *Édouard Daladier, chef de gouvernement* (Paris: Fondation Nationale des Sciences Politiques, 1977).

———, ed., *La France et les Français en 1938–1939* (Paris: Fondation Nationale des Sciences Politiques, 1978).

Reynolds, David, "Churchill and the British 'Decision' to Fight On in 1940: Right Policy, Wrong Reasons," in Langhorne, ed., *Diplomacy and Intelligence*, pp. 147–67.

Reynolds, Nicholas, *Treason Was No Crime: Ludwig Beck, Chief of the German General Staff* (London: William Kimber, 1976).

Richards, Denis, *Portal of Hungerford: The Life of Marshal of the Royal Air Force Viscount Portal of Hungerford* (London: Heinemann, 1977).

———, and H. St. G. Saunders, *The Royal Air Force, 1939–1945*, vol. 1, *The Fight at Odds* (London: HMSO, 1953).

Richardson, J. O., "French Plans for Allied Attacks on the Caucasus Oil Fields," *FHS*, no. 1, 1973, pp. 130–56.

Richer, Philippe, *La Drôle de guerre des Français, 2 september 1939–10 mai 1940* (Paris: Olivier Orban, 1990).

Ritchie, Sebastian, *Industry and Air Power: The Expansion of British Aircraft Production, 1935–41* (London: Fran Cass, 1997).

Ritter, Gerhard, *Carl Goerdeler und die deutsche Widerstandsbewegung* (Stuttgart: Deutsche Verlags-Anstalt, 1955); trans. R. T. Clark, *The German Resistance: Carl Goerdeler's Struggle Against Tyranny* (New York: Frederick A. Praeger, 1958).

Roberts, Andrew, *"The Holy Fox": A Biography of Lord Halifax* (London: Weidenfeld and Nicolson, 1991).

Robertson, E. M., *Hitler's Pre-War Policy and Military Plans, 1933–1939* (London: Longmans, 1963).

Robineau, Lucien, "La Conduite de la guerre aérienne contre l'Allemagne, de septembre 1939 à juin 1940," *RHA*, no. 3, 1989, pp. 102–12.

Rocolle, Pierre, *La Guerre de 1940*, 2 vols. (Paris: Armand Colin, 1990).

Rogers, H.C.B, "Arras, Mai 1940," *Connaissance de l'histoire*, Sept. 1982, pp. 46–51.

Rohwehr, Jürgen, *Die Funkaufklärung und ihre Rolle im Zweiten Weltkrieg* (Stuttgart: Motorbuch, 1979).

Rollot, Gen., "Les Rapports Franco-Belges au moment de l'offensive allemande de Sedan le 10 mai 1940," *RHDGM*, April 1960, pp. 1–14.

Rönnefarth, Helmuth K. G., *Die Sudetenkrise in der internationalen Politik*, 2 vols. (Wiesbaden: Steiner, 1961).

Rosar, Wolfgang, *Deutsche Gemeinschaft: Seyss Inquart und der Anschluss* (Vienna: Europa, 1971).

Rose, Norman, *Vansittart: Study of a Diplomat* (London: Heinemann, 1978).

Rosenbaum, Ron, *Explaining Hitler: The Search for the Origins of His Evil* (New York: Random House, 1998).

Rosinski, Herbert, *The German Army* (Washington, D.C.: Infantry Journal, 1944).

Roskill, S. W., *Hankey, Man of Secrets*, 3 vols. (London: Collins, 1972–74).

———, *Naval Policy Between the Wars*, 2 vols. (London: Collins, 1968–76).

Ross, Steven, "French Net Assessment," in Murray and Millett, eds., *Calculations*, pp. 136–74.

Rossi-Landi, Guy, *La Drôle de guerre: La Vie politique en France, 2 septembre 1939–10 mai 1940* (Paris: Armand Colin, 1971).

Rothbrust, Florian K., *Guderian's XIXth Panzer Corps and the Battle of France: Breakthrough in the Ardennes, May 1940* (Westport, Conn.: Greenwood, 1990).

Rottgardt, Dirk, "Die deutsche Panzertruppe am 10.5.1940," *Zeitschrift für Heereskunde*, May–June 1985, pp. 61–67.

Rowe, V., *The Great Wall of France* (New York: G. P. Putnam, 1960).

Ruby, Marcel, *La Vie et oeuvre de Jean Zay* (Paris: n.p., 1969).

Ruland, Bernd, *Spionin für Deutschland: Zwischen den Fronten des zweiten Weltkrieges* (Bayreuth: Hestia, 1974).

Salesse, Lt. Col., *L'Aviation de chasse française en 1939–1940* (Paris: Berger-Levrault, 1948).

Salewski, Michael, *Die deutsche Seekriegsleitung, 1935–1945*, 3 vols. (Frankfurt am Main: Bernard & Graefe, 1970–73).

Salmon, Patrick, "British Strategy in Norway," in Salmon, ed., *Britain and Norway*, pp. 3–14.

———, ed., *Britain and Norway in the Second World War* (London: HMSO, 1995).

Sanson, Rosemonde, *Les 14 juillet, fête et conscience nationale, 1789–1975* (Paris: Flammarion, 1976).

Sasse, Heinz Günther, "Das Problem des diplomatischen Nachwuchses im Dritten Reich," in Dietrich and Oestreich, eds., *Forschungen*, pp. 367–84.

Sauvy, Alfred, *Histoire économique de la France entre les deux guerres*, 2 vols. (Paris: Economica, 1965–67).

Scheibert, Horst, *Das war Guderian* (Friedberg: Podzun-Pallas, 1980).

———, *Die Gespensterdivision: Eine deutsche Panzer-division (7) im Zweiten Weltkrieg* (Friedberg: Podzun-Pallas, 1981).

Schellendorf, Bronsart von, *The Duties of the General Staff* (orig. ed., 1875; 3rd ed., 1893); trans. W. A. H. Hare (London: HMSO, n.d.).

Schellendorf, Fabian von, *The Secret War Against Hitler* (New York: Pitman, 1965).

Scheurig, Bodo, *Alfred Jodl: Gehorsam und Verhängnis: Biographie* (Berlin: Propyläen, 1991).

———, *Ewald von Kleist-Schmenzin: Ein Konservativer gegen Hitler* (Oldenburg: Stalling, 1968).

———, *Henning von Tresckow: Ein Preusse gegen Hitler: Biographie* (Berlin: Propyläen, 1987).

Schmidl, Erwin A., *März 38: Der deutsche Einmarsch in Österreich* (Vienna: Österreichischer Bundesverlag, 1987).

Schmidt, Gustav, "The Domestic Background to British Appeasement Policy," in Mommsen and Kettenacker, eds., *Fascist Challenge*, pp. 101–24.

Schneider-Kostalski, Capt., "Tank Battle," *Field Artillery Journal*, Oct. 1941, pp. 769–72.

Schoenbaum, David, *Hitler's Social Revolution: Class and Status in Modern Germany* (New York: Doubleday, 1966).

Schöllgen, Gregor, "Das Problem einer Hitler-Biographie," in Bracher, Funke, and Jacobsen, eds., *Nationalsozialistische Diktatur*, pp. 687–705.

Schott, Franz Josef, *Der Wehrmachtführungstab im Führerhauptquartier, 1939–1945* (Bonn: Rheinische Friedrich-Wilhelms-Universität, 1980).

Schramm, Percy Ernst, *Hitler, the Man and the Military Leader* (Chicago: Quadrangle Books, 1971).

Schramm, Wilhelm v., *Sprich vom Frieden, wenn du den Krieg willst: Die psychlogischen Offensiven Hitlers gegen die Franzosen 1993 bis 1939* (Mainz: Hase und Köhler, 1973).

Schrodek, Gustav, *Ihr Glaube galt dem Vaterland: Geschichte des Panzer-Regiments 15* (Munich: Schild, 1976).

Schuker, Stephen A., "France and the Remilitarization of the Rhineland, 1936." *FHS*, 1986, pp. 299–338.

Schustereit, Hartmut, "Heeresrüstung und 'Blitzkriegskonzept': Fakten zur Materiallage im Herbst 1939," *Soldat und Technik*, 1990, pp. 126–32.

Schwoerer, Lois G., "Lord Halifax's Visit to Germany, November 1937," *The Historian*, May 1970, pp. 353–75.

Seabury, Paul, *The Wilhelmstrasse: A Study of German Diplomats Under the Nazi Regime* (Berkeley: University of California Press, 1954).

Sereny, Gitta, *Albert Speer: His Battle with Truth* (New York: Alfred A. Knopf, 1995).

Servais, Commandant A., *La Coopération militaire franco-belge 1920–1940* (Brussels: Centre de Documentation Historique des Forces Armées, 1978).

Sesonske, Alexander, *Jean Renoir: The French Films, 1924–1939* (Cambridge, Mass.: Harvard University Press, 1980).

SHAA, *Recueil d'articles et études, 1976–1978* (Château de Vincennes: Service Historique de l'Armée de l'Air: 1984).

Shay, Robert Paul, Jr., *British Rearmament in the Thirties: Politics and Profits* (Princeton, N.J.: Princeton University Press, 1977).

Shepperd, Alan, *France 1940: Blitzkrieg in the West* (London: Osprey, 1990).

Sherwood, John M., *Georges Mandel and the Third Republic* (Stanford: Stanford University Press, 1970).

Shirer, William L., *The Collapse of the Third Republic: An Inquiry into the Fall of France in 1940* (New York: Simon & Schuster, 1969).

———, *The Nightmare Years, 1930–1940* (Boston: Little, Brown, 1984).

———, *The Rise and Fall of the Third Reich* (New York: Simon & Schuster, 1960).

Shore, Zach, "Hitler, Intelligence and the Decision to Remilitarize the Rhine," *JCH*, no. 1, 1999, pp. 5–18.

Siewert, Curt, *Schuldig? Die Generale unter Hitler: Stellung und Einfluss der hohen militärischen Führung im nationalsozialistischen Staat* (Bad Nauheim: Podzun, 1968).

Simiot, Bernard, *De Lattre* (Paris: Flammarion, 1953).

Simon, Herbert, *Administrative Behavior* (New York: Macmillan, 1947).

Skidmore, Ellen Towne, *Pierre Cot: Apostle of Collective Security, 1919–1939* (Knoxville: University of Tennessee Press, 1980).

Smelser, Ronald M., "Nazi Dynamics, German Foreign Policy and Appeasement," in Mommsen and Kettenacker, eds., *Fascist Challenge*.

———, *The Sudeten Problem, 1933–1938: Volkstumpolitik and the Formulation of Nazi Foreign Policy* (Middletown, Conn.: Wesleyan University Press, 1975).

Smith, Bradley F., "Die Überlieferung des Hossbach-Niederschrift im Lichte neuer Quellen," *VfZ*, no. 2, 1990, pp. 329–36.

Smith, Malcolm, *British Air Strategy Between the Wars* (Oxford: Clarendon Press, 1984).

Sobel, Robert, *The Origins of Interventionism: The United States and the Russo-Finnish War* (New York: Bookman Associates, 1960).

Sormail, Isabelle, "Le Haut Commandement aérien français et la participation de la RAF à la bataille de France: Une Note du Géneral Vuillemin du 8 juillet 1940," *RHA*, no. 168, 1987, pp. 2–8.

Soulié, Michel, *La Vie Politique d'Édouard Herriot* (Paris: Armand Colin, 1962).

Spaeter, Helmuth, *Die Geschichte des Panzerkorps Grossdeutschland*, 3 vols. (Neckargemünd: Kurt Vowinckel, 1958).

Sprengling, G., "How Eben Emael Was Taken," *Field Artillery Journal*, June 1941, pp. 358–59.

Stead, Philip John, *Second Bureau* (London: Evans, 1959).

Stegemann, Bernd, "Hitlers Ziele im ersten Kriegsjahr 1939/40: Ein Beitrag zur Quellenkritik," *MGM*, no. 1, 1980, pp. 93–106.

Steiger, Rudolf, *Panzertaktik im Spiegel deutscher Kriegstagebücher 1939 bis 1941* (Freiburg: Rombach, 1973).

Stein, Janice Gross, "Building Politics into Psychology: The Misperception of Threat," *Political Psychology*, no. 2, 1988, pp. 245–71.

Steinbruner, John D., *The Cybernetic Theory of Decision* (Princeton, N.J.: Princeton University Press, 1974).

Steinert, Marlis G., "Deutsche im Krieg: Kollektivmeinungen, Verhaltensmuster und Mentalitäten," in Bracher, Funke, and Jacobsen, *Nazionalsozialistische Diktatur 1933–1945*, pp. 474–87.

———, *Hitler* (Paris: Fayard, 1991), trans. Steven Randall, *Hitler, a Biography* (New York: W. W. Norton, 1997).

———, *Hitlers Krieg und die Deutschen* (Düsseldorf: Econ, 1970); trans. and ed. Thomas E. J. de Witt, *Hitler's War and the Germans: Public Mood and Attitude During the Second World War* (Athens, Ohio: Ohio University Press, 1977).

Stengers, Jean, "Enigma, the French, the Poles and the British, 1931–1940," in Andrew and Dilks, eds., *Missing Dimension*, pp. 126–37.

———, *Léopold III et le gouvernement: Les Deux Politiques belges de 1940* (Paris: Duculot, 1980).

Stolfi, R.H.S., "Equipment for Victory in France in 1940," *History*, Feb. 1970, pp. 1–20.

———, "Reality and Myth: French and German Preparations for War, 1933–1940," Ph.D. dissertation, Stanford University, 1966.

Stourzh, Gerald, and Birgitta Zaar, eds., *Österreich, Deutschland und die Mächte: Internationale und Österreichische Aspekte des "Anschlusses" vom Marz 1938* (Vienna: Österreichischen Akademie der Wissenschaften, 1990).

Stoves, Rolf, *Die gepanzerten und motorisierten deutschen Grossverbände (Divisionen und selbständige Brigaden) 1935–1945* (Friedberg: Podzun-Pallas, 1986).

Strabogli, Lord, *The Campaign in the Low Countries* (London: Hutchinson, 1940).

Strong, General Sir Kenneth, *Men of Intelligence: A Study of the Roles and Decisions of Chiefs of Intelligence from World War I to the Present Day* (London: Cassell, 1970).

Stumpf, Reinhard, *Die Wehrmacht-Elite: Rang- und Herkunftsstruktur der deutschen Generale und Admirale 1933–1945* (Boppard am Rhein: Boldt, 1982).

Suchenwirth, Richard, *The Development of the German Air Force, 1919–1939* (Maxwell Air Force Base, Ala.: USAF Historical Division, 1968).

Susbielle, B. de, "Chasseurs à pied, cavaliers et blindés au combat: Canal des Ardennes 16–23 mai 1940," *RHA*, no. 2, 1972, pp. 75–99.

Taubert, Friedrich, *Französische Linke und Hitlerdeutschland: Deutschlandbilder und Strategieentwurfe, 1933–1939* (Bern, New York: Peter Lang, 1991).

Taylor, Telford, *The March of Conquest: The German Victories in Western Europe, 1940* (New York: Simon & Schuster, 1967).

———, *Sword and Swastika: Generals and Nazis in the Third Reich* (New York: Simon & Schuster, 1952).

Teyssier, Arnaud, "Le Général Vuillemin, Chef d'État–major Général de l'Armée de l'Air (1938–1939)," *RHA*, no. 167, June 1987, pp. 104–13.

Theisinger, Hugo, *Die Sudetendeutschen: Herkunft, die Zeit unter Konrad Henlein und Adolf Hitler, Vertreibung: Ein Beitrag zur sudetendeutschen Geschichte* (Buchloe: Druckerei H. Obermayer, 1987).

Thielenhaus, Marion, *Zwischen Anpassung und Widerstand: Deutsche Diplomaten 1938–1941* (Paderborn: Ferdinand Schöningh, 1984).

Thies, Jochen, *Architekt der Weltherrschaft: Die Endziele Hitlers* (Düsseldorf: Droste, 1976).

Thomas, Georg, *Geschichte der deutschen Wehr- und Rüstungswirtschaft (1918–1945)* (Boppard am Rhein: Boldt, 1966).

Thomas, Martin, *Britain, France and Appeasement: Anglo-French Relations in the Popular Front Era* (Oxford: Berg, 1996).

Thun-Hohenstein, Romedio Galeazzo, Graf von, *Der Verschwörer: General Oster und die Militäropposition* (Berlin: Severin & Seidler, 1982).

Tippelskirch, Kurt von, *Geschichte der Zweiten Weltkrieges* (Bonn: Athenäum, 1951).

Toland, John, *Hitler: The Pictorial Documentary of His Life* (Garden City, N.Y.: Doubleday, 1978).

Tournoux, J. R., *L'Histoire secrète: La Cagoule, le Front Populaire, Vichy, Londres, Deuxième Bureau, L'Algérie française* (Paris: Plon, 1962).

Tournoux, Gen. Paul-Émile, *Haut-Commandement: Gouvernement et défense des frontières du Nord et de l'Est, 1919–1939* (Paris: Nouvelles Éditions Latines, 1960).

———, "Pouvait-on prévoir l'attaque allemande des Ardennes en mai 1940? Un Général avait dit 'oui,' " *RHA*, no. 2, 1971, pp. 130–41.

Trythall, A. J., "The Downfall of Leslie Hore-Belisha," *JCH*, 1981, pp. 391–411.

Turlotte, Michel, "L'Alliance polonaise à travers les archives de l'état-major de l'Armée," *RHA*, no. 4, 1985, pp. 70–83.

Turnbull, Patrick, *Dunkirk: Anatomy of Disaster* (London: Botsford, 1978).

Turner, Henry Ashby, Jr., *Hitler's Thirty Days to Power, January 1933* (Reading, Mass.: Addison-Wesley, 1996).

Ueberschär, Gerd R., "Ansätze und Hindernisse der Militäropposition gegen Hitler in den ersten beiden Kriegsjahren (1939–1941)," in Walle, ed., *Aufstand des Gewissens*, pp. 365–93.

———, *Generaloberst Franz Halder* (Göttingen: Musterschmidt, 1991).

———, "Generaloberst Halder im militärischen Widerstand 1938–1940," *Wehrforschung*, Jan.–Feb. 1973, pp. 20–31.

Uexküll, Rönn von, *Unser Mann in Berlin: Die Tätigkeit der deutschen und schweizerïschen Geheimdienste, 1933–1945* (Lucerne: Steinach, 1976).

U.S. War Department, Military Intelligence Division, *German Military Intelligence* (Washington, D.C.: War Department, 1944).

Vaïsse, Maurice, "Against Appeasement: French Advocates of Firmness, 1933–1938," in Mommsen and Kettenacker, eds., *Fascist Challenge*, pp. 227–35.

———, "Der Pazifismus und die Sicherheit Frankreichs," *VfZ*, 1985, pp. 590–616.

———, "La Perception de la puissance soviétique par les militaires françaises en 1938," *RHA*, no. 3, 1983, pp. 18–25.

———, ed., *Ardennes 1940* (Paris: Henri Veyrier, 1991).

———, ed., "Histoire du renseignement," *Cahiers du Centre d'Études d'Histoire de la Défense*, no. 1, 1996.

———, ed., *Le Pacifisme en Europe des années 1920 aux années 1950* (Brussels: Bruylant, 1993).

Vallette, Geneviève, and Jacques Bouillon, *Munich 1938* (Paris: Armand Colin, 1964).

Van Kleffens, Eelco Nicolaas, *Juggernaut over Holland* (New York: Columbia University Press, 1941).

Van Langenhove, Fernand, *La Belgique en quête de sécurité, 1920–1940* (Brussels: Renaissance du Livre, 1969).

Vanwelkenhuyzen, Jean, *Les Avertissements qui venaient de Berlin (9 octobre 1939–10 mai 1940)* (Paris: Duculot, 1982).

———, *Miracle à Dunkerque: La Fin d'un mythe* (Brussels: Racine, 1994).

———, *Neutralité armée: La Politique militaire de la Belgique pendant la "Drôle de Guerre"* (Brussels: Renaissance du Livre, 1979).

———, "Les Plans belges de défense des Ardennes," in Vaïsse, ed., *Ardennes*, pp. 33–56.

Verhoeyen, E., " 'Honorables Correspondants': Citoyens belges et services de renseignements 'alliés' en période de neutralité (septembre 1939–mai 1940)," *RBHM*, 1992, pp. 449–62, 511–33.

Vertzberger, Yaacov Y. I., *Misperceptions in Foreign Policymaking: The Sino-Indian Conflict 1959–1962* (Boulder, Colo.: Westview, 1984).

———, *Risk-taking and Decisionmaking: Foreign Military Interventions* (Stanford: Stanford University Press, 1998).

———, *The World in Their Minds: Information Processing, Cognition, and Perception in Foreign Policy Decisionmaking* (Stanford: Stanford University Press, 1990).

Verzat, Jean, "À propos du P.C. Gamelin," *RHA*, no. 2, 1982, pp. 98–109.

Vial, Jean, "La défense nationale: Son organisation entre les deux guerres," *RHDGM*, no. 18, 1955, pp. 17–34.

———, "Une Semaine décisive sur la Somme, 18–25 mai 1940," *RHA*, Dec. 1949, pp. 45–58; March 1950, pp. 46–60.

Viault, B. S., "Les Démarches pour le rétablissement de la paix (sept 1939–août 1940)," *RHDGM*, no. 67, 1967, pp. 13–30.

Vickers, Sir Geoffrey, *The Art of Judgment: A Study of Policy-Making*, centenary ed. (Thousand Oaks, Calif.: Sage Publications, 1995).

Vidalenc, Jean, "Les Divisions de série 'B' dans l'armée française pendant la campagne de France 1939–1940," *RHA*, no. 4, 1980, pp. 106–26.

Vivier, Thierry, "L'Aviation française en Pologne (janvier 1936–septembre 1939," *RHA*, no. 4, 1993, pp. 60–70.

————, "La Coopération aéronautique franco-tchécoslovaque (janvier 1933–septembre 1938)," *RHA*, no. 1, 1993, pp. 70–79.

————, "Le Douhétisme français entre tradition et innovation (1933–1939)," *RHA*, no. 3, 1991, pp. 89–99.

Völker, Karl-Heinz, *Die deutsche Luftwaffe, 1933–1939: Aufbau, Führung, Rüstung* (Stuttgart: Deutsche Verlags-Anstalt, 1967).

Vollmacht des Gewissens, ed. Helmut Krausnick, 2nd ed., 2 vols. (Frankfurt am Main: A. Metzner, 1960).

Vormann, Nikolaus v., *Der Feldzug 1939 in Polen* (Weissenburg: Prinz Eugen, 1958).

Waites, Neville, ed., *Troubled Neighbors: Franco-British Relations in the Twentieth Century* (London: Weidenfeld and Nicolson, 1971).

Walde, Karl J., *Guderian* (Frankfurt am Main: Ullstein, 1976).

Walle, Heinrich, ed., *Aufstand des Gewissens: Militärischer Widerstand gegen Hitler und das NS-Regime 1933–1945* (Berlin: E. S. Mittler, 1994).

Walther, Simone, "Die Versorgungslage in Berlin im Januar 1940 und das politische Verhalten der Bevölkerung," *Zeitschrift fur Geschichtswissenschaft*, no. 5, 1986, pp. 427–32.

Wanty, Gen. Emile, "From Polish Bomba to British Bombe: The Birth of Ultra," *INS*, no. 1, Jan. 1986, pp. 71–110.

Wark, Wesley K., "Sir Edmund Ironside: The Fate of Churchill's First General, 1939–1940," in Bond, ed., *Fallen Stars*, pp. 141–63.

————, "Something Very Stern: British Political Intelligence, Moralism and Grand Strategy in 1939," *INS*, Jan. 1990, pp. 150–70.

————, "Three Military Attachés at Berlin in the 1930s: Soldier-Statesmen and the Limits of Ambiguity," *International History Review*, no. 4, 1987, pp. 586–611.

————, *The Ultimate Enemy: British Intelligence and Nazi Germany, 1933–1939* (Ithaca, N.Y.: Cornell University Press, 1985).

Warusfel, Bertrand, "Histoire de l'organisation du contre-espionnage français entre 1871 et 1945," in Vaïsse, ed., "Histoire du renseignement," pp. 13–40.

Watt, Donald Cameron, "Anglo-German Naval Negotiations on the Eve of the Second World War," *Journal of the Royal United Services Institute*, 1958, pp. 201–7, 384–91.

————, "British Intelligence and the Coming of the Second World War in Europe," in May, ed., *Knowing One's Enemies*, pp. 237–70.

————, "An Earlier Model for the Pact of Steel: The Draft Treaties Exchanged Between Germany and Italy During Hitler's Visit to Rome in May 1938," *International Affairs*, April 1957, pp. 185–97.

————, "Hitler's Visit to Rome and the May Weekend Crisis: A Study in Hitler's Response to External Stimuli," *JCH*, Jan. 1974, pp. 23–32.

————, *How War Came: The Immediate Origins of the Second World War, 1938–1939* (New York: Pantheon, 1989).

————, "The Initiation of Negotiations Leading to the Nazi-Soviet Pact: A Historical Problem," in Abransky, ed., *Essays*, pp. 157–70.

————, "The May Crisis of 1938: A Rejoinder to Mr. Wallace," *Slavonic and East European Review*, July 1966, pp. 475–80.

————, "Le moral de l'armée française tel que se représentaient les Britanniques en 1939 et 1940: Une faillité des services de renseignements," in *Français et britanniques dans la drôle de guerre*, pp. 197–213.

————, *Personalities and Policies* (London: Longmans, 1965).

————, "The Rome-Berlin Axis, 1936–1940: Myth and Reality," *Review of Politics*, no. 4, 1960, pp. 519–43.

————, *Too Serious a Business: European Armed Forces and the Approach to the Second World War* (London: Maurice Temple Smith, 1975).

Weber, Eugen, *The Hollow Years: France in the 1930s* (New York: W. W. Norton, 1994).

Wehner, Gerd, "Die militärischen Verhandlungen im Anschluss an die britisch-polnische Garantie vom 31. März 1939," *MGM*, no. 2, 1988, pp. 51–60.

Weinberg, Gerhard L., "Die deutsche Aussenpolitik und Österreich 1937/38," in Stourzh and Zaar, eds., *Österreich, Deutschland und die Mächte*, pp. 61–74.

————, *The Foreign Policy of Hitler's Germany*, 2 vols. (Chicago: University of Chicago Press, 1970–80).

————, "The German Generals and the Outbreak of War," in Preston, ed., *General Staffs*, pp. 24–40.

————., *Der gewaltsame Anschluss 1938: Die deutsche Aussenpolitik und Österreich* (Vienna: Bundespressedienst, 1988).

————, "Hitler's Image of the United States," *American Historical Review*, July 1964, pp. 1006–21.

————, "The May Crisis 1938," *JMH*, Sept. 1957, pp. 213–25.

————, *World at Arms: A Global History of World War II* (New York: Cambridge University Press, 1994).

Weitz, John, *Joachim von Ribbentrop, Hitler's Diplomat* (London: Weidenfeld and Nicolson, 1992).

Wendt, Bernd-Jürgen, *Grossdeutschland: Aussenpolitik und Kriegsvorbereitung des Hitler-Regimes* (Munich: Deutscher Taschenbuch, 1987).

————, *München 1938: England zwischen Hitler und Preussen* (Frankfurt am Main: Europäische Verlagsanstalt, 1965).

Werth, Alexander, *France and Munich* (London: Hamish Hamilton, 1939).

Westerfield, H. Bradford, ed., *Inside CIA's Private World* (New Haven, Conn.: Yale University Press, 1995).

Whaley, Barton, *Codeword BARBAROSSA* (Cambridge, Mass.: MIT Press, 1973).

Wheeler-Bennett, John W., *John Anderson, Viscount Waverley* (New York: St. Martin's Press, 1962).

————, *Munich, Prologue to Tragedy* (New York: The Viking Press, 1964).

————, *Nemesis of Power: The German Army in Politics, 1918–1945* (London: Macmillan, 1964).

Whiting, Charles, *Jener September: Europa beim Kriegsausbruch 1939: Ein Bild/Text-Band* (Düsseldorf: Droste, 1979).

Wieland, Volker, *Zur Problematik der französischen Militärpolitik und Militärdoktrin in der Zeit zwischen den Weltkriegen* (Boppard am Rhein: Boldt, 1973).

Wighton, C., *They Spied on England, Based on the German Secret Service War Diary of General von Lahousen* (London: Odhams, 1958).

Wildhagen, Karl-Heinz, ed., *Erich Fellgiebel* (Hannover: Wildhagen, 1970).

Wilensky, Harold, *Organizational Intelligence* (New York: Basic Books, 1967).

Willequet, Jacques, *Paul-Henri Spaak: Un Homme, des combats* (Brussels: Renaissance du Livre, 1975).

Williams, John, *The Ides of May: The Defeat of France. May–June 1940* (London: Constable, 1968).

Winock, Michel, *La Fièvre hexagonale: Les Grandes Crises politiques, 1871–1968* (Paris: Calmann Lévy, 1986).

Wohlstetter, Roberta, *Pearl Harbor: Warning and Decision* (Stanford: Stanford University Press, 1962).

Woodward, Sir Llewellyn, *British Foreign Policy in the Second World War*, vol. 1 (London: HMSO, 1970).

Wormser, Georges, *Georges Mandel, l'homme politique* (Paris: Plon, 1967).

Woytak, Richard A., *On the Border of War and Peace: Polish Intelligence Diplomacy in 1938–1939 and the Origins of the Ultra Secret* (Boulder, Colo.: East European Quarterly, 1979).

Wright, Jonathan, and Paul Stafford, "Hitler and the Hossbach Memorandum," *History Today*, March 1988, pp. 11–17.

———, "Hitler, Britain, and the Hossbach Memorandum," *MGM*, no. 2, 1987, pp. 77–123.

Wullus-Rudiger, J., *La Défense de la Belgique en 1940* (Villeneuve sur Lot: Alfred Bador, 1940).

Young, Robert J., "The Aftermath of Munich: The Course of French Diplomacy, October 1938 to March 1939," *FHS*, Fall 1973, pp. 305–22.

———, *France and the Origins of the Second World War* (New York: St. Martin's Press, 1996).

———, "French Military Intelligence and Nazi Germany," in May, ed., *Knowing One's Enemies*, pp. 271–309.

———, "La Guerre de Longue Durée: Some Reflections on French Strategy and Diplomacy in the 1930s," in Preston, ed., *General Staffs*, pp. 41–64.

———, *In Command of France: French Foreign Policy and Military Planning, 1933–1940* (Cambridge, Mass.: Harvard University Press, 1978).

———, "Preparations for Defeat: French War Doctrine in the Inter-War Period," *Journal of European Studies*, no. 2, June 1972, pp. 155–72.

———, "The Strategic Dream: French Air Doctrine in the Inter-War Period, 1919–1939," *JCH*, Oct. 1974, pp. 31–42.

———, "The Use and Abuse of Fear: France and the Air Menace in the 1930s," *INS*, no. 4, 1987, pp. 88–109.

Zelikow, Philip, "Foreign Policy Engineering: From Theory to Practice and Back Again," *International Security*, Spring 1994, pp. 143–71.

Zentner, Christian, *Der Frankreichfeldzug—10. Mai 1940* (Frankfurt am Main: Ullstein, 1980).

———, *Illustrierte Geschichte des Dritten Reiches* (Munich: Südwest, 1983).

Zimmer, Lucien, *Un Septennat policier: Dessous et secrets de la police républicaine* (Paris: Fayard, 1967).

Zitelmann, Rainer, *Hitler: Selbsverständnis eines Revolutionärs* (Hamburg: Berg, 1987).

Zorach, Jonathan, "The British View of the Czechs in the Era Before the Munich Crisis," *Slavonic and East European Review*, no. 1, Jan. 1979, pp. 56–70.

———, "Czechoslovakia's Fortifications: Their Development and Role in the Munich Crisis," *MGM*, no. 2, 1976, pp. 81–94.

Zuylen, Pierre van, *Les Mains libres: Politique extérieure de la Belgique, 1914–1940* (Paris: Desclée de Brouwer, 1950).

ACKNOWLEDGMENTS

If I thanked everyone who deserves thanks, this would be the longest chapter in the book. So, many people go unthanked, except in my bosom.

I am forever indebted to five friends who read the whole manuscript at a late stage and set me right about facts or interpretations or concepts: Richard E. Neustadt, Donald Cameron Watt, Gerhard Weinberg, Robert J. Young, and Philip D. Zelikow. Needless to say, they bear no responsibility for the text that survived their scrutiny—especially since, in some instances, I stubbornly resisted advice.

Among others who did research in my behalf, I have to single out, in the United States, George F. Williamson; in Britain, John Herman; in France, Christian Bachelier, Scott G. Blair, Vincent Desjuzeur, and Lori Maguire Zuber; and in Germany, Hans-Jürgen Schraut. In France, Maurice Vaïsse, now chief historian for the Ministry of Defense, was wonderfully helpful. For assistance with German records, I am indebted to Manfred Messerschmidt, Wilhelm Deist, and Wolfgang Krieger. Charles Cogan and Mary Saratte vetted some of my translations, and Charles, a veteran of the U.S. clandestine service, also set me right about some operational intelligence issues.

My obligations to institutions are immense. The Harvard College Library is a treasure house for this subject as for most others. I also made use of the Library of Congress and the Columbia University and University of Pennsylvania libraries in the United States, the Bodleian and Queen's College libraries in Oxford, and the Bibliothèque Nationale in Paris. I owe obvious debts also to the U.S. National Archives and Records Service, the British Public Record Office, the Services Historique of the Armée de l'Air and the Armée de Terre in France, and the Bundesarchiv-Militärarchiv in Freiburg and the Bundesarchiv in Koblenz; to the Birmingham University Library, Churchill College, Cambridge, King's College, London, and the Fondation Nationale des Sciences Politiques in Paris for access to manuscript sources; and to Colonel Paul Paillole for sharing with me the diary of General Louis Rivet.

Generous research support came to me initially from Andrew W. Marshall's Office of Net Assessment in the Office of the Secretary of Defense and later from the C.I.A.'s Center for the Study of Intelligence, headed successively by David Gries, Brian Latell, and Lloyd Salvetti. None of these sponsors ever even asked, "Why is it taking so long?," let alone hinted at any desire to shape it. At a crucial moment, Peter Kovler of the Kovler Foundation surprised me with an unsolicited grant.

The last debts to be acknowledged are those to my agent, Sterling Lord; to my wonderful editor, Elisabeth Sifton; and to my wife, Susan Wood, who joined me in exploring the Ardennes Forest and who now has an answer, I hope, to her insistent question: "And the point?"

INDEX

Abwehr: Ardennes deception plan organized by, 266; Canaris as head of, 103; as filter for reports to Hitler, 103–4; Hitler's control of, 103; Hitler's overthrow plotted by officers in, 88; invasion plans betrayed by resistance in, 226; Piekenbrock in, 243; role of, in Plan Yellow, 243–44; SR penetration of, 136; *see also* intelligence, German
Achtung Panzer! (Guderian), 88, 234, 353
air forces: *see* French air force; Luftwaffe; Royal Air Force
Albert Canal (Belgium), 305, 373, 374
Alias, Col. Henri, 420
Allies, inactivity of: after Czech and Polish conflicts, 455; French army's frustration over, 330; Germans surprised by, 252–53; at start of war, 306; *see also* Allies/Allied forces
Allies/Allied forces: Beck's concern regarding, 70–72; declarations of war by, 93; flawed decision-making process of, 453–54; German assessment of, 252, 257; initial emphasis on economic warfare by, 286–87; initial presumption of victory by, 287–88; and lack of cooperation between French and British, 450; obsolescence of battle plans, 346; Oster's betrayal of German plans to, 226, 283, 284, 315; Soviet alliance considered by, 197–98; withdrawal from Norway by, 267; *see also* Allies, inactivity of; balance of forces; Belgian army; British military power; French air force; French ground forces; Royal Air Force

Altmayer, Gen. Marie-Robert, 131
Amouroux, Henri, 208
Anschluss: French reaction to, 153–54, 211–12; Gamelin's warnings about, 145–46; German public's approval of, 63; Halder's enthusiasm for, 87–88; Halifax's refusal to denounce, 149–50; Hitler's plans for, 58–60; Mussolini on, 54–55, 59; Paillole on, 145; Weizsäcker's enthusiasm for, 79; *see also* Austria; Nazi Party, Austrian
anti-Semitism: in France, 155, 159, 180; of Hitler, 97–98; and *Kristallnacht,* 180; and murder of Polish Jews, 21
Archen, Ferdinand, 3–4, 360, 383
Ardennes offensive: and Allies' misunderstanding of German strategy, 412; Chasseurs Ardennais redeployed during, 394, 395, 405, 406, 421; Corap's defensive line established in, 404–6; and Corap's retreat from Semois to Meuse, 407–8; and demolition of Yvoir bridge, 423; and distintegration of Huntziger's Fifth DLC, 412; and German crossing of Meuse, 408, 412, 423–24; and German deception plan, 266; and German entry into Ardennes, 399; German logistical problems in, 418–19; Guderian's troops airlifted in, 421; Halder's apprehension about, 264; Hitler's enthusiasm for, 236–37; and Huntziger's planned defense of Maginot Line, 408, 409–10; Huntziger's retreat and request for reinforcements during, 410; Germans' Luxembourg-to-Ardennes thrust ignored in, 358, 360, 361; Meuse